Palgrave Macmillan Transnational History Series

Series Editors: Akira Iriye, Professor of History at Harvard University, and Rana Mitter, Professor of the History and Politics of Modern China at the University of Oxford

This distinguished series seeks to develop scholarship on the transnational connections of societies and peoples in the nineteenth and twentieth centuries; provide a forum in which work on transnational history from different periods, subjects, and regions of the world can be brought together in fruitful connection; and explore the theoretical and methodological links between transnational and other related approaches such as comparative history and world history.

Editorial Board: Thomas Bender, University Professor of the Humanities, Professor of History, and Director of the International Center for Advanced Studies, New York University; Jane Carruthers, Professor of History, University of South Africa; Mariano Plotkin, Professor, Universidad Nacional de Tres de Febrero, Buenos Aires, and member of the National Council of Scientific and Technological Research, Argentina; Pierre-Yves Saunier, Researcher at the Centre National de la Recherche Scientifique, France, and Visiting Professor at the University of Montreal; Ian Tyrrell, Professor of History, University of New South Wales

Titles include:

Gregor Benton and Edmund Terence Gomez
THE CHINESE IN BRITAIN, 1800–PRESENT
Economy, Transnationalism and Identity

Sugata Bose and Kris Manjapra (*editors*)
COSMOPOLITAN THOUGHT ZONES
South Asia and the Global Circulation of Ideas

Sebastian Conrad and Dominic Sachsenmaier (*editors*)
COMPETING VISIONS OF WORLD ORDER
Global Moments and Movements, 1880s–1930s

Martin Conway and Kiran Klaus Patel (*editors*)
EUROPEANIZATION IN THE TWENTIETH CENTURY
Historical Approaches

Joy Damousi, Mariano Ben Plotkin (*editors*)
THE TRANSNATIONAL UNCONSCIOUS
Essays in the History of Psychoanalysis and Transnationalism

Desley Deacon, Penny Russell and Angela Woollacott (*editors*)
TRANSNATIONAL LIVES
Biographies of Global Modernity, 1700–present

Jonathan Gantt
IRISH TERRORISM IN THE ATLANTIC COMMUNITY, 1865–1922

Abigail Green and Vincent Viaene (*editors*)
RELIGIOUS INTERNATIONALS IN THE MODERN WORLD

Eric Hotta
PAN-ASIANISM AND JAPAN'S WAR, 1931–45

Martin Klimbe and Joachim Scharloth (*editors*)
1968 IN EUROPE
A History of Protest and Activism, 1956–77

Erika Kuhlman
RECONSTRUCTING PATRIARCHY AFTER THE GREAT WAR
Women, Gender and Postwar Reconciliation between Nations

Deep Kanta Lahiri Choudhury
TELEGRAPHIC IMPERIALISM
Crisis and Panic in the Indian Empire, c. 1830–1920

Bruce Mazlish
THE IDEA OF HUMANITY IN THE GLOBAL ERA

Giles Scott-Smith
WESTERN ANTI-COMMUNISM AND THE INTERDOC NETWORK
Cold War Internationale

Glenda Sluga
THE NATION, PSYCHOLOGY, AND INTERNATIONAL POLITICS, 1870–1919

Mark Tilse
TRANSNATIONALISM IN THE PRUSSIAN EAST
From National Conflict to Synthesis, 1871–1914

The Palgrave Macmillan Transnational History Series
Series Standing Order ISBN 978–0–230–50746–3 Hardback
978–0–230–50747–0 Paperback
(*outside North America only*)

You can receive future titles in this series as they are published by placing a standing order. Please contact your bookseller or, in case of difficulty, write to us at the address below with your name and address, the title of the series and the ISBN quoted above.

Customer Services Department, Macmillan Distribution Ltd, Houndmills, Basingstoke, Hampshire RG21 6XS, England

Western Anti-Communism and the Interdoc Network

Cold War Internationale

Giles Scott-Smith
Roosevelt Study Center/Leiden University, The Netherlands

© Giles Scott-Smith 2012

All rights reserved. No reproduction, copy or transmission of this publication may be made without written permission.

No portion of this publication may be reproduced, copied or transmitted save with written permission or in accordance with the provisions of the Copyright, Designs and Patents Act 1988, or under the terms of any licence permitting limited copying issued by the Copyright Licensing Agency, Saffron House, 6–10 Kirby Street, London EC1N 8TS.

Any person who does any unauthorized act in relation to this publication may be liable to criminal prosecution and civil claims for damages.

The author has asserted his right to be identified as the author of this work in accordance with the Copyright, Designs and Patents Act 1988.

First published 2012 by
PALGRAVE MACMILLAN

Palgrave Macmillan in the UK is an imprint of Macmillan Publishers Limited, registered in England, company number 785998, of Houndmills, Basingstoke, Hampshire RG21 6XS.

Palgrave Macmillan in the US is a division of St Martin's Press LLC, 175 Fifth Avenue, New York, NY 10010.

Palgrave Macmillan is the global academic imprint of the above companies and has companies and representatives throughout the world.

Palgrave® and Macmillan® are registered trademarks in the United States, the United Kingdom, Europe and other countries.

ISBN 978–0–230–22126–0

This book is printed on paper suitable for recycling and made from fully managed and sustained forest sources. Logging, pulping and manufacturing processes are expected to conform to the environmental regulations of the country of origin.

A catalogue record for this book is available from the British Library.

A catalog record for this book is available from the Library of Congress.

10 9 8 7 6 5 4 3 2 1
21 20 19 18 17 16 15 14 13 12

Printed and bound in Great Britain by
CPI Antony Rowe, Chippenham and Eastbourne

Contents

List of Plates	vi
Series Foreword	ix
Acknowledgements	xi
List of Abbreviations	xiii
Introduction: The Communist Challenge	1
1 Anti-Communism and PsyWar in the 1950s	13
2 Building the Network	44
3 A Dutch–German Cabal	85
4 The European Web	108
5 East–West Engagement and Interdoc Youth	134
6 The Fallout from *Ostpolitik*	168
7 Bringing the Americans Back In	189
8 Interdoc Reconfigures: The 1970s and Détente	209
Conclusion: Assessing the Legacy	243
Appendix I: Interdoc Conferences	250
Appendix II: Interdoc Publications	253
Appendix III: Interdoc Contacts in Eastern Europe	261
Notes	264
Bibliography	341
Index	352

Plates

1. Antoine Bonnemaison's original plan for Franco-German cooperation in anti-communism, 1958. Einthoven has added in ink in the middle: "Holland dit zijn wij HBVD HKO" (Holland, that's us, Chief BVD, Chief Training)
2. The Interdoc apparatus as envisaged by the French delegation for the May 1960 planning meeting in The Hague: Hollande, Allemagne, France
3. The German proposal of 1960: note the inclusion of the British and Italians
4. A more detailed working of the German proposal
5. Laan Copes van Cattenburch 38, the location of the BVD's training division (KO: kader opleiding) in the 1950s and 1960s. Cees van den Heuvel led this division from 1949 up to his departure from the service on 1 January 1962
6. The training division of the BVD, circa 1959. From the left, back row: C.C. van den Heuvel, Ottolini, Boske, Boomsluiter, Bolten, Couwenberg. Front row: Van der Lee, secretary, Cea Slager, secretary, Mennes
7. The Economic League in action: Helen Bailey speaking to London dockworkers during their lunch break, 1959
8. Plaats 11a (the white building), opposite the Dutch parliament building in the centre of The Hague, the first official location for SOEV in 1961–62
9. "Les Galeries" at Gevers Deynootplein, Scheveningen, the location of the SOEV offices in 1962–63
10. Van Stolkweg 10 (the "rabbit hole"), the nerve centre for Van den Heuvel's many operations from 1962 to 1986
11. Felix A.C. Guépin, a director (1950–1959) and board member (1959–1966) of Royal Dutch Shell, and a valuable supporter of the SOEV–OWI–Interdoc apparatus
12. K.Chr. de Pous (dark suit, arms folded), chief of security for Dutch Railways, at a dinner in honour of his retirement in mid-1963, in private discussion with his successor, B.F.A. Mikx (on De Pous's right). The Dutch Railways was a valuable client for SOEV and OWI in the early 1960s
13. Rue de la Pépinière 14, close to the Gare St-Lazare in Paris, the address Antoine Bonnemaison was using during the formation of Interdoc

List of Plates vii

14. Pössenbacherstraße 21, Pullach (the "villa"), the location of Rolf Geyer's IIIF during the 1960s
15. Rolf Geyer in the late 1960s
16. Habsburgerplatz 1/1, Munich, the location of Nicolas von Grote's Verein zur Erforschung Sozialpolitischer Verhältnisse, the "public front" for Geyer's IIIF. It was renamed the Deutsche Arbeitsgruppe für West-Ost Beziehungen e.V. in 1966
17. Nicolas von Grote (centre), the head of the Verein/Arbeitsgruppe bureau in Munich
18. The Haus der Zukunft on Goethestraße in Zehlendorf, Berlin. This was used for training courses for participants from the Netherlands and other countries during the 1960s
19. Hans Beuker (with fist raised) in West Berlin, circa 1961
20. The opening of the 8th World Youth Festival in Helsinki, August 1962, the site of the first Interdoc "counter-action": Hans Beuker's anti-Soviet speech
21. Pieter Koerts (centre) on the Kurfürstendamm, West Berlin, during a training course in the summer of 1962
22. Pieter Koerts (at the microphone) confronting the board of the WFDY-sponsored Conference of Youth and Students for Disarmament, Peace and National Independence in Florence in February 1964
23. Mont-St-Michel, the location of the final Interdoc *colloque* involving the French as official participants, 1962
24. Antoine Bonnemaison in the late 1950s
25. Diego Guicciardi, Shell's representative in Genoa, who played a key role in developing contacts in Italy
26. An Interdoc conference in the mid-1960s. Louis Einthoven is seated on the left at the front. Front row from the right: Herman Mennes, F.C. Spits, J.M.M. Hornix, unidentified. Raimute von Hassell is two rows behind Mennes. Sitting next to the aisle directly behind the front row on the right is Claus Kernig, two seats behind him is Uwe Holl, and behind Holl is Cees de Niet
27. Louis Einthoven in 1965. Einthoven devoted his full attention to developing the Interdoc network after his retirement from the BVD in 1961
28. Raimute von Hassell, Dietmar Töppel, and Andreas von Weiss outside Van Stolkweg 10, 17 November 1966
29. Dietmar Töppel and Andreas von Weiss on the beach at Scheveningen, 17 November 1966
30. Rolf Buchow, the anti-Soviet activist who ran Interdoc Berlin

viii *List of Plates*

31. Charles Howard (Dick) Ellis, the Australian MI6 officer who ran the Interdoc UK office from Norfolk Street in London during the 1960s
32. The University Arms Hotel, Cambridge, location of the second Interdoc conference on British soil, in September 1966
33. Bertil Häggman (far left), Interdoc's main contact in Sweden, seen here honouring an East German refugee killed while trying to escape to the West, Trelleborg, 1964. Much of the work of the Inform group – some of it funded by the West Germans – concentrated on counter-acting GDR propaganda in Sweden
34. Frans A.M. Alting von Geusau, who created and led the John F. Kennedy Institute at Tilburg University from 1967 to 1985
35. H.G. (Dik) Groenewald at a reception for OSS veterans at Huis ten Bosch, 16 September 1974, organized by the Netherlands–US Foundation. Prince Bernhard is behind his left shoulder. Together with Cees van den Heuvel, in the mid-1970s Groenewald led the attempt to mobilize the Federation of European–American Organizations into a more active body
36. Rio Praaning at a JASON reception. A protégé of Cees van den Heuvel, Praaning played a vital role in transforming the Atlantische Commissie during the 1980s
37. Cees van den Heuvel at the reception marking his retirement from the Atlantische Commissie, 1986. Behind him on the right is his son Christiaan
38. Members of IIIF reunited: Peter Becker (left) and Dietmar Töppel, Munich, June 2008
39. Members of SOEV-OWI reunited – Willem Couwenberg (left), Lyda van der Bree and Christiaan van den Heuvel outside Van Stolkweg 10, January 2006

Series Foreword

We have published a number of studies in the *Palgrave Macmillan Transnational History Series* that examine the ways in which transnational history and national history intersect – that is, when certain national developments become linked to global phenomena, and when transnational themes take on domestic significance in some countries. Thus, for instance, *The Chinese in Britain, 1800–Present* by Gregor Benton and Edmund Terence Gomez gives a detailed description of Chinese migrants and residents in Britain, but the subject is relevant not just to British or to Chinese history but to global affairs (economic, cultural, military) in which overseas Chinese played important roles. To take another example, *Telegraphic Imperialism* by Deep Kanta Lahiri Choudhury establishes fascinating connections between the development of the telegraph, a transnational phenomenon, and social and political movements in India that were facilitated by the new means of communication. It is clear that both the national and the transnational offer crucial contexts for understanding the past, and for this reason the intersection between the two perspectives is one of the most interesting areas for historical inquiry.

This book also deals with national affairs – in particular the history of the Netherlands – in relation to such transnational themes as ideology, cooperative research, and international conferences. But the primary context for the discussion of these themes is the Cold War, an international, geopolitical phenomenon. The relationship, therefore, between international history and transnational history is presented in all its richness and complexity.

We call our series "transnational history" rather than "international history" because we believe there are some important differences between the two. International history usually deals with interrelations among nations, in particular at the political and strategic level. The key questions in international relations relate to diplomacy and war. Nations seek to protect themselves against would-be enemies; they define their respective national interests and hope they may be reconciled through diplomatic efforts; they seek to construct some sort of a stable "international system" through the balance of power and other mechanisms; and when such balance breaks down, war can result. All these are subjects of study in international history. It is not surprising that many studies in that genre deal with origins of wars, both hot and cold, and efforts to re-establish peace, however short-lived it might prove to be.

Transnational history, in contrast, is concerned less with affairs among sovereign states than with interactions among individuals and their communities. These are "non-state actors" and so often act without restraint by governments. Moreover, they pursue objectives little related to geopolitical questions (military balance, national security, war), such as the cure of diseases, control of drugs, prevention of human rights abuses, and the protection of the natural environment. Transnational actors and themes tend to develop with their own momentum, thus following their own chronologies separate from ones that privilege national or international geopolitical affairs.

This book offers a fascinating instance in which international and transnational themes come together. Its overall framework is the Cold War, a quintessentially geopolitical phenomenon, but the volume contains a discussion of private and semi-private networks of intellectuals in the Netherlands and elsewhere in Europe who sought to understand and to influence their Soviet counterparts. The focus is on the International Documentation and Information Centre (Interdoc) that was established in The Hague and was active during the 1960s in engaging in ideological research and campaigns to counter Soviet propaganda. Former intelligence officials were involved in Interdoc's founding. There is little doubt, then, that this story forms a part of Cold War history, an aspect that is relatable to psychological warfare. The transnational significance lies in the way in which various meetings and research projects came to focus on "Western values" that were to be formulated and protected, and to seek to establish global networks of like-minded individuals and organizations. In time, during the 1970s, Interdoc served as an instrument for reaching out to intellectuals in Soviet-bloc countries.

Some volumes in our series have documented the growing contact between both sides of the Iron Curtain during the 1960s and beyond. This book offers additional insight into the ways in which a geopolitical "reality" (Cold War) was steadily transformed into a transnational phenomenon.

Akira Iriye
Rana Mitter
Jeff Michaels

Acknowledgements

This book is largely based on the papers of C.C. van den Heuvel located at the National Archives in The Hague. The papers are extensive but incomplete: some files were destroyed for security reasons even during his lifetime. Files on Denmark and Royal Dutch Shell, for instance, are no longer present, and records of Interdoc board meetings are scarce. These gaps could be filled by making use of other archival sources in Europe and the US. It is probably impossible to compile a fully comprehensive history of Interdoc, such was the diversity of its activities and the semi-clandestine nature of much of its business. Nevertheless, it has been possible to put together the Interdoc story, the people and ideas that drove it, and its place within Cold War history.

In completing this book I have benefited greatly from the support of many people along the way. First, I would like to thank the Van den Heuvel family members, Christiaan, Elme, and Marona, who did everything they could to encourage my progress and to assist the research. Special thanks also goes to the archivist at the National Archives, Robbert Jan Hageman, who accommodated without any problem my erratic visits to The Hague over a period of seven years. The Roosevelt Study Center in Middelburg has been the perfect base for this project, providing the encouragement, financial support, and research time without which none of this would ever have come about. Of the many people whom I interviewed, I would particularly like to thank Peter Becker, Willem Couwenberg, and Pieter Koerts for their willingness to share their recollections on several occasions. I am grateful to those who provided me with personal papers that added greatly to the final story: Gunhild Bohm-Geyer, Willem Couwenberg, Edo Groenewald, Bertil Häggman, and Uwe Holl.

I also must thank those who assisted in the research along the way with useful advice and documents: Bernard Ludwig, Adrian Hänni, and Erich Schmidt-Eenboom. Paul Koedijk opened up the Interdoc story back in the mid-1990s, making this book possible – thank you, Paul; I hope the result meets your expectations. Bram Boxhoorn kindly allowed me to access the archive of the Atlantische Commissie, a vital component in the 1970s, for which I am thankful. Many other colleagues have offered their time, advice, help, and valuable information since the project began, for which I am very grateful: Pierre Abramovici, Scott Anthony, Valérie Aubourg, Oliver Bange, Robert Crommelin, Dennis Bos, Olivier Cabon, Helge Danielsen, Luc van Dongen, Dick Engelen, Thomas Gijswijt, Johannes Grossman, Peer Henrik Hansen, Constant Hijzen, Mike Kender, Stefan Kieninger, Joni Krekola, Rob Lawa, Denis Leroux, Kristian Marsch, Donald Marsh, Holger Nehring, Idelle

Nissila, Karen Paget, Ingeborg Philipsen, Nick Rutter, Thomas Scheuer, David Snyder, Han Verduin, Stephanie Waske.

Finally, thanks must go to the publishers at Palgrave Macmillan (English edition) in Britain and Boom (Dutch edition) in the Netherlands, who remained admirably patient, and to two anonymous referees who provided very useful comments and advice which definitely improved the manuscript. Of course, responsibility for the final version rests entirely with me.

Abbreviations

IIIF	Section F (Psychological Warfare) of the BND's Research and Analysis Division
AAEE	American–Asian Educational Exchange
AC	Atlantische Commissie/Atlantic Commission
AESP	Académie Européenne de Sciences Politiques
AFL–CIO	American Federation of Labor–Congress of Industrial Organizations
AfO	Arbeitsgemeinschaft für Ostfragen
AIVD	Algemene Inlichtingen en Veiligheidsdienst (successor to the BVD in 2002)
AKU	Algemene Kunstzijde Unie, later AkzoNobel
ANJV	Algemeen Nederlandse Jeugd Verbond/Dutch Youth League
APACL	Asian People's Anti-Communist League
ASIS	American Society for Industrial Security
ATA	Atlantic Treaty Association
AWF	Aktionskomitee Wahret die Freiheit/Action Committee for Truth and Freedom
BBC	British Broadcasting Corporation
BDJ	Bund Deutscher Jugend
BMG	Bundesministerium für gesamtdeutsche Fragen
BND	Bundesnachrichtendienst
BPM	Batavische Petroleum Maatschappij (a division of Royal Dutch Shell)
BRFA	British Reserve Forces Association
BSC	British Security Coordination
BUI	British United Industrialists
BVD	Binnenlands Veiligheidsdienst/Dutch Security Service (1949–2002)
CAS	Committee on Atlantic Studies
CC	Common Cause
CCF	Congress for Cultural Freedom
CDU	Christlich Demokratische Union
CEDI	Centre Européen de Documentation et d'Information
CESES	Centro di studi e ricerche sui problemi economico-sociali/ Centre for Research on Socio-Economic Problems
CEVS	Centrum voor Europese Veiligheid en Samenwerking/ Centre for European Security and Cooperation
CIA	Central Intelligence Agency
CIAS	Comité International d'Information et d'Action Sociale
CIDA	Centre d'Information et de Documentation Atlantique

xiv List of Abbreviations

CIDCC	Comité International pour la Défense de la Civilisation Chrétienne
Cominform	Communist Information Bureau
Comintern	Communist International
Confindustria	Confederazione Generale dell'Industria Italiana/General Confederation of Italian Industry
COSEC	Coordinating Secretariat of the International Student Conference
CPN	Communistische Partij Nederland
CSCE	Conference on Security and Cooperation in Europe
CSU	Christlich-Soziale Union
DM	Deutsche Mark/deutschmark
DSC	Defensie Studie Centrum/Defence Study Centre
EC	European Community
ECCS	European Union of Christian Democratic and Conservative Students
EDS	European Democratic Students
EEC	European Economic Community
EL	Economic League
EPPC	Ethics and Public Policy Center
FBI	Federal Bureau of Investigation
FDP	Freie Demokratische Partei/German Liberal Party
FEAO	Federation of European–American Organizations
FEC	Free Europe Committee
FHO	Fremde Heere Ost
FIR	Fédération Internationale des Résistants
FWF	Forum World Features
G-2	US Army Intelligence
GDR	German Democratic Republic
ICCS	International Union of Christian Democratic and Conservative Students
ICTO	Interkerkelijk Comité Tweezijdige Ontwapening/Interdenominational Committee for Bilateral Disarmament
IKV	Interkerkelijk Vredesberaad/Interdenominational Peace Commission
Interdoc	International Documentation and Information Centre
InVoLu	Interne Voorlichting Luchtmacht/Internal Information Service of the Dutch Air Force
IPC	International Preparatory Committee (for WFDY–IUS festivals)
IRD	Information Research Department of the British Foreign Office
ISAY	International Secretariat for Atlantic Youth
ISC	International Student Conference

List of Abbreviations xv

ISoC	Institute for the Study of Conflict
ISMUN	International Student Movement for the UN
ISS	Institute for Strategic Studies
IUS	International Union of Students
IY	Interdoc Youth
JASON	Jong Atlantisch Samenwerkings Orgaan Nederland
JFK	John F. Kennedy Institute (Tilburg)
KGB	Komitet gosoedarstvennoj bezopasnosti (Committee for State Security)
KLM	Koninklijke Luchtvaart Maatschappij/Dutch Airlines
KVP	Katholieke Volkspartij/Catholic People's Party
LDP	Liberal Democratic Party (Japan)
MDIC	Multilateral Disarmament Information Centre
MIT	Massachusetts Institute of Technology
NAM	National Association of Manufacturers (US)
NATIS	NATO Information Service
NATO	North Atlantic Treaty Organization
NFR	Nationale Federatieve Raad van het Voormalige Verzet Nederland
NIVV	Nederlands Instituut voor Vredesvraagstukken/Netherlands Institute for Peace Research
NJG	Nederlandse Jeugd Gemeenschap/Netherlands Youth Association
NRC	Nieuwe Rotterdamse Courant
NS	Nederlandse Spoorwegen/Dutch Railways
NSA	National Student Association
NSC	National Security Council
NSIC	National Strategy Information Center
NSR	Nederlandse Studenten Raad/Netherlands Student Council
NTS	Narodno-Trudovoy Soyuz Rossiyskikh Solidarstov/National Alliance of Russian Solidarists
NUPI	Norwegian Institute of Foreign Affairs
OAS	Organisation Armée Secrète
OGEM	Overzeese Gas- en Elektriciteitsmaatschappij
OI	Ost-Institut (Switzerland)
OPSJ	Organisatie van Progressieve Studerende Jeugd/Organisation of Progressive Student Youth
OSS	Office of Strategic Services
OWI	Oost-West Instituut/East–West Institute
PCI	Partito Comunista Italiano
PSB	Psychological Strategy Board
PTT	Staatsbedrijf der Posterijen, Telegrafie en Telefonie/National Post, Telegraph, and Telephone Company
RGR	Rassemblement des gauches républicaines
RHSA	Reichssicherheitshauptamt/Reich Security Office

SCESC	Soviet Committee for European Security and Cooperation
SDECE	Service de Documentation Extérieure et de Contre-Espionnage
SDES	Société pour le Développement de l'Economie Suisse
SFMO	Stichting Fondsenwerving Militaire Oorlogs- en Dienstslachtoffers/Foundation for Fundraising for Military Casualties in War
SHAPE	Supreme Headquarters Allied Powers Europe
SIB	Studentenvereniging voor Internationale Betrekkingen/Student Society for International Relations
SIHE	Society for the Investigation of Human Ecology
SOEV	Stichting voor Onderzoek van Ecologische Vraagstukken/Foundation for the Investigation of Problems of Ecology
SORELS	Société Coopérative d'Etude et de Promotion des Echanges Economiques et Culturels
SPD	Sozialdemokratische Partei Deutschlands/German Social Democratic Party
SV	Staatsveiligheid/State Security (Belgium)
SVP	Stichting Vredespolitiek/Foundation for Peace Politics
SYL	Suomen ylioppilaskuntien liitto/Finnish Student Association
SYS	Scandinavian Youth Service
TD	Technischer Dienst (of the Bund Deutscher Jugend)
TUC	Trades Union Congress
UCID	Unione Cristiana Imprenditori Dirigenti/Christian Union of Business Executives
UDHR	Universal Declaration of Human Rights
UIRD	Union internationale de la résistance et de la déportation/International Union of Resistance and Deportee Movements
UN	United Nations
UNESCO	United Nations Educational, Scientific and Cultural Organization
USIA	US Information Agency
VFF	Volksbund für Frieden und Freiheit
VV	Vrede en Vrijheid
WACL	World Anti-Communist League
WASC	World Alliance for Student Cooperation
WAY	World Assembly of Youth
WCDE	Werkcomité voor Opvoeding tot Democratie/Working Committee for Democratic Education
WFDY	World Federation of Democratic Youth
WVF	World Veterans Federation
ZWO	Nederlandse Organisatie voor Zuiver-Wetenschappelijk Onderzoek/Netherlands Organization for Pure Research

Introduction: The Communist Challenge

> How do you tell a communist? Well, it's someone who reads Marx and Lenin. And how do you tell an anti-communist? It's someone who understands Marx and Lenin.
>
> President Ronald Reagan, Arlington, 1987

> Karl Marx stated that theories and ideas become material power as soon as they have conquered the consciousness of the masses. Let us see that this dictum proves true in our sense and in accordance with our intentions.
>
> Rolf Geyer, 1968[1]

From George Kennan's description of the Soviet government as "a conspiracy within a conspiracy" in 1946 to President Reagan's vilification of the USSR as an "evil empire" in 1983, US–Soviet relations were marked during the Cold War by deep aversion and distrust.[2] Attempts to normalize these relations through diplomacy proved difficult, if not impossible. Leaders in both East and West occasionally recognized the futility of the superpower contest, but convictions on both sides that they represented "a superior way of life" ultimately prevented any real concessions.[3] In this fundamental clash of interests, both sides "needed to change the world in order to prove the universal applicability of their ideologies".[4] The existence of an enemy also served useful purposes. Stalinist propaganda directed its criticism at a duplicitous West encircling and threatening the Soviet Union, thereby justifying the Soviet empire abroad and the repression of dissent at home.[5] This "war on the mind" was driven by fear – fear of defeat, of destruction, of being inferior and second-best to a despised adversary.[6] This fear was expressed on both sides, from the witch-hunts of Senator McCarthy and the House Un-American Activities Committee in the 1950s through to the silencing of Sakharov and other Soviet dissidents in the 1970s and 1980s. "Don't talk to communists," the message went in the West, "because if you do, you'll lose the debate and become brainwashed." The only way to deal with this fear was to deny everything that the adversary stood for.

The Cold War was above all a war of ideologies. "Power", in the words of British historian Nigel Gould-Davis, "came in large measure to be defined in ideological terms, gains or losses during the Cold War being measured by the global advance or retreat of regime types."[7] But, while the struggle for supremacy continued, there were those who saw it as a negative, highly dangerous zero-sum game and who looked for ways to overcome it. This book is about a network of individuals and institutes based in Western Europe that sought to end the fear and pave the way for an end to the Cold War. At the centre of this network was Interdoc, the International Documentation and Information Centre, located from 1962 to 1986 in the plush suburban street Van Stolkweg in The Hague, the Netherlands seat of government. Interdoc was the result of discussions in the late 1950s between Western European intelligence officers, political philosophers, and businessmen, who were determined to deal with communism as an intellectual adversary, not a paranoid existential threat. With French–Dutch–German cooperation at its core, it facilitated a trans-European network of allied institutions that included the British, the Belgians, the Danes, the Italians, the Swiss, the Swedes – and, of course, the Americans. This remarkable exercise in European integration aimed to consolidate resistance to communist infiltration and to respond in kind by promoting "Western values" in the East. The Central Intelligence Agency (CIA) was present all along – "present at the creation", one might say – but Interdoc was predominantly a European operation that reflected European Cold War concerns.

At the time of Interdoc's founding, following the debacle of the Hungarian uprising in 1956, the Cold War division between East and West was looking more and more permanent, and the dangers of nuclear conflagration – Berlin, Cuba, or by accident – were ever more present. There had to be a way out that would avoid conflict. But how? The US was the dominant force in the West when it came to opposing communist influence, be that militarily or in the field of information and propaganda. By the late 1950s this was becoming counterproductive, because "the overarching nature of US power" determined that "the strategic values of Washington held sway, and the emergence of a specifically European strategic culture was further constrained".[8] The Western Europeans largely regarded US military commitment as a necessity – even de Gaulle did not want the US to withdraw fully from the continent – but the result was a struggle to find a European voice on security concerns. CIA operations intervened in all aspects of Western civil society, so that every identifiable social group became a target in the ideological war.[9] Managing opinion and waging the war of ideas against communism by both covert and overt methods was a top priority – if not the very contest that defined the Cold War itself. "By the early 1950s," writes Richard Aldrich, "operations to influence the world by unseen methods – the hidden hand – became ubiquitous and seemed to transform even everyday aspects of society into an extension of this battleground."[10]

The story of Interdoc not only supports this claim, it also expands our understanding of how the ideological war was fought. CIA control and its determination to take more than it gave to its Western partners prevented any joint Western effort. National rivalries, lack of trust, and concerns over security leaks largely excluded a coordinated response to Soviet-bloc psychological warfare. Western intelligence and security services were as much occupied with each other's activities as they were with those of their Soviet-bloc adversaries. As the maxim goes, "there are no friendly secret services, only the secret services of friendly states".[11] The issue of strategic intelligence cooperation remains controversial, right up to recent studies that have questioned the reliance of US national security on faulty intelligence from allied nations prior to 9/11.[12] Intelligence cooperation says a great deal about the state of play between allies. As Wesley Wark has argued, "the secret underside of alliance systems bears study for what it reveals of common perceptions of threats, degrees of mutual trust and confidence, the development of mechanisms for information exchange, and the status of intelligence within partner states."[13] The Interdoc project exposes how difficult it was to achieve a broad consensus on an anti-communist strategy. It was problematic for the Western Europeans to develop their own collective response to the Soviet threat – their own "strategic culture" – and attempts to overcome these obstacles through multilateral cooperation via North Atlantic Treaty Organization (NATO) had mixed success.[14] How could a response be organized?

The Soviet challenge: Peaceful coexistence

Interdoc was created because the West was on the defensive in the ideological war. Leninist thinking had pioneered the notion of the political vanguard leading and educating the rest of society, and the use of front organizations to garner support, mobilize public opinion, and seize the moral high ground had already been perfected by Willi Münzenberg in the 1920s. Capitalizing on the widespread wish for peace in the 1920s and 1930s as a way to broaden popular support for Soviet interests – effectively "packaging" Marxist–Leninist principles and protagonists within a morally appealing "united front" – was a central part of Münzenberg's activities for the Comintern (Communist International) in those years.[15] This approach was consolidated after World War II by the revival of the international communist movement through the Cominform (Communist Information Bureau) in September 1947. The US National Security Council (NSC) reported in December that year that Moscow aimed "not merely to undermine the prestige of the US and the effectiveness of its national policy but to weaken and divide world opinion to a point where effective opposition to Soviet designs [would be] no longer attainable".[16] With hindsight it seems remarkable that a one-party political system that made large-scale use of terror and the negation of individual rights could ever attain wide appeal. Surely the exposure of the gulag, the show trial, and the lack of individual freedoms undermined Soviet claims of "progress"? Yet for a while it seemed as if "the wind was blowing our way", in the words of Italian communist Fausto Gallo.[17] Soviet propaganda played cleverly on people's concerns and desires – and their mistrust of American motives. Fear of nuclear warfare enabled the Soviet-orchestrated Peace campaign to garner widespread support from March 1950 onwards, thanks also to the prestige it gained from Pablo Picasso's initial involvement.[18] Communist propaganda skilfully connected with the hopes and wishes of a nervous populace and an progressive intelligentsia. Castigating America as the leader of soulless warmongering capitalism resonated with much European opinion.

Following Stalin's death in 1953, the Soviet Union under first Malenkov and then Bulganin and Khrushchev adopted a strategy of "peaceful coexistence". Stalin's policies had generated widespread fear in the West, and his successors "wanted to dismantle this foundation, reduce anti-Soviet fears among the middle classes of Western Europe, and encourage pacifist elements within NATO member countries".[19] The Kremlin's sudden search for stability in international affairs, including peace proposals for a demilitarized, unified Germany, brought pressure to bear on Western governments adamantly opposing such overtures.[20] The advent of the thermonuclear age – marked by the detonation of US hydrogen bombs on Bikini Atoll during February–May 1954, code-named Operation Castle – brought home the hanging threat of "the termination of all life on earth".[21] The Kremlin seized the opportunity to shift the emphasis of the East–West contest towards a competitive struggle between communism and capitalism: "peaceful coexistence" between rival systems. Drawing from Lenin and Bukharin, Khrushchev spoke out at the infamous Twentieth Party Congress in 1956 and thereafter against the assumption of inevitable war with the forces of capitalism and in favour of a relentless contest for economic superiority. Cooperation and competition with the West would necessarily operate side by side as the class struggle was pursued unabated, any gesture of reconciliation being no more than a tactical manoeuvre on the way to communist victory. Meanwhile revolutionary war would be waged as appropriate in the decolonizing parts of the globe.[22]

The launch of the first Sputnik satellite on 4 October 1957 illustrated the technological prowess of the Soviet Union. In October 1959 Khrushchev followed this up by outlining his position in no less than the journal of the US Council on Foreign Relations, *Foreign Affairs*:

> In its simplest expression it signifies the repudiation of war as a means of solving controversial issues [...] We say to the leaders of the capitalist states: Let us try out in practice whose system is better, let us compete without war [...] The main thing is to keep to the positions of

ideological struggle, without resorting to arms in order to prove that one is right [...] We believe that ultimately that system will be victorious on the globe which will offer the nations greater opportunities for improving their material and spiritual life.[23]

Such a message was persuasive, and the new approach raised many questions about the anti-communist strategy of the West. It was much easier for Western leaders to confront an obviously bellicose enemy than one apparently keen on international accommodation. Soviet strategy turned the tables on the West and made the excesses of American anti-communism seem like the main threat to international peace. US NSC memorandum 5501, issued in January 1955, declared that the potential consequences of the peaceful coexistence strategy "will probably present the free world with its most serious challenge and greatest danger in the next few years". Fear, as US Secretary of State John Foster Dulles realized, would no longer be enough to hold the broad anti-communist coalition together. President Eisenhower tried to convince the world of the peaceful outlook of the US by means of a series of counter-initiatives during the 1950s. The President's inner circle "interpreted 'peaceful coexistence' as a psychological warfare strategy more menacing than Stalin's confrontational diplomacy because it enhanced Soviet prestige at the same time that it fed doubts about the prudence of American anti-communism".[24] The US Information Agency (USIA) admitted in 1957 that "Soviet-Style 'socialism' has increasing attractive power throughout the world and can defeat capitalism in a peaceful competition in the world market place of ideas".[25] It was now a question of which socio-economic system was superior, not just which bomb was more destructive. What was at stake was the guiding image for the future. Which provided the best hopes for progress, justice, and equality: communism or capitalism? And which side could transmit its message the most effectively to make it at least *appear* as if it was winning?

The American response illustrated once again the shortcomings of the West in the psychological contest. Increased efforts on all fronts to display the superiority of Western freedoms, good intentions, and desire for peace simply negated the Soviet Union as the source of all tyranny, duplicity, and lies. The aim to "contain" the Soviet Union was too one-dimensional and limited because it viewed all global politics from a single perspective. The potential for propelling political change in the East through increased contacts was recognized, but so were the dangers.[26] Meanwhile, attempts to craft a counter-rhetoric were also ineffective. The British Foreign Office's Information Research Department (IRD), the government unit responsible for developing and distributing the anti-communist message, went through a whole range of possibilities – Peaceful Cooperation, Constructive Cooperation, Cooperation in Freedom, Cooperation in One World – before deciding on Coexistence Plus.[27] It was difficult to fix on "a superior alternative concept" to compete on ground already staked out by Moscow.[28] The British were stuck: "We ought I am sure to steer absolutely clear of any attempt to sell Western democratic forms, while remaining true to democratic principles."[29] There was only the forlorn hope that "the Harvard and Columbia intellectuals" would solve this dilemma.[30] But the Americans were in a similar state. Dean Rusk, President Kennedy's Secretary of State, spoke unconvincingly of the "world of free choice and free cooperation" as opposed to "the world of coercion".[31] Lucius Battle, looking back in 1971, admitted that "The same sort of speeches were still being made, the same kind of arguments were still being advanced in the early 1960s that were advanced in the late 1940s."[32] Interdoc represented an alternative path. The European security and intelligence establishment was concerned about the long-term effects on Western morale of public support for a relaxation of East–West tensions. A new approach was needed. As one German official put it, "it is in no way sufficient to approach communism by negating its ideological theses".[33] Or another: if Moscow wanted to fight out the Cold War as an ideological contest of peaceful coexistence and dialogue, "then we would fight".[34]

The Interdoc circle

Several figures played key roles in bringing Interdoc together. There was Louis Einthoven, the first post-war chief of the Dutch security service (BVD: Binnenlands Veiligheidsdienst), who wrote in his autobiography that "above all international cooperation was necessary in order to exchange details on the global movement being directed from one or other central point (Moscow and later Peking)".[35] His West German counterpart was Reinhard Gehlen, who established the Bundesnachrichtendienst (BND) under the tutelage of the Americans but focused on specifically German security concerns. There were the French psychological warfare expert Antoine Bonnemaison, who saw that the best Western response to peaceful coexistence involved reversing the principles of Leninism; Brian Crozier, the "free agent" who worked with (not for) the American, British, and French services in the pursuit of an effective anti-communism; and Allen Dulles, the CIA director from 1953 to 1961 who prompted Einthoven to seek greater European intelligence cooperation but who did not want to pay for it. Various other exotic Cold Warriors crossed the Interdoc path: Count Carl Armfelt, the Finnish-American son of a diplomat whose support for anti-Soviet sabotage operations remains shrouded in mystery; Geoffrey Stewart-Smith, the Cold War entrepreneur regarded as a "crank" by the British government services he disparaged; and Georges Albertini, the Vichy sympathizer who continued his anti-communism unabated via *Est-Ouest* after World War II.

At the centre of this group were two individuals who for the first decade of Interdoc's existence put their stamp on its ideas and operations. One was Rolf Geyer, who, as the youngest officer in the general staff of the Wehrmacht's

Army Group East, knew Gehlen from World War II. Geyer did not come from a military background but had been driven by a sense of national duty, signing up with the artillery already in March 1929 and graduating as an officer from the *Kriegsakademie* in 1938. Having served in both France and on the Eastern Front, Geyer was able to avoid the Russians in 1945 and ended up in a British prisoner of war camp, eventually being released in 1947. Economic and family privations undermined his ambitions for a university career in philosophy, and he was eventually brought into the BND by Gehlen in 1959 for the specific purpose of developing the psychological warfare section.[36] Nicknamed "the professor" and a follower of Rudolph Steiner, Geyer pursued the cause of East–West rapprochement with well-read and erudite sophistication – some would say *over*-sophistication. Central to this outlook was the anomaly of two Germanies, an artificial division situated at the heart of Europe's tense Cold War balance, and a division that had to be overcome to achieve any lasting peace.

Geyer's main associate in the Interdoc endeavour, paradoxically enough, was a former World War II resistance fighter, the Dutchman Cees Cornelis (C.C.) van den Heuvel. The common mission against communist totalitarianism overcame any obstacles in this regard. If Geyer was the brains, Van den Heuvel was the perfect operator. Those who knew him speak of his powers of persuasion, his talents for entrepreneurship and networking, and his ability to turn ideas into reality. The Dutchman was a "warhorse" seeped in the theory and practice of psychological warfare, but he loved Graham Greene and maintained a British style in humour, language, and demeanour.[37] The son of a powerful Protestant politician, Van den Heuvel was 21 and a member of the coastal artillery at the outbreak of the war. From March 1943 to May 1945 he was a member of the resistance network known as the Albrecht Group, working underground and constantly on the run. Throughout this period Albrecht would provide valuable information on German positions to the Dutch intelligence service in London.[38] Like many from this strongly Protestant network, he joined the Dutch security apparatus after the war: the Bureau Nationale Veiligheid in 1945 and its successor the Centrale Veiligheidsdienst in 1947, where he undertook the task of checking the *bona fides* of the service's new recruits. When Einthoven became chief of the newly formed BVD in 1949 he immediately made Van den Heuvel the head of training. With a rock-solid self-belief grounded in the resistance experience and the Calvinist faith, he seemed destined for the top of the service.[39] Instead, together with Einthoven, he laid out the plans for Interdoc and went private to pursue a new kind of campaign. His BVD past would ensure that he remained a controversial figure in Dutch public life thereafter, everyone assuming that he worked for *someone*: "I had a very good contact with the CIA [...] But my relationship was that I was absolutely free. They asked me to do things, not in their service but just in my own orbit. Many speculated that I was a CIA agent but I wasn't." Van den Heuvel's links with the CIA were so close that in the 1980s a word from him would secure direct access to CIA director William Casey.[40] The joke was that, while half of The Hague thought he *was* CIA, the other half thought he was Committee for State Security (KGB: Komitet gosoedarstvennoj bezopasnosti).[41]

In the BVD Van den Heuvel sank himself into the Marxist way of thinking and impressed on his trainees how communists thought and the methods they used to infiltrate organizations across Western civil society. The "Cold War" – the war of ideologies – represented a new phase in human conflict. For the first time in history the destructive potential of military conflict meant that "non-violent weapons" – the weapons of psychological warfare and propaganda – were now of crucial importance, so much so that they could even decide the outcome.[42] Training courses run by the CIA and MI6 took him and many others from the BVD to Washington, DC, and London. Directly involved in anti-communist propaganda and dirty tricks operations during the 1950s, by the end of that decade he was convinced that such capers were insufficient to deal with the implications of peaceful coexistence.[43] Khrushchev wanted the West to believe that the Cold War was over, but "peaceful coexistence" only meant that the contest had been shifted from a military to an ideological front. "Soviet society is organized", as Isaiah Berlin eloquently wrote in 1957, "not for happiness, comfort, liberty, justice, or personal relationships, but for combat."[44] For Western security services the danger was that the new message from Moscow would obscure this and lull many into a false sense of security, allowing communism surreptitiously to gain more converts. As Van den Heuvel wrote in 1959, "the gap between communists and non-communists is narrowing, making it easier for communism to influence the non-communists".[45] Thus "the containment policy which was an appropriate course at the time of the cold war, can no longer be the general policy in a time when the Communist world – whatever the reasons may be – tries to establish better relations with the Western world".[46] But there was only so much that a security service could do from behind the scenes. A network of public institutes was needed to openly engage civil society and steer public opinion in the right direction. People in the West needed to be reminded of the basic values that held their societies together, and the security services – via Interdoc – would remind them. To make this credible it had to be based on the actual improvement of people's material and social conditions. This gave the operation something of a progressive air:

> Interdoc represents the view that the intellectual discussion with world communism, and the political and economic defence of the democratic system in government, society, and the economy against attack by totalitarian world communism, also includes the full realization of our own freedoms. The protection, preservation, development and defence of our way of life is the best anti-communism.[47]

Understanding the enemy was therefore only part of the story. By the late 1950s the Soviet Studies community in the US was vast, being well funded by a government and a military keen to learn about every aspect of the adversary. Yet the sheer scale of the American "military-intellectual complex", with its diversity of expertise across the humanities and social sciences, prevented any wholly consistent message from emerging. Neither was it particularly geared towards producing a coherent policy response.[48] In contrast Interdoc operated on a much smaller scale, designed to act as a "clearing house" to facilitate and distribute research on the communist world, its methods of subversion, and the appropriate response, all in one integrated apparatus. The analysis was to be as objective and non-judgemental as possible. Communism was not going to disappear in the short term, and the actualities, drives, possibilities, and shifts within the communist world therefore needed to be tracked and understood in detail. Communism was a fact of modern life, not a temporary security threat. At its peak Interdoc was distributing 25 periodicals in four languages (English, German, French, and Spanish), ranging from the weekly *Notes on Communist and Communist-Sponsored Activities as reported by Communist Sources* to the monthly *Religion and Church in the Communist Orbit*, the bimonthly *East–West Contacts*, and the trimonthly *Activities of the Communist World Organizations* and *Beiträge zur psychopolitischen Lage der europäischen Ostblockländer*. Selected publications, such as *The Position of Top Ranking General Officers in the Leadership of the Soviet Union* (1969), were issued in Japanese. Some of Interdoc's output would go out under its own imprint; other material would be "unattributable" (no source being stated). The material for these digests was gathered by the intelligence world, making use of researchers wholly separate from, connected with or wholly within the services involved. One nation's output would be translated and circulated via another nation's network. Conferences were regularly organized to bring the intelligence world together with the worlds of academia, journalism, and government to consider issues of common interest in the Cold War contest: transatlantic relations, East–West exchanges, political radicalism, guerrilla warfare, the situation in Africa. Alongside these activities Interdoc also involved a *training* component: it was deeply involved with the whole issue of citizenship, rights, and duties, and with how to nurture the "free individual" in a time of ideological (if not existential) crisis.

Interdoc was a European response to European dilemmas, eschewing dependence on the US and deeply imbued with an offensive outlook. Khrushchev had announced at the Twentieth Party Congress that "countries with differing social systems can do more than exist side by side. It is necessary to proceed further, to improve relations, to strengthen confidence among countries."[49] The Germans, Dutch, and French at the centre of Interdoc took him at his word, looking to turn the tables on Moscow's call for dialogue. Peaceful coexistence should neither be exposed and rejected as a con trick nor accepted as simply a new form of cooperation, but must be engaged with precisely as the ideological struggle that Lenin intended. Liberal democratic values would be exported, individual by individual, with the goal of gradually wearing down the aggressive edges of Soviet thought and action, strengthening revisionist tendencies and undermining the stereotypical negative image of the West.[50] In this way the Cold War divisions could be overcome, step by step, as this statement from Van den Heuvel's East–West Institute in 1965 makes clear:

> The West [...] has an opportunity to improve its image in the communist world. It can also favourably influence positive developments there, to its advantage. Through this the chances of decreasing tension between East and West will also be increased. If Western ideas are able to penetrate more and more in the communist world, this can have – in combination with liberalisation and a weakening of ideology – a moderating effect on the aggressive totalitarian drives of that system.[51]

For Geyer, the foremost mission was to deal with the existence of the German Democratic Republic (GDR), moving from denial and rejection to dialogue and engagement in a sure-footed process to overcome the Cold War division. Van den Heuvel accepted that the West German link – and West German finance – was the basis of Interdoc's existence, but he refused to be boxed in by the demands of any other power. Dutch efforts to bridge national interests to form a trans-European and even transatlantic network were central to what Interdoc was all about. He summed it up in this way:

> The effort should be international. In the first place because Communism is operating internationally. Therefore it should be met internationally. In the second place because Western values have a far wider range than the Western world. The "Universal Declaration of Human Rights of Man" is for the greater part based on Western values.[52]

How should Interdoc as an organization be classified? It was certainly more than a mere front for hidden interests (although there was definitely an awareness and usage of Münzenberg's strategies and tactics).[53] In some ways it acted as a "state-private network": a private organization brought into being by a state apparatus to project a world view in civil society in support of Western interests (freedom, democracy, anti-communism).[54] The CIA's arsenal of state-private networks reached into all areas of society to ensure that non-communist cultural ideas were active and visible. The most notorious example from this campaign, the Congress for Cultural Freedom (CCF), acted as a framework through which a Cold War intellectual consensus could be projected through books, journals, and conferences that rejected the Marxist–Leninist world view.[55] But Interdoc was more complex than this suggests. First, it occupied a "grey area" somewhere between the public and private worlds. While the intelligence and security services brought it into existence, they did so in a way that blurred the boundary between the "secret state" and the general public. Personnel actually left the intelligence world to join Interdoc, or at least occupied positions deliberately on the edge of the intelligence world in an attempt to achieve public credibility. In contrast to the CCF, which was dedicated above all to funding, organizing, and amplifying the "right" voices in the Cold War, Interdoc was intended to act as a revolving door between the secret and non-secret worlds, allowing ideas to travel in both directions and acting as a public distribution point for material collected by the intelligence establishment's own research base.

Second, it is not possible to reduce Interdoc to nothing more than the designs of one particular nation state, because it sought to overcome and *transcend* national differences for the sake of the Western Alliance. Only then could the West effectively meet the Soviet challenge of peaceful coexistence, which was bent on sowing division. In this sense it was a transnational organization, offering its services to national clients ranging across government and society. This distinction is important because "transnational political activities [...] do not derive their power and authority from the state" – they are (or at least attempt to be) more flexible in purpose and outlook.[56] Third, it was as much an elite "policy network" as it was an attempt to mould public opinion. Policy networks possess "similar compatible values and world views", "broadly agree on desirable policy developments" and aim to "pool resources, form coalitions and influence media reporting and public communication within and beyond nation-states".[57] Fourth, while the intelligence and security establishment was instrumental in bringing Interdoc about, the new network always acted according to a strong commercial drive: it would provide services for others – be they information, training, or organization – but at a price. Interdoc was supposed to be *self-supporting*, or at the very least it was meant to use its expertise to sustain itself on a mix of public and private money. Fifth, the training aspect of Interdoc – literally "cadre formation" – indicates that this was far more than simply an effort to manipulate opinion. The ambition was literally to make selected individuals aware of what they and their society stood for in the Cold War ideological contest, and to get them to pass that on to others as "multipliers". Finally, Interdoc also had a covert action side, using "dirty tricks" and sometimes direct action to disrupt communist front organizations. The origins and activities of Interdoc therefore fit the claim that the Cold War was primarily an ideological struggle – a battle of ideas. As Ken Osgood put it, for this community "psychological warfare had become, in essence, a synonym for cold war".[58] But this was psychological warfare in its broadest possible sense: not propaganda alone, but a genuine contest between competing ways of life.

There were of course many other anti-communist networks active during the Cold War, but each had their limitations. Some, such as Paix et Liberté, its successor the Comité International d'Information et d'Action Sociale (CIAS) and the World Anti-Communist League (WACL), were simply too negative in their approach. Others, such as Otto von Habsburg's Centre Européen de Documentation et d'Information (CEDI) and Paul van Zeeland's Comité International pour la Défense de la Civilisation Chrétienne (CIDCC), were extensive in membership but founded on Catholic values that caused them to be too exclusionary. Then there were groups, such as the Pinay Circle (Le Cercle) around French Prime Minister Antoine Pinay, which were too private and behind-the-scenes. From the mid-1950s onwards the informal Bilderberg meetings of the transatlantic policy-making and business elites were useful for informal liaison and the sharing of ideas, even as a subtle pressure group, but this owed more to the intrinsic power of such a high-level network.[59] To understand the significance of entities such as Bilderberg and Interdoc necessarily requires a transnational approach, since "the distinction between the private and official realms, civil society and the state, seem to collapse altogether, as indeed does the very concept of nationality".[60] Interdoc interacted with all of the above, but often at a distance and sometimes in ways that simply made use of what these networks had to offer. Sometimes it was not even clear who was really using whom. As Interdoc's director wrote to the WACL's secretary general in 1968, dealing with peaceful coexistence was different from "a direct Communist Cold War strategy [...] This is one of the reasons that we do not want to be labelled as an anti-communist organization [or] listed together with known anti-communist organizations."[61] All of these private groups, with their overlapping memberships, agendas at times converging and at times diverging, and different access points to the traditional world of politics, contributed to "the diversification, privatization and growing complexity of the foreign policy decision-making process".[62] Needless to say, Interdoc sought to become the *central point* through which all the others could link up and, ideally, coordinate their message. And that was an ambitious goal.

1
Anti-Communism and PsyWar in the 1950s

> It is only common sense to respect the strength of the Communist adversary and in particular his extraordinary pertinacity, but it is equal sense to remember that he is the slave of his own theory.
>
> Information Research Department, 1963[1]

While the input for Interdoc came from various nationalities and institutions through the 1950s, the origins can best be located in West Germany, the front-line state of the Cold War, and it was the Germans who became the driving force behind the institution in the 1960s. The reasons for this are not hard to find. The establishment of the Federal Republic of Germany in May 1949 had been followed by that of the German Democratic Republic (GDR) in October of the same year. The occupying forces of the Americans, British, French, and Russians were still effectively in charge, but from this point on the relations between the two Germanies would be at the centre of East–West relations. The regimes in Bonn and East Berlin would regard each other as illegitimate upstarts, equally claiming the mantle of the one true Germany. They would also work hard to undermine each other. The Federal Republic's first chancellor, Konrad Adenauer, wasted no time in setting out the basis for the Western attitude. Germany was divided only because of Soviet design, not popular will, and until it could be reunited only the government in Bonn would be its legitimate representative. For the time being the GDR – referred to as "The Zone" or "Pankow" – must be denied recognition and diplomatically isolated. This approach was codified in the mid-1950s by the so-called Hallstein doctrine, named after State Secretary Walter Hallstein of the Federal Republic's Foreign Ministry. The doctrine vowed to break relations with any nation state that had the temerity to recognize the GDR.[2]

Of course, this state of affairs was complicated by the presence of the occupying powers in the two Germanies. Fortunately for Adenauer, London, Paris, and Washington all agreed that the GDR should not be granted *de jure* nor be able to claim *de facto* recognition, which meant opposing diplomatic and consular relations and allowing only trade relations via non-governmental outlets. The outbreak of the Korean War also highlighted the need to fast-track a Federal Republic contribution to NATO. In September 1950 Washington sanctioned Adenauer's claim to speak for all German people and not just those in the West, as part of its containment strategy. Yet, while this support was welcome, it also demonstrated where the rules were really being set. Greater concerns over East–West relations and Moscow's attitude would always overshadow the Allies' direct interest in West Germany's wishes. Thus a United Nations (UN) meeting in late 1951 revealed clearly that "The task of blocking East Germany's admission to international conferences fell to the Western Allies; West German delegations were instructed to offer no more than a few sentences of support in favor of positions argued by the American, British, or French delegates."[3] The threat of Moscow capitalizing on relations with newly independent countries across Asia and Africa did provoke London and Paris to say they would intervene in foreign capitals if necessary. But the Federal Republic would have to carve out a diplomatic space for itself and develop its own means to counteract the presence of the East Berlin regime.

Adenauer was determined to build a position of strength in the West that would, together with the policy of isolation, eventually force the GDR into reunification on the West's terms. But this approach did not envisage any real contact between the peoples of the two Germanies themselves. The Social Democrats (SPD) especially found this difficult to accept, due to the traumatic circumstances of the formation of the GDR, when the party's fusion with the communists in 1946 led to dissenters either fleeing to the West or being imprisoned in former World War II concentration camps. When the Soviet Union granted formal sovereignty to the GDR in a treaty in September 1955, the SPD's Erich Ollenhauer argued that the East Berlin regime was becoming a fact and that Bonn had to get used to dealing with it. While recognition remained unacceptable, Ollenhauer supported arranging deals to allow cross-border economic and social contacts.[4] The rigid, dogmatic policy propagated by Hallstein could potentially lead to the isolation of West Germany itself. A further field of interest was the fact that the Eastern European region had been a valuable trading partner for Germany before World War II. From the Eastern side, increased trade would be a useful channel through which to normalize relations with the West, gain industrial products in short supply, and contribute to the Soviet aim for a general increase in East–West interchange. From the late 1950s onwards, trade between the Federal Republic and Czechoslovakia, Hungary, Poland, and Romania showed a steadily upward trend. Eastern Europe represented only 5 per cent of West German trade, but the market had potential. What is more, interdependence via trade could be a means to open up the East to political influence.[5] From the late 1950s onwards political, social, and economic interest groups were therefore pressing for an easing of restrictions on contacts with the East.

Gehlen and the BND

The formation of the Bundesnachrichtendienst (BND), the foreign intelligence service, on 1 April 1956 was an important mark of full sovereignty for West Germany. But the BND was of course not created out of thin air. The man who had been at the centre of its gestation was Reinhard Gehlen, a former member of the Wehrmacht General Staff, who prior to 1956 had been running the prototype for the BND, the Gehlen Organization. For more than fifteen years he had been preoccupied with monitoring developments in the East. With the arrival of the BND, this task took on new dimensions.

Gehlen had been appointed Head of Operations of the General Staff's Eastern Group in late 1940, placing him at the centre of preparations for the invasion of the Soviet Union. In April 1942 he received a fateful reassignment, becoming chief of Fremde Heere Ost (FHO), the General Staff's intelligence service on the Eastern front. From this position he built a reputation as a good organizer and cool evaluator who ran the FHO as an efficient outfit.[6] By late 1943 Gehlen seemed convinced that the entry of the US into the war had made it impossible for Germany to win. Instead of joining anti-Hitler plots such as the failed assassination attempt of 20 July 1944, he began to make different plans. A Europe divided and under the occupation of the US and the USSR looked a highly likely outcome. In these circumstances, the information held by the FHO on Soviet forces was potentially of great significance. Gehlen, confiding in his closest associates, sought to preserve both material and personnel from his organization for a post-war era where the US should value what they had to offer.[7]

Following his surrender to US forces in Bavaria in late May 1945, Gehlen and his colleagues went through several nerve-racking years trying to establish themselves as a recognized asset for US security interests. Fortunately, certain key individuals saw the merits of Gehlen's plan early on. In the summer of 1945 G-2 (US army intelligence) officer John Boker and his superior General Sibert tried to initiate "Operation X" to allow Gehlen's group to reassemble and show what they could produce. When Gehlen and six others were suddenly flown to Washington for interrogation at US army intelligence headquarters, Sibert continued to gather other Gehlen associates and former Abwehr (German military intelligence) personnel at the US Detention and Interrogation Center in Oberursel. Operation X became Operation Rusty. Following Sibert's departure in 1946, the G-2 apparatus maintained its hold over the Gehlen Organization via its liaison officers John Deane and Eric Waldman. It was Waldman, wanting to give the scattered and vulnerable outfit a secure location, who first heard of the former Nazi party compound in Pullach, south of Munich. In December 1947 the Organization began to move into what would be the base for West German intelligence for the rest of the Cold War.[8] Two decades later Waldman, by then an academic based in Canada, would reappear as a participant in the Interdoc network.

Although this sounds like a straightforward development, the confused period after the war made it anything but. US intelligence was being reformed, with the winding up of the Office of Strategic Services in September 1945 followed by the creation of the Central Intelligence Group in January 1946, the first stepping stone towards the Central Intelligence Agency a year and a half later. US security goals were undefined immediately after the war, and there were differences of opinion over how harsh the retribution should be towards former members of the German General Staff. What is more, General Sibert had more or less run Operation Rusty as a separate outfit, disconnected from the rest of the US intelligence infrastructure in Germany at that time. Sibert's intention that the Gehlen Organization would simply become part of the US intelligence infrastructure also did not fit with what Gehlen himself was aiming for:

> He intended to develop the FHO into a national intelligence service supported by the Americans but possessing a German character that would be amenable to a future German government. He planned to move his organization as rapidly as possible into some defined legal status within a new German government. In the meantime he would limit U.S. access to information about his organization, its members, and its operations.[9]

To this end Gehlen assembled as many members as he could of the former General Staff and Abwehr to form a core of personnel for the future security apparatus of an independent Germany. In July 1949, when the Federal Republic of Germany was founded, responsibility for the Gehlen Organization was passed from the US Army to the CIA, with James Critchfield as head of the CIA's Pullach Operations Base. Gehlen's network was considered too valuable as a source of information on the situation in the East for it to be abandoned. A working relationship was hammered out whereby Critchfield would set the requirements for operations and oversee the results. There were plenty of risks involved. For Gehlen this was no more than a "trusteeship arrangement" for a future of complete independence. Critchfield had established that the 300 individuals linked to the organization had come out of the war "with reasonably clean slates" and were not on the Nuremberg arrest list.[10] But others further down the chain of command were not so clean. Not only did Gehlen try to prevent the CIA from obtaining full information on his personnel and agent network, but he also consciously developed the political outlook of his service. The result was a feeling of suspicion and mistrust within both the CIA and the US Army as to Gehlen's real motives. Donald Galloway of the CIA wrote in December 1948 that "we do not know very much about the inner workings of the RUSTY organization [the Gehlen Organization's code name], and it is probable that the [US] Army does not either".[11] In the mid-1950s this even led to a wide-ranging investigation (code-named Operation Campus) by an Army G-2 unit that strongly suspected Gehlen's organization of being riddled with former Nazis and communist spies. The exposure of many Gehlen agents by the East Germans in Operation Hacke in 1953 only confirmed the worst thoughts of many: that the Pullach set-up was completely penetrated. Campus was right, but the bungling of this unauthorized investigation meant that the problem would not be dealt with for several more years.[12] This would have a direct impact on US participation in Interdoc.

Psychological warfare against the East

While Gehlen was trying to establish his *bona fides* with the CIA in Pullach, discussions were being held elsewhere in the fledgling West German government on how to deal with the threat from the East. Anti-communism was far more than simply a policy option, since "For Bonn's political elites, the very *raison d'être* of the infant West German state was to act as a bulwark against Soviet expansionism", and the portrayal of the Federal Republic as a vital Western rampart against the Soviet threat is constantly repeated in official documents from that time.[13] The trigger for these first moves came in 1951, due to concerns within German industry about the threat posed by communist-inspired agitation among the workforce.[14] By late 1952, in the wake of Stalin's proposal for a settlement of the German question that March, the first steps were taken towards a comprehensive psychological warfare strategy for the Federal Republic.[15]

The starting point for the Germans was the global mission of the US to combat Bolshevism, from which followed opportunities for the Federal Republic to utilize this strategy for its own national interests. First and foremost, the West German mission was to secure Soviet withdrawal from the "Zone" and prepare for a "favourable decision" on unification and the Eastern borders "beyond the Oder–Neisse". To be successful, the US–West German strategy had to be "tuned" (*abgestimmt*) to Soviet methods: the use of "fifth column" supporters in non-communist organizations, the coordinated manoeuvring of communist parties, the development of a "war economy", and the constant dissemination of propaganda. In response, Bonn's specific goals towards the Soviet Zone involved the undermining of its administrative and economic infrastructure, monitoring the level of resistance of the populace, and carrying out acts of sabotage to reduce the credibility of the regime. Within the Federal Republic itself it was vital to educate the citizenry on the situation in the East and the constant need to identify and repel communist infiltration. Most important here was the need to coordinate the many already-existing private organizations that were active in anti-communist agitation, and to redirect counter-propaganda towards "a comprehensive banishment of the communist movement" (*eine allgemeine Ächtung der kommunistischen Bewegung*) from public consciousness. For this, print media and radio were insufficient: mass organization was required.

In late 1952 it was proposed to set up a German–American committee to coordinate the mobilization of civilian resistance, with representatives from the US High Commission and, under the leadership of the Ministry for All-German Affairs (BMG: Bundesministerium für gesamtdeutsche Fragen), representatives from the German Foreign Ministry, the Ministry of the Interior, the Federal Office for the Protection of the Constitution (Bundesamt für Verfassungsschutz), and the Chancellery. This committee, which had to ensure a complete separation from existing military activities in this field, would define the overall strategy, the potential of each organization in that strategy, and the financial means required to carry it out. This also involved ensuring that selected private organizations would be "necessarily subordinated under official German supervision", including where appropriate a change of leadership and tasks. A list of 43 anti-communist organizations was assembled, 15 of which were located in Berlin. Responsibilities were now being shared out between the Germans and the Americans, and official liaison channels established. The BMG, with its mission to "maintain a national consciousness" and promote democratic principles as an essential part of the process of reunification, took on a leading role.[16]

The implications of this document for German government involvement in the Cold War were considerable, not least in terms of expanding official responsibilities and defining who was to lead this mobilization and how it would be carried out. Over the next few years a running discussion was held, involving the Ministry for All-German Affairs, the Chancellery (particularly State Secretary Hans Globke), and the Ministry of the Interior (particularly Dr Toyka), on how best to run this extensive state–private network, whereby organizations became a sort of extended government department or remained private but received all or part of their finances from Bonn.[17] The necessary expertise on how to run this was still lacking. The sensitivity of these developments meant there was a great need to keep those involved to a minimum, even though participation was spread across several departments. In October 1953 a proposal was put forward for a committee of experts to fill this gap. The author, Rudolf Grüner, remarked how the openness of democratic society left it vulnerable to the kinds of subversion practised by communist parties and their fellow-travellers. There was a great need for an organization, "on the basis of mass psychology", to intervene in German society at an earlier stage than the security service and the courts. Grüner emphasized that the communist threat was changing from a simplistic "on the barricades" radicalism led by the Communist Party to a sophisticated network of front organizations. This required nothing less than a broad "vaccination" (*Schutzimpfung*) of the people to help them understand and withstand the threat. A counter-network, directed from a central bureau, was required to supervise this. While the communist infiltration of Western civil society was expanding into all areas of social activity ("from film production to pigeon-breeding associations"), Grüner remarked that the response up till then had been simplistic, ineffective, or, due to scandal, badly discredited.[18]

The scandal Grüner was referring to concerned the Bund Deutscher Jugend (BDJ), an anti-communist youth movement established in June 1950 (just prior to the outbreak of the Korean War) by World War II veterans. The BDJ, which received financial support from the Ministry for All-German Affairs and Chancellor Adenauer's office, ran operations to confront and disrupt the activities of the East German Freie Deutsche Jugend and related pro-communist or neutral front organizations. Yet the activities of the BDJ were wound up in October 1952 when it was discovered that it also maintained a paramilitary wing known as the Technischer Dienst (TD), a stay-behind network that would run reconnaissance and guerrilla operations in the event of a Soviet invasion. While the BDJ was a German affair, the TD was largely a creation of US Army Counter-Intelligence and the Office of Policy Coordination (the US government's covert action unit that was absorbed by the CIA in 1952), who provided funds, training, and weapons. What turned this into a serious scandal was the fact that members of the TD assembled a "Proscription list" of potential enemies to the nation, and this included not only suspected communists but also members of the SPD. While the TD's actual intentions with this list were never clarified, the fact that the TD was operating under the orders of the US, an occupying power, meant that its members could not be prosecuted under German law. The US security establishment, in the interest of strengthening anti-communist forces, was therefore backing a ramshackle network of former Nazis and nationalists who, despite involvement in criminal activity, were immune from prosecution. This caused serious outrage from the SPD, and the ramifications for German sovereignty and democratic stability were obviously immense. It also seriously undermined the credibility of American intentions to promote a democratic Germany, and the arrogant manner with which US authorities responded to the German investigation further damaged relations.[19] In short, the affair demonstrated the need for the German authorities to develop their own approach to deal with the communist threat. Allowing the CIA to run its own programmes without German control was no longer acceptable. It also showed the necessity for centralized coordination to ensure a clear strategy, clear goals, and reliable personnel. The German roots of what would later become Interdoc lie in the response to the BDJ–TD fiasco.

Through 1953–54, as the Federal Republic headed towards full sovereignty, discussions with the US authorities on the sharing of responsibilities in psychological warfare continued. The US position was clarified in a "Statement of Intentions vis-à-vis Resistance Groups" passed to State Secretary Ewert von Dellingshausen, the BMG official now responsible for this dossier, in October 1954.[20] The document, which updated a previous Statement of Intent from October 1952 (following the BDJ–TD affair), described six organizations which received US support "as instruments of psychological warfare". Two of them, the Investigating Committee of Free Jurists (Untersuchungsausschuss Freiheitlicher Juristen) and the Fighting Group against Inhumanity (Kampfgruppe gegen Unmenschlichkeit), were in terms of finance and direction more or less direct extensions of US covert action aimed at exposing injustice and undermining the functioning of East German authorities. The others – the Association of Political Refugees from the East, the Marbach Group of writers (under Karl-Heinz Marbach), the satirical magazine *Tarantel*, and the People's League for Peace and Freedom (Volksbund für Frieden und Freiheit) – received to varying degrees US funding and supervision. The Statement emphasized that it was the intention to ensure these activities "recognize a valid official German interest", that there would be sufficient liaison and exchange of information, and that "the coordination of policy guidance for such operations" would continue, "looking forward to the time when the Federal Government will be in a position to play a more direct role in the management of the organizations mentioned herein". But much ground still had to be covered.[21] Who was going to be responsible for coordination, both on a national and on an international level? And how would it be carried out?

International liaison: NATO and Bilderberg

The entry of West Germany into NATO in May 1955 took these discussions on to a higher plane. The Soviet shift to peaceful coexistence and the renewal of diplomacy with the Geneva Conference in 1955 presented dangers for an Alliance that could not coordinate a response. As Canadian Foreign Minister Lester Pearson put it, the Soviet leaders "hope NATO will fall apart in détente".[22] Thinking ahead to Germany's involvement, in October 1954 von Dellingshausen, who saw the Soviet propaganda threat as a common problem requiring greater coordination at the international level, was writing of the need for a "General Staff" within NATO to define the goals, methods, and means required to run a collective psychological warfare campaign.[23] The development of diplomatic relations between the Federal Republic and the Soviet Union, exemplified by Chancellor Adenauer's visit to Moscow in 1955, only emphasized this further. The new coordination apparatus must be civilian, not military – a separation of tasks was necessary. A new kind of war demanded new kinds of organization. Working through NATO would also allay the fears of others that the Federal Republic was getting too keen on upgrading its propaganda capabilities.

Propaganda and counter-propaganda had been a live issue within NATO since its beginning. While Article 2 of the North Atlantic Treaty highlighted the need for the signatories to strengthen "their free institutions, by bringing about a better understanding of the principles upon which these institutions are founded", there was disagreement on whether NATO's public information activities should also involve anti-communist counter-propaganda.[24] Two issues were contentious. One was the suggestion that NATO project its anti-Soviet activities to the East. General Kruls, until 1951 Chief of the Dutch General Staff, wrote of the need for a collective psychological warfare strategy to project the West's message of support for "liberation" to the oppressed peoples of the Eastern bloc. Despite support from Field Marshal Montgomery, who became the Deputy Supreme Allied Commander Europe in 1951, this was a step too far because it did not fit with the Alliance's posture as a defensive organization.[25] The second issue was to what extent NATO should actually function as a centre to coordinate psychological warfare activities. Among the supporters were the French, who proposed exploring the practice of "ideological warfare" at the NATO level in early 1951.[26] In November 1951 a more moderate American proposal was put forward for a high-level Information Advisory Committee to advise the North Atlantic Council on strengthening morale. The committee, made up of "individuals of the highest standing [...] from science, education, business or labour groups" should "consider the psychological problems of public opinion in the free nations of the West."[27] This initiative was an extension of the newly formed Psychological Strategy Board (PSB) in the US, which was meant to coordinate all anti-communist psychological operations abroad.[28] But even this was not widely accepted, precisely because it threatened to override national prerogatives. For the moment any effort in this field would have to be undertaken either through private initiatives or at the national level, with NATO acting as no more than a supportive institution.

It was during this period that French politician Jean-Paul David, with the backing of the French government, attempted to fill the gap. His organization, Paix et Liberté, made its appearance in France in September 1950. Prime Minister René Pleven had called a meeting of like-minded political leaders to propose the formation of a new organization to confront communist "fifth column" infiltration in French society. David, at 37 the leader of the Rassemblement des gauches républicaines (RGR), deputy for Seine et Oise, and mayor of Mantes-la-Jolie, "was not an intellectual but an organizing genius, a courageous man endowed with some straightforward ideas, notably an urgent need to combat Marxist influence". Finance in the region of two to three million francs a year was assembled from French industry and banks, and a high-profile campaign was begun utilizing posters, brochures explaining the communist threat and the reality of concentration camps, radio transmissions, and even a film, *Crève-Coeur*, about the French battalion fighting in the Korean War.[29] Links were also made with like-minded groups across Western Europe. A key role in this was played by Eberhard Taubert, the former Reichsministerium für Volksaufklärung und Propaganda official and the inspiration behind the Antikomintern, who had already proposed the blueprint for the Volksbund für Frieden und Freiheit (VFF) to US occupation authorities in Germany in 1947.[30] By August 1951 a European coordination committee had been formed with representatives from France, Belgium, Italy, the Netherlands, and West Germany, with meetings held in Paris every two months. All national affiliations were equal and acted separately according to local circumstances, but the intention was certainly to respond to communist propaganda strategy in unison across the West, thereby rebuffing Soviet-bloc efforts to cause divisions inside NATO by playing member states off against each other. By January 1955 there were 20 affiliates, ranging across Europe and beyond.[31]

In the international context Paix et Liberté was therefore decentralized, the goal being to maintain regular contacts between its affiliates. Nevertheless David, who gained notoriety as the network's spokesman, became the point man for a determined attempt in 1952–53 to take it a step further by establishing a psychological warfare section within NATO itself. With the backing of French Foreign Minister Georges Bidault, David carried out an intensive rolling tour of NATO countries during this period in order to raise governmental understanding and support for psychological warfare activities.[32] Always received at the highest levels, David's visit to the US in February 1952 was recorded in the *New York Times* and was intended to link up with like-minded American organizations and send a strong message that Europe was rearming not only militarily but also psychologically in the struggle against communism.[33] But responses were mixed. While the Greeks and the Turks were enthusiastic, a report of David's visit to the Netherlands in mid-1953 suggested that his goal was to combine "psychological defence" (sustaining morale within NATO countries) and "psychological warfare" (behind the Iron Curtain) within a single centralized coordinating body, a proposal the Dutch were not prepared to accept. The report also confirms that David's efforts were carried out without holding any contact with the NATO Information Service (NATIS) itself, so much so that NATIS officials were afraid he was actually doing more harm than good. Neither was there official recognition from the North Atlantic Council.[34]

David's second trip to the US in September 1953 involved meetings with Allen Dulles, Walter Bedell Smith, and members of the Operations Coordinating Board (the successor to the PSB), but the Americans were also unwilling to back Paix et Liberté as a NATO venture. The US wanted to maintain its own strategy of psychological warfare and maintain it as *primus inter pares*; it did not want to officially democratize Western strategy via NATO meetings, which would only limit its freedom of action.[35] There has always been strong suspicion of American covert funding for David's network, but this link has never been categorically proven.[36] Also, the actual links between the national committees remained obscure. In France Paix et Liberté did function with the aid of a "brains trust" consisting of high-up figures within the French state, including members of the Service de Documentation Extérieure et de Contre-Espionnage (SDECE), France's external intelligence agency, but David has flatly denied that there were ever any representatives from other NATO countries involved in those twice-monthly meetings. Each national committee went its own way.

David's ambitions were never fully realized. The organization's message remained simple: communism was evil, and the Soviet Union, through its proxy organizations in politics, the trade unions, and across society at large, propagated lies to cover this up by presenting itself as promoting peace and freedom. Whereas this had a function in the tense days of 1950–51 when the Korean War broke out, by the mid-1950s the complexities of peaceful coexistence had undermined Paix et Liberté's usefulness. Reacting to the Geneva Conference of 1955, the international committee could only announce that the Soviet leaders continued with "their slanderous accusations, resulting in the creation of an atmosphere of distrust and hatred among the people in a political war with the aim to expand the rule of the USSR over the world".[37] The BVD came to the conclusion much sooner that such an outfit as Vrede en Vrijheid (VV) – the Dutch wing of Paix et Liberté – had a limited reach and shelf-life. VV had been established in August 1951 to "publicize and defend the sentiments of peace and freedom" by means of various media outlets: a newspaper (*De Echte Waarheid*), pamphlets, posters, exhibitions, TV and radio spots, and lectures.[38] The movement was initially fully supported by the BVD, since Einthoven knew its secretary, E.W.P. van Dam van Isselt, from his days as Rotterdam police chief in the 1930s.[39] Cooperation and financial support came from major Dutch companies, the trade union leadership, and politicians, but the message was too basic. An intelligence assessment from June 1953 of a VV press conference in Eindhoven concluded that the event "had a quite hopeless organization" and made "a very poor impression". It also managed to stimulate negative media interest in where funding for such an event could possibly come from.[40] Nevertheless *De Echte Waarheid* still continued until 1966, and Vrede en Vrijheid itself – at least on paper – only closed its doors in 1986.[41]

In 1956 the French government ceased its support and the organization was renamed, the Paris bureau continuing as the Office National d'Information pour la Démocratie Française and the international committee as the Comité International d'Information et d'Action Sociale (CIAS). The remnants of this network would provide one of the foundations for the development of Interdoc in a few years' time. Paix et Liberté's national committees functioned as "a sort of vigilance, of conscience" in the war of ideas, but the changing East–West environment demanded a new approach.[42] This would ultimately involve not only a network separate from

NATO and – significantly – US direction, but also an outlook more profound than the negative propaganda of David and his associates, which offered no alternative beyond the need for Western anti-communist solidarity.

The discussions within NATO did not proceed very far. At the request of the Danes and the Greeks, a Special Committee on Information (AC/46) was formed in June 1952 for "the exchange of information" between intelligence and counter-intelligence services "on experiences in their efforts to counteract subversive activities".[43] In September the British, looking to break the deadlock on the NATO role, proposed a new committee to concentrate on both "positive information work designed to find ways and means of convincing the peoples of NATO countries of the value of NATO" (such as television and radio interviews with government officials, newsreels, exchange of journalists and students, and youth camps) and a direct use of counter-propaganda. This involved focusing on "indirect Communist propaganda" from front organizations such as the World Peace Movement by unmasking their communist origin. To be effective, the organs for achieving this would not be in the government but "non-official persons and organizations".[44] These two positive–negative, offensive–defensive strands fed into the formation of the permanent Committee on Information and Cultural Relations (AC/52) in June 1953. It was a neat compromise, but differences of opinion prevented anything further than this. The Committee on Non-Military Cooperation, assembled in 1956 to assess how to improve cooperation and a sense of unity, would soon recommend that "coordinated policy [in the information field] should cover also replies to anti-NATO propaganda and the analysis of Communist moves and statements which affect NATO".[45] Disagreements between member states prevented any progress. Lord Ismay, NATO's first Secretary General, had this to say on the matter in 1955:

> On the one hand, there is a feeling in some quarters that member countries should examine in NATO the methods of combating the massive anti-NATO propaganda made by the Communists and others hostile to the Alliance. On the other hand, it is argued that this is a matter which must remain the prerogative of each government. Between the two points of view a compromise has been reached whereby NATO can act as a forum for consultation about psychological warfare. Such consultation is, however, restricted to matters affecting member countries only: NATO, as an international organization, has never envisaged carrying on propaganda to the peoples of the Soviet Union or of the satellite countries.[46]

A further site of discussion on international cooperation in anti-communism and counter-propaganda were the Bilderberg conferences, begun in Oosterbeek, Netherlands, in May 1954 as a meeting place for European and American political, business, and media elites to discuss matters of mutual concern. In particular the second conference, held in Barbizon in March 1955, devoted time to the communist challenge. Since Stalin's death peaceful coexistence had improved the image of the communist world by highlighting its cultural prowess and apparent willingness to negotiate with the West. Resonant terms such as "peace" and "disarmament" had been appropriated by communist information programmes and forced the Western nations on to the defensive. Three options were put forward to regain the initiative: treat communism as a security threat to the state; improve coordination in counter-propaganda; approach communism as a political and economic challenge to democratic capitalism. While the first option was considered too repressive and (with McCarthy fresh in everyone's mind) controversial, the second drew mixed responses. Paul Rijkens, former chair of Unilever, proposed forming a joint organization – a sort of "democintern" – but others disliked its implications. NATO was already doing enough to expose front organizations, a standardized operation would not fit into national contexts, and, according to Denis Healey, "a single Western organization would be perceived as an operation run by the Americans, which would destroy its credibility in many European countries". Instead, it was more important to consider the message that the West needed to convey. The real differences between communism and democracy had to be spelled out. As the Norwegian Justice Minister Jens Christian Hauge said, many doubters could be swayed if they were presented with "objective information as to the degree to which the communist system really denies the very basis of their existence, namely free science, free art, free literature".[47] This was a significant comment. The propaganda war had to be shifted on to terrain that would expose the weaknesses of the communist bloc. It had to be done in a way that ensured maximum credibility – not based on obvious propaganda, but on objective, factual research. This was to be the way forward. Following Barbizon, Bilderberg chairman Prince Bernhard of the Netherlands forwarded the transcripts of the discussion to BVD chief Louis Einthoven for consideration: "We shall certainly be glad to have a series of propositions which we can recommend to relevant countries for a genuinely effective response to this propaganda."[48] While the Bilderberg meetings would not play a further role in this story, the Prince certainly would.

The *colloques* and the Studienbüro

The 1956 was a key year on the road to Interdoc at both national and international levels. In West Germany proposals were put forward to establish an institute for the scientific study of Marxist ideology. With the usefulness of the VFF in question following the outlawing of the Kommunistische Partei Deutschlands (the controversial Taubert was more or less forced out of his leadership position), and the Kampfgruppe likewise undergoing an audit by the BMG and the CIA, it was time for a new direction. While institutes such as the Osteuropa-Institut in Munich and the Büro für heimatvertriebene Ausländer in Düsseldorf studied the history, economics, culture, and political developments of the Eastern bloc, a site was required to examine the practice of dialectical materialism and its actual effects in the region.[49] As a German official remarked, "this is why we need a research institute working on a philosophical level".[50] Inter-departmental discussions on this issue had begun already in late 1955, and in May 1956 a proposal was sent to Chancellor Adenauer for "the foundation of an institute for scientific discussion with dialectical materialism", a kind of Western counterpart to the Marx–Engels Institute in Moscow. This was to be coupled with an increased mobilization of civil society groups against communist propaganda, and the creation of an "elite school" to educate key sections of society (*Multiplikatoren*) in both the theoretical and practical workings of communism and "the worth of our ideology of freedom and the powerful potential of the free world".[51] The plan was well received in the Chancellery, particularly by Dr Hans Globke, a state secretary and trusted adviser on government organization to Adenauer who had played a key role in introducing Gehlen to the Chancellor. Gehlen worked hard to secure a favourable audience in Bonn, particularly within the opposition Social Democratic party.[52] An Inter-Ministerial Working Group (*Arbeitskreis*) was duly established in June to assess the next steps, but the move triggered something of a contest between the Ministry of Defence, the Ministry of the Interior, and the Ministry for All-German Affairs over who would take the lead in terms of jurisdiction, personnel, and funding. By October 1957 von Dellingshausen had to admit that the hoped-for "General Staff for the Cold War" to coordinate the private anti-communist groups active in German society (he used the Operations Coordinating Board as an example) was still a long way off: "in my opinion the entire coordination effort has got stuck".[53] Instead, separate initiatives from different parts of the government were confusing things.[54] In July 1958 the Foreign Ministry, concerned about the dangers of peaceful coexistence, created the inter-ministerial, public–private Arbeitskreis für Ost-West Fragen, a "Political Advisory Board" modelled on the US State Department's Policy Planning Staff.[55] Meanwhile, under the leadership of the Ministry of the Interior, the secret Arbeitsgruppe für geistig-politische Auseinandersetzung mit dem Kommunismus was assembled in January 1959. The BND, seen by the other departments as a provider of information but not yet a full partner, would pursue its own plans.

In April 1956, less than a year after the occupation of the Federal Republic was ended by the Bonn–Paris conventions, Gehlen's BND was officially invested as the federal government's intelligence service. One of Gehlen's key partners in laying out the future BND had been Hermann Foertsch, formerly the chief of staff of the German army in the Balkans. Foertsch, "among the most intellectual of the German generals", was closely involved (with

Globke and others) with plans for German remilitarization, and it was he who began a monthly publication, *Orientierung*, to circulate news and analysis within the military and the Gehlen Organization and foster an *esprit de corps* and allegiance to the new German state.[56] After 1956, with remilitarization secured, Foertsch shifted his attention to psychological warfare and played a key role in the preparations for Interdoc. In his sombre assessment of October 1957 von Dellingshausen had also remarked that "a closer connection with military and civilian intelligence services" would lead to a more comprehensive understanding of communist strategies and methods. The BND was becoming an accepted partner to the political discussions, although before 1960 they were still excluded from the Inter-Ministerial Abeitskreis.

The first meeting on the road to what would become Interdoc took place in Paris in April 1956 – the same month that the BND officially came into existence – between the French and the Dutch. One of the participants was journalist Jerome Heldring, asked to attend by Louis Einthoven. Fifty-five years later Heldring remembered that it involved a series of meetings with the French and a group of Czech military defectors about communism and the situation in the Soviet bloc.[57] In the previous year Einthoven had met Colonel Antoine Bonnemaison, chief of the Guerre/Action Psychologique section of the Service de Documentation Extérieure et de Contre-Espionnage. An expert on Soviet tactics, Bonnemaison was closely involved in developing psychological warfare capabilities in the French military during the Algerian War.[58] His role in SDECE was as coordinator of a network of psychological warfare organizations – the Cinquième Bureau – via a public front, the Centre de Recherche du Bien Politique, run out of Bonnemaison's residence, 14 rue de la Pépinière in Paris.[59] A return visit by the French to the Netherlands was hindered by the Hungarian uprising in November 1956 (and presumably by Suez as well).[60] Einthoven then went to Nigel Clive, then head of MI6's Special Political Action section, to assess his interest in the following question: "To what extent can an intelligence service assist in the conduct of psychological warfare?" Van den Heuvel went to Paris to discuss the same question. In May 1958, following the accession to power of de Gaulle, Bonnemaison finally replied that a meeting to discuss the matter would be held later that year. General Jean Olié, de Gaulle's Chief of the General Staff, would lead the French delegation, but Bonnemaison was the brains behind it.[61]

The SDECE did have intelligence-sharing arrangements with other services (CIA, BND, MI6, Italy, Belgium) under an agreement system known as TOTEM but, as Bonnemaison's chief remarked later, "these remained too informal and limited in scope".[62] Bonnemaison's venture was to be more far-reaching. He had already sought out contact with the Germans, initiating in early 1957 a series of discussions or *colloques* as a forum for Franco-German intelligence cooperation. This was a significant extra step in the gathering rapprochement between the two countries, aided by the processes of European integration, German rearmament within NATO, and the French focus post-Suez on finding European solutions to common strategic problems. The Suez crisis "created the impression that the United States was willing to sacrifice Western European interests" in the context of its overarching global contest with the Soviet Union in the Third World, and suggestions that the US military commitment to Western Europe was fragile caused doubts among the Germans as well.[63] For Reinhard Gehlen, who had nurtured contacts with French intelligence for several years, the Franco-German meetings represented a further step towards legitimacy and prestige for the BND.[64] However, the Franco-German relationship was severely complicated by the Algerian War and the determination of the French secret service to eliminate support from German businesses for the Algerian nationalists. Long-running suspicions would not so easily be overcome.[65] Nevertheless in late 1958 the French, Germans, and Dutch came together for the first time at Jouy-en-Josas, to the south-west of Paris.

In summer 1958 events took a new turn when Minister of Defence Franz-Josef Strauss announced plans for a "psychological defence department" under Lieutenant Colonel Mittelstaedt, an entity that, according to the *Frankfurter Allgemeine Zeitung*, "carried a strong American accent" although Strauss openly compared it to the French Cinquième Bureau and "similar institutions in Switzerland and Sweden".[66] This openness notwithstanding, the paper predicted "a whirlwind of objections", and it was right – the SPD's press service was soon sending out an article that accused Strauss's initiative of potentially bringing McCarthyism to Germany in order to silence opposition to the CDU (Christlich Demokratische Union)–CSU (Christlich-Soziale Union) government.[67] The timing was significant, because the stakes in the contest between East and West Germany were rising. In October 1957 Tito's Yugoslavia became the first country outside the Sino-Soviet bloc to officially recognize East Germany. In November 1958 Nikita Khrushchev issued his first ultimatum on Berlin, threatening to end Soviet responsibilities as an occupying power and hand them to the GDR authorities, thereby forcing Western recognition. Emboldened by these moves, during 1958–59 the GDR carried out a major diplomatic campaign across Asia and Africa to obtain greater recognition.[68] The Hallstein doctrine was under pressure. Not surprisingly, therefore, Strauss's move re-energized discussions within the federal government on the coordination of anti-communist measures. By September 1958 a unit had been set up in the Chancellery to oversee the Inter-Ministerial Working Group, and one month later the Ministry of the Interior, via the Verband für Wirtschaftsförderer in Deutschland, established an "Information Centre" to work closely with German industry on psychological warfare, with an annual budget of DM (Deutsche Mark (deutschmark)) 300,000. Strauss's new department also became the reference point for planning similar national bureaux with the same concerns.

Throughout the 1950s there was much talk of the necessity of "immunizing" the West German citizenry against communist influence, but that was easier said than done. Clarifying the organizational structure of this emerging network of anti-communist activity kept all of the participants busy in meeting after meeting.[69] Meanwhile the BND kept the *colloques* as a separate affair, and revealed neither their purpose nor their very existence to its governmental "partners".

A network – or, better said, networks – were beginning to form. Alongside the French initiative – or "right through the middle of it", as Einthoven put it with some indignation – came the Studienbüro Berlin, established by the Ministry for All-German Affairs in late 1956 as a means to bypass bureaucratic obstacles. This was part of the Ministry's network of "outreach institutes" involved in research, information, and liaison activities, which by the early 1960s included the Haus der Zukunft and the Europahaus in West Berlin, the Büro für politische Studien and the Verein zur Förderung der Wiedervereinigung Deutschlands in Bonn, and the Gesellschaft für Wirtschafts- und Sozialpolitik at Haus Rissen in Hamburg. Von Dellingshausen described the Studienbüro as a meeting point for "politically interested individuals in West Germany and West Berlin" to facilitate the trans-European study of communist strategy and tactics. Van den Heuvel first attended in autumn 1957, and other invitees came from France, Denmark, Sweden, Switzerland, Luxembourg, Austria, and the US.[70] Von Dellingshausen noted that the special place of the Federal Republic in this scenario meant that the Berlin Büro would maintain leadership of the group, although locations outside of West Germany were used – such as in Denmark in early 1963.[71] Also, "cooperation with American institutions is guaranteed". While NATO still offered the most logical location for developing a Western response to communist propaganda, the preferable way forward was exactly via a private initiative such as the Studienbüro, as this offered a solution that was not only less bureaucratic but also – crucially – open to participation from neutral states (Switzerland and Sweden being of special importance in this regard).[72]

The sixth Büro meeting, held in September 1961, which discussed the activities of communist parties and the various responses to them, indicates that its clientele consisted mainly of officials working for government or government-assisted public information bureaux, giving it more of a strict policy orientation that the broader themes dealt with by the original *colloques*.[73] From the beginning, therefore, the *colloques* and the Studienbüro were overlapping – if not parallel – informal arrangements with similar international goals initiated around the same time, the former by the French and the latter by the Germans. Both were initiated as responses to the lack of such a meeting point within NATO. Both represented attempts by different wings of the German government – the Ministry for All-German Affairs and the BND – to fill this gap. But the Büro was meant as a fully German initiative, with a central theme being the mapping of Soviet initiatives to influence West German public opinion through "devious routes" via other Western countries.[74] In contrast the *colloques* began as a common Franco-German operation and were intended to be a multinational endeavour. This, from day one, was the view of the Dutch, although German dominance later caused them to compromise. There was undoubtedly some competition over who would lead these trans-European ventures into intelligence and psychological warfare cooperation.

Fact-finding missions 1958–59

European cooperation had of course begun much earlier. The British Foreign Office's Information Research Department (IRD), making use of the multinational platforms provided by the Brussels Treaty and NATO, took on a leading role in disseminating information on communist front organizations and manipulation in the public sphere. However, this was largely limited to the sharing of information and definitely did not extend into the realm of coordinated responses, as this would undermine national control over sensitive anti-communist activities.[75] Through the 1950s the Dutch, in contrast, began to search out ways in which coordination in anti-communist activities could be achieved as a common enterprise. In February 1953 a BVD delegation had attended a seminar in London on intelligence-gathering on communist parties and the ways and means of undermining their popular support. One method discussed was the possibility of spreading dissent within the party by creating opposition to the leadership. In November 1953 Einthoven took up these ideas with his governmental superior, Minister of the Interior Louis Beel, and was able to convince him that the BVD should be able to go on the offensive in this manner, even if it was not strictly covered by its official mandate. Beel reluctantly agreed, and Dutch psychological warfare was given the green light.

Van den Heuvel became the coordinator of these efforts to undermine the Dutch Communist Party (CPN: Communistische Partij Nederland). Alongside acting as BVD liaison with Vrede en Vrijheid (the Dutch wing of Paix et Liberté), Van den Heuvel regularly fed selected journalists useful information and was directly involved in "Project Toekomst" (Future), a sustained and surreptitious plan to cause division within the communist movement in 1956–58. The success of this last venture prompted further interest in the internationalization of offensive anti-communist activities. Already in 1954 Van den Heuvel had been directed by contacts in business circles to visit one of the annual meetings of Moral Rearmament, held in Caux, in Switzerland. He returned impressed and convinced that "the only effective response to communism is to oppose it with a superior ideology".[76] In April 1958, with both the *colloques* and the Studienbüro in mind, Einthoven was able to secure the support of Interior Minister Teun Struycken for continuing these efforts, now termed Phoenix, in a European setting.[77] While BVD historian Dick Engelen is correct in taking note of this development, he based his analysis wholly on BVD files, in particular those of H.C. Neervoort, head of the BVD's operations section. What is clear from other sources is that by 1958 Einthoven and Van den Heuvel were already developing plans for future operations outside of official BVD channels. Interdoc was being nurtured three to four years before either of them left the BVD to pursue it full time.

Both the *colloques* and the Studienbüro meetings were held twice a year, and both invited similar clientele: representatives from the military, politics, business, academia, and the media, as well as intelligence personnel. From 1959, in a similar way to the Büro, the *colloques* brought in participants from Britain, Belgium, Italy, the Netherlands, and Switzerland.[78] It is clear that for Einthoven and Van den Heuvel the *colloques* were their primary venue. The BND was excluded from the Büro meetings, and while they proved to be a useful site for exchange of information they did not represent – nor were they meant to evolve into – a permanent centre. From here on, unless otherwise mentioned, the *colloques* will be discussed. The locations for the meetings that are known were as follows:

1958 Jouy-en-Josas (France)
1959 Wolfheze (The Netherlands) and Ettal (West Germany)
1960 Aix-en-Provence (France) and Heelsum (The Netherlands)
1961 Bad Soden (West Germany) and Barbizon (France)
1962 Mont-St-Michel (France) and Noordwijk (The Netherlands)
1963 Bad Godesberg (West Germany).

In 1958 Foertsch put forward a proposal for the *colloques* with the aim of inventarizing the purpose, methods, and targets of all communist entities – formal and informal, open and "front" organizations, and non-communist organizations "that consciously or unconsciously support the spirit of international communism" – that each participating nation could identify. Based on this, the possibilities for developing a response in each case could be clarified.[79] In a meeting between Einthoven and Van den Heuvel in mid-December 1958, it was decided to put forward three themes for the *colloque* the following April: the cultural offensive of the Soviet Union under "peaceful coexistence"; revisionism on the left; and, significantly, the possibility of a "central documentation bureau" to back up anti-communist psychological warfare in Europe. Einthoven went off to Munich a few days later to discuss further contact with Gehlen, Foertsch, and BND liaison officer Harald Mors.[80]

In his subsequent report on peaceful coexistence, Van den Heuvel emphasized that, while the Soviet approach proposed peaceful relations and economic competition among states, it still held on to the irreconcilable differences between ideologies. While most people in the West were taken in by what appeared to be a new positive outlook on East–West relations, the hidden reality was "the continuation of the Cold War by other means".[81] The threat had not diminished: it had only taken on new and more subtle forms, making it harder to differentiate and appreciate. While opposition to communism in the Netherlands remained strong, increasing political, economic, and cultural contacts with the Soviet Union and the Eastern bloc were altering perceptions: "As the communist party in the Netherlands decreases as a political factor, the feeling that communism is a real danger also declines." As East–West contacts increased, particularly in non-political fields, "the situation arises that many no longer believe in the aggressive intentions of communism and are no longer prepared to offer resistance. When this point is reached, communism has won the Cold War."[82] Economic convergence was also a factor. The impressive achievements of Soviet industry, coupled with the introduction of de-Stalinization under Khrushchev, suggested that over time the differences between the Soviet-bloc command economy and Western social democracy could gradually be reduced. This was amplified by the fact that, in a broad social sense, there were common tendencies at work in the US, Europe, and the Soviet Union that marked the twentieth century as one of contact, communication, and collectivity (as opposed to the nineteenth century's individualism and subjectivism). Under the conditions of modernity, similarities between East and West could not be denied.[83] One of the *colloques*, held in Aix-en-Provence in 1960, involved a presentation by Raymond Aron on the convergence of the different systems caused by industrialization and technological development.[84]

Van den Heuvel, increasingly taking a leading role in this process of internationalization, also devoted 1958–59 to organizing a series of fact-finding missions. The goal of these missions was twofold: to gather a core group of Dutch employers and businessmen and attract their support for a national institute to further the anti-communist ambitions of the *colloques*; to report back to the *colloques* on what was learnt, for future reference. Contacts with Dutch business circles had already been nurtured for several years via regular conferences in Heelsum on the communist threat and security issues, run by the BVD. Extending the investigation to see what others were doing was therefore logical. The first trip was to West Germany in November–December 1958, taking in Haus Rissen (Institut für Wirtschafts- und Sozialpolitik) in Hamburg and the Haus der Zukunft, located in the Berlin suburbs of Zehlendorf and Grunewald. The group of nine included the chair of Vrede en Vrijheid, Ruud van der Beek, and those responsible for internal security at business concerns such as the railways, postal services, mining, Unilever, the oil industry, and the employers' union. The head of the Haus der Zukunft, Herbert Scheffler, was chair of the Studienbüro, and the director of Haus Rissen was also a Büro participant. Both worked together with the Volksbund für Frieden und Freiheit, the German wing of the Paix et Liberté/CIAS network.[85] Zukunft had been set up by the BMG in 1955 as a study centre on the GDR and East–West questions in general, hiring in experts to run specific courses for both Germans and those from abroad (amounting to around 15,000 participants between 1955 and 1958). Haus Rissen was a conference centre dedicated to the study of socioeconomic issues and promoting the responsibilities of particular professions and groups in a free society.

The one-week visit to these institutes, which involved a VFF lecture in Hamburg and a course on communist infiltration in German industry in Berlin, greatly impressed the Dutch group in the quality and depth of information provided on the socio-economic reality in the two Germanies (the GDR of course being referred to as "the Zone") and the methods used to penetrate the West. The scale of GDR infiltration and subversion in West German industry struck the Dutch, particularly since this well-orchestrated campaign had been escalated after the outlawing of the Kommunistische Partei Deutschlands in 1956. The Berlin visit, which included meeting some of the more than 700 refugees coming west every day, also had a stark impact on the group. Khrushchev had made his first ultimatum only three weeks previously, causing an extra-tense atmosphere. G. Diepenhorst of the Dutch employers' union (and formerly of the BVD) spoke of being "confronted from close up with *un*freedom. The sight of East Berlin behind the Iron Curtain made an oppressive impression." Van den Heuvel himself remarked how "a stay on the East–West front" strengthened the resolve to oppose communist activities.[86] The visit lay the grounds for what would later become Interdoc Berlin, an attempt to organize regular study trips to the beleaguered city on the reality and consequences of Germany's division. No further structural link was developed with Haus der Zukunft until 1968, when study trips were once again organised in cooperation with Rolf Buchow and Interdoc Berlin.[87]

The second trip was to the US, in February 1959. This was made by a smaller group of experts: Van den Heuvel, director of the State Psychology Service F.J.E. Hogewind, Leiden professor J.H. van den Berg, sociologist and psychological warfare researcher J.M.M. Hornix, and head of railway security K.D. de Pous. Van den Berg was an important member of the group, having opened up the field of historical psychology – the study of how ways of life altered human thought and self-understanding over time – with his book *Metabletica* in 1956.[88] Einthoven's good friend Frans den Hollander, director of the Dutch Railways, became the financier, and although Shell agreed to contribute Den Hollander was unable to convince Frits Philips that he should do likewise.[89] While problems with securing the money delayed the trip, Van den Heuvel's preparatory planning was clear: an in-depth survey of methods to oppose communist influence as practised by US research institutes, the media, education, in the military, and in business circles. Indeed, US society as a whole was of interest, because of the strong belief in self-help, resistance to government interference, "freedom of thought and action", and what could be learnt from these traits for application elsewhere.[90] It was clearly a fact-finding trip not so much for the case of the Netherlands, but for the case of the ideological contest between West and East as a whole.[91] The Dutch were acting as pathfinders for the European operation.

Enquiries by Einthoven with the CIA led him to Dr John Gittinger, a psychologist with the Agency, who was able to arrange a visit to the Society for the Investigation of Human Ecology (SIHE) in New York.[92] Established at Cornell University Medical College by Professor Harold Wolff and his colleague Lawrence Hinkle in 1955, and with Adolf A. Berle Jr. on the board, the Society was run as a legitimate research centre while it carried out studies for the CIA. The focus was on "human ecology", or what has since become known more derogatively as "mind control": the study of ways to control the interaction between humans and their immediate environment, and the consequent possibilities for manipulating behaviour.[93] CIA interest in this field, ranging from sensory deprivation to experimental drug concoctions, had begun seriously in 1949 following the Cardinal Mindszenty show trial in Hungary, a process stimulated further by the scare during the Korean War about US prisoners of war undergoing Chinese brainwashing techniques and renouncing their homeland as a result (a scare partly fuelled by CIA propagandist-journalist Edward Hunter, who gave us the term "brainwashing" in his exposé of this phenomenon in 1950).[94] The Society's report for 1957 spelled out the main concern:

> Basic beliefs have apparently been altered by Communist indoctrination methods. It must certainly be recognized as a distinct possibility that the human personality is not as stable as we often assume; that, in fact, it is susceptible to marked change if the right environmental conditions exist.[95]

By the late 1950s the "brainwashing" scare – a real fear that "the 'Reds' had cracked the problem of controlling human behaviour" – had shifted to a more objective interest in "immunization". Social science was keen to "demystify" the processes involved in order "to undermine the popular image of the robotic brainwashee."[96] In the Federal Republic the Grüner Report of October 1953 still spoke of "vaccination", but von Dellingshausen was referring to the "necessary immunization" of German society from 1957 onwards.[97] It was not always used in public documents: Einthoven had written to James Monroe at SIHE that he wanted to develop an "Adult Education program on Communism" – but the issue was the same.[98] Writing to Monroe prior to departure, Van den Heuvel set the following questions:

> What effect has the Soviet offensive in the field of peace, science, culture, and sports on the different strata of the population, in particular the working classes, intellectuals, youth, and the military?

In what ways could these groups be immunized against this psychological offensive? What conditions should be fulfilled for an institution – and above all its collaborators – to be successful in the field of counter-influencing?[99]

The resulting itinerary, with SIHE personnel James Monroe and Walter Pasternak as the group's guides, was impressive. Learning more about the techniques of brainwashing was at the centre of the trip.[100] A "special conference" on this subject was held at the SIHE office on Connecticut Avenue in Washington, DC, involving various scientists connected with US Air Force research programmes on prisoners of war. The reason for this interest was clear:

> Brainwashing in its narrow sense (as applied by Chinese and Russian communists to prisoners) is assumed to be related in some way or other to brainwashing in its wider sense (such as the political indoctrination of the Chinese people) and with brainwashing in its widest sense (such as the communist propaganda to the non-communist world).[101]

Brainwashing had potential if it could offer blueprints for the appliance of influence on a societal basis. The key was to link the micro and macro levels of analysis – to study the forces used to maintain the cohesion of communist societies (and their efforts to influence outsiders) from the perspective of the individual in a controlled environment.

In the Western world these techniques are questioned, especially in the field of freedom and ethics. Indeed they are contrary to Human Rights.
Nevertheless, the Western world has seriously to reckon with these methods, both in cold and hot war.
The microscopic contemplation of the whole non-communist world as one large prisoner-of-war camp – with communist camp-leaders applying "brainwash" techniques in the sense of psychological warfare and propaganda techniques – can afford elucidating insight into the tactical and strategical [sic] methodologies of the communists.[102]

Yet, while the danger was recognized, the micro–macro link was difficult to define, and further advances in social psychology research were needed before definitive conclusions could be drawn. The report noted that humans had made use of a whole variety of forms of influence for centuries, perhaps increasing vulnerabilities: "Are not we, Western people, for this reason, if for no other, more susceptible to the system practiced by the communists both in micro and macro situation [sic]?"[103]

The Dutch group attended several other meetings. One, with invited academics and journalists, degenerated into a wayward discussion on the meaning of "American", but another, the All-American Conference to Combat Communism, was more useful. While it certainly did not produce unanimous positions, the All-American Conference did show the Dutch the added value of gathering like-minded organizations into one movement, which allowed for the information and research generated to be spread first among a wide field of supporters, and beyond via the press. Having said that, the conclusion was "it seems to be extremely difficult to rouse people for a positive cause."[104] Lectures by managers of General Electric and Du Pont explained the ins and outs of American corporate culture and their contributions to fostering a positive business climate, both amongst their workforce and beyond in the community at large.[105] The visitors then attended MIT (Massachusetts Institute of Technology) and the Russian Research Center at Harvard, discussing with Daniel Lerner, Adam Ulam, Max Millikan, and others the extent of US research on Soviet society, before going on to meet with representatives of the FBI (Federal Bureau of Investigation) (William C. Sullivan and his staff) to talk over the contribution a security service could make to "psychological defence" in society as a whole. The Department of State provided an overview of their course for government personnel on communist theory, Sino-Soviet foreign and domestic policies, their influence in various regions, and counter-measures. The Dutch group then met Colonel John Broger, head of the Pentagon's Office of Armed Forces Information and Education. Broger had been the instigator of the Militant Liberty programme, a plan to train "freedom cadres" to proselytize the values of the democratic, capitalist, self-reliant, god-fearing way of life around the world.[106] Using a straightforward logic, Broger argued that since "Communism is a dynamic ideology" it "can only be defeated by a stronger dynamic ideology".[107] Although Militant Liberty was not adopted beyond one or two pilot projects, in 1956 Broger was given the task of educating armed forces personnel on communism. Positive references to this approach did appear in the Dutch group's subsequent attempts to define "Western values" and how to proselytize them (discussed in Chapter 2), but Broger also triggered some questions on how much information should be provided and by whom (for example, was it effective for a military officer to lecture at universities on anti-communism?).

The report from the trip, which was compiled collectively by the group members after meeting at Hotel Wolfheze in Heelsum, concluded with some lessons learnt. Counter-measures against communist influence must be of both a defensive and offensive nature, but the accent was on the defensive: no moves could be made without first conducting a thorough study of the theory and practice of the opponent. A careful appreciation of the strengths and weaknesses of communist ideology was needed: "ethically no goal can be attacked which has as its principal element 'everyone gets what he needs'". Different forms of "political education" must be adapted for each segment of society, but, because communist strategy focused on disintegrating capitalism by highlighting its contrasts and contradictions, the initial emphasis lay on "immunizing" the working classes as the most vulnerable group. To carry this out, a national institute predominantly funded by big business was required to study, connect, advise, and train, building networks throughout the media, trade unions, universities, churches, and the armed forces. If Western nations would pursue this, "these centres will coordinate their activities in such a way that international communism will be met with truly international opposition".[108]

Following the trip, contacts were maintained between the Society's executive secretary, James Monroe, and the Dutch. The Dutch report was sent around to many of those who had participated in the visit, eliciting various responses: Lewis Galantière (Free Europe Committee) disliked the way "the Team took its whole view of America from the businessmen it talked to", while Glen Perry of Du Pont felt they should focus more on "a process of enlightenment than 'immunization' against undesirable influences". Arthur Barron of Columbia's Russian Institute commented that any Dutch institute should "work effectively with the non-communist Left", and this could be complicated if the main source of income was business. He also commented that the whole focus on immunization and brainwashing was directed at the "working class", whereas "the pivotal group" was probably the intellectuals. The strongest response came from the FBI, who objected to the claim that the value of the Communist Party of the US for the Soviet Union was declining. An addendum was added to the US version of the report that insisted the party "remains a serious threat to the internal security of that country".[109]

Monroe himself visited the Netherlands with Gittinger and Samuel Lyerly from SIHE in October 1959 (which included a side-trip to "our refugee project in Nijmegen") and returned to the US with plans for cooperation with several institutes in Scandinavia and elsewhere.[110] Monroe also became a conduit for soliciting support for the Dutch initiative in various US business and military circles, a shrewd move considering that SIHE already had a foothold in the Netherlands. In November 1959 Monroe reported that the National War College's seminar on national strategy (closely linked to the Foreign Policy Institute at the University of Pennsylvania) had established an association which, he hoped, would "provide a ready-made 'US Committee' and a continuing source of financial support" for the proposed Dutch institute.[111] Van den Heuvel remarked that European activities in psychological warfare remained scattered and post-Nazi reservations about centralizing these kinds of activities had led to bureaucratic obstacles in the Federal Republic, but "If American and European forces join in such a project, much could be achieved." By May 1960 Van den Heuvel could report that the *colloques* were expanding in membership to include others from "Free Europe", so that "the time will come when there will be insistence on the invitation of an American observer for a general conference". Looking to move things along, a "working party" of two Germans, two French, and two Dutch (Van den

Heuvel and Hornix), under the leadership of Einthoven, had been formed to push forward the plans for an international institute.[112]

But things did not work out so smoothly thereafter. Monroe pointed out that there was "a real potential for cooperation" with the Institute for American Strategy, part of the American Security Council's network, but Monroe was now working for the African Research Foundation as well as SIHE and he had little time to set this up.[113] Einthoven went to the US in late 1960 to generate US financial interest, but the Dutch were now being held back by the problem of having to provide specific details for the Americans on the planned purpose and activities of the international institute, whereas the delicate business of securing inter-European cooperation prevented this. There is a strong suggestion that Einthoven, who had aimed to retire as head of the BVD and transfer his activities to the new institute in April 1961, now delayed this precisely because of the lack of American backing. Einthoven instead spent several months securing support in France, Italy, and the Federal Republic before returning to the US in November. By the end of 1961 a financial commitment had been obtained from French, German, and Dutch companies, but the start did not happen in January 1962 as intended.[114] By this stage Monroe had left SIHE (renamed the Human Ecology Fund) to become a consultant for the US Air Force and the Bureau of Social Science Research.[115] However, the developments Monroe had referred to did lead to the formation of the National Strategy Information Center, later to become Interdoc's main US partner.

Following the US came Britain, where Van den Heuvel visited the Economic League in November 1959 with an eleven-man delegation similar to the group that went to Hamburg and Berlin. The League was established as a private organization in 1919 by a group of industrialists (and the former head of naval intelligence) who were concerned that the combined effects of post-World-War-I demobilization and the Russian Revolution could lead to socio-economic disturbance in Britain. It aimed to counter disruptive activity by the left (or right) within the working class through "constructive economic education", which focused on opposing radical claims with facts, generating positive employer–employee relations, and creating "an atmosphere in which it would be difficult for extremists to make any headway". This was carried out by means of a variety of factual publications and by training programmes for lower management positions.[116] The two-day visit was appreciated by the Dutch, who were able to see the League at work when Helen Bailey, one of its public speakers, addressed London dockworkers leaving the harbour for lunch.[117] The training programmes in particular attracted Van den Heuvel's attention, and a return visit by the League's director general, John Dettmer, and publicity director, John Baker White, took place in November 1960. They participated in sessions on anti-communist tactics in Dutch industry at De Baak, the employers' union's conference and training centre at Noordwijk. Soon after, Van den Heuvel brought

Dettmer into contact with Günter Triesch of the Deutsches Industrie-Institut to share information on their respective campaigns, and the following year both Dettmer and Baker White were invited to the *colloque* in Barbizon.[118] The British example brought home to the Dutch an important point best summed up by historian Scott Anthony: for any anti-communist campaign, "no matter how ideologically motivated, reaching a broad adult audience in the early Cold War period depended on aligning yourself with material concerns against abstract interests".[119]

With these fact-finding trips laying the basis, during 1959 the *colloques* started to plan ahead to take the French–Dutch–German meetings to the next level. Leading the way, Van den Heuvel drew particular conclusions from his new-found knowledge on British and American "psychological defence". The British in general were somewhat lackadaisical about the Soviet threat, but their information services – particularly the BBC (British Broadcasting Corporation) – provided excellent examples of impartiality and truthfulness in reporting, building valuable credibility as a result. The Americans understood the Cold War as a global confrontation with communism, but were at times drawn to excessive responses to oppose it. Both nations offered inspiration, but also signs of what to avoid. In particular, Van den Heuvel stressed their understanding of anti-communist activities as defensive, a mentality which needed to be reversed in order to highlight the Western world and what it stood for as a vibrant alternative.[120] In October two proposals were put forward: one from Hermann Foertsch for a Documentation and Information Centre, and the other from the Dutch. Both proposals foresaw a network of national institutes along the lines of the Dutch proposal from the US trip. Connecting these efforts would be a new international institute to integrate and distribute the results from the national level, particularly to nations outside of Western Europe, who were increasingly the target of communist propaganda. A public apparatus separate both from the intelligence services and from existing organizations was needed to act as a collecting point and outlet for the research produced on communism. It would also serve as a means to link up with professional elites from the private sector and the military, in order to identify vulnerabilities in their working environment that required attention, to act as channels for the dissemination of material, and to provide funding from outside government. Looking to distance the enterprise from government, Van den Heuvel looked towards the (Dutch and American) multinationals and hoped that "the international institute might be financed by funds placed at its disposal by private enterprises of a world-wide scope (Royal Dutch, Unilever, Standard Oil, Philips, etc.), and well-known foundations (Carnegie, Ford etc.)".[121]

Foertsch foresaw the Centre's role in the fields of research, planning and implementation, and networking and distribution, making the *colloques* into a concrete form of cooperation.[122] For this apparatus he also sketched a defensive/offensive strategy, whereby the limiting of communist influence in "vulnerable" areas of Western society (religion, the economy, and the arts were mentioned) would ideally be combined with an offensive counter-campaign on a broad front, ranging from publishing the experiences of Eastern-bloc refugees to deliberately disrupting the gatherings of peace and youth congresses through "the transmission of Western opinions, influencing susceptible participants, influencing the final resolutions".[123] Special attention was also reserved for those travelling to communist countries, such as businessmen. Both Einthoven and Van den Heuvel saw opportunities to turn the tables on peaceful coexistence:

> This does not mean that contact with the Soviet Union should be as little as possible. Those who hold this opinion point to the disadvantageous influence that visits of Western delegations to countries behind the Iron Curtain can have. The assumption is that these contacts are more to the advantage of communism. This is often the case when Western delegations are not sufficiently prepared for meeting the communist world, and meanwhile insufficient attention is given to the ways in which communist delegations visiting the Western world can best be received.[124]

Such an offensive would require the careful training of those chosen to carry out such measures, and there was general agreement that this was still a few years ahead. Reacting to Foertsch's deliberate plan, Van den Heuvel was more ambitious. The new institute should reach beyond Europe, and it should look to coordinate all existing anti-communist organizations: the lack of such a body was precisely the problem. The French wanted to improve cooperation to assist rather than centralize or control: "It is more urgent to improve what exists, to extend, enhance efficiency, than to create an additional body trying more or less to empty the substance of that which already exists."[125] The Germans agreed:

> Interdoc does *not* step on the space of already-existing institutions and organisations that are dedicated to similar missions. There shall be much more mediation and connection between existing institutions and organisations in order to achieve a far-reaching collective result for the fight on the broadest possible basis across Europe.[126]

NATO was still regarded as the most logical location to attempt this. The Khrushchev ultimatum on Berlin on 10 November 1958 put Western unity to the test, and Adenauer discovered that both the Americans and the British seemed prepared to put negotiations with Moscow ahead of support for the Federal Republic's hard-line non-recognition stance towards the GDR.[127] Through 1959 Soviet propaganda was exploiting intra-alliance disagreements by portraying Adenauer as a "frustrated and embittered supporter of continued East–West tension and revanchist policies". Only de Gaulle backed the Chancellor's position.[128] In March 1960, under the instigation of Strauss, the West German delegation circulated an official proposal within the North Atlantic Council entitled "NATO-Wide Co-operation and Co-ordination in the Field of Psychological Warfare".[129] The proposal claimed that the "political and ideological attacks" of the Soviet Union were aimed at undermining the belief in collective defence, solidarity, and mutual confidence that NATO rested upon by creating mistrust towards German ambitions. There was also the fear that partial reconciliation with the East would undermine the Federal Republic's own identity and cohesion. Referring to the changing nature of the Soviet threat, from potential military attack to actual ideological subversion, the German proposal even invoked Article 5 of the North Atlantic Treaty because "in this psychological war, that attack against one NATO ally is also an attack against *them all* and against NATO as a whole". There was no point, as Strauss explained to his NATO colleagues, in equipping Western armies with the latest weaponry if no effort was made to simultaneously establish "a moral solidarity".[130]

The West German initiative did lead to a Working Group on Psychological Warfare in October 1960 (which included Strauss's psychological warfare expert Lieutenant Colonel Mittelstaedt), but resistance from other NATO nations (including Britain and the Netherlands) prevented the creation of a new body to coordinate Western "counter-measures". There was too much concern that such a centralization would make effective security impossible and would take control away from the national governments. The German delegation's call for an offensive psychological strategy towards the East also made others nervous about potential consequences. Von Dellingshausen noted in early 1961 that American proposals for a common NATO programme did not address any of the central issues of concern for the Federal Republic itself.[131] The last remaining outcome of the German attempt, a study group of experts meeting irregularly to discuss psychological warfare and youth, was disbanded in April 1963.[132] By that stage it was perfectly clear that other arrangements would have to be made to establish the desired permanent contact points. The Netherlands may have opposed German plans within NATO, but the BVD was active in realizing them elsewhere. Nevertheless NATO would always stay in the picture as the ideal "base" for a common Western anti-communist initiative, however cautious and unwilling the organization itself proved to be.

An American role?

Although the Gehlen Organization had been incorporated into the CIA's European operations, after 1956 the relationship changed. For one thing, in line with the Federal Republic gaining almost complete sovereignty in 1955, the CIA was prepared to allow Bonn to play a greater role in anti-communist psychological warfare within Germany itself, with the Germans accepting full political responsibility for any future actions taken.[133] What is more, according to Gehlen the CIA played a decisive role in establishing the BND as an accepted partner within Western intelligence circles as part of the political rehabilitation of the Federal Republic.[134] The CIA certainly contributed by connecting MI6 with the BND and so undermining the long-running British mistrust of Gehlen, but others have suggested that the value of the German service actually declined for the Americans, both in terms of the quality of its intelligence and its liability for security leaks.[135] While a semblance of trust was built up between the Americans and several other Allied services (including the British and Dutch), "such trust had not developed with the BND, except between a few individuals at the Pullach level".[136] A gradual rapprochement between British and German political and business elites had been achieved through the important informal Königswinter conferences from 1950 onwards, but these did not stretch to include the Gehlen group.[137] The ground was not fertile enough for substantial cooperation, and this goes some way to explain why the BND was so keen to trade whatever information it could with its US ally in order to maintain its position.[138]

But the misgivings were two-way. Whereas the Studienbüro, according to von Dellingshausen, "guaranteed" American participation (although this was not always the case), the *colloques* were different. The influence of Gaullism is noticeable here, as well as the deep mistrust of the CIA within the SDECE due to the Americans' secret involvement in shipping arms to the Algerian rebels in the late 1950s.[139] The Germans may not have been so militant about it, but similar negative sentiments certainly existed. Foertsch's proposal for an Information Centre from October 1959 includes a significant aside. Referring to the necessity of obtaining funding and experienced personnel, the document remarks that ideally this could be arranged through "the authority of one or more 'major promoters' (a personality of the Catholic Church, a prominent Jewish personality, not an American)".[140] There were practicalities involved here, since the aim was to avoid the new venture immediately being stamped as a CIA operation. But it also reveals the extent to which Interdoc was intended to move away from a US-centric outlook on Cold War ideology. In this sense BND interest in Interdoc exactly represented a bold move towards propagating its own perspective on the division of Germany in particular and the Cold War ideological contest in general. Van den Heuvel's response to Foertsch was revealing:

> It seems to me decidedly *incorrect* to exclude the Americans. In the first place because of their position as leader in the Western world. In the second place because that is precisely where we will find a great willingness to support this project. In the third place because the possibility for material help is predominantly present there. I am not so concerned for the label "American help"; the communists will call it that anyway.[141]

The US was present in these deliberations, albeit at a distance. According to a letter from Einthoven to Prince Bernhard from early 1962, the Dutchman had undertaken the task of establishing Interdoc due to requests from "French, German, and American friends (Allen Dulles)" to make use of his remarkable array of contacts in both NATO and the neutrals (Sweden and Switzerland).[142] It was to be expected, therefore, that at the very least the CIA would be fully informed of developments, if not as an actual partner. The Dutch also had a trump card in hand. In discussing possible locations for the institute, Foertsch remarked that "as neutral a site as possible is desired, to counter national misgivings". Two possibilities were mentioned: The Hague or Geneva. What is most interesting in this regard is that the Netherlands was far from being a neutral country in official diplomatic terms. Foertsch was clearly referring to neutrality in a more general sense, as in how others would perceive a leading role for the Dutch and the local reactions that such an institute might trigger. In this sense The Hague was ideal. It made use of both the networking and the informal international bridge-building skills of the Dutch (think of Bilderberg), and it recognized the value of the BVD in developing the project as a whole. It reflected the long-running concern of both Einthoven and Van den Heuvel to bring greater cohesion to Western anti-communism, and their lack of any great power pretentions. The other nations (particularly the Americans) saw the Dutch as useful arbitrators and "middle-men" and *not* as competitors. For Foertsch, it also indicated the willingness of the Dutch to act as a front site for German interests.

But the Dutch had their own agenda as well. The close relations between the Dutch and American intelligence services did suggest that a greater American involvement in the new organization would be inevitable. As ex-BVD officer Fritz Hoekstra has recorded, "in the 1950s the Americans started to strengthen their ties with the Dutch services by providing aid: They simply purchased a more or less 'master–servant relationship' with a substantial amount of dollars."[143] CIA technical and financial support provided up to 10 per cent of the total BVD budget through the 1950s and 1960s, BVD personnel took part in CIA training programmes, and the Dutch willingly supplied intelligence to the Americans without there being a *quid pro quo* arrangement (or, for that matter, a formal governmental authorization for such an exchange).[144] It is understandable, therefore, that the Dutch made consistent efforts in the following years to bring the Americans in.

2
Building the Network

> So that I can devote myself to the immense task of influencing people: to inform them about the dangers, to show them the darkness in order to make them appreciate the light.
>
> Louis Einthoven, 1961[1]

Defining Western values

Communist strategy focused on speeding the disintegration of the capitalist West by undermining the sense of threat within society – that was what peaceful coexistence was all about. In these circumstances the military origins of psychological warfare had to be abandoned in order to emphasize that this was now a matter of everyday concern within every sector of civilian life. Western values, once taken for granted, now needed to be clarified, amplified, and literally ingrained into those sectors of the population who were most likely to come into contact with proselytizers of communism: businessmen, trade unionists, students, religious officials, the military. The problem was this: how to define Western values, and how to promote them?

This had obviously been a major issue in post-war West Germany, but it also occupied the BVD and its associates from the early 1950s onwards.[2] Einthoven had sought out expert help on the issue of why, in a well-off and stable country such as the Netherlands, people would still vote communist and sympathize with communism's standpoints: "What diagnosis could be put forward for this disease? And the following question: what kinds of psychopolitical therapy are available to turn this extremism around?"[3] In 1954–55 Einthoven (with Van den Heuvel and H.C. Neervoort, head of the BVD's operations section) arranged regular meetings at the home of the German émigré Professor Kurt Baschwitz (mass psychology and public opinion research), together with Jan Barents (political science) and Evert Hofstee (sociology), to discuss the problem. Barents had contributed to Van den Heuvel's book *De Grondslagen van het Communisme* (The Foundations of Communism), which he used in the training of BVD personnel.[4]

Unfortunately, the poor health of both Barents and Hofstee prevented much progress, but Einthoven looked positively on this first attempt to link up with outside experts, even if "it was sometimes painful to note how little researchers knew of practical work".[5]

The next opportunity arose via the Defence Study Centre (DSC: Defensie Studie Centrum), established in 1951 by General Michaël Calmeyer to promote research and training on the strategy of modern warfare and the role of the Netherlands in the Western defence apparatus. In 1953–54, under the supporting leadership of DSC director Vice-Admiral F.J. Kist, Van den Heuvel was brought in via Einthoven to provide a course on the communist ideological threat and the need to activate the "moral power" of the Dutch population as the best response. "An equally concrete social goal" based on the realization of democratic potential and material well-being was essential, because while "the creation of a favourable climate for the spiritual realization of each individual" was the desired outcome, it was also the individualization of Western society that made it vulnerable (the West is "threatened from *inside* out"). Discussions took place during 1954–55 on a possible "separate service" to use civil society organizations to promote psychological stamina in the face of war, but the focus remained limited, whereas Einthoven and Van den Heuvel wanted to broaden the approach as a fundamental aspect of everyday life in the Cold War. The replacement of Kist (who became the coordinator of the intelligence and security services in the Minister-President's office) by General Mathon in April 1956 also signalled a change of tack, Mathon being less charmed by the input of the BVD men. Van den Heuvel lost his instructor position and the connection with the DSC was broken until Mathon was succeeded as director in the early 1960s by first Admiral Bos (who attended the Interdoc *colloque* in Oxford in September 1963) and then Max Broekmeijer.[6]

The arrival of the *colloques* gave these efforts new impetus. The fact-finding trips to Germany and Britain had brought together a group of around twelve representatives of Dutch big business (Shell, KLM (Koninklijke Luchtvaart Maatschappij (Dutch Airlines)), Unilever, the State Mining Company, Philips, the Dutch Railways, the Dutch Post and Telephone Company, and the employers' union). With Frans den Hollander as the lynchpin, the intention was that he would "peddle these ideas around his fifteen corporate boardrooms" to generate interest in a new institute. As Einthoven put it, "let's please not join up with Vrede en Vrijheid".[7] The first Dutch delegation to a *colloque* in 1958 included Hornix, H.J. Rijks of the Batavische Petroleum Maatschappij (Shell), theologian Zacharias Anthonisse, and *Vrije Volk* editor H. van Hulst. Anthonisse had trained as a Catholic missionary in the 1930s with the intention of forming a mission in Russia (he made it as far as Estonia by 1940); after the war he worked with East European refugees in Munich before being appointed professor in Nijmegen. He would become a fixed part of the wider BVD circle for the next decade. The US trip in early 1959 added the intellectual talents of Hogewind and Van den Berg, as well as consolidating the practical link with the railways via De Pous.[8] By 1960, therefore, the network had been assembled for justifying and promoting a Dutch national institute, a cause given a major boost by the US trip. The next move was to define its message. Einthoven, looking back in his autobiography more than a decade later, offered the following:

> The need for a public alert and able to defend itself against a regime striving for world domination, so that people at least appreciate the preservation of its democratic freedoms, the "values of the West". Vague concepts, partly because they are difficult to describe in simple terms [...] Many believe Western values can be summarized in a slogan: democracy. But I am convinced that democracy is never an end in itself. It is only a means to achieve freedom of conscience, *liberté de conscience*. This is the highest good.[9]

In September 1959 Hornix and Van den Heuvel compiled a think-piece report for a *colloque* on Western values and how they might be promoted within society. Hornix began by stressing the general dissatisfaction with many definitions for being either too simplistic or opaque. There was also the problem of ambiguity. The Soviet Union used Marxist–Leninist ideology to claim ownership of "freedom", "individual respect", and "justice", causing misunderstandings in trying to differentiate East from West (which was precisely one of the Soviet goals). But there were ways to differentiate, and to make the public aware of the difference. Van den Heuvel emphasized that communism "provides a logical answer – based on its ideology and world view – to every problem [...] The feeling of being 'chosen' as the vanguard of humanity, to have an answer to everything, an absolutist doctrine, leads to the desire to lead and control everything."[10] Using the work of André Philip in response, Hornix waxed lyrical: European culture is *exactly* incomplete, impossible to realize, open to doubt, and contradictory beyond any hope of synthesis. It was this sense of *ongoing* development, never finished, which created the space for free individuals to fulfil their potential in all walks of life.

> Each Western value is a paradox, an open value [...] Life is ultimately a game. He who does not know how to smile, is not alive. This is, in relation to a streamlined, organized, complete lifestyle, a substantial deficit. A deficit, however, that the West insists makes life liveable. The West sets behind all values, after the so-called Western values as well as the values of the Soviet Union, a comma. This comma is the value of the West, that is really Western, provided that the sentence after the comma remains incomplete.[11]

Western values were essentially defined as the right of free choice for every individual, balanced by the responsibility to take the rights, opinions, and beliefs of others into account. Taking a social democratic stance, this should represent the "right to education and social, political and economic development under equal protection of the law". By making citizens aware that these values were under threat – especially as the threat was largely unnoticed – it would be possible to develop a "resilient freedom", a freedom that was grounded in the conscience of each individual and not taken for granted. At the centre of this value system lay the UN's Universal Declaration of Human Rights (UDHR). The editorial for the first issue of *Oost-West*, the journal established by Van den Heuvel's circle in 1962 (see chapter 3), stated that the publication aimed to oppose the communist position by supporting "objective scientific method, democracy, law, equality (in the sense of a rejection of any form of discrimination) and social justice". *Oost-West* editor Willem Couwenberg saw the journal as representing "the underlying interrelationship" between these values as portrayed in the UDHR. The communist desire for an ideal society effectively "trampled on" this set of values.[12] As East–West relations relaxed further and the Détente era took shape in the early 1970s, the UDHR was increasingly taken up by both Van den Heuvel and Couwenberg – in their own particular ways – as the guiding theme by which to define "the West" from "the East".

Van den Heuvel focused on the practical issues of how to get this message across. "*Voorlichting*" – literally "information" – covers many meanings: instructing, advising, informing, pleading for, promoting, or propagandizing. All were appropriate for the job at hand: to ensure that the essential values of Western society were consciously appreciated as a guide for beliefs and behaviour. This had to be a subtle business, tuning in on existing psychological and emotional motivations of those to be informed: "The more he sees – or still better: feels – a connection with the things that he deals with every day, the better the impact will be."[13] Communism did not play so much on the existence of poverty as on a sense of dissatisfaction or exclusion among individuals. It sought to split the non-communist world along lines of mistrust and anger: workers from capitalists, Europe from the US, the developing world from the West. The response had to involve providing a higher goal, a future perspective, with which individuals could identify and around which they could orientate themselves. The best way to achieve this was first to demonstrate that communist theory and practice were fundamentally contradictory, since no "perfect society" could be created via the violence and repression of dictatorship and class war. With this as the basis, the goal was to set in motion the "training and forming of individuals" who could spread this "value consciousness" throughout society. Only in this way could the distinction between West and East, which was crumbling under the influence of Soviet "peaceful coexistence", be reinstated. Thus Van den Heuvel, betraying something of his Protestant background, remarked that "one really values light as light if one also knows the dark".[14]

Proselytizing Western values in a meaningful way was the necessary move from negative to positive anti-communism. This had been a long-running problem in the West since the late 1940s. C.D. Jackson, Eisenhower's special adviser on psychological warfare, had bemoaned the fact that it was apparently so difficult for the West to project "a positive rather than a negative approach" to the peoples of the Soviet bloc, despite the realities of communist rule. Nelson Rockefeller had been trying to formulate a positive "constructive diplomacy" approach since 1955 with the Quantico meetings, but with mixed success.[15] European developments offered one way forward. Von Dellingshausen, writing in 1957, spoke of the importance of "the European idea and the necessity of European integration and the design of the future European territories in the East" for transforming the Western message "from the negative of anti-communism [...] to the positive state of democratic education".[16] The *colloques*, and subsequently Interdoc, were to base their whole approach on this shift from negative to positive. The communist challenge as represented by peaceful coexistence demanded some self-reflection in the West on what it stood for. This must not be "pressed into the constraints" of a one-sided, black-and-white ideology or degenerate "into an uncensored glorification of our own system", but "must also point out the defects of democracy, and must not ignore the truths which every movement – communism included – possesses".[17] Writing in 1967, Van den Heuvel emphasized how peaceful coexistence could be "a double-edged sword", but the West had to be careful:

> The West can exploit this situation but this should be done in an intelligent way. If we – in our contact with the Communist world – boast proudly about our superior values and achievements, and if we expose disdainfully the evils, weaknesses and shortcomings of Communism, we shall only contribute to frustration and aggressiveness, and we shall gain nothing. We should develop more modest ways in explaining the foundations and institutions of our society.[18]

As Couwenberg put it decades later, "we conceived of communism as a challenge to our society, to improve the structure and the development of our society".[19]

The formation of a Dutch National Institute

Intelligence services such as the BVD possessed a great deal of information and analytical expertise on communist methods, but the problem lay in channelling this material into the public arena to achieve the desired influence and effect on wider opinion. There was resistance to the idea that the BVD would take on such a direct role in influencing people's opinions, as it fuelled fears of a police state. Yet the BVD was the best informed about the strategy, tactics, and methods employed by communist forces to infiltrate and undermine Western society. What to do about this?[20] Vrede en Vrijheid was a first attempt, but its methods were quite simplistic. Looking for other possibilities, in 1954 Van den Heuvel stated the following:

> What the BVD does is gather information on communism and the activities of its supporters that are dangerous for the state, and promotes security measures in response. This more or less indirect response to communism – albeit an important one – is only one side of the total response. Without a goal-driven offensive psychological warfare approach, the West will always be on the defensive and at a disadvantage.[21]

Of the various means to combat communism – politically, economically, with weapons – it was the ideological–psychological realm that was by far the most important "because it is positive [...] it maintains the possibility of attracting supporters from among its opponents". His conclusion points the way ahead: "Although the ideological warfare against communism is not a task of the BVD, I believe that there is every reason to be better informed about this."[22] By the late 1950s he was receiving an increasing number of requests for help in crafting anti-communist information, from the military, from business, from the police.[23] The problem was that intelligence and security services obviously needed to work in secret. They could channel information to the press, but this was indirect. It would be far better to have an institute, in the public realm, directly occupied with the study of communism and ways to oppose it. But official governmental support for this initiative had been ruled out before. Einthoven's contacts with Minister-President Drees and his successor De Quay brought only the message that direct governmental involvement was impossible. The BVD was not going to touch it either, it being outside its official responsibility. The only way forward was to go private, since, as Einthoven remarked, "psychological defence or attack" could sometimes "be better taken by a private institution than by Government services", for instance "if this action would be based on classified information".[24] Logical, but still, it was unknown territory.

The result was the Stichting voor Onderzoek van Ecologische Vraagstukken (SOEV – Foundation for the Investigation of Problems of Ecology), created in April 1960. Van den Heuvel was still in the BVD at the time, and he ran it initially from his front room in Mechelsestraat, The Hague, in order to maintain a distance – an element of deniability – from official government structures. SOEV's name clearly betrayed the influence of the CIA-funded Society for the Investigation of Human Ecology in New York, and the Dutch followed the American example, "albeit with a different accent".[25] The name was something of a problem, because the phrase "human ecology" was not so well known in Dutch (or European) public life at the time. With Van den Heuvel as director, the initial plan was to begin with a group of researchers, but financial constraints reduced this to one member of staff, the psychologist J. Ibelings, with other expertise hired in as necessary. (Ibelings went on to join the social research department of Unilever in 1962.[26])

SOEV presented itself as a centre devoted to researching the "human ecology" of communism: how it determined the socio-political and economic environment of individuals, and how individuals responded psychologically. Built into this was attention to the methods used to expand communist influence through psychological warfare (the "very misleading" theme of peaceful coexistence), and the best methods for "neutralizing" it.[27] In 1961 SOEV shifted its attention to "cadre forming" – the training of others to act as sentinels for Western values throughout society. The complications of the modern world (with the evolving East–West division at its centre) required that the fundamentals be clearly explained. During the 1959 US trip the Dutch visitors had been impressed by American business ethics and corporate social responsibility and the ways in which US corporations were running socio-economic improvement projects for their workers and, in cooperation with local residents, for their immediate environment. The US model, based as it was on strong feelings of anti-statism and self-help, could not be adopted wholesale outside of its social context, but the visitors came away convinced that "there is yet great scope for the Dutch manager".[28] The aim was to develop a programme that would place the psychological warfare aspects of anti-communism ("immunization") and the promotion of Western values within a broad promotion of "civil education" and active citizenship.[29] In this way the sense of propaganda would be reduced, since the message was fully grounded in an understanding of democracy, democratic freedoms, and the role and responsibilities of the individual. For many in the West the political environment was becoming confusing. Peaceful coexistence was blurring the concept of "freedom" and the difference between West and East, and reducing the will to defend the core values and interests of free society. Ibelings' study among Dutch students had shown that there was a lack of understanding over what "the West" still stood for: "on the political level the result is tolerance, as a reflection of insecurity".[30] In these circumstances it was far from guaranteed that individuals would receive sufficient guidance or make the right decisions:

> If it is considered desirable that man in the West correctly judges communism and, in the present-day pluriform and polyvalent society, knowledgeably makes his political choice for the Western democratic system, then he needs knowledge of the one and the other. He can obtain this knowledge in various ways. Experience shows, however, that private initiative generally falls short.[31]

SOEV was a wholly private venture with private financial support, much of it from the Dutch Railways and from Shell. Shell provided finance, staff, property, and even one of its best translators, Willem de Boer, to work on Interdoc materials. H.J. Rijks (head of the Royal Dutch Shell Laboratory in Amsterdam up to 1960) and Cees de Niet (head of the Central Administrative Services Division until 1964), both Shell employees, acted as successive SOEV treasurers, indicating the strong mutual interest in consolidating the links between SOEV and the multinational. Before moving to Shell, De Niet had been a BVD officer in Section D, responsible for preventive measures against espionage, infiltration, sabotage, and other subversive tactics, and he knew Van den Heuvel from the war years.[32] SOEV moved from Van den Heuvel's front room to rented office space at Plaats 11a in central The Hague in 1961–62, followed by a temporary location at the Shell offices in "Les Galeries", an impressive former hotel complex at Gevers Deynootplein, on the coast in Scheveningen, during late 1962 and early 1963. Among the five Shell sections housed there was the personnel department where De Niet worked.[33] Shell, as SOEV secretary Lyda de Bree put it much later, was "very important" for the whole operation, and the multinational remained the main Dutch benefactor of the whole operation throughout the 1960s and into the 1970s. In 1963 Van den Heuvel was able to move all activities to the spacious (rented) villa at Van Stolkweg 10, taking all the furniture from Les Galeries with him. This was a real advantage since, as De Bree remarked, "we now had the space to hold meetings". Van den Heuvel would remain in business there until 1 September 1986.[34] In all three locations Louis Einthoven had his own office, and in Van Stolkweg he even took a bedroom on the top floor, so that he did not always have to return in the evening to his home in Lunteren, in the east of the Netherlands.

While SOEV's original board (Hornix, Van den Heuvel, Rijks, and Hogewind) and advisers (Van den Berg, Zacharias, and Major F.C. Spits of the air force information service) included the usual suspects, other contacts were developing. K.J. Hahn, international secretary for the Catholic People's Party (KVP: Katholieke Volkspartij), the largest party in the Netherlands at the time, was a regular contact. A Belgian connection was opened up when Professor Max Lamberty of Leuven University (author of the 1961 book *Wat is Westerse cultuur?*) joined the board in 1962. When SOEV was created, Van den Heuvel took with him several members of his training team from the BVD: S.W. (Willem) Couwenberg and Herman Mennes (who both joined SOEV's staff in 1962), and C. Ottolini. They were joined by, among others, the journalists Max Nord (*Het Parool*) and J.R.G. Verreijdt (*Het Vaderland*), the BVD officer turned employers' union security expert G. Diepenhorst, the BVD officer turned Shell personnel manager Cees de Niet, and the wartime resistance hero Lieutenant Colonel J.J.F. Borghouts ("Peter Zuid") to form a study group on how to transfer SOEV research into practical effect. During 1960–61 this group developed a series of 20 discussion seminars for media and government personnel, covering the theory and the practice, the strengths and the weaknesses, of communist ideology and peaceful coexistence, followed by a series on Western values.

The ideas and the approach were getting sharper. Mennes, who had joined the BVD to become an agent runner but was soon taken under Van den Heuvel's wing in the training section, concentrated on the Militant Liberty programme as an example of an attempt to mobilize support in society, translating it into "Weerbare Vrijheid" (Resilient Freedom).[35] Couwenberg, a journalist and director of the Catholic trade union's training school, had come to prominence in 1956 with the publication of *De Vereenzaming van de Moderne Mens* (The Alienation of Modern Man), a socio-philosophical tract that traced the effects of ongoing individualization, its political consequences, and possible solutions to reconstruct social relations, including a section on "cadre forming" in the workplace.[36] As Couwenberg recalled later, Van den Heuvel "contacted me and came to my house and asked me if I was prepared to cooperate with him in founding some courses on all sorts of things. So our relationship started with developing courses on sociological and political issues for members of the BVD."[37] At the time the idea that two individuals from strong Catholic and Protestant backgrounds would work together on such a project was highly unusual in the stratified society of 1950s Netherlands. But both were freethinkers, and both refused to be hemmed in by petty faith-based barriers.

In the Western values project Couwenberg contributed a more historically grounded vision than the previous elegiac prose of Hornix. Focusing on the essential nature of the "independent free personality" in Western thought, Couwenberg emphasized that "the individual is a goal in himself" and is not to be undermined by a greater plan for social progress.[38] But there were problems when faced with how to defend these values. First, individual rights were being challenged in the mid-twentieth century by the social rights of equality and the welfare state, causing many to remark on the gradual convergence of communist and state capitalist systems. As if this did not pose enough difficulty, the Western world suffered from an unmistakeable political apathy.

> While in the time of Roosevelt the greatest threat was fear, which had taken over the American people in the 1930s, for Kennedy it is the spirit of self-satisfaction and the consequent inertia, which is highly dangerous in the struggle against world communism.[39]

Hornix developed this by emphasizing how modern society was in a state of flux, with traditional values no longer offering sufficient guidelines in the maelstrom of information that individuals were faced with. In this context, a coherent value system – such as communism – can become appealing as an all-inclusive answer. At this point Van den Heuvel came in with the counter-strategy, not for an alternative one-dimensional Western ideology, but for raising awareness of the necessarily open, developing character of Western society in which all groups could contribute to a better existence.[40] At the centre of this approach was an appreciation of Leninism and its goals. It had been Lenin who crafted a political strategy to respond to the critique of capitalism provided by Marx and Engels. This involved not only the analysis and optimization of contradictions in the enemy's society, but also, crucially, the training of cadres in the workplace and society at large to enable them to understand their "true consciousness" and their role in political action (or their role in history, as it were). As one study put it, Leninist propaganda was "only one aspect of a total program of action which ranges from primary education to industrial and agricultural production, and which encompasses all literature, art and leisure. The entire life of the citizen becomes the object of propaganda."[41] The Comintern had put this into action at the Lenin School in Moscow during 1926–38, transforming through "systematic study and suitable political education" the leadership of foreign communist parties into "an iron elite of disciplined Leninist cadres".[42] For the group around Van den Heuvel, the task was to take the principles of Leninism and turn them around – literally, to use them against the Marxist–Leninist state itself. Cadre training lay at the centre of this vision. As the historian Robert Service put it in 1989:

> Great political changes, [Lenin] maintained, do not come about only because large social groups will them; leaders have to supply the decisions and the direction. Nor is leadership an innate gift. Training and experience are vital, and any effective party – or, by implication, any substantial modern organization – has to husband its personnel as a vital resource. Stability of cadres, too, was necessary [...] [Lenin] repeatedly asserted that a determinant role in the preparation of mass opinion would have to be played by serious thinkers and the popularizers of their thought. By implication, leaders with correct doctrine could tip the balance of history.[43]

Bonnemaison played a vital role in this thinking process. As he explained to Brian Crozier, "Marxism is a philosophy. It has a right to exist. Leninism is activism and a threat to the State."[44] The best way to defeat Leninism was to use the same methods, but coming from a different direction. The defensive–offensive psychological warfare strategy of SOEV – the combination of enhancing awareness of the communist threat with the clarification and projection of the values that best opposed it – would later be a constant motif of Interdoc. Van den Heuvel wrote at the time: "psychological warfare has two sides: the build-up of moral strength within one's own side and the undermining of the morale of the opposing side".[45]

SOEV was just the first step. While its training programmes were intended to raise the necessary finance to make it self-sustainable, it also sought to become the centre of all anti-communist activities in the Netherlands. This was a delicate business, since other institutions already had a claim on this terrain. SOEV's 1962 Annual Report presented the institute as being at the centre of a national network (Defence Study Centre, National Federal Council of the Former Resistance, Volk en Verdediging, Vrede en Vrijheid, Werkcomité voor Opvoeding tot Democratie) and of an international network (covering West Germany, France, Britain, Italy, Switzerland, and the US). But initial plans for expanding SOEV's board to include members of other national institutions had to be abandoned in 1962–63 in favour of regular but informal meetings for the sharing of information on activities.[46] Clearly some existing institutions did not appreciate being marshalled by a newcomer, even if there was agreement on the greater cause.

Some partnerships did develop, as with the National Federal Council of the Former Resistance in the Netherlands (NFR: Nationale Federatieve Raad van het Voormalige Verzet Nederland). The NFR had been formed in 1947 to represent the interests of those who had worked in the resistance during World War II. Van den Heuvel, as a prominent member of the Albrecht Group, was active in the NFR. He had a close ally in Borghouts, who led a movement for change within NFR that produced a resolution at the 1958 annual conference to expand its influence and propagate its wartime legacy throughout Dutch society. A committee under Borghouts was formed to develop a programme, with Moral Rearmament as a source of inspiration (the hand of Van den Heuvel is clear here). Prince Bernhard was asked to lead the campaign, but he declined.[47] Nevertheless in May 1959 Borghouts became NFR chair and placed the new campaign, now termed "Geestelijke Weerbaarheid" (Psychological Defence), at the centre of NFR activities. Speaking after his appointment, Borghouts emphasized that, while the members of the NFR would die out, their ideals and their spirit must not, otherwise "the Netherlands is as good as lost". Borghouts led from the front, giving lectures around the country to revive the values fought for in World War II.[48] The response was positive, particularly among those NFR members who "are involved in educational activities with the youth".[49] The NFR's members knew what it meant to be confronted with a threat to their way of life, and they understood the importance of passing on this understanding to other generations – and its relevance in the Cold War context. As Borghouts said in 1958,"the battle still rages today, perhaps more severely than before".[50]

In March 1961 Van den Heuvel (communism), together with Hornix (spiritual defence of the Western world), Spits (the East–West situation), and army pastor C.M. Graafstal (Western values), ran a conference on the theme for NFR members in Hilversum, and the NFR agreed to work closely with SOEV to spread the message further.[51] The NFR added its membership to local councils and secondary schools, exactly the areas of interest for enabling SOEV to reach a wide cross-section of Dutch youth and society. A list of possible speakers to spread the Psychological Defence message was drawn up, which included European Agriculture Commissioner Sicco Mansholt (European unity) and the young academic Frans Alting von Geusau (the UN). Van den Heuvel was initially listed as an expert on psychological warfare, but his name was crossed out – the second thoughts probably coming from this being too out in the open for someone still with the BVD. Nevertheless, having left the service on 1 January 1962, he immediately joined the NFR's board and from there, with the full support of Borghouts, coordinated the linkage of the NFR and SOEV. Soon after, the Federation's publication duly changed its name from *VVN* to *GW-VVN* and then *Geestelijke Weerbaarheid*, with Van den Heuvel adapting its content to expand its readership beyond NFR members.[52]

Relations were also built up with the Dutch Railways (NS: Nederlandse Spoorwegen). In August 1950 it had been decided that the BVD could make use of personnel working in "vital and vulnerable government and private institutions" in order to fulfil its mission of national security. As a result, since the early 1950s Van den Heuvel had been directly involved in training railway police personnel in intelligence and observation work and agent running, to enable them to monitor the activities of communist trade union members.[53] The head of the railway police, De Pous, belonged to the "club" of security officers from the major companies (National Post, Telegraph, and Telephone Company (PTT: Staatsbedrijf der Posterijen, Telegrafie en Telefonie), Philips, the State Mining Company, Unilever, BPM (Batavische Petroleum Maatschappij) -Shell, KLM, and Fokker) who met about once every two months to discuss common concerns. In this connection De Pous had already travelled to the US in May 1956, to examine American methods in railway security with an eye on possible West European cooperation in this field.[54] De Pous himself was fully aware of what the Cold War meant in practice. He quoted Clausewitz's dictum on the political dimensions of warfare in his service's 1956 annual report, and he agreed that "attention must be given to the points and areas where an enemy has good offensive possibilities, as much in a material sense as in a political, ideological, and psychological sense".[55] With the positive influence of NS chief den Hollander in the background, De Pous oversaw the gradual expansion from 1957 onwards by Van den Heuvel and his colleagues of their access to NS personnel, with cadre training and orientation lectures on communism. By September 1960 senior NS staff were offered a six-month course run by Couwenberg (still with the BVD), and by 1962, with SOEV backed by NS finance, the institute was providing in return a series of courses for top, middle, and lower management in the pleasant surroundings of the village of Laage Vuursche, near Utrecht.[56]

Alongside the NFR and the NS, SOEV continued to broaden its presence in Dutch public life. A positive article in the newspaper *Trouw* in February 1962 announced the arrival of SOEV as a public institution. Van den Heuvel was quoted on the need for an "offensive coexistence" with the communist world, whereby his institute would provide the necessary information and clarity on how to deal with the Soviet bloc: "We want to function as a kind of signpost for others. Communism presents as much a challenge as a threat for us."[57] In the same year Van den Heuvel published a series of three articles on psychological warfare in the main journal for Dutch armed services personnel.[58] Civil–military relations were at the centre of the SOEV network. In August 1962 it was joined by the Stichting Volk en Verdediging (Foundation for Citizens and Defence). Under the symbolic leadership of Prince Bernhard and with Hornix as secretary, Volk en Verdediging sought to maintain close relations between the Dutch people and its military services, and to generate appreciation of their continuing importance for the well-being of the Netherlands. With its royal patronage and impressive non-partisan list of political supporters, Volk en Verdediging provided the perfect large-scale backdrop for the more focused activities of SOEV and its allies.[59] The link with the military was further cemented when Borghouts, who had been involved in air force training programmes since 1951, became head of personnel welfare in that service in 1961, followed by overall chief of air force personnel in 1964 and, from July 1965 until his untimely death in February 1966, State Secretary for Defence. Van den Heuvel had powerful allies – often World War II resistance veterans – through which he could broaden out SOEV's anti-communist mission.

Preliminary plans for Interdoc 1960–61

SOEV showed what could be done, and it encouraged the Dutch to push for similar success at the international level. At the sixth *colloque*, in Aix-en-Provence on 25–26 March 1960, a couple of weeks before SOEV officially came into existence, a working group was established to pave the way towards an international institute. With Einthoven as chair, it consisted of Theodor Krause (BND) and Günter Triesch (Deutsches Industrie-Institut) from the Federal Republic, Guy Lemonnier (a member of Georges Albertini's *Est-Ouest* group) and L. Préchac from France, plus the Dutchmen Van den Heuvel and Hornix. Meetings were held in The Hague in May and in Cologne in July. The group first produced the outline for a documentation centre. Activities would include compiling a card-index system to list all known organizations and publications related to the study of communism, and a regular bulletin covering the latest developments in international communism and up-to-date bibliographic details of books and articles on this subject.[60] No group or individual publically active in the field of communist studies and anti-communism in Western Europe, the US, and (gradually) the rest of the world was to be left out of this comprehensive overview. By the time of the following *colloque*, in Heelsum on 30 September 1960, a draft set of statutes had been drawn up. There was as yet no name, and the organization's purpose was described as "the promotion of research and the study of environmental [ecological] influences on the individual, from both social and material surroundings".[61] The working group came out in favour of creating the institute by a step-by-step process instead of "with a fixed design" (*met een forse opzet*). A four-phase development was therefore planned out, with each phase taking one year and involving a gradual increase in staff to a total of 22: documentation and indexation, evaluation, "action", and expansion.[62] "All the centre's activities and those of the national centres must eventually lead to action. Such action must be developed directly or indirectly by the international centre [...] [and] may take various forms, such as: information, training or special campaigns."[63] While it was anticipated that the institute's provision of advice and training (part of "action") would produce revenue, "one should not be too optimistic, this will not bring in more than 10–15 per cent of the total needed to cover annual costs".[64] The annual budget in these preliminary schemes ranged from 150,000 to 500,000 guilders (DM 167,000 to 550,000). Everything remained provisional – "the political situation, the cooperation, the available resources, the choice of location, etc." – but it was starting to take shape:

> Concerning the location for the proposed documentation centre, there was at first no unanimity in the committee [...] A place that was more or less centrally situated between the three cooperating nations was suggested. In this respect Brussels was considered, a neutral country such as Switzerland was also mentioned, where Geneva might be a possibility. In the beginning it seems necessary to ensure constant oversight of the centre. In relation to this, it seems most desirable if this work could be carried out in the immediate environment of the chairman of the committee, which means The Hague. This location also has the advantage that local influence will make specific facilities available.[65]

Einthoven was beginning to get his way, but there were plenty of glitches to sort out in the coming months. At the instigation of Foertsch, the legal status of the institute had to be clarified, as did the rights of any future employees.[66] This was new ground for all concerned, and careful steps had to be taken. Foremost was the fact that a Dutch foundation (*stichting*), the intended form, had different meanings in both France and Germany, causing some confusion. The Germans eventually agreed to it, since establishing a link with an equivalent *eingetragener Verein* was possible. The French remained unconvinced due to their different legal requirements, but the decisive factor was that favourable tax rebates could be gained in this way in the Federal Republic and, in particular, in the Netherlands. Next came the relationship with the national institutes: how would they be represented? To avoid giving away too much autonomy, the French emphasized that the international institute should always be seen as an addition to the national institutes. If this unique form of cooperation was going to work, it had to involve close oversight – which in the intelligence world meant everyone watching everyone else. The danger was that the international institute would become too powerful, overshadowing interests at the national level. By December 1960 it was agreed that the new institute would be in the Netherlands, but only on the condition that there would be a French and a German representative working with the Dutch director.[67]

As 1960 turned into 1961, there was a real sense of momentum. Within the Federal Republic the BND launched an action plan which stressed the need to shift from a strategic defensive to a tactical offensive posture. This required integrated contacts both nationally (centring on the Chancellery) and internationally (with other Western powers and NATO). Listing a batch of themes to be addressed, "the USSR's neo-imperialism and neo-colonialism" – a topic that would feature highly in Interdoc's first "counter-action" – was the main issue of importance for international audiences. The fundamental aim of the proposal was to take the initiative away from the GDR in the field of propaganda. Every contradiction in every message coming out of "the Zone" would have to be taken apart, critically repackaged, and thrown back. This would be done not so much by priming the mass media, but literally by making use of "other viable channels":

> These are available if the principle is followed that the goal justifies a higher expense. If the desired discussion is first mobilized from below, the mass media will not be able to escape participating.[68]

These were the ideas being presented at the *colloques*, floated here for the first time within the German discussions. The aim was not to fall back on the media but to address the very question of how to influence the way (key sections of) society thought about communism, the Soviet Union, China, the Cold War – and Western values. From that, everything else – defensively and offensively – would follow. Crucially the BND document admitted that the service "cannot have a leading but only an assistance role (provision of documents and *Wirkungskontrolle*)". Did this assistance role fully encompass what the *colloques* were proposing? The BND clearly thought so, and was now an equal player within the German discussions (which by 1961 involved five ministries, the Chancellery, the Bundesverfassungsschutz, and the service). Others would soon question the service's mandate on this terrain.

The Aix-en-Provence and Heelsum *colloques* had given the proposed institute a name: Interdoc, reflecting its principal task of gathering international documentation. But there was still some way to go. Van den Heuvel sent the *colloques*' plans to colleagues in the CIA for comment, only to hear that it was still unclear "to what extent the Institute is supposed to be a support or an action mechanism, whether it is an independent Europe-wide organization or a co-ordinating body of national organizations, and so forth". The Americans were also unimpressed that the proposed bibliographic bulletin covered only Dutch, French, and German publications (with a few British and American ones): "How can anybody concern himself with international Communism without knowing about publications in Russian?"[69] Nevertheless, step-by-step Interdoc was put together. In the attempt to avoid an over-ambitious agenda, attention turned to training, referred to as the "primary task" for producing Western "cadres". The national institutes needed to focus on those groups most vulnerable to and affected by communist infiltration, with Interdoc coordinating these activities and providing a focal point for the cadre trainers in the different countries. Whereas only a few years previously the focus had still been on the working class, by 1961 it was felt that "communist influence today is proportionately greater in certain scientific, religious and cultural circles". But the emphasis lay on business and industry, and on the need to convince the managers that more needed to be done to promote politically aware citizenship. Among the managers themselves, those coming into contact with communists at international congresses were important both defensively and offensively for "transmitting western ideas into the Communist camp". The training would involve the ideology and practice of communism, communist psychological warfare, Western values, and possibilities for defensive and offensive anti-communism.[70] Since cadre formation was the main goal, it was decided to turn the two *colloques* in 1962 over to comparing training practices in the participating nations and to generating interest and support among international business leaders. With training as the priority, Van den Heuvel's ten years of experience in this field with the BVD placed him in pole position to become Interdoc director.[71]

Einthoven retired from the BVD at the end of March 1961. Ideally he would have moved directly into Interdoc work, but the organization was still not in existence. The goal was put back to 1 January 1962.[72] Getting somewhat impatient with his European colleagues, Einthoven devoted the following six months to travelling in France, Germany, Italy, Britain, and Switzerland to generate the necessary financial and logistical support for a definite positive decision. After the first round of talks in April–June he reported the following: the Germans, thanks to the efforts of Foertsch, were fully on board; the French were supportive but somewhat chaotic and there were "many difficulties to overcome"; contacts with business and the Catholic church were leading towards Italy becoming the fourth participating nation.[73] In the Federal Republic Foertsch had now entered the inter-departmental debates and was taking a leading role. Western values needed to be promoted more in order to confront "one of the strongest communist weapons, the theatrical celebration of victory that 'subliminally' works more and more on the consciousness of people in the Federal Republic. If this influence is not immobilized, all other efforts are futile."[74] But first Westerners needed to understand what their political identity was. As Gerhard von Mende (closely connected with the German émigré community via the government-initiated contact body Forschungsdienst

Osteuropa) remarked, the clarifying of communist theory and practice at venues such as the Ostkolleg also carried the danger that individuals might appreciate it all the more.[75]

The French, having initiated the *colloques*, were now proving to be difficult partners. Einthoven remarked that "the people and groups who are fully occupied with anti-communism in France are either extreme right-wing Catholics or [World War II] collaborators [...] and those who for want of income have turned anti-communism into a profession". Among this last category were Russian émigré Boris Souvarine and Pierre Rostini, David's successor as chief of the former Paix et Liberté organization. Visiting with Bonnemaison, Einthoven saw for himself how Rostini ran a rather ramshackle but well-funded operation as an "anonymous information centre" supported by the SDECE and later by de Gaulle's prime minister Michel Debré to propagate anti-communist and pro-government propaganda, particularly for French policy in Africa. Despite Rostini's limitations (Einthoven described him as "at the most an average man [...] without prestige or leadership"), the model of an "independent organization that produced everything and anything for defending democracy" was "an excellent cover" and not to be dismissed.[76]

Contacts with the Catholics (de Fabrègues, Jean Madiran) were disappointing. For these activists there was no such thing as a trustworthy leftist, preventing them from making any contact with Catholic trade unions. Einthoven recognized that progressive elements of the Catholic hierarchy were considering making concessions to the communists in order to open up a dialogue, alienating those, including Madiran, who saw this as a dereliction of values. Yet this led only to a hardening of opposition instead of to an awareness of what needed to be done. Einthoven knew full well that mobilizing the Catholic church in both France and Italy would be an essential component of the international project. The Dutchman also sought out Georges Albertini, who, together with fellow wartime collaborator Guy Lemonnier and de Gaulle's former intelligence chief in London, André de Wavrin, ran an anti-communist headquarters funded by the Worms company.[77] Albertini wrote high-quality articles in his self-produced pamphlet *Est-Ouest*, but his wartime reputation meant that he would never reach beyond his existing circle of enthusiasts. Einthoven summed him up as *"een gevaarlijke wroeter"* (a dangerous scavenger) with strong fascist tendencies – an unlikely candidate with whom to join forces to defend democracy. A meeting with former socialist premier Guy Mollet produced mixed feelings of a different kind. Thanks to the influence of Prince Bernhard, Mollet granted Einthoven 45 minutes between other obligations, and although he appreciated the Dutchman's efforts he saw it only as incidental (*lapwerk*). Only full economic democracy, involving a fair distribution of wealth and worker participation in planning, could provide a future perspective that could compete with communism. Mollet was very dismissive of the

Americans, who had "an indescribable lack of psychological insight". What is more, he claimed that the Socialist party did quite enough of its own cadre training and did not require any more.[78] On the positive side, Einthoven did make some headway in French business circles. Herman van Karnebeek of Esso Netherlands set up a link with De Scheer of the company's French wing, and Frits Philips did the same with his French subsidiary via its president Haver Droeze and technical director Tal Larsen in France. Under the guiding hand of Shell chief F.A.C. (Felix) Guépin, Shell Française opened its doors for Bonnemaison to give a series of lectures on cadre formation, and this led the way for offering similar services elsewhere. Einthoven saw a chance to reach out to a whole swathe of middle management cadres in French big business, so that after ten years "throughout these companies there will be young people *able* and *keen* to get into a discussion with the communists, whereas at the moment there is an unbridgeable gap". He was also encouraged by meeting Georges de Lagarde, a Catholic lawyer who acted as a corporate adviser to the French employers' association. To Einthoven's delight, de Lagarde joined the Interdoc working group and planned to join him in Italy later that year to talk to the employers' association, the Christian Union of Business Executives (UCID).[79] But the overall impression of the French situation was sombre. The French people were "more divided and more confused than ever". The wartime division between the Gaullists and the supporters of Vichy remained critical: "In *this* France everything and anything can happen, also because nobody is busy with the *only* real enemy: communism." For the majority, the French Communist Party was seen as more or less an accepted part of the political scene and not as an arm of Russian influence.

> The French intelligence and security service, which anyway wasn't so well informed about the subversive activities of the communists, has its hands so completely full for the moment with the illegal Algerian movement and with the totally unacceptable ultra-right French groups that the communists have more or less an open playing field.[80]

De Gaulle himself had "too one-sided a view of Russian imperialism".[81] Bonnemaison was a good ally, but he was clearly isolated. Einthoven's negative view of the French situation would prove correct a year later.

The Dutch spy chief began a second round of travels in September 1961. Accompanied by the BND's vice-president, Horst Wendland, and Theodor Krause, he met von Dellingshausen, the Interior Ministry's security chief Dr Toyka, Heinrich Köppler of the Central Catholic Committee, Drs Merker and Küffner from the Chancellery, Triesch from the Industrie-Institut, and the Defence Ministry's psychological warfare experts. Einthoven's pitch, which emphasized the necessity of working together with existing institutes such as the Ostkolleg and the Studienbüro, went down well: "It is almost certain that the Germans will contribute to a large extent towards the financing of Interdoc", he stated, yet it would remain unclear for a while which part of the state would give what amount.[82] By the time of the Barbizon *colloque* in early October 1961, which included representatives from the Netherlands, France, West Germany, Italy, Britain, and Belgium (Professor Lamberty from Louvain), Einthoven had a full overview of the situation. In France and Italy, anti-communism was too much associated with the far right. Contacts in Italy rested on UCID, the Catholic employers' association, "since special services (and government in general) are afraid of being considered as fascists if they cooperate with Interdoc". In West Germany the level of anti-communist activity was such that no one really knew all the organizations working in this field, yet this was also the country that suffered the most from communist infiltration. Switzerland was a revelation due to the high level of public information and training already taking place, particularly by the Schweizerischer Aufklärungsdienst and Peter Sager's private Ost-Institut in Bern. Sager had given up academia to devote all his time to running the Institute's information service on everything occurring in the Soviet bloc, producing an anti-communist news weekly *Der Klare Blick* and providing 300 English-language newspapers in Asia and Africa with news updates.[83]

Einthoven's report on his travels at the Barbizon *colloque* concluded that there was no need for a large-scale international institute as originally envisaged, since so much was already being done in the documentation and evaluation field. Instead he saw the value of a "small braintrust in The Hague", "an estate agent's office, a clearing house", with representatives from each participating country who would, through the direct links with the national institutes, oversee and direct (where necessary) the wide terrain of anti-communist psychological warfare in Europe and elsewhere.[84] Above all, "there is a complete lack everywhere of good centres for starting 'untainted' actions in the field of psychological warfare, press campaigns, trade union resolutions, political party declarations, and even governmental activities".[85]

Anti-communism needed a new start, and this was Interdoc's mission. Van den Heuvel, now chosen to be director (Einthoven had been offered the position but turned it down – "The creation of a completely new organization required youthful energy"), was set to leave the BVD and take up his new post on 1 January 1962. In the first place this meant facilitating the training of cadres, "the framework of our Western society". West Germany had excellent facilities such as the Ostkolleg in Cologne, already up and running, but they needed to be made accessible to the French, British, and Italians, and then they could serve the West as a whole, not just one nation. Likewise the Studienbüro, with its perfect location in West Berlin: "In Germany one can, thanks to the unlimited number of practical examples, show what the reality really is to those who think that anti-communism is a hobby for a few fanatics." Sager's Ost-Institut produced excellent material, but much of it remained within the relatively small German-speaking community in Switzerland – it would be far better to support and spread his institute's work via Interdoc than to create something entirely new, and "moreover, *everything* that comes out of neutral Switzerland will be believed sooner than NATO propaganda, which our activity will no doubt be stamped with". Apart from coordination and amplification, Interdoc must still clarify what the Western message is, not by fixing some kind of Western ideology, but "by formulating a few principles that one can put forward against communism". Western youth were not going to be motivated by uncertain feelings and vague relativism alone.[86]

But Einthoven's final point was the most remarkable. Picking up on Mollet's call for greater economic democracy, the Dutchman made a plea for a genuine social democracy in order to provide a supportive ground for Western values of equality and justice. University study should be available for all. Talented individuals from any class or race should have equal opportunities to rise to the top, especially within business. Without this, training in Western values was an empty shell, communist propaganda would always hit home, and those who could have joined the Western cause would instead become disillusioned and join its opponents.

> It is vitally important for the West to maintain its form of society but to introduce within the bounds of the existing social order such changes that are deemed necessary to undermine the appeal of communism.
>
> These changes are not to be differentiated on the basis of Marxist theories, but on the basis of Christianity and democracy in the highest sense of the word.[87]

The last thing Einthoven wanted was a rejuvenated insistence on Western superiority. Interdoc and its associated national institutes must also look at how Western society itself could be improved and fully realize its own noble values of freedom, equality, and justice. Such a self-critical stance would remove any danger of repeating the one-sided simplistic propaganda that was the hallmark of the 1950s. This double-sided approach was fully shared by the BND's Rolf Geyer and to some extent by Van den Heuvel, although his SOEV colleague Willem Couwenberg would subsequently pursue it with more conviction in the pages of his journal *Oost-West*. Einthoven's sermon-like message ended with a call to arms:

> I am convinced that Van den Heuvel and his colleagues from the contributing nations will be of great benefit for the Western world when they put this plan into action. All the signs indicate that they will succeed. They will need all our cooperation and support. Let us promise to give this to them.[88]

Barbizon went well, despite the unfortunate call from Claus Kernig (soon to be Interdoc's vice-president) for Interdoc to be "a sort of private MI5" or "political Interpol", which was tactfully ignored by everyone.[89] But, despite Einthoven's optimism, the structure was still fragile. "The two embryonic national groups in Germany and France depend from [sic] Gehlen and [Paul] Grossin [SDECE chief]", meaning that continuing covert support was essential. The focus still lay on Europe, but the Americans were kept fully informed by the Dutchman, and he left for Washington on 8 November 1961 with the expectation of "a contribution from the United States specifically for Interdoc since this organization will be in a better position than any other group of people to start special anti-communist actions of a general character in Europe".[90] Whether the CIA would provide support – and whether all the parties to Interdoc actually wanted this support – remained open.

Britain

According to Brian Crozier's own (unlikely) account, he met Bonnemaison on a flight from Algiers to Paris in February 1958. Crozier, a journalist with *The Economist* who spoke flawless French, engaged his neighbour on the plane and received an in-depth assessment of the rise of the militarist right in French politics. The chance meeting, nurtured by Crozier as a new source, led him to be invited to the Frankfurt *colloque* the following year – as a member of the French delegation. (He describes a "mysterious and intriguing" meeting of about 35 people which was "very productive in terms of facts, background, analysis, and intelligent discussion".[91]) Crozier became a regular at these meetings. He soon took on an informal liaison role with the British Foreign Office and MI6, and arranged for British participation. Thanks to him, the British delegation at Barbizon included his *Economist* colleague Christopher Layton (son of European Movement supporter Lord Layton), Federation of British Industry official F.W. Hazeldine, and former MP Aidan Crawley.[92] But Crozier always had his own interests at heart, and he would not take on the desired role of Interdoc linkman.

A more formal link had been established in 1959 with the visit to the Economic League, which eventually led to the invitation to the League's top officials to join the *colloques* in 1961. But although the League was a potentially useful partner with specific expertise – particularly from Hugh Welton, the author of *Subversion in Industry* (1958) and *The Agitators: Extremist Activities in British Industry* (1963) – it was not a site for an Interdoc office in the UK. Searching for advice, Einthoven was directed by MI6 to Charles Howard (Dick) Ellis. Ellis, an Australian by birth, had joined the SIS (Secret Intelligence Service, better known as MI6) in 1924, and under cover as a journalist he became the service's main liaison with anti-communist émigrés in Paris during the 1930s. In 1940 he was posted to New York to act as deputy to

William Stephenson ("Intrepid") at British Security Coordination (BSC), the MI6 outfit charged with "engineering" America away from isolation towards support for Britain's war effort. By the time Ellis returned to London in 1944, he had assisted with the creation of the American Office of Strategic Services, and he soon became MI6's head of Western Hemisphere and Far East operations.[93] But Ellis had enemies, and suspicions began to arise that his émigré work (he married a White Russian) had entangled him as a source of leaked intelligence for the German Abwehr. MI6 rebuffed MI5's initial accusations, based on claims made by Soviet defectors Walter Krivitsky and Igor Gouzenko, but in 1953 Ellis did retreat to Australia to became adviser to his home country's Security Intelligence Organisation, and quietly retired from MI6 (he turned 58 in 1953). Yet within a year he had returned to Britain, ostensibly for relationship reasons, and he was reassigned on a part-time basis by MI6. In 1963 – the year that Kim Philby defected to the Soviet Union – Ellis was assigned to organize the records of BSC for future historical use, a move that gave him access to the service's archives, a remarkable task for someone still under suspicion.[94]

MI5 finally gained its chance to reopen the Ellis case after Philby's departure. Brought in for interrogation in 1965, Ellis eventually admitted that he had been drawn into trading information to the Germans via his brother-in-law Alexander Zilenski, an activity which brought much-needed income to augment his meagre MI6 salary. But Zilenski was selling information to the Russians as well, and MI5 were convinced that Ellis was also a Soviet spy of a rank higher than Philby. This part he denied, and no conclusive evidence could be produced, least of all from MI6 records which Ellis himself had so recently "sterilized". Not wanting another "Soviet mole" case to damage the service, MI6 successfully suppressed the details of the case. Disaffected MI5 officers, foremost among them Peter Wright, ensured that the information eventually emerged, first via Chapman Pincher and later via Wright's own *Spycatcher*.[95]

The controversy surrounding Ellis does not seem to have affected in any way his involvement with Interdoc. Ellis wrote the following candid note to Van den Heuvel at the end of 1967: "I told [MI6] that I would stand no more nonsense about myself, and demanded that they put their cards on the table or shut up. I have been told that 'no action is contemplated'; they regret having embarrassed me (and others) but in view of the seriousness of the Philby and Blake cases (there is more to come!) they have to examine every possibility, however remote."[96] Van den Heuvel, responding to the publication of *Spycatcher* in 1987, defended his former colleague: "He perhaps went too far in his attempts to exchange information, which has therefore given a false impression. He was a remarkably active man. I have personally never doubted his loyalty."[97] Ellis entered the Interdoc circle through MI6 chief Dick White, whom Einthoven approached in June 1961 for "some participants from MI6" for the Barbizon *colloque* in October. White picked out Ellis as the most appropriate linkman due to his experiences in the 1930s, a move that had significance as well as repercussions.[98] White's decision seems to indicate a lack of interest in the Interdoc operation, it being more a convenient way of keeping Ellis occupied and using him as a channel for information on what was going on. Einthoven had hoped that MI6 would function as the "Central Point" in Britain, a similar role to those of the BND and SDECE, but this was too high a hope.[99] As reported at Barbizon, "the observer from M.I.6 [Ellis] [...] agreed on being the British liaison with the other delegates".[100] Ellis would collect and distribute relevant materials and act as "a sort of 'talent spotter' ", but he could do little beyond that because MI6 insisted he avoid giving the impression that his "old service was the real motor behind these activities".[101]

> The most important limitation is that I am still related to my old service [MI6] and I participate in the colloques as representative of this service. I therefore have to follow their policy and that is: don't be in the foreground too much and avoid creating a link between my activities arising out of the colloques and the old service. Otherwise the impression could be given that the old service is actually the real motor behind those activities.[102]

Ellis's suspect reputation in the Foreign Office also complicated matters. Writing to "a retired intelligence chief" [MI6's wartime chief, Sir Stewart Menzies] in 1963, Ellis reported that "I am kept busy with this INTERDOC organization [...] several of us are now doing privately what [the Foreign Office] have never succeeded in doing – getting an 'action group' going".[103] Writing to Van den Heuvel in the same year, Ellis stressed that "it is essential that my name should not be mentioned" in connection with the Foreign Office's efforts to link SOEV with "high-level contacts in the industrial and managerial world".[104]

Alongside MI6, these negotiations involved another player: the Foreign Office's Information Research Department (IRD). Established in 1947, its purpose was to "counter Sino-Soviet propaganda and to expose Communist ideology and tactics". In doing so it mirrored the US approach in "the need for factual, truthful and forceful presentation", so that IRD claimed "our principles offer the best and most efficient way of life", such that "we have a rival ideology to that of Communism" based on civil liberties, human rights, and democratic and Christian values.[105] Close relations were maintained with the Americans from the beginning.[106] In no way was its output meant to be linked to the British government, both for the sake of deniability and because "the fact that H.M.G. is responsible for compiling and issuing material attacking governments with which it is friendly is secret." This unattributable status ("an added value") created "a reasonably confidential relationship with the recipient", communication with whom needed to be classified.[107] Printed materials were disseminated through British embassies and via the NATO Information Committee meetings.[108] IRD was also prepared to give advice on measures to counter communist subversion "outside the limited field of counter-propaganda". Although its research sections would feed information to other Foreign Office departments "when an assessment is being made of any aspect of the communist threat, locally or internationally", it is clear that the liaison between IRD and other units of the Foreign Office itself left a lot to be desired.[109]

The Netherlands, which lacked a major domestic communist threat, was not high on the list of IRD targets. However, an official enquiry by the Dutch in 1957 prompted this reply from IRD to the British Embassy in The Hague:

> [T]he principle with imprintless papers is that copies should only be given to personal contacts who can be relied on not to reveal the source [...] If the Ministry of Foreign Affairs gives you names and addresses and you can make contact direct well and good. If, on the other hand, they suggest that they should act as intermediary and pass the material on, we would not object so long as our and your security is not jeopardised. The best thing, of course, would be to find some local Dutch organisation official or unofficial, which would be prepared to issue our material – preferably re-edited and in Dutch – under their own imprint, but this may not be easy to arrange and the need for it in Holland is not so great as in many other countries.[110]

The exchange did prompt more press contacts and renewed contact with the Coordinating Secretariat of the International Student Conference (COSEC) in Leiden.[111] But real change came only when Van den Heuvel made contact in April 1961 with the IRD head office in London and its liaison officer at the British Embassy in The Hague. Out of this came an agreement that IRD publications would be translated into Dutch, for use in SOEV training programmes.[112] Van den Heuvel provided an overview of his personal network in the Netherlands: head of training for the BVD, director of SOEV, instructor at the Defence Study Centre, provision of material for Vrede en Vrijheid and the Study Centre for Military Leadership, and contacts with "security officers of the biggest companies". The *colloques* were referred to obliquely as "the international group" engaged with "psychological defence against communism".[113] The London office felt that "contact with van den Heuvel appears most promising", and deals were struck.[114] The publisher Nijgh and van Ditmar agreed to create a Dutch-language series of IRD books, and despite the expectation that it would run at a loss the series opened with editions of *The Writer and the Commissar* and Hugh Seton-Watson's *The New Imperialism*.[115] IRD's publishing outlet, Ampersand, would in return be made available for English-language versions of Interdoc publications. Despite these apparent signs of growing cooperation, the foundations of what became Interdoc UK, which rested on MI6–IRD cooperation, were shaky from the start.

Switzerland

In the 1950s the Swiss Interior Ministry had encouraged various private organizations to coordinate their activities in "maintaining the national spiritual heritage", with anti-communism being an essential aspect of this. The so-called Gurten Group that emerged (named after the Hotel auf den Gurten near Bern) included the government's civilian information service (Aufklärungsdienst), the military information and *"politische Bildung"* apparatus Heer und Haus, Pro Liberta (which organized travelling photo exhibitions with titles such as "Berlin – Test Case for the Free World"), the public information operations Action Civique (French-speaking) and Aktion freier Staatsbürger (German-speaking) which were both connected via the Liga für Freiheit to the CIAS network, and the Ost-Institut in Bern, "undoubtedly the most important member". While Heer und Haus was created in 1940 to counter Nazi propaganda, the other organizations were all from the post-WW II period. Financial support and oversight – to ensure that the organizations did not unnecessarily overlap or compete – was provided by the Interior Ministry and the Société pour le Développement de l'Economie Suisse (SDES), based in Geneva.[116] By the time Einthoven made his first fact-finding missions to Switzerland in July–August 1961, Swiss anti-communism was already very well organized. While Pro Liberta in particular maintained close relations with German contacts (including, it seems, future Interdoc Berlin front-man Rolf Buchow in West Berlin) Swiss neutrality made any proposal for international cooperation very delicate.

Einthoven went first to discuss the lie of the land with Olivier Reverdin, an old family friend who was the editor of the *Journal de Genève*. Together the two assembled a list of likely participants for the anti-communist venture: Raymond Déonna, director of SDES; Dr Albert Münst of the Liga für Freiheit; Hans Huber of Heer und Haus (and, usefully, the publisher Huber & Co.); Professor Josef Bochenski of the University of Fribourg; and Peter Sager, head of the Ost-Institut in Bern. Bochenski, a Polish Dominican, was a major figure in the field of Sovietology and the study of communist doctrine. A professor of history at Fribourg, Bochenski had built up considerable influence as director (from 1957) of the Institute of East European Research. He was the author (with Gerhart Niemeyer) of *Handbuch des Weltkommunismus* (1958) and founder-publisher of the journal *Studies in Soviet Thought* (from 1961) and the series *Sovietica* (from 1959). Bochenski was definitely on the Interdoc radar from early on: Einthoven knew him personally, referring to him in a memo to Prince Bernhard as "one of the most important experts in the field of communist doctrine".[117] Active at the Ostkolleg, Bochenski was also considered as a possible Bilderberg participant. Yet Reverdin clearly did not think much of Bochenski's academic approach and saved his highest praise for Sager, who had used the Ost-Institut to build up an impressive network of activities and influence in the public realm: "not very scientific, but a first-rate propagandist". Bochenski, who valued Sager's intellect, also regretted the fact that the latter had become too much of a journalist. Nevertheless Einthoven found Bochenski understanding of the need for international coordination of anti-communism due to the serious lack of quality Sovietologists. The Pole was particularly dismissive of American contributions to this field, as a German Interior Ministry report from 1962 noted:

> On the scientific level the study of contemporary communist ideology and its development process can only be described, due to a shortage of resources and experts, as inadequate. Beyond the network in West Germany, in Rome (Professor [Gustav] Wetter), and the Institute led by Professor Bochenski in Fribourg, where something like half of all Western researchers on contemporary Soviet philosophy are active, there exists in the West – even in France and the USA – hardly anyone who is scientifically involved with this central problem.[118]

Bochenski was also pivotal in the debate on Western values, having put together five theses that could be used in response to communist ideology: scientific method (human authority over defining reality); humanism (autonomous development of the individual); social democracy (fundamental equality of rights); democratic politics (to ensure justice); economic pluralism (opposed to the "enslavement" of state monopoly).

Sager was a unique character in other ways. Active in research on international communism since 1949 and a student at Harvard's Russian Research Center during 1952–54, he established the Osteuropa-Bibliothek and the Ost-Institut in 1959. In the mid-1950s Sager was also closely involved with the Free Europe Committee's Free Europe University in Exile in Strasbourg. He ran the Institute as an Aktiengesellschaft (a corporation with shareholders) involving newspaper editors, academics, and representatives from political parties. Its productivity was impressive: weekly and bi-weekly compendiums from the Soviet-bloc press covering political and economic developments, the anti-communist bulletin *Der Klare Blick: Schweizer Kommentare für Freiheit, Gerechtigkeit und ein starkes Europa*, a book series, and around 120 meetings a year throughout the country. Two-thirds of the Institute's annual income of 300,000 Swiss francs came from subscriptions, and no money from abroad was accepted. Sager was increasingly turning his attention towards influencing opinion in Asia, Africa, and Latin America, making use of Swiss credibility as a neutral nation lacking a colonial past. He had triggered a major debate within the government with a plan for attracting more foreign (predominantly African) students to study there as an alternative to the Lumumba University in Moscow (and even as an alternative to going to France, where they often came under the influence of communist agitators). He even expressed the wish to enter parliament itself, the advantages of which Einthoven doubted because it would undermine the "neutrality" of the Institute. The Dutchman came away from his meetings with Sager with the strong impression that linkages with Interdoc would be ideal, particularly in terms of simply expanding the international reach of Sager's Institute. Beyond this it was unclear, because Sager was already running a completely self-contained, self-sustaining operation, and he could be something of a "loose cannon": "very skilled, but also very wild".[119]

Nevertheless it is obvious that for a while Einthoven thought he had discovered the anti-communist holy grail. In late 1961 Einthoven pursued a plan to link Déonna's organization with American business interests located in Switzerland ("Caltex, Esso, etc.") with the purpose of "discreetly" channelling extra finance to expand Sager's operations. The intention was to multiply the Ost-Institut's researchers and translators, expand its outlets across Latin America, Asia, and Africa, and "gradually make this neutral Swiss institute a world center for information about democracy and communism". With Déonna and SDES president Georges Fischer on board as local support, and the CIA backing the venture, everything looked set to go ahead. Brazil was seen as the first target, with Philips and Unilever also interested in pursuing information activities in Africa. At some point Sager must have baulked at losing control of his institute, because the line goes dead. Einthoven did not give up, the advantages of a Swiss outlet such as Sager's being too good. In early 1962 the Dutchman tried to link up with James Monroe and SIHE. Later that year he tried again, this time via the New York-based Latin American Information Committee, which included representatives "of very important companies with great financial interest in Latin America" (Esso being prominent among them). Einthoven tried to launch a plan to bring "hand-picked university-trained Latin American boys" to Fribourg to be trained by Bochenski in Western values and sent back "to form scientific anti-communist nuclei independent from the United States or Europe". It was a nice if costly idea, and Einthoven hoped it would open up other avenues with Sager. But the Swiss man was not impressed about suddenly being "discovered" by Einthoven and then through 1961–62 facing his operations being hijacked by a cabal of US corporations. Einthoven, carried away by the chance to build a transatlantic apparatus, had misjudged Sager entirely.[120]

As Einthoven noticed, there were plenty of opportunities "in der kleine Schweiz". Nevertheless there were obstacles to overcome. It was one thing to agree that international cooperation was a good idea, but quite another to implement it. The level of existing anti-communist organization in Switzerland was in this sense actually an impediment. Sager preferred not to receive funding from outside Switzerland. Relations between Sager, Huber, and Münst were also problematic, making a united front unlikely. Huber admitted that "after fifteen years of resisting relations with the communist world, it is not easy today to switch to positive psychological warfare in terms of East–West contacts".[121] Added to this was the fact that, according to Einthoven, the Swiss were "very suspicious", causing him to take care to explain to his counterparts in the domestic security service exactly what he was doing on his trips to Bern and Zurich.[122] Swiss reservations about cooperating internationally on anti-communism remained very strong. The most that could be achieved at the time of Interdoc's formation, therefore, was a case-by-case working relationship with Münst, who agreed to function as the main contact.[123] Once again, the old Paix et Liberté/CIAS network proved useful in times of need.[124]

Italy

From the very beginning it was difficult to find reliable partners in Italy. In contrast to the over-organized Swiss, the Italians had surprisingly little to offer. The early 1960s was the period of the "Opening to the Left", when the Socialist party under Pietro Nenni, edging away from its alliance with the communists, gradually entered a productive dialogue with the Christian Democrats.[125] This confused the political atmosphere and caused many to adopt a "wait-and-see" approach. The first time Italian representatives attended the *colloques* seems to have been in September 1959 in the small Bavarian village of Ettal. By the time of the Aix-en-Provence meeting the following year there were hopes that Mme A.M. Battista, a researcher whom Bonnemaison had met in Paris, would form the basis for an Italian group, but apart from flirting with Einthoven ("you have the spirit of a dictator ... to be directed by 'a dictator' as intelligent and kind as you is very pleasant") she did little and the contact faded out.[126] Bonnemaison started to broaden the net, concentrating on the military, big business (Fiat), and networks around the Catholic church.[127] It proved difficult to find individuals who were both reliable and willing to invest in the relationship. What was at stake was not money – there was plenty of that – but finding an individual "who could deal with the most prominent institutions in Italy and with representatives from other nations on an equal footing in The Hague".[128] Whereas Van den Heuvel took responsibility for Britain and Belgium early on, it was Einthoven who took on the task of developing the Italian connection. The CIA's input is very clear on this issue. In his notes from Barbizon Einthoven had remarked that "during my visit to Washington in Nov./Dec. 1960 I got the impression that C.I.A. was very much interested in the situation in Italy." The Americans were keen to use the Dutch to try and bring some coordination to Italian anti-communism, but it would prove a tough task.[129]

The Dutchman made the first real breakthrough through Diego Guicciardi, the chief of Shell's operations in Genoa, who opened the way to Vittorio Vaccari, head of the Christian Union of Business Executives (UCID). Vaccari was close to the Vatican and very active internationally, particularly in Latin America, but Guicciardi eventually brought him into contact with

Einthoven via a meeting of the three in Nice in October 1960.[130] Vaccari also apparently had direct contact with Allen Dulles at this time.[131] At the end of January 1961 Einthoven introduced Vaccari to Bonnemaison in Paris. The Italian was certainly of the right mindset, writing at the time that "the situation in Italy gives us real concerns; I believe that the communists here exploit the 'misunderstandings' and uncertainties of the other political parties and economic classes".[132] Vaccari seemed to be the perfect partner for other representatives of national industry who attended the *colloques*, such as Delagarde of France and Triesch from the Federal Republic. But UCID was not the official Italian employers' association, and since it relied on individual and not corporate membership it also lacked funds.

Meanwhile, looking to establish direct channels with the Catholic church, Einthoven called on Cardinal Alfrink and the Pax Christi organization before making his way to Rome. Einthoven wanted to avoid ending up with only Jesuits on his list – they may have been committed, but they would also alienate moderate Catholics from the Interdoc circle.[133] Einthoven also paid a preparatory visit to Gehlen in Munich, who made some calls and provided considerable background information to pave the way.[134] Since 1948 the BND chief's brother, Hans "Giovanni" Gehlen, had been the service's direct liaison with the Vatican and the Maltese Order in Rome, another useful contact point for gaining introductions ("Giovanni" was later described by the CIA as "a brilliant man" in the sciences who had unfortunately become an undisciplined "Roman lounge-lizard").[135] The Dutchman travelled to Rome in June 1961 to meet up with the church's main social organizations, Catholic Action (Gioventù italiana di Azione cattolica) and Comitato Civico. With Jesuit Fathers van Gestel and Martegani as his ideological and theological guides, Einthoven did the rounds. His first meeting was with Catholic Action's president, Professor Maltarello, who immediately highlighted the fears about compromise with the Socialists and Nenni. While some in the church saw this as "a drift to the left, from where there is no possible way back", the Christian Democrats were prepared to risk it, causing major divisions in their ranks. The picture was sombre: the government dared not act against the strong communist movement, and the "ruling class" and the employers were unwilling to embrace the reforms required for an open democratic society. Instead of Catholic Action, which was more occupied with ethical issues, Maltarello recommended contacting Professor Luigi Gedda of Comitato Civico, a political movement that seemed to fit Einthoven's ideas on anti-communist training. Gedda, a geneticist, is notorious for being head of the Gregor Mendel Institute in Rome and holding a close association with Mankind Quarterly, a journal accused of scientific racism. As the head of Comitato Civico, Gedda ran an organization with 1700 "ideological shock troops" spread across Italy, and he saw the only hope in a "United Europe" as a future ideal. As Einthoven put it delicately, "this man is determinedly no democrat".[136] But the real problem was that many among the clergy accepted communism "as merely an economic system and thus [do] not bother about it". It was thus possible to be simultaneously a good Catholic and a communist.[137] The Dutchman's hopes were somewhat raised by a visit to a Catholic training school in Frascati, outside Rome, geared solely to explaining the realities of communism and its goals to parish priests. Yet a dilemma was becoming clear: since the Italian employers were doing very little against the communist influence, the church's efforts would run up against strong economic interests.[138] Repeated efforts by Einthoven to discover if there were any Sovietologists in Italy produced only one name: Professor Gustav Wetter of the Pontifical Institute for Oriental Studies in Rome, someone he had already met back in 1951.

Subsequently put under pressure by Einthoven, Vaccari eventually produced a meeting for Einthoven with Cardinal Siri in Rome in August 1961. Siri was renowned for his conservative opinions within the church, but he was well connected with the top of Italian business (Fiat, Olivetti) and he was one of the few who were interested at that time in reviving the Vatican's contacts in the Soviet bloc.[139] Einthoven, warming to the cause of "economic democracy", homed in on the possibility that the church could make more use of edicts such as the Rerum Novarum of 1891 and the Mater et Magistra of May 1961.[140] Einthoven tried some conspiratorial logic ("een oud adagium") on the Cardinal:

> When one finds oneself in a revolutionary situation, in order to avoid the outbreak of a dangerous revolution it is better to actually provoke such a disturbance so that its direction could be controlled. This movement should, even though it would also have a revolutionary accent, nevertheless be based on principles that were completely the opposite of those of the enemy. While communism claims that a satisfactory situation for the working class can only be achieved via the way of Marx and Lenin, Mater et Magister proposes in contrast that it can also go the way of Gospel.[141]

What Siri made of this piece of intricate wisdom is not recorded, but the Cardinal did agree that the industrial "ruling class" should introduce reforms before "they face the prospect of being overwhelmed by a system that neither of us want to see". The meeting produced an agreement that Alfrink would keep the Italian informed of developments so that "the two Eminences [can] consult when they meet in Rome".[142] Einthoven also looked into duplicating the "Frascati system" for Catholic priests in both the Netherlands (via Alfrink) and France (via Pater Calvez, a Jesuit in Strasbourg).[143]

Einthoven returned to Rome once again in September for further talks with Vaccari, UCID, and the "red Jesuits" of Father Castelli in Milan, who felt that the church could do much more to pursue the Mater et Magistra and undermine communist support.[144] These efforts eventually generated an Italian contingent for the Barbizon meeting that October. Although Vaccari, Wetter, and Gedda formed the core of the group, all three failed to make it. Instead the delegation consisted of Dr Giorgio Filippi (Comitato Civico), Dr L. d'Amato (editor of the weekly Vita), Professor Mariano Gabriele, R. Pavetto (Edison Volta Office of Economic Studies, Milan), and I. Papa and A. Zappi of Catholic Action. Vaccari, who proved difficult to reach when Einthoven was in Rome in September, made amends by coming to The Hague at the end of November 1961, bringing with him Monsignor Leopoldo Teofili, the Pope's representative to the Netherlands. The outcome was that Vaccari, despite agreeing on the need for Interdoc, would lay the ground for an Italian national institute but backed away from leading it himself due to too many other commitments.[145]

By March 1962 Einthoven returned to Rome to discuss with Vaccari "the foundation of an Italian national centre", formed out of a core of UCID, Comitato Civico, and Catholic Action representatives. But Vaccari was once again absent despite prior agreements, and Einthoven heard from several sources that it would be impossible to create an Italian SOEV in the coming few years. The Vatican was looking more towards a reconciliation with the governments of Poland and Hungary, which required being moderate towards the left in Italy itself. To add to the disappointment, Guicciardi felt he had to turn down Einthoven's request to replace Vaccari as the "focal point" in Italy due to concerns that it would conflict with his official role for Shell (even though Shell director Lijkle Schepers gave the green light from The Hague). As Einthoven had remarked on the Italian context after Barbizon, "I had to put many of these groups under a certain pressure in order to make them move in our direction".[146] The Italian venture still lacked someone to pull it together.

Interdoc founded 1962–63

By late 1961 it was clear that the West German push to create a new psychological warfare infrastructure within NATO had failed. This was no surprise, and anyway an organization being run from NATO did not prevent the formation of an independent private agency. There were too many advantages in being independent from official bureaucracy.[147] In discussion with Professor Bassani, the head of the Italian Atlantic Institute in Milan, Einthoven

> asked him in all honesty if he believed that NATO could carry out psychological warfare from its large bureaucratic secretariat, led by diplomats, who themselves are dependent on other diplomats in the permanent council, who receive their instructions from national politicians, who can be replaced at every election.[148]

Yet the disagreements over Interdoc's purpose dragged on. Preparations on the German side were delayed by the 1961 national elections holding up budgetary decisions well into 1962. There were also bureaucratic difficulties. Within the Federal Republic, the tasks of the Chancellery's national Informationszentrum were only clarified in mid-1961. The BND insisted that it be a public institute, to demonstrate the government's wish to respond openly to the communist threat. Then, after years of deliberations, in a classic case of defending departmental turf, the Ministry of the Interior suddenly questioned its necessity, triggering a new round of deliberations.[149] The BND drew its conclusions and decided it was best to proceed on its own, but of course it did not inform the other parties involved. On the international level there was a tussle over whether the chief location for liaison with The Hague should be Bonn or Munich. Both the BND and the SDECE insisted on Munich, the French stating that keeping it wholly within the services would prevent "being penetrated by the wrong elements", but this was not fully resolved until 1962. Then Foertsch died suddenly in late 1961 at the age of 66. His place was largely taken by Colonel Rolf Geyer, recruited to the BND by Gehlen in 1959 to join the psychological warfare discussions going on in Bonn. It was Geyer who would build on Foertsch's legacy and create the BND's psychological warfare apparatus in his own image. An aside in a meeting between Gehlen and two CIA liaison officers in September 1966 gives an insight into the BND view of the governmental deliberations on this issue:

> [Gehlen] thinks that there is a cultural penetration going on in Germany carried out by the Soviet Bloc [...] In earlier days he said he had suggested in high government quarters that some sort of an effort should be made to fight this Eastern Bloc action. He said that there were various meetings and it was agreed that ministries and organs of the government which were to deal with this danger should submit plans. The committee met. CATUSK [BND] was the only one that had a plan ready [the Aktionspläne of December 1960]. This led to further discussions which never got off the ground. UTILITY [Gehlen] said, "finally I left the committee and let myself be represented by Holm [Horst Wendland]". At this Holm laughingly blushed and said, "Oh I'm sorry, I forgot to report, I have left the committee and turned it over to (alias) Goslar [Geyer]." Goslar is the psychological situation man who works for alias Degehardt [Dethleffsen].[150]

The BND remained committed, shielding the Interdoc project from unnecessary influence from the ministries in Bonn (particularly the BMG), but also imposing additional conditions. Interdoc must not run any activities or maintain any direct contacts in the territories of other participating nations, and must not run any independent cadre training. No contacts were to be made within the Federal Republic without BND sanction, something which Van den Heuvel, running around making connections for SOEV, initially contravened (but he was allowed to continue nevertheless). Interdoc would serve the documentation needs and planning requests of the national institutes, and "work as much as possible in the background". If the Dutch agreed to this narrowing of Interdoc's mission, the French were also willing to maintain regular contact with The Hague via their still-to-be-created national institute. The Dutch had done the hard work, but the major powers were now calling the shots. To overcome Einthoven's frustration that he now had to wait for budgetary decisions in Bonn (which even had the consequence that "an appropriate location" for the international venture could not be chosen), Generals Dethleffsen (Geyer's direct superior) and Horst Wendland (BND vice-president) agreed to send BND researcher Andreas von Weiss (code name Weber) to The Hague to deal with immediate Dutch needs.[151]

However, the French contribution was by this time very shaky. Grossin, SDECE chief since 1957, retired in 1962. A resistance leader with a special relationship with de Gaulle, Grossin had overseen a transformation of the SDECE from an organization recruiting according to class and privilege to one interested in higher education and merit. Only under Grossin could someone like Bonnemaison operate and develop the *colloques*, so Grossin's departure inevitably spelled the end of a productive international relationship. As early as January 1962 Einthoven learnt from his BND partners that French cooperation could no longer be guaranteed, and "that France could only 'symbolically' join in with Interdoc".[152] What is more, there was strong mistrust between the SDECE and the Gaullists. The sinister group the Red Hand, which perpetrated a series of bombings and assassinations against German and Arab targets during 1959–61 in order to halt the sale of arms to the Algerian rebels, had close ties with certain elements in the SDECE, which was committed to Algeria remaining part of France. De Gaulle's u-turn on Algerian independence caused some in the service to support the Organisation Armée Secrète (OAS), and these views also penetrated the Cinquième Bureau, making them vulnerable to Gaullist wrath. Aside from the threat to the French state, de Gaulle also had little time for SDECE operations, which he referred to derogatively as *"ces affaires de basse police"*.[153] Within de Gaulle's reconfiguration of Atlantic affairs and a possible rapprochement with Moscow, the activities of the SDECE, especially direct involvement in an international coalition developing anti-communist psychological warfare, were decidedly expendable.

Between 29 March and 1 April 1962 the last international *colloque* on French soil took place in the picturesque surroundings of Mont-St-Michel. Backed by the Conseil national du patronat français (National Council of French Employers), it was in many ways Bonnemaison's intellectual swansong for the *colloques*, and the political situation in France meant that it was put together in something of a rush. The programme, entitled "The Attitude of Industry towards Marxist–Leninist Propaganda among the Cadres," was an ideological and strategic call to arms for positive anti-communism – and an attempt to bring together representatives of French, Dutch, and German big business to support it. Based on eight years of French experience in training military cadres against subversive warfare, it emphasized that, while the focus up till then had been on protecting "the masses" against communist subversion, it now had to respond to changing communist tactics and instead raise awareness and organize the "leaders" (*les dirigeants*) in all sections of society. Marxism based its critique not just on capitalist exploitation but also on a claim over the future, particularly in terms of the apparent convergence of East and West as two industrial civilizations. This had a persuasive effect on an increasingly disorientated (and indifferent) Western public. But it was Lenin and not Marx who was "the genius of action and the creator of an apparatus" to bring this to fruition. The Leninist approach must be reversed to reinforce and diffuse the ethics, economics, and politics of the West throughout all social structures, restore its political forces, and provide "a seductive force on equal terms with the appeal of the Soviet Union". Society was changing: the middle classes were growing, and were becoming more materialistic and more isolated according to their (technical) professions. In relation to Western society becoming more atomized and vulnerable, it was Marxism which "is more capable of re-establishing all the links of the human personality, of guiding human consciousness beyond the alienation which it suffers in our society and of leading towards the decisive ethical–political selections". In response to this challenge, the industrial cadres – the key to success – needed to understand their role as the "shepherds of being" (Bochenski). Input from a whole range of thinkers – from de Tocqueville and Toynbee to Aron, Teilhard de Chardin, and even Proust – was used to construct a remarkably dense response to the Marxist–Leninist challenge. Interdoc would facilitate the process of cadre formation by enabling them to "find in themselves the certainties to regain their confidence in the world in which they live, materially, intellectually, and morally".[154] It is worth quoting the thinking behind this at length:

> It would be committing a fatal error, if the reply opposed by [sic] the West to communist pressure would be inspired by principles of "direct action" by which the adversary himself is inspired. The western reply will be efficient in the measure only, in which it is truly "western", that is to say, in conformity with the values of our civil tradition. Experience has shown that, among the various formulas tried out in the programs of formation of the cadres, the most efficient is the one, that, according to the canons of the Socratic "maieutica", (Socratic measures), carries the individual to the attainment of the "truth"; (that is to say: to be

absolutely conscious of the real basis of ones convictions and argument, of the real nature and the realistic dimensions of the problems) the truth, won through personal effort of research and ascent and not through passive absorbing from outside and unconsciously adopting this truth as one's own.[155]

Details of the practical application of cadre formation through regular self-educative group discussions were presented from both an anonymous French enterprise (the fact that "the future of petroleum" was one of the subjects suggests again that it was Shell or one of its corporate allies)[156] and the Italian Christian Democratic and Communist parties. The models existed. It was now time to apply them on a broad scale.

With French participation in doubt, the Dutch and Germans pushed ahead undeterred, but there were final complications to sort out within the Federal Republic itself. The reason was that von Dellingshausen suddenly discovered what the BND was up to. Together with Europahaus director Herbert Scheffler he travelled to The Hague in May 1962 to clarify the situation with Einthoven and Van den Heuvel face to face. Von Dellingshausen stressed that Interdoc "needs a very precise and careful construction" and must only act as a clearing house, to avoid duplicating existing arrangements in the field of documentation. The fine details of which institute should provide which information to which client were, for the Germans, of vital importance. Neither was Interdoc to perform any cadre training of its own – unless it made use of the BMG's network, run through the Büro für politische Studien in Bonn.[157] Von Dellingshausen's concern that things could get out of hand is palpably obvious from this discussion. The visit indicated that the question of who exactly was going to hold the responsibility for working with the Dutch and Interdoc had not been resolved in the Federal Republic itself. Both Einthoven and von Dellingshausen would travel to Munich in June to sort this out once and for all. Relations between von Dellingshausen and Geyer, who held regular liaison meetings, were apparently very good, making this episode stand out.[158] Nevertheless there was also a clear view on the value of this new, public, scientifically grounded venture. Even an Interdoc limited in powers was heading in the right direction towards improved Western cooperation.[159]

The June meetings did not prevent an official agreement between SOEV and its BND counterpart, the newly formed Verein zur Erforschung sozialpolitischer Verhältnisse im Ausland e.V., in June 1962. The Verein was Geyer's creation, an institute to gather together a broad-based anti-communist coalition in civil society that could blend together different viewpoints for the common cause.[160] Von Dellingshausen knew nothing about the Verein at the time of his visit to The Hague, and only by "obtaining certain documents" around this time did he discover the agreement made at the Heelsum *colloque* in October 1960 to create Interdoc. Not surprisingly, he felt that the BND had overstepped its mandate, ignored the careful inter-departmental planning of the previous years, and "placed its realization above all in doubt". The international cooperation pursued by von Dellingshausen – the Studienbüro – was after all more effective politically than this other Foertsch–Einthoven arrangement.[161] The BND had moved ahead regardless of agreements – or, more accurately, disagreements – with Bonn, but von Dellingshausen now reined it in. At the end of June 1962 he sealed an agreement with Geyer that gave the BMG sole responsibility for cadre training in cooperation with SOEV. The Verein and Interdoc were thus blocked from entering the territory claimed by the Ministry and its associated institutes, but Geyer was prepared to cede this to guarantee Interdoc's documentation-dissemination role. Von Dellingshausen also wanted to join the Verein's board as an associate member, and whereas the Verein would financially be the sole responsibility of the BND he even proposed that the Ministry would channel up to DM 10,000 a month through the Verein to Interdoc. This was a rash attempt to appropriate the entire Interdoc set-up, and he was unable to produce the funds. For the moment the BMG man got his way. Even the BND's hidden controlling role over the two institutions as a way of presenting them as independent entities separate from government was questioned. The tendency of intelligence services "to spread a haze of secrecy" over their activities did not sit well, according to von Dellingshausen, with the attempt to forge international cooperation in a public information campaign.[162]

The von Dellingshausen–Geyer agreement opened the way for Munich to pursue the practical arrangements with The Hague. While German funds would cover the staffing and premises, it was expected that the Dutch would near enough match the Federal Republic's financial contribution in order to maintain Interdoc as a shared enterprise. The "provisional office" would open on 1 September 1962 and its legal status as a foundation would be fixed by 31 December. Van den Heuvel would from then on devote 25 per cent of his time to Interdoc, and it would be up to him to decide in the future whether he was still able to function simultaneously as director of both SOEV and Interdoc. Official representatives for the Verein were Professor Hans Lades (now with the University of Erlangen), Claus Kernig (a researcher with the Herder publishing house), and Nicolas von Grote. Over the previous six years Lades, formerly with the Ministry of the Interior and then the Ministry for Families and Youth, had participated in the inter-departmental discussions on a psychological response to communism, so his switch to become chair of the Verein's board was a logical move. Kernig had become a key proponent of the Interdoc operation, providing it with academic respectability. Von Grote was another veteran of Army Group East (liaison officer on propaganda with German Army High Command) who after the war joined Triesch at the Deutsche Industrie-Institut in Cologne before retiring to run the Verein. On the other side were Einthoven and

"1 representative from Royal Dutch [Shell]". It was initially proposed that this would be Guépin himself (as chairman even), but discretion made him make way for H.J. Rijks, the head of Shell's laboratories in Amsterdam. He was joined by Hornix to complete the Dutch contingent. The agreement closed with the remark that "orientation by Dr Einthoven and Mr Geyer with the French delegation would follow", sealed with the signatures of Van den Heuvel and Geyer.[163] The Netherlands was chosen "because it is anticipated that the inconspicuous image of this country will make it a success".[164]

Inevitably, money proved the last obstacle. Despite the support from Shell and interest from other Dutch multinationals, funds in the Netherlands remained severely limited. To force a solution, Einthoven turned to Prince Bernhard for support. The former BVD chief referred to his role in military education in 1939–40, explaining to the forces the values they must defend against Nazism. This had to be repeated, but now "the entire population" needed to be indoctrinated against communist propaganda. "Very strong support" from Shell, together with Philips, AKU (AkzoNobel), and Unilever, laid the basis for SOEV. Shell commissioner Felix Guépin and director Lijkle Schepers proposed gathering together other captains of industry for an "inside information" session on the national and international communist threat.[165] Bernhard obliged, and a meeting attended by the top ranks of Shell, AKU, the Dutch Railways, Philips, the main steel, coal, and shipyard companies, and the employers' associations took place at Soestdijk Palace on 10 February 1962. The mood was good: "everybody agreed we should start as soon as possible with our attempt to defend the Western world against psychological influence from Moscow".[166] The immediate result was a series of training courses for the Railways, Unilever, and Shell from September onwards, and the initiation of two research projects to explore why, now that the Netherlands had reached a level of post-war prosperity, certain Dutch citizens continued to vote communist.[167]

Despite this royal input, in August 1962 Van den Heuvel let it be known that the Dutch contribution would not be more than 20,000 guilders a year in the beginning, something which drew the response "unacceptable" from Geyer. This amounted to no more than 1666 guilders a month, a "merely symbolic" amount and not the 50–60,000 a year that Einthoven had proposed at the Mont-St-Michel *colloque*. If this was going to be a genuine form of international cooperation it had to be on a more equal basis, otherwise Geyer would insist on a German and not a Dutch director and move the operation to Munich, where there would be more oversight of the use of the funds, in line with German tax laws. This would also avoid the impression that Interdoc was "a German instrument of agitation under the camouflage of a Dutch flag" or that German taxpayers were funding a Dutch institute. Besides, the possibilities for administrative, legal, and financial confusion between SOEV and Interdoc, both with the same director and operating in the same location, were considerable.[168] But the stakes were too high to pull out now, and the differences were resolved at the end of September: Interdoc would only begin when the Dutch could guarantee 20,000 guilders for 1963. A German deputy director in The Hague would ensure a direct role in the running of Interdoc. SOEV and Interdoc each would have their own separate staff, requiring some inventive book-keeping from the Dutch.[169]

American financial support could have solved this problem in one go, but it proved elusive. Einthoven's close relationship with Allen Dulles did not translate into direct support from either the CIA or from the US private sector, despite the fact that Dulles had initially encouraged the Interdoc idea.[170] A primary reason for this lay in the Federal Republic, where two major scandals rocked the BND during 1961–62. Heinz Felfe, a former SS officer and member of Walter Schellenberg's Reich Security Office (RHSA), was recruited by the KGB in 1951. Soon afterwards he joined the counter-intelligence wing of Gehlen's BND, and over the next ten years he manoeuvred himself into a place of utmost confidence next to Gehlen. Despite growing suspicions over the next decade, it took the revelations of Polish intelligence defector Michal Goleniewski in 1961 to finally convince the CIA that Felfe was a traitor – and, in turn, convince Gehlen. Felfe's arrest and interrogation during 1962 then coincided with a serious confrontation between the BND and the German Ministry of Defence, which ended with Gehlen being summoned to Adenauer's Chancellery in November for his alleged involvement in leaking information to *Der Spiegel* to undermine Franz Joseph Strauss.[171] The combination of these two events ensured that the BND looked like badly damaged goods, and it is not surprising that there was hesitation on the part of the CIA to undertake a new cooperative venture at that time.

Einthoven persisted nonetheless. He approached both the Ford and Carnegie Foundations – the latter thanks to Bernhard's contact with Joseph Johnson, both Carnegie representative and "honorary secretary" of the American wing of Bilderberg – but was refused financial support on the basis that "we are not 'neutral' enough".[172] An earlier attempt by Einthoven to gain $10,000 from the Free Europe Committee – probably connected with a larger proposal on covert operations in Europe – was also turned down.[173] He did not give up. In January 1963 Einthoven discussed with Dulles a three-page memo with the title "The Dialogue between West and East" which discussed the "unavoidable" intensifying of relations with the Soviet bloc and the need to avoid providing only "naive scientists and even more naive young enthusiasts" for such a dialogue. Integrating instruction in communist ideology and Western values in university curricula was essential, and "the institute to carry this out exists, the experts are ready, but the necessary funding to begin this work is missing". Einthoven also emphasized the special role that the Netherlands could play:

> If I speak above all about the Netherlands I do this not because I am Dutch but because I am convinced that a discussion between a communist from behind the Iron Curtain and a representative from a small country will have a greater impact than such a discussion with an American, Englishman, Frenchman, or German, in other words with a representative of an "imperialist" power.[174]

Following their meeting in Washington, Einthoven refined the memo. The necessary finance had to come from the private sector, to avoid the inevitable political disagreements over public money. SOEV intended to develop a network of student representatives in each Dutch university to promote the institute's courses, study materials, and contacts in Germany (including study trips to West Berlin and contacts with students from Eastern-bloc countries). Einthoven was convinced of the great potential for strengthening Western resolve and spreading uncertainty and dissent behind the Iron Curtain in this way. SOEV, with a staff of four full-timers and five part-timers, could not take this on without a major expansion, and the groups requesting their services – predominantly from the student world – did not have the money to pay for it.[175] He duly asked Dulles for an annual contribution of 350,000 guilders (around $80,000 at the time), with a start-up amount of 150,000 guilders to get things moving. The reaction was negative: "he eventually let me know that there was no money available for these goals".[176] Einthoven further reported to Bernhard that via Dulles he had "tried to gain an entrance to the smaller funds, but was told that Europe must now pod its own peas [*zijn eigen boontjes maar moest doppen*]".[177] The American angle now seemed exhausted. Van den Heuvel would pursue it further, but it would never work out as hoped.

After six years of deliberations, on 7 February 1963 the official statutes of Interdoc were finally signed in a Hague solicitor's office. Einthoven was chairman, with Kernig vice-chairman, von Grote secretary, and Rijks treasurer.[178] The real work could begin, and the emphasis now rested on applying a new direction:

> The adoption of a positive anti-communist tactic to replace the existing largely negative approach [...] [An] Offensive attitude, in connection with which opportunities are presented which can be utilised to extend Western knowledge of the Communist world by visits to countries behind the Curtain, and by establishing suitable contacts with visitors from communist countries (professors, scientists, students, etc.).[179]

Yet the original French–German–Dutch triangle had been broken, and the relationship with the British, Swiss, Italians, and Belgians remained somewhat ad hoc. Bonnemaison had been involved in the drafting of the articles of association but no official French representative or participation was referred to in the document. The articles were signed just 16 days after the declaration of the Franco-German Treaty of Friendship, an event which Gehlen himself regarded as "a historic event [which] meant a formalization of our long-standing and friendly relations with the French foreign intelligence service, the SDECE".[180] Crozier has recorded how General Olié and a small French delegation made the gesture of attending the first Interdoc *colloque* in Bad Godesberg in March 1963, as if this was the end of the line. In a way it was. In early 1963, with Grossin now out of the picture, de Gaulle closed down the Cinquième Bureau. Crozier would refer to this withdrawal as "the first breach in the Allied united front against Soviet Active Measures", a well-meaning but remarkable exaggeration of the level of Western cooperation at the time. Bonnemaison went private, lecturing at the Ecole Supérieure de Commerce in Paris and creating the Centre d'Observation du Mouvement des Idées to run *"clubs de pensées"* on free-market thinking and the future of France after de Gaulle.[181] SDECE channels – discreet yet active – were definitely kept open, even if they were played down for the outside world ("confined to liaison and some coordination of effort in the information field").[182]

The Dutch certainly persevered with the French, since Einthoven, who took on responsibility for liaising with the French due to his personal contacts, used Lemmonnier's Institut d'Histoire Sociale et de Soviétologie as a base "to replace the gap in France created by the departure of Mr. Bonnemaison". (Ellis would once report, having attended a lunch between Bonnemaison and Crozier, that the Frenchman "regretted very much not being able to attend meetings".[184]) But Lemonnier was essentially a frontman for Albertini, and through the 1960s it would be Albertini's right-hand man, Nicolas Lang, who would be the liaison.[185] By the end of the decade he was joined by Jean Violet, an international lawyer close to Antoine Pinay, who under Grossin became a kind of political "fixer" for the SDECE and behind-the-scenes roving ambassador for the Conseil National du Patronat, the French business association.[186] While Bonnemaison, in the words of Brian Crozier, focused on "personally briefing leaders", Violet was "more concerned that the right attitudes were taken by certain publications", and it was to Crozier that Violet – and the Pinay Circle – offered their financial and organizational support.[187] In early 1966 Van den Heuvel reported to Geyer that Einthoven had received "an extraordinarily friendly letter" from Grossin's successor, Paul Jacquier, that thanked the Dutchman for his understanding of SDECE's predicament in Gaullist France and stated that the informal connection with Interdoc would undoubtedly continue under his successor (Eugène Guibaud). Despite the awkward circumstances the French made sure that they remained part of the Interdoc circuit throughout the 1960s, attending Interdoc *colloques* as individuals and off the record. The French circle was quite small, since Einthoven reported to an Interdoc board meeting in April 1967 that "the only group which dealt with communism were far-right Catholics".[188] And their official absence did have consequences: from 1964 the *colloques* would no longer have French as one of their official languages, the intermittent French participation not justifying the extra cost of simultaneous translation.[189]

3
A Dutch–German Cabal

Die Felder sind reif für die Ernte, aber die Arbeiter sind wenige.
Cees van den Heuvel, 1966[1]

Interdoc goes public: *Tasks for the Free World, The Challenge of Coexistence*, and *Oost-West*

In 1964 *Tasks for the Free World Today* was published in English and German under the Interdoc imprint.[2] *Tasks* was intended to take Interdoc's views to a wider public. It was not intended as yet another analysis of communist ideology, but as a discussion on "the need to discover and to define the response of the Free World in its confrontation with the world of communism". The motive for this was not that Western values were deemed inferior, since, as Van den Heuvel stated in the Introduction, "there is a wealth of living intellectual, social and political values, which far surpass dialectical materialism". Instead the purpose was exactly to emphasize the great need for such a discussion as relations between East and West entered a period of more relaxed détente. Paralysed by self-assertive communist propaganda and a wish for peace, many in the West – particularly the youth (as Alfred Münst put it: "we give our youth neither ideals nor objectives") – saw less and less need to stress the differences or declare the inherent superiority "of our concepts of human dignity, freedom, justice and other values". Just when Marxism–Leninism was entering a critical phase (the Sino-Soviet split, the Third World challenge, economic setbacks), the Western resolve to push home its advantage was being lost. That this was a discussion and not a declaration was essential, since not only the strengths but also the weaknesses of the Western position would be pointed out, and the intention was that Western citizens would once again become engaged with the major questions of their time. In short, *Tasks* wanted to awaken and engage the public of Western nations who were forgetting that the Cold War contest still existed.[3]

Tasks was predominantly a work of political philosophy, with the ever-practical Van den Heuvel rounding it off with a concluding chapter on what it all meant in practice. The dominant theme throughout the book was the need to shift from a negative to a positive anti-communism, as laid out in the preface:

> Negative anti-communism tends to picture things in connection to communism in terms of black and white. It only wants to criticize communism, which is often done in a purely negative and emotional manner. It is usually not inclined to see any improvements in relations with the Communist World or inside that orbit.
>
> Positive anti-communism wants to study communism as objectively as possible, in order to base its criticism on scientific research. It maintains an open mind regarding the possibility of favourable changes in communism and in East–West relations. Through the confrontation with communism it wants to stress the basic values of the West.[4]

Originally ambitious in scope, the book's first line-up of contributors included Adlai Stevenson and Reinhold Niebuhr and the *Economist*'s Barbara Ward.[5] The final outcome, consisting of texts from two German, three Dutch, a Belgian, and a Swiss contributor, was deliberately inconsistent in its approach precisely to reflect the diversity of opinion in free societies. Thus Lamberty began his chapter by simply saying that both positive and negative anti-communism stemmed from "perfectly understandable reasons", and Albert Münst felt that "the boundary between positive and negative anti-communism need not place anyone in a quandary".[6] But several themes dominate the book. First there is the value of founding documents for encapsulating the Western position, in particular the Preamble to the North Atlantic Treaty and the UN's Universal Declaration of Human Rights. These were not doctrines but expressions of the best possible conditions for allowing human life to prosper in every way. Second there is Christianity and its fundamental contribution to the Western position opposing communism, even in a period of increasing secularization. Third there are the expectations of what increasing East–West contacts were supposed to bring. On the one hand it was recognized that necessary reforms within Western liberal capitalism needed to be pushed forward to undermine the communist critique (Münst: "the elimination of alienation", Couwenberg: "the extension of democracy in the social–economic sphere"), while on the other hand there was the opportunity for picking up on developments in the communist world and achieving real change. Thus von Grote talked of the need to promote new forms of international cooperation that would take the initiative away from the limited ideological designs of peaceful coexistence, Münst called for genuine freedom of movement across borders, and Couwenberg distanced himself from the negative outbursts of those who wanted to destroy the enemy: "positive constructive anti-communism sets itself a more realistic aim, namely: the transformation of communism". Following up on this, Van den Heuvel concluded on the necessity of preparing "equipped representatives of the West" to highlight the Western concept of human dignity both at home and abroad.[7] The book ended with some short texts from Arnold Buchholz, Nicolai Berdyaev, and Teilhard de Chardin for additional inspiration.

The following year *The Challenge of Coexistence* was published as a kind of "spiritual continuance" (von Hahn) of *Tasks*.[8] In some ways this is a follow-up to *The God That Failed*, the infamous collection published in 1950 containing soul-searching reflections by former communists on why they had turned away from their political faith. *Challenge* had a less impressive line-up of former communist intellectuals, but a more profound engagement with the reality of communism. If 1950 was the height of Stalinism and *The God That Failed* of all the reasons for rejecting communism, 1965 was a time of tentative East–West rapprochement and *Challenge* a recognition that Western influence could gradually lead to "the erosion of communist ideology". This was an extension of what both Couwenberg and von Grote had said in *Tasks*: by constantly highlighting on a factual basis the gap between theory and practice in the communist world, rigid doctrine could be edged towards self-reflective compromise. Van den Heuvel summed it up: "If this should help to bring an end to the more aggressive and totalitarian traits of communism, the effort would be more than justified, and hopes for a more peaceful world would be enhanced."[9] The demands for recognisable rights as citizens and the desire of scientists and artists to escape from the needless limitations of dialectical materialism were opening up spaces of dissent within Soviet society, however vulnerable and short-lived, which were creating fertile ground for Western ideas. As the former Soviet communist Abdurakhman Avtorkhanov put it, in a passage that reads a little like an advertisement for Interdoc itself, the West had to get organized:

> It is often said that the communists have a positive programme while we in the West have nothing but anti-communism; that we have nothing with which to oppose the communists. This is not only a false argument, it is a harmful prejudice. The West has certain values which act like a gigantic magnet to the people and like poison to dictators of all shades; it has political and spiritual freedom, guaranteed rights for citizens and a state of law [...] After taking up the challenge the West must shift from its amateurish operations, its dilettantism and its lack of co-ordination to an organised and systematic exporting to the East of its most precious commodity, that commodity which free mankind has at its disposal – *the idea of freedom*. The preliminary conditions for the popularity and success of this commodity is [sic] not its organisation by governmental organs of

any of the states of the West, but its organisation by the social institutions of independent Western intellectuals.[10]

Books are important for spreading ideas, but they do not build an intellectual community: that could better be achieved by holding conferences and, more importantly, by publishing a journal which individuals could contribute to, enter into debate with, and associate with. In late 1960 a plan started to take shape within Vrede en Vrijheid's editorial board for "the creation of a studious monthly, aimed at the intelligentsia and focused on the study of international communism". The heavy anti-communist tone of *Echte Waarheid* and the more business-orientated *Feiten* were no longer sufficient for the changing political landscape, which required more objective analysis and commentary. Since Van den Heuvel oversaw Vrede en Vrijheid's activities for the BVD, he certainly had a hand in stimulating this move. The original plan was to compile a *Digest* making use of quality analysis from foreign sources on the Soviet Union and communism: *Orientierung* and *Ost-Probleme* from Munich, the *Economist*'s Foreign Report, IRD's *Interpreter*, *Est et Ouest*, and *Problems of Communism* from the US. Couwenberg, who had been responsible for *Feiten*, would continue on the Vrede en Vrijheid payroll but shift his attention to selecting articles for translation into Dutch, to be reissued on a monthly basis. The sense that the newly created SOEV was taking over the anti-communist cause led to some resistance within Vrede en Vrijheid's board, but the message from Van den Heuvel that there was a growing interest among government and business in greater insights into the communist world, along with the changing nature of communist influence via peaceful coexistence, clinched the argument.[11]

By late 1961, with Vrede en Vrijheid's hesitation causing delays, Einthoven and Van den Heuvel decided to replace the *Digest* with a proper Dutch-language journal, *Oost-West*, containing commissioned articles from Dutch and foreign authors. As Van den Heuvel wrote at the time, "I ask myself if the time hasn't come that we, who launched the idea and provided the editor, damn well reclaim the whole plan and begin ourselves." The new platform to enable this would be the Foundation for Information on East–West Relations (Stichting ter Voorlichting over de Oost-West Verhouding), on paper separate from SOEV and with a good Van den Heuvel acquaintance, former *Het Parool* editor P.J. Koets, as chair.[12] *Oost-West* was the perfect vehicle to establish Couwenberg as a more independent voice separate from employment by either the BVD or Vrede en Vrijheid, and it set out "to give objective information on East–West problems, on [the] basis of the values of the West as these have been formulated in the 'Universal Declaration of Human Rights'".[13] The journal further widened the scope of the SOEV network, strengthening its claim to be a genuine research institute and its scholarly legitimacy. While the NFR's Psychological Defence activities were aimed at the "lower cadres", *Oost-West* was definitely intellectually highbrow. When the first issue appeared in March 1962 the new management structure had not yet been finalized. Couwenberg was named as editor, but the journal's address was his own private house and the identity of the publication appeared somewhat obscure.[14] As Willem Banning wrote to Couwenberg, "In our nation, with its deep mistrust of clericalism, people want to know: what money is behind this, and which groups?"[15] The journal's first print run of 7000 had an immediate impact, with newspapers such as the *Volkskrant*, *NRC* (*Nieuwe Rotterdamse Courant*), *Het Vrije Volk*, and *Algemeen Handelsblad* noting its arrival, but it was a costly business. With only 1563 subscriptions in the first year, the SOEV had to subsidize the journal with 19,803 guilders.[16]

Was *Oost-West* the Dutch *Encounter*, the high-profile British culture-and-politics bi-monthly that was crippled when it was revealed in the late 1960s, along with the Congress for Cultural Freedom (CCF), to be part of the CIA's anti-communist intellectual empire? There are definitely similarities. *Encounter*, *Preuves*, *Tempo Presente*, and the other journals from the CCF–CIA stable provided the inspiration, and there was no equivalent in the Netherlands at the time.[17] *Oost-West*, like the CCF journals, attempted to position itself above domestic partisan divisions in order to provide a broader, more objective view of national and international political developments. Whereas most of those in the Interdoc circle were on the conservative right, the journal genuinely sought to build bridges with the centre left, more the terrain of the CCF. The first editorial of *Oost-West* made clear that it opposed neutralism as "a refusal to engage with actual history" and "particularly dangerous" in relations with communism.[18] Parts of the Dutch press thought they smelled a rat. *De Brug* reported in June 1962 that the financial background to *Oost-West* was obscure, and the journal's intention to represent "human dignity, rule of law, equality (in terms of rejecting all forms of discrimination)" was suspect when put against the fact that chief editor Couwenberg "has definitely already earned his spurs as a diligent communist expert from [...] the Domestic Security Service".[19] But there are also major differences. Couwenberg has confirmed his awareness of the CCF's output but stated that there were no links with the CCF apparatus, and indeed the CCF never gained any meaningful foothold in the Netherlands at all.[20] *Oost-West* was subsidized via SOEV, and SOEV received its funding from big business and not from the BVD. Van den Heuvel's successor as the BVD's head of training (and responsible for liaison), Nico van Rest, responded unequivocally in an internal memo to BVD chief Sinninghe Damsté:

> It cannot be excluded [...] that questions will be asked in parliament. The question [of BVD support] can be categorically denied. Unless you decide otherwise, I propose that should the *bona-fide* press turn to me for further information in this matter, I will inform them along the lines of the above.[21]

While the links with the intelligence and security world were very close, the journal was being put together exactly by a group who wanted to achieve a level of influence without relying on that world. *Encounter* and the CCF journals were assembled by intellectuals who were drawn into the CIA's network for the sake of the greater cause of anti-communism (and, of course, patronage), whereas *Oost-West* was assembled by intellectuals such as Couwenberg who were wanting on the contrary to move outside the BVD circuit. This was not easy to achieve. At a SOEV board meeting in September 1962 Van den Heuvel commented:

> In the first place there is a rumour circulating that "Oost-West" is a tool of the BVD. Alongside this is the claim that it is an instrument of American psychological warfare. Both rumours are completely unjustified. In relation to the BVD, the only support from them is that they have taken out a few subscriptions.[22]

The main consequence of this reputation, which would always hang in the air around the journal, was that while it did reach an appreciative public it was not able to expand its market as much as was hoped. The first issue had included articles from Hugh Seton-Watson (Communism and the intellectuals) and Barbara Ward (in place of negative anti-communism) alongside expositions by Van den Heuvel and Couwenberg on peaceful coexistence and psychological warfare, giving it a strong "anti-communist manifesto" feel. But it soon broadened its scope, and a survey held after the first year brought much praise for the breadth of topics covered, particularly "The West and Communism and special issues on China, religion and communism, and East–West trade. While there was criticism of the style (articles were too long, or too academic, or too journalistic), there was no doubt that the journal had an active readership, although the question must be asked whether the journal's controversial reputation prevented it from doing more than "preaching to the converted". Nevertheless its approach was quite novel for the time. In the Netherlands still socially divided according to religious and political stripe, *Oost-West* was praised for standing above this and offering a variety of perspectives. Under Couwenberg's leadership it was a deliberate part of the "*verzuiling*" process, whereby the social "pillars" were being broken down in a more modern socially mobile meritocracy. This was not an easy process: as Couwenberg put it, quite correctly, "my misfortune is that I have always advocated ideas at the wrong time, always too early".[23] As with *Tasks*, the outlook stemmed from promoting Western values as encapsulated in the UN's Universal Declaration of Human Rights, but the aim, as the first editorial had hinted, was for anti-propaganda through genuine critical self-assessment of West as well as East. Western society and the values that guided it were dynamic and in constant need of reappraisal. Black-and-white thinking was symptomatic of the negative approach the journal wanted to supersede.

Einthoven added his weight to obtaining more subscriptions, and despite rising costs the journal was temporarily issued as a monthly from March 1964.[24] By the end of 1964 it was accepted that SOEV would have to provide between 30,000 and 35,000 guilders annually to keep the journal going.[25] It was a valuable publication holding on to a niche market, with its occasional successes (the brochure "Problems of Democracy" in 1965) insufficient compensation for the fact that it was not going to take over the mainstream.[26] Insult was added to injury because Einthoven, Van den Heuvel, and Couwenberg all felt they were fulfilling tasks that the government should be doing for the sake of the nation. Neither the Ministry for Foreign Affairs nor the Ministry of Education had the personnel to provide this kind of public information on international affairs, civic training, and preparation for contacts with the East among students and businessmen, all of which was becoming more and more necessary. SOEV was trying to manage all of this on a commercial basis, so the least that could be provided was some form of subsidy in recompense. What is more, as Couwenberg put it, "in the sixties to get a good reputation you had to be funded by the government, not by private enterprises". The new journal was also "an intrusion on vested interests": established institutes such as the elitist Netherlands Society for International Affairs, its journal *Internationale Spectator*, and the Oost-Europa Instituut at the University of Amsterdam regarded *Oost-West* as a suspect upstart and not as an addition to their field. Attempts to obtain funding from the Prince Bernhard Fund, the Ministry of Education, and the Netherlands Organization for Pure Research (ZWO) all ended in failure. Even Einthoven's direct appeals to the highest levels of government did not result in anything.[27]

In an attempt to improve the journal's image and escape "the irritating judgement against us that we are occupied with indoctrination and not responsible scientific research and information", Couwenberg proposed changing the name of SOEV to highlight more strongly the focus on East–West relations, a subject that was after all gaining more attention in public life. In 1965 this resulted in SOEV merging with *Oost-West*'s management structure to form the Oost-West Instituut (OWI: East–West Institute), joining the training and advisory functions of SOEV with the scholarly–intellectual output of the journal. In practical terms this meant the SOEV board taking over the journal and the journal board becoming an advisory council. But the move was far more significant than that, because it signalled the end of the start-up phase for the Dutch operation and the turn towards a concentration on the social, political, and economic consequences of rapidly changing East–West relations. Ecology and "brainwashing" were out; détente was in. The "daughter of SOEV", as Van den Heuvel termed it, was replacing the parent. While in the coming decade Van den Heuvel would increasingly orientate his activities around détente, for Couwenberg, trying to establish his journal in an unforgiving marketplace, this was only the first of more changes to come.[28]

The Netherlands: the BVD

As SOEV and OWI looked to consolidate their position in the Dutch intellectual landscape, their relationship with the BVD had to be clarified. Einthoven had after all been the BVD's first chief and Van den Heuvel one of his most prominent lieutenants. Although they left the service in 1961 and 1962, respectively, it could be expected that contacts – even significant contacts – would remain. Was not SOEV, and indeed Interdoc itself, simply a further extension of BVD activities? A document from Einthoven's secret memoirs sheds some light on the relationship. On 18 December 1961 a meeting took place that divided up responsibilities. SOEV–BVD contacts were to be handled in face-to-face contact between Van den Heuvel and his successor as head of training at the service. Van den Heuvel could take his contacts with him to SOEV, so long as they were "pure". Any uncertainty, and the BVD would claim priority over subjects related to communist subversion and counter-intelligence in the Netherlands, leaving psychological warfare to the foundation. The BVD's monthly report would still be sent to Van den Heuvel for "background information".[29] Beyond this, there was surprisingly little contact. Einthoven was determined to maintain a low profile and not influence matters following his retirement, and anyway his successor, Sinninghe Damsté, possessed a different style and was uninterested in psychological warfare. BVD personnel did not take part in the training activities run by SOEV despite the fact that Van den Heuvel had been head of training for the service.[30]

Joop van der Wilden, a long-time friend of Van den Heuvel who rose to be head of the BVD's Section C (Counter-intelligence), recalled later that the transfer of BVD money to the new operation was "strictly forbidden [...] they wanted to avoid a central office for psychological warfare".[31] Peter Keller, responsible during the 1980s for liaison with Van den Heuvel, emphasized that the latter's "secret propaganda" activities meant that the BVD did not want "unchecked channels of communication" or BVD personnel being involved in ways that the service had no control over.[32] But there were major sensitivities to be overcome. Van den Heuvel (and Einthoven) after all had direct relations with CIA personnel in both The Hague and Washington, DC, and the BVD, despite its close relations with the Americans, was very wary of US activities on its patch. In 1965 CIA Chief of Station Gordon Mason had been asked to leave by Sinninghe Damsté precisely because he did not abide by the rules of working via the BVD within the Netherlands itself.[33] Van den Heuvel was also not above occasionally trying to make use of his former colleagues. Van der Wilden recounted one episode from the late 1960s when he was asked to initiate a disinformation exercise against the Russian Embassy in The Hague, only to discover later that BVD deputy director Hans "Hassan" Neervoort had already vetoed the request. Such attempts only hardened the service's determination to maintain a distance.

One should not discount the element of rivalry in this situation. With Einthoven's departure looming, Van den Heuvel was certainly a competitor of both Neervoort and Andries Kuipers, head of Section B (Operations), for the top jobs in the service. It was Kuipers who became Sinninghe Damsté's deputy in 1961, fully expecting to take over later as BVD chief, and when he did so in 1967 it was Neervoort who followed him into the vacant deputy position. While Neervoort did maintain informal relations for old time's sake, Kuipers had initiated a more softly-softly approach towards the Dutch Communist Party in 1959 that to some extent clashed with the direction Van den Heuvel was then moving in.[34] As a memo from 1967 demonstrates, Kuipers was also prepared to act in case SOEV's successor, the Oost-West Instituut, brought any unwelcome negative publicity for the service. For observers such as the KGB it was almost certainly considered a branch of the BVD. Remarkable in this memo is the comment that "our information about what East–West actually does is very limited", which points to more than an arm's-length distance between the two.[35] Did Van den Heuvel set out on his own with SOEV and Interdoc because he knew at a certain point that his career path within the BVD was blocked? It is possible, but unlikely. He was neither the conventional career type nor someone who would bend his convictions according to the needs of an institution – even the BVD – that did not necessarily agree with the direction he wanted to take. Going out on his own meant breaking new ground, and avoiding the intrusion of those (such as Kuipers) who did not approve of his methods.

The Netherlands: big business

In the business field, SOEV struggled to establish itself. Such a private organization was not been seen before, and potential financiers needed to be convinced. Cooperation with Shell was by far the most extensive. Wolfgang Buchow, active in Interdoc Youth in the late 1960s, recalled that "Van den Heuvel was Shell, he got a lot of money from Shell for Interdoc".[36] How this was done comes out of a letter from Einthoven to Prince Bernhard in July 1963, which states that "we are busy training the higher cadres from all divisions of Royal Shell in Netherlands, from the laboratories to the oil fields and refineries and also marketing and tankers". The Railways, Unilever, and the Air Force Staff College were also regular clients, but little was developing with Hoogovens (steel), the coal mines, or the trade unions.[37] An insight into the financial situation at this time is given by documents from the company archives of Philips. Initial contacts between the company and SOEV date from 1961, with Einthoven the initiator.[38] A notation from a meeting of the major Dutch businesses in January 1964 provides some details: Shell was the main contributor with 35,000 guilders a year, followed by Philips, Unilever, and AKU (the predecessor of the chemical conglomerate AkzoNobel) with 25,000 each. Smaller contributions came from Hoogovens and the mines.

"Courses and other services" brought in a further 49,000 guilders. The most revealing item is a subsidy of 98,911.66 guilders – probably the equivalent of $25,000 at the time – from an unnamed *"Amerikaanse stichting"* (American foundation). This is the only evidence so far found anywhere that the Hague operation actually received US funds in the early phase.[39]

Despite funding SOEV since the beginning Philips had never shown any interest in the training option, which raises the suspicion that they were contributing simply as part of the Dutch big-business club. To remedy this, board member J.R. Schaafsma called a meeting of Philips management on 26 February 1964 at Chalet Royal in Den Bosch, involving lectures by Van den Heuvel on East–West relations and by Couwenberg on Western values. The evaluation was mixed: neither speaker was able to convince the Philips audience of the value of SOEV for the company, although "the general opinion" was that "it is occupied with important questions" that deserve attention. Further discussion within "De Grote Vier" (The Big Four: Shell, Unilever, Philips, and AKU) was necessary to decide SOEV's future potential. A visit to Van Stolkweg by Philips' political adviser led to the conclusion that it was difficult "to take the foundation's work *au sérieux*".[40] Philips took their time, but by mid-1965 they had decided to reduce the annual subsidy over a period of three years to 10,000 guilders. Another meeting at Van Stolkweg that summer revealed that SOEV was still struggling to gain a foothold in the business world. While the courses for air force staff had already been running for three years, no similar entry had been achieved with either the army or the navy, despite the influence of Borghouts. The general conclusion of all concerned was that more focus should be laid on the promotion of Western values. The Philips representatives were especially dubious about East–West relations because things were changing so fast that informed opinion was very difficult (adding the scathing comment that "the employees of the foundation know scarcely more about communist China than what is to be found in the *NRC*"[41]).

The result was a further meeting on 3 November 1965 to discuss establishing a National Institute for Civic Education, with representatives from the military, education, the unions, and business, funded by government and with Couwenberg as director. The ground had already been laid for this. In 1961 Van den Heuvel had made contact with the Werkcomité voor Opvoeding tot Democratie (Working Committee for Democratic Education, WCDE), an independent pedagogical foundation established to promote "the consolidation of Western-based democratic values in society, both nationally and internationally".[42] Couwenberg had already been active in this field for a decade, and in the early period of SOEV there were real ambitions to pursue cadre formation in three key areas: business, the military, and education, the last being seen in terms of developing a resilient form of democratic citizenship attuned to the ideological East–West contest. Its members were invited to the *colloques* of the early 1960s, and the chair of the WCDE, J.J. Schokking, was invited on to the OWI board. Two *colloques* were used to try to forge both a national (around OWI) and an international (around Interdoc) consensus on the need for more coordination and attention to training in democratic citizenship: Noordwijk in September 1962 on education and industry (uniting two key interest groups) and Lunteren in May 1964 on youth and communism.[43]

The *Oost-West* special issue on Problems of Democracy (which included an article by the Minister of Education) was used by Einthoven to generate interest from Minister-President Cals in the National Institute idea. Yet once again the wish to become the central point around which to organize others generated resistance. The meeting in November 1965 brought this out in the open, since SOEV's attempt to hijack the agenda was encroaching directly on the interests of existing institutions such as the WCDE. These negative responses "were not handled so tactfully by Mr. van den Heuvel", who clearly showed his frustration at the lack of progress, and the plan was passed to a "research committee".[44] Keeping the proposal alive, Couwenberg did succeed in setting up the Nederlands Centrum voor Democratische Burgerschapsvorming (Centre for Democratic Citizenship) in July 1967 in partnership with the WCDE. Successful in attracting subsidy from the Ministry for Culture, Recreation, and Society, it acted as a useful catalyst for expanding OWI activities in this direction.[45] But the November 1965 meeting marked the end point of serious interest from Philips, beyond the company's sense of obligation, as one of the "Big Four", to continue a level of funding. Van den Heuvel did soon bring in a staff member to cover China, former Lieutenant Colonel H.A. (Henry) van Oort, but he was actually a specialist on Chinese porcelain who admitted after a visit to the Ostkolleg in 1966 to his "limited knowledge of communism".[46] He proved to be a quick learner, but whether this would have satisfied the observers from Philips is highly questionable.

Another temporary setback came from the railways in 1964. Although De Pous had been an important supporter, he still had to respond to the specific needs of his police force – and the evaluations of the 1962 training courses were mixed. De Pous expressed disappointment that the content of the courses did not connect very well with the actual tasks of the railway police. Van den Heuvel was required to explain once again the principles of "human ecology" that lay behind the course manuals, but the purpose was clearly not getting across to its audience.[47] The relationship was therefore already in doubt when De Pous retired on 14 June 1963. While his successor, B.F.A. de Mikx, emphasized that the purpose of the railway police was to act for "justice, state security, and the company itself", it was not clear where the training courses fitted in his outlook. On 17 March 1964 de Mikx met with his top officers to discuss future relations with SOEV. Strangely enough, the page of the minutes explaining the outcome of this part of the meeting is inexplicably missing from the archive.[48] The SOEV Annual Report for

1964 tellingly remarks that the training courses had not been taken up as hoped. In 1965 Rijks bemoaned the fact that the Institute had not been able to secure corporate support over the longer term, with Shell being the only financial mainstay. After SOEV transformed itself into the OWI in 1965 it shifted emphasis away from instruction in communist thinking (too abstract for the Dutch audiences) towards more practical matters of corporate interest, such as the fostering of democratic citizenship and, from 1965, courses for those in higher management "directly involved in East–West traffic".[49] In this way it was able to maintain a diverse array of clients for courses and training sessions, including AKU, the PTT (post office personnel), and the national airline KLM.

Much was expected of Prince Bernhard. In his role as Inspector General of the Dutch Armed Forces, Bernhard did promote the idea of including East–West relations in the training programme of the Royal Military Academy. There were also moves to utilize the Prince's Bilderberg network in support of a major conference in The Hague on the German Question.[50] But Bernhard proved unable – or unwilling – to force things through. In July 1963 Van den Heuvel made an official request for funding for the *Oost-West* periodical from the Prince Bernhard Fund, originally established in 1940 with starting capital from Shell to contribute towards Spitfire production. Despite having as its post-war goal "the promotion of spiritual resilience through cultural self-sufficiency", objections from members of the Fund's board that the SOEV–*Oost-West* operation had "a clearly controversial character" led to the request being turned down. Pleading for *Oost-West*'s academic credentials, Van den Heuvel then discovered that a negative article in the leftist weekly *Vrij Nederland* had led to the decision. Further applications also proved unsuccessful.[51] In general, Van den Heuvel did not feel that the Prince was committed enough; personally, he did not feel that Bernhard gave him the recognition he deserved. The fact that Van den Heuvel never received the Willems Orde, the highest decoration for service to the nation, for his role in the wartime Albrecht Group was a sore point.[52]

Other avenues gradually opened up, including within the government. Einthoven managed to convince the Ministry of Foreign Affairs that its trainee diplomats needed a course on communism and Western values, providing finance and enhanced credibility for SOEV. Begun in 1964, these courses were continued by the Oost-West Instituut into the 1970s. The Ministry of Defence proved a more reliable partner. Air force personnel were from the beginning a key constituency, being the most likely section of the armed forces to fall into enemy hands during a conflict (the army and navy were anyway far less interested). Through Spits and Borghouts SOEV–OWI developed a close working relationship with the Dutch Air Force's Internal Information Service (Interne Voorlichting Luchtmacht or InVoLu), established in 1962. Under the leadership of the freethinking Lieutenant Colonel Rob van Hoof, InVoLu's semi-autonomous status generated "a lot of suspicion" within the air force, it being something of a competitor for the more hierarchical Defence Study Centre. Nevertheless the unit maintained its close link with Van Stolkweg until budget cuts forced its closure in 1974. Several influences fed into the formation of InVoLu: the concerns over brainwashing dating back to the Korean War, the formation of the Bundeswehr and German methods of fostering a new military under democratic civilian control, and Borghouts' belief that officers should understand domestic and international political developments and their public and professional role in a broader context. While the early courses were heavily weighted towards studies on communism, by the late 1960s OWI was hiring in prominent speakers (Jerome Heldring, Karel van het Reve, Jan Willem Schulte Nordholt, Ernst van der Beugel) around seven or eight times a year, at 100 guilders a time, to deliver lectures on international politics and the East–West situation to InVoLu officers who would then take this material with them as they themselves made speaking tours around air force bases.

There is no doubt that the InVoLu courses were a valuable regular source of income for OWI (36,000 guilders in 1967) and there is a suggestion that the relationship was allowed to continue for so long as a way of directing funds to Van Stolkweg outside of official funding channels.[53] With corporate subsidies drying up, in 1967–68 Van den Heuvel approached first the Minister of Defence and then Minister-President Piet de Jong to try to expand OWI services to the other armed forces. He made the point that not only was OWI fulfilling the task of government at a lower cost, but that it "possesses good foreign connections, one of which has extended an interest-free loan to cover the negative balance for 1967 and has offered to do the same for 1968". Lack of interest from either the army or the navy prevented any new courses, but the Minister-President was clearly moved to action at the thought that foreigners were subsidizing such a unique Dutch enterprise. A one-off contract was quickly generated (worth 25,000 guilders, the level of OWI's deficit for 1968) for a study on détente and East–West relations for the Ministry of Defence.[54] Van den Heuvel would continue to press for subsidies from the Ministry through the 1970s, with mixed success.

The veterans' organizations also continued to provide a useful network. In 1965 Van den Heuvel succeeded Borghouts as chairman of the NFR after the latter's death, and he maintained the emphasis on the Psychological Defence campaign for his entire term up to 1978. While this campaign brought new energy to sections of the NFR network, it was not such a simple business to make contact with and transmit the legacies of World War II to Dutch youth, as various annual reports admit.[55] With uncertainty beginning to creep into the NFR board, in 1969 Van den Heuvel split the activities and formed the Stichting Geestelijke Weerbaarheid (Institute for Psychological Defence) in order to maintain momentum and prevent further loss of interest. The new foundation, which produced the publication *Basis*, maintained Van den Heuvel's long-running interest in civic education programmes. The statutes state that it sought "the willingness to maintain, develop and defend if necessary the values and achievements that are among other things anchored in the Dutch constitutional monarchy and parliamentary democracy".[56] The times were changing and a new impulse was needed to protect society from threats coming from both left and right:

> We live in a time of increasing uncertainty. A bewildering array of developments force themselves upon us and a stream of information flows over us to explain these developments. Feelings of frustration increase, we are unable to gain a complete picture, we have the sense that we know less when more and more is happening. One becomes discouraged, believes everything, and falls silent. The silent majority is created [...] The Institute for Psychological Defence wants to become the voice of the real majority and wants to mobilize this majority with a more conscious experience of democracy.[57]

The Institute immediately became the new platform for Van den Heuvel to unite with other national veterans' organizations, such as Veteranen Legioen Nederland and Expogé (Nederlandse Vereniging van Ex-Politieke Gevangenen), something which had been difficult before.[58] With support coming from F.J. (Frits) Philips and Willem Drees, the Institute became the central point (with the Centre for Democratic Citizenship and later, in 1978, the Centre for Active Democracy) for the effort to encourage social awareness of democratic values. The new development did not go unnoticed by the Dutch media, who suspected a right-wing club, especially as Van den Heuvel could be a little loose-lipped about the use of violence against youthful protesters. By 1972 it claimed to have around 15,000 members.[59] Looking to develop the campaign internationally, in 1967 Van den Heuvel also became Vice-President of the International Union of Resistance and Deportee Movements (UIRD). It was from this platform, taking inspiration from similar initiatives in Switzerland and Sweden, that he sought to internationalize the Psychological Defence programme in the 1970s.[60]

A Dutch–German cabal

To ensure smooth Dutch–German liaison, Geyer's Verein was represented in The Hague through the position of deputy director. Official lines of authority were traversed by this arrangement, since from 1964 there was also a BND station chief in The Hague: Hans Büchler (code name Brock). The first person designated for deputy director was Oberstleutnant Hiltmann, a member of military intelligence based in Ems, but despite his salary being agreed and his involvement in the preparations he never made it to The Hague.[61] Instead, someone from outside the intelligence world was chosen: Baron Wilhelm von Hahn. Von Hahn, born to a German family in

Russia, had fled the country in 1917, aged 22, to become a journalist. During the war he was head of the Ministry of Propaganda's German News Bureau in Rome. After one and a half years in a prisoner-of-war camp he worked with the Interior Ministry's Bundeszentrale für den Heimatdienst in Bonn (renamed the Bundeszentrale für Politische Bildung in 1963) and then with the German government's cultural exchange service Inter Nationes. His placement as deputy director of Interdoc in early 1963 (initially for a trial period of five months) was due to "his knowledge of international affairs, communist affairs, and languages (including Russian)" and his usefulness in knowing his way around the German government. Both von Grote and von Dellingshausen were close friends of his.[62] Von Hahn was already 67 when he arrived in The Hague, proof that he was brought in temporarily to consolidate the arrangement early on. Yet his role, which involved building up the research and public information links with organizations such as the Institut zur Erforschung der UdSSR in Munich, the Institut für Sowjetologie (Bundesinstitut für Erforschung des Marxismus-Leninismus) in Cologne, and the Otto Suhr Institut in Berlin, soon focused on enhancing the reach of German Cold War analysis and opinion via Interdoc to the English-speaking world.[63] This took on such importance that he soon gave up other commitments for a full-time position with Interdoc.[64] During his three years in The Hague von Hahn pursued two main lines of research. One, entitled "Konfrontation", built on Geyer's *Strategie des Friedens* and explored the actualities of engaging in contact with the East. The other, also with an eye on the future, was a major survey of the effects of Soviet propaganda on the Federal Republic's image in other West European nations, assessing its impact in the media and on public opinion, and how it might be dealt with.[65]

The core of Interdoc was obviously small, and its foundation and functioning rested entirely on the successful mix of personalities of the main players. Einthoven's mixture of passionate belief and genial bonhomie was a positive factor in developing trust on both the German and French sides during the crucial preparation phase. The person in charge of the Munich end of the operation, and the brains behind its whole approach, was the BND's Rolf Geyer. Geyer had been the youngest colonel in the Wehrmacht's Army Group East general staff, so connections with Gehlen went back to the war. After time in a US prisoner-of-war camp Geyer went through various jobs in Marburg before being recruited specifically for psychological warfare by Gehlen in 1959. Gunhild Bohm-Geyer, who met Geyer for the first time in 1966, when he came to speak to her student group at the Institut für Gesellschaft und Wissenschaft (Hans Lades' institute in Erlangen), described him as a natural teacher who "always had respect for the other side – respect, not necessarily acceptance. If you know yourself and the other side you are in control of the situation."[66] Einthoven concurred: "a type of philosopher. Once a career officer, now with long shoulder-length artist-like hair. Knowledgeable in Buddhism, Hinduism, and a follower of Rudolf Steiner.

Despite all this philosophy he does not give the impression that he is 'floating around'."[67] Geyer was a well-read auto-didact, an interesting mix of authoritarian Prussian officer and anthroposophical guru who deserved his nickname "The Professor". As his IIIF colleagues remembered, Geyer was an "exotic figure" who treated his hair as "antennae".[68]

Geyer was the chief of section IIIF, the psychological warfare subdivision of the BND's analysis and evaluation branch III. Although Geyer's immediate superior was the head of III branch, General Erich Dethleffsen, Geyer was given full responsibility by Gehlen to run IIIF as he chose, and he reported directly to the BND chief.[69] While it was Foertsch who laid the foundations for the BND's involvement in psychological warfare, it was Geyer who built the apparatus and provided the philosophy behind it. Geyer was on first-name terms with Allen Dulles and was obviously familiar with American approaches in this field, but IIIF has all the hallmarks of his own particular world view. It was Geyer's initiative (sanctioned by Gehlen) to run IIIF as an *Aussenstelle*, a unit situated outside of the BND's own compound – the only part of the III branch apparatus that had this status. It was located as a self-contained operation at Pössenbacherstraße 21, a spacious address not far from the service's headquarters in the Munich suburb of Pullach. To the general public IIIF was the Studienstelle für Auslandsfragen, as stated on a plaque in the doorway of the villa, but this was just a cover name and nothing was produced under this imprint. With a staff of around 50 people, IIIF was divided up into subsections, with groups of experts concentrating on specific regions: the Soviet Union, the GDR, Poland, religion, and world communism.

The emphasis lay on the analysis and evaluation of open-source and classified materials to cover the attitude of the Soviet and communist media towards West Germany and a broad assessment of social, economic, and political trends in the East. This would then be articulated via anonymous (or pseudonymous) articles in the monthly *Orientierung* and other periodicals distributed through the Interdoc network. Since communist rule was always imposed from above on the majority of the population – it was always Leninism, not Marxism – psychological analysis of popular opinion could give insights into the extent of loyalty towards the regimes. Attention was also given to "targeting" specific conferences and other meetings of interest, to expand the knowledge network and gather information on potential new recruits (otherwise known as "operational research"). Contact was maintained from the villa with the "Operational Groups", which included von Grote's Verein (later Arbeitsgruppe) and the Ilmgau Verlag in Pfaffenhofen, which published IIIF–Verein output. The link was semi-clandestine: only von Grote from the Verein would come to the villa, and only Geyer from IIIF would go to BND headquarters. Code names were used – Geyer's was "Goslar" after the town in Hesse, and he ran *Orientierung* under the name of "Michael" – but within the villa itself a collegial atmosphere was maintained.

Aristocratic titles (there were quite a few) and academic degrees were freely displayed, in contrast to the anonymity of the BND compound. The intent was to present the entire set-up – the Verein, the publishing house, the link with international contacts via Interdoc – as a public entity engaged in scholarly research (which of course they were). This allowed the intelligence community to use these channels to influence public opinion and civil society in a disguised way. Geyer ran a tight operation, on the one hand maintaining strict tradecraft by running the villa as a unit closed off from the rest of the world to prevent GDR penetration, and on the other building a camaraderie amongst its workforce. It was a diverse crowd, with "exiles" from East Prussia and the Baltic states and veterans of Gehlen's Army Group East and the anti-Soviet Vlasov army mixing with younger analysts of the post-war generation, including Herman Foertsch's son Volker.[70]

An insight into Geyer's outlook is provided by a speech he gave to the villa's staff for Christmas 1968. With references ranging from Lao Tse and a fourteenth-century Japanese emperor to St John the Evangelist, Oswald Spengler, and the German artillery field manual from 1907, Geyer roused his team with a mixture of sermon and statistics. In the previous year they had produced ("controlled or at least influenced") 19 publications in 33 different editions. They had added Spanish to their linguistic lexicon, opening up access to Latin America. Theodor Krause's opinions on the Soviet press and Soviet strategy were now being taken up by West German press attachés. Andreas von Weiss was requested by the federal government to write a study on the New Left. He placed the total budget for the whole network at a substantial DM 2.2 million, a sum which, in the context of the federal budget of more than DM 80 billion, was small. But it was still "tax money", and Geyer demanded self-criticism about what they were doing at every turn. The cause was not just a striving for knowledge or the search for truth, but also a will to act. Using Marx as inspiration (*Theses on Feuerbach*: "The philosophers have only interpreted the world, in various ways; the point is to change it"), Geyer linked the two sides:

> And you can see, my friends, that we are a house in which knowledge is cultivated, where knowledge must be cultivated as the basis for the other side of our mission, when we turn our work into action. We are a place where thoughts shall become and have already become deeds; and as long as I remain the leader of this unit I will use all my abilities to safeguard this linkage of thoughts and deeds, and I ask you once again to work with me in this task.[71]

Despite the Dutch–German agreement to establish Interdoc, the specific budgetary details still needed to be worked out. Von Hahn, having spoken to von Grote, informed Van den Heuvel in May 1963 that Interdoc's finances should not be taken for granted. The initial plan from the Germans had been to wait until an operation of sufficient quality had been assembled before committing for the long term.[72] Initially Geyer was only authorized to dispense funds for actual expenses or specifically notified goals, beyond which Interdoc's budget did not exist.[73] Von Dellingshausen's proposal for DM 10,000 a month in mid-1962 could not be realized, creating a confused financial situation as a result. However, Geyer's authorization to issue larger amounts in advance (*"quasi als Vorschuss"*) offered a way forward. The aim was to calculate, at the end of 1963, the total costs from February–December, and compare this sum with the total amount authorized by the board for that year: 90,000 guilders (approximately $20,000 at the exchange rate of the time). Von Grote's plan was to be careful and efficient in that first period, to allow Geyer the space to react positively and grant an increase of 10 per cent or more for 1964. In this way, the result would be both to strengthen Geyer's position with Interdoc and to create the conditions to justify a considerable annual increase in Interdoc's budget.[74] This approach, which von Hahn referred to as "clever" and "necessary", proved to be a success. As he stated in his notes for a talk in Bonn in mid-1965: "Finances: no government control", indicating that the BMG was no longer part of the story and that Interdoc was now fully a BND issue.[75] That did not mean a free-for-all, especially not from the Dutch side. This is clear from an exchange in 1966, in which Rijks berated both Einthoven and Van den Heuvel for not sufficiently declaring their foreign travel expenses to him.[76] The agreed ratio of funding in 1963 between German and Dutch sources was 4:1 (which means, based on the total budget of 90,000 Dutch guilders for 1963, roughly 18,000 from the Dutch and 72,000 from the Germans). However, this 4:1 ratio was broken in the following years. While the Dutch contribution was increased to 45,000 guilders, this was the highest that could be achieved. In contrast the German contribution would expand to more than 500,000 guilders by 1969.[77]

Once Interdoc was up and running Van den Heuvel operated with a lot of freedom. A balance was always needed between specific German interests and the wider ambitions of the Dutch, and Van den Heuvel would sometimes reject proposals that were too narrow in outlook. As von Hahn wrote to Van den Heuvel in mid-1964:

> More and more I begin to realize that we in The Hague have to shoulder the full responsibility for our work, out of our own initiative, asking our friends in Munich only when our loyalty to them is at stake. As the frame of Interdoc is internationally broadening [sic], we have to do what we feel necessary without asking for help or wisdom from others as long as we can manage alone.[78]

Correspondence between Geyer and Van den Heuvel offers a slightly different view. Both Geyer and von Grote were fully aware of the potential psychological strain (*"psychologische Belastung"*) that heavy dependence on German financial support could have on a supposedly equal Dutch–German cooperative venture. The freedom to manoeuvre in The Hague was an attempt to compensate for this. Geyer was deeply concerned that he nevertheless experienced "atmospheric disturbances" (*"atmosphärische Störungen"*) from Dutch colleagues in The Hague. He could not understand how by mid-1965 such anti-German sentiment could still exist among partners who had already been cooperating for eight years in a common cause. Geyer understood that the dominance of German funding could be a "psychological weight", but both he and von Grote were determined not to use it as a means of always getting their way. The "Interdoc family" was turning into a success and issues of nationality should no longer be relevant.[79]

Van den Heuvel brushed Geyer's concerns aside, claiming that the occasional irritations were not based on anti-German sentiment but were comparable to any institutional set-up. He also emphasized that the inner circle of "Geyer–Grote–Hahn–Heuvel" was an exception in that they operated together as the single unit that Geyer imagined they should. The Dutchman emphasized this again at the end of that year; aside from cordiality, it is clear that the German benefactor needed to be reassured.[80] Others remembered it differently. Dietmar Töppel, who regularly joined Geyer on his trips up the autobahn to The Hague (often to deliver the cash), remembered Geyer having an attitude along the lines of "I give you the money and you do what I say." Although contact with the French was maintained "at the working level", the official withdrawal of the SDECE from Interdoc allowed the set-up to be run according to "the German order". Van den Heuvel's free-wheeling autonomy was not above criticism in this arrangement, and he made Machiavellian use of any available extra leverage. Töppel has suggested that the Dutchman "intrigued" against Geyer with the BND station chief in The Hague, Hans Büchler, because Büchler did not appreciate interference on "his" territory from another BND unit in Munich.[81] But these issues were not enough to derail the partnership, since the benefits for the Germans were considerable, and the Van den Heuvel–Geyer correspondence is replete with determinations of friendship and unity against the common enemy. The Netherlands was an ideal "front country" base which could avoid suspicion in a way that West Germany could not. The lingering resentment of many Dutch people towards the Germans from World War II was also a perfect cover, especially considering Van den Heuvel's own activities amongst the networks of resistance veterans. The West German (BND-Verein) analysis of East–West relations was distributed throughout the worldwide Interdoc network with little or no attribution to its origin. And for ten years students, journalists, and trainee diplomats from the Netherlands and elsewhere were instructed in those views by German experts at the Ostkolleg in Cologne and on study trips to West Berlin.

The training network

The first SOEV Annual Report to refer directly to the importance of the student community was that of 1963. These leaders of tomorrow were travelling east on study trips in increasing numbers and receiving Soviet-bloc guests in return. Preparation was needed.[82] Initial ideas about establishing a new training facility in the Netherlands were rejected as too costly, leading to a search for stable partners in the Federal Republic. The focus soon lay on the Ostkolleg, located on the Stadtwaldgürtel in Cologne. The Ostkolleg, established in 1957, worked closely with the Interior Ministry's Bundeszentrale für den Heimatdienst (later the Bundeszentrale für politische Bildung) to promote the study and understanding of Soviet communism and East–West relations in the Federal Republic. Its clientele included members of the BND and the Bundesamt für Verfassungsschutz (Protection of the Constitution). Van den Heuvel had learnt about it from German colleagues as early as 1960, while still head of training at the BVD, and in 1961 he met the Ostkolleg's Dr Karl-Heinz Ruffman in Cologne to learn more about the set-up.[83]

In January 1962, at a meeting in Munich, Einthoven secured a BVD–BND agreement for small groups of selected Dutch "representatives" to visit selected German institutes and assess the quality of various German publications with an eye to future collaboration. Van den Heuvel returned to Cologne the same month to ask for 16 seminar places (two places each on eight week-long seminars) for that year as a trial run, choosing participants from among government information personnel, political officials (cadres), and the BVD. The reply was that, so long as those attending were involved with East–West questions, they would be welcome.[84] In January 1963 the number was increased to 20, with the addition of British and French participants if it could be arranged.[85] This was not all: via von Dellingshausen, who could provide financial support for activities within the Federal Republic, Van den Heuvel arranged SOEV-organized study trips to West Berlin and two conferences, one for students and one for trade unionists. Via Günter Triesch he also planned a meeting of Dutch and German corporate management to discuss the state of citizenship education in their respective businesses. Van den Heuvel, aware of Geyer's insistence that all contacts in the Federal Republic should be known and sanctioned by the BND, kept his German colleague informed.[86]

Differences of opinion did exist within the German camp. Von Dellingshausen would not support the Ostkolleg connection, regarding its "scientific education" as "unnecessary ballast" and devoid of any value, and the chances of his direct involvement in Interdoc were deemed to be "low".[87] He also expressed doubts as to the merits of von Hahn's "Konfrontation" study on how best to prepare students, tourists, businessmen, and the like for their increasing contacts with Eastern-bloc societies, suggesting once again a division of opinion on this issue between BND circles and the civilian ministries.[88] But the Cologne connection, stimulated by von Hahn's personal contacts with the Institut für Sowjetologie's Boris Meissner, Arnold Buchholz, and (from 1964) director Dr Berner, became a central part of the Dutch–German network during the 1960s. Meissner in particular was convinced that the world-revolutionary character of communist ideology meant that peaceful coexistence was no more than a dangerous illusion, a view which fitted with the outlook of the BND–BVD circle behind Interdoc.[89] Buchholz in turn was sensitive to shifts in the communist world and the need to move beyond a simple "two camp" approach.[90]

Laying the basis for cooperation, Van den Heuvel decided that all those working with SOEV should attend the Ostkolleg in order to raise their level of awareness for their operation in the Netherlands.[91] He then passed responsibility for its management to his deputies at Van Stolkweg, Herman Mennes and Bart van der Laan (a teacher from the military training school in Den Helder). The first SOEV contingent, consisting of Frank Spits and Van der Laan, returned in May 1962 with a very positive report. The quality of the speakers was high, the focus was broader and more useful than just on the "German question", and the course provoked some reflection on both the need for equally high-qualified experts in the Netherlands and the level of understanding of communism within SOEV itself.[92] Mennes, Couwenberg, and Van den Heuvel's nephew Pieter Koerts soon followed, and from then on the net grew wider. Van der Laan contacted Einthoven's intellectual mentor, Willem Banning, to spread the word on the Ostkolleg via Labour Party circles and the Protestant Church's study and training centre Kerk en Wereld.[93] Another satisfied client was Lieutenant Colonel Van der Pol from the Air Force Staff School, who praised the "remarkable level" of the course in October 1962.[94]

Opinion leaders on two influential liberal–secular newspapers, the *Algemeen Handelsblad* and the *Nieuwe Rotterdamse Courant* (Dries Steketee, Henk Hofland, Jerome Heldring, Karel van der Poll), and *Vrij Nederland*'s Dries Ekker were brought in. Heldring attended a week's seminar in December 1962 with much reserve, expecting "a thoroughly anticommunist indoctrination or, at best, propaganda for the return of the lost German territories in the East". Instead he returned very satisfied with the quality and impartiality of the information provided, so much so that he recommended the course to his paper's foreign affairs editor, Fritz Dekker.[95] Not all participants were convinced. Captain Benist of the Dutch Marine reported to the chief of the Marine Staff that all aspects of communist ideology were studied in relation to "the Soviet Zone" and the Berlin question. The issues split the auditorium between the older generation, orientated around German nationalism, and the younger generation, with a more democratic outlook. Benist finished his observations by remarking that these nationalist tendencies maintained West Germany as a threat to world peace, so much so that he advised "resistance against the provision of nuclear weapons to the Bundeswehr under national controls, be they tactical or strategic".[96] Nevertheless, by early 1964 small student groups from Leiden and Utrecht, particularly from the law faculties (a prime site for the Dutch elites), were attending on a regular basis.[97] SOEV and its successor, the Oost-West Instituut, continued to advertise these study trips via the relevant student organizations in Leiden and Utrecht up to 1972. The last group to attend travelled in November 1972 via the Leidse Studentenbeweging voor Internationale Betrekkingen.

The internationalization of the Ostkolleg through SOEV/Interdoc led the Germans to attempt more of a coordinating role. In December 1964 a multinational conference was held in Cologne under the heading *Ostforschung und politische Bildung* (Eastern studies and political education), the intention being to gather together practitioners in political education from NATO and neutral countries to share research and experiences.[98] With 22 delegates from eleven nations attending, the event became something of a showcase for the efforts of the Germans and SOEV (with Van den Heuvel delivering a paper on the Dutch situation) to upgrade public awareness of the threat.[99] As the opening statements claimed, the "immunization" of Western populations was impossible without first providing a full understanding of the Soviet system. This should involve not "state training" (*staatliche Schulung*) but the possibility for the informed citizen to make an enlightened choice. Of course, it was assumed that the correct approach would ensure that the enlightened citizen would end up always going in the desired (anticommunist) direction. This was not to everyone's liking. While the Danish (Noemi Eskul-Jensen) and French (F. de Liencourt) speakers agreed that something needed to be done to connect the concerned elites with the indifferent mass of the population, the British were sceptical.[100] Neither were the rather ethereal discussions of Swiss professor Joseph Bochenski on "spiritual engagement with communist ideology" what some practitioners wanted to hear. Peter Foster of the British Embassy in Bonn reported to IRD afterwards that he "found the proceedings rather dull and unreal", involving too much of an overview of existing anti-communist research and too little attention to "the effectiveness of the press, radio and television as the only media capable of reaching a broad public". Van den Heuvel agreed that the organization was substandard, the discussions below par, and – more importantly – "the heterogeneous character of the group was clear". The SOEV/Interdoc model of institutes acting as essential intermediaries between scientific study and more general political education was not considered by everyone to be necessary. Comments by the British delegates (who included Edward McCabe, Jane Degras from Chatham House, and Walter Laqueur) on the absence of any need for instruction on communism in Britain "was taken by some of the Germans present as evidence of a lack of toughness and determination and perhaps of woolly-mindedness". Foster added the comment that German "attitudes towards Communism tend to be more in tune with the views of the late Mr. Foster Dulles than with current thinking in London and Washington".[101] The reply from London was telling:

> If we were to produce British delegates who made the sort of noises these particular Germans would like to hear, I am afraid they would be very unrepresentative and liable in the long run to do a certain amount of damage by wild assertions [...] Communism is most effectively countered by people to the left of centre, whereas those on the right can usually do no more than preach to the converted.[102]

Not surprisingly, plans for a follow-up conference disintegrated in disagreements between those who wanted to focus on educational methods and those more interested in how to take the offensive against communist influence. Despite the obvious merits of this kind of gathering for Interdoc, Van den Heuvel lacked the time (and the money) to pursue it himself.

By 1965 Geyer was already looking to replace von Hahn with "a young academic who has completed their studies and who has the best possible knowledge of the English language", but no suitable candidate appeared.[103] Instead von Hahn, who moved to be Interdoc liaison in Bonn, was eventually replaced on 1 November 1966 by Raimute von Hassell-von Caprivi, the niece of German diplomat and 20 July plotter Ulrich von Hassell and granddaughter of Bismarck's successor as German Chancellor, Leo Caprivi.[104] In the 1950s von Hassell had been active with the Abendländische Akademie, a Munich-based evangelical Catholic group led by notables throughout federal and national politics.[105] The task laid out for her was considerable: coordination with von Grote's Verein (renamed in that year the Deutsche Arbeitsgruppe für West-Ost Beziehungen) and Geyer's Studienstelle für Auslandsfragen in Munich; future planning of activities with Van den Heuvel; organization and maintenance of all research materials and publications for use by Interdoc and its associated institutes in the Federal Republic; maintaining contacts with Interdoc's international network.[106] She may not have been the first choice, but von Hassell proved to be very popular in The Hague as a constant source of constructive criticism.[107]

4
The European Web

> If the psychological war against communism is really going to be won, a defensive posture is insufficient and an offensive outlook is required. That means psychological warfare that reaches out to the communist sphere of influence. The Free World has yet to achieve effective and coordinated activity on this terrain.
>
> Cees van den Heuvel, October 1959[1]

Interdoc UK

By early 1962 the relationship with the Information Research Department (IRD) in London had become clearer: the British would provide all necessary information regarding communist meetings and organizations, in particular youth festivals.[2] Working relations were soon tested. Foreign Office cutbacks that year meant that the embassy in The Hague lost its IRD post. As a result the ambassador, Sir Andrew Noble, proposed that all IRD material should be sent direct to Van den Heuvel, "leaving Interdoc and the Dutch themselves to fight the anti-Communist battle".[3] The response from London was unanimously negative. Reversing the opinion expressed in 1957, the new head of IRD, C.F.R. (Kit) Barclay, protested that all direct contacts with "influentials" in Dutch society should be maintained.[4] Passing control over the recipient list to Interdoc would also make the credibility of the material more opaque for the recipient. Further, "In no country in the world do we rely solely on a local anti-Communist organisation to undertake distribution."[5] Views were decidedly mixed:

> We do not think very highly of Interdoc [...] moreover Interdoc clearly resents French and German tendencies to regard them mainly or primarily as a convenient clearing house, a translation bureau, and a distribution centre for research material and information [...] It does not appear from this that they would take great interest in distributing our material.[6]

According to Josephine O'Connor Howe, a member of IRD's editorial staff from 1953 until the department's closure in 1978, suspicions of Interdoc had more to do with their practices than their motives. Also, IRD's focus on the non-communist left did not correspond with Interdoc's broader outlook. For these reasons, the establishment of a UK office for Interdoc was not considered a threat to IRD operations, simply because there was no belief that it would achieve anything.[7] Nevertheless there were mutual benefits in working out a deal. Parcels of IRD publications would be sent to the British Embassy in The Hague without any classification, and Van den Heuvel would take over the distribution from there. So long as IRD knew where their material was going, this arrangement was satisfactory.[8] But for those in London Interdoc was a client, not a partner. Since IRD received its finance from the Secret Vote (the annual sum granted by parliament for intelligence activities) it could have produced financial support if there had been a conviction that it was worthwhile. In this case it was never considered.[9]

Efforts to establish an equivalent to SOEV and the Verein in Britain continued nonetheless, with the Economic League (EL) and IRD as the basis and Dick Ellis as the "central point" around which plans could evolve.[10] Along with Crozier, both EL and IRD were singled out for invitations to the Noordwijk *colloque* in September 1962, which had the theme of cooperation between education and industry to promote the political education of cadres. (No one from the League could attend, but Baker White did submit a paper.[11]) Likewise for the Bad Godesberg *colloque* in early 1963: EL's Dettmer and Baker White, Crozier, Ellis, and IRD's Colin Barclay. The League was by then combining resources with SOEV for training programmes for industry, such as the programme on communist subversion in industry held for IBM in Amsterdam in the same year.[12] IRD chief Colin Barclay started sounding out potential allies for Interdoc in parliament, among the employers' associations, and at the Institute for Strategic Studies (ISS). Contacts with ISS already existed via R. Gould-Adams and would improve further when the Swiss Curt Gasteyger, a friend of Kernig, became director of programmes in 1965. Lijkle Schepers, on Shells' board of directors, opened the door to Shell UK executive Brian Trench, who responded positively.[13] In early 1963 Einthoven still hoped for "the closest possible British cooperation" in Interdoc's management and financing.[14] British involvement was essential to ensure a global reach. But Van den Heuvel could only comment that "The English are extraordinarily difficult to get moving [...] they hate coordinating, and they hate being coordinated even more."[15]

Widening the net to academia, contacts were made with St Anthony's College, Oxford, respected for its foreign affairs experts and notorious for links with MI6. The first reactions were cautious.[16] To galvanize interest, preparations were made for a *colloque* to bring together the Economic League and IRD with other interested parties such as the Multilateral Disarmament Information Centre (MDIC) and Common Cause (CC), the latter associated with the Paix et Liberté/CIAS network. Arranged via the contacts of CC's Neil Elles, it was held in April 1963 in Christ Church College, Oxford, under the title "Britain and the East–West Conflict".[17] While Common Cause had an impressive board of military top brass and other notables, at the time it was not regarded as a serious player by the Interdoc circle, although this would change later. Formed in January 1952 by an American, Natalie Paine, as an offshoot of the US-based organization of the same name, CC's aim was "the defeat of the Communist Party in Great Britain".[18] Attempts to turn CC into the national umbrella organization for anti-communist activities in Britain failed, and a bitter leadership struggle in the late 1950s had left it largely moribund. Its limited value as a partner is revealed in Van den Heuvel's comments that it was "a very small […] outspoken anti-communist organisation" and "based on an out-moded cold war mentality."[19] Nevertheless its contacts were useful. When Elles was asked to join a new international board for CIAS in late 1963 Van den Heuvel had no objection. The following May Elles arranged for Van den Heuvel to deliver a lecture to the British European Movement at the House of Commons on communism in Western Europe.[20]

Shell UK figured prominently in the Christ Church funding plans via Brian Trench, albeit "in strict confidence". The conference was a major boost, giving Van den Heuvel the impression that all parties, including the Foreign Office, were finally "really interested".[21] Italian, Swiss, and Dutch delegates participated alongside strong French (including de Lagarde, Guy Lemonnier, Préchac, and General Olié), British (including Crozier, MP Aidan Crawley, and Hugh Seton-Watson), and German delegations (including Geyer, von Grote, Dethleffsen, von Dellingshausen, Kernig, Lades, and Triesch). Responses from Oxford were "in general very favourable", although some expressed surprise at the number of French and German participants in military uniform. One delegate, Labour MP G.W. Reynolds, recommended that the trade union movement should hold a similar meeting, and there were hopes for bringing in the influential Federation of British Industries. The creation of a British foundation was now at the top of the agenda, along with the need for a UK frontman to assist Ellis. The first candidate was Leslie Sheridan, a Special Operations Executive veteran from World War II who went on to join IRD, running its Ampersand Books imprint and otherwise being active as a "public relations consultant".[22] The benefits were obvious, and by August 1963, following meetings with Geyer, von Grote, von Hahn, and Einthoven in Scheveningen, Sheridan accepted a one-year payroll of £720 (plus £300 expenses) to devote one day a week to developing contacts, strengthening "a financial basis", and functioning as the two-way channel between Interdoc in The Hague and associated institutions in Britain.[23] Still, the grounds for action were fragile, because no existing institution wanted their activities to be curtailed in any way by a new arrival, a predicament which also caused a reluctance to fund it.[24] Inter-departmental dissonance appeared again when Ellis let it be known that MI6 did not want "operational" reports meant for them also being passed via Sheridan to IRD, as this created a security risk.[25] Van den Heuvel cleared this up on a trip to London in November, and from then on IRD was given the code name "Power" in all correspondence. MI6 was in turn referred to as "Johnson".

Efforts to get Interdoc UK together were delayed when Sheridan failed to follow up on the success of the Christ Church meeting. His sudden death in January 1964 further complicated matters. Successors were discussed, but Van den Heuvel then made a logical proposal: wouldn't Ellis like to become the new representative? He knew all the right people, and he knew the cause.[26] Ellis was 70 and not keen on a full-time position. However his job categorizing British Security Coordination (BSC) records for MI6 came to an end as of 1 March 1964, so he accepted, taking the same financial reward as Sheridan. With revived elan, the two crafted a specific proposal for Interdoc UK. Ellis secured the use of office space at 2–3 Norfolk Street in central London (also the address, interestingly enough, of Common Cause). With these items in place, they then called a meeting for 20 July 1964 to secure the deal. Everyone invited was present: EL's Dettmer, three representatives from Common Cause, one from MDIC, Crozier, and W. Bertram Hesmondhalgh of Shell's public relations department in London. It was envisaged that the existing level of cooperation on publications and *colloque* participants would be upgraded, with the establishment of a board, an overt presence in British intellectual–political life, and ultimately an equal place alongside the Dutch and Germans to "determine Interdoc policy".[27] Everyone agreed on the added value that Interdoc UK would bring, and the board was set as James Duffy (MDIC), John Dettmer (EL), Neil Elles (CC), and Brian Crozier, with Ellis as secretary. Finance would come from Shell through Hesmondhalgh on a one-year trial basis, on the assumption that the new outfit's worth for business interests still needed to be tested. (In the interests of discretion it was also considered wise that he should not become a board member.) Shell did have doubts, since EL was receiving criticism from Labour MPs who felt it was too pro-business, making it a potential liability as a partner.[28] Enforced limitations were present from the beginning: as Ellis outlined, Interdoc UK would neither seek to coordinate existing organizations nor "concern itself with activities of a domestic character".[29] IRD was not represented, to ensure deniability for the Foreign Office, but remained in the background "as the most valuable contact in the United Kingdom". Its interest and influence was clear in two areas: the ongoing focus on communist-controlled peace and youth meetings, and greater attention being given to communist infiltration in sub-Saharan Africa.[30] This also interested Shell, not surprisingly considering the opening and rapid expansion of its oil production operations in Nigeria after 1958.[31]

Other contacts crossed the Interdoc path in this period. One was Geoffrey Stewart-Smith, a wealthy self-styled anti-communist activist and secretary to the Foreign Affairs Circle, formed in 1962 to focus attention on opposition movements in communist countries. Stewart-Smith's personal ambition already placed him outside any Interdoc plans, since by 1964 he had begun his own journal, *East West Digest*, and was functioning as a one-man pressure group within British politics. His 1966 critical study of British anti-communism, *No Vision Here*, actually made no reference to Interdoc at all.[32] IRD regarded him as a "crank", Ellis thought he was stuck "using the slogans and weapons of 1927", and his association with Suzanne Labin's high-profile but largely inactive Conférence Internationale sur la Guerre Politique des Soviets, the far-right John Birch Society, and the ultra-nationalist National Alliance of Russian Solidarists (NTS: Narodno-Trudovoy Soyuz Rossiyskikh Solidarstov) did not improve his reputation either.[33] The closest Interdoc came to cooperation was in late 1966, when Van den Heuvel and Geyer floated the idea of taking a subscription for several hundred copies of the *Digest*, on the condition that Stewart-Smith stop his criticism of British government inaction since "he has not the slightest idea of what they are actually doing", but it went no further than that.[34] Another contact was the Czech émigré Josef Josten, who ran the influential Free Central European News Agency and distributed a regular bulletin from an office in Kensington. A respected source and useful for checking the bona fides of individuals in the East, Josten was immediately keen on an association with Interdoc. Yet his reputation blocked any official link: "he is considered in Fleet St. and by Power as someone who is sometimes talking too much and a little bit obtrusive." For the British, Josten was not "one of us". The Czech did attend the Christ Church conference and a plan to produce guide books for visitors to the East temporarily caught Van den Heuvel's attention, but the contact faded out quite rapidly.[35]

The intention was that Interdoc UK would soon pay for itself and even generate money for The Hague – the key to full British membership on the Interdoc board. Einthoven travelled to London once more in August 1964 to urge Dick White to sanction MI6 financial support. Ellis was bullish over finding the necessary funds, but a reason for his lack of success was now surfacing: IRD in particular felt that the material coming out of the Federal Republic was far from objective and the constant focus on the German Question too narrow. The German dominance in material and *colloques* also caused doubts within Common Cause as to the merits of Interdoc for other parties. The Eschwege *colloque* in October 1964, dominated by West German concerns over relations with the GDR and Geyer's "Strategy of Peace", lay behind much of the discontent. Both the Economic League and Common Cause felt this showed "the German tail wagging the Interdoc dog" and that "our German friends are using it as a channel to present their own political case and not as an instrument against Communism as such."[36] This was correct, although it missed the urge of the Germans to want *everyone* to associate with their cause as a common endeavour. Van den Heuvel objected to the suggestion that he was no more than a German front, and Einthoven countered that full British participation would bring with it greater influence in the Interdoc outlook, whereas carping from the sidelines would bring nothing at all.[37] Planning continued. Ampersand proved an ideal outlet, publishing both Interdoc's mission statement, *Tasks for the Free World Today*, in 1964 and its follow-up, *The Challenge of Coexistence*, in 1965, as well as an English-language version of the Büro für politische Studien's Helsinki dossier, *Frieden und Freundschaft?* But patience was running thin. The message was passed to Ellis that The Hague (i.e. the Germans) would no longer financially support Interdoc UK as of 1 August 1965. Interdoc UK still lacked a convincing mission. "I must say," lamented Van den Heuvel, "that I don't quite understand the attitude of Power–Johnson (especially Power). There is an obvious advantage for them in a close cooperation with Interdoc."[38] Van den Heuvel strongly recommended that IRD make use of Interdoc channels for distributing their materials: von Grote, Triesch, Herbert Scheffler at the Büro für politische Studien, and the federal government's press and information service.[39] But British cooperation with the West Germans in the information field was already quite good. From 1960 onwards Anglo-German Information Talks, triggered by mutual concerns over NATO and West Berlin, involved IRD, the Bundespresseamt, and the respective Foreign Offices, and covered the full range of Soviet activities in Western Europe, in front organizations, and in the developing world.[40] These talks also involved mutual interest in old networks such as CIAS, as well as more recent additions including the Comité International pour la Défense de la Civilisation Chrétienne (CIDCC).[41] As of July 1963 the British Embassy in Bonn was distributing IRD materials to around 200 "outlets" across West German government and society, and specific items were even sent further afield via West German embassies abroad. Staffing limitations prevented the British Embassy in Bonn from expanding its responsibilities in this direction (especially as the Embassy's main concern was not so much "the menace of communism" as "insidious French propaganda about our suitability as a member of the European club"), and Van den Heuvel was unable to persuade IRD of the added benefits he could provide. Nevertheless he did agree to pass "certain background material" from IRD to Dutch journalists when required.[42]

It is also true that IRD's purpose was under constant review during the 1960s. In August 1960 a policy paper entitled "Current trends in Soviet Policy" had called for the Department to be "more positive in urging the virtues of Western systems, [...] the dangers of Russian and Chinese imperialist expansion", and the need to contrast peaceful coexistence with "Western constructive cooperation".[43] Asked to offer advice, the retired diplomat Lord William Strang reported in July 1963 that IRD was failing to take full advantage of the splits in the communist world.[44] Efforts were made to rectify this by focusing on the Sino-Soviet "struggle for power in the developing world", yet this did not stem the criticism.[45] At the end of 1966 the internal paper

"Current Trends in the Policies of Communist Powers and Implications for our Propaganda" still saw IRD as "an experienced and efficient machine for unattributable effort against the undeclared 'enemies of the Queen'", whereas former director John Peck responded that the developing "polycentrism" in the communist world meant the department was "busily flogging a dead horse".[46]

The period 1964–65 was frustrating. In some ways Interdoc UK was making headway. The Economic League was mobilized to put together a 15-day trip for British trade unionists to the Netherlands, Denmark, and West Germany, and Ellis made fruitful contact with the head of the Trades Union Congress's information section, Edward Pierce, who agreed to distribute Interdoc materials. Links were also building with the Young Conservatives via Nicholas Scott.[47] EL was keen to revive links with Confindustria (Confederazione Generale dell'Industria Italiana (General Confederation of Italian Industry); dormant for the previous ten years) in the form of a training course for a group of Italian middle managers.[48] But the League would not part with much of its annual budget of £250,000, reserved purely for national and not international activities. Once again "Shell is the only one who are willing to provide financial support", but even Hesmondhalgh doubted Shell UK's continuing role without a major push to assemble some prominent public figures to back the venture up.[49] MI6 had originally made clear that they would only pay for "specific tasks of mutual interest, as they arise", meaning that together with IRD they would cover "a small retainer" for Ellis but no office. Instead, via Hesmondhalgh, they pressured Shell, which grudgingly agreed to extend its support for another year.[50] Einthoven had discussed with Shell director Gerrit Wagner the possibility of Royal Dutch Shell mobilizing to bring its British partner and other international corporations together for a fact-finding/fund-raising meeting, similar to what Prince Bernhard had arranged in the Netherlands two years before.[51] If this could be related to a specific field that no one else dealt with, such as advising on the increasing opportunities for East–West contacts, the chances looked better, particularly from the side of the Foreign Office and the Federation of British Industries. The existence of the Great Britain–USSR Association, which was funded by the government to pursue civil contacts, did not prevent this because of its formal nature and determination to appear as neutral as possible. There would be more room for manoeuvre for a private organization.[52]

All of this was costing Van den Heuvel a lot of time, time which could have been devoted to other projects, but his productive relations with Ellis led him to plead with Geyer for more patience:

> Our connections and our cooperation with these institutions are good, but their level of financial help is so little. Nevertheless I am convinced that it is of great importance to maintain Interdoc UK even if that means that we completely fund the London office and reimburse Ellis

for his services there. I would even be willing to let other projects go to achieve this.[53]

The Dutchman won out. A breakthrough of sorts was achieved when IRD finally agreed to take over the rent of the Norfolk Street office from 1 April 1966, allowing The Hague to reduce its monthly input from £50 to £20.[54] Yet even this move in the right direction was to be little more than an April Fool. Shell remained unconvinced, and IRD and MI6 were disappointed by Interdoc's failure to generate more "special actions" against front organizations in the youth and student field. While cooperation in planning and publications continued, Interdoc UK in this form would last less than three more years.

Interdoc Switzerland

The most logical "central point" (*Mittelpunkt*) in Switzerland for an Interdoc working group (*Arbeitskreis*) was Sager and the Ost-Institut, but Sager was heavily preoccupied with his own affairs and there was an air of controversy surrounding him.[55] An opening suddenly appeared in 1964, when Sager reported to Claus Kernig that he was in serious financial difficulties and offered Interdoc the opportunity to take over the Ost-Institut by buying up all the company's shares for 50,000 Swiss francs. Sager literally "blamed the atom test stop" (the Limited Test Ban Treaty of October 1963) for his problems, since "people thought that the communist danger was over" and subscriptions to *Klare Blick* had fallen by 25 per cent. But what seemed like a golden opportunity did not get very far. Einthoven responded in May that year that Interdoc was mainly interested in the weekly *Swiss Press Review and News Report*, distributed in English, French, and Spanish throughout Asia, Africa, and Latin America. Déonna agreed to act as middleman to channel the finance to Sager, so that Interdoc's role could be kept secret. But the deal was never closed. Sager protested that it was impossible to split his activities up, making it an all-or-nothing offer. There was also the reputation of Sager himself, raising doubts as to how this headstrong figure would function as an "employee" of Interdoc. Einthoven had to inform Sager in July that the Interdoc board had turned down the idea of buying a stake in the Ost-Institut because "that would mean a certain responsibility for your domestic affairs" and they were not prepared to take that risk. This prevented what looked like a perfect opportunity from going through.[56]

The Locarno *colloque* in April 1965 provided the opportunity for drafting something new. While Münst was tasked with running the organization, an invitation was given to Ernst Kux, the Soviet specialist from the *Neue Zürcher Zeitung*, to introduce the *colloque*'s theme of "Thoughts, Ideas and Values that can be projected to the East".[57] But tensions were around every corner: Münst disliked the more easy-going attitude of Gasteyger and Herbert Lüthy (the academic/journalist attached to the Congress for Cultural Freedom network) towards East–West contacts and refused them a place on the programme; Gasteyger was not convinced about Kux as spokesperson; and everyone had an opinion on Sager. Münst had his own problems, since for years he had pursued the view that contacts with the East were taboo and now he had to reverse this and still maintain his credibility.[58] With 21 Swiss participants, Locarno gave Interdoc's position in the country a major boost, but it also exposed the fragility of the ground for Interdoc activities in that country. Some unwanted publicity on the conference did leak out in the form of articles in *Der Bund*, *National Zeitung*, and *Schweiz*, and there was some speculation that the telephone conversations between Einthoven and IIIF's Theodor Krause had been eavesdropped on by the security establishment and fed to the press. Despite Einthoven's personal contacts, it was hard to undermine local suspicions.[59]

The event provided the basis for a new attempt to craft an *Arbeitskreis*. Previous attempts – including by Curt Gasteyger, a friend of Kernig and at the time director of programmes at the London-based International Institute for Strategic Studies – had foundered on the strongly differing attitudes among the Swiss towards contacts with the Soviet bloc.[60] There had already been a running national debate on the pros and cons of trade with the East. To what extent, asked the critics, would this conflict with Swiss neutrality? The Aufklärungsdienst had been actively campaigning against East–West trade as late as 1961, but was prepared to change tack if it could be used to make the Soviet bloc vulnerable. Van den Heuvel also needed to overcome some personal scepticism, since the hierarchically minded Swiss had up till then been dealing largely with Einthoven and did not understand why the Dutch intelligence chief had now taken a back seat. Nevertheless, with Sager providing administrative back-up (rather than leadership), and with the Swiss Foreign Ministry and the Schweizerische Aufklärungsdienst both giving a favourable nod from behind the scenes, Hans-Peter Ming of the Aktionskomitee Wahret die Freiheit was chosen as the *Mittelpunkt*. The Aktionskomitee, an outgrowth of student activism following the Hungarian revolution of 1956, was formed in Zurich in 1959 to promote the Swiss view on freedom and democracy among Third World students at the major international youth festivals, and by 1965 it had developed a solid reputation.[61] Views were divided on whether to include Münst, due to "his negative anti-communism" and the fact that he had acted "very difficult" with other Swiss participants. Münst had contributed to *Tasks for the Free World*, and Van den Heuvel remarked ruefully that "he is obviously disappointed that he is not our only man in Switzerland." Nevertheless his contacts and drive made him indispensable. In contrast, Sager had risen in the Dutchman's estimation, despite his desire to appropriate everything for his own goals.[62] In June Van den Heuvel sought to press the advantage in a meeting with Ming and others from the Aktionskomitee and the Ost-Institut. The mood was good and there was general agreement that the time was right for direct Swiss involvement in Interdoc's *Konfrontation* with the East, despite "the morbid fear of the Swiss authorities" of putting neutrality in danger. But yet again the plan fell apart. Ming backed off from being the "central point" and there were few candidates who fitted Van den Heuvel's wish for "a young dynamic person" to take the helm and lead a committed team with "no big names".[63]

The only solution was to persuade the group Aktionskomitee Wahret die Freiheit, and in particular its 25-year-old president Hans Graf, to become the Interdoc base in Switzerland. There were problems with this, since Wahret was only a rolling committee rather than a fixed organization, but the burden was made lighter by a change of approach from The Hague and Munich. The aim was no longer an *Arbeitskreis* but simply the intensification and expansion of Interdoc's distribution network. The Swiss anti-communist apparatus was being shaken up as the decline of East–West tensions reduced the demand for such activities. One victim was Münst's Aktion Freier Staatsbürger, which lost its funding from 1 January 1966, although many of its members soon reformed into the Aktion für freie Demokratie, focusing on the threat of espionage and subversion in Swiss society. In contrast Wahret die Freiheit, with its positive attitude towards East–West exchange, was more influential in the new circumstances, and Sager's fortunes with the Ost-Institut also picked up once business interests realized that he was actually in favour of East–West trade.

Both Graf and Sager participated in the Zandvoort *colloque* in September 1965, covering the theme "Preparation for East–West Contacts". Van den Heuvel visited the Ost-Institut in November 1965 and could not have been more impressed by Sager's ability to maintain such an efficiently run organization with 21 staff despite the severe cutbacks of the previous year. Plans were made for a follow-up to Locarno, in the form of a two-day event for travel agencies entitled "Introduction to the Problem of Contacts with the East", involving among others Geyer and Ellis.[64] As Graf and Ming hesitated, Sager once again entered the picture as a serious partner, and in December 1965 he agreed to take over most of Interdoc's Swiss distribution. The aim was to build it up to 100–200 addresses (similar to the number in the Netherlands) from a cross-section of the political parties, business, government, the media, and the churches.[65] By 1966, therefore, Van den Heuvel had to admit that, although the original hope for a Swiss *Arbeitskreis* never came together, the level of cooperation with Swiss individuals and institutions was excellent. Interdoc had at least established itself as an important "clearing house" within the Swiss context.[66] Contacts with Graf would continue to intensify in the youth and student field in the coming years.

Interdoc Italy

In the summer of 1963 lengthy discussions in the Interdoc circle produced the decision to shift the focus away from UCID, Comitato Civico, and Catholic Action and towards Italian industry. A trip by von Hahn and Van den Heuvel was planned for October, centred on meetings in Milan and Rome. The preparation was carefully laid – this was a trip in search of "practical, concrete, enduring cooperation" and not money. The message was that "Interdoc is the only institution on an international level today that aims to combine all the forces pursuing an active intellectual war against communism." Von Hahn's personal connections played a major role in setting this up.[67] The Milan meeting was hosted by the head of Pirelli, Emanuele Dubini, and brought in members of the Associazione Industriale Lombarda, Confindustria, the Società Edison Volta chemicals–metallurgy conglomerate, and Ideal-Standard. After a long discussion the Italians agreed that Interdoc could provide them with useful insights into the communist threat, particularly in terms of sharing "best-practice" methods of cadre formation in Britain, France, and West Germany. With the full backing of Confindustria the head of Società Edison, de Biasi, assigned his chief of research, Renato Pavetto, the task of putting the Italian apparatus together. Pavetto was a good choice: he had attended the Barbizon *colloque* and was up to speed about Interdoc's methods and goals.[68]

The Rome leg of the trip was focused on picking up the leads from Einthoven's 1961 visits, but again von Hahn had direct contacts of his own: the "Nr. 2 of the Papal Nunciate", Monsignor Mosconi, the Swiss apostolic representative for Scandinavia, Archbishop Heim, and notably Professor Ratzinger, the future Pope Benedict XVI, who at the time was "said to have a decisive influence" as adviser to the influential Cardinal Frings.[69] The results of the Rome meetings are not recorded. The Second Vatican Council, convened by Pope John XXIII, had started its deliberations on the relations between the Roman Catholic Church and the modern world in October 1962 and ran for more than three years, occupying the attention of the church's hierarchy. In contrast, Milan would produce a major breakthrough.

In December 1963 Pavetto announced that a research centre was going to be established in Milan as the first step towards building an Italian organization. Van den Heuvel was positive, considering "it is astonishing to learn how little has been done in the country where the communist danger is greater than in any other Western country."[70] The Van den Heuvel–von Hahn mission had triggered an immediate response. During the second week of January 1964 a series of meetings took place in The Hague with Pavetto and the person tasked with getting the centre off the ground, Renato Mieli. Mieli was a very interesting character for this role. A zealous anti-fascist, he was drawn to joining the Italian Communist Party (PCI: Partito Comunista Italiano) in 1945 (or perhaps earlier) after having worked as a journalist and, during the last year of the war, for the Psychological Warfare Branch of the US Office of War Information. An obvious talent, by 1947 he was running the Milan branch of *L'Unità* and by 1949 he had taken over the party's Office of Propaganda in Rome. At the time of his break with the Communist Party in 1958 Mieli was deputy chief of the party's Foreign Section, reporting directly to leader Palmiro Togliatti. The reasons for his disillusionment seemed to be Khrushchev's anti-Stalinism speech at the 20th Party Congress and the invasion of Hungary in 1956, although the CIA reported to Van den Heuvel that "the ideological and motivational factors which impelled Mieli to leave the PCI are far from clear to us."[71] By 1964 Mieli was openly challenging Togliatti's position on revisionism by questioning the party leader's behaviour during the purges in the late 1930s, and he joined a committee of ex-communists under the leadership of Ignazio Silone to investigate Stalinist crimes. In terms of having someone who understood the workings of communism in Italy, there was no one better.

Pavetto and Mieli's visit to The Hague included briefings over five days from Einthoven, Van den Heuvel, Geyer, and von Grote on the whole SOEV–Verein–Interdoc set-up. In turn the Italians explained their own plan. With DM 800,000 guaranteed from Confindustria and other business sources as starting capital for 1964, the Centro di studi e ricerche sui problemi economico-sociali (CESES: Centre for Research on Socio-Economic Problems) would begin by building a documentation library on Soviet ideology and strategy and then, with a projected staff of 20, shift to cadre training. Pavetto and Mieli emphasized that the anti-communist struggle had to include "enhanced strengthening of Italian democracy, of a healthy and conscious acceptance of democratic responsibility, and the carrying out of indispensable domestic reforms". Cooperation with Interdoc was deemed essential for their task, but full membership was ruled out for the time being. As the next step a travel plan was arranged with Geyer and von Grote for the Italians to tour the West German institutional network in Munich, Bonn, Cologne, and Freiburg.[72] Britain, the Netherlands, and France were also on the agenda, although Bonnemaison, who made a special trip to The Hague for this purpose, met the Italians at Hotel Terminus and not at Van Stolkweg, to maintain the official distance that the SDECE had to keep.[73] CESES had now supplanted UCID as Interdoc's Italian base, requiring some delicate correspondence from Van den Heuvel to avoid unnecessary fallout.[74] At the end of March Van den Heuvel travelled to Milan to check on progress. Mieli admitted that SOEV was the basic model for CESES, and they even wanted to create an Italian version of *Oost-West*. At this stage both he and Pavetto were keen to join the *colloques* on a regular basis.[75]

The only concern was that Confindustria wanted results fast, and this was putting pressure on the still understaffed institute. By early 1965 this was becoming apparent. The Hague was trying to incorporate Mieli more and more in their operations: attending Interdoc board meetings, linking up with the Economic League, organizing the Italian delegation for the Locarno *colloque* in April on East–West contacts, contributing a chapter for *The Challenge of Coexistence*, participation in the "Luxembourg Group" on youth and student movements. Einthoven tried repeatedly to bring Mieli into contact with Guicciardi to cement the Italian link.[76] But Mieli had been told by the CESES board that he could only do this on a personal basis, and official association with Interdoc was out of the question.[77] He still made it to an Interdoc meeting in The Hague in November 1964 despite putting together CESES' first seminar, on Soviet economic planning, in Rome in the same month. Von Grote (one of the speakers) reported that the seminar, which brought in 29 participants from Britain, Belgium, France, Italy, West Germany, and the US, was a great success due to the quality and level of participants, the large budget, and the "wonderful weather".[78] Joking aside, there was a growing sense that Interdoc needed Mieli more than Mieli, after the initial start-up phase of CESES, needed Interdoc. The approach of the two was the same: Mieli described at the seminar the need to examine the Soviet experience "with a scientific rigour and systematic adherence to actual reality" and not from "passionate judgements" or "personal ideological inclinations".[79] But their interests were diverging because Mieli was forced by his Confindustria benefactors to focus on their immediate interests in Italy. The Hague had no choice but to start looking for an alternative "focal point" alongside CESES.[80] Lines had got crossed between the "Vaccari-group" and the "Mieli-group" and Vaccari felt he had been sidelined despite his efforts to make progress. Someone was needed to try to pull this all together.

The Locarno *colloque* was important: with 65 participants it was one of the larger Interdoc conferences, the intention being to consolidate links with the Swiss and the Italians. With the Swiss it succeeded, but with the Italians, as Van den Heuvel ruefully remarked to Lamberty, "you are never sure".[81] Ever since Einthoven's early trips to Switzerland there had seemed to be real potential to use the Swiss (particularly Sager) as a way of reaching the Italians, both in terms of providing information and making contacts, but Locarno proved how difficult it was to set up this link. Mieli did show up and gave a badly prepared paper, but other Italians failed to make it. Further evidence of the confused state of affairs came from Bertram Hesmondhalgh, who stunned Van den Heuvel by remarking cheerfully that he had heard Interdoc Italy was being financed by Shell's offices there. When the Dutchman replied that Interdoc Italy didn't exist, investigations revealed that a group using the name, with contact person a certain Miss M. Rocchiero, was indeed receiving Shell money. Rocchiero turned out to be Vaccari's secretary.[82] The finance had been cleared by Shell Italy's chief, Count Guido Zucchini, in liaison with Shell UK. Even though Zucchini (who had taken over the Interdoc dossier from Guicciardi) showed once again the commitment of Shell to this enterprise, it demonstrated the problems of dealing with Italian partners who neither communicated nor followed agreements.[83]

Nevertheless, following Locarno Van den Heuvel refocused his attention on Vaccari and the UCID group. Alongside Vaccari, fruitful cooperation with the chief of UCID's Bologna chapter, Gianfranco Galletti, was also a good sign. Galletti was the editor of the political monthly *Cronaca Politica*, and through 1964–65 he published a series of articles supplied by Van den Heuvel giving brief analyses of the West European communist parties.[84] Meanwhile exasperation began to creep into the correspondence with Mieli, with von Hahn blurting out in September 1965 that "we really wonder here again and again why it is so extremely difficult for you to answer our letters".[85] Mieli continued to profess genuine interest in Interdoc, but from mid-1965 it became a standard tale of invitations being sent to Milan that either remained unanswered or were turned down (with regrets). Although he was asked to join Interdoc's advisory board in 1967 (along with Vaccari), all reports suggest that he did not attend another *colloque* after Locarno. Visiting Mieli in March 1967, Van den Heuvel noted that CESES and Interdoc had parted company because "his institute is more and more developing into a scientific program", running postgraduate training and academic seminars on economics, law, and history for participants from both East and West. The Dutchman noted the results:

> Propaganda does not enter the discussion openly, but Mieli still holds the view that by exactly reporting what the representatives of the East-European countries have said or written, the result is propaganda for the West, as usually what the communists have to offer is inferior to what the West can offer [...] Mieli is very satisfied about his highly sophisticated psychological action which is possible because of his scientific program.[86]

The activity of CESES must be seen in the context of a drift towards the expansion of the state's role in the Italian economy, in terms of both ownership and planning. While this was being done in the name of efficiency, critics feared that the ruling Christian Democrats (and the Vatican in the background) were effectively justifying the PCI and undermining free society as a result. "Ultimately," Van den Heuvel concluded, Mieli's aim was "actually to help to train a new young democratic intellectual elite in Italy."

The centrality of the Vaccari group was revived with a visit by Van den Heuvel to Milan in June 1965. Somehow repeating the exercise of October 1963 (which had led directly to the formation of CESES), a group of Italian industrialists met to discuss forming a national committee. Out of this came a prime candidate: Giorgio Barbieri, chief of the Bologna Industrial Association and someone tipped to be the next head of Confindustria. Barbieri made no promises, but he confirmed after long discussions that August at von Hahn's residence in Bad Gastein that he would bring Interdoc into direct contact with the Confindustria secretariat and its General Secretary, Melotti. CESES would have to be bypassed. Barbieri saved his deepest critique for Vaccari, "a very dangerous man" who belonged to the influential circle around Cardinal Siri at the top of the Vatican that was prepared to compromise with the PCI and accept their presence in a government in return for the unhindered propagation of the Catholic faith.[87] This put Einthoven's discussions with Siri in 1961 in a new light. But once again there was a difference between an Italian discussing Interdoc face to face and an Italian who had to go and put the ideas into action. A planned trip for von Hahn and Van den Heuvel to Milan and Bologna in November 1965 to follow up with Barbieri fell through, and contact with the Italian, as with most of his compatriots, faded out. Einthoven wrote to Van Gestel that same month that the chances of him returning to Italy to pick up the leads again for the first time since 1962 were nil: "Cooperation with the Italians is so difficult that it is not worth the effort to make such a long and expensive trip."[88] Von Hahn saw darker motives at work: "Apparently there are forces which are not inclined to accept cooperation with Interdoc."[89]

Throughout this period of disillusionment Vaccari continued to act as a promoter of Interdoc at every opportunity. He put forward useful contacts with International Christian Leadership in Washington, DC, and the Fédération des Jeunes Chefs d'Entreprises d'Europe in Brussels, and then in June 1966 he wrote to Van den Heuvel about a noteworthy group of interested parties wanting to receive Interdoc publications.[90] The list of right-wing Catholics included Archduke Otto von Habsburg of the Paneuropean Union, Jean Violet (mentioned as a member of Synthèses-Avenir), and the controversial theologian Jean Madiran.[91] Vaccari was above all determined that Van den Heuvel should meet Violet, the notorious "fixer" for the SDECE. The Italian experience had been an all-round disappointment. It had been impossible to establish any lasting relationships; the formation of CESES – which Van den Heuvel and von Hahn had triggered – effectively occupied the space that Interdoc had wanted; and it was clear that interests in Confindustria, for whatever reason, were not willing to share it. Only Vaccari continued to offer occasional assistance and, although he proved useful in the US, he operated in the kinds of right-wing circles that Interdoc, with its positive anti-communism, would rather avoid. A similar experience would be repeated in Belgium.

Interdoc Belgium

On paper the Belgians would be a logical partner for the Dutch–French–German enterprise that was Interdoc, sandwiched as they are in between these three countries. It was also agreed early on that contacts in Belgium, as in France, would be a prime responsibility for Einthoven. The Dutchman originally saw the logic of arranging a Belgian director for Interdoc who could share the task with Van den Heuvel.[92] Yet the process of including the Belgians was never an easy one. An insight into the difficulties is given by a letter from Colonel Margot of the Belgian Staatsveiligheid (SV, the domestic security service) to Einthoven in 1962. Margot, picked out by SV chief Ludovicus Caeymaex to assist in the matter, had been sounding out the possibility of governmental support for the Interdoc venture, but the response was that only a NATO-run operation would be acceptable. Meanwhile Belgian politics was taking a turn to the left, and a large chunk of Belgian business was fully tied up with operations in Eastern Europe, making all moves increasingly awkward. Then there was the linguistic split, making the chances of a *national* institute even lower. This left only the more extreme elements on the right, who had the financial power (Margot referred to a Belgian banker who funded the Suzanne Labin network)[93] but who were nonetheless unreliable. Margot even ended with a note of criticism: why had this request not been made sooner, in 1957? Was this not another example of exclusiveness from "les sphères anglo-saxonnes spécialement", who anyway often achieved little despite the large sums of money distributed?[94]

Nevertheless the search continued. The first contact was Professor Nabor (Urbain August) Devolder of the Catholic University in Leuven, a member of the Vrede en Vrijheid network whom Van den Heuvel also knew from his 1957 book *De Communistische Propaganda: Theorie, Strategie en Methode*.[95] Devolder was invited to join the *colloque* scene, but it was the more respected Max Lamberty, social science professor at the Royal Military School, who was asked to join the SOEV board in November 1962 and *Oost-West* a year later. From 1963 to 1965 Lamberty, a renowned humanist "bridge-builder" between Belgian socialists and Catholics and Flemish nationalists, functioned as an important contact person for Interdoc planning.[96] His position on the advisory board for Elsevier publishers brought him regularly to the Netherlands, and in turn Van den Heuvel worked hard to secure both English (translated by a Shell employee) and German versions of his book *Wat is Westerse Cultuur?* that could be spread through the IRD and Interdoc networks, particularly in Asia and Africa.[97] By the mid-1960s the gradual loosening of East–West divisions made the theme of Lamberty's book more relevant than when it was originally published in 1961. Lamberty also contributed to *Tasks for the Free World Today* and Couwenberg's journal *Oost-West*, where he wrote (rather vaguely) of the need for a dialogue with the Soviets precisely to undermine the antagonistic falsities of communist ideology.[98] He was stronger in language when writing to Van den Heuvel in mid-1964:

> "We", the carriers of a particular conviction, who are not tied to governments, have more to do than simply make up the balance in the evolution of relations between Moscow, Peking, and New York. We, Interdoc, must give a direction, set out principles, prepare a message that can then be spread [...] In the midst of the confusion and uncertainty that is noticeable in both the West and the East, there is still a task to fulfil, a decisive task: *lay out those principles which are ours*.[99]

Lamberty was soon curious about the "German relations" Van den Heuvel referred to, and in early 1964 the Dutchman arranged for him to deliver a lecture in Munich on his version of positive anti-communism. By May Lamberty was fully up to speed, talking of "the friends in Munich" and "the friends in The Hague" with evident enthusiasm.[100] Yet despite his obvious commitment and valuable prestige, Lamberty did not want to function as the sole central point for Interdoc Belgium: turning 70 in 1963, he simply had too many other commitments.

Van den Heuvel continued looking for a critical mass of Belgian partners. A visit from Stewart-Smith to The Hague in 1964 brought him into contact with Dr F.J. Thomson from Antwerp, a researcher on communist infiltration in religious circles. Pater van Gestel, who had already assisted with Einthoven's itineraries in Rome, suggested Professor Florent Peeters of Ghent University and the Institut de recherches de l'Europe centrale in Leuven. Lamberty brought in Professor Emmanuel Coppeters, Director General of the Royal Institute for International Affairs, a close collaborator with the Dutch equivalent, the Nederlandse Genootschap voor Internationale Zaken (they issued the journal *Internationale Spectator* together). Coppeters was willing to join a national committee, but put forward another name as possible "central point": Jacques-Henri Pirenne, in his late 40s, head of both the NATO-orientated Centre d'Information et de Documentation Atlantique (CIDA) and the Société Coopérative d'Etude et de Promotion des Echanges Economiques et Culturels (SORELS), and possessor of an enviable network of contacts. With Lamberty, Devolder, Coppeters, and Pirenne, the basis for a Belgian committee with a reasonable Flemish–Walloon balance was in sight, especially as Pirenne, a member of a respectable family and "one of the best-known names" in the country, was prepared to act as chair. By late March 1965 the Interdoc board had agreed to support the venture with 10,000 guilders towards creating "a self-supporting 'Interdoc-Belgium' " within one year.[101]

The signs were therefore good, but as with Britain they proved deceptive. Pirenne's initial wish to use Interdoc to promote "les relations humaines" and a general rapprochement between East and West made Van den Heuvel worried: Interdoc was all about confronting the false pretences of peaceful coexistence, not overseeing its ultimate success.[102] A planning meeting between Pirenne, Lamberty, and Van den Heuvel in The Hague on 1 April thrashed out a schedule: Pirenne would use both CIDA and SORELS as a basis for preparing the way to a national committee within a year. A revised mandate was soon issued that stressed the need to "prepare individuals to intervene at international youth meetings, or with the underdeveloped nations, to expose the weaknesses of Soviet propaganda" and "prepare specialized individuals for East–West contacts". Useful publications could be obtained via both *Oost-West* (Couwenberg) and *Est-Ouest* (Albertini, with German sources coming on line if things worked out satisfactorily).[103] Lamberty had doubts about his colleague, whose aristocrat-fallen-on-hard-times demeanour suggested that he was in this largely for the money. But

Van den Heuvel was prepared to go ahead on the basis of Pirenne so far being "businesslike and 'to the point' ".[104] Einthoven made some calls to the secretary of Shell's board, Willem Snouck Hurgronje, to arrange an entry for Pirenne to its Belgian offices, and he brought Caeymaex up to date.[105]

Pirenne duly teamed up with Robert Nieuwenhuys, president of the Association Atlantique Belge (the Belgian wing of the US-based Atlantic Council), to organize the first preparatory meeting on 7 May. The results were encouraging: 18 participants (including Peeters, but without Lamberty) from the military, academia, the press, and the foreign ministry discussed the need for "an appropriate psychological display" from the West. But Van den Heuvel saw things he didn't like. There was an over-emphasis on the potential for East–West trade to bring positive change, and Pirenne had summed up the importance of "maintaining the division of Germany" in order to prevent a new threat from pan-Germanism.[106] This would not go down well in Munich. Pirenne had to clarify: a divided Germany was indeed less of a threat to the balance of power in Europe than a unified Germany, but this also required easing the GDR away from its close relations with Moscow. Besides, the success of the Communist Party in the Belgian elections of early 1963 had begun to focus the attention of business leaders on the continuing threat, making the environment favourable for action.[107] Nevertheless Einthoven travelled to Brussels to read Pirenne the riot act:

> I explained to Pirenne that the Interdoc circle had agreed in principle not to criticize those things which were held dear by another nation and instead to concentrate on forming a united front against communism. When I asked him how *he* would feel if a significant part of Belgium was under the control of another state with a completely opposed ideology, he replied that his remarks were only meant as an attempt to escape from the impasse [...][108]

Pirenne continued, his ability to achieve entrance to the highest circles of Belgian politics and society a distinct advantage. A lunch hosted by the director of Shell Belgium on 25 June brought together a cross-section of industrialists and politicians (including Marcel de Roover, through his position with Brufina) to raise awareness. Einthoven prompted the idea of a lecture series to publicize Interdoc's purpose, involving Bonnemaison, ex-communist Douglas Hyde, and Mieli. Momentum would then be secured with a major *colloque* at the Collège de l'Europe in Bruges in 1966. The mood seemed right. There was widespread confusion as to the significance of the Moscow–Beijing split, suggesting that an Interdoc Belgium could reach a wide audience looking for clarification.

Yet during the summer of 1965 the plan fell apart. Lamberty was never convinced, observing that Pirenne's "mondaine French-language Brussels world" could provide the money but it was a world where he, Peeters, and "intellectuals in general who find East–West relations important [...] do not feel at home". This Francophone elite also ignored anything coming out of the Netherlands, making it an option for Lamberty to follow "what the Jesuit order has done for years" and simply establish separate Walloon and Flemish organizations.[109] While Geyer was prepared to offer finance for two years to enable a Belgian committee to establish itself, and Einthoven returned from his meeting in June with the feeling that Pirenne was moving in the right direction, Van den Heuvel and Lamberty shared concerns through the summer of 1965. Pirenne was taking the money without making a move on either a national committee or a distribution network for Interdoc materials. A decision was taken in early October to end the financial relationship by 1 January 1966, and "Operation Pirenne", as Lamberty called it, came to an end. In the words of von Hahn, Pirenne had "so far failed to recognize the structure, methods and mission of Interdoc".[110] Neither was Pirenne, who understood only French, at all suited to either bridging the cultural divisions of Belgium or joining the transnational network of Interdoc.[111]

Pirenne protested and countered that he was in the middle of putting together yet another preparatory meeting on 5 November under the 1950s-style heading "la défense psychologique de l'Ouest contre la contagion de l'idéologie communiste". Van den Heuvel, who considered "psychological defence" to be "as old as NATO itself", decided to seize the opportunity. Together with von Hahn he hijacked the agenda in Brussels by turning it into a discussion on Interdoc's role in pursuing a new form of anti-communism. A vibrant discussion ensued, out of which came an embryonic committee led by the "dynamic, hard-working", and just retired G.A. Kestelin of Brabant Provincial Council. Concerns that the committee was full of old men – considering Van den Heuvel's explicit call for engaging with youth in both West and East – were only partially allayed by the participation of Lamberty's son, a lawyer in Brussels.[112] The failure with Pirenne evidently caused doubts in both The Hague and Munich. Everything seemed to be in place, but nothing developed. Geyer wrote to Van den Heuvel in October that more guidance and attention was needed to ensure success: "We should – also in relation to Italy and Switzerland – think through thoroughly the problem of 'group formation'."[113]

Interdoc Belgium struggled on. Kestelin visited The Hague for a full briefing in December, but his tenure was cut short by a mountaineering accident on Mont Blanc in the following month. His replacement was Robert Nieuwenhuys, a banker with the Brufina holding company, Chairman of the Belgian Atlantic Association, and a prominent society figure. But by the end of the year Nieuwenhuys had proved to be as completely unreliable as Pirenne. Lamberty stayed in the picture – he was a special guest at the Interdoc meeting in Freiburg im Breisgau in April 1966 to discuss Kernig's project for an encyclopaedia of communism – but his input was increasingly limited. Efforts to bring in the World War II resistance leader and Fédéralistes Démocrates Francophones Senator Jean Fosty failed. Einthoven made a bid to interest Caeymaex in Interdoc's potential for countering Chinese communist propaganda among African students in Brussels and Louvain. Even though it would replace US activities in this field with a local response backed by The Hague, it came to little.[114]

The only factor that revived the Belgian story was the reappearance of Florent Peeters. Initially ignored as a central point because he lacked national status, Peeters continued to show genuine interest in Interdoc. Peeters saw the hand of "cryptocommunists" and international communism, specifically the International Union of Students, behind the disturbances in Leuven that led to the splitting of the university into French- and Flemish-speaking parts, and still felt in early 1967 that "a focused working group between Flanders and the Netherlands on combating communism is definitely necessary."[115] Van den Heuvel was convinced enough, after all the other disappointments, to invite Peeters to the Interdoc conference in Bad Tönisstein in September on "The Communist Reassessment of Capitalism and the Western Response". By the following year the Belgian was functioning as the long-sought-after linkman, arranging for groups of Ghent students to attend Interdoc Berlin seminars and introducing The Hague to potential new partners. One of these was the well-funded Ligue Internationale de la Liberté of Paul Vankerkhoven and Suzanne Labin, with around 2000 members in Belgium alone. In a meeting with Mennes in Ghent, Vankerkhoven agreed to distribute Interdoc publications.[116]

In one way the contact with the Ligue was a step back, since it represented the simplistic kind of right-wing anti-communism that Van den Heuvel and Einthoven had been trying to escape from. Van den Heuvel reported to Geyer after a trip to Brussels in January 1970 that, while the Ligue and its associated network (the anti-subversion Centre de Défense Nationale, partner groups in France and Italy) were useful for contacts, conference contributions, and special actions "that officially are better not carried out by Interdoc", official links had to be limited with an organization that saw communist conspiracy everywhere. For these reasons he declined the offer to join the Ligue's advisory board "with polite and careful words".[117] On the other hand, these kinds of groups represented a new direction which Interdoc would focus more on during the 1970s: the promotion of human rights. Other Belgian-based right-wing anti-communist groups, all of them interlinked, would also cross the Interdoc path in this area, such as Vankerkhoven's Cercle des Nations, Marcel De Roover's Brussels office of the Centre Européen de Documentation et d'Information (CEDI) and Florimond Damman's Académie Européenne de Sciences Politiques. According to David Teacher, "together with a few close friends, Damman represented the Belgian end of almost all the international right-wing networks such as the PEU [Paneuropean Union], CEDI, and WACL [World Anti-Communist League]".[118] CEDI was the transnational

Catholic network with Archduke Otto von Habsburg at its head, and there were close ties to the BND. The WACL was especially active in Asia, and it would provide some useful contacts there – Peeters spent the summer of 1968 doing research in Taipei, partly funded by Interdoc. But for an institute like Interdoc, attempting above all to establish itself as a credible voice, these were dangerous waters. Moderate anti-communists were hard to find in the late 1960s.

Scandinavia

The first contacts in Scandinavia related to Interdoc seem to have made through the Swedes, from 1958 onwards, although it is quite possible that relations with the Danes were already active at that stage. The first Swedish contact was Colonel Ivar Göthberg, formerly head of the Swedish Home Guard, who between 1947 and 1957 had run the Centralförbundet Folk och Försvar, the Swedish equivalent of the German (Arbeitskreise für Volk und Verteidigung) and Dutch (Volk en Verdediging) organizations promoting closer relations between the citizenry and the military. Göthberg was soon invited to become a member of the Studienbüro meetings in West Berlin.[119] By the early 1960s Van den Heuvel was in contact with a determined student group known as the Fight Communism Committee, formed in 1963 at the University of Lund.[120] The group, which renamed itself *Inform* in January 1964, spoke out against communist infiltration, torture, and "the enslavement of nations" and was keen to oppose the strong leftist tendencies prevalent at Lund, also the site of the important annual International Student Course that attracted participants from Eastern Europe and the third world. Mennes visited the course in September 1963 and returned with the conclusion that the event showed no signs of deliberate leftist propaganda or indoctrination but was "vulnerable" to communist infiltration. The *Inform* group's intention of running a counter-conference for "dedicated anti-communists" appeared to the Dutch a little heavy-handed, giving the impression that they tended to represent the direct-action style of anti-communism that Interdoc wanted to escape from.[121]

Options for a Swedish SOEV were taken up by Einthoven with Birger Hagård, leader of the Young Conservative movement, in late 1964. Hagård was well connected across Scandinavia and via the Conservative and Christian Democratic Youth Community, a trans-European movement formed on 1 May 1964(!) under the leadership of future Conservative MP John MacGregor. Initial investigations led Hagård to recommend the *Inform* group as the best option for Interdoc: it had by then "between 5 and 10 different groups all over the country" and "close contacts with Denmark". Hagård described Bertil Häggman, "one of the most prominent young conservatives in southern Sweden", as the best contact. Van den Heuvel was not impressed: *Inform* was "a purely negative anti-Communist organisation" and an unsuitable partner.[122] A lawyer by trade, Häggman was an admirer of Barry Goldwater, James Burnham, and the *National Review*, and he visited Van Stolkweg in January 1965 to discuss possibilities with Einthoven. Häggman possessed contacts in student circles throughout Denmark, Norway, and Finland, and could be a real asset.[123] Not surprisingly Van den Heuvel changed his mind, and Häggman would remain a part of the wider Interdoc circle into the 1970s. But no real impetus for pursuing a Swedish Interdoc office existed. The experiences in Belgium, Italy, and Switzerland had convinced both Van den Heuvel and Geyer that it was a better arrangement instead to use all available contacts to increase the distribution of Interdoc materials and form ad hoc partnerships according to specific projects.

One such contact was Åke Sparring, a respected researcher at the Swedish Institute of International Affairs who also visited Van Stolkweg with serious intent, after meeting Van den Heuvel at the Ostkolleg in late 1964. Sparring, whom Van den Heuvel described to Geyer as "the first quality Swedish contact", came with a proposal for a new English-language periodical covering the communist presence in the smaller European countries, in an effort to raise awareness across the continent. Despite fruitful contact with some of Sparring's colleagues, nothing materialized out of either the plan or his determination to join forces with Interdoc.[124] Swedish contacts in early 1965 therefore included *Inform*, Göthberg, Hagård, Sparring, Gunnar Dahlander (formerly chief of the Swedish trade union press office and lecturer in psychological warfare at the Defence College), J. Rydström of Jernkontoret (the Swedish steel producers' association), and Arvo Horm, secretary of the Scandinavian Youth Service. Horm and Häggman knew each other through the Baltic Committee formed to organize opposition to the visit of Nikita Khrushchev in 1964.[125] Anti-communist activities were already difficult due to the leftist atmosphere in Swedish politics and society, perpetuated by successive Social Democratic governments, and from 1965, led by the young Olof Palme, Sweden's politicians would demonstrate their country's neutrality by vocally opposing the Vietnam War.[126] As Häggman put it much later, "being an anti-communist in Sweden in those years was quite controversial", since even in the Conservative Party "anti-communists were looked at with some suspicion". Police intelligence in Sweden (predominantly social democratic in orientation) was "a very powerful force", and the extent of surveillance and harassment of anti-communists has only been revealed in recent years.[127]

One of the more exotic characters to cross the Interdoc path was Carl Armfelt. Armfelt was the scion of a proud Swedish noble line that stretched back to holding military commands in the army of Gustaf Adolf II during the Thirty Years' War. In the following centuries the family held high positions in both Sweden and Finland, and when Armfelt was born in New York in 1918 his father, a Finnish diplomat, was on a mission to the US to elicit support (from, among others, Henry Ford) for Finnish independence. Possessing US and Finnish nationality, Armfelt signed up with the US Army Air Corps in 1938 but was detained following Pearl Harbour due to suspected Nazi sympathies.[128] Following World War II Armfelt's life becomes one full of rumour and counter-rumour. He was apparently recruited by Frank Wisner's Office of Policy Coordination, the original covert action wing of the CIA, and worked with William Colby in Sweden in 1951 to establish anti-communist cells – the stay-behind network, otherwise known as Gladio.[129] Armfelt's involvement in anti-Soviet campaigns included running guerrilla and sabotage operations around the time of the Hungarian uprising of 1956.[130] By his own account he first met Van den Heuvel in the late 1950s in Scheveningen, but it was always a personal relationship, since the flamboyant aristocrat was too much of a potential liability for the Interdoc circle's credibility. Even though it was Armfelt who brought Hagård into contact with Interdoc, both Einthoven and Van den Heuvel insisted that neither Hagård nor Häggman should pass any details of their discussions on to the aristocrat, and Hagård himself noted that there was considerable mistrust of Armfelt in Swedish and German refugee circles.[131] His association with the controversial NTS (Narodno-Trudovoy Soyuz Rossiyskikh Solidarstov, the National Alliance of Russian Solidarists), the émigré group established in 1930 to work for a postcommunist Russia whose members were harassed and assassinated by the KGB, did not help matters. Between 1934 and 1956 MI6 had invested a great deal in a host of "resistance groups" in the Ukraine and the Baltic states, only to discover too late that they had all been rounded up and either "turned" or executed by the KGB. MI6 contact with the NTS was cut in 1956, but Armfelt maintained his links with the organization into the 1990s.[132] Nevertheless Häggman has spoken of meeting with Armfelt and Wedin to discuss ways and means of opposing Soviet control of the Baltic states, although it is unclear if anything came of this. When there were difficulties over Häggman and his colleague Bertil Wedin's expenses after an Interdoc meeting in The Hague in early 1969, it was Armfelt who stepped in to insist on a full explanation.[133]

In 1968 Armfelt, aided by Van den Heuvel, moved to Knokke on the Belgian coast, conveniently on the Dutch–Belgian border. Armfelt and Van den Heuvel were good friends, but this did not mean unquestioning support for each other's activities. Ellis had been asked by MI6 in mid-1965 to keep tabs on Armfelt, and he reported to Van den Heuvel all contacts with the Finn: "I am not too keen on that link unless I have clearance from you."[134] Over the next few years Armfelt used his new base to run infiltration operations against radical student groups, anti-Soviet propaganda stunts, and contacts with various émigré groups. The rather reckless nature of these activities probably led the CIA to distance itself from Armfelt, who felt that the Agency was trying to blacklist him to disrupt his movements in the US. Armfelt was involved with the Freedom Studies Center of the Institute for

American Strategy in Virginia, opened on 1 October 1966 in Boston, Virginia under the leadership of the Ukrainian-American professor of economic Lev Dobriansky. He was also active in promoting the World Anti-Communist League (WACL) across Western Europe, a task which brought him into close association with the likes of CEDI's Otto von Habsburg and the Belgian right-wing lynchpins Marcel De Roover and Paul Vankerkhoven. One typical Armfelt action from that period involved Vik van Branteghem, a Ghent University student activist and founder of the Flemish Action Committee for Eastern Europe, who was arrested in Red Square in January 1970 for handing out dissident literature. (He was released after one year and in the 1980s he joined the Vatican's press bureau.) Another was something Armfelt himself referred to as the "Pepperdine operation", connected with the Los Angeles-based Pepperdine College's year-in-Europe programme, then being run at its new Heidelberg campus. Armfelt called in on Ellis and Common Cause in early 1969 and described the set-up: "This college was connected to the 'Church of Christ' and its financial support was confidential! A. said the American students at the Heidelberg 'college' would engage in a research into student affairs in Europe [...] When we asked who would be the recipients of the outcome of the college's efforts, A. was equally vague." Ellis, who then heard Armfelt describe openly how he wanted to contact right-wing Conservatives about "changing" the Labour government, admitted to being "uneasy" with him: "It seemed all rather amateurish and Middle-West American."[135] Armfelt's secretary, Hans Cornelder, investigated the US Vietnam deserters scene in Amsterdam and other European cities. Another of Armfelt's activities was a media operation, News Perspective International, together with US journalist William J. Gill.[136]

Van den Heuvel, interviewed about Armfelt in 1996, admitted that the Swede was active in creating "cells" to form a "strong anti-communist front", probably in line with his WACL activities, but WACL was deeply divided during the 1970s between far-rightists and moderates. Blatant attempts to undermine leftist politicians by linking them with the KGB were one result.[137] From 1973 onwards he was also running activities opposing Swedish Prime Minister Olof Palme, whom he accused of being a Soviet agent supporting a Cuban international terrorist network.[138] In 1985 he returned to Canada, but his link with Van den Heuvel continued up to their joint 80th birthday celebration in 1998 in The Hague.[139] Armfelt was always a loner and independent operator; he had many contacts but he was trusted by few of them. While he was constantly presenting new projects, it is highly uncertain how many of them actually went ahead.[140]

Denmark was part of the Interdoc circle from early on. The Danes played host to Studienbüro meetings, and document distribution notations indicate that Arne Nielsen, the head of the Danish police intelligence service in the early 1960s, was kept fully informed of the Interdoc plans. In 1963 Leslie Sheridan would declare that "Interdoc has a very close tie with some Danish organizations through which they can, and do, get much information".[141] Two specific organizations were involved. One was the network of the former resistance fighter turned anti-communist organizer Arne Sejr. Sejr was the initiator of a range of activities, from the "private intelligence service" the Firm to the establishment of the Society for Freedom and Culture, associated with the Congress for Cultural Freedom (CCF), in 1953.[142] Sejr insisted on maintaining an autonomous position separate from the CCF, and the same attitude was adopted with Interdoc.[143] Next to Sejr was Frihed og Folkestyr (Freedom and Democracy), referred to through the 1960s as the sole Danish contact.[144] From 1960 Frihed og Folkestyr published *International Analyse*, a periodical of unattributable material on international communism that was upgraded to a more lavish layout in 1964. This was undoubtedly used as an outlet for Interdoc research in Denmark. The youth organization Demokratisk Alliance (Democratic Alliance), led by Sören Steen, was by the late 1960s deemed unsuitable for Interdoc liaison due to its radical right-wing outlook (although for a short while Häggman hoped to use it as a base for a Scandinavian network). Neither of these last two organizations had much money or many followers.[145]

More public links were maintained with the writer Noemi Eskul-Jensen (author of *Is a Soviet revolution imaginable?* in 1952) and P.A. Heegård-Poulsen, both members of Frihed og Folkestyr. Eskul-Jensen, a close associate of Münst in Switzerland, had represented Denmark at the Ostkolleg conference of December 1964. Heegård-Poulsen was a consultant to the elite Hjemmeværnet (Home Guard), who played a key role as a Danish linkman for Interdoc Youth in the late 1960s. Heegård-Poulsen was writing for *International Analyse* (which had both Sejr and Knud Rosdahl of Interdoc Youth on the board) at least from 1967 onwards and wrote the periodical's special issue on youth radicalism in January 1970, which referred to Interdoc as a source.[146] The Danes were part of the network but did not want to appear so, and strenuous efforts were made to maintain this distance.

Norway entered the Interdoc circle mainly through Interdoc Youth (IY). Contacts with the West German Ministry of Defence had brought in the Krigsskolen (Military Academy) in Oslo as a welcome host institution for civilian–military IY seminars, so long as Ernst Riggert's Volk und Verteidigung could arrange free transport with Luftwaffe planes. Per Paust, who later joined the diplomatic service, became an enthusiastic IY representative and a possible frontman for expanding Interdoc work in Norway. Another contact, the historian and security analyst Dr Nils Ørvik of Oslo University, was asked to join Interdoc's advisory board. Several of the Norwegian IY crowd went on to find positions in international affairs, including Sverre Lodgaard, who later became the director of the Norwegian Institute of Foreign Affairs (NUPI). Aside from some project-based contacts in the 1970s Interdoc Youth proved to be the high point of this Nordic country's involvement.[147]

Portugal and Greece

One of the most direct links between Interdoc and the anti-communist hard right is represented by Aginter Press, a front set up by former French captain Ralf Guérin-Sérac (Yves Guillou) in Lisbon in 1966 to gather together French neo-fascists and disillusioned military personnel from the Organisation Armée Secrète (OAS). Until the Carnation Revolution of April 1974, which deposed the Salazar regime, Aginter functioned as a front for a covert action network of the far right (particularly Ordine Nuovo), with direct involvement in the terrorist campaign of the "strategy of tension" in Italy during the 1970s.[148] Initial contacts in Portugal had been provided through Vittorio Vaccari's UCID network, but from late 1967 Interdoc publications (*Religion and Church in the Communist Orbit*, *Red China*) were being sent direct to Guérin-Sérac. Through the Italian Ivan Matteo Lombardo (a member of the World Anti-Communist League) a further set of contacts was provided in 1969, including with the Salazarist organization Convergência Occidental.[149] That Interdoc's contacts with Portugal were in general pragmatic is shown by the way they continued after the revolution. Van den Heuvel visited the country in March 1975 as part of "an international study of the revolutionary developments" and actually wrote to Minister of Foreign Affairs, Max van der Stoel, over his concerns about the increasing influence of the Communist Party. Plans took more concrete shape through the Dutch Catholic priest and part-time journalist Jan Habets, a resident of Portugal who approached the OWI in 1976 to assist in creating an information centre in Lisbon to counter communist propaganda in the country. Despite failure to gain government funding, Habets used his own income to pursue his plan independently.[150]

As in Portugal, Interdoc also attempted to secure contacts in Greece during the right-wing regime that followed the coup of 21 April 1967. Once again Lombardo was a useful source of contacts. Through the international veterans' network Van den Heuvel approached General Pierre Nicolopoulos prior to a visit to Athens in April 1969 with the intention of building up ties, but links with Greece were intermittent and anyway highly controversial in the Netherlands following the April 1967 military coup.[151]

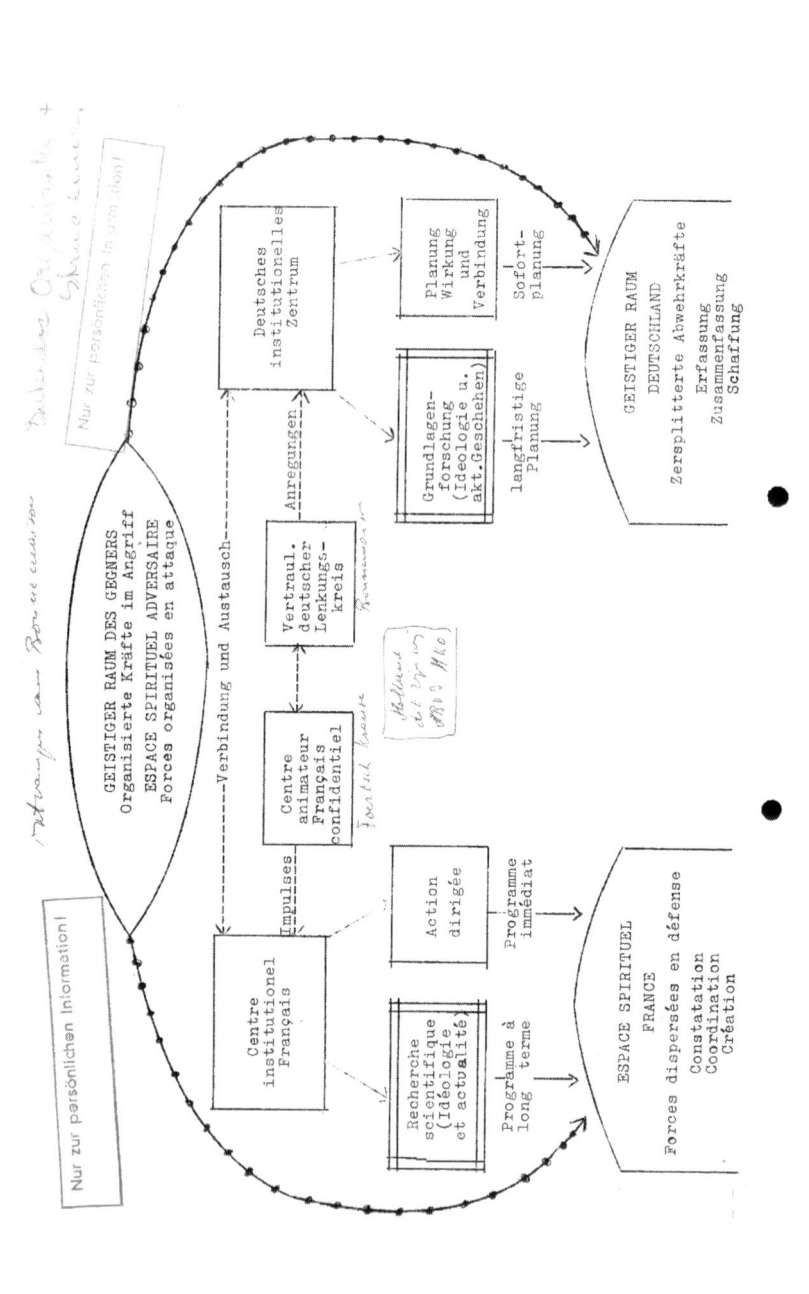

Plate 1. Antoine Bonnemaison's original plan for Franco-German cooperation in anti-communism, 1958. Einthoven has added in ink in the middle: "Holland dit zijn wij HBVD HKO" (Holland, that's us, Chief BVD, Chief Training) (Source: Archive "Voorgeschiedenis Interdoc")

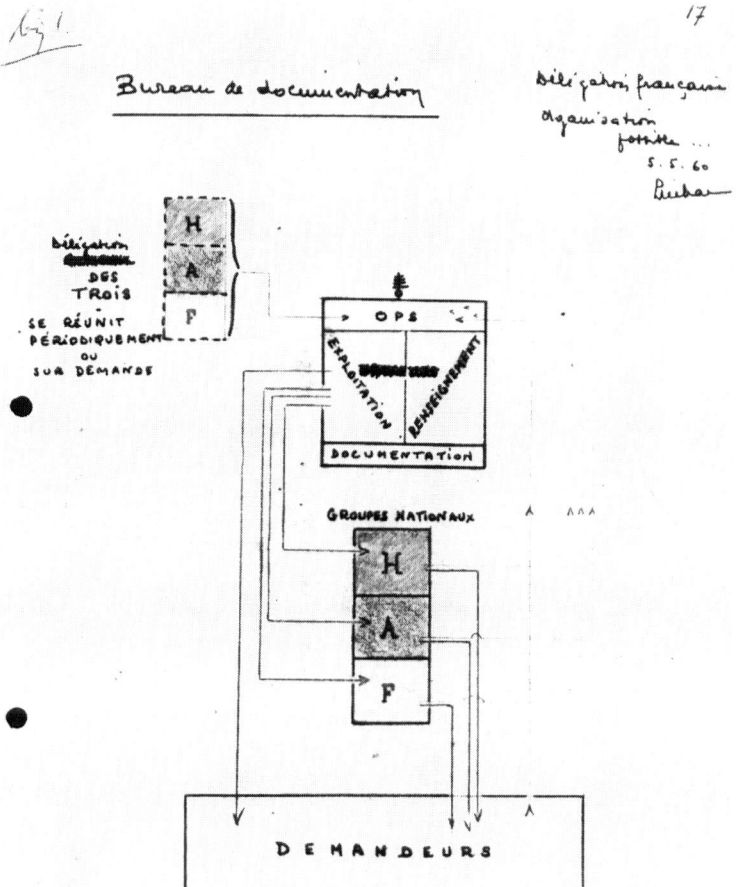

Plate 2. The Interdoc apparatus as envisaged by the French delegation for the May 1960 planning meeting in The Hague: Hollande, Allemagne, France (Source: Archive "Voorgeschiedenis Interdoc")

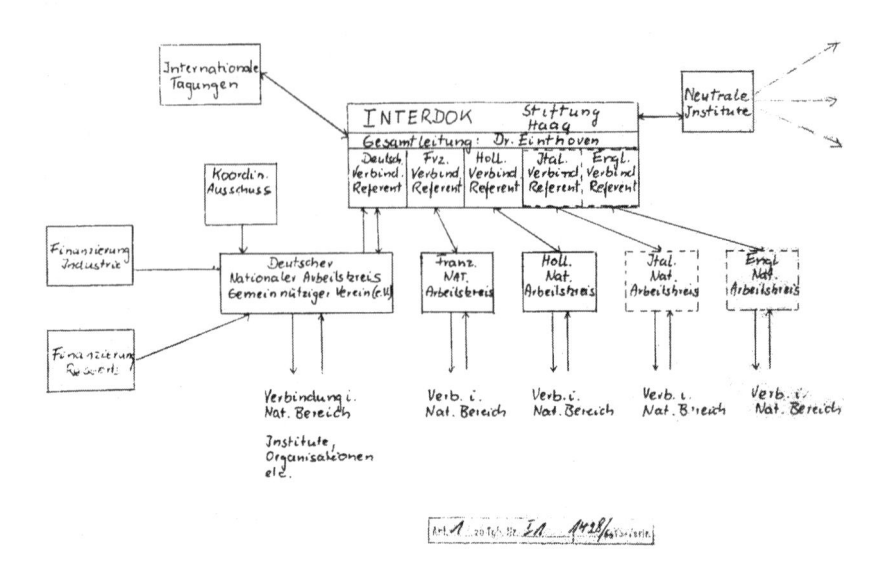

Plate 3. The German proposal of 1960: note the inclusion of the British and Italians (Source: Archive "Voorgeschiedenis Interdoc")

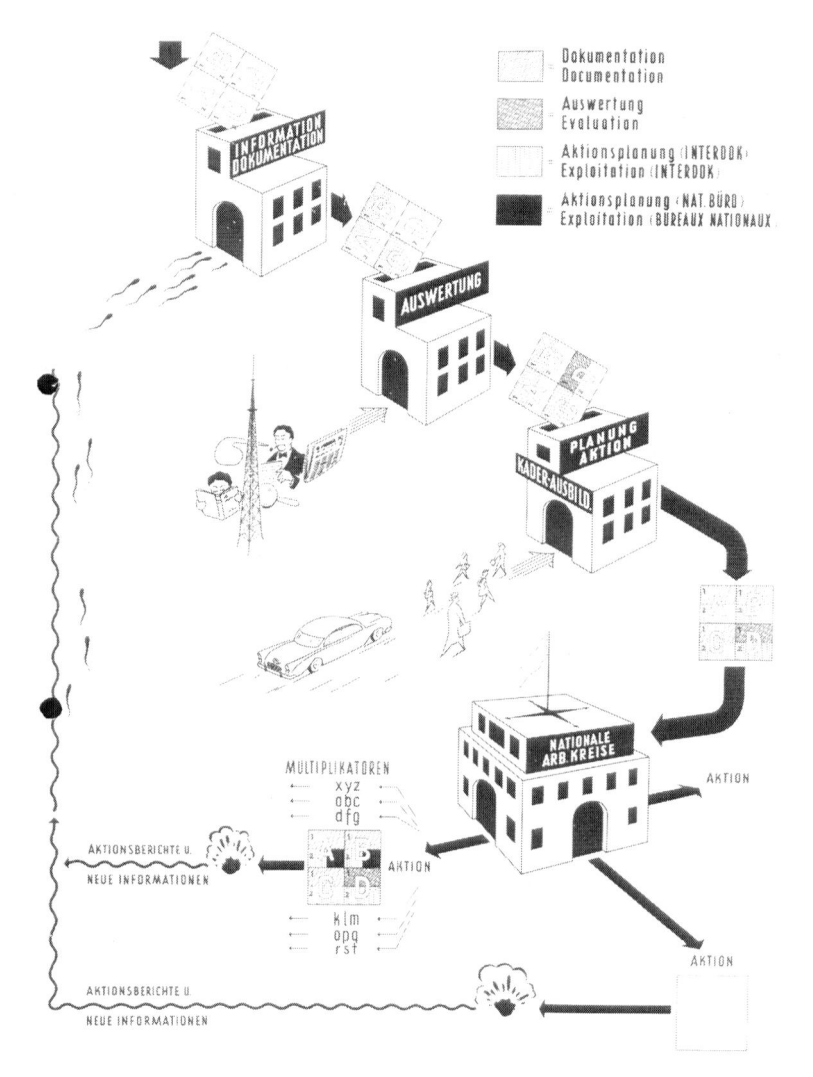

Plate 4. A more detailed working of the German proposal (Source: Archive "Voorgeschiedenis Interdoc")

Plate 5. Laan Copes van Cattenburch 38, the location of the BVD's training division (KO: kader opleiding) in the 1950s and 1960s. Cees van den Heuvel led this division from 1949 up to his departure from the service on 1 January 1962 (Source: author)

Plate 6. The training division of the BVD, circa 1959. From the left, back row: C.C. van den Heuvel, Ottolini, Boske, Boomsluiter, Bolten, Couwenberg. Front row: Van der Lee, secretary, Cea Slager, secretary, Mennes (Source: Christiaan van den Heuvel)

Plate 7. The Economic League in action: Helen Bailey speaking to London dockworkers during their lunch break, 1959 (Source: Planet News Ltd)

Plate 8. Plaats 11a (the white building), opposite the Dutch parliament building in the centre of The Hague, the first official location for SOEV in 1961–62 (Source: author)

Plate 9. "Les Galeries" at Gevers Deynootplein, Scheveningen, the location of the SOEV offices in 1962–63 (Source: Haags Gemeentearchief)

Plate 10. Van Stolkweg 10 (the "rabbit hole"), the nerve centre for Van den Heuvel's many operations from 1962 to 1986 (Source: author)

Plate 11. Felix A.C. Guépin, a director (1950–1959) and board member (1959–1966) of Royal Dutch Shell, and a valuable supporter of the SOEV–OWI–Interdoc apparatus (Source: Photograph by Walter Bird, Shell archive)

Plate 12. K.Chr. de Pous (dark suit, arms folded), chief of security for Dutch Railways, at a dinner in honour of his retirement in mid-1963, in private discussion with his successor, B.F.A. Mikx (on De Pous's right). The Dutch Railways was a valuable client for SOEV and OWI in the early 1960s (Source: Utrechts Archief)

Plate 13. Rue de la Pépinière 14, close to the Gare St-Lazare in Paris, the address Antoine Bonnemaison was using during the formation of Interdoc (Source: author)

Plate 14. Pössenbacherstraße 21, Pullach (the "villa"), the location of Rolf Geyer's IIIF during the 1960s (Source: author)

Plate 15. Rolf Geyer in the late 1960s (Source: Gunhild Bohm-Geyer)

Plate 16. Habsburgerplatz 1/1, Munich, the location of Nicolas von Grote's Verein zur Erforschung Sozialpolitischer Verhältnisse, the "public front" for Geyer's IIIF. It was renamed the Deutsche Arbeitsgruppe für West-Ost Beziehungen e.V. in 1966 (Source: author)

Plate 17. Nicolas von Grote (centre), the head of the Verein/Arbeitsgruppe bureau in Munich (Source: Dietmar Töppel)

Plate 18. The Haus der Zukunft on Goethestraße in Zehlendorf, Berlin. This was used for training courses for participants from the Netherlands and other countries during the 1960s (Source: author)

Plate 19. Hans Beuker (with fist raised) in West Berlin, circa 1961 (Source: Hans Beuker)

Plate 20. The opening of the 8th World Youth Festival in Helsinki, August 1962, the site of the first Interdoc "counter-action": Hans Beuker's anti-Soviet speech (Source: Pieter Koerts)

Plate 21. Pieter Koerts (centre) on the Kurfürstendamm, West Berlin, during a training course in the summer of 1962 (Source: Pieter Koerts)

Plate 22. Pieter Koerts (at the microphone) confronting the board of the WFDY-sponsored Conference of Youth and Students for Disarmament, Peace and National Independence in Florence in February 1964 (Source: Pieter Koerts)

Plate 23. Mont-St-Michel, the location of the final Interdoc *colloque* involving the French as official participants, 1962 (Source: author)

Plate 24. Antoine Bonnemaison in the late 1950s (Source: Marie Hélène Bonnemaison)

Plate 25. Diego Guicciardi, Shell's representative in Genoa, who played a key role in developing contacts in Italy (Source: Shell archive)

Plate 26. An Interdoc conference in the mid-1960s. Louis Einthoven is seated on the left at the front. Front row from the right: Herman Mennes, F.C. Spits, J.M.M. Hornix, unidentified. Raimute von Hassell is two rows behind Mennes. Sitting next to the aisle directly behind the front row on the right is Claus Kernig, two seats behind him is Uwe Holl, and behind Holl is Cees de Niet (Source: Christiaan van den Heuvel)

Plate 27. Louis Einthoven in 1965. Einthoven devoted his full attention to developing the Interdoc network after his retirement from the BVD in 1961 (Source: J.C. Einthoven)

Plate 28. Raimute von Hassell, Dietmar Töppel, and Andreas von Weiss outside Van Stolkweg 10, 17 November 1966 (Source: Dietmar Töppel)

Plate 29. Dietmar Töppel and Andreas von Weiss on the beach at Scheveningen, 17 November 1966 (Source: Dietmar Töppel)

Plate 30. Rolf Buchow, the anti-Soviet activist who ran Interdoc Berlin (Source: Wolfgang Buchow)

Plate 31. Charles Howard (Dick) Ellis, the Australian MI6 officer who ran the Interdoc UK office from Norfolk Street in London during the 1960s (Source: C.H. Ellis, *The Transcaspian Episode 1918–1919*, London: Hutchinson, 1963)

Plate 32. The University Arms Hotel, Cambridge, location of the second Interdoc conference on British soil, in September 1966 (Source: author)

Plate 33. Bertil Häggman (far left), Interdoc's main contact in Sweden, seen here honouring an East German refugee killed while trying to escape to the West, Trelleborg, 1964. Much of the work of the Inform group – some of it funded by the West Germans – concentrated on counter-acting GDR propaganda in Sweden (Source: Bertil Häggman)

Plate 34. Frans A.M. Alting von Geusau, who created and led the John F. Kennedy Institute at Tilburg University from 1967 to 1985 (Source: JASON papers)

Plate 35. H.G. (Dik) Groenewald at a reception for OSS veterans at Huis ten Bosch, 16 September 1974, organized by the Netherlands–US Foundation. Prince Bernhard is behind his left shoulder. Together with Cees van den Heuvel, in the mid-1970s Groenewald led the attempt to mobilize the Federation of European–American Organizations into a more active body (Source: Groenewald family archive)

Plate 36. Rio Praaning at a JASON reception. A protégé of Cees van den Heuvel, Praaning played a vital role in transforming the Atlantische Commissie during the 1980s (Source: JASON papers)

Plate 37. Cees van den Heuvel at the reception marking his retirement from the Atlantische Commissie, 1986. Behind him on the right is his son Christiaan (Source: Box 238, Atlantische Commissie archive)

Plate 38. Members of IIIF reunited: Peter Becker (left) and Dietmar Töppel, Munich, June 2008 (Source: author)

Plate 39. Members of SOEV-OWI reunited – Willem Couwenberg (left), Lyda van der Bree and Christiaan van den Heuvel outside Van Stolkweg 10, January 2006 (Source: author)

5
East–West Engagement and Interdoc Youth

> Transforming a mentality is a long term business.
>
> Louis Einthoven, 1962[1]

The relevance of youth to international politics during the Cold War, and particularly the impact of an increasing transnational radicalism during the 1960s, has been noted in recent years. Jeremi Suri wrote of the growing "international language of dissent", claiming that popular dissatisfaction with the static reality of the East–West divide pushed world leaders into the accommodations of détente. More recently, Martin Klimke has demonstrated how the radical "transnational subcultures" of the decade saw themselves as being part of a cause that transcended national divisions. Governments, looking for evidence of outside influence in domestic upheaval, tried to trace and respond to these transnational networks. This chapter covers the involvement of Interdoc in youth politics, beginning with its attempts to employ students in the East–West contest and ending with its analysis of and efforts to counter the New Left. While Suri claims that détente was deeply conservative in outlook, for the Interdoc circle any rapprochement with the East necessarily offered new opportunities for cross-border engagement and the possibility of fomenting social change. In this sense the need of the West Germans to adapt to recognizing a permanent German Democratic Republic combined with the Dutch wish to unpack and dismantle communist ideology. Youth was a prime element within this strategy.[2]

From the beginning Interdoc's activities were to include more than just information. A background paper written around the time of Interdoc's formation stated that it intended to "provide background data, advise, and in certain cases to inaugurate operations to counteract communist infiltration and subversion tactics".[3] Although the BND's caution prevented this last field of activity from being fully developed, Interdoc (and Van den Heuvel in particular) did become very active in youth and student affairs. The catalyst for this was the development of the large-scale Soviet-sponsored international youth festivals run by the front organizations World Federation of Democratic Youth (WFDY) and International Union of Students (IUS). Soviet management was hardly disguised, since the average age of the top management of these organizations was surprisingly high, and the vice-president of the WFDY in the late 1950s was none other than A.N. Shelepin, soon to become the chief of the Soviet security police. Nevertheless, following the first youth festival in Prague in 1947, similar events held every two years had attracted increasing participation from around the world.[4] The sense of momentum produced by the success of the 1957 Moscow festival led to the decision to go on the offensive and hold the following events outside of the communist bloc, so that "peaceful coexistence opened the venues of Vienna and Helsinki for the cultural Cold War encounters at the festivals".[5] The Helsinki event was regarded by many Finns, wary of antagonizing their powerful neighbour, "as a symbol of how the Soviet Union, unhindered, could extend its ideological impact across the Finnish border".[6] Both the Austrian and Finnish governments remained neutral and treated the respective festivals as private affairs. A 1962 study by the Norwegian International Youth Service noted that, while the early festivals had been orientated more towards communist-bloc youth, the later events had targeted "politically mature youth from colonial or former colonial areas" and "a real effort has been made to influence non-Communist youth in position [sic] of responsibility in youth and student organisations in non-Communist countries".[7] Neither the Vienna nor the Helsinki event was backed by the respective national student union. The (CIA-backed) Coordinating Secretariat (COSEC) of the International Student Conference (ISC), with its base in Leiden, attempted to keep the WFDY and IUS out of Helsinki by making contact with Pennti Mahlamaki, the president of the Finnish student association SYL, soon after the decision was taken in 1960. Wanting to keep his visit to Leiden "as confidential as possible," Mahlamaki agreed to issue a statement of protest (written by COSEC) against the festival, but ultimately the SYL could do little for fear of becoming partisan itself and undermining its exchange agreements with the Soviet bloc.[8]

The CIA was active from the late 1950s onwards in trying to disrupt the smooth operation of these festivals, making use of the Independent Research Service front created alongside the National Student Association (NSA) to participate in Vienna in 1959 and Helsinki in 1962.[9] But, as with Interdoc in general, European initiatives outside of CIA direction were also coming together. For Vienna a study group consisting of "about 60 young people from Germany and other European countries" was assembled under German direction for the purpose of participating in and observing the festival. This was deemed a useful exercise, so that when the Eighth World Youth Festival in Helsinki was announced for August 1962 a similar operation was planned, except that this time it would focus more on the "practical political" than the "scientific psychological". Vienna had shown that more in-depth preparation was required in order to reap the most rewards from countering the attempts of the festivals to conjure a united front of world youth. The Germans, having taken the leading role in Vienna, this time asked Van den Heuvel to do so.[10] This request was made to him strictly as an individual: von Dellingshausen had stressed that it was essential for this type of activity not to be connected with Interdoc. Van den Heuvel's role as *Generalkoordinator* would thereafter continue on a case-by-case basis according to the need and the value of taking special action.[11] Although there were discreet contacts with the Leiden-based COSEC, the central office of the ISC, it is clear that the Interdoc network aimed to establish its own particular presence in the international student field. An unstated "firewall" existed between the two organizations, so that information and logistical support was provided only discreetly to maintain a safe distance.

In 1961 Van den Heuvel therefore began "to act as a sort of team-leader of the European group" of about 30 Dutch, British, French, German, and Belgian students. The German veterans of Vienna would provide the "directives" for Helsinki, and each national group was meant to have a student leader who would themselves instruct the members in the basics of their task.[12] British involvement was shaky from the start. Neither Ellis nor the Economic League could find a suitable group leader, despite serious interest from MI6 and IRD, who told Einthoven that it would be appreciated if the Dutch "could get some coloureds to Helsinki (for instance Surinamers or Papoas)".[13] Via Comitato Civico Einthoven tried to arrange for a group of ten Italian students to join, including "some coloureds" to facilitate contacts with African participants (and to invite them on a trip to Italy afterwards).[14] The Swiss, represented by Aktionskomitee Wahret die Freiheit and its exhibition "Frontstellung Kommunismus – Free West", also offered their support.[15] Reports have come out since of the "counter-festival" (with jazz bands) and other disruptive activities being organized and paid for by the CIA via the Independent Research Service front (which included author Gloria Steinem).[16] The Van den Heuvel group, on the other hand, set out to tackle the festival's way of thinking.

At the core of the European group was a three-man Dutch student team which Van den Heuvel hand-picked through family ties and close friends. One of them, Hans Beuker, had been in contact with Van den Heuvel for several years, and had already travelled to Warsaw (1957) and Sofia (1961) as a member of the Dutch student fencing team. According to Beuker, Van den Heuvel attempted to work through the non-communist student organizations for Helsinki but was rebuffed, leading him to form an independent "band of Gideon". The group took part in a training programme at the SOEV offices at Plaats in central The Hague, starting some seven or eight months before the Helsinki event in August. This involved meetings on a Saturday, once a fortnight, where the students were instructed by Van den Heuvel,

Mennes, and others from the SOEV circle in the workings of communist ideology, the organization and propaganda methods used by communist fronts, and the realities of life behind the Iron Curtain. Literature included Willem Banning, Arthur Koestler, Robert Carew-Hunt (*The Theory and Practice of Communism*), Wolfgang Leonard (*Die Revolution entläßt ihre Kinder*), and Van den Heuvel's own BVD training manual.[17] It was above all practical information, so that the students could understand, withstand, and literally dismantle the arguments they would encounter from pro-Soviet delegates in order "to form a certain counterpoise to the influence of this Youth Festival". This kind of off-the-record response was deemed far more appropriate than sending official national delegations, since it would seem all the more spontaneous and genuine.[18] Van den Heuvel knew that the students held the right anti-communist credentials, but the training took them several steps further along the line of Western-style "indoctrination". Helsinki was to be "a case study" for the embryonic Interdoc on how this kind of communist-controlled event functioned (methods of manipulation, use of different media, ways of organizing meetings, and so on) and how it could best be combated.[19]

The group of three – Hans Beuker, Pieter Koerts, and George van der Pluim – signed up for the festival in the early summer of 1962. The majority of the 200 or so Dutch participants came from the leftist Dutch Youth League (ANJV: Algemeen Nederlandse Jeugd Verbond), the Organisation of Progressive Student Youth (OPSJ: Organisatie van Progressieve Studerende Jeugd), and the Amsterdam Pericles group. In this suspicious environment the three had to avoid at all costs the impression that they were working together. Both the Netherlands Youth Association (NJG: Nederlandse Jeugd Gemeenschap) and the Netherlands Student Council (NSR: Nederlandse Studenten Raad), the principal national student bodies, rejected official participation but did "recognise the value of individual participation by young people and students from the Netherlands, who are prepared to defend their views at the festival". Likewise the Dutch and German governments had discreetly signed off on a study group attending "providing they do not attend officially and do not make public their going there".[20]

Van den Heuvel held a meeting of the various national team leaders in Heverlee (Belgium) on 6 June to ensure that preparations were complete.[21] Alongside the core group were others picked from the NSR who were also involved in an attempt to bring African students back to the Netherlands after the festival.[22] The students made the trip to Finland by train, with a stop in East Berlin (as guests of the Freie Deutsche Jugend), a visit to the former Sachsenhausen concentration camp, and another stop in Brest-Litovsk. Van den Heuvel travelled to Helsinki by car through Denmark and Sweden, with other SOEV staff (and his son Christiaan), while Mennes took a different route. Once in Helsinki they communicated with the group via the SOEV couriers ("cut-outs") and never directly. For Beuker, an economics student in Rotterdam who wanted to enter military intelligence, it was quite an experience:

> It was such an unbelievable thing, to sit in that Olympic stadium in Helsinki, next to American people, students, and when Cuba came in: "Yankee, No!" it was amazing! We had to walk there on the street with communist groups of course, with all these red balloons, I had "No Nukes in the Netherlands", as a second lieutenant in the Dutch army![23]

Communication was arranged via "spontaneous" liaison on the dance floor with two SOEV secretaries who had travelled to Helsinki with the coordinators. At some point the decision was taken "to make a point" and not just to observe, causing one of the Dutch group, Hans Beuker, to register to speak during a festival colloquium on the role of students in solving problems related to the third world. This was a mistake by the festival organizers because Beuker was not an official member of the Dutch delegation. The speech was prepared by Van den Heuvel ("I am sure he had help from the German delegation") and passed secretly to Beuker before the session.[24] Beuker approached one of the NSR group who knew Russian, Chel Mertens, to ask if he would participate in a joint English/Russian presentation, but Mertens was aware of the risks ("it was a very hostile environment") and declined.[25] When Beuker's time came, he took the podium before an audience of around 300 and denounced the one-sided focus of the meeting on Western imperialism, instead criticizing the expanding Soviet domination of Central Asia, the Baltic States, and Eastern Europe, ending with Hungary in 1956. Interestingly enough, he also protested against the communist campaigns against Islam in the Soviet republics. In contrast to the decolonization of the Western empires, the continuing forms of Soviet oppression deserved more attention.[26]

Soviet imperialism had been singled out in the German deliberations on an anti-communist "action plan" as a central theme to be exploited, and the speech was very much in line with publications of the period that sought to turn the tables on Moscow's criticisms of the West: Arthur Bottomley's *The Two Roads of Colonialism* (1959), Hugh Seton-Watson's *The New Colonialism* (1963), Brian Crozier's *Neocolonialism* (1964), and Ellis's own brochure *The Expansion of Russia* (1965).[27] But Beuker's action was effectively taking the argument into the lion's den, and he had difficulty finishing his speech amongst the loud denunciations, accusations of "fascist!", and cat-calls from the hall. This orchestrated event, designed to present a united anti-Western anti-capitalist voice, had suddenly been thrown on to the defensive, and a series of speakers from the Soviet Union and the Eastern bloc came forward to respond. The following day, Beuker returned to the continuing session to hear speaker after speaker denounce him. (He was not even supported by the non-communist students in the Dutch delegation, because he had acted without permission of the group's leaders!) To avoid appearing as an agent provocateur, Beuker, after some discussion with his colleagues, decided to return to the Netherlands by train as planned instead of making a swift exit by plane. Surrounded by suspicious and hostile students, Beuker nervously made the three-day trip back to Amsterdam, trusting that the publicity surrounding his statement would protect him. It did, but others were apparently not so lucky.[28]

Beuker's speech made it into the pages of *Komsomolskaja Pravda* and the *New York Herald Tribune*, and was widely reported in the Dutch press (*Het Vaderland, Het Parool*, Jacques Verreijdt in *Het Binnenhof, Panorama*). He even made it into the CBS TV series "The Twentieth Century", broadcast in February 1963, there being, not coincidentally, an American film crew present at the time. Much was made of the tumult that Beuker caused in the session, with his words "If this is a democratic forum, why can't I finish my speech?" being widely quoted.[29] Friso Endt's article in *Het Parool*, which included an interview with Beuker, was sent to the CIA by Van den Heuvel himself "as proof that it had worked".[30] There were suspicions, and not just with *Pravda* noting the "coincidence" of a US camera crew being present. Friso Endt queried what Beuker was doing in Helsinki in the first place, but the article accepted Beuker's explanation of a student driven to action. The Dutch communist daily *De Waarheid*, on the other hand, smelled a "stunt" and "NATO's answer to the festival", which had taken over the front pages at the expense of the "real" message of the event.[31] But the heaviest criticism came from the Dutch non-communist Christian students (around forty out of the two hundred who went) whom Beuker typecast as naive and playing into the communists' hands by assuming that a one-on-one equal dialogue could be achieved. The response of the chief editor of *Pharetra*, the student paper of the Free University in Amsterdam, is telling:

> More serious is that Beuker's speech was drawn up and handed over to him by the ecological institute – the research counterpart of the BVD, so that these anti-communist arrows were actually fired by the Dutch government. One of the other Dutch students refused to give a Russian translation of this deeply one-sided speech, but Beuker clearly had no complaints because it was a "stunt" which earned him a "hero's role".[32]

Beuker was allowed to respond to this remarkably well-informed critique, claiming that "my relations with the Society for Research into Ecological Questions are limited to reading the bi-monthly journal 'Oost-West'." But the Dutch Christians were mainly unhappy about Beuker's one-sided speech. Frijda, pointing to George Kennan's *Russia and the West during Lenin and Stalin* (1961), remonstrated that such a festival required not only answering the communists but also recognizing the mistakes of the West, because "the communists are sometimes right and the wishes of the developing world usually justified".[33] Beuker's speech provided a good anti-Soviet message, but it didn't succeed with many from the third world. This was an important conclusion for Interdoc to take on board.[34] Although the national media's reporting was dominated by the positive views in *Het Parool*, *Panorama*, and *Het Vaderland*, the leftist press started to check up on SOEV's identity. *Vrij Nederland* reported in May 1963 that Van den Heuvel had requested 21 changes to an interview with *Pharetra* in order to tone down the links with the BVD. He explained:

> From the "public relations" perspective I would prefer that my former position does not get mentioned (and this applies obviously to Mr Mennes as well). In reality this is not so serious, but a rumour continues to circulate that the Ecology Foundation is an instrument of the BVD.[35]

The rumour would continue to circulate for many years to come.

Once back in the Netherlands, Beuker and the others took part in an evaluation of the Helsinki operation. The successful on-site counter-action had been well covered by the media and there was every reason for satisfaction. Van den Heuvel's subsequent report made clear that the delicacy of Finnish-Russian relations had originally ruled out any "counter-activities", but that "during the festival it seemed possible to do something in that field", suggesting a spontaneous action decided on the spot. The report outlined the "policing" of the event by the "festival disciplinary service" (Finnish communists) and the careful choreography of everything from Yuri Gagarin's celebrity visit to pantomime shows lambasting "rich capitalists, hypocritical clergymen and Helsinki teddy-boys". It is hard to see from this description how anything could have been attempted at all, which of course highlighted the contribution of those such as Beuker who opposed the festival's goals. Following Vienna and Helsinki, the report ended by looking ahead, saying that "the ninth [youth festival] in a country outside the Communist sphere of influence might well mean the end of Communist world youth festivals old style".[36] For public consumption the Büro für politische Studien in Bonn put together a comprehensive study of the event entitled *Freiheit und Freundschaft?*, which included the text of Beuker's speech.[37] Beuker himself drifted away from the SOEV–Interdoc scene. Apart from attending the Ostkolleg in 1963, Beuker no longer took part in their activities, instead completing his studies and emigrating to South Africa in 1968. His was now a well-known face, prone to attracting unwanted attention.

Van den Heuvel continued his coordinator role from Helsinki for the West European student network, referred to initially as the Strasbourg and then the Luxembourg Group. Dick Ellis attended the meetings and provided liaison with IRD and MI6, both of which were interested in this venture. Although Strasbourg University was the home of the CIA-backed Free Europe Committee's Summer School (formerly the Collège de l'Europe Libre), there was no connection. The change of name indicated the withdrawal of official French involvement, similar to their withdrawal from Interdoc as a whole, although meetings still took place in Strasbourg itself. While Strasbourg/Luxembourg looks at first like either a CIA or MI6 operation, evidence points to a special Interdoc operation run at the behest of the Germans, with sign-offs and inputs from elsewhere. In a letter to Van den Heuvel in May 1965 Ellis remarked in passing that IRD was not happy about "Pålsson's organisation" (the *Inform* group of Sten Pålsson and Bertil Häggman based in Lund) and "its financial dependence on Bonn", a remarkable and revealing claim – all the more so because by early 1965 Van den Heuvel stated that the Swedes were the most active element within the Luxembourg Group.[38] Pålsson himself has since confirmed this: "whatever we could get from reasonably acceptable sources we would accept". According to the Swede, who attended Luxembourg meetings in January and May 1965 as well as the Locarno conference, Luxembourg was run by Van den Heuvel together with Herbert Scheffler of the Europa Haus organization. Carl Armfelt was part of this picture, having arranged for the Swedish participant, Birger Hagård, to become involved with the initial Luxembourg planning meeting on 14 November 1964. But correspondence sent to Hagård indicates that Armfelt was *not* to be told of this specific Luxembourg meeting on 14 November 1964. Neither Einthoven nor Van den Heuvel wanted Armfelt to know about the Luxembourg Group operation. Involvement in these counter-festival actions could put individuals at risk in locations such as Algiers, and Armfelt was clearly regarded as a liability.[39]

Over the following five to six years the Group functioned as an ad hoc action committee, called into operation as needs and interests required. The Helsinki operation had generated several fruitful links for future cooperation with like-minded groups such as Hans Graf's Aktionskomitee Wahret die Freiheit (AWF: Action Committee for Truth and Freedom), the World Alliance for Student Cooperation (WASC, a "front" for the Fribourg-based international federation of Catholic intellectuals, Pax Romana, which also had close links with the Free Europe Committee), the International Student Conference, and the Scandinavian Youth Service (SYS), founded expressly to engage with the youth festivals and "train the technique of discussing international issues with hostile or neutral delegates". Another contact was Bertil Häggman, described as "one of the leaders of the last adventure in H[elsinki]", who was in the middle of the Swedish anti-communist activist community revolving around Armfelt, Bertil Wedin, the Baltic Committee, and the SYS.[40] Häggman sent his *Inform* colleague Sten Pålsson to the second Luxembourg meeting on 20 January 1965, and representatives of all of the above would meet via the Strasbourg/Luxembourg network. The WASC had achieved wide publicity by running a popular café on board the Dutch ship *Mathilde* in Helsinki harbour, attracting many students from Eastern-bloc nations and ultimately departing with a group of African and Asian students for a tour of Western Europe. WASC would be active in the coming years in organizing tours of Western Europe for African and Asian students studying in the Soviet bloc, as a way of undermining communist propaganda. Ad hoc meetings were the best arrangement for all involved. The Helsinki report ended with an important caveat: "the differing aims, as well as the differing composition of the groups, make very close cooperation impossible, and indeed undesirable".[41]

Within the Netherlands itself Van den Heuvel sought to establish relations with the National Student Council, the loose coordinating body for the various university societies, and for several years he looked to coordinate and influence those student groups active in international affairs and East–West exchanges. From 1962 to 1965 a key role was played in this by Gert van Maanen, who served as international secretary and then president of the NSR during this period. Van Maanen had first encountered the East in 1960 via a World Council of Churches' international meeting of Christian students in Berlin (organized by a cousin of his mother), but it was a trip to Warsaw in 1963 for a meeting of European student councils that fully exposed him to the machinations of Soviet fronts run by "students" above the age of 40 taking every opportunity to denigrate the "fascist" West. He described being present in West Berlin in August 1961, when the Wall went up, as "putting a fingerprint on your life", and as "an amateur, young, and full of hope" Van Maanen was drawn to finding out more. Van den Heuvel contacted him soon afterwards. Family relations again played a role, since H.J. Rijks was a cousin of Van Maanen's father. The intention was that this connection would lead to the SOEV–NSR relationship becoming more "institutionalized", but obstacles were present here as well. For many students Van den Heuvel was simply too much of a "cloak and dagger" type to make it an easy relationship.[42]

On the other side was a wary government. In the early 1960s Van den Heuvel manoeuvred his way on to the ad hoc advisory group on international student issues at the Ministry of Foreign Affairs, which oversaw the international contacts of Dutch student organizations. This group was run by Ministry Secretary General Van Tuyll van Serooskerken and including the establishment figures Ernst van der Beugel and B.H.M. Vlekke of the Netherlands Society for International Affairs. Van Maanen witnessed how the group reacted negatively, in the presence of Van den Heuvel, to the suggestion that the former BVD man would join them, and Van der Beugel strongly opposed Van den Heuvel's encouraging student groups to take an active role in international politics. Yet Van den Heuvel remained an active member of the group for several years.[43] These activities were picked up by the BVD itself, which reported at the end of 1964 that SOEV, despite "good contacts in the student world" and the availability of financial resources, was not widely appreciated within the NSR. Sinninghe Damsté ("H.BVD") added tellingly that, while SOEV was free to claim this information task, "this does not mean that they have a monopoly".[44]

On the fringes of the Helsinki operation and aware of the Strasbourg/ Luxembourg Group, Van Maanen's main value came from his involvement in the official international student movement. Having seen the way the Soviet sympathizers worked at IUS meetings, he was convinced of the need for ISC to provide an answer, and in the mid-1960s he was even a candidate for ISC president. Van Maanen insists that he did not function as Van Stolkweg's liaison with the ISC, and it is almost certainly true that he functioned more as an individual contact for Van den Heuvel, who wanted him "to be an ambassador for the Interdoc philosophy". For a while he was, responding to third-world anti-Western sentiment at ISC conferences and travelling widely (Tunisia, Iraq, India, Cambodia, South Vietnam). But their views did diverge. Van den Heuvel saw East–West contacts as "a battlefield": "he was the Cold War type, so everything that happened would be measured against that yardstick". Students were "easy victims" for communist ideological propaganda, and exchanges with the East should only go ahead after the necessary training (provided, of course, by SOEV–OWI). From his experience with the Christian student networks Van Maanen found such a "warning" approach unnecessary. Western students who visited Moscow did not necessarily return as communists, and Van den Heuvel "overrated the skills of the other side to convince young people". The NSR, wanting to represent students of all political stripes, had the view that all individuals should find out for themselves what it was like on the other side. It was from this more easy-going perspective that he attended his one *colloque*, in Locarno in 1965, to give a talk on East–West exchanges. The text of Van Maanen's contribution to Locarno pushes all the right Interdoc buttons, stressing in detail the kinds of preparation needed before contacts with the East should be pursued and emphasizing in several places how essential the coordination of Western efforts in this field actually were. But hints of a generational divide were present in the Summary, which indicated that, while some participants saw the danger of such contacts as a tactic of peaceful coexistence "to undermine our will to resist Communism", "especially the younger participants felt that much more could be done", and "on a much larger scale".[45] More problematic was an extended version of Van Maanen's Locarno essay which he published in *Internationale Spectator*. The longer introduction to this version is more easy-going in approach than the tightly presented conference paper. The goal "to present oneself as a human being who wants to learn about the other, and not as an opponent who wants to convince the other" did not reflect the inevitable risks involved, and Van den Heuvel and Mennes attempted to get this version changed before publication.[46] Van Maanen refused.

This divergence of views, plus Van Maanen's wish to leave student politics, caused a parting of ways, although he remained "in the loop" for several years to come.[47] His last major involvement was during 1965–66, when he spent eight months researching and writing a comprehensive

English-language history of the ISC and its struggle with the IUS.[48] This appeared just before the ISC was "exposed" by *Ramparts* and the *New York Times*. Van den Heuvel announced that "through our international student contacts, we shall send it all over the world", and it was an important riposte to the critics of CIA skulduggery. For some it was a long riposte: IRD found its 350 pages of detail "too long and too historical" and MI6 sat on the manuscript for months before announcing that they were not going to follow through with plans for producing a shorter version. (Ellis wanted to pressure MI6, in recompense, to buy several hundred copies when the book was eventually produced by a Dutch publisher.)[49] For his trouble, in March 1967 Van Maanen was inevitably accused of being a kind of CIA stooge in the leftist weekly *Radicaal*, which described Interdoc as "part of the secret service of the Netherlands Ministry of Foreign Affairs".[50] Yet his work would remain the most detailed study of ISC's mission for the next 35 years.[51]

A smaller WFDY-sponsored Conference of Youth and Students for Disarmament, Peace and National Independence in Florence in February 1964 was the scene of the first follow-up action after Helsinki, this time under the direction of Herman Mennes, who ran the operation on site. Other partners were again brought in: Comitato Civico was contacted to provide local logistical support and Renato Mieli was requested to supply some press contacts for publicity. From Switzerland came an "experienced" member of the Schweizerischer Studentenverein and Münst's trusted lieutenant from the Helsinki operation, Peter Hess, as back-up.[52] Both IRD and MI6 were particularly interested in the Florence action, providing information materials to be distributed on site by the student group. Point-man for the Dutch students was this time Pieter Koerts, who not only delivered a prepared statement similar to Beuker's in Helsinki but also took things a step further by locating and sabotaging the local university printing press, to prevent conference materials from being reproduced during the event.[53] The Florence action may have gathered less publicity that Helsinki, but it maintained the momentum for international cooperation. Van den Heuvel remarked to Ellis that Florence "has been very successful for our group", since it proved once again to partners such as the CIA and MI6 what could be achieved by "a well-motivated, well-instructed group (however small it may be)", all on a limited budget.[54] He was also very impressed with the level of Swiss organization and decided to work with Ming, Graf, and the AWF at any future opportunity. The arrival of Hess was a bonus, as he teamed up well with Mennes and provided an article on the event for the *Neue Zürcher Zeitung*. Hess, who attended the Lunteren *colloque* in May, worked for Aare publishers, an outlet established by "young intellectuals" who wanted to promote "a progressive, positive, dynamic neutrality" for Switzerland. In practice this meant bringing out titles on communist front organizations. Van den Heuvel was interested in Aare as a channel for Interdoc publications (including *Tasks*), but Hess's departure for India in December 1964 seems to have ended the discussion.[55]

Koerts was another family connection, a nephew of Van den Heuvel who was studying economics at the Free University in Amsterdam at the time of the Helsinki operation. For a period he was at the centre of the student activism being fostered out of Van Stolkweg.[56] As well as Helsinki and Florence, during 1962–64 Koerts attended seminars at the Ostkolleg (Cologne), the Haus der Zukunft (West Berlin), and the Fight Communism Group in Lund. Despite being the international secretary of the Free University's Political Society, Koerts really "had no zeal to do anything political" and was soon "sick of all those stupid communists – come on guys, get real!" The attitudes of the Germans in the Interdoc circle, whose ideas he described as "antique", also put him off. Instead Koerts decided to study the Soviet economy and monetary policy for his Master's, and out of this came the Interdoc periodical *East–West Contacts* and a publication on trade for the OWI. Koerts felt that business could be the most effective way to open the Soviet bloc up to Western influence, something which Van den Heuvel would start to look at seriously with the Americans. After graduating in 1968 he moved on into the business world himself.[57]

There was a sense after Florence that the time was right to press home the advantage. Ming and the AWF had for a while been considering launching a plan for a major East–West youth festival "under neutral patronage".[58] The idea resurfaced at a meeting between Van den Heuvel, Münst, and several Swiss student representatives (including Hess) in Zurich in September 1964, at which the Swiss floated UNESCO (United Nations Educational, Scientific and Cultural Organization) as a potential sponsor. The Sino-Soviet split was making it difficult for Moscow and its allies to control the direction of its fronts, and the proposal aimed to make the most of Moscow's "tricky situation".[59] But, if Helsinki was a high point for the fledgling Interdoc, Florence was already something of a valedictory statement. Efforts to get a Dutch observer to the Christian Peace Conference held in Prague in the summer of 1964 were unsuccessful (Interdoc adviser Zacharias Anthonisse was turned down by the organizers and a back-up failed to materialize).[60] IRD prompting to attempt something at the European Disarmament Conference in Salzburg in November 1964 also came to nothing when the meeting was cancelled. All attention was on whether the WFDY would organize another large-scale festival so that the Helsinki operation could be repeated, but this movement was itself in disarray, largely due to the Sino-Soviet split. IRD reported in early 1963 that it was likely "we have seen the last of the Monster jamborees on the lines of last summer's Helsinki Youth Festival and the Moscow Peace Congress, and that in future the Russians will try to lay on smaller regional meetings in which it will be easier to control proceedings and from which the Chinese can be excluded".[61] The first attempt to rejuvenate the movement centred on Algiers, where the Festival Mondial de la Jeunesse et des Etudiants pour la Solidarité, la Paix et l'Amitié was planned in the summer of 1965 to take advantage of Algerian elan as a newly independent nation.

The prospect of an Algiers action provided the real basis for codifying the Luxembourg Group's purpose.[62] Van den Heuvel reported to Mieli in early 1965 that the Group, consisting of representatives from the US, Britain, West Germany, Switzerland, Sweden, the Netherlands, and "an international student-organization" (either the ISC, WASC, or the World Assembly of Youth), was preparing to send small groups of students to put the Western point of view and "aggravate contradictions and tensions in the meeting".[63] Denmark was also active, via the Democratic Alliance, but they were held outside the Luxembourg umbrella. Western governments did not support any official involvement, but Van den Heuvel thought "a way might be found to countenance non-attributable action".[64] Plans went ahead to send Herman Mennes to Algiers on a reconnaissance mission prior to the festival, and the Dutch National Student Council started to prepare an unofficial delegation.[65] Wahret die Freiheit occupied a vital position in this process, since it also held the dominant position in the Swiss group connected with the youth festival's International Preparatory Committee (IPC). Swiss neutrality allowed the AWF greater freedom of action in this situation. In plans similar to those surrounding Helsinki '62, Graf's organization aimed to take a group of 20 African students from the Algiers festival on a three-week round trip through Switzerland, West Germany, the Netherlands, and Britain to defuse any anti-Western propaganda they might have picked up.[66] Van den Heuvel's "American friends in the Embassy" (CIA) recommended that the Independent Research Service, the anti-festival arm of the US National Student Association, should join the Luxembourg Group, which the Dutchman, always keen to bring in the Americans, found to be "an excellent idea".[67]

But this gathering of forces was stopped in its tracks by the fall of Algerian leader Ben Bella in June and the subsequent cancellation of the event. Following this disappointment, and with the festival organizers in disarray, Ming and AWF president Hans Graf tried to seize the initiative by presenting their plan for a joint East–West festival (without UNESCO, which the Luxembourg Group saw as "communist infiltrated") to the IPC. The purpose was to force the Soviet fronts, faced with increasing interest in Beijing from developing countries, into a compromise that would mean a genuine 50–50 organization: WFDY and IUS on one side, ISC and the World Assembly of Youth (with which Wahret die Freiheit had excellent relations) on the other. Peaceful coexistence would be fully tested out in the youth field. Opposition from the Luxembourg Group and the ISC forced Graf and Ming to abandon the proposal, which had already caused serious divisions within the IPC.[68] A hasty compromise was reached by the IPC in Vienna in January 1966 with the choice of Accra in Ghana for a smaller festival that September. With this stretching logistics to the limit, Van den Heuvel gathered together "the reconstituted Interdoc committee", this time consisting of student representatives from Britain, the Netherlands, West Germany,

Switzerland, and the ISC ("à titre privé"), with a meeting at Van Stolkweg in February 1966. That it was now an Interdoc committee and no longer referred to as the Luxembourg Group is an interesting detail, considering the previous German demand to keep a distance between the two. The absence of the Swedes is notable considering the previous contributions of Häggman, Pålsson, and Wedin, but by 1967 the *Inform* group had fragmented. The fall of Nkrumah in the same month brought planning to a halt once again.[69]

The IPC, increasingly divided between communist/non-communist, communist/communist, and developed/developing nations, eventually chose to hold a full festival in Sofia in 1968. Both Graf and Van den Heuvel were "convinced that the chances were very limited in this case", Bulgaria being a very different proposal from Helsinki or even Algiers. Ellis likewise passed on advice from London that any participants "should be chary of attempting, or seeking to attempt, any kind of disruptive activity themselves and that their image should not appear to be emphatically anti-communist".[70] The idea of holding a Western festival was revived, but once again the ISC was needed to back this up, and in March 1967, the very month that Van den Heuvel and Graf discussed this option, its status was damaged beyond repair by the *Ramparts* article that exposed the CIA's links with the US National Student Association and ISC itself.[71] A festival in a communist country placed too heavy a demand on the Luxembourg Group's abilities, but Van den Heuvel did arrange for two law/political science students from Leiden, Antoinette Gosses and Michiel Verschoor van Nisse, to attend as observers. The idea was that they would produce a report with photos that could be worked into a full-length study for public consumption, along the lines of Van Maanen's book or the Helsinki festival's *Frieden und Freundschaft*. Described as "very enthusiastic" in the background notes, both students were "fully briefed" before departure, with the special instruction that all papers from Van Stolkweg had to be destroyed to avoid possessing any incriminating evidence.

A preliminary visit to the World Federalists conference in Vienna in July 1968 provided a training run for the students. Graf, who attended the Sofia event as a tourist, offered his support on site. But once in Bulgaria the plan came under intense pressure. The Sofia festival was chaotic, disrupted by disputes within the socialist ranks as the Czechoslovaks, Romanians, and Yugoslavs organized a counter-festival of their own, and the attendance of non-communist and New Left groups from West Germany caused a running confrontation with their counterparts from the East. The two students came under suspicion from the rest of the Dutch group, on the lookout for a Helsinki-type situation. Despite the preparations, Gosses felt later that she had "just stumbled into it" and was unprepared to be treated as a "suspect" by the leaders of the Dutch student groups Socialist Youth (Socialistische Jeugd) and Politeia. Verschoor van Nisse channelled reports to *De Telegraaf* describing the "psychotic fear of the BVD" among the group and the divisions this had caused. The atmosphere was poisonous, and having endured this unexpectedly harsh ordeal neither participant produced the intended book-length report.[72]

The final involvement in this field took place at the tenth festival, in East Berlin in 1973. Cautious of upsetting the improving relations with the GDR, Van den Heuvel received agreement and financial support from the Ministry for Inner-German Relations (Bundesministerium für innerdeutsche Beziehungen) for a "counter-action" so long as the participants were trained in advance by Ministry-specified experts (including Hans Lades).[73] This allowed for a final gathering of the Interdoc Youth (IY) network. Henri Starckx came in from Belgium, and Rolf Buchow's colleague from Interdoc Berlin, Klaus Riedel, provided support on location. Bertil Häggman agreed to use his Foundation for Conflict Analysis as a cover for two Interdoc brochures published for distribution at the festival (when Van den Heuvel was unable to take the 500 copies into East Berlin he handed them out at Checkpoint Charlie himself).[74] Van den Heuvel's son Christiaan, then a politics student at the Free University in Amsterdam, was this time designated to give a prepared speech after it had been delivered by a "runner" from West Berlin. He recalled later that his ten-minute call for the free movement of people and ideas at one of the festival's sessions in Humboldt University met with a "dead silent" audience.[75] As Van den Heuvel senior remarked afterwards, "contrary to the three previous festivals, there was no opposition of any significance, which made it a rather dull event".[76] Once again, publicity was provided via an article fed to journalist Philip Mok at *Elsevier Magazine* that emphasized the disruptive nature of the festival in a time of East–West détente.[77] Interdoc's counter-crusade at the world youth festivals had come to a relatively quiet end, although it would be revived on a minor scale later in the 1970s.

Konfrontation: meeting the East

To achieve what it set out to accomplish, Interdoc needed to craft a position on East–West contacts that would be widely accepted, something that could not be taken for granted. The Studienbüro meeting of September 1961 highlighted two fundamentally different approaches to the issue: the Swiss model, which rejected all contacts to prevent their abuse; and the Dutch model, "the systematic search for contacts and their use for offensive purposes".[78] The Dutch would win out. As early as 1963 SOEV's Annual Report referred to the opportunity for introducing Western ideas into the communist world by rising to the challenge and effectively turning the "openness" of peaceful coexistence inside out.[79] Over the previous six years the *colloques* had focused on the methods and requirements of a defensive strategy: the long-term goals, ideological basis, and tactical manoeuvring of communist activities in the West, and the different methods employed to withstand these threats (such as the development of civic responsibility and the formation of cadres within key sectors of industry). From 1963 onwards, fuelled by the existence of Interdoc as an institutional base, the outlook switched to the offensive. The Luxembourg Group signified that it was time to think in terms of not "counter-action" but simply action. In the Netherlands lack of funds had prevented SOEV from really fulfilling its ambitions in this direction, causing Einthoven to plead with Prince Bernhard for more support in influencing "the 'future framework' (*skelet*) of our society".[80] But during 1964–65 Interdoc, with growing self-confidence, ran a series of conferences on the strategic development of East–West contacts and its own place in this scenario.

In May 1964, in Lunteren near Utrecht (Einthoven's home town), a seminar was held on the relationship between youth and communism in the West. This was followed later the same year in Eschwege (West Germany) with "Considerations for an Active Peace Policy". Eschwege marked a critical point in the Interdoc deliberations. First, there was a reaction to the heavy West German stamp on the discussions. Both the IRD and Ellis, supported by Van den Heuvel, wanted to move the *colloque* away from Eschwege, located close to the East–West German border, to West Berlin, "*the* most important neuralgic point in world politics".[81] Second, Geyer's background text for the Eschwege discussions – "The Strategy of Peace" – drew mixed reactions. Geyer emphasized how "peaceful coexistence" and signs of liberalization among communist regimes were undermining Western fear of "world communism" and isolating West Germany as a nation still unwilling to take steps to legitimize the Soviet bloc. Basing his position on Walt Rostow's declaration of a "Great Act of Persuasion" to redirect Soviet attention away from ideologically driven world domination towards Russian national interest in cooperation and arms control, Geyer insisted that up to that point no response had yet fully answered the "strategic challenge" to Western political consciousness posed by Moscow.[82] The only way forward seemed to be to take Moscow's peaceful overtures at face value, thereby playing the game according to their tune. Searching for a way of shifting the West's approach from negative to positive and "from reaction to action", Geyer proposed "a dynamic intellectual action in person-to-person encounters" that would lock on to the national sentiments of peoples in the East and nudge them towards the realization that "material security" and Marxism–Leninism were incompatible. To achieve this, a flexible but guided approach "to confront the people of the Soviet bloc with the wealth of Western intellectual–political life", using all public and private means, must be initiated.[83]

Geyer's text was a 25-page treatise that tried to identify the most effective entry points into the communist mind, but it was not to everyone's taste (talk of "the ineradicable 'interdependence' between consciousness-building and political praxis" did not go down too well with the British participants). Van den Heuvel also found the text "much too long". As he commented to

Mieli, "It is still very difficult for the Germans to see the East–West conflict in the right perspective, they are too much involved, emotionally involved."[84] Eschwege went ahead, after two planning meetings in Munich (June) and The Hague (July) to iron out the differences. Even then, Geyer's insistence on highlighting "the special problems of the Federal Republic of Germany" at the *colloque* had a negative effect on other participants.[85]

Taking over the direction of the conferences, Van den Heuvel guided the 1965 gatherings – at the Grand Hotel in Locarno (Switzerland) and in Zandvoort (Netherlands) – towards getting a grip on what such a Strategy of Freedom meant in practice, particularly from different national perspectives. Inspiration for this came from the US in the form of Polish émigré and Columbia professor Zbigniew Brzezinski, the author of *Alternative to Partition* (1965) and one of the leading voices in favour of a full engagement with the East. *Oost-West* had already introduced Brzezinski to its Dutch audience in early 1963.[86] Brzezinski argued that the partition of Europe was in no one's interests, yet the balance of nuclear weapons and superpower spheres of interest caused it to appear permanent. Looking for a way ahead to break the deadlock, he sketched possibilities for promoting and taking advantage of "the internal liberalization of East European societies" in order to peacefully erode the artificial division of East and West.[87] A special role could be played by expanding East–West trade:

> In the expansion of East–West trade, the West should attempt to erode the narrow ideological perspectives of the ruling communist elites and to prevent them from restricting closer contact exclusively to the economic realm, thus resolving their economic difficulties while consolidating their power and perpetuating the present partition of Europe. The communist leaders, with their public pleas for closer commercial relations (including Western credits), have been successful in representing themselves as the apostles of international cooperation. Western statesmen should be as vocal in stressing that concrete improvements in cultural relations, more intellectual dialogue and freedom of expression are as important as trade in creating genuine international cooperation. The two should always be related in every Western statement, comment, or negotiation with the East.[88]

Locarno built on Geyer's vision and Brzezinski's practical proposals. Which ideas and values were most suitable to be taken into the East? How should the people behind the Iron Curtain best be approached? The starting point for Interdoc was above all that "we *affirm* these contacts rather than oppose them, *provided* that certain prerequisites are met".[89] The resulting conference booklet – the first to be issued as a public document, a sign of growing confidence – includes British, Dutch, French, German, Italian, and Swiss perspectives. It expresses an awareness of the major opportunity to engage with a communist world in disarray through Sino-Soviet splits and societies eager for knowledge of the West, but also a definite caution as to the continuing dangers. The problem was twofold: organization and mentality. Educational and scientific contacts, sports tours, and tourist tours were controlled by arms of the Soviet state apparatus for political and economic gain, whereas in the West they were allowed to take place in the private sector without any central guidance, often on the assumption that more was better. The result was that the communist world still held the advantage even if it was crumbling from within. The solution, of course, was for Interdoc to provide the necessary services:

> Everyone participating in congresses and meetings in the Communist bloc must prepare himself by ideological training, not only for the purpose of being able to defend his viewpoints in the discussion but in order to comprehend Communist tactics and the real Communist everyday life.[90]

The potential was there, but the means were limited. Western nations were responding to the overtures of "peaceful coexistence" by signing cultural exchange and trade agreements, and even the Swiss, for whom all contacts with the East were taboo prior to 1962, were loosening up. But the overall picture was one of haphazard moves and unclear motives. The French delegate described the possibility of changing the Soviet system through exchanges as "the drop of water in the sea", but it still represented "the limited possibility of 'basic' contacts between East and West, and is thus far from being negligible". Even Renato Mieli, a sceptic who wanted to concentrate on the national level and not formulate grandiose pan-Western responses, saw their value for opposing the Communist Party's "cultural diplomacy": "All these movements for peace and so on should not be a monopoly of communism, should be infiltrated [...] and possibly transformed little by little, so that the discussion on disarmament, for instance, on peace should not be left to them and should be carried [out] with our contribution."[91]

Interdoc's role was now to both warn of the dangers and provide the solutions, including supplying factual information and training a new set of cadres (tour guides, businessmen) to undertake "prepared East–West contacts".[92] By pooling the resources available within the Interdoc network – the Ostkolleg, Ost-West Instituut, IRD – the "clearing house" function could come to fruition. But the politicians still had to be convinced. The Locarno report circulated widely at the top of the British government (including the British Council, the Trades Union Congress, even reaching Foreign Secretary Michael Stewart and Prime Minister Harold Wilson), the topic being in vogue with the signing at the time of a new three-year cultural exchange agreement with the Soviet Union.[93] But getting government support still proved elusive. In a lecture in Bonn in June 1965 von Hahn outlined his understanding of *Konfrontation* with the East, which he saw as "a new targeted approach for contacts with the East, previously neglected by the anxious and insecure

Bonn ministries".[94] He argued that, while East–West contacts were increasing at all levels as part of an "irreversible process", little attention was being given in the West to their scope, purpose, or importance despite the fact that the communists saw all such activities as a logical extension of political struggle. But "all contacts have an awareness-raising effect in both directions", and growing dissatisfaction within societies behind the Iron Curtain, caused by the gap between communist ideology and daily political and economic reality, meant that the possibilities for Western influence would also only increase. The best way to interact with these dissatisfactions and introduce alternative "models and thought processes" (*Leitbilder, Denkprozesse*) was through "personal discussion" (*das persönliche Gespräch*). The Soviet Union and its satellite states, eager to gain foreign currency, were being forced into a "slow opening of the door" (*langsamen Öffnen der Tür*) to investments and tourists. Von Hahn reckoned that around 1.6 million Westerners travelled to Czechoslovakia alone in 1964, so that "the 'mass tourist' is increasingly the ruler of the situation". Thanks to mass media representations, those in the East had preformed negative ideas of the West – and particularly of capitalism – but they were "hungry for knowledge" (*erkenntnishungrig*) on all aspects of Western life.[95] Von Hahn had suggestions for the way such contact should proceed:

> A discussion about ideological differences is also not very popular with a communist. It often degenerates from their side into the repetition of Soviet political arguments.
> (For the rest the discussion tends to remain unfruitful, because
>   a. from the communist side it is conducted by experienced dialecticians
>   b. the German side all too often does not know the communist definition of their common terms – e.g. self-determination, freedom, coexistence...)
> Therefore, it is usually more sensible to concentrate on communism "in practice" in order to question the theory.
> Discussion partners from nations behind the Iron Curtain are the most vulnerable to criticism [...] In a longer talk – especially with intellectuals or scientists – sooner or later the "discomfort", the "awareness of the empty fields" (Buchholz), the "cultural malaise" and the wish for an evolution of social life towards greater individual freedom and economic and cultural development (which can only be achieved at the expense of the Party) becomes more apparent.[96]

Ordinary citizens had to become channels of information – and influence. Since the closure of the border in Berlin in 1961 the BND had looked to West German citizens going East for information on the situation in the GDR. Interdoc was now aiming to utilize this resource on a coordinated European scale.

The Zandvoort meeting in September 1965 built on Locarno under the guidance of "Lenin's famous question: What are we to do?" The conference report emphasized the "psychological preparation" necessary for going East: "What can I expect when I go there" and, crucially, "what can I offer my opposite number in a confrontation?" Since communism would always seek to expand its influence, "it is the task of all freedom-loving forces to preserve their own order" by providing "a clearer view of our Western life and values". The goal was to reduce tensions and – potentially – transform attitudes:

> It is not by ideological discussion that we are going to persuade the Soviet Communist Party and other communist parties to give up their monopoly of power. What we can do and ought to do is to create doubt in as many minds as possible. If a sufficient number of people within the Soviet Union are convinced that the system no longer works and if this doubt spreads f.[or] i.[nstance] to the Armed Forces, then it is possible that their may be a change, but it is difficult to see this change coming simply as a result of discussion.[97]

The language is careful, but it cannot fully hide the intent, and behind the scenes the optimism was growing. Both IRD and MI6 were positive about the direction Interdoc was going in. Geyer declared to Van den Heuvel at the end of 1965 that he could look back on the previous year with some satisfaction. Interdoc's policy of waiting with patience until its overall approach was fully formed and coherently built up was now paying off. The British, Italians, and Swiss were contributing to the debates, even if they were not full members. Geyer described a plan for a youth exchange programme between the Federal Republic and the USSR in 1966, which would ambitiously seek to bring forty groups of 25 participants to the West in one year. Calculating the "multiplication" factor of the way people passed on their experiences to others, Geyer gleefully wrote of directly and indirectly influencing around 200,000 Russians.[98]

Van den Heuvel, tuning in to Geyer's more philosophical approach, wholeheartedly agreed:

> It is a bold undertaking that we now switch over from the defensive to the offensive. On our way we often faced resistance and needed to battle against conservative thinking. Often we ran ahead of the "music"; by "music" I mean official government policy. We did not follow its twists and turns, but hoped that the "music" would catch up with us. Our greatest advantage is that on the whole the youth stand on our side. On the other hand this gives us a great responsibility concerning the education and training [*Heranbildung*] of this youth.[99]

Other partners were appearing on this terrain. Although the Free Europe Committee (FEC) had proved unwilling to provide financial support to

Interdoc, it was now interested in combining forces. Van den Heuvel had run into Eugene Metz of the FEC's Paris office at the Ostkolleg conference in December 1964, and he reported to Geyer soon after that the Committee was looking to expand its operations for influencing Eastern Europeans beyond the efforts of Radio Free Europe. The most appropriate site for this was the University of Strasbourg, where since 1960 the FEC had been running summer courses for participants from the Soviet bloc and, increasingly, from the developing world. In July 1965 Van den Heuvel lectured to 150 participants there on East–West relations, most of them being Africans studying at Soviet-bloc universities who had been invited for a "holiday" in the West which included the course. He returned enthusiastic: "I had long debates with them on the Vietnam situation, the Congo, the peaceful coexistence […]"[100] Nevertheless contacts remained discreet: when Metz and his FEC colleagues attended the Locarno *colloque* in 1965, they did so as "interested Americans" and not as Committee representatives.[101]

Van den Heuvel also made it on to the speakers' list for a NATO summer course on East–West coexistence, held in Oxford in July 1965. The Dutchman delivered a talk on "Subversion and Counter-Subversion" which outlined the separate tasks of security services (preventing sabotage, espionage, and infiltration) and private organizations (counter-propaganda), emphasizing once again the need for a new phase in the struggle:

> The word "counter" is becoming more and more unpopular. It is realized that Soviet Communism in its present appearance cannot be met in the old way. New attitudes and new approaches are necessary […] These organisations do not only want to expose the dangers of Communism, but they also have an open eye for certain favourable developments taking place inside Communism. Developments which could eventually lead to the changing of Communism, to such an extent that Communism is no longer Communism, that means that it has lost its agressive [sic] and totalitarian traits.[102]

Van den Heuvel's talk went down particularly well with one member of the audience: Brigadier General Wilson, then the head of NATO's Information Division at Supreme Headquarters Allied Powers Europe (SHAPE). Wilson visited Van Stolkweg later the same year with two other staff officers to discuss how to utilize Interdoc's ideas for improving the image of NATO among Western youth ("wie man mithilfe der Presse die notwendige Widerstandskraft hervorrufen kann"). The meeting generated a return invitation for Van den Heuvel and von Hahn to Fontainebleau to speak to his team and sample the "special international collegial atmosphere of SHAPE".[103] This chance encounter laid the basis for a relationship with NATO which Van den Heuvel would take much further in the following decade.

Not all parties were so convinced. IRD in particular felt that Western institutions were telegraphing too strongly their wish to exploit contacts with the East, causing Moscow to introduce restrictions. The case of Gerald Brooke was used as an example. Brooke, a teacher from London, was arrested with his wife in the Soviet Union in April 1965 for smuggling in anti-Soviet propaganda. Sentenced to five years in a Soviet detention centre, he was eventually released in 1969 through a spy swap. Brooke admitted in court to acting as a courier for the anti-communist National Alliance of Russian Solidarists (NTS), and his case was turned into a *cause célèbre* by Moscow as a way of highlighting the underhand agenda of the West in promoting civilian contacts.[104] But Van den Heuvel remained a believer: "the Russians try to scare us because these cultural exchanges are going beyond their control."[105]

The New Left and Interdoc Youth

By the late 1960s Interdoc's developing view on East–West relations was suddenly challenged by disruptive developments within the West itself. Carefully laid plans on how to turn détente to the West's advantage were now being challenged by the rise of youth radicalism, fuelled by the US civil rights movement and opposition to the Vietnam War, which complicated the whole approach of utilizing student contacts to open up the East. The arrival of the New Left demanded new analysis, since it complicated the original thesis from the early 1960s that Western youth were susceptible to communist influence. There was now emerging a vocal, active, and radical leftism that considered Eastern and Western regimes as equally oppressive. The disruptiveness of New Left activists at the Sofia festival in 1968 demonstrated their determination to be independent from both sides of the ideological Cold War.

Looking to gather together expert opinion on these developments, a conference on the New Left was held in September 1968 in Zandvoort (following a preparatory "experts" meeting in Murnau in March), with a series of papers offering theoretical and country-based studies on youth, radical politics, and violence. Seventy participants from eleven countries attended, and "for the first time in the history of Interdoc it could be said that there was real participation by the Americans", including Cleveland Cram, the CIA station chief in The Hague from 1965 to 1969.[106] Some of the papers from the Zandvoort conference were published, soon followed by a second short volume in early 1969 that concentrated on the New Left phenomenon in Britain, West Germany, and the US, and a third in 1970 focusing on France.[107] A further conference in April 1970 – "Radicalism and Security" – assessed the threat of right- and left-wing extremism on Western societies and their armed forces. There was no unanimity in these conferences and publications on either the extent or the nature of the threat. Positions ranged from Brian Crozier's focus on the "new inspirers of violence" as "a major threat to civilised life in advanced industrial societies" and Swedish political scientist Niels-Eric Brodin's fear that the US faced "real threats posed against its foundations of security and order" to Stephen Kreppel's comment that "the danger [...] to British defence policy from political extremism is not very real" and Ministry of Defence official Hans Joachim Wohl's judgement that "vis-à-vis the defence of the Federal Republic [...] left-wing radicalism constitutes a danger that cannot be taken too seriously".[108]

Interdoc therefore served as a genuine meeting point for those involved in Western security to exchange views on the different kinds of threat posed by both the New Left (and, indeed, the New Right) across the West. Having said this, the one issue that did unite this crowd was the ever-present danger that the forces of Soviet communism could take advantage of New Left disruption. In Zandvoort, only a month after the ending of the "Prague Spring" by the Warsaw Pact, the Arbeitsgruppe's expert on youth politics, Andreas von Weiss, agreed that the motives, arguments, and goals of student unrest in the West and the East were very different, but he still saw the New Left as a dangerous "reserve for the activities of world revolutionary thought in the West". Kernig saw a general urge for social reform generated by a reaction to the traditions and structures of universities, but he could not see any organization or "uniform authority" behind these international phenomena, "let alone a communist one".[109] Van den Heuvel also rejected the right-wing notion of "an international communist conspiracy", instead highlighting the shifting alliances and contradictions between orthodox communism and its radical youthful variants which needed to be monitored for their effects on East–West relations. But the possibility for combined action always existed, not least in opposition to NATO, and by the time of the Radicalism and Security conference Interdoc's shift to the right allowed Ivan Matteo Lombardo to talk of the New Left as the "shock troops" for a leftist agenda: "the essential threat is posed by the whole leftist alignment of which the New Left is merely an active component".[110] Von Grote, Interdoc's resident hard-line conservative, concluded the Zandvoort publication with the following:

> The New Left has a complicating effect on the East–West confrontation and on the dialogue between the two, as, on the one hand, it may give rise to confusion in the Eastern camp, and on the other hand it may be a potential reserve for polycentrist communism in its competitive policy of subversion.[111]

This divergence of opinion is confirmed by a young journalist who joined the Interdoc scene around this time. Karel van Wolferen's father, a World War II veteran, had been a member of Van den Heuvel's Psychological Defence Committee in the NFR veterans' organization during the early 1960s, and in 1969 Van Wolferen Jr. was brought in to sort out the piles of information then gathering at Van Stolkweg on student movements and youth radicalism. This developed into a full-length study on student radicalism in the West, *Student Revolutionaries of the 1960s*, published in 1970.[112] Taking a sociological approach to social change and the causes of rebellion (technological advances and dehumanization, a cultural malaise, obsolescence of values, anti-authoritarianism, the generation gap), the main conclusion of this well-received study was that there was no worldwide radical conspiracy, only localized disturbances with wide-ranging but similar characteristics: "those who organized the struggle had not the slightest intention of arriving at tangible goals. Reaching one's goal would have meant an end to the all-important struggle."[113] Van Wolferen attended the Interdoc conference on Radicalism and Security at Noordwijk in April 1970 and recalled later that there were clearly two camps: those like himself with a more sanguine attitude and those, especially among the older German representatives, who insisted on the need to be constantly alert against the ever-present, all-encompassing subversive threat from the East. For Van Wolferen there was a "push to make things more threatening than was justified". The BND and their associates were "chasing ghosts" and making connections that did not exist to justify their anti-communist world view.[114]

Nevertheless, from these meetings plans were set in motion for a more substantial response to the New Left and youth activism. The impulse came from West Germany and particularly from Geyer and Lades, who wanted to establish a new apparatus to creatively mobilize Western youth in a time of fragmenting value systems and student agitation. The New Left, as an "anti-movement" (van den Heuvel) with "diffuse elements" that possessed "a hostility to organization" (Geyer), was a difficult target. The best response seemed to be the formation of a counter-organization to gather together those students who were prepared to stand up for the democratic values that the New Left were denigrating. Reinventing the link between Western youth and the armed forces as the defenders of Western society was a vital part of this. Communist "psychopolitics" sought to provoke and benefit from social disillusionment with and resentment of the military in the West, and in September 1968 Interdoc devoted a conference – "The Armed Forces in the Psycho-Political East–West Confrontation" – to examining the nature of this threat across Europe.[115] In 1967 Lades approached Rob van Hoof, the head of the Dutch Air Force's InVoLu unit, with a plan for "an international seminar for students and officers" as a first step towards breaking down the increasingly critical attitude of youth and students towards the armed forces and military service. At the Interdoc board meeting in December that year it was once again noted with approval that "Holland, as neutral ground, could function as an intermediary".[116] The first result of this was a symposium for around fifty Belgian, British, Dutch, German, Swedish, and Scandinavian students and officers in Amersfoort in April 1968, entitled "Perspectives on

European and Atlantic Integration from different National Interests", supported by Van Hoof and specifically for "students and well-educated young officers" from around Europe. A follow-up meeting was held in Oslo that August. Van den Heuvel remarked that an "Interdok der Jugend" was coming into being.[117] It was now time to find someone to run it.

In June 1968 von Hassell was officially replaced by 27-year-old Uwe Holl, who had already been working at Van Stolkweg since August 1967. The need to bring in a new generation was very clear by this stage, with many of the main players either beyond retirement age (Einthoven, von Grote, von Hahn, Ellis) or in their forties and fifties (Van den Heuvel, Couwenberg, Geyer).[118] Holl, like many in the German Interdoc circle (von Hahn, von Grote), came from a German family from the East (Danzig), and the experience of fleeing from the Soviet advance and being a refugee in Denmark after the war had a profound effect on him as a child. Attending the same school as Raimute von Hassell's son, Holl was already known to Munich when the search for a new deputy in The Hague was being made. The first project he dealt with did not bode well for the future. Holl was asked to draw up a full audit of the costs and infrastructure of the Van Stolkweg set-up, to be presented to the Interdoc board meeting in late 1967. He duly produced a report that suggested some cost-cutting measures, which Van den Heuvel supported but for some reason von Hassell did not. Holl ended up in the middle of a Hague–Munich tussle over the rising budget, which resulted in von Hassell undermining his credibility with Geyer and von Grote. From then on Holl's path to becoming deputy director was blocked, and he was instead given a heavy portfolio of administrative tasks (all the correspondence, and the collection and control of research materials). From this vantage point he gained the strong impression that Van den Heuvel was skilled at manoeuvring between the clashing German viewpoints to create space and time for himself. At the same time, it was perfectly in Munich's interests to allow the Dutchman this freedom to pursue "German work with a Dutch hat on". Geyer was still coming to The Hague around four times a year during Holl's period at Van Stolkweg, for both board meetings and private liaison. Holl also remembers that Einthoven was still in the Interdoc picture during the late 1960s: "when he said something he was always listened to".[119]

With the departure of von Hassell in 1968 Holl became assistant director (not deputy director as originally intended). Munich would only be fully represented in The Hague again with the arrival of Johannes Hoheisel in 1969, after von Hassell had returned once again to cover some of the extra workload during April–July 1969. Another Easterner (from Tuckum, Lithuania) and colleague of Gehlen's from Army Group East, Hoheisel had joined the BND in 1956 and became chief of the political evaluation section in III branch in 1963. The need for someone to cover the administration in Van Stolkweg was evident, because by late 1968 Holl was given a new task on top of his already bulging portfolio: to build Interdoc's youth project.

It was Holl's mission to bridge the gaping generation gap that was opening up between the World War II veterans and Western youth, and with it the lack of communication, mistrust, and absence of consensus on social and political values. This was similar to what Van den Heuvel was increasingly attempting via the veterans' groups and his Institute for Psychological Defence (Geestelijke Weerbaarheid) through the 1960s and 1970s, but Holl was to operate with a different mandate on the international level. The first major step was taken with a preliminary meeting at Erlangen in January 1969 involving Norwegian, Swedish, German, Dutch, and Swiss representatives, and it was there that the draft articles of association were drawn up under the guidance of Hans Graf. Erlangen's student-run Collegia Politica group of activist students, centred on Hans Lades and his Institut für Gesellschaft und Wissenschaft in Mitteldeutschland, was a major catalyst for the Interdoc Youth organization. Von Dellingshausen had referred to the importance of nurturing such groups at universities during the inter-departmental coordination meetings of 1960–61 (the idea of promoting student groups devoted to democratic citizenship had originated already in the late 1950s), and under Lades – who had also participated in those meetings – Erlangen became a key site.[120] Gunhild Bohm-Geyer joined Lades' group in 1966 after her involvement in a similar venture in Hamburg. Ostensibly there to study the literature and politics of the GDR, Bohm-Geyer participated in the Erlangen Collegia's drive to take over the student association by applying Leninist tactics against the New Left themselves.[121] The impulse for the Collegia came once again from the challenge of the GDR:

In East Germany students must devote a large part of their time to socio-scientific studies aimed at producing a militant political awareness as defined by world revolutionary Communist aims. Spurred on by this fact and out of responsibility for our society students in the collegia politica feel obliged to cultivate a frank attitude to world affairs and a positive sense of freedom, German unity and European solidarity, in addition to acquiring a good specialised knowledge of their subjects.

The realisation that they live in the better system is not, in itself, sufficient.[122]

One of its members, Wolfgang Buchow, recalls that there was another impulse behind this than mere "confrontation": "I think the mind [of Interdoc] changed [...] From the position of telling the people how terrible communism is, it changed into how can we work on [communist thinking] to overcome this situation." This reflected the views of Lades, whom Buchow saw as an *Ausgleichender* (Equalizer, Reconciler) aiming "to close the gap" between East and West.[123] The Erlangen group foresaw three levels of participation, whereby someone would "graduate" from attending study groups to carrying out specialized studies comparing East and West through to being able to deliver lectures themselves. On the basis of tolerance, mutual intellectual understanding, and interdependence, and backed by "democratic values in accordance with the United Nations Charter", Interdoc Youth aimed to "eliminate sources of friction in [East–West] political discussion in order to stabilize international relations". There was some awareness of the scale of the task: "That Interdoc Youth is undaunted by the magnitude of this undertaking is no proof of an estrangement from reality, but rather of a high regard for the individual and his personal effort."[124]

A follow-up gathering from Erlangen took place in The Hague during 29–30 March to consolidate the organization. Holl wrote to Ellis soon afterwards that "we are still wondering about the best name: Interdoc Youth, Interdoc of Youth, Interdoc Junior, Interdoc of the younger generation? Since we are also involving people up to 40 years of age I am afraid that neither [sic] of these names hits the point and is equally short and appealing [...] For the time being we run under the flag 'Interdoc Youth'."[125] Eighteen participants from eight countries in Western Europe attended the event at Hotel Op Gouden Wieken (On Golden Wings) in The Hague, where Holl was named secretary general and Mennes took on the role of chairman representing "Interdoc Senior". The new organization would "act as a basis for information and not indoctrination" and aimed "to inform and cooperate, with those people of the younger generation who share the view that Western democratic values need protection against dangers from outside as well as from within". The board of Interdoc Youth (IY), with a strong Scandinavian component, consisted of the following: Mennes (chair), Holl (general secretary), Wolfgang Buchow (son of Interdoc Berlin's Rolf Buchow), Per Paust (Norway), Bertil Wedin (Sweden, with Bertil Häggman as alternate), and Hans Graf (Switzerland), who played a key role in drawing up the statutes. Advisers to the board were Jim Daly (UK, formerly assistant general secretary of the National Union of Students and ISC) and the Bundeswehr officer Peter von Geyso, with additional student representatives from Belgium (Henri Starckx and Raoul Syts from Ghent University) and France (Gisèle Loc'h, a member of the Collegia in Erlangen).

Mixing students and young military officers was already one of the background themes to IY at the Amersfoort meeting in April 1968, as a way of dealing with the increasingly critical attitude of Western youth towards the armed forces in the late 1960s. Lieutenant Geyso was the contact man for German military support, and Volk und Verteidigung, the German equivalent of Hornix's Volk en Verdediging, oversaw the arrangements for the student–military seminars. Bundeswehr aircraft were literally used to fly participants to locations such as the Military Academy in Oslo, whose liaison officer, Captain Saebøe, also attended IY conferences. IY was intended to be a self-contained unit within Interdoc, so long as it remained fully accountable and answerable for its activities. An ambitious roster of activities was planned, including regular seminars, a periodical (*Youth Forum*), the formation of national working groups based on the Erlangen model, and exchanges with the Eastern bloc. Holl took over an office on the top floor of Van Stolkweg 10 and officially began operations on 1 April 1969. Although IY replicated the general purpose of Interdoc as a clearing house for improving transnational cooperation and information, Holl's mission also included "to interest and engage the younger generation of the Third World in Interdoc Youth's activities". The inevitable full recognition of the GDR as a nation state caused much concern within the BND during the late 1960s and the expansion of Interdoc was a sign of this. A budget of 30,000 guilders was agreed for the first year.[126] Doubts remained about Holl's abilities to manage his role, most notably from Geyer, who felt that he was unable to concentrate on the most important tasks. The BND man despaired that the much younger Holl could not fulfil the tasks that the 72-year-old von Grote pursued with vigour. Concluding that Holl needed to be guided along "the path of virtue", Geyer took the patient route and gave the whole operation two to three years to prove itself.[127]

During 1968–69 Holl was assisted by trainee diplomat Alexander Heldring. Heldring had followed the one-week course for young diplomats run by the Oost-West Instituut, which included a study trip to Interdoc Berlin, but his entry to Interdoc was provided by his aunt, a member of the BVD. Van den Heuvel, at the time increasing his involvement in World War II veterans' organizations, gave Heldring the project of researching the Fédération Internationale des Résistants (FIR), a World War II veterans' organization founded in 1951, and "unmasking" it as a communist front.[128] Alongside his research Heldring was active in the start-up phase of IY, assisting with the Amersfoort seminar in April 1968 and taking responsibility for running the Nijenrode study trips to Interdoc Berlin. He was also Van den Heuvel's first choice to be the Interdoc observer at the World Youth Festival in Sofia, but concerns over how this might affect his future diplomatic career meant that he turned it down.[129] Drawing on Van Stolkweg's extensive library, Heldring completed his book on the FIR in 1969 (it was subsequently produced in English, Dutch, and French versions) and left to join the diplomatic service, which would take him to postings in Poland, Washington, DC, and Czechoslovakia.

Holl set out by trying to encourage the formation of Collegia Politica in each of the participating nations, which consisted mainly of Belgium, Britain, the Netherlands, Norway, Sweden, Switzerland, and West Germany. Denmark and France remained on the edges (rather as they did with Interdoc as a whole), while Italy was never involved.[130] IY would have no members, but would act as a clearing-house facilitator bringing others together, in the Interdoc mould. When Bertil Wedin proposed an official link with the right-wing Democratic Alliance of which he was a member, Holl let it be known that Interdoc maintained contacts of "different political shades in various countries" but direct contacts with the Alliance had deliberately been stopped in 1965.[131] IY wanted to avoid becoming a right-wing club, but the need for "alliances of convenience" sometimes put this under stress. Thus Gerald Howarth, an important student contact in Britain early on, was excluded from official representation because of his extreme political views, but cooperation was sought with the Austrian student body FOEST despite its relations with the nationalist Österreichische Volkspartei (ÖVP).[132] Yet at the same time Per Paust was discouraged from bringing in "revolutionary participants": IY was not meant to become an ideological war zone but on the contrary to be an activist community dedicated to *realisieren nicht theorisieren* and the defence of democratic values. Paust understood: "We are all members of a society for which we want to stand up."[133] There was also an effort to ensure IY's independence. At the IY board meeting in Hamburg in June 1969 (held at the Bundeswehr officers' school) it was decided that "for psychological reasons nobody from the older generation shall attend the board meeting" even though both Geyer and Van den Heuvel were also in town.[134]

Some, such as the Swiss, were already well organized. Hans Ulmer of the Aufklärungsdienst, present at the Erlangen meeting, soon handed over to philosophy student Kurt Bütikofer.[135] In the Netherlands contacts with the National Student Council had been in existence since the early 1960s, and links with the Student Society for International Relations (SIB: Studentenvereniging voor Internationale Betrekkingen), originally laid with the Ostkolleg seminars, were revived. Student study seminars with Interdoc Berlin were arranged, and IY subsidized an SIB group of 20 on a visit to the Soviet Union in May 1970 (on the condition that each participant write a report on the attitude of Russians towards the West). A similar arrangement was made with the Free University in Amsterdam to subsidize their exchange with the Polish Student Association at the Jagiellonian University in Krakow.[136] The SIB was also involved in opposing radical student influence via international bodies such as the International Union of Christian Democrat and Conservative Students (ICCS).[137] Overall, though, IY had a low opinion of the SIB and its members and did not see them as reliable partners. Other contacts in the Netherlands were more fruitful. A lecture series on East–West relations for students at the prestigious international business school in Nijenrode, near Utrecht, became a regular feature, with IY arranging for groups of American students to attend Interdoc Berlin seminars as an added benefit. Relations were opened with the Nederlandse Jeugd Gemeenschap (NJG), the Dutch wing of the World Assembly of Youth (WAY), through exchange of periodicals and participation at IY events.[138]

Britain, as ever, was another story. A meeting in London in early June 1969 between Holl, Ellis, Jim Daly, and Southampton law student Gerald Howarth discussed the possibilities in Britain. Undergraduates there were younger than their European counterparts and were attached to a party if politically active, and "it is difficult to win over English youth with in-depth theoretical analyses of broad themes". Any movement would have to be built gradually by inviting individuals to specific seminars and linking them with their continental counterparts. Sixties libertarianism, left-wing suspicions, and the fallout from the exposure of the ISC meant that "students were no longer prepared to accept the authority of any governing body", but a reconfiguration was taking place as several key National Union of Students activists took on positions with the international department of Transport House, at the time the home of the Labour Party and the Transport and General Workers' Union. Daly, who returned from a seminar in West Berlin in February 1969 enthusiastic for "an institute which would bring together young political, educational, managerial and military people", was determined to mobilize a British contingent for IY over the ensuing months. The demise of the ISC had shown that "professional institutional student unionism" was "a mixed blessing" for both the US and the USSR, and more flexible, limited but focused arrangements were the way to go. Daly also attended the conference of the International Association of Cultural Freedom (the successor to the CCF) on Student Rebellion and the Future of Western Industrial Society, held in Sardinia in April 1969.[139]

Holl began to widen the scope beyond Europe, introducing IY to those already receiving Interdoc periodicals (in Asia, and particularly in India) and establishing new links with the International Student Movement for the UN (ISMUN) in Geneva, the Malaysian Youth Council, the Kojimachi Institute in Tokyo, the Asian Peoples' Anti-Communist League and the Nehru Institute of Youth Affairs in New Delhi, and the Association of Latin American Christian Democrats in Europe. For IY's constituency North–South relations were as important as East–West. A visit by Asian youth leaders organized by the German wing of WAY offered another opportunity. While the West Berlin visit as always made a "deep impression", an interesting message was delivered by the head of the Indian National Council of University Students (which already received Interdoc publications): "some of the translations from the communist press give the impression that Interdoc is doing the work of the Communists by distributing English translations of communist propaganda". What was self-evident for a European audience attuned to communist contradiction was not the case for an Asian audience lacking the immediate context.[140] Always on the lookout for antagonistic developments, Holl contacted Bjørn Iversen in Copenhagen about artist Asger Jorn's Scandinavian Institute for Comparative Vandalism, presumably thinking that this project chronicling Viking folk art was somehow linked to disruptive elements of the New Left.[141]

The meeting of representatives held at the Richmond Hill Hotel in West London in October 1969, announced as the first international conference of IY, was intended to cover the "social demands of the younger generation in East and West".[142] Geyer gave an introductory "call to arms" presentation entitled "The Situation of the Youth in West and East". Analysing the destructive motivations that lay behind the youthful protests of the time, Geyer pointed out the need for "new, generally applicable objectives capable of positively activating the political enthusiasm potentially present in us all." "Self-realisation" was the general goal in both East and West, but the motivation behind it differed: "here in the west a distant utopia which is to be achieved by means of the destruction... of former values and former forms of organisation of society; there in the east the desire to relax a straight-jacket which is felt to be inadequate." While "counter-forces against the radical New Left" were thus essential, the prime target had to be "arousing [the] consciousness" of the "quiet majority" to reform society in both East and West. Geyer refrained from saying how: "As an older person I shall give no answer – I expect it from you, from the conference".[143]

Geyer was followed by studies from participating nations (France: Loc'h, Sweden: Wedin, Netherlands: Cees Spaan, a journalist from Utrecht) that assessed the broad range of concerns felt by contemporary youth and the urge for "democratization", the common denominator being "that radical, violent solutions [...] should be rejected". The younger generations had lost interest in the Cold War, and it was necessary to emphasize that "the political East–West confrontation" still lay at the centre of world affairs.[144] Among the fifty or so participants were representatives from the German ministries of Defence and Family and Youth, as well as Roy Godson of the National Strategy Information Center (NSIC), who flew in as the only representative from the US. Von Geyso organized transport by Bundeswehr aircraft in Europe to RAF Northolt (the nearest available airfield) for all participants except the Swiss, for whom this was a step too far; the Dutch flew from Valkenburg airfield, near The Hague.

Richmond was not an easy meeting. Journalists from the Dutch Catholic broadcaster KRO heard of the meeting and started asking questions, which Holl parried as best he could, but no members of the press were invited and it was difficult to avoid raising suspicions.[145] At the conference "the Board of Interdoc Youth found itself in the situation to explain, discuss and even to defend the aims and the purpose" of the new organization. To add to the difficulties, two journalists from KRO confronted Holl and Mennes after the conference, wanting an interview.[146] It was evident that basic questions such as "who is Interdoc Youth?" and "what does Interdoc Youth want?" still had to be answered, not just for the outside world but for the members themselves. An extraordinary board meeting was planned for the end of November in St Niklaas Waas, outside Brussels, to try to iron out these fundamentals, and it did produce a renewed sense of purpose. The central tasks would be *Youth Forum*, facilitating the Berlin seminars, and holding an annual international conference. The origins of IY would be sustained by establishing wider dialogue between students and young officers through seminars at military colleges, for which a meeting with German Ministry of Defence officials in The Hague in early February clarified the details.[147]

Added to this was the continuing ambition to focus on developments outside of Europe, with a conference on "Communist Strategy and Tactics towards the Third World" (focusing on Chinese and Soviet competition in the Subcontinent and the Indian ocean) planned for autumn 1970 in Oslo.[148] With Chou En-lai touring Africa during that same period, the timing was highly opportune. Holl duly stepped up his promotion of IY, showing a special interest in Sri Lanka and Japan.

Other issues split the group. Wolfgang Buchow recalled "a hard discussion" within Interdoc concerning the pros and cons of direct contacts with the East, a discussion which Van den Heuvel, Lades, and those "who wanted to solve the problem" eventually won against the "Cold Warriors".[149] There were also ambitions to extend IY to the US. It was Frank Barnett who suggested Roy Godson, then active with the NSIC and Assistant Professor of Government at Georgetown University, as the most appropriate contact.[150] Godson proved to be a willing linkman. He put Holl in touch with Irving Brown, the infamous trade union chief of the AFL–CIO's (American Federation of Labor–Congress of Industrial Organizations') International Affairs division, and tried to set up a visit by Americans to Sweden to counter the influence of a left-wing conference on the Vietnam War.[151] He then developed a film project, intending to interview refugees from the GDR with the Wall as a scenic backdrop. This became a joint NSIC–IY project designed to bring home to American audiences the reasons for a continuing US military presence in Western Europe, a position that was under threat from Senator Mike Mansfield's attempts to reduce US force levels there. Production was planned for September 1970 with Airlie Productions, and Holl did a lot of the groundwork to get official permission and prepare a group of Erlangen students to help out. With everything set to roll, Godson had to report in August that the project had to be postponed, and it never went ahead. Holl was justifiably upset: he had asked assistance from around 20 people and used all available contacts to secure political consent at both federal and regional levels.[152] While Godson was part of the Interdoc circle for a while – he attended the Noordwijk conference on "Radicalism and Security" in early 1970 – it was a similar story to the stop-start involvement of the Americans throughout Interdoc's existence. Godson confirmed what for Wolfgang Buchow was a hopeless attempt to bring the US in as a partner: "it is too far away with its thoughts and philosophies. I don't think the Americans were very interested, they always do their own thing."[153]

IY made gradual progress. Looking to generate publicity, Mennes and Holl sent a "Declaration of Interdoc Youth" to the EEC's (European Economic Community's) Hague Summit in December 1969 which announced that "consolidation of the EEC requires democratic direction through elected political representatives, and accordingly institutions such as the European Parliament and the Council of Ministers should operate with an appropriate constitution" and the Treaty of Rome should be amended accordingly.[154]

The first national IY conference was held by the Belgians at Leuven University at the end of January, with the intention that this would serve as a model for others. Holl was satisfied afterwards that "we have been accepted by the left students as discussion partners".[155] In March the IY board met in Strasbourg specifically to build links with the Council of Europe, involving presentations by the Council's human rights and youth commissions and a talk by Ian Tickle from Sager's Ost-Institut on clashing Soviet and Chinese approaches towards the third world (Tickle was also a key speaker for the planned autumn conference). Holl was especially pleased with the Council's hospitality, a positive sign that "will do no harm to our image".[156] The invitation for Holl and Mennes to attend the ICCS executive committee meeting in Vienna as observers that summer was an added token of international recognition.[157]

But indications of change were already brewing. With the arrival of the SPD government in 1969, it was no longer possible to assume automatic cooperation from Bonn. The autumn conference came under threat because Bundeswehr officers were now increasingly occupied with information campaigns in schools, and aircraft could no longer be guaranteed for transporting participants. Since the Norwegian Military Academy was not in tune with the proposed conference theme either, Oslo was abandoned as a location and the search began for an alternative (with Gutenfels Castle on the Rhine, used by the Willi Maurer Foundation-supported German–French Youth Association, the first choice).[158] Nevertheless, at the end of May 1970 a week-long IY seminar was held in West Berlin, where Rolf Buchow, Mennes, and Holl decided to cover not only the political identity of the city, as was usual, but also to plan ahead on *Kaderformung* and widening the recruitment of capable representatives.[159] Riots in West Berlin during early May, in protest against President Nixon's decision to bomb Cambodia, turned the divided city into a prime site for observing both New Left radicalism and old-style communism, since there was also a "visit to East Berlin for those who want to go there".[160] By June *Youth Forum*, which had been delayed due to higher-than-expected production costs, was ready to proceed with a print run of 6000 (in English, German, and French) to be distributed to schools, universities, public libraries, youth and student organizations, trade unions, and the media across Western Europe and beyond. But *Forum* would only go into full production when the IY board members had provided the necessary addresses from their respective countries, and this took time. Holl eventually announced at the end of August that the target of 6000 addresses had been reached, and the first issue was duly scheduled for October.[161]

From the beginning Interdoc Youth had faced a difficult task. Although interest in its purpose and activities did begin to spread, thanks to the promotional work of Holl, the constantly shifting locations and involvement of its members and the variable demands of student and working life meant that it was almost impossible to create a consistent, coherent organization with a stable base. Exams would literally get in the way of regular attendance for board members.[162] The task of holding this all together was beyond the means of one individual (Herman Mennes maintained IY contacts in the Netherlands but Holl maintained 90 per cent of the network), and administration absorbed time which should have been used for travelling and organizing. And just when there was optimism that something worthwhile was being created, the whole set-up came apart.

6
The Fallout from *Ostpolitik*

> Was Deutschland betrifft, so kann ich mich des Eindrucks nicht erwehren, dass es einem recht schwierigen Jahr entgegengeht. Übrigens möchte ich noch die Hoffnung aussprechen, dass die neue Regierungskoalition sich günstig auf die Entfaltung Deiner Arbeit auswirkt.
>
> Cees van den Heuvel, 1966[1]

The largest share of the Interdoc budget between 1963 and 1971 was provided by the Germans. In 1970 the German contribution was 605,300 guilders (about $150,000), more than 90 per cent of the total.[2] Despite a six-fold increase on the 1963 budget, Geyer was well aware that this was not enough to cover the necessary support staff in The Hague, hampering the ability of Interdoc to function as intended. Geyer also had trouble justifying the rising costs from early on.[3] The expansion of Interdoc Youth was an extra draw on resources. To cap it all, at the height of its activities, Interdoc's operations were suddenly placed under serious threat. This decision came suddenly and was wholly connected with the shift in West German foreign policy towards a rapprochement with the East.

Ostpolitik came out of a need for the Germans to grasp the German Question for themselves. The hardening of the East–West border, exemplified by the construction of the Berlin Wall in 1961, gave a false air of permanence to a situation which was untenable in the long term. The development of the European Economic Community raised the question of trade with the Soviet bloc. The shift in US nuclear strategy from "massive retaliation" to "flexible response" under President Kennedy had raised doubts about Washington's commitment to the all-out defence of Western Europe. No one understood this better than de Gaulle, who tried to ease Bonn's reliance on Washington through the Franco-German Treaty of January 1963 and initiated his own search for détente with a visit to Moscow in June 1966.[4] Looking to nudge Bonn towards more flexibility, President Lyndon Johnson publicly encouraged the West Germans to embrace détente. He subsequently delivered two "bridge-building" speeches, in May 1964 and again in October 1966, on the subject of improving East–West relations, referring in the first to building "bridges of increased trade, of ideas, of visitors, and of humanitarian aid", and in the second to "making Europe whole again" by achieving "a reconciliation with the East – a shift from the narrow concept of coexistence to the broader vision of peaceful engagement".[5] The US was not necessarily in the best position to lead this process, either. The CIA's response to Johnson's opening recognized that certain Western European allies "by virtue of history and economic factors" were "better qualified to undertake some aspects of the 'bridge building' and could be encouraged to expand their current role".[6] A major source for this way of thinking was Zbigniew Brzezinski, who had introduced the phrase "peaceful engagement" in an article with former Radio Free Europe adviser William Griffith in *Foreign Affairs* as early as 1961. Brzezinski saw the active stimulation of social change in the East as the only way to move away from both aggressive "liberation" and rigid status quo, and he pursued this line further as a member of the State Department's Policy Planning Staff during 1967.[7] Brzezinski was certainly a hardliner, seeing détente from the perspective of his Polish roots as a means to both undermine the Soviet Union and if necessary maintain the division of Germany.[8] But centripetal trends were certainly evident in the East. Romania under Nikolae Ceauşescu sought a more independent path within the Warsaw Pact, Yugoslavia continued to chart its own path, and Albania sided with Mao's China. Alliances were loosening, and Europeans began to look for ways to deal with their own predicament. At the forefront of this development were leading members of the German Social Democratic Party (SPD: Sozialdemokratische Partei Deutschlands).

In July 1963 – five months after the formation of Interdoc – the Mayor of West Berlin, Willy Brandt, and his adviser Egon Bahr spoke at a conference at the Tutzing Evangelical Academy, south of Munich. They took the opportunity to lay out the vision behind what would become *Neue Ostpolitik* under Brandt's leadership six years later. Since 1949 Bonn had held on to a negative, defensive approach to the East that offered no concessions and relied on the three Western occupying powers to maintain a "position of strength" against the Soviet Union. This had been severely tested during the Berlin crisis of 1958–61, when it appeared that Bonn's interests could potentially be negotiated away in the interest of European security. Brandt, who became Mayor of West Berlin in October 1957, had already used the term *Ostpolitik* in January 1958, and in a speech at Chatham House in March of that year he called for an "active coexistence" that meant abandoning the West's defensiveness and fear of communism.[9] In Tutzing Brandt aimed to seize the initiative and "break through the frozen front between East and West" by increasing social and economic contacts with the GDR and the rest of Central Europe. Bahr emphasized in turn the need for East and West to recognize each other's mutual interests, in doing so opening new paths to overcome diplomatic and military deadlock. He still referred to "the Zone", to stay within the limits of Bonn's official policy of non-recognition, but he saw a chance for "change through rapprochement" (*Wandel durch Annäherung*) and a transformation of the East by peaceful means. The status quo would be overcome through an approach of engagement that answered the needs of the people on both sides of the divide. It was to be a strategy of transformation simultaneously pursued both in the chambers of diplomacy and in German households themselves.[10]

Right from the beginning, therefore, the *colloques* and the emergence of Interdoc seemed to follow a path in synchronicity with the thinking of Brandt and Bahr. Others agreed that it was time to pursue change, both in the East and in the West. A European settlement required that Bonn abandon the Hallstein doctrine and its isolation of the GDR. The Protestant Church issued a memorandum in October 1965 that called for acceptance of the post-war boundaries (particularly Oder–Neisse) to reduce fears in the East (and, not incidentally, in the West) of a recidivist German nationalism. In the following years the Catholic Church – in the form of the Bensberger Kreis intellectual forum, which included Josef Ratzinger – sought a similar reconciliation with its Polish counterpart. By 1966 the German Liberal Party (FDP: Freie Demokratische Partei) had joined the SPD in rejecting German possession of nuclear weapons and calling for increased East–West trade.[11]

Trade was the principal avenue along which the ruling Christian Democrats (CDU) in the Federal Republic could contemplate change. With their coalition partner, the Christian Socialists (CSU), more determined to lay claim to the "lost lands" to the East, the CDU had little room for manoeuvre. Foreign trade between West Germany and Czechoslovakia, Hungary, Poland, and Romania was on an upward trend: from $371 million in 1958 to $603 million in 1964. Trade missions were established in 1963–64 in Warsaw, Budapest, Bucharest, and Sofia, staying within the bounds of the Hallstein doctrine but opening up the possibility of full diplomatic relations. During 1963–66 the CDU Chancellor Ludwig Erhard, unwilling to abandon Adenauer's "position of strength" policy of no compromise, sent mixed messages on what the purpose of these new links was. Various political and business interests were involved: connecting East and West, extending West German influence, increasing the East's dependence, and pure economic gain. Foreign Minister Gerhard Schröder defended the government's progress but cautiously stressed that the main danger "lies not so much in the fact that we might overlook but that we might overrate the changes in Eastern Europe and their significance".[12] Meanwhile, in the Soviet bloc itself the increasing need for West German credits and investments was causing intricate arguments on why such capitalist tendencies were beneficial.[13] The CIA had noted in late 1964 that Schroeder's "policy of movement" was a new development, but there was still no clear vision in Bonn as to how best to exploit the "ferment and fluidity in Eastern Europe".[14] It was exactly this dynamic of liberalization – disorientating as it was for the communist ideologues – that Interdoc wanted to engage with for the West's benefit. The 1966 information booklet *Ost-West-Begegnung in Frage und Antwort*, produced by von Grote's Arbeitsgruppe, proved a popular document in the Federal Republic at this time. The West German government was falling behind the opinion of its main Western allies and was in danger of becoming isolated. The BND and Interdoc, ahead of the politicians, were planning the way forward – but to implement it they needed support from Bonn.

The CDU–SPD "Grand Coalition" of December 1966 to September 1969, with Willy Brandt as Foreign Minister, registered the abandonment of Bonn's right to sole representation of the German people, a significant move that marked the official end of the Hallstein doctrine. The doctrine had been fully hollowed out by then anyway, and the view among West German intellectual circles in 1965–66 was that the time was right for a *geistige Auseinandersetzung*:

> Bonn should defend its social and political model aggressively in an open exchange of views with East German representatives. Free traffic in theatre ensembles, films, books, and newspapers across the borders would help diminish the creeping alienation of the divided German population.[15]

The delicacies of coalition politics, the GDR's counter-strategy to strengthen its own relations with Eastern European capitals, and the intransigence of the Brezhnev regime prevented major breakthroughs. Brandt did succeed in securing diplomatic relations with Romania in January 1967, but the hoped-for follow-up with the Czechs was ended by the Warsaw Pact invasion of August 1968.[16] The arrival of the SPD in government did bring a major reappraisal of the BND's role and purpose, as Gehlen noted in his memoirs.[17] As a result, uncertainties over the budget for Geyer's IIIF and von Grote's Arbeitsgruppe forced a temporary halt to the flow of cash from Munich to The Hague in early 1967.[18] But this was soon overcome and the confident outlook in Pullach was resumed. There was little expectation among the Interdoc circle that the SPD would go on to assume power on its own, or that this would mean a drastic reappraisal of their activities.

Interdoc could provide useful services in the context of a developing *Ostpolitik*: provision of factual information on the East, preparation for the increasing number of social contacts, opinion surveys on the effects of Soviet propaganda.[19] Wasn't this, after all, its very purpose? Hadn't they spent the previous decade refining their outlook towards this goal?[20] There was an air of optimism from 1966 onwards, with the expectation that Interdoc's approach could start to coincide with the official West German position. Von Hahn wrote jubilantly to Zanchi in August 1966 that the German Foreign Office under Schröder was showing signs of "a new Eastern policy".[21] Later that year von Hahn left The Hague for Bonn, where he became the

Deutsche Arbeitsgruppe representative tracking Grand Coalition policy from up close. An international Interdoc Advisory Council, first convened at the Zandvoort conference in September 1968, was assembled to give the network a more official appearance: the names included Crozier, Neil Elles of Common Cause, Nicolas Lang, Renato Mieli, Vittorio Vaccari, and Richard V. Allen of the Hoover Institution (Allen joined Henry Kissinger's National Security Council staff in late 1969). The September 1967 *colloque* at Bad Tönisstein, entitled 'Communist Reassessment of Capitalism, its Resultant Strategy and the Western Response", outlined the weaknesses of the other side. Soviet policy was now regarded as being deeply contradictory. Peaceful coexistence had evolved into on the one hand a search for cooperation by Western communist parties and international fronts with their non-communist counterparts, but on the other hand a hardening of intolerance towards deviationist tendencies within the bloc itself. While efforts could be made to ensure the continued isolation of communist groups in the West, the situation in the East paradoxically offered increasing opportunities to make an impact. As Geyer stated,

> This "meeting with the West" is taking place at a time when, in spite of the consolidation of the political systems, the ideological coordination of the population within the sphere of the satellite states is stagnant, and in the case of the Soviet Union, a frustration among the intelligentsia, or what is more significant, a certain ideological weariness is becoming noticeable. There is sufficient evidence for this statement [...][22]

Yet the Interdoc inner circle was not unanimous on this point. An interesting insight is given by a "Stasi" (GDR Ministry for State Security) report on the board meeting in Zandvoort prior to the conference on the New Left. This indicates that, while some felt Interdoc should provide "to a greater extent analysis and proposals for the politicians in dealing with the socialist countries", a majority insisted on maintaining an independent role as an information clearing house. Günter Triesch (mainly in opposition to Lades) stressed that contacts with the East had to be conducted "from a conception of 'confrontation' and not from a pathological search for the last remains of common feeling", but most of those present accepted that such contacts had to be pursued with a positive, offensive attitude and not defensively.[23]

Nevertheless the GDR still remained a dictatorship with a nefarious agenda to undermine the West. With Brandt taking Bonn in a new direction towards rapprochement, in 1967 Interdoc Berlin was officially established. For the next five years the Berlin office would run its own tours and training sessions for foreign visitors precisely to highlight the continuing negative consequences of the GDR regime, in contrast to the more emollient official line coming out of Bonn. From 1968 onwards Interdoc came under increasing surveillance from the GDR's national security apparatus. Following the ministerial council's issue of Befehl 40/68 ("the implementation of politically operative measures to eliminate the element of surprise and detect in time an acute threat of war"), Van Stolkweg and its many activities were placed under regular observation. From the perspective of GDR security, Interdoc represented exactly the "strengthened coordination of enemy intelligence, military and state agencies with the centres and institutions of political–ideological diversion and the increasing influence of their inflammatory and slanderous activities against the GDR and other socialist states".[24]

The hope that Interdoc could play a central role in the Federal Republic's new approach turned out to be seriously misguided. Gehlen's service remained distant from those at the centre of West German policy-making. The CDU–CSU governments of Adenauer and Erhard both refused to work closely with the BND, considering it neither important nor reliable. Erhard had deliberately removed the BND's liaison office from the Chancellery to emphasize the distance. In 1968 the first full review of BND activities was initiated by Karl Carstens, chief of staff of Chancellor Kurt Kiesinger's office, who felt that Gehlen had to step down to enable a fresh start. The Grand Coalition showed, as Kissinger put it, that the Social Democrats "were fit to govern", and after 1969 they were in the driving seat.[25] The untimely death of Fritz Erler in February 1967 also removed one of the principal contact persons for the BND at the top of the SPD. Erler's colleagues had much less interest in working closely with the BND, and the long-running suspicions harboured between Bonn and Munich – and the socialists and the security services – took a heavier turn. Not for nothing was the BND referred to as the *Bayern Nachrichtendienst*, especially as its main political contacts existed in the Christian Socialist Party (CSU). Parliamentary oversight via the Vertrauensmännergremium (oversight committee) increased dramatically during the first years of the SPD government. In an attempt to break down the barriers, Gehlen resigned in 1968 and his replacement, long-time adjutant Gerhard Wessel, initiated his own reorganization of the BND (carried out by the chief of section IV Administration, Eberhard Blum) and invited the SPD to appoint a vice-president. This was to be Dieter Blötz, the influential SPD politician from Hamburg. Geyer's apparatus was safe under Blum and Wessel. However, once the SPD assumed power at the end of 1969, Blötz and Horst Ehmke, the powerful successor to Carstens at the Chancellery and Federal Minister for Special Affairs, would oversee a more radical restructuring of the service.[26]

The collapse and rebirth of Interdoc UK

From late 1965 onwards Interdoc UK was a holding operation with Ellis as "central point", receiving minimal support from IRD and Common Cause (CC) to keep the office ticking over. British business was simply not interested enough in *international* communism to make Interdoc a viable venture. Looking to interact more with British government, corporate, and academic interests, a conference was held at the University Arms Hotel in Cambridge in September 1966. The topic – "East–West Confrontation in Africa" – reflected the ongoing interest of both IRD and big business in the threat posed by Soviet and Chinese communist strategy on that continent, and it involved surveys of these subversive activities and British, French, and German responses. The result was an in-depth assessment that highlighted on the one hand Russian and Chinese failures to benefit more from the processes of decolonization and on the other the dangers of Western complacency in response.[27] With financial backing from IRD, Shell, Unilever, CC, and the Economic League (EL), Cambridge went well. Brian Biggin, IRD's participant in the event, noted that the Germans seemed "obsessed unduly with Soviet achievements" and "the French and the Dutch still feel the grave sense of the loss of their colonial empires", but he was impressed by the range of Interdoc academic, business, and military contacts in the UK. He concluded that "it was useful for us to show our face there for the first time" (no IRD representative had attended an Interdoc conference before).[28]

Nevertheless the conference was not enough to consolidate the Interdoc UK situation. The first problem was personnel. Ellis was forced to retire from his Interdoc post in early 1967. He planned to continue as board member and work from the Norfolk Street office, but finding a suitable replacement turned out to be a difficult business. While Ellis's withdrawal was presented as being on health grounds, there is more than a hint in the documents that both MI6 and IRD suddenly wanted to withdraw from the set-up agreed in 1964. Not given a specific reason, Van den Heuvel speculated that "they became afraid after what happened to their American colleagues and that they want to lie low for some time", a reference to the fallout from revelations in *Ramparts* and the *New York Times* of CIA links with the National Student Association, the Congress for Cultural Freedom, and other public organizations.[29] But there were other reasons, which Ellis openly shared with Van den Heuvel: doubts about Ellis's past had not gone away easily, and during the transition of MI6 leadership from Dick White to John Rennie in 1967 Ellis was once again the target of an investigation "in which inquiries were made regarding me of your people, and in US and among other former colleagues, which might have done me a great deal of harm".[30]

Since Interdoc shared the Norfolk Street address with Common Cause, the latter agreed to maintain the office, and at a CC board meeting in May (with Van den Heuvel and von Grote both present) it was agreed that Common Cause would become Interdoc's London representative. Although a logical move, it neither solved the main problem of the loss of the personal link with both IRD and MI6, nor recognized the fact that neither were keen on direct contact with Common Cause. Contacts with the National Union of Students, the Labour Party, and the trade unions would not be assisted by this arrangement. Negotiations with MI6's Dennis Ambler led to a communications channel via the British Embassy in The Hague, but Van den Heuvel was very dissatisfied.[31] The British operation was slipping from merely ad hoc to outright messy.

With Interdoc as a whole stepping up operations in the late 1960s, Van den Heuvel remained resolutely determined that Britain should be a part of this expansion. Time after time he lamented the lack of local support and the fact that IRD, MI6, and the Economic League failed to recognize the value of the Dutch OWI or the German Verein. It took almost a year to find a replacement for Ellis as London contact man, and significantly enough it was Shell who provided him. Brian Trench was sounded out first, but it was Bertram Hesmondhalgh who agreed to take on the role for one year for a fee of £1000 plus expenses. A former Foreign Office employee and with multiple business contacts via Shell, Hesmondhalgh seemed ideal to drum up support. It proved to be another false dawn. IRD, facing increasing scrutiny of its budget and "under more or less direct Johnson [MI6] control", backed off from guaranteeing his salary, which would have to be covered from The Hague.[32] Interdoc UK had been unable to ground itself in the British scene, despite the valiant efforts of Ellis. IRD felt it added little to their cause, and MI6 avoided too close an association.

A distribution list for Interdoc publications in Britain dating from 1968 indicates a limited but influential collection of names: Brigadier W.F.K. Thompson and David Floyd of the *Daily Telegraph*, the MPs John Biggs-Davison and Geoffrey Rippon, Walter Laqueur, Edward Shils of *Minerva*, the *Observer*'s Edward Crankshaw, and Robert Conquest, while the Griffin Press Bureau (also located at 2–3 Norfolk Street) was used to channel materials to the international departments of the Labour (Gwyn Morgan), Liberal, and Conservative parties, the Trades Union Congress (TUC), and the National Union of Students (Geoff Martin). Distribution of materials across UK universities – particularly through the expanding Eastern European and Soviet Studies network at the newer universities (Warwick, Essex, Sussex, Reading, Southampton, Leeds) – was increasing.[33] With a tentative committee in mind that would include Crozier, Conquest, Leonard Shapiro, and representatives from the Institute for Strategic Studies (ISS), the TUC, and the Conservative Party, Hesmondhalgh set to work to sound out interest in such an East–West Study Group. The effects of communist propaganda on trade and investments were now the key, as he explained: "Companies, particularly international ones, will be interested in an organization which by exposing the ill consequences of Marxist economic theory and practice helps to protect their investments overseas and to counter the dangerously growing semi-marxist attitude to economic and commercial affairs by a number of Western governments." Yet the opposite happened: business and government baulked at an "anti-communist drive" that "might militate against trade interests with the East". He received the predictable response from the Foreign Office: they were already doing enough in this field, either through IRD or the Great Britain–USSR and Great Britain–Eastern Europe Associations. Hesmondhalgh's request for £10,000 was out of the question, since only £500 a year for specific projects could be made available. Hesmondhalgh then approached the British United Industrialists, a discreet funding channel for both the Economic League and the Conservative Party, but instructed Van den Heuvel: "Please do not talk to others about the BUI organisation."[34] Once again, Interdoc was being pushed to the right in its search for partners.

In August 1968 the situation was already deemed hopeless. Hesmondhalgh's position was set to be terminated at the end of the year, three months early, with little achieved, and Ellis was once again holding the fort.[35] In the same month Van den Heuvel's relations with IRD took a turn for the worse. The Dutchman had been distributing IRD material without their authorization to contacts abroad: Bertil Häggman in Sweden, Knut Rosdahl in Denmark, Hans Graf in Zurich, and Liu Yuan-tao in Taiwan. IRD's distribution was carefully monitored, and the personnel who oversaw it abroad were often MI6 or, in the Commonwealth, MI5. Interdoc agreed to stop doing this if IRD would continue to send the material direct, but that would mean revealing that The Hague had in fact been distributing unattributable Foreign Office papers, a serious faux pas.[36] The incident increased the determination of Nigel Clive, the head of IRD since 1966, to break off relations. In late 1968 the Foreign Office's Colin Maclaren made a tour of IRD's West European operations to assess their continuing value and "purge" the distribution list, under orders of Nigel Clive.[37] A frank talk with Van den Heuvel followed in January 1969, after which Maclaren set in motion the end of the working relationship, "although there was no reason to distrust Interdoc or its manager", and he actually reported back being "most impressed" by the Interdoc operation.[38] By October the British Embassy had regained full responsibility for sending out IRD material to Dutch recipients. Although the Netherlands was still seen as "a strong bridgehead in our campaign to extend our European role", Interdoc was no longer considered part of this ambition.[39]

Matters improved somewhat when Clive retired in late 1969. Encouraged by James Welser and Colin Maclaren, Geyer visited London with Van den Heuvel in October to meet up with IRD and Common Cause and set the record straight.[40] The visit coincided with the appointment on 1 October of a reliable successor to Ellis as Interdoc representative: Walter Bell. Bell and Ellis knew each other from British Security Coordination days in New York in 1941, when Bell was MI6 liaison officer with Bill Donovan's Office of Strategic Services. Bell had moved on to be private secretary to Lord Inverchapel in Washington in 1946–49 before holding several appointments across Africa, India, and the Caribbean. Bell came out of retirement for a "probation" period with Ellis in early 1969.[41] Holl described him as an ideal softly-softly frontman who "made a living of keeping quiet", but Bell also developed strong opinions, soon distancing himself from Common Cause and abandoning the Norfolk Street office to work from home. Ellis stayed in the background as part of the network, continuing with translation work and information gathering as health permitted, and was even asked by the CIA to write "a confidential history of the early days of OSS".[42]

There was enough reason for Geyer's optimism. A carefully worded letter to von Grote from early 1968 had revealed not only Geyer's dismay with Clive's leadership of IRD, but also his intention "to go over his head to influence the course of events". By early 1970, with Clive gone, Geyer could remark that "it seems as if we have now achieved a breakthrough in England".[43] Yet within three years IRD would have its budget cut by 60 per cent, ending its effectiveness.[44] And within two months Geyer himself was out of the BND.

The end of BND involvement

The impending election victory of the SPD created a noticeable difference in attitude from the German side of Interdoc. Crozier already noted more caution with regard to the Soviet Union at the Deidesheim conference in September 1969.[45] Interdoc showed that it was moving with the times, holding a conference in West Berlin in March 1970 (*"Anerkennung der DDR?"*) that brought together various perspectives from around Europe on the implications of diplomatic recognition of the GDR.[46] But the first victim of the SPD's heavy hand, after Gehlen, was to be Geyer himself. IIIF's views on East–West *Konfrontation* did not fit in with the SPD's outlook of "change through rapprochement". Above all, Geyer's attitude that large-scale contacts with the East should be conducted did not fit with the more restricted political manoeuvring of the SPD leadership, and it is obvious that the Social Democrats in Bonn would not tolerate part of the intelligence apparatus propagating views that did not necessarily support the government line. The late 1960s were rife with stories of CIA manipulation of public opinion, and the SPD was determined to control any similar activities in the Federal Republic. Positive contacts between Geyer, former CDU chancellor Kurt Kiesinger, and SPD party chair Herbert Wehner were not enough to bridge the divide, and the fallout was swift. Still optimistic in February 1970, by April – having contributed to Interdoc's Radicalism and Security conference that month – Geyer had resigned. Deeply disappointed about the changed political attitude, he departed under cover of poor health to avoid the professional and institutional upheaval he knew was coming. For Geyer, the loss of Interdoc was especially bitter, as he observed the continuation of *Ostpolitik* and the improvement of relations between the Federal Republic and the GDR without any apparent awareness of the dangers involved. He continued lecturing and writing in the security field on a freelance basis with the Munzinger Archive and the Ost-Akademie in Munich. Although he remained on friendly terms with both Kernig and Lades there was no further working relationship with them, and Geyer's contacts with the BND were well and truly cut.[47] Out of respect, his former BND colleagues retained the term "Goslar" to designate the International Communism working group within headquarters. Geyer did follow closely Van den Heuvel's efforts to keep Interdoc afloat, but they drifted apart. His last letter among Van den Heuvel's papers fittingly quotes Bonnemaison: *"survivre, c'est vaincre"*.[48]

In April 1970 Van den Heuvel, together with von Hassell and von Grote, had a meeting with "K" (BND) to discuss the future without Geyer. A discussion paper for the meeting emphasized the necessity of "an instrument for psychopolitical debate" in a situation where the West sought "the expansion of freedom" in the East while the East intensified its "ideological subversion" of the West. Van den Heuvel made the case that Interdoc had served Bonn's interests well by spreading "German information and documentation – without a German stamp – over the whole world". "K" agreed, but the biggest doubts concerned the role of the BND in this setup. Geyer's section IIIF was going to be split, with responsibilities and staff transferred to either BND headquarters or private bodies, such as Kernig's outfit in Freiburg and the Stiftung Wissenschaft und Politik, founded by Gehlen's former chief of analysis, Klaus Ritter, in 1962.[49] Asked about possible successors, the Dutchman could only say that the removal of Geyer was "not only a personal tragedy but also a serious professional loss" and no one could come close to replacing him. The meeting was conducted in "a very open atmosphere" and Van den Heuvel came away encouraged that the future was secure.[50] Blötz confirmed in May that Interdoc was going to be "outsourced" (*ausgegliedert*) but it was uncertain exactly to where.[51] Geyer was devastated. A letter to Van den Heuvel the following month reveals a deeply disappointed and disillusioned man, defeated by political machinations in Bonn and Munich and saddened that he had left his friend with Interdoc "in a critical situation".[52]

In June 1970 Geyer's successor, Herr Wiggers, announced that the intended budget for 1970, 600,000 guilders, would be guaranteed (as was the income of 1,000,000 guilders for the Arbeitsgruppe), but within a week of this meeting the amount was reduced to 540,000, with everything being shifted to a month-by-month evaluation of running projects.[53] Wiggers added the following:

> The salaries would ideally be paid not in cash but by bank transaction and that due to the increasing insecurity Mr Spruijt [a former BVD officer who became OWI's accountant], if he should collect larger amounts from the bank, should be accompanied by a second person (ideally in a car).[54]

Dietmar Töppel's drives up the autobahn with bags of money for The Hague were now definitely over.

By September the situation was looking much more serious, with German funding as a whole now in doubt. In response Johannes Hoheisel stated that "Interdoc's work will have to be made more commercial", and "a financial contribution from the American side must be striven for". Even the Germans were now forced to accept that this predominantly European operation had to turn across the Atlantic to maintain itself. Research, publications, and conferences would have to be shared with "friendly institutes": Crozier's Institute for the Study of Conflict (ISoC), Sager's Ost-Institut (OI), Albertini's *Est-Ouest*, and Barnett's NSIC.[55] The reality of the situation was only presented to the wider Interdoc circle at the Rimini conference on "Soviet Activities in the Mediterranean" in October 1970.

The background to Rimini is worth recording. The first *colloque* to take place in Italy – the intention to meet in that country had been there since 1963[56] – it turned out to be the last for the organization in its original form. Yet the initial push for a Mediterranean focus came from Spain. While Vaccari had provided some early contacts, Van den Heuvel did not make a visit himself until February 1969. The contacts were then coming through the Centre Européen de Documentation et d'Information (CEDI), the transnational pan-European Catholic organization with Otto von Habsburg at its centre. BND–CEDI links had a long history, including a deal to use Radio Nacional de España for German-language broadcasts to Eastern Europe from 1956 onwards.[57] Van den Heuvel's principal host in 1969 was CEDI's Manuel Thomas de Carranza, the head of the Ministry of Foreign Affairs' Servicio Exterior del Movimiento, an outreach organization aimed at promoting orderly political life in Spain. Carranza, who was also connected with the WACL, proposed a conference bringing together various national perspectives on the Mediterranean as a contested region in East–West relations.[58] Ultimately it was the unresolved problem of Gibraltar that led the Spanish to withdraw as the conference hosts, and de Carranza passed the responsibility of acting as host to Ivan Matteo Lombardo, the Italian Atlantic Committee chairman and Ligue Internationale de la Liberté/European Freedom Council frontman.[59] The speakers were a mix of Interdoc stalwarts, such as Rostini's associate Nicolas Lang and Brian Crozier, with new partners including Israeli diplomat Katriel Katz and Lebanese publisher/author Jebran Chamieh. Another was Eric Waldman, the man who had initially secured the link with the Gehlen Organization and the US Army back in 1946. Waldman, an Austrian by birth, had left US Army Intelligence in 1949 and become an academic. By the late 1960s he was an expert in post-World War II German affairs at the University of Calgary, and he became a regular speaker at Interdoc conferences during 1969–70.[60]

Other speakers were Brigadier W.F.K. Thompson, former Italian Ambassador to the USSR Carlo Alberto Straneo, and German journalist Dr Wolfgang Höpker. Foreign affairs correspondent for *Christ und Welt* since 1958, for the previous decade Höpker had concentrated on the expansion of Soviet influence in Africa and the Mediterranean region.[61] Overall the conference emphasized the need for more NATO attention towards its southern flank and an appreciation of the linkage between Soviet strategy across the whole European theatre (for the Soviet General Staff, northern and southern Europe were "the pincers of the nutcracker encircling Western Europe"). Western divisions and weakness caused as much concern as the relative strength of the USSR itself, and the conference's effort to strike unity among representatives of Mediterranean nations – including Franco's Spain – and to overcome the Arab–Israeli divide was the real message: the need to oppose Soviet manoeuvres should trump all other issues.[62]

Rimini could have provided a stepping stone for Interdoc to branch out in new directions, but the event was instead overshadowed by a crisis board meeting chaired by Einthoven. The message was given that the Deutsche Arbeitsgruppe could not guarantee any funds for 1971, so that Interdoc had no choice but to find new financial sources (as the board minutes bluntly put it: "(USA!)"). The number of regular periodicals would be reduced to one (*East–West Contacts*), special publications would be continued predominantly in English only, the Berlin courses would be cut back, and Interdoc Youth would be reorganized. Determined on the continuing value of their project in the context of *Ostpolitik* and détente, all present agreed to reconstruct Interdoc and maintain the coordinating function among the various national institutes. Van den Heuvel reckoned that the immediate audience for Interdoc's information services via its international network was around 30,000 people. Walter Bell kept spirits up with the intention of organizing a conference in Brighton the following year, and interest was now coming from Spain.[63] Nevertheless it was a genuine crisis, as Van den Heuvel admitted to Hans Ulmer of the Swiss Aufklärungsdienst: "we have no idea how things will develop and what the outcome will be".[64]

Prior to his US trip in November 1970 Van den Heuvel wrote to Ehmke at the Chancellery to explain Interdoc's purpose and his conviction that "the goal of Interdoc fitted well into the thinking of German *Ostpolitik*, through dealing on the one hand with a realistic analysis of the East–West problematic and on the other hand with the promotion of East–West contacts". The intention was to compensate for the loss of German finance from American sources: if the German contribution could be maintained, there was even a chance to expand operations. The reply was hopeful: discussions were being conducted within the government to find a solution.[65] On 3 December 1970 a meeting took place in The Hague between Einthoven, Van den Heuvel, Hoheisel, and Gerhard Wessel, Gehlen's successor as head of the BND, with Dr Meier (chief of BND Acquisitions section) and Hans Büchler (BND station chief in The Hague and liaison officer with the BVD) in attendance. Wessel declared that Interdoc had come about through a personal agreement between Einthoven, Gehlen, and "a leading member of the French Service", but times had now changed. Both he and Ehmke were convinced of the value of Interdoc's work, but the link with the BND would have to be broken and another apparatus (*Aufhänger*) had to be found. Future cooperation in terms of the provision of information for Interdoc periodicals was not ruled out, but would have to be assessed on a case-by-case basis. The BND would grant a further 300,000 guilders for 1971, the last such payment. The BND represented not only money but also the prime source of information and analysis on the communist world. Van den Heuvel tried to keep the door open to the German Service's expertise, but the message was clear: you are now on your own. Wessel's last act was to invite Einthoven and Van den Heuvel to a lunch on 1 March 1972 – almost exactly nine years after the official signing of the Interdoc statutes – to celebrate their former cooperation. Needless to say, he offered to pay their travel costs.[66]

This set in train discussions with Ehmke, the Chancellery, and the Ministry of Science for a new institutional–financial construction. The outcome was that Claus Kernig's new centre in Freiburg, the Institut für Sozialgeschichte und Systemvergleich (Institute for Social History and System Analysis), would take over some of IIIF's functions and become the new go-between with Interdoc. Kernig held great prestige through his publications with Herder Verlag, and this was cemented further thanks to the epic six-volume *Sowjetsystem und demokratische Gesellschaft: eine vergleichende Enzyklopädie*, which appeared during 1968–72. The funding, channelled from the Deutsche Forschungsgesellschaft through the Ministry, would include an annual sum of around 300,000 guilders for Interdoc to act as the Freiburg Institute's international wing. In anticipation of this development Van den Heuvel opened a bank account in West Berlin for future transactions. The Arbeitsgruppe would remain in existence, leaving its Habsburgerplatz address for a new location on Munich's Schleißheimerstraße. The Interdoc board was reconstituted to reflect a leaner institution (both Crozier and Neil Elles withdrew) and members of the Interdoc–OWI team sought alternative appointments: Holl returned to Germany, to Triesch's Deutsches Industrie-Institut (soon to become the Institut des Deutsches Wirtschaft), Couwenberg occupied a professorial chair in the philosophy of politics, culture, and religion at the Erasmus University in Rotterdam, Mennes went to the Dutch Defence Study Centre, and Van Oort joined the University of Amsterdam.[67] It looked as if Interdoc's German base had been secured, with ambitions for being the international wing of the Institut für Sozialgeschichte and continuing as the fulcrum between various national institutes (including plans for a European journal).

A Stasi report on these deliberations – probably coming from an *Inoffizieller Mitarbeiter* (IM) working with Kernig – made a telling observation:

> If no satisfactory solution regarding the West German financial grants for supporting the work of Interdoc is found, the view of the West German political scientists involved [Kernig and Lades] was that Interdoc

would increasingly become financed by the American secret services, which would complicate cooperation between Interdoc and West German institutions.[68]

In December 1971 Kernig announced that, while there was no serious problem, it would not be possible to provide funding from his Institute immediately in January 1972. Thinking that the 300,000-guilder budget was only delayed, van den Heuvel continued Interdoc business as normal, but requested from Kernig a clarification of the working relationship between Freiburg and The Hague.[69] This never came. Instead Kernig, who had said as late as April 1972 that everything was proceeding according to plan, eventually let it be known in June that the Deutsche Forschungsgesellschaft would after all not allow any of the funding going to Freiburg to be channelled to Interdoc. Kernig had received a definitive no from the Chancellery, and he saw his own budget for Freiburg collapse from DM 1.3 m to DM 300,000. For the first six months of 1972, Interdoc and the OWI had been running on an assumed budget of 437,000 guilders, when only 137,000 would now be available. Since the OWI had already provided Interdoc with a loan of 60,000 guilders to keep it afloat during this period, both institutes were facing bankruptcy and closure by the end of September.[70]

Van den Heuvel could not hide his frustration with Kernig's lack of urgency and clearly felt let down by his long-time German partners. Desperate measures were called for. Support staff in Van Stolkweg were laid off and publications brought to a halt. Einthoven reached out to Prince Bernhard one more time, reminding him of his support ten years before to get the show on the road in the Netherlands. Van den Heuvel urged Brigadier Thompson to persuade Prime Minister Edward Heath to sanction a British contribution (Thompson tried, but to no avail) and wrote directly to Ehmke to explain the predicament he was in as a result of the broken German budgetary promise. As a legitimate damages claim he requested the sum of 60,000 guilders from the minister to literally save the institutes.[71] It was Ehmke who saved the day, when in a letter at the end of September he regretted the situation and claimed it came from "developments outside of my sphere of business". The one-off payment of 60,000 would go through.[72] It was the minimum Ehmke could have done, since although he became Federal Minister for Research and Technology later the same year he did not intend to offer any further help. Nevertheless it was enough to bring Interdoc back from the brink. The accounts for 1972 ultimately showed receipts amounting to the equivalent of £31,000 and costs totalling £36,000, leaving a deficit of £5000 that was duly picked up by the OWI. On paper Interdoc in 1973 would consist of no more than Van den Heuvel, two clerical staff, and Bell. The goal now was to rebuild by bringing in an equal annual financial contribution from the US, the UK, West Germany, and the Netherlands.[73] Looking ahead and ever optimistic, Van den Heuvel noted in 1972 that

> It is realized more and more in responsible circles that the work of Interdoc is useful and absolutely necessary in a time of changing East–West relations. The problem for Interdoc is how these feelings can be turned into material support.[74]

Interdoc Berlin

The fact that the contest over Berlin attracted an increasing number of Western, Asian, and African visitors to the city turned it into a location of supreme importance in the Cold War information field. In the inter-departmental discussions of the late 1950s West Berlin was marked out for a special role in psychological operations. Writing in 1957, von Dellingshausen saw not only the need to work closely with the private sector in this endeavour, but also that "a connection with intelligence-related missions would be avoided". The Studienbüro, with the BMG directing it via the Büro für politische Studien in Cologne, was originally intended to make the most of Berlin as a showcase for the East–West confrontation.[75] DM 9 million were invested annually by the Federal Republic to accommodate foreign visitors to West Berlin, as a way of demonstrating the clear distinction between East and West to the outside world (an approach obviously enhanced by the arrival of the Berlin Wall in August 1961).[76] SOEV ran its first study trip to West Berlin (involving 11 Dutch students, among them Pieter Koerts) as early as 1963.[77]

In January 1967 a further expansion was secured with the opening of "Interdoc Berlin", a seminar centre under the supervision of Rolf Buchow established by the Verein specifically for the visits of international groups. Buchow, a freelance journalist focusing on the GDR and a Berliner by origin, had close relations with the BND. A Russian-speaking civil servant in the information service during World War II, he moved to the American sector of the city when released from a Russian prisoner-of-war camp in 1946. Buchow worked with the BBC's West Berlin office and often wrote for the press, but much of this was done anonymously to avoid unwelcome publicity. Working officially out of his Büro (private office) on the Possweg in Zehlendorf, he was deeply involved with the community of refugees from the East and was also involved in getting people over the Wall. This was a very stressful existence – his son Wolfgang remembers West Berlin police keeping their home under observation to avoid a kidnapping – and it meant "dealing with people who are always in danger [...] this was a ride on a razorblade".[78] Einthoven, referring to the personnel who would join Geyer and von Grote in IIIF and the Verein, remarked in January 1962 that "whether Buchow will join us is uncertain".[79] But Buchow's local knowledge and contacts were too valuable, and he did not want to transfer to the BND apparatus in Munich.

How tense Buchow's existence was can be gauged from documents obtained from the archives of the Ministry for State Security (the Stasi) in Berlin. Buchow was under observation by GDR agents from the early 1950s onwards due to his association with Werner Bader and his so-called Publikationsgruppe B, a well-organized semi-clandestine group that distributed anti-communist brochures. Bader's group was well funded by the CIA and soon developed close relations with the BMG.[80] Already active during the WFDY Festival in Berlin in the summer of 1951, Buchow and Bader formed the group's editorial committee. A series of reports by Stasi *Gesellschaftlicher Mitarbeiter* (GM) "Heinz" (Heinz Gellner), who associated himself with the group, indicate that repeated attempts were made to discover how they functioned and by what means they smuggled materials into the GDR.[81] In 1954 Buchow, together with Bader and five others, established the Arbeitsgemeinschaft für Ostfragen (AfO), an official non-governmental organization designed to extend the impact of their work via official channels. The impulse was clear: "The fact that a majority of the members of this group are displaced persons explains the theme of these discussions: Ostpolitik." The Stasi was on top of it from the beginning, since the secretary in whose house the meetings were held – Heinz Gellner – was an informer. The AfO, which focused on issues such as the Oder–Neisse border, "Agents–Saboteurs–Schemers", "the tasks for a civil movement for the reunification of Germany in Berlin and the Soviet-occupied zone", and "Is Resistance still possible?", had close relations with the large community of Germans forced out of Central and Eastern Europe at the end of World War II, as well as with the West Berlin wings of the SPD and the BMG. Politically this was a highly fractious group, and disputes over the unrelenting recidivism of some (for instance, the Berliner Landesverband der Heimatvertriebenen) caused the untimely dissolution of the AfO in October 1955.

Buchow comes across as a very cautious operator with quite some knowledge of intelligence tradecraft. Gellner described him as "by nature a very closed-off person, more of a scientific analyst who says no more than necessary for the immediate work at hand".[82] By 1959 he was being tracked under the Stasi's enemies-of-the-state "Reichskanzler" programme, in which it was stated that he had been "Agent des englischen Geheimdienstes" – or at least of one or other "imperialistischen Geheimdienstes" – for the previous ten years. After the AfO Buchow teamed up with the Volksbund für Frieden und Freiheit and joined the Studienbüro, maintaining his anti-GDR information work under cover of his status as a journalist. Constant surveillance and the dangers of West Berlin caused him to spend much of his time on the road in West Germany, an existence which made him a difficult target for the GDR's services.[83]

By keeping his West Berlin base Buchow became a central point for Interdoc and the BND, so that he, Lades, and Kernig formed a kind of "brain trust" on the German side of the network, with von Grote the titular head of the group and Geyer and Van den Heuvel the organizers. As Wolfgang put it years later, "they used his knowledge on the GDR, its politics, communism, Leninism, everything. Berlin was to see it in reality, not just to talk about it [...] to have seminars and then show the Wall to see what results communist politics can bring."[84] The Berlin outpost became central to Interdoc's purpose, as is evident from Uwe Holl's comments in March 1970:

> It is emphasized that a visit to Berlin, in particular for young people, makes possible a "practical investigation of the object", namely what it means for all people if two different ideologies are based in a cramped space [...] Our activity in Berlin is preoccupied with providing practical visual lessons of the totality of the East–West problematic.[85]

By drawing on the expertise of Berliners from local government, business, academia, and the media, the seminars connected theoretical discussions on Cold War "confrontation" directly with day-to-day reality. Interdoc Berlin was essentially Buchow and one other staff member (Klaus Riedel), and they made use of both the Europa-Haus on the Bismarckallee and the Haus der Zukunft in Zehlendorf for group seminars. Interdoc Berlin began with six seminars in 1967 for Dutch, American, British, Belgian, and Danish participants, expanding to nine by 1969 (involving 250 participants from 13 countries).[86] Rolf Buchow also had close relations with the Swiss Aufklärungsdienst (Hans Ulmer), who wanted to learn everything they could about communist infiltration methods and the reality of the threat. Regular trips were made between West Berlin and Zurich.

In 1968, 1969, and 1970 the OWI ran training courses for the new intake of trainee diplomats at the Dutch Ministry of Foreign Affairs, which included participation in the Interdoc Berlin seminars.[87] The Dutch SIB organized group visits, and annual trips of American students from the elite Nijenrode Business School (at the time still known as the Nederlands Opleidings Instituut voor het Buitenland) were run by Buchow and hosted by the Europa-Haus in Berlin from 1967 onwards.[88] The Nijenrode visits ("the high point of their year in Europe") continued at least up to 1977, hosted by the European Academy (the former Europa-Haus).[89] The unique location of West Berlin made these study trips a popular item, and with the arrival of Interdoc Youth the Interdoc office under Buchow was envisaged as a "key link" between the junior and senior apparatus.[90] However, an assessment at the end of 1969 raised the point that some participants either did not know enough German or showed little interest in the political dimension, leading Uwe Holl to complain that "we must find ways to improve the quality of participants".[91]

The end of Interdoc Berlin and Interdoc Youth

In mid-October 1970, with location fixed (the Europahaus in Bad Marienberg) and promotion in full swing (Holl had invited Professor Richard Löwenthal as keynote speaker), Holl was told that the Interdoc Youth (IY) conference would have to be postponed until 1971.[92] The message was that no further developments could take place before the main Interdoc conference in Rimini, Italy, at the end of October. Holl, already forced to backtrack on the film project, now somehow had to save face and tell all IY participants, with one month to go, that the long-awaited event had to wait. But Rimini brought far worse news. Interdoc Berlin was praised for its services, with Buchow having run 32 seminars for 740 participants (students, politicians, military officers, and academics) from Britain, Norway, Denmark, Switzerland, Belgium, and the Netherlands over the previous four years. Interdoc Youth, on the other hand, was considered expendable, and no further funds would be available as of 31 December 1970. *Youth Forum*, ready to roll off the press, had to be abandoned, the conference would not take place, and Holl would be out of a job. The future of the 35,000 guilders still in the IY budget was "unclear", and Holl remarked bitterly that "the question of the relation between Interdoc and Interdoc Youth has become irrelevant".[93]

Holl later recalled being taken completely by surprise, and it was a major blow.[94] IY had been a BND creation, and it was now the BND that cut it down after less than two years, just when it was starting to make real progress. Others were less affected. Before Rimini, Van den Heuvel admitted to having been a sceptic from the beginning. The purpose of IY had originally been to support Interdoc Senior in the same activities, but its shift to dealing with third-world issues was "much too wide, much too vague, and diverged from the real purpose: East–West relations". This had already been evident at the Richmond conference, and a separate IY prevented its leading figures from playing a full role in Interdoc proper (something that Jim Daly also disliked). Van den Heuvel clearly felt that Holl had been given too much unsupervised freedom to go his own way. If IY was to continue in any form, it would be fully under his own direction.[95]

Determined not to lose what they had created, the IY board members present in Rimini talked of contingency plans to maintain their circle in a new arrangement centred on C.E. Riggert (Volk und Verteidigung, the sister organization to Hornix's Dutch outfit) and Hans Lades, and "should a financial basis be found, it is planned to establish IY as a separate organization under another name".[96] Holl, reckoning that around 100,000 guilders a year were necessary to maintain IY "at the present level of activities", saw no real options apart from contingency plans. Lades soon proposed hosting three seminars in 1971 in Erlangen to keep the group together, and Holl decided that all efforts needed to be focused on getting *Youth Forum* out, in order to "secure continuity between conferences without a permanent office as we have now".⁹⁷ Holl drafted a contingency plan. IY would become the Den Haager Kreis (The Hague Study Group), and the emphasis drew heavily on the 1969 EEC summit in The Hague to which Holl and Mennes had sent a resolution:

> The "Den Haager Kreis" exists of a group of scholars [sic], students, young executives (originally the IY-Board) who aim at: collecting, analysing and spreading news on Europe's future position between/with East and West [...] It is the aim of the group:
>
> – to foster the European idea
> – to analyse prospects and dangers of European unity
> – to create a consciousness for European terms of reference
> – to create an understanding for the problems of all European countries affected by this process.⁹⁸

Holl remained positive: "there is no reason to believe that 'all is over' as we thought under the first impression of the shock", he wrote to Per Paust in mid-November, "I think that we derived enough strength from the fat years which will help us to survive the meagre years".⁹⁹ A meeting in Erlangen between Wolfgang Buchow, Gläsker, von Grote, Lades, his Erlangen colleagues Baron von und zu Aufseß and Dietrich Grille, Mennes, Holl, and Jim Daly (the only one outside the German–Dutch circle present) in mid-December decided that, while Mennes would take over IY documentation and Benelux activities at Van Stolkweg, operations would be moved to Erlangen and run by Grille, Gläsker, and Buchow. Dr Grille, a refugee from the GDR and a friend of Rolf Buchow, had coordinated work on political citizenship and youth work at Erlangen since 1965, later becoming professor of political science and philosophy in Nuremberg. Support would be sought via the Friedrich Ebert Foundation and the Deutsche Gesellschaft für auswärtige Politik. Beyond this, however, there is a sense that the group lacked any real direction. Talk of "an exchange-agency for political scientists" based on "Promotion of Peace" or "Inter-Governmental Studies" was vague and unlikely to attract much interest from potential financial benefactors.¹⁰⁰ Of necessity, priorities changed, and people started to move on. Holl returned to Triesch's Deutsches Industrie-Institut in Cologne and, together with his Collegia colleagues Wolfgang Buchow and Gunhild Bohm, worked on a Ph.D. under professor Hans Lades. Even in Erlangen the normalization of relations between East and West Germany under *Ostpolitik* took away the momentum of the Collegia Politica, but Lades, whose brother Heinrich was CSU Mayor of Erlangen from 1959 to 1972, had "a broad base" from which to continue in other directions via his Institut für Gesellschaft und Wissenschaft. Interdoc Youth would remain unfinished business.¹⁰¹

Everyone wanted to keep Interdoc Berlin functioning. While this succeeded through 1971, Van den Heuvel was forced by financial pressures to undertake the "sad task" of closing the office down in July 1972.[102] Looking back, Wolfgang Buchow remarked that in the context of *Ostpolitik* the SPD had decided it "would not be very clever to prolong the Cold War stories which might disturb the discussion between East and West". In any case "the politicians wanted to make it on their own, they thought it was better to work in an official way and not underground. [Interdoc] was just a bit subversive."[103] Rolf Buchow took these developments very hard. Having spent the best part of his life trying to get the truth out about life in the East, he found that his work was being taken away from him. Once again Geyer tried to get Buchow to Munich to secure his future, but the Berliner turned him down. When Van den Heuvel went to Berlin that July, the office was being run by Buchow's associate Claus Riedel. Buchow had committed suicide in 1971, aged 61.

7
Bringing the Americans Back In

> But now to be truthful about CIA, I've told you already, I was not in the service of the CIA […] people thought that I was in the service of CIA and I was not. I had a right to tell them that I didn't want to be involved in projects. And on the other hand they helped me several times also in financial things, if that agreed with their ideas. I had my own Institute, and if they agreed with certain things and wanted to contribute financially I never said no. [And] the Mellon Foundation! They helped me.
>
> Cees van den Heuvel, 2002[1]

The fact that there was no regular source of funding from across the Atlantic at the time of Interdoc's foundation did not prevent continuing efforts to bring the Americans in. This became primarily the concern of the Dutch, keen to play the middlemen and craft a pan-Western front out of the diverse activities occurring at the various national levels. The French had never been interested in American input and the Germans were equally unenthusiastic. It was the Dutch all along who tried to turn Interdoc into a transatlantic affair. This was for ideological reasons (the ingrained Atlanticism and anti-communism of many Dutch people) and for reasons of efficiency (the desire for a combined Western effort, the hope for US funding, and the ability to fulfil a mediating role that no other nation could). It also had to do with the fact that Allen Dulles had encouraged Einthoven and the Dutch to take on this role as coordinators of a pan-European anti-communist network alongside (but separate from) CIA activities. For the French and the Germans it was precisely the opposite: American thinking on the Cold War and relations with the East were going nowhere, and this was preventing Europe from finding solutions that could overcome its own division. Nevertheless, the Dutch–German relationship within Interdoc during the 1960s does not seem to have been undermined by the efforts from The Hague to maintain the transatlantic bridge.

After the initial contacts with Allen Dulles in 1961–62, the focus soon lay on the National Strategy Information Center (NSIC). Founded in 1962 "to conduct educational programs on national defence", this was an outgrowth of the national strategy seminar mentioned by James Monroe in collaboration with several neoconservative institutions such as the Institute for American Strategy and the American Strategy Council, the latter stemming originally from informal contacts between the likes of Henry Luce, Clair Booth Luce, and Jay Lovestone. The NSIC was led by Frank Barnett, who was previously the director of research for the Smith Richardson Foundation, and the Center's early directors and advisers included Joseph Coors of the brewing conglomerate, Frank Shakespeare (later of USIA and the Heritage Foundation), and William J. Casey. From the early 1970s (and probably earlier) the NSIC began to receive large-scale funding from Richard Scaife's various philanthropic outlets, and it worked closely with the Committee on the Present Danger as part of the right-wing anti-détente movement that was active in the US during that decade. At the time of writing the NSIC was led by Roy Godson, Emeritus Professor of Government at Georgetown University and a well-known linkman in the Iran-Contra apparatus. Godson's contacts with the Centre (and with a whole host of other similar institutions on the political right) go back to the late 1960s, when he had also joined the Interdoc network.[2]

In short, Interdoc's initial contacts in the US were firmly planted in the right-wing think-tank milieu, and here lay the central problem. The basis for Dutch–German thinking on relations with the East, as developed within Interdoc circles, was strongly related to the transformative power of an enlightened *Ostpolitik*. This required – once the necessary preparations had been made – actively pursuing increased contacts with the East at all levels and in all fields, in order, literally, to spread "Western values" and weaken communist rule. For the conservative right, however, (and this did not just apply to the Americans, of course) such contacts were anathema and betrayed the necessity to contain the communist world by rejecting it wholesale. Dutch entrepreneurship in looking to the Americans was therefore potentially divisive for the Interdoc operation itself. In 1961 Barnett explained his position in *Military Review*:

> Political warfare, in short, is warfare – not public relations [...] The aim of political warfare is *not* to promote "mutual understanding" between different points of view; it is to discredit, displace, and neutralize an opponent, to destroy a competing ideology, and to reduce the adherents to political impotence.[3]

Nevertheless, the approach Barnett laid out in this article did connect with the deliberations going on in Western Europe on how best to inform the public and make them aware of the continuing threat from the East. Barnett spoke of the Institute for American Strategy as a kind of "travelling civilian war college", holding public and professional seminars around the country to promote the continuing study of the Cold War confrontation. There are connections here with similar ideas in Europe – particularly in Germany – on the need to encourage a responsible citizenry as part of the process of maintaining a democratic society. Interdoc would make use of the network of political citizenship academies (such as the Akademie für politische Bildung and the Ostkolleg in Cologne) for the purpose of training students, journalists, academics, and members of the military in the finer points of the ideological contest. But Barnett's more radical neoconservative perspective did jar with the views expressed in Europe.

The link with Barnett continued through the 1960s. In May–June 1966 Van den Heuvel made a three-week trip to North America, stopping off in Montreal, New York, and Washington, DC. Contacts were established for him via Dick Ellis (who suggested Ernest Cuneo, the former OSS (Office of Strategic Services) liaison officer between Franklin Roosevelt and William Donovan, who had good relations with Lyndon Johnson) and K. Donaldson of Foundation International Services Ltd, a frontman for US philanthropy (Ford, Rockefeller) in London.[4] Although Donaldson did not come through with any sources, Van den Heuvel felt confident enough to report before his departure: "I have so many contacts now in the US that it will be difficult to restrict myself to the most valuable ones."[5] New avenues for cooperation were opening up. Recent contacts with the Hoover Institution at Stanford University had produced an agreement that Interdoc would supply material on the Netherlands and Belgium for their *Yearbook on International Communist Affairs*, opening up in the US. With this came increased intellectual respectability.

On 31 May 1966 Van den Heuvel attended a meeting at the offices of the National Association of Manufacturers (NAM) in New York, presided over by Stewart Baeder (head of the NAM's International Affairs division) and with both Barnett and Admiral (retired) William C. Mott of NSIC (and Vice-President of the Independent Telephone Association) present. It was actually Vittorio Vaccari, the elusive head of UCID, who had recommended to Van den Heuvel in late 1964 that he should approach Baeder and the NAM. Meanwhile the Dutchman had Barnett's bona fides checked out via his CIA friends from Langley.[6] Baeder was pivotal in persuading Barnett "to act as a focal point for Interdoc, provided the necessary funds could be found for the extra work" for NSIC.[7] In July the Dutchman reported to Ellis that "both Baeder and Mott are pressing Barnett to come to a more definite arrangement with Interdoc".[8] The chances of an Interdoc office in New York were never better, but Barnett, as Uwe Holl put it, was "someone who […] I would not like to have as a partner" (and Mott was simply "crude" – or, as Walter Bell put it later, "just a PR man").[9] Baeder's departure from the NAM later that year undermined the momentum, but his move to Europe as representative of Boyden International (the pioneer in executive headhunting) in Geneva opened potential new avenues for cooperation.[10]

Back in the US attention shifted to Baeder's successor, Russell Davis, and William Searle, an NAM official greatly interested in the implications of East–West trade and the potential role of businessmen "through their contribution to the infiltration of Western ideas into the Eastern bloc". Searle was supportive, and once again Van den Heuvel was optimistic about a US base.[11] The problem was now Barnett, as the Dutchman explained to Ellis:

> What I expected has come true; Barnett who was – as you will remember – rather critical is even more now. Obviously he is still thinking entirely in terms of cold war and does not think much of the positive opportunities the West has in regard to increasing East–West contacts [...] we shall have to look for someone else who is inclined to act as a focal point for Interdoc in the United States. I would not regret this development as I have always had my doubts about Barnett in regard to the right attitude towards the present East–West situation. Searle would be a good man, and so would Theroux.[12]

"Theroux" was Eugene Theroux, brother of novelist Paul and a member of the CIA front the Independent Research Service, which functioned together with the US National Student Association (NSA). The Independent Research Service was seen as a potentially ideal distribution network for Interdoc publications.[13] Meanwhile Barnett, travelling around Europe, met up with Crozier in Madrid at Van den Heuvel's suggestion. Crozier apparently declared afterwards that "Barnett was rather a reactionary type, convinced that no real change had taken place in the communist world and that the club was the only weapon". But the two hit it off. Barnett introduced Crozier to Dan McMichael, who handled the sizeable philanthropic wealth of the Mellon heir and Gulf Oil shareholder Richard Mellon Scaife. Through the 1960s and 1970s Scaife became a key financier of the conservative New Right, particularly for projects influencing public opinion. This would lay the basis for a new venture that saw Interdoc as a useful addition and not an equal partner.[14]

The pros and cons of trade with the East were a subject of much debate in the mid-1960s. Although President Truman had initially been positive towards economic relations with the Soviet Union, the rising tensions of 1948–49 due to the Czech coup and the Berlin blockade caused a restrictive trade regime to be introduced, limiting both US and West European exports on national security grounds. Western coordination under US leadership was established with the Consultative Commission – Coordinating Council (CoCom), while US policy itself was heavily determined by Congress through the Export Control Act. Both were driven by the principle that trade was essentially detrimental to US interests since it assisted adversarial communist regimes. The result was that US trade with the Soviet Union and communist regimes remained minimal (apart from Poland and Yugoslavia, and with the general exception of wheat sales, "a non-strategic commodity"), while others – particularly West Germany and increasingly the UK – looked to expand economic relations for both financial gain and, potentially, political leverage.[15]

President Johnson's overtures for "bridge-building" in April 1964 and October 1966 looked to move forward "peaceful engagement" instead of peaceful coexistence, and both speeches were a recognition of the evolution of the alliance systems in both East and West. East–West trade was a prime channel for opening this up further. The October 1966 speech was partly inspired by Brzezinski, who considered its importance to be that "it fundamentally reversed the post-war priorities of the United States and Europe": change could come first through gradual East–West reconciliation instead of the demand for German reunification.[16] Johnson triggered renewed discussion on whether US credit and export licences should be loosened to propel reformist trends in the Soviet bloc.[17] Eastern European regimes needed Western credits in order to improve economic development and competitiveness and "capture the national feeling of their people".[18] While the State Department saw the political advantages, the problem remained that for many "peaceful engagement" still equalled "soft on communism", and Congress was largely hostile to "trading with the enemy".[19] It was also a competitive field between nations within the West, there being "no clearly defined ideological attitude to trade with Socialist countries".[20]

The NAM took a middle position in this debate. Although its domestic audience was strongly conservative, US companies involved in international trade did have a more open view, and it was on this group that Baeder and the NAM's International Affairs division hoped to build.[21] A 1965 study sponsored by the NAM emphasized that most of the economic and political benefits of a relaxation of restrictions lay with the Soviet Union. Soviet policy regarded trade as no more than a potential extra tool through which to perpetuate its ideological struggle and ultimately achieve "the destruction of the United States". Nevertheless the study proposed in response that the US should adapt its policies to draw the maximum political gains from East–West trade through attaching conditions, promoting liberalization, and playing on Soviet economic weaknesses. The expectations were limited, but the importance of this study comes from its understanding of trade as an extended part of the Cold War struggle and the need to respond to the USSR in kind, and not as a potential means to achieve a peaceful world through greater interdependence.[22] This fitted well with the general outlook of the Interdoc circle, albeit with reservations. Some felt that the trade issue was either misguided Liberalism or no more than a distraction: Communism should be exposed, not supported by the West. Van den Heuvel, on the other hand, saw a meeting of minds with the NAM and was convinced of the merits of trade if it could be appropriated as another channel for Western influence: "I believe that increasing economic East–West relations are essential for the acceleration of the disintegration of the communist system."[23] But he avoided any confrontation on the issue. An OWI study from this period carefully avoided dealing with the "political implications" in order to analyse the nature of the Soviet-bloc economies and "the basic economic problems of East–West trade".[24]

By early 1967 there seemed to be some movement on Interdoc in the US. Ellis, referring to recent correspondence from Barnett, remarked that "it looks as though he has had a change of heart[…]I am a bit suspicious of US 'mergers' but there may be something in the concept of a closer link between 'certain European groups' and a sort of combined US organization."[25] Barnett now seemed interested in joining forces, sealing the cooperation with a Euro-American conference of like-minded security institutes in Brussels in late 1967. Ellis reported a week later that MI6 had no objections to talks with the Americans proceeding "provided you are certain that you are not going to be merged into something too big, and liable to be political".[26] But Barnett's plan clashed with a counter-proposal from Van den Heuvel and Baeder for a conference on East–West trade in Vienna. The Vienna meeting would be fully business-orientated, covering the transatlantic investment environment, the US–Europe technology gap, and the contribution that corporate know-how could make in general towards improving East–West relations. Baeder arranged full backing from the American Chamber of Commerce in Vienna, and there was talk of asking Prince Bernhard and Prince Philip to act as conference chairs. This Van den Heuvel–Baeder plan would continue simmering for the next few years, but a lack of consensus on its merits in the American camp caused endless postponement.[27]

During June–August 1967 Van den Heuvel had the opportunity to take these discussions further, thanks to an invitation to participate in the US Embassy's International Visitor Program, a public diplomacy tool for bringing influential individuals to the US for a mix of consultation with their professional counterparts and a tour through American society. Van den Heuvel was nominated by the CIA to enable him to strengthen Interdoc's links in the US.[28] In his own words, the invitation was "a sort of reward for the things I'd done, under strong pressure from the CIA".[29] Donald Norland, at the time a political officer at the US Embassy in The Hague, later recalled that the invitation "would have been something of an imperative, given the role of his Institute as a platform for US foreign policy positions".[30] A cable to the State Department on 17 April 1967 described the OWI as an "important organization in field of political education" and "sponsored by Ministry of Defense". Van den Heuvel put forward three principal study themes for his 45-day trip: the behavioural sciences, youth movements ("with particular attention to left wing activities") and race relations ("psychological effects of integration"). He also put Brzezinski (along with Kennan and Kissinger) at the top of his list of people to meet, although these meetings could not be arranged.[31]

The trip took the Dutchman from Washington through Philadelphia, New Orleans, Los Angeles, San Francisco, Las Vegas, Boston, and New York (as well as the Grand Canyon). Along the way he visited a host of "American institutions dealing with East–West problems" and sounded out attitudes towards the "bridge-building" approach, taking every opportunity to expand the Interdoc periodical mailing list and distribute invitations to Interdoc conferences. He encountered much scepticism on the effectiveness of contacts (and trade) with the communist world. The strong impression was that US public opinion "in general still regards Communism as the enemy who should be treated accordingly". The room for manoeuvre was therefore limited, against which Van den Heuvel pushed the Interdoc view at every opportunity: if these kinds of contacts could be applied with tactical nous, results, however limited, could still be achieved. But it was not clear what the US role in this should be. At a meeting with Barnett, Mott, and friends from the Pentagon, government, and the press on 6 July the view was put forward that "thinking and activity in regard to influencing the Communist world was more advanced in Europe than in America". A week before, Eugene Theroux, who had by then joined Sargent Shriver's Office of Economic Opportunity, had expressed the view that revelations of CIA support for NSA, the Congress for Cultural Freedom, and other anti-communist organisations meant that "for the time being American organizations cannot do very much in the field of psychological warfare against Communism. European organisations have to take over this task, but they should be supported (not overtly) by American organisations."[32]

The majority of Van den Heuvel's hosts were supplied by Barnett and the NAM and were solidly on the conservative right: the Hoover Institution, the Freedoms Foundation, the Institute for American Strategy, Robert Strausz-Hupé at the University of Pennsylvania, the Research Institute on Communist Strategy and Propaganda at the University of Southern California. A meeting with James Pratt of the State Department's Soviet desk set up an appointment with Eugene Staples of the Ford Foundation's International Affairs division. Staples showed interest in Interdoc but wondered openly about Van den Heuvel's approach, as the Dutchman reported afterwards:

> [that] the general public was still anti-Communist and that the intellectuals were divided. He believed that during my trip I had spoken more to conservative representatives of the intelligentsia interested in East–West affairs than to the more progressive ones. He did not think the first group has a majority, in any case its influence on American foreign policy is much less than that of the other group.[33]

Van den Heuvel did drop the idea of possible funding for Interdoc activities, but the Ford people were wary. After a follow-up meeting Peter de Janosi of the Education and Research division remarked that:

> The [Oost-West] Institute according to Mr van den Heuvel is supported by Dutch big business, and my quick impression was that politically it is somewhat on the right. Perhaps that is one explanation why Mr van den Heuvel's American contacts are primarily based on the National Association of Manufacturers. Surprisingly, van den Heuvel was not well-acquainted with scholarly US research organizations dealing with international relations, for example, he did not know about the existence of the Council on Foreign Relations.[34]

Aside from the scepticism at Ford, Van den Heuvel did make some headway with his principal hosts, the NSIC and NAM. Whereas the Van den Heuvel–Baeder conference proposal focused on generating US business interest for "bridge-building" and "the role of businessmen and non-governmental organizations in the East–West confrontation", Barnett remained rigidly focused on the Soviet military–psychological threat, and although a compromise was somehow forged the event was postponed to early 1968. Relations with the NAM were close at this time, so much so that it was Van den Heuvel who introduced Baeder and Davis to the Dutch Employers' Federation in The Hague in June 1967, just prior to his US trip. A linkage between the NAM and European manufacturing associations could have had major implications for Interdoc's status. In September 1964 an orientation meeting had been organized for the Netherlands Centre for Directors (commercial managers from wholesalers and trading houses) prior to their fact-finding group tour to Moscow, Leningrad, and Kiev later that month. Von Grote had arranged for Helmut Klocke, a Soviet economy expert at the University of Göttingen, to deliver a talk on Soviet business operations, and the information provided was well received.[35] An expansion of interest in East–West trade could make such meetings more common – and potentially lucrative. But Dutch interest in this trade remained below that of its European neighbours, and the NAM ultimately went its own way.[36] A proposal that Interdoc produce a detailed, business-friendly book "on how to do business in the East" was supported by both Davis and Searle, but did not leave the drawing-board stage.

Van den Heuvel did return from the US with one breakthrough: Crosby Kelly of NAM's Foreign Relations Committee agreed to function as a "promoter" of Interdoc interests and a distributor of its material within the US, although he backed away from being "*the* Interdoc representative". The goal was still to find a suitable American who would function as Ellis did in Britain, but Kelly, a well-known PR guru with Litton Industries and a member of the famed right-wing network the Pinay Circle, was an excellent temporary solution.[37] He explained that there were several influential individuals in the NAM who "favour East–West trade, not in the first place because of the expectation of any considerable profits, but as this trade will contribute to reinforce the structural changes now apparent in Communist countries". He was supportive of the Vienna conference plan so long as it provided the kind of practical information US businessmen would need, and did not "preach".[38] In search of US partners, Van den Heuvel by necessity moved in right-wing circles that were certainly beyond the pale for some Europeans. This was sometimes a difficult balancing act to manage. In 1970 Couwenberg produced a special issue of *Oost-West* on radicalism with the deliberate aim of including critical viewpoints, one of which described the American Security Council as "one of the most important Nazi organizations in the US". Van den Heuvel was understandably not very happy. The Council was certainly "right-wing, nationalist and anti-communist" but not anti-Semitic. "I find it decidedly dangerous of the author to stamp right-wing organizations as Nazi. That is what the communists do!"[39]

The Vietnam projects

As the Vietnam War damaged the image of the US in Europe, particularly among the youth, it became imperative for Washington to balance the "negative press" with more nuanced views on the conflict. In discussions with the CIA in September–October 1966 Reinhard Gehlen had offered "to plant some Vietnamese material in the German press" by providing trusted journalists with an "exclusive".[40] A string of publications issued by Interdoc at the end of the 1960s indicate that the operation in The Hague – either with or without Gehlen as intermediary – also participated in this process. The principal stance of these books is that the conflict should be regarded as a human tragedy for which all parties are responsible, thereby moving the blame away from a simple condemnation of US aggression. Such a stance was broadly in line with President Johnson's aim of internationalizing the war by involving more allies, thereby sharing the burden.

Van den Heuvel had already been active in running "study sessions" and information on Vietnam in 1965, in close cooperation with the US Embassy. In late 1966 he started to look for translation opportunities for *Een Dag in Vietnam*, an even-handed travelogue covering South-East Asia by Dutch journalist Max Nord that made use of pictorial material to emphasize the human side of the conflict.[41] Looking to counteract the vivid negative images of the war that were beginning to dominate press and television news, Van den Heuvel then rapidly assembled a collection of essays that provided observations on the war from a variety of angles, incorporating official statements from the US, Moscow, and Beijing with views from political, military, ethical, and peace research perspectives.[42] The text marked a fruitful collaboration with Major-General Max Broekmeijer, a useful ally of Van den Heuvel as director of the Defence Study Centre. The two went on to produce a more combative book, *South Vietnam: Victim of Misunderstanding*, to raise interest in Saigon's side of the conflict (this book was also published in Mandarin).[43] The "tragedy" book series was completed by a follow-up project with Nord, *Vietnam is our World*, a predominantly pictorial (and graphic) depiction of everyday life in North and South amidst the violence and human suffering.[44]

Attempts to broaden this campaign met with less success. With the Tet offensive still ongoing, in February 1968 Van den Heuvel's OWI deputy, Henry van Oort, sought backing for a public campaign to aid the South Vietnamese as the community that was facing the brunt of the war. In contrast to the many Western private support groups formed to direct money, medicine, and food to the North Vietnamese, Van Oort lamented that "there is no group that is devoted to organizing support for the people of *South Vietnam*", but he was unable to persuade prominent figures to join the cause.[45] Van den Heuvel pitched the "tragedy" books as an open attempt to counter the dominance of a predominantly critical media, providing "objective facts" to enable readers to weigh up this highly contentious war fairly. Interdoc's use of Dutch authors in the production of English-language (and Chinese) publications on Vietnam is yet another example of the Netherlands being used as a more acceptable "front" for other interests (in this case American ones).

Interdoc's focus on the Far East was further strengthened through other ventures. In December 1968 Van Oort established the Asia Institute, the goal being the "promotion of good cultural, economic and political relations between the Netherlands and the countries of Asia". Van Oort undertook a four-month trip to Asia in 1969 to build up a contact network, and the Institute produced an irregular periodical before Van Oort passed control in mid-1973 to Broekmeijer, who relaunched it through an *Asia Bulletin* (1974) and the quarterly *Asian Perspectives* (1975).[46] Alongside the Asia Institute came the Sun Yat Sen Center, established in 1973 by businessman and former director of the Dutch Red Cross Hans van Ketwich Verschuur with Fredrick F. Chen (later Taiwanese representative to the US and a member of the Club of Rome). The Netherlands was Taiwan's second most important trading partner in Europe at the time, and Van Ketwich Verschuur, who also acted as president of the Netherlands–Free China Foundation, hired an office on the second floor of Van Stolkweg (for 6000 guilders a year) to stimulate bilateral business contacts and simplify the issuing of visas. The office became such a busy thoroughfare that it was upgraded into the Far East Trade Organization and moved to its own premises.[47] The venture was significant because there were no official diplomatic relations between The Hague and Taipei, and in May 1972 the Netherlands recognized the People's Republic of China, effectively blocking official diplomatic links with Taiwan.

The Vietnam books, the Asia Institute and the Sun Yat Sen Center are definite indications of a US influence on Interdoc/OWI activities, but there was more involved at this time. In 1967, exactly in the period when Interdoc was looking to extend its international reach, Van den Heuvel attended the inaugural meeting of the World Anti-Communist League (WACL), held in Taipei, and he would remain associated with the League up to 1973. While WACL was useful for gaining new contacts around the world, the association was never a close one. WACL, which came out of the Taiwan-based Asian People's Anti-Communist League and had close ties to the US-based anti-Beijing "China lobby", was an attempt at an umbrella organization for anti-communist factions across the globe. Its shift to the right in the 1970s, including the involvement of neo-Nazis (the far right Anti-Bolshevik Bloc of Nations, led by the Ukrainian Yaroslav Stetsko, was also involved), led Van den Heuvel to drop out. He had already written to WACL secretary general José Hernandez in 1968 that "our approach to Communism is different from yours [...] confrontation with Communism may need different methods in different parts of the world".[48] Broekmeijer would remain part of the moderate wing that split off to form the European Council for Freedom and Human Rights in 1978.[49] Through this turmoil the link with Taiwan was maintained, and at the time of writing the Taiwanese delegation to the Netherlands was located in an impressive mansion only a few doors down the road from Van Stolkweg 10.

Interdoc goes global: 1967–70

One of Raimute von Hassell-von Caprivi's principal tasks following her appointment as deputy director in The Hague in November 1966 was to pursue a rapid expansion of Interdoc's contacts and increase the number of recipients of its publications worldwide. Special attention was given to the decolonized regions of Africa, the Middle East, and Asia. Contacts were maintained with South Africa, both publicly and behind the scenes.[50] Contacts in Latin America had already been secured via the Vatican and especially the good offices of the Jesuit Pater van Gestel, who in early 1962 had supplied Einthoven with a detailed list of individuals and institutions directly involved in social work across the continent (significantly, many of those on Van Gestel's list were directly connected with the Comité International d'Information et d'Action Sociale, the successor to the Paix et Liberté network).[51] By the late 1960s the failure to establish national committees in Belgium, Italy, Sweden, and Switzerland had caused a rethink on strategy, and it was now considered more effective financially (and less time-consuming) to gain exposure through existing outlets than to try to organize new ones. The drive met with some success: the Progress Report for 1968 reported 1300 contacts (an 80 per cent increase over 1967) in around 100 countries (an increase of 100 per cent). By 1969 these new demands led to an extra building being requisitioned behind the Van Stolkweg premises for an expanding Interdoc staff.[52] Many contacts (South Vietnam, South Korea, India) came through Van den Heuvel's link with the WACL.

The most interesting contacts to come out of this expansion drive concern Lebanon, Japan, India, and Indonesia. In late 1967 von Hassell received a long letter from Jebran Chamieh, a journalist who ran the Research and Publishing House in Beirut and sent out the Arabic monthly *Record of Political Events in the Arab World* to several thousand subscribers. Chamieh's outlook coincided closely with that of Interdoc, since his publications presented "the basic values of the Western civilization on the one hand, and expose the fallacies and weaknesses of the communist-oriented regimes in the Arab countries".[53] The Lebanese not only provided a list of contacts across North Africa and the Middle East (including in Saudi Arabia several close family members of King Faisal), but also proposed an Arabic translation of Broekmeijer's *South Vietnam: Victim of Misunderstanding* to counter "Viet-Cong" propaganda in the region (he had already arranged Arabic versions of George Orwell's *Animal Farm* and *1984*). Van den Heuvel was unable to produce the necessary funds (estimated at 10,800 guilders for 5000 copies), even though Interdoc did not possess any up-to-date material for the Arabic-speaking world.[54] Chamieh visited The Hague in November 1968 and the WACL conference in Saigon the following month, and for a while he was genuinely interested in expanding Interdoc's reach across the Middle East (including Einthoven's suggestion for distributing French publications via Saudi networks across Muslim Africa). The high point of cooperation came with the Rimini conference in October 1970, when Chamieh acted as pointman for arranging Arabic participation. With Interdoc insisting on Israeli participation, it was hoped that the conference theme of the Soviet threat would bridge the Arab–Israeli divide, but it didn't. As Van den Heuvel ruefully admitted, "Arab unity is a myth. Hostility towards Israel unites the Arabs."[55] In the end Chamieh was the only Arab present. The subsequent concentration of Interdoc activities on Europe and Asia broke the contact thereafter.

In Japan the main contact was Etsuo Kohtani, a retired colonel of the Imperial Japanese Army who ran the Kojimachi Institute, a research centre on domestic and international communist activities supported by the Liberal Democratic Party (LDP). Kohtani, who came into contact with Interdoc via the Hoover Institution at Stanford, had previously worked together with the Public Security Investigation Agency (Koancho), an agency of the Ministry of Justice set up in 1952 as a counter-espionage and surveillance unit focusing on left-wing subversion.[56] In September 1969 he gave a paper on peaceful coexistence and Asia at the Interdoc conference "National Views on Neutralism and East–West Detente" in Deidesheim, after which he visited Van Stolkweg to discuss linking Interdoc Youth with the LDP's youth wing and contributing to a third volume on the New Left around the world (which never materialized due to the loss of German funding).[57]

India was a special case due to the debate there during 1968–69 on whether to formally recognize the GDR. Prime Minister Jawaharlal Nehru had determinedly maintained the nation's non-aligned status, and considerable West German trade and investment made the consequences of such a move potentially harmful. Nevertheless, increasing activities by the GDR in the late 1960s to bolster its international position, a campaign which resulted in some successes (the announcement by General Nasser that Egypt recognized the GDR in July 1969 being foremost among them), led Bonn to fear that India might give way.[58] Interdoc engaged in this debate by distributing publications on GDR policies and society through various Indian proxies, including the local branch of the Congress for Cultural Freedom and the J.K. Organisation in Bombay (a business conglomerate contact of Frank Barnett's). By October 1967 a list of 40 Indian addresses had been compiled, key among them being the journalist P.N. Agarwala, who offered to act as the local "Interdoc correspondent", and the active Asian People's Anti-Communist League (APACL) representative Rana Swarup, who had been linked to Häggman's *Inform* group in Lund back in 1963. Agarwala's offer was turned down ("his material is of limited use"), although he did publish on Eastern-bloc activities in India in the BND journal *Orientierung*.[59] In contrast, in 1969 Swarup was granted $75 a month for planting unattributed Interdoc material into APACL publications and his own *Free News and Feature Service* paper. By 1971, under the imprint of his newly founded East–West Centre in New Delhi, Swarup was distributing several thousand copies of the BND pamphlet "Activities of the GDR in India" to coincide with a renewed political debate on Indian recognition of the GDR. Contacts with Swarup would continue up to 1974. The Indian episode demonstrates a remarkable temporary alignment of official West German foreign policy, Interdoc, and the APACL network around the goal of isolating the GDR internationally.[60]

Indonesia played an important role in Interdoc's internationalization phase due to its colonial relationship with the Netherlands up to 1949. Following the elimination of the Communist Party in 1965–66 and the appointment of Suharto as acting president in March 1967, Interdoc immediately established links with two new contacts: H. Sitompoel, the representative in the Netherlands of the Jakarta-based right-wing newspaper *Nusantara* (previously banned under Sukarno), and General Simatupang, the Indonesian delegate to the World Council of Churches.[61] The linkman here was Professor Verkuyl, an uncle of Van den Heuvel and at the time the General Secretary of the Dutch Protestant Mission Council, who brought in both Sitompoel and Simatupang for a meeting in The Hague in April 1967. Sitompoel, who wanted to know if Interdoc would arrange a training programme for two of his colleagues, held long discussions on the possibilities with Mennes, Couwenberg, Ellis, and von Grote. Due to the sensitive nature of Dutch–Indonesian relations at this time and the need to avoid any impression of interfering in Indonesian affairs, Einthoven quietly cleared it with the Ministry of Foreign Affairs.[62] Einthoven, who was running this project himself, then raised the necessary funds from Shell, Unilever, Akzo (the successor to AKU), and Philips (18,800 guilders in total), and the two candidates – Dharmawan Tjondonegro and Domingus Nanlohy – arrived in April 1970 for a four-month training period in the Netherlands. The project was to be a first small step towards breaking down Indonesia's political and cultural isolation and re-engaging the country with Western ideas, but by 1970 the ambitions had grown to forming a regional information centre for South-East Asia, with OWI and the Kohtani Institute as models. As Tjondonegro and Nanlohy remarked, the Communist Party had been neutralized as a military force but it now also needed to be confronted on the "psycho-political" level. There were serious hopes that, via De Niet, Shell would fund such a venture.[63]

In October 1968 another avenue opened up via Oejeng Soewargana, an expert in communist strategy and an instructor at the military staff colleges in Jakarta. Soewargana was given the task by the Suharto government of establishing an Institute for International Studies, making him the first non-communist allowed to instruct high government officials in the theory and practice of communism, and he contacted Interdoc for assistance. A lengthy fact-funding mission followed, which took him across the US and Europe (including visits to von Grote's Arbeitsgruppe and Stiftung Wissenschaft und Politik) and included a partly subsidized stay in the Netherlands to study materials on China. Significantly Soewargana also wanted to concentrate on Islam and modern society, which "will become the main problem in the near future".[64] There is no record that these contacts were continued after 1971, or whether the desired South-East Asia centre was established. Nevertheless the opening up of these contacts with Indonesia enabled OWI to position itself at the vanguard of renewing bilateral relations, holding a one-day conference in The Hague in February 1970 on Indonesia out of which Couwenberg produced a special issue of *Oost-West*. The conference, which triggered an active discussion on Indonesian political developments and what Dutch development aid could contribute, gathered considerable publicity and was a useful way to build a still-weak bridge to the Dutch Ministry of Foreign Affairs. Einthoven was deeply disappointed that the Ministry had not seized this major opportunity to use Interdoc as a post-colonial intermediary with Indonesia.[65] In September 1970 Suharto would make an important state visit to the Netherlands, effectively normalizing official bilateral relations.

Brian Crozier, the Institute for the Study of Conflict, and the American phase: 1968–1972

In November 1967 Van den Heuvel reported to Vaccari that an organizing committee meeting involving himself, Baeder, and Triesch would be held at the Hotel Sacher in Vienna at the end of the month, to prepare the way for the Barnett–Baeder–Van den Heuvel transatlantic event (Vaccari was invited to be the fourth man, but was once again unable to attend). Van den Heuvel was the leader: "I realize that most of the work has to be done by me, but that is all in the game."[66] The Euro-American gathering in Vienna was again postponed, to late 1968, and at some point must have been cancelled.[67] The reason for this lies with the contact between Barnett and Crozier, which took on a more concrete form through 1968. Crozier, who had resigned from the *Economist*'s Foreign Report in December 1963 to escape the "increasingly burdensome and counter-productive" editorial control over the publication, was keen on building his own institute on his own terms.[68] He became more interested in the New Left and the threat of violent subversion in the West, seeing the hand of the Kremlin behind these developments, and this was to be the motif for his new venture. He wrote about these subjects for both the Congress for Cultural Freedom's (CCF) press agency, Forum World Features (FWF, where he was editor from 1965) and IRD, and also contributed to Interdoc's Zandvoort conference on the New Left in September.

Crozier now wanted to go further and establish (in his own words) "a research centre which would produce studies on the ever-widening range of groups and forces bringing violence, chaos and disruption into our societies, but always in the context of Soviet strategy". The first move, in May 1969, was to issue a monthly series of *Conflict Studies* under the imprint of the Current Affairs Research Services Centre. The following year, together with Sovietologist Leonard Shapiro of the London School of Economics and other notables (academics Max Beloff and Hugh Seton-Watson, diplomat and CCF affiliate Adam Watson, counter-insurgency expert Sir Robert Thompson), he created the Institute for the Study of Conflict (ISoC). What is most interesting about ISoC is its funding base. According to Crozier, he received initial grants from Shell (£5000 a year for three years) and British Petroleum (£4000 a year for two years), and via the CIA he secured direct access to the philanthropist Richard Mellon Scaife, who duly delivered $100,000 a year. Scaife was clearly influenced by McMichael in this decision, as someone who, Crozier noted with more than a hint of self-satisfaction, "picked the right outlets for the funds at his disposal".[69] CIA money was transferred through FWF as well, but ISoC, both in terms of funds and staff, would also have very close links with MI6.[70]

This was the kind of money that Van den Heuvel had been after for the previous five years, in both Britain and the US, and which had remained stubbornly out of reach. Instead it was Crozier who found the right approach to the right connections. The result was that Interdoc had to manoeuvre within this new constellation of forces to find a secure role. Van den Heuvel and Geyer travelled together to the US in November 1968. The trip, marked by optimism following the success of the Zandvoort conference on the New Left in September, sought to intensify collaboration and secure funding, and to push forward for an "Interdoc-USA". The fact that Geyer accompanied the Dutchman indicates that this was a serious move towards closing some kind of partnership deal with associates in the US, since Geyer, in the words of his IIIF colleague Dietmar Töppel, "didn't trust the Americans".[71] But Geyer showed real interest in the Anglo-American connection during this period, also visiting London in late 1969, and the Annual Report for 1967 claims that "a number of concrete cooperation points" were secured on the US trip. There were hopes of setting up an "Interdoc Canada" in Ottawa thanks to an old contact of Einthoven's, former diplomat A.H.J. (Tony) Lovink. Lovink, who had a prestigious if not always successful career behind him (including being head of the Centrale Inlichtingendienst in London during 1942–43 and the first Dutch High Commissioner to the newly-independent Indonesia in 1949), had retired in Canada in 1967 following his second stint as ambassador in Ottawa.[72] Interdoc's "Progress Report 1968" stated clearly that top of the list for this trip was "to accelerate the realisation of an Interdoc-USA". The report also mentioned an aim "to submit one or two projects to the Ford Foundation in the course of 1969", but no record of any proposal exists in the Ford archives.[73]

By 1969 the American presence within Interdoc was becoming clearer. The Progress Report for that year concluded:

> Despite the abundance of institutes in America concerned with East–West affairs it appears that, in very many cases, particular interest is still being shown in Interdoc work and Interdoc publications. Interdoc has such good connections with some of these institutes and people that an Interdoc office in the United States can already be considered. To set up a permanent central office in the United States still remains the object of Interdoc aspirations.[74]

Van den Heuvel continued to expand his American network, meeting NSIC founding member William Casey for the first time in June 1970. But the hoped-for breakthrough of an official Interdoc office was never achieved.[75] Crozier – who had met Casey in 1968 – was ahead of the game. After the failure of Hesmondhalgh and the breakdown of the link between Interdoc and IRD in 1968, Crozier also backed off from taking on any extra responsibilities for The Hague.[76] The 1968–69 period has all the markings of positioning Interdoc as a useful extension of the new transatlantic NSIC–ISoC apparatus. Both Barnett and Crozier would for the moment remain on good terms with Van den Heuvel. Crozier accepted the invitation to join the Interdoc board when Ellis wound down his involvement in 1967, remaining active until 1971. He also used the Interdoc Deidesheim conference in September 1969 to spread the word on *Conflict Studies*, and in turn channelled FWF material to The Hague and Munich.[77] But this was all strictly on a business footing.

Crozier's correspondence with Van den Heuvel is filled as much with receipts and requests for payment as with any sense of a genuine meeting of minds or sharing of ideas. In 1970 he teamed up with a revived Common Cause, which under the leadership of Peter Crane began to expand its corporate support, for his own multi-author study on the New Left.[78] Agendas were now being set, and Crozier wanted to call the shots.

Van den Heuvel stepped up his attempts to secure US input following the Rimini conference in October 1970 and the announcement of the German withdrawal. Travelling immediately to the US in November, he put a proposal to Barnett and Dan McMichael for an annual contribution of between $25,000 and $70,000 annually, depending on what the Germans were going to do. It was envisaged that Interdoc would continue as an international clearing house for information and maintain a presence in London and Berlin, and that both Barnett and Mott would subsequently join the board.[79] Special attention would be given to training participants for East–West conferences and publishing work by Soviet dissidents "exposing negative traits and defending basic human rights" that could be smuggled to the West. Operationally Interdoc would function as the international extension of the NSIC–ISoC–OI apparatus (Albertini was not included in this set-up). The Americans agreed to make "a serious effort" to get the necessary funds.[80] But Crozier's ISoC, which opened that June and held its first conference (on the Arab–Israeli conflict) at Sidney Sussex College, Cambridge, in December, was already occupying this space.[81] One incident sums up the relationship. Van den Heuvel, stretched for funds for Interdoc's Brighton conference in September 1971 on European and American approaches towards the Soviet bloc, asked the ISoC to help out, but was turned down. Crozier spoke of operating "a skeleton staff" with "meagre funds", and the motto was that the Institute "is going to be strictly a receiving, not a donating, organization".[82] This was clearly a limited form of partnership. An alternative route was the French. Einthoven had tried to revive the link with Paris once the Germans announced their withdrawal, and the Brighton conference did see the presence of General Jacques Puech, the former head of personnel for the French Army. Lang, reporting on the event for Albertini, remarked that this showed the hand of the new post-Gaullist head of SDECE, Alexandre de Marenches. There are signs that in the 1970s the French may actually have channelled funding to Interdoc as well.[83]

Barnett came up with an alternative, directing Van den Heuvel to make a request for $30,000 from American–Asian Educational Exchange (AAEE), an "anti-totalitarian" outfit established in 1957 to pursue mutual understanding between Americans and "the independent nations of Asia" (a polite way of saying that it was part of the right-wing pro-Taiwan "China Lobby" in the US). The Dutchman made good use of Van Oort's Asia Institute, the Interdoc Vietnam publications, and the increasing attention given to China to make his case, and in March the reply came that the request had been granted. With the American funding came new demands. Van den Heuvel, aware of the success of ISoC's approach with the Americans, had pitched a series of publications on the theory and practice of Chinese influence in the Middle East and Indonesia, and a conference on guerrilla warfare in Asia to be held later that year. The AAEE was satisfied, but like all US Cold Warriors they also wanted to see more attention given to what Moscow was up to. With the June 1971 Brighton conference on Guerrilla Warfare in Asia going ahead, Van den Heuvel invited AAEE chairman and former NSIC director of studies Frank Trager to give a paper on the Asia situation.[84] Other contributions came from Kernig, Brigadier W.F.K. Thompson, USIA's Vietnam specialist Douglas Pike, and from University of Kent academic Dennis Duncanson (a close associate of counter-insurgency expert Robert Thompson) on the lessons from Malaya in the 1950s. The pitch of the event was clear: the Vietnam War should be seen within the context of global communist strategy to make use of "national liberation wars" as an essential element of peaceful coexistence. As Trager put it, Vietnam was "a *front* in a global war".[85] Any criticism of the US military response was therefore missing the point entirely. The conservative, pro-American tone of the event was a sign of things to come. Van den Heuvel let Ellis know in mid-1971 that "I expect an increasing American cooperation", and after a further trip to the US in May he could report that his workload had increased considerably because "the new American support also includes certain tasks".[86] A string of Interdoc publications during 1971–72 indicate this new American input: *Activities of the GDR in India* (1971), *The Indonesian Communist Party and its relations with the Soviet Union and the People's Republic of China* (1972), *Soviet Aid to India* (1973), and *Soviet Views on Japanese Expansion* (1973). A publication on the "International Communist Student Movement", despite "very good inside information", does not seem to have reached fruition. The American contribution for 1972 would be a further $22,500 (around 100,000 guilders).[87]

The $30,000 for 1971 was a vital lifeline, but the total collapse of German funding in 1972 was a serious crisis. McMichael reported in August that there was no possibility of new funds from the Scaife network and that neither Barnett nor Trager could produce anything in the short term.[88] It was impossible for Van den Heuvel, faced with severe staff cutbacks, suddenly to shift Interdoc's attention towards the Far East as his new American patrons wanted.[89] Instead the focus now rested on a major conference, together with the American Bar Association's Committee on Education about Communism, to be held in November at the Freedoms Foundation's Airlie House in Valley Forge, Pennsylvania. Under the title "American–European Relations vis-à-vis Communist Objectives in Europe", this was intended to consolidate the Interdoc operation in the US and pave the way ahead. But, with two months to go, it was looking more like the last hurrah. Despite some promises of alternative channels being found, German funds had after all dried up entirely. Van den Heuvel was quite forthcoming to Crozier about the American connection:

> I think that practically all of us want to consolidate the American link with Interdoc. One or two may have small reservations as they fear that the Americans might get a too predominant position in Interdoc. I do not share that fear, Interdoc is in the first place a European organization and it will stay that. However, for many reasons, a close co-operation with the Americans is essential. Western Europe and North America form the Western world. The unity of this Western World is all important and should be promoted with all possible means, also by Interdoc.[90]

The conference that should have consolidated the US link went ahead in November 1972, being insulated from the financial tribulations of that year by the guarantee of US funding secured by Mott via the American Bar Association. As W.F.K. Thompson remarked afterwards, "the holding of a major INTERDOC conference for the first time in the United States was in itself of great significance".[91] Van den Heuvel was determined to make an impact, inviting the Secretary General of NATO, Joseph Luns, one of his predecessors, Manlio Brosio (then head of the Atlantic Treaty Association), and Atlantic Institute deputy director and former associate Curt Gasteyger, in a bid to unite Interdoc with established transatlantic networks.[92] Walter Bell used the event to interest Jeremy Russell of Shell UK, an expert on Eastern Europe, in Interdoc's continuing relevance in international affairs, and the Shell man willingly participated as a discussant. Including contributions from former Secretary of State Dean Rusk (on "Negotiating with the East") and Under Secretary of State for Political Affairs U. Alexis Johnson (on "East Policy of the West"), the event had a high enough profile to raise the stature of Interdoc across the Atlantic. Sizeable British, Dutch, and German delegations attended – along with two French delegates, General Puech and Battalion Commander Robert Monguilan.[93] Other panel sessions addressed "The US Presence in Europe" and "Frictions within the Alliance", and the conference addressed the changing transatlantic relationship in an era of détente and US–China rapprochement. As a local report put it, "long discussions centred on Soviet objectives in Europe, which were ranked from outright communization as a maximum Soviet goal to 'Finlandization' (neutralization of Western Europe like Finland, with a Soviet veto over its policies) as a minimum one".[94] The Stasi, still keeping tabs on Interdoc despite the withdrawal of the BND, reported quite correctly on the conference's message that "the strength and unity of the Western alliance was a crucial prerequisite for successful negotiations with the East", an essential part of which was represented by the continuing presence of US forces in Western Europe.[95]

But tensions were never far below the surface. Despite this being an Interdoc conference, Barnett had invited Europeans to attend without clearing it with Thompson, Bell, or Van den Heuvel. Barnett closed the conference by initiating a discussion on "what next?", himself indicating that his real interest lay in "a new international setup, perhaps funded by multi-national companies, which would study the problems of international security". For Bell this was the problem: "Barnett is *paid* to adopt an uncompromising negative attitude" in which "action" meant "founding and supporting Cold War societies and institutions". On the other side Van den Heuvel took the opportunity to state once more that The Hague was a perfect location for a briefing centre for those doing business or otherwise travelling across the Iron Curtain. Writing afterwards to Kernig, Lades, and von Grote (none of whom had been present), he emphasized the plan for an Interdoc desk to pool expertise on negotiating with the East, to be paid for 50–50 by Americans and Europeans. The original plan discussed with Baeder and Barnett back in 1967 was still there, but so were the sharp divisions, and they would only get worse.[96]

8
Interdoc Reconfigures: The 1970s and Détente

> Hostility which is met with hostility can never create anything positive, but only hate, and relations based on hate easily lead to aggression. It may be too much to expect that we can turn an adversary into a friend as that will take a very long time. What we can try however is to change him to such an extent that he gradually loses his hostility. He must realize that through the better relations he will gain rather than lose. If the West proceeds along these lines it will make a substantial contribution to peace.
>
> Cees van den Heuvel, 1967[1]

In October 1974 Cees van den Heuvel went to Moscow. It was to be the first of several trips to capitals in Eastern Europe, each time involving visits to institutes of international affairs, foreign policy think tanks, and foreign ministries. Through the decade he established strong links in Poland and the Soviet Union in particular. He travelled alone and arranged all the details himself. These were fact-finding missions, to learn more about communist perceptions of the West in a period when the diplomatic and security negotiations of détente were in full swing. East and West were jousting for position at the Conference on Security and Cooperation in Europe (CSCE) in Helsinki, the Mutual Balanced Force Reductions negotiations in Vienna, and the Washington–Moscow Strategic Arms Limitations Talks. Having spent the previous decade or more warning and instructing others via SOEV, the OWI, and Interdoc on the intricacies of East–West contacts, Van den Heuvel now wanted to see for himself. Geyer would no doubt have approved. The Dutchman's trips east lay at the centre of an Interdoc that was changing with the times – but equally determined to fulfil its mission. "What is the use of our military and diplomatic assumptions if we don't understand the Soviet perception of strategic and political reality?" he had written in 1967: "This is first of all a psychological question."[2] Recent research has begun to focus more on the role of private groups in the détente process, particularly the way they pursued a human rights agenda before

Western governments officially took up this cause.[3] This chapter builds on this research by exploring the dimensions of the Interdoc network into the 1970s and the differences of opinion on détente that lay at its heart.

In the aftermath of the BND's withdrawal Interdoc was refashioned as more of a loose multinational enterprise, with the board agreeing in 1973 to function "as the international branch of the East–West Institute".[4] Contacts with West Germany were maintained throughout the 1970s, but Interdoc was now separated from the German fixation with the GDR. In 1971 the board was reconstituted, with the now ailing Einthoven replaced as chairman by Brigadier W.F.K. "Sheriff" Thompson. Thompson, a close associate of Crozier, Stewart "Paddy" Menaul (Royal United Services Institute for Defence Studies), and Frank Kitson, used his column in the *Daily Telegraph* to warn of the dangers of complacency in an era of détente. "Extremist groups determined on undermining established institutions are willingly or unwittingly exploited by external Powers", he wrote in August 1972: "the danger is less in the effectiveness of the forces of subversion than that we, through excessive liberalism, may, like the German Weimar Republic, bring about our own downfall."[5] Both Kernig (vice-president) and Lades remained on the board (at least on paper) until 1979, joined by De Niet (treasurer), Hornix, and Bell, and the Americans Barnett and Mott. Kernig – *à la* Crozier – was now occupied with a multi-national study of "urban violence in highly developed, modern societies", whereas Lades pursued a comparative study of education in East and West Germany.[6] With Kernig and Lades occupied elsewhere, Van den Heuvel renewed his contacts with Haus Rissen in Hamburg and, in tandem with Hornix and the Nation and Defence Foundation (Stichting Volk en Verdediging), secured new partners at the West German Ministry of Defence and its main publishing outlet, Markus Verlag.[7] In 1973 a new relationship was forged with the Ministry's Arbeitskreis für Landesverteidigung, a public institute established to improve support for a continuing defence capability in a period of détente and popular support for demilitarization.[8] The following year the OWI and the Arbeitskreis ran a joint two-day conference in Noordwijk covering the need to maintain military preparedness in the NATO countries. Remarkably, the entire conference at the Hotel Noordzee was conducted in German.[9]

Financially Shell continued to be a faithful supporter, as accounts for 1978 still indicate a sum of 30,000 guilders coming from the multinational (alongside 10,000 from Philips and 5000 from Unilever).[10] Van den Heuvel's long-running battle to obtain a subsidy from the Ministry of Defence continued. He possessed strong allies, in particular Gerard Peijnenburg, the Ministry's Secretary General from 1969 to 1984, and Liberal politician Harm van Riel (an OWI board member), who raised concerns in parliament over the declining motivation of Dutch military personnel. Peijnenburg, as a board member of Stichting Fondsenwerving Militaire Oorlogs- en Dienstslachtoffers (SFMO: Foundation for Fundraising for Military Casualties in War) was in a key position to direct its large-scale funds (over 70 million guilders in the 1980s) to several of Van den Heuvel's projects, including the Institute for Psychological Defence (Geestelijke Weerbaarheid) and its efforts to promote the ideals of democratic citizenship via its publication *Basis*.[11] But input was coming from elsewhere in the 1970s, as the OWI's financial reports indicate: in 1976 "foreign funds" (*buitenlandse fondsen*) provided 90,000 guilders, half of the total received from benefactors as a whole, and this continued through 1977 (92,000 guilders) and 1978 (71,000). The most likely source of this support is the Americans (with an outside possibility being the French, although there was no French member of the board). The American contribution was $25,000 in 1974 and Van den Heuvel, constantly on the lookout for how to maintain this source, would refer to "our Pittsburgh friends" (Scaife) in a letter to Bell, but the relationship was fractious and the source of the "foreign funds" remains unclear.[12]

An overview of the OWI's most important partners prior to its dissolution at the end of 1978 shows that the coalition put together to keep Interdoc afloat in the early 1970s still held (Crozier's ISoC, Sager's Ost-Institut, Haus Rissen, and the Hoover Institution), at least on paper, but deep rifts had been opened up during the decade. Van den Heuvel developed good working relations with Rissen and its director, Gerhard Merzyn, through their common interest in promoting East–West trade, especially for Americans. Notable absentees from the list are the NSIC and the American Bar Association, and an attempt to gather a final Interdoc conference in 1978 was abandoned due to lack of cohesion among the former partners. Other groups on the anti-communist right – WACL, CEDI, the Pinay Circle – had gradually faded away from Interdoc's circle by the late 1970s. Wanting to abandon the "psychological warfare" tag for a new era, Bell argued that "the extreme right-wing element must be eliminated. But I can see that is not so easy [...]". By the end of 1976 he had ended his role as Interdoc UK representative, disappointed with the result.[13]

The 1973 public prospectus declared that "Interdoc seeks to serve the Atlantic Community. Firmly rooted in Europe, with headquarters in The Hague, Interdoc has reached out across the Atlantic and established firm relationships in the United States."[14] With Couwenberg increasingly occupied with *Civis Mundi* and his role at the Erasmus University, throughout the decade Van den Heuvel was supported by two new partners, the journalist-turned-communications-entrepreneur A.C.A. (Tony) Dake and the well-connected businessman Ernst H. van Eeghen. In 1973 Dake shifted from a career in the media (*Het Parool* and *NRC Handelsblad* correspondent in Moscow and Bonn, followed by political adviser to the Netherlands public broadcasting company NOS) to run his cable infrastructure business (Delta Kabel), which benefited from the needs of the growing commercial television market. The Dake family's Haëlla Foundation was a crucial new source of funds for Van den Heuvel's activities, providing 30,000 guilders in 1976 alone.[15] Van Eeghen, whose family business interests included the oldest private bank in the Netherlands (Oyers & Van Eeghen, established 1797) and the foodstuffs conglomerate the Van Eeghen Group (established 1662), was another formidable independent operator. Inspired both by his Mennonite beliefs and by the example of the informal Dartmouth conferences between Soviet and American representatives, in the 1970s Van Eeghen used the World Council of Churches and World War II veterans' channels to establish his own contacts with the Soviet security establishment and ran a series of informal seminars at his Berkenrode estate in Haarlem.[16]

The range of activities pursued during the 1970s to strengthen the transatlantic bond operated along the same lines of defence and offence which had been the trademark of the Interdoc circle since its inception. On the defensive side, efforts were made to bolster public opinion in support of the Atlantic alliance embodied by NATO and the presence of US forces in Western Europe. This was pursued in the Netherlands particularly via the Atlantic Committee, its youthful off-shoot, JASON (Jong Atlantisch Samenwerkings Orgaan Nederland), and new ventures designed for the purpose, such as the Netherlands–US Foundation. Youth and student affairs were once again central in these efforts to build bridges with upcoming generations and promote the values that the alliance stood for. Connected with this was a continuing analysis of political violence and terrorism in the West, in conjunction with partner institutes around Europe. The offensive aspect was exemplified by Van den Heuvel's increasing dialogue with and facilitation of contacts in the East. Meanwhile he became something of a roving consultant and speaker within the circles of US big business and academia. With US interest in East–West trade increasing, he was regularly invited to lecture on its significance as a tool for change, becoming a "faculty member" of the International Management and Development Institute (a Washington, DC, non-profit organization promoting government–business contacts).[17] He also acted as a security consultant to US big business, for example, with the security seminar on East–West trade for Esso Belgium (arranged via De Niet) in December 1973 (which included insights into KGB entrapment tactics) and a similar set-up for the American Society for Industrial Security (ASIS) in Brussels in March 1974.[18] The East–West Trade Center in Vienna, established by the US government in 1974, became a regular port of call, and Van den Heuvel was even invited to the Mont Pelerin Society's annual meeting in Amsterdam in April 1977 to hear Friedrich von Hayek speak to this free-market advocacy group on the value of "denationalizing money". The US-sponsored lecture circuit was an ideal way to maintain the profile of Interdoc among potential funders, but financial constraints still forced the last Interdoc journal, *East–West Contacts*, to cease publication in 1974.

A more far-reaching development at this time was the attempt to refashion the OWI into a monitoring institution for the aftermath of the Helsinki

Accords. The Accords' 7th Principle was here of vital importance: "The participating states [...] make it their aim to facilitate freer movement and contacts, individually and collectively, whether privately or officially, among persons, institutions and organizations of the participating states." In 1979 Van den Heuvel would throw all his efforts into a new venture – the Centre for European Security and Cooperation (CEVS: Centrum voor Europese Veiligheid en Samenwerking) – which sought to become an official outlet enabling Western governments to track the implementation of the Accords. It was a bold move, but once again it foundered on government intransigence.

Oost-West went through its own particular transformation in this period. At the end of 1969 Couwenberg initiated yet another discussion on the identity of the journal, arguing that it was time to let the focus on East–West relations go and replace it with a broader framework centred on the "fundamental trends" of the coming decade: participation (changes in national politics, the role of the citizen, and youth activism) and interdependence (the undermining of nation states as single political and economic units). A global framework beyond the orthodox US–Europe–USSR Cold War dilemmas was needed. Recent books such as John Burton's *World Society* were already pointing in this direction. For Couwenberg détente was out; global citizenship was in. In 1971 *Oost-West* duly became *Civis Mundi*, and Couwenberg set out to congregate existing journals and institutes around this project as part of a combined effort through conferences, in education, and in the media.[19] With the goal being "the development of a citizenship that experiences its rights and duties from the perspective of a global solidarity (interdependence) and responsibility", Couwenberg lamented the narrow-mindedness of contemporary politics and the false benefits of the "information explosion", and expressed the need for "an upheaval (revolution) in human consciousness". Needless to say, other parties – including the Netherlands Centre for Democratic Citizenship (Nederlands Centrum voor Democratische Burgerschapsvorming), which Couwenberg had himself initiated – suspected the OWI of "imperialist motives", and plans for new foundations and societies were shelved. Couwenberg also had to deal with the fact that Koets' successor as chair of the journal's Advisory Council, Henri Baudet, found *burgerschapsvorming* a "monstrous term".[20]

Couwenberg eventually succeeded in casting *Civis Mundi* free from its original moorings by creating a separate foundation in January 1975. By then he had been asked to join the advisory board of the prestigious Netherlands Institute for Peace Research (NIVV: Nederlands Instituut voor Vredesvraagstukken, one of the predecessors of the Clingendael Institute of International Relations) and invited to visit Japan by its government. A free thinker, he always courted controversy. In the 1950s he called for the formation of a national Christian Democratic Party ten years before it was seriously discussed. In the 1960s and 1970s he focused on the issues of citizenship and national identity long before they were considered matters of serious concern. He was at the forefront of a movement in the late 1970s to improve the democratic system by introducing referenda. His outspoken rejection of all taboos earned him the reputation of a right-wing agitator, but that is a major misjudgement of Couwenberg's non-conformist drive for social reform. The shadow of the BVD, which had unjustly plagued the first decade of the journal, would gradually recede. The separate foundation finally opened the way for a successful application for a subsidy from the Ministry of Culture (40,000 guilders). By the mid-1970s Couwenberg was a fully independent operator, and he would keep the journal going into the twenty-first century (it went digital in 2010).[21]

Defensive manoeuvres: strengthening transatlantic ties

Van den Heuvel's most remarkable coup in the 1970s was his successful takeover of the Atlantic Committee (AC: Atlantische Commissie). Established in 1951, the Dutch Atlantic Committee formed part of the transatlantic network of institutes created to explain and promote the North Atlantic alliance within Western societies. In 1953 the Dutch group played a role in the formation of the Atlantic Treaty Association (ATA), the umbrella organization for all national committees.[22] By the early 1970s the AC was badly in need of renewal, the average age of its board members being noticeably high and its financial records in corrupt disarray. The reconstruction that took place in 1974–75 saw Dake become treasurer and Van den Heuvel brought in as a communications adviser. The two had known each other since Dake returned from being Moscow correspondent for *Het Parool* in 1963, as he was a good source on up-to-date Soviet thinking.[23] The official record of the AC's history describes how in rapid tempo the AC's information campaign was revamped to focus more on the bonds between the US and Europe – as much psychological and military – and to explain Moscow's standpoint on détente to the Dutch public. The periodical *Atlantische Tijden* was modernized and a string of brochures presented the facts on Eurocommunism, the CSCE, and other contemporary topics. Dake led a successful fund-raising campaign in the Dutch business world. People began to notice that this formerly stuffy and out-of-date group was now actually producing interesting material.[24]

This version is correct, but it leaves out the background to the enforced changes at the Atlantic Committee. Dake had already found himself a useful role when in October 1971 he was asked by Defence Minister H.J. de Koster to act as adviser on the Ministry's information policy. Writing about the ATA, Dake expressed the view that "information [...] can be more than an instrument to ward off real or supposed dangers from the outside [...] it offers other options [...] it can be used not only passively but also actively". It was Dake and Van den Heuvel who, as the most critical board members, prompted the

Ministry of Foreign Affairs, the main subsidizer, to start an investigation that led to the dismissal of the Committee's secretary, J. Kortenhorst, in 1975. It was Van den Heuvel who encouraged his journalist friend Henk Aben to make the details of Kortenhorst's mismanagement public in the *Algemeen Dagblad*, a move deliberately designed to force Kortenhorst's hand. And it was Dake – as the new treasurer – who played a key role in persuading the board in 1974 to offer Van den Heuvel and the OWI the contract for the information task, worth 30,000 guilders a year.[25] This was a considerable sum considering the financial crisis OWI had been in less than two years previously. From then on Dake and Van den Heuvel worked in tandem on the board and on the education and exhibitions subcommittees to modernize and professionalize the AC's public role. The official account also leaves out much of the revealing debate within the Committee itself on Van den Heuvel's efforts to get a grip on its activities, and it glides over probably his most lasting achievement: the creation of the youth wing, JASON.

Van den Heuvel's reputation preceded him, and he consistently had to battle against sceptics on the board who mistrusted his motives. He could take on an active role with the AC only after his old nemesis from the Defence Study Centre, General Mathon, stepped down as chairman in 1973, and it was no coincidence that the impending arrival of Labour Party security expert Piet Dankert as chairman in 1987 marked Van den Heuvel's own exit. The first text he wrote to present his understanding of NATO's situation, which focused on the widespread confusion concerning its role in pursuing either defence or détente (or both), was met with a dismissive remark from Mathon warning that "he shouldn't run before he can walk" and anyway "NATO will never be a popular organization".[26] In 1976 Van den Heuvel's move from "adviser" to full board member generated direct criticism from both the Dutch European Movement's chairman, J.H.C. Molenaar, and Dankert, who felt that the role of the OWI in effectively running the Committee's information campaign (for a fee) had the look of an unaccountable backroom take-over by a "political secretariat".[27] Likewise Van den Heuvel's attempt to focus more on the question "what are we defending?" – a theme which harked back to SOEV's original Western-values debates – was rejected.[28] Neither was he always very diplomatic, once provoking his critics during a board meeting with "the problem is that [...] in the Netherlands it seems as though there is no one outside the BVD who really knows and understands communism".[29]

For both Dake and Van den Heuvel it was clear where the money should be invested. Détente had changed the whole context of East–West relations. NATO having been in existence for 27 years, the whole point of the organization and the continuing need for defence needed to be re-explained to a largely indifferent public and above all to an increasingly critical youth. Central to this approach was a rejection of propaganda methods in favour of presenting objective facts, since "it is not enough to be right, one needs to be put in the right by others. For this purpose subtle approaches are necessary which do not conceal the message but present it in an acceptable way." This involved not only the nurturing of "opinion moulders" in the media and academia but also listening to and directly engaging with critics in debate, something unheard of by the Committee up to then. For this purpose another classic method of "information control" was employed: a young member of the Van den Heuvel entourage, Kees Nederlof, was contracted to produce a lexicon of political, military, and strategic terms to enable the public to follow what East and West were saying to each other.[30] Van den Heuvel was now able to apply Interdoc thinking to promoting NATO, something that he had wanted to do since the late 1950s. International channels were also approached for this: the European Movement, the Paris-based Atlantic Institute (where Curt Gasteyger was now deputy director), and especially the ATA. In 1966 Einthoven, Barnett, and Ellis had attempted to generate interest in the ATA for "a new psychological NATO strategy towards the Eastern world" and the role that Interdoc could play in this, but the various national committees proved to be either unwilling or unfriendly.[31] In the 1970s a serious effort was made by Dake and Van den Heuvel to make the Association's role more political through its Information Working Group, more or less aiming to transform it from a loose collection of well-meaning Atlanticists into a structured public relations apparatus for promoting the alliance. But such views were not widely shared within the Association. Van den Heuvel's determination that "The ATA should not, as is now the case, walk behind NATO politics, but on the contrary give indications for the future" also stumbled over resistance within the AC itself. Such talk raised concerns about how far one could go before "information" became "propaganda". Van den Heuvel remained resolute, admitting to Walter Bell: "what [the ATA] need is new blood, young people who are positively inclined towards NATO, but who approach matters[…] with different concepts from those of the early fifties."[32]

By 1976 Van den Heuvel had abandoned the ATA as "a club of old boys" that "does not mean a thing".[33] In contrast, motivated young people were ready and available. Leiden University's International Relations Society had originally formed the basis of the AC's youth wing AJCON (Atlantisch Jongeren Comité Nederland), in 1963, but this had disbanded in 1971 due to lack of interest. It reappeared a year later, and in 1974 Van den Heuvel set in motion a deliberate plan to take the group over and create a platform that would eventually capture the Atlantic Committee itself. At the centre of this move was Leiden law student Rio Praaning. Praaning had already taken over the national Student International Relations Society (Studentenvereniging voor Internationale Betrekkingen: SIB) and set up its first student-run East–West exchange with Poland in 1973. Attracting the attention of Van den Heuvel, Praaning was invited to join the OWI staff the following year. From his Van Stolkweg base Praaning gathered a like-minded team together and established JASON (Jong Atlantisch Samenwerkings Orgaan Nederland) in September 1975. The first issue of its periodical appeared in December that year, with Van den Heuvel contributing a short piece on the necessity of East–West contacts as a way of influencing Soviet-bloc decision-making. Praaning later described Van den Heuvel's approach as "impressive, personal, very stylish", and the mentor would have a major impact on the younger man's thinking from then on.[34]

Since the early 1970s both Dake and Van den Heuvel had been agitating on the board and in the ministries to improve the Committee's NATO-promotion activities (and relevance) at the university and school levels, but JASON was much more. Applying the Van den Heuvel credo of engaging with the opponent, Praaning attempted to break down JASON's image as a right-wing club for NATO propaganda by inviting other views into its newsletter, something that was not appreciated by NATO itself.[35] Within a year Praaning had set up the International Secretariat for Atlantic Youth (ISAY) as "a documentation and information centre for Atlantic (and other) youth" with his British counterparts and sought out further alliances via the ATA, European Democratic Students, and other Atlanticist fora. Two JASON representatives attended the WFDY's Conference on Security and Cooperation meeting in Warsaw in order deliberately to present the Western viewpoint on security issues at this predominantly pro-Soviet meeting.[36] Van den Heuvel had effectively called a new Interdoc Youth into being, and this time with a very clear set of goals. Admittedly, the hoped-for international coordination was never realized. Praaning's French and Belgian counterparts failed to back ISAY, and their national representatives also blocked his attempt to become assistant secretary general for information at the ATA.[37] The same suspicions and limitations that plagued Interdoc were still present. Within the Netherlands, however, Praaning's drive, charm, and enthusiasm proved unstoppable. With a committed core of supporters JASON soon grew to challenge its status of subservience to the Atlantic Committee.[38] In 1976 Van den Heuvel made Praaning the OWI's assistant director and in November 1978, at the age of 26, he was appointed director of the Atlantic Committee. At the same time Van den Heuvel replaced Dake as treasurer, and between 1978 and 1982 the Committee operated out of offices at Van Stolkweg 10. The take-over was complete, as some observers noticed.[39]

As the relaxation effect of détente continued to loosen alliance ties, it put pressure on the reasons for stationing a large proportion of the US military in Western Europe. Senator Mike Mansfield's amendment to Congress in May 1971 to halve the number of US forces stationed Western Europe to 150,000 was defeated 61–36 in the Senate, and President Nixon had no intention of supporting this move while US forces in Europe were a perfect bargaining tool against Moscow.[40] But it was a sign that "burden-sharing" was a serious issue and that the US military presence guaranteeing European security could no longer be taken for granted. In 1971–72, while

Dake was agitating at the ATA for an information campaign to oppose this trend, Crozier proposed forming something new, "a sort of pressure group to keep the Americans in Europe", a plan that Van den Heuvel took up with enthusiasm.[41] Crozier mobilized retired diplomat Joe Godson (father of IY associate Roy), Labour Party chairman Douglas Houghton, and Alan Lee Williams, director of the British Atlantic Committee, and then retired into the background while this group assembled a major conference in Amsterdam in March 1973 on the common problems facing Europe and the US. Although Bell kept in touch with this group, to Van den Heuvel's dismay it took place in his own back yard with little Interdoc input.[42] This is all the more startling considering that Frank Barnett was one of the speakers at the event, which included a hard-hitting Anglo-American line-up of Brzezinski, Dean Rusk, Cyrus Vance, Harlan Cleveland, Shephard Stone, and Alfred Wohlstetter, with Prince Bernhard as overall chairman.[43] Just over six months after the Freedom House conference, Van den Heuvel was completely sidelined by his American and British "partners". Roy Godson, acting as Barnett's contact with the conference group in London, was also at the centre of this division. If anything gives an indication of the fractious Interdoc–US relationship, it is this event.[44]

But a Dutch wing of the proposed Europe-wide organization – which Van den Heuvel envisaged "to counteract anti-American propaganda in Europe in the press, in television", with similar committees in Belgium, Italy, Norway, and West Germany – was nevertheless established in June 1973. This was the Foundation for Solidarity and Alliance Netherlands–United States (Stichting Solidariteit en Verbondenheid Nederland-Verenigde Staten). The person Van den Heuvel found to run the new foundation was Henk Hergarden, a retired military officer who had joined the Zuid Nederlands publishing house in 1970. The two already had a clandestine working relationship: Van den Heuvel used the publisher to produce English- and Russian-language books to be sent to addresses in the USSR. Others working at Van Stolkweg at that time also recall this book programme, which was run by Mennes and involved sending the titles together with a covering letter from a "Dutch student" to make it appear spontaneous and innocent. Where the addresses came from is not clear, but this has all the markings of a CIA-funded task.[45]

The new foundation mixed what Van den Heuvel had been busy with for many years via the veterans' groups – highlighting the continuing importance of the values fought for in World War II – with a contemporary celebration of bilateral relations through anniversaries, memorials, and exchanges. The foundation admitted the negative effects of the Vietnam War in fuelling the prevalent anti-Americanism of the times, but wanted to balance this by reviving respect and understanding for what the US stood for in the world, and especially in Europe. Corporate sponsorship was received from, among others, the American Chamber of Commerce in Rotterdam,

Heineken Breweries, and KLM, which led to a joint campaign promoting tours of the US during the 1976 bicentennial year.[46] Frits Philips was also on the advisory board. Inevitably the foundation was run from Van Stolkweg 10, and it included a youth wing to counteract the way the image of America among the younger generations had shifted from "liberator" to "imperialist power", fuelled by a "one-sided, subjective, and emotional" media.[47] With Prince Bernhard agreeing to act as president, in the ensuing years the foundation ran a host of high-profile events: a visit by OSS veterans to the Netherlands in September 1974; a trip to Washington, DC, for the 1982 Netherlands–US bicentennial celebrations (including a dinner at the Army and Navy Club with Prince Bernhard and Bill Casey, then head of the CIA); the presentation of a bust and annual memorial dedicated to President Eisenhower at the military academy in Breda in 1990; Friendship dinners to celebrate Dutch–American Friendship Day (19 April); and many exchanges with US World War II veterans.[48] Away from the spotlight the foundation also ran large-scale information programmes on US history and society for Dutch schools. This was a major exercise in both public relations and public education.

By 1976–77 attention turned to new tasks, which included (reflecting once again the corporate sponsorship) teaming up with chambers of commerce to promote transatlantic trade. A working group was even formed to examine the issues of unemployment and inflation. But the main effort was to push for an effective organization at the European level "to ensure a continuing presence of the US in Europe".[49] Van den Heuvel remained in the background while close associates took a leading role. One was Jack Fieyra, a World War II resistance veteran who maintained excellent links with US military veterans' organizations.[50] Another was the former resistance leader turned businessman-cum-artist H.G. (Dik) Groenewald, who became a key channel for contacts in the US (he knew Bill Casey personally, staying with him during a US trip in late 1974) and organizations across Europe. In October 1976 Groenewald attended a meeting of the Federation of European–American Organizations (FEAO) in Paris. Originally the Council of European–American Associations, it had been created as an offshoot of the Salzburg Seminar in Austria in 1950 to promote transatlantic ties through the formation of national friendship societies. With delegates from 11 nations attending (including Romania), the chairperson, former resistance leader and Gaullist Jacques Chaban-Delmas, seemed open to developing the level of European coordination. Setting an example with the dynamic Dutch foundation, Groenewald, the cosmopolitan contact man, and Van den Heuvel, the behind-the-scenes "organizational guru", together set out to mobilize the FEAO into an effective lobby organization on current-day issues. A new set of principles was produced, stating that mutual understanding between Americans and Europeans "is no longer a matter of local or optional interest, but a common duty". A public relations campaign was drafted, complete with "policy steering committee", "position papers", and the issuing of occasional "balanced but pithy" public statements on everything from tariff barriers to NATO's military procurement policy. The aim was to make the FEAO "an authoritative voice in European–American relations". But the plan never came to fruition, despite Prince Bernhard's moral support as "Honorary European President". Due to illness Groenewald missed a "meeting of experts" in Strasbourg in January 1978, and there is no evidence that he attended the next board meeting in Paris the following July. Support from various national institutions was not enough to convince Chaban-Delmas. Elected President of the French Assembly in 1978, he had no intention of letting FEAO be taken over by others while he was occupied elsewhere, and the plans were shelved.[51]

Defensive manoeuvres: countering extremism

The veterans' organization Union Internationale de la Résistance et de la Déportation (UIRD – International Union of Resistance and Deportee Movements) was the platform for another Van den Heuvel initiative. The UIRD had been formed in July 1961, an amalgamation of its predecessors, the Comité d'Action Interallié de la Résistance (founded in 1953 in Brussels) and the Commission Internationale de Liaison et de Coordination de la Résistance (founded in 1957). The UIRD, which included members from Israel, was formed to try to bring together the main strands of the World War II veterans' movement to oppose the resurgence of fascism and promote the cause of human rights (in January 1974 Van den Heuvel would visit Israel as part of a UIRD delegation).[52] As chair of the Dutch NFR Van den Heuvel soon became UIRD vice-president and he presided over its conference in Amsterdam in May 1970, at which Prince Bernhard emphasized the organization's ongoing role to pass on the values of the Universal Declaration of Human Rights to the younger generation.[53] It was there that Van den Heuvel set up a Commission for Resistance and Youth to promulgate an educational and media campaign "to make Youth aware of particular violations of human rights in the world to-day", with "particular regard to the operation of totalitarian regimes". A logical extension of Interdoc Youth and the Institute for Psychological Defence, the aim was to unite the generations in a common struggle for democratic rights:

> Resisting the established order is in itself a healthy development [...] The youth of the 1970s have an ideal opportunity to synthesise the good elements of both the experiences of the resistance in World War II and the youthful resistance of the second half of the 1960s. These were, respectively, the defence and maintenance of democratic values and achievements, and their further development. Democracy is not an end point but a social form that is constantly in movement.[54]

Interdoc was officially called in to provide the central point for this new movement, but the upheavals of 1971–72 prevented much being done beyond the announcement of a new international committee for the defence of human rights in the Soviet Union. It was not until 1973 that the initiative began to take shape.

The analysis of political violence in the West had been an Interdoc priority since its focus on the New Left during the late 1960s. Conferences on Radicalism and Security (Noordwijk, April 1968) and Guerrilla Warfare in Asia (Noordwijk, June 1970) had explored this terrain, as had two publications on irregular warfare and terrorism in Latin America by Alphonse Max, the Bulgarian-born political commentator based in Montevideo.[55] The influence of the Americans and Crozier here is evident, the aim being to focus Interdoc meetings on specific issues and involve experts in tactical and strategic discussion, but the 1970 Noordwijk conference also involved a partnership with the West German Defence Ministry. As Van den Heuvel explained, "radicalism [both left and right] is affecting our defence effort".[56] By 1971 the OWI was even providing courses for the Amsterdam police on political extremism in the Netherlands.[57] Crozier duly enlisted Van den Heuvel's network to provide material for his multinational Study Group analysis on counter-subversion during this period.[58]

In 1973 the UIRD plan launched in Amsterdam produced its first results, with a conference in The Hague entitled "Resistance and the New Generation", involving (mainly student) participants from the Netherlands, Belgium, Britain, and Germany. The event also marked the arrival of a new partner, the Resistance and Psychological Operations Committee of the British Reserve Forces Association (BRFA), which had approached Interdoc with the conference proposal. The main force behind the BRFA was Major Gordon Lett, a World War II Special Operations Executive veteran who wanted to develop the Association via links in France and Italy into a multinational enterprise tracking psychological warfare and communist subversion.[59] Another BRFA member was Arnhem veteran, *Daily Telegraph* military correspondent, and ISoC board member Brigadier W.F. Thompson, who in replacing Louis Einthoven as the new president of Interdoc became an important linkman in the ISoC–Interdoc constellation.[60] The BRFA's Committee proposed that Interdoc become the base for a research programme into what was termed "International Revolutionary Anarchy", including "the teaching of hostile ideologies in our State schools and Universities", the "interference by revolutionary groups from abroad in the affairs of our countries" (with, for the British, particular reference to Northern Ireland) and "the deliberate use of drugs to undermine the structure of the State" (particularly the armed forces). The proposal was adamant that

> We are NOT trying to set up any kind of "secret" organization. What we want is material that has been given publicity and is obviously

aimed at creating doubt and unrest in the minds of the public owing to exaggeration and the distortion of facts.[61]

Lett outlined a proposal for concentrating efforts in Britain, Belgium, Denmark, and the Netherlands, with Interdoc as a central point, so that after a year enough evidence would have been compiled to enable the group's representatives to go public and expose examples of subversion.[62] Van den Heuvel saw possibilities in Lett's proposal, not least because it strengthened ongoing alliances: "Frank Barnett," he added in a handwritten note, "is strongly in favour of doing something in this area. No analysis, more action. A field-manual which includes what must be done."[63] Bell was more doubtful, wanting to leave the violence and subversion work to the likes of Crozier and Barnett's associate "Paddy" Menaul while Interdoc shifted its attention to the Atlantic Committee and the European Movement to concentrate on sustaining NATO and European integration.[64] But Van den Heuvel could not let it drop entirely. The one concrete sign that anything came out of the BRFA/Lett proposal was a film project that briefly reunited Van den Heuvel with Bertil Häggman, by this time a lawyer and high-profile anti-communist activist in Sweden. Following the Fight Communism/*Inform* group in Lund, Häggman had been asked to act as Swedish representative in the Luxembourg Group (his colleague Sten Pålsson attended instead) and later (with Bertil Wedin) in Interdoc Youth, for which he attended the conference in The Hague in March 1969.[65] Via the Baltic Committee, formed to support those who had left the Baltic States to escape Soviet control, Häggman also became involved with various exile groups, such as the European Freedom Council (formed in 1967) and the Anti-Bolshevik Bloc of Nations (whose leader, Yaroslav Stetsko, came to Stockholm in 1964 to oppose Nikita Khrushchev's visit). Together with Wedin, Häggman then formed the Committee for a Free Asia to respond to the Bertrand Russell–Jean-Paul Sartre International War Crimes Tribunal, which in late 1966 began its high-profile condemnation of the US military intervention in Vietnam. Between 1967 and 1971 Häggman initiated a scheme to improve America's image in Sweden and (supported by, among others, the US Information Agency and the South Vietnam Foreign Affairs Council) travelled to South Vietnam three times, becoming in the process an important media contact on the war (he remains adamant to this day that the war was justified and winnable if the US military had been allowed to act unhindered). A participant at Interdoc's New Left (1968) and Guerrilla Warfare in Asia (1971) conferences, in 1972 he formed Stiftelsen för Konfliktanalys (Foundation for Conflict Analysis), which had a similar outlook to Brian Crozier's ISoC (they worked together in the 1970s), focusing on communist infiltration and support for terrorism. In the 1980s Häggman also renewed working relations with another contact from the past, Roy Godson – they two knew each other from Interdoc Youth and counter-actions against the anti-Vietnam-War lobby – and they would combine on various anti-terrorism studies via NSIC in the 1980s.[66] Having worked with Häggman again on the Berlin Youth Festival action in 1973 Van den Heuvel approached him to join in a project with the Norwegian Libertas group, a cross between the OWI and the Institute for Psychological Defence that publicized critical analyses of socialism via the Elingaard publishing house. Following a lecture at Van Stolkweg in September 1975 by Libertas chief Trygve de Lange on leftist infiltration of Norwegian TV and radio networks, a plan emerged for an exposé of left-wing bias in the media and leftist extremism in democratic society in general. This was originally conceived to include Belgium and Sweden (Häggman reacted enthusiastically to the proposal), and Van den Heuvel travelled to Oslo and Helsingborg via Hamburg (Haus Rissen) in February 1976 to discuss the details. It was ultimately decided to make a film for television (budget: $16,000) focusing only on the Netherlands and Norway but drawing out comparisons with the experience of other Western countries. Whether it was ever made is not recorded. The proposal was the last form of cooperation between the Dutchman and the Swede. Van den Heuvel's opinion of Häggman's work had definitely improved over the years. Writing to elicit assistance for Häggman's study of Chinese intelligence, Van den Heuvel praised the way "he is doing a very good job in a very difficult situation and environment [...] Unlike others in similar positions in Western countries, he has survived, and he has more than just survived. He is now active in such a way that he is even accepted by circles who have quite different views, without having given up his basic principles and ideas."[67] Could the same be said of Van den Heuvel? It is certainly true that he held on to his principles, but wider acceptance – at least in the Netherlands – would always remain problematic.

Offensive gambits: Helsinki, Eastern contacts and the JFK Institute

Analysing the direction of Soviet policies and Moscow's understanding of détente had been high on the Interdoc agenda since the Bad Tönisstein conference of September 1967 on communist strategy. Cold warriors had consistently rejected the Soviet proposals for a European security conference, first floated by Foreign Minister Molotov in 1954 and revived at the Bucharest summit of the Warsaw Pact in March 1967, as a sham designed to undermine Western resolve. Opinion in Interdoc was more divided, aware of the dangers as much as the opportunities these developments posed. At Bad Tönisstein Geyer had pointed out, in response to those commentators in the West who argued that it was no longer possible to discern a coherent Soviet policy in the "polycentrism" of the communist world, that the Soviet drive for a new European security system aimed to divide NATO, disengage the US from Western Europe, and fend off West Germany's emerging new *Ostpolitik*. Even if the capitalist collapse had not arrived as planned and the communist world appeared in disarray, Eastern proposals for dialogue and the efforts by the Western communist parties to enter the political mainstream through classic "popular front" tactics (in the trade unions, the peace movement, religious groups) required constant vigilance in a time when the public in many Western nations felt – or wanted to feel – that the communist threat was rapidly diminishing. As Hans Lades pointed out, Brezhnev had only recently made the revealing statement that "the hand of the political barometer moves to the left during an international détente" at the April 1967 pan-European gathering of communist parties in Karlsbad (Lades was opposed to recognition of the GDR). While most observers were tracking diplomatic meetings and official announcements, Van den Heuvel emphasized that the crucial battleground was civil society, both to rebuff communist tactics in the West and to influence opinion in the East.[68] In a survey for the Dutch Ministry of Defence prepared two years later (the result of the one-off 1968 subsidy of 25,000 guilders) Van den Heuvel came back on the point: a process of "de-ideologization" was certainly apparent in the East but it would be a mistake to assume it was complete, since "in the study and training programmes in education, in the armed forces, in youth and other organizations, indoctrination has a fixed place".[69]

These views were expressed more fully at the Deidesheim conference, "Neutralism and East–West Détente: Wishful Thinking or Reality?", in September 1969. Once again Geyer spelled out how the major international conference of communist parties held in Moscow the previous June indicated an apparent willingness to reduce East–West tensions, yet "in the overall context of long-term Communist aims [...] the proposed security conference or a security system resulting from it would then also appear to be a means of demolishing the status quo" by propelling the fragmentation of the West and the continuation of worldwide class struggle. Détente was no more than a useful temporary tool to engineer a communist victory in the future. Geyer's caution was balanced only by the hope that Western advocacy of "Liberalisation in the Soviet bloc – however one may understand this term" would lead to an equal "socio-political upheaval" through "the opening of frontiers, widening of contacts and reduction in outward manifestations of tension".[70] Summing up the many national viewpoints put forward at the conference, Geyer concluded that "our aim for the future should be a policy directed towards détente and consequently a 'policy of movement'". Interdoc had to seize the opportunity "to engage in all discussions with the other side [...] We have attempted to explain the situation – it is now up to us to change it."[71] According to Holl, Van den Heuvel in particular saw that détente could "create a new battlefield" for Interdoc's "intelligent anti-communism".[72] The signing of the Helsinki Accords on 1 August 1975 meant that "for the first time a document, signed by the representatives of East and West, lays down principles and intentions to promote peace, security, cooperation and human rights. This offers a unique opportunity."[73] The upheavals within Interdoc during 1970–72 had been a temporary setback to Geyer's vision, but from 1973 Van den Heuvel set out to realize those goals as a "policy entrepreneur" in his own right by establishing contacts and exchanging opinion with those from the Central and Eastern European foreign policy community.

On a small scale his initiatives fitted with the later proposals of the high-profile Independent Commission on Disarmament and Security (Palme Commission), which aimed to break down East–West antagonism on the basis of a common security framework for Europe as a whole.[74] From 1974 to 1985 the OWI, CEVS, and JASON ran a public lecture series at Van Stolkweg involving prominent Soviet, East German, and Polish international relations experts to explain the intricacies of Moscow's world view, in doing so offering a platform for debate. While the turnout was not always as hoped, Shell employees were often present to pick up on the latest developments behind the Iron Curtain.[75] The new direction was emphasized at the Interdoc conference "Development of East–West Relations through Freer Movement of People, Ideas and Information" (Noordwijk, September 1973). Still reeling from the financial shortfalls of 1971–72, Van den Heuvel turned to the business networks of Ernst van Eeghen and Hans van Ketwich Verschuur (Sun Yat-Sen Center) to raise the necessary funds, which produced a positive response from Overzeese Gas- en Elektriciteitsmaatschappij (OGEM), Heineken, and the ABN bank, among others, as well as the Ministry of Foreign Affairs.[76] With finance secured and an eye on making an impact within the Dutch political scene in particular, a noteworthy line-up of speakers was arranged which included a paper by the First Secretary of the Russian Embassy in The Hague, Vladimir Kuznetsov.

Van den Heuvel had been keen to invite East Europeans to Interdoc conferences but was aware of opposition to this from Barnett and von Grote in particular. East European delegates had been invited for the first time to the World Veterans Federation congress in Belgrade in 1970, and he saw the value in creating new fora for contacts. He had originally invited the Soviet Ambassador to Noordwijk, but he passed the buck to Kuznetsov. The Russian's involvement is interesting considering that the conference focused on the central issue in the Helsinki negotiations that caused a problem for the Soviet Union. As he said in his contribution, "The USSR sees as quite natural in the circumstances of détente the broadening of contacts, exchange of spiritual values and information, [and the] development of ties between the public of various countries, provided strict conditions of respect for sovereign rights and non-interference into domestic affairs of states are observed." Western proposals for a an unrestricted flow of people and information between East and West had been "openly and crudely extended to include overt interference in domestic affairs" and "subversive activities against the system which exists in these countries", activities exemplified by Radio Free Europe and the clandestine smuggling of books by citizens "acting on the instructions of the anti-Soviet centres still existing in Western Europe" – surely a direct critical reference, with Van den Heuvel next to him, to what Interdoc itself had been doing. Kuznetsov, as his presence at the conference showed, also fully appreciated the need for dialogue at all levels: "Détente in Europe is a common problem of all Europeans." Nevertheless, the overall tone of the event was predictable. Kuznetsov's "hard-line" contribution in the subsequent publication was bracketed by those of Cornelis Berkhouwer of the European Parliament ("the efforts for détente, security and cooperation in Europe will have no lasting success [...] if we do not succeed in creating an increasing measure of freedom of movement") and Boris Meissner ("To characterize long-term coexistence as 'peaceful' is to imply that the extension of communism in the world should take place without international wars and, if possible, through peaceful means, in order to bring about a painless transition from capitalism to socialism"). And, while the official diplomacy continued, "the object of unofficial activity is to use ingenuity to satisfy the desire for information existing in the East and to keep alive hopes that the system will change".[77]

Kuznetsov was clearly not put off by the experience. He duly smoothed the way for Van den Heuvel to arrange a visit to Moscow, although the Dutchman emphasized to his Foreign Ministry that it was his initiative, which was no more than facilitated by the Soviet Embassy. The visit was hosted by the Soviet Committee for European Security and Cooperation (SCESC), the mix of academics and foreign policy experts founded to represent Moscow's views during the Helsinki process, but Van den Heuvel's "leap into the dark" had the benefit of Kuznetsov as interpreter, guide, and entertainment manager while in the Soviet Union. The tour took in the Moscow Institute of International Relations, Gyorgy Arbatov's Institute of the United States of America, the Institute of World Economy, and a meeting with the foreign editor of *Pravda*, and Van den Heuvel returned genuinely thankful for this week-long insight into Soviet thinking.[78] For someone who had studied Soviet perceptions of the West for more than 20 years, these one-on-one discussions in Moscow itself were unique in value:

> To hold a conversation with others, who regard East–West relations as relations between two opposite systems, is also a psychological problem. This is the more so if this view includes the ideological irreconcilability of the two systems and the continuation of the class struggle at an international level. This shapes a certain attitude to the West and this attitude is often reinforced by reading the studies of Western Sovietologists. I have been holding this sort of talks [sic] for a long time already and I know the limitations all too well. However, I still believe in the use of these talks.[79]

What did he discover? The predictable mistrust of Western motives, particularly on human rights and the free movement of people and ideas, but this was accompanied by open admittance that adopting these measures "would undermine their system considerably". NATO was an "obsolete institution" blocking any breakthrough for peace. Western policy was dominated by a military–industrial complex (referred to as "certain circles") that was the main threat of an outbreak of war. Despite these traditional ripostes, Van den Heuvel saw "signs of improvement". The very fact that he was in Moscow, able to conduct these talks and provide a counterpoint to the "often distorted views of the West", was in itself progress. Increasing dialogue and contact – with an awareness of what it was for – should be the next goal.[80] Several of those he met would make their way to Van Stolkweg as guests of the OWI in the future. Back in the Netherlands his contacts in the media – and there were many by this stage – ensured some welcome publicity.[81]

Imbued with confidence, Van den Heuvel continued with his "unofficial activity" in the ensuing three years. Contacts via the World War II veterans' network were crucial. In the context of détente, the common bond of the anti-Nazi effort was a perfect "calling card" for Van den Heuvel to exploit.[82] At the end of the 1960s, increasingly active as Vice-President of the International Union of Resistance and Deportee Movements (UIRD), Van den Heuvel sought to defend his involvement to Geyer by emphasizing the uses of these networks for Interdoc.[83] These links now came into their own.[84]

At the World Veterans Federation (WVF) conference in Belgrade in October 1970 Western and Eastern veterans and resistance fighters met to discuss "European Security", and it was there that Van den Heuvel – making his first trip to the Eastern bloc – established links with SUBNOR, the Yugoslav association many of whose 1.2 million members held influential positions in that country. Using this as a springboard, in September 1975 he made a trip to Belgrade to meet up with the Institute for International Politics and Economics.[85] In 1977 he made three more brief visits: to ADIRI, the international law and international relations research centre in Bucharest (February); to the Foreign Ministry and the Institute for International Relations and Foreign Policy in Sofia (May); and to the Foreign Ministry and the Polish Institute of International Relations in Warsaw, with a brief trip to the GDR (September). In the autumn of 1978 it was Czechoslovakia and Hungary, again taking in the Foreign Ministries, main foreign policy think tanks, and Helsinki-related Committees for European Security and Cooperation. On each occasion Van den Heuvel sought out his hosts' foreign policy perspectives and attitudes towards the West, writing detailed reports on the non-alignment of the Yugoslavs, the independence of the Romanians, and the solid pro-Moscow line of the Bulgarians. These were calculated networking missions to build links for the OWI and draw in partners for its Helsinki Monitor Project, which would require up-to-date information from as many nations as possible. If the OWI could position itself as the principal

East–West meeting point – making use of the Netherlands as a go-between location – ministerial support could be assured. The WVF was an additional platform, enabling stronger ties with the Yugoslav and Polish groups (the 600,000-member ZBOWID – Association of Fighters for Freedom and Democracy) in a joint CSCE implementation session at the conference in Maastricht in October 1976, and Van den Heuvel became an adviser to the WVF on disarmament.[86]

At times it does appear that Van den Heuvel went too far in his efforts to curry favourable relations, perhaps to balance the negative image the Netherlands had in the East through the hard-line attitude of its government – particularly Foreign Minister Max van der Stoel – on the human rights issue. Having built up "a particularly good contact" with the Bulgarian ambassador to the Netherlands, Ivan Kiulev, Van den Heuvel coaxed the foreign editor of the *Algemeen Dagblad*, Henk Aben, into an interview. "It is repeatedly suggested to me from the East European side that I should some time write an article about the good relations between their country and the Netherlands", he explained: "I never pass this on to anyone else, but in this case I want to make an exception."[87] But the most insightful comments concern the meeting with the Polish Institute's deputy director, Janusz Symonides, and scientific secretary, Wojcieck Multar. Noting the "liberal views" of his hosts, Van den Heuvel pointed out that they still used the entire communist lexicon on international affairs (peaceful coexistence, class struggle, proletarian internationalism, etc.). They explained that, even though their Institute avoided ideological issues, "after all their basic philosophy is Marxism".[88] Van den Heuvel had encountered the limits of East European "liberalization".

There were of course others making similar trips, including in the late 1960s from an unexpected quarter: Tilburg. Contacts with Tilburg had always been present via Hornix, and Mieli's interest in Soviet planning caused Van den Heuvel to link him up with the Tilburg Economics College (Economische Hogeschool) in 1965.[89] But Tilburg's ambitions to expand its presence internationally led in 1967 to the creation of the John F. Kennedy Institute (JFK), an academic body with a strong leaning towards policy-relevant research. Like the OWI, the JFK would look both West and East.

The JFK was the brainchild of Frans A.M. Alting von Geusau, a graduate in law from Leiden University who was made Professor of International Law at the Catholic University Brabant (later the University of Tilburg) in 1965. He had also studied under Henri Brugmans at the Europa College in Bruges, following which, during 1959–60, he had worked closely with Ernst B. Haass at the University of California in Berkeley. Having completed his Ph.D. in 1962 on "European Organizations and the Foreign Relations of States", he criticized the way the study of International Relations in Europe was largely focused on problems related to European integration. As a result, "a systematic study of problems in their Atlantic context is therefore lacking".

Since "Atlantic problems" necessarily required an interdisciplinary approach involving "at least the faculties of law, economics, the social sciences, and the arts (including political and historical science)", the best solution was to run such a set-up from an independent institute unburdened by faculty boundaries. Alting von Geusau names Brugmans among his most important intellectual influences, along with Leiden international law professor Frederick van Asbeck, an expert in human rights. Ultimately, his interests lay in the contribution that international organizations could make to ending the "absurd artificial" division of Europe and creating a viable post-war peace system.[90] It was time to realize that "the obsolescence of the sovereign nation state, especially in Europe, is such that its continued existence increasingly endangers international peace".[91] It was the goal of the JFK Institute to contribute towards overcoming this situation. With Dutch security policy built entirely around a functioning Atlantic alliance, there was a strong feeling that "the Netherlands [...] offers the best political climate in Western Europe for establishing this institute".[92]

The arrival of the JFK was both a blessing and a curse for the OWI. The academic and political ground in the Netherlands was already difficult for the Van Stolkweg institute. Alting von Geusau possessed excellent relations with the Foreign Ministry and the upper reaches of The Hague, something that had been denied to Van den Heuvel and his team, and the JFK pursued an issue-based, policy-relevant approach (monetarism, energy, nuclear non-proliferation) within a solidly Atlanticist framework that appealed to government circles. Alting von Geusau was also "proud of his true academic credentials" and looked down somewhat on the presumptions of the Van Stolkweg crew.[93] George Embree, an American journalist who made use of office space at Van Stolkweg and who worked on various projects with the JFK, recalled later that the two institutes never really "gelled".[94] Van den Heuvel admitted to Geyer that the JFK's project was completely within OWI's field of work, and he asked if his Munich colleague could "do something" to promote a partnership and benefit from JFK's "good reputation and many valuable contacts". Geyer was not able to produce the necessary funds.[95] Nevertheless the opportunities for cooperation were more than evident. Alting von Geusau joined the *Oost-West* advisory board in 1970, giving the journal some welcome academic credibility, and in September that year he proposed joining forces with other Dutch institutes active in the field of East–West relations to stimulate a national debate. Alting von Geusau was effectively doing what the OWI had aspired to but been unable to realize. He even floated the prospect of taking over the blue-chip *Internationale Spectator*.[96]

Alting von Geusau's credentials were extensive. The Institute's research board included Jean Monnet's confidant Max Kohnstamm, the Bilderberg meetings' international secretary Ernst van der Beugel, and Alting von Geusau's intellectual mentor Henri Brugmans. Close cooperation was also established from the start with the Dutch Atlantic Committee and the Nederlandse Genootschap voor Internationale Zaken (Netherlands Institute for International Affairs). As a member of the European wing of the Ford-Foundation-funded Committee on Atlantic Studies (CAS) he was at the centre of a transatlantic academic network ideal for the JFK's purposes. A grant in 1965 from the Carnegie Endowment for International Peace meant that Alting von Geusau was already pursuing a research agenda on the role of international organizations in the implementation of treaties before the JFK was even founded. In November 1966 a grant of 25,000 guilders from Jean Monnet's Institut de la Communauté Européenne pour les Etudes Universitaires enabled the Institute to hold its first symposium on "Non-Proliferation and Nuclear Sharing in NATO as a Problem for Dutch Foreign Policy".[97] It was through this colloquium that Alting von Geusau came into contact with the transatlantic network he considers to be the most important for his professional activities, the International Institute of Strategic Studies in London.[98] Similar symposia would follow: Atlantic Relations after the Kennedy Round (December 1967); The Future of the Atlantic Alliance (following a request from NATO – July 1968); The Future of the International Monetary System (January 1969); NATO and Security in the 1970s (October 1969). The aim was always to provide a space for the mixing of theoretical and practical approaches and academic and policy-making circles, thereby building "a more policy-attuned environment".[99]

The first structural contacts between Tilburg and the Eastern bloc occurred in 1967, when a group of staff and students from the Economics Department went to Moscow, followed by a trip to Prague in April the following year.[100] This developed further in 1970, when Alting von Geusau was approached by the Polish Embassy in The Hague with an offer to bring him into contact with the Institute of International Affairs in Warsaw. The first "round table conference" took place in Warsaw in January 1971, the Dutch delegation consisting of Alting von Geusau, journalist Jerome Heldring, Catholic Party MP Jozef Mommersteeg, Labour Party MP and future Foreign Minister Max van der Stoel, Director of the Institute for Peace Research (NIVV) Hendrik Neuman, and Leo Kraland representing the trade interests of the East–West Trade Commission of the Netherlands Wholesale Association. A similar event took place in Budapest in June 1971 under the auspices of the Hungarian Scientific Council for World Economy. The same Dutch group was then joined by a new player in this field, Rudolf Jurrjens, creator of the Foundation for the Promotion of East–West Contacts at the Free University Amsterdam and also a member of the *Oost-West* advisory board. Contact with the Yugoslav Institute for International Relations followed a year later. Between 1971 and 1985 a total of 17 bilateral East–West round tables were held with Polish, Hungarian, and Yugoslav delegations representing both government and academic institutions.

The JFK, the OWI, and Jurrjens' Foundation would function as a triumvirate throughout the 1970s, a kind of private conglomerate making use of détente to further the cause of peace in Europe through East–West contacts, and both competing and cooperating as they saw fit. The closest they came to a common approach was at the major conference "East–West Perspectives: Theories and Policies" set up by Jurrjens in September 1975. With the main speakers being Zbigniew Brzezinski and Gyorgy Arbatov (from the Institute for United States Studies in Moscow), Alting von Geusau and Van den Heuvel participated alongside 36 guests from 12 countries (including the GDR, Poland, Hungary, Czechoslovakia, Romania, and Yugoslavia) to discuss the European security situation in the immediate wake of the Helsinki Accords.[101] Jurrjens studied with Brzezinski at Columbia University during 1975–76 and wrote his Ph.D. on "the interchange between Socialist and non-Socialist countries" in the Helsinki era.

All three of these figures came at the issue from different perspectives. Van den Heuvel was motivated by Cold War psychological warfare approaches that required understanding the position of the opponent and then engaging it through dialogue, avoiding any sense of superiority in the process. Alting von Geusau was more the academic practitioner, imbued with the thinking of Ernst Haass, the transformative role of institutions, and the practicalities of interdependence among nations, but he never really articulated this fully in his writings.[102] Of the three, it was Jurrjens who worked out his vision of East–West contacts most deeply in his study of "psychological operations", methods of political control, and the attitude of the Soviet Union towards the free flow of people and ideas. Despite the obvious similarities in their activities, others could not resist taking a jab at Van den Heuvel as a "loose cannon". Jerome Heldring was quoted criticizing the OWI's lecture series by Soviet experts: "Are they so dumb at that institute or do they receive convertible roubles in exchange?"[103] Ultimately, however, all three were motivated by the wish to escape the bipolar Cold War system by initiating a new system of peaceful relations that could overcome interstate (and inter-ideological) rivalry. In the words of Alting von Geusau, "the three of us had in common that contacts were right and necessary, but don't give up your principles in the process".[104] But there were differences. For Alting von Geusau the aim was to reduce policy-related tensions, whereas for Jurrjens the accent lay on the human rights component within the Helsinki process:

> Universal respect for human rights and the process of détente cannot be considered as incompatible concepts. It is only in a world which generally accepts a free flow of people, ideas and information as an unchallenged and natural phenomenon that a stable, firm and lasting relationship of detent can flourish.[105]

The determination to push through a strong human rights agenda in the CSCE negotiations became a central plank of many groups on the right in this period. As a result, after the initial contacts in the late 1960s, Interdoc came into the same waters as the Académie Européenne de Sciences Politiques (AESP), a venture established by the Belgian Florimond Damman but with Jean Violet as an important patron. Together with CEDI, the Pinay Circle, and the Cercle des Nations, during 1972–74 the Académie coordinated a series of high-profile conferences and declarations in support of Peace without Frontiers, an agenda for European confederation and the free movement of people and ideas to "let everyone breathe the sweet air of liberty" across the continent. While some of the wider Interdoc circle participated – the Académie's March 1974 conference in Lucerne on the Rights of Man and self-determination of peoples included contributions from Ernest Kux, Josef Bochenski, Boris Meissner, and Geoffrey Stewart-Smith – Van den Heuvel kept his distance and avoided any open association even if the goals were the same as his own. Of course, this careful nurturing of Interdoc's public image did not exclude cooperation behind the scenes.[106] In 1984 these links surfaced when a letter from Damman to Violet, which described a meeting at the US Embassy in Brussels in 1973 between these two, Van den Heuvel, Paul Vankerkhoven, and Alain de Villegas, surfaced in the Dutch press. Interdoc was referred to as the group's Dutch "cell", something which Van den Heuvel was obviously forced to deny.[107]

Brian Crozier, teaming up with Violet in this period for an anti-détente campaign, was deeply suspicious of the Helsinki process as a cover for Soviet subversion. The Soviet push for a European Security Conference was described in an ISoC report as a means "to split and in other ways weaken the Western Alliance": "The danger of the Western belief in the possibility of 'detente' lies in the temptation to make concessions to achieve it, which the Russians will either not reciprocate, or will meet only with concessions that would be withdrawn as a result of a crisis engineered to that end." Likewise *Ostpolitik* was dangerous and "clearly in line with Soviet policies". Presumptions that the Soviet approach could be modified or weakened in this way were self-defeating illusions.[108] While Van den Heuvel sought ways to exploit the Helsinki process by opening up the East, Crozier became increasingly stringent with his warnings, regarding the OWI's activities as no more than a platform for Soviet propaganda. Bell warned in October 1974 that "Brian is very worried about your new friends", and Van den Heuvel's Moscow visit proved to be a major breaking point with the anti-détente crowd at the NSIC.[109] Looking to consolidate these views, Crozier gathered forces for a conference at Ditchley Park in April 1975 to cover "New Dimensions of Security in Europe", from Soviet nuclear strategy to energy supplies, terrorism, and clandestine support for subversion in the West. The event, which was attended by a host of British and American military analysts as well as Van den Heuvel, Bell, Gasteyger, Sager, and Violet, drew a mixed response from the Dutchman, who did not agree with the hard-line "conclusions in regard to Soviet intentions and Soviet policy". In return he engaged in some one-upmanship, letting the ISoC man know that Interdoc's latest study on Helsinki – Boris Meissner's *The Soviet Concept of Coexistence and the Conference on Security and Cooperation in Europe* – explained "the guiding communist principles as applied to that conference" and had "found already its way to Western delegates".[110] The two were competing on the same ground, but from very different perspectives.

Van den Heuvel's optimism and insistence on taking every step, however small, towards altering the perceptions of the other side through engagement did not go down well with hardliners such as Crozier. But the opponents of dialogue missed the purpose of the OWI–Interdoc conferences and publications. It continued the original purpose of Interdoc to unmask the realities of Soviet doctrine, putting their representatives under the critical spotlight, and defusing their damaging stereotypes of the West. Thus Meissner, unpacking Soviet ideology in relation to Helsinki, still emphasized that "the description of coexistence in the long term as 'peaceful' merely means that communism is to be spread in the world by the avoidance of international wars, wherever possible by non-warlike methods, thereby causing the least possible suffering in the transition from capitalism to socialism". This was the same perspective that Zacharias Anthonisse had put forward ten years before in the SOEV publication *Communistische Vreedzame Coëxistentie*.[111] But by the mid-1970s Van den Heuvel had moved beyond this to search for ways to appreciate the European security situation as a set of common problems shared by both sides, which only both sides could solve together. The challenge was to escape the zero-sum game of accusatory East–West diplomacy, and here the private sector could play a vital role in gradually nudging things along. The fact that there was a certain democratization of foreign policy in the East, whereby "the opinions of those who have studied international relations are increasingly being listened to", offered more contact points that only the private sector could take advantage of.[112] Van den Heuvel and his like-minded colleagues had no illusions about achieving a decisive breakthrough in this process, but they did believe in the value of incremental efforts to take the edge off the tensions and suspicions on both sides by increasing the opportunities for dialogue.

The difference of opinion came to a head at an NSIC-sponsored conference in Winchester in late 1976. In his autobiography Crozier suggests that he had already broken with Interdoc around 1972 because its "value had decreased sharply".[113] In Winchester he went further, openly accusing the Dutchman (who was not present) of becoming "soft on communism" and a tool of Soviet propaganda. With Barnett, Trager, and Paddy Menaul present, Crozier effectively ostracized Van den Heuvel from "the circle of anti-communists to which he and the others belonged". The Dutchman was indignant, responding that Crozier did not understand OWI–Interdoc's role in explaining and understanding the Eastern position and from that aiming "to try to influence certain wrong or distorted views which they have on Western values [and] institutions". Confrontation was not the answer any more. These were not secret contacts either, since Van den Heuvel published his findings in *NATO Review* and *Atlantische Tijden* and spoke about them at conferences. The accusations triggered some immediate fire-fighting, with Ernst van Eeghen rebutting Crozier's words to Frank Barnett. But the rift was unbridgeable. Couwenberg would report at the end of that year that "the conceptions of both institutes on East–West relations have grown apart so much that there is no more contact between them".[114] Crozier was not invited to participate in Van den Heuvel's 80th birthday *liber amicorum*, despite their close working relationship from the late 1950s to the mid-1970s. As Bertil Häggman summed it up much later, "if one wanted to grade Mr Crozier and Mr van den Heuvel, Mr Crozier was more anti-communist because his opinion was that you couldn't talk to those people".[115]

By the late 1970s the OWI had become a recognized discussion partner for Soviet delegations.[116] The first meeting between the Institute and the Soviet Committee for European Security and Cooperation took place in November 1974, following Van den Heuvel's Moscow trip, and the role of the OWI was appreciated due to the "stubborn policy" of the Dutch government on the human rights issue and the lack of any meaningful Dutch CSCE Committee as counterpart.[117] Ensuing exchanges led to the Soviet side providing information for the OWI's Helsinki Monitor Project, a collaborative venture between the Dutch and their associates in the US, Britain, and West Germany to track the implementation of the Helsinki Accords.[118] The project produced a string of publications during 1976–78, monitoring responses to the Accords and social developments in Eastern Europe, and the final Interdoc conference, held in Noordwijk in September 1976, also covered this theme.[119] By 1978 the Soviet delegates admitted freely that the Institute "tries hard to improve détente" and that its step-by-step approach was effective. The debate over the deployment of the neutron bomb by US forces in Europe was raging at the time, and the Soviet participants insisted on linking progress on human rights with moves towards disarmament. This drew a classic softly-softly response from Van Eeghen, who listed the problems Western societies were facing and suggested that they "help each other in solving these problems. We are living in a world which is impossible to live in without cooperation."[120] The OWI's activities were not immune from criticism within the Netherlands itself, and it was described as "the mouthpiece of the Kremlin" in an *Internationale Spectator* article in 1976.[121] It is remarkable that Van den Heuvel, for years under suspicion in the Netherlands because of his BVD background, was now generating controversy because of his contacts with the East. But détente was not accepted at any price. The last Interdoc publication, which mirrored a title from the Vietnam projects of the late 1960s, was *Afghanistan is Our World*, issued in 1981. A study of the background and consequences of the Soviet invasion of that country in December 1979, the publication began with language reminiscent of Crozier's ISoC publications: "After years of Détente, the invasion of Afghanistan brought the non communist world to the sobering realization that a policy which had aimed for a long time at cooperation and mutual understanding had come to nought." Afghanistan was "renewed proof of lasting offensive Soviet communism and its unrelenting efforts to achieve world hegemony".[122] The reorientation of OWI–Interdoc was noticed elsewhere with interest. In 1974 Carl Bildt, then Vice-Chairman of the European Union of Christian Democratic and Conservative Students (ECCS, which Henri Starckx had dismissed as largely ineffective in 1970) wrote to Van den Heuvel about ECCS activities in East–West exchanges and stated that he was "very interested in the work that Interdoc is doing". An exchange of letters followed, leading to the attendance of Bildt (by then ECCS chairman) and Vice-Chair Colin Maltby at Interdoc's September 1974 conference on ' "Europe and the North Atlantic Alliance" at the Hotel Noordzee in Noordwijk. The two also came to Van Stolkweg in December for further talks, including the preparation of a 15-strong ECCS delegation to the WFDY Conference on Security and Cooperation in Warsaw in 1975 for "counter-action" to oppose "incorrect Eastern perspectives" on the West. The Warsaw conference was postponed (a sign of the Soviet bloc authorities' difficulties over how to control it), and Bildt shifted the attention of ECCS (renamed European Democratic Students – EDS – in 1975) to supporting "democratic non-socialist groups" in Portugal, Spain, and Greece. A final meeting took place between Van den Heuvel and Bildt in Amsterdam in August 1975, when it was once again agreed that "to influence that [Warsaw] meeting as much as possible, the EDS delegation will have its own preparatory meeting, preferably in Holland". It is not clear if Bildt went through with this plan – certainly two members of JASON, closely associated with the EDS at the time, did attend the event. The arrival of ECCS made it look for a while as if the heady days of Helsinki 1962 were going to be revived, but Bildt moved on to become elected to the Swedish parliament in 1979 and Van den Heuvel turned his attention elsewhere.[123]

Into the 1980s: CEVS, the Atlantic Commission, and the Memorial Cross

The redirection of the OWI and its Post-Helsinki Monitor Project took more concrete shape in 1978, when the Institute was finally wound up and replaced as of 1 January 1979 by the Centre for European Security and Cooperation (CEVS: Centrum voor Europese Veiligheid en Samenwerking). A fresh start was needed to leave behind the baggage of two decades of OWI and Interdoc activity, and corporate support – including Shell's – was terminated in 1978.[124] CEVS was intended first to unite all relevant Dutch institutes engaged with "Basket III" issues and then to internationalize to coordinate like-minded European allies under one umbrella. This was more than ever before a bid for official recognition by aligning the OWI's focus with Dutch government policy. During the Helsinki follow-up conferences in Belgrade (1977–78) and Madrid (1980–82) Dutch diplomats continued to call for the implementation of Basket III and the safeguarding of human rights. In 1979 the promotion of human rights was taken up as an official goal of Dutch foreign policy. While the Dutch Foreign Ministry was prepared to act alone in this regard, it preferred to try to coordinate a common Western viewpoint towards Moscow.[125] A private institute could achieve such coordination more flexibly than diplomats. The OWI was at the time the only institute in the Netherlands that was specifically active in tracking developments in this area. What is more, the Foreign Ministry wanted to rationalize the number of non-governmental institutes active in the field of foreign affairs by using its subsidy policy to enforce greater cooperation. It therefore appeared that the ground was perfect for the CEVS proposal.

An initiative committee consisting of Dake, Van den Heuvel, Couwenberg, Alting von Geusau, former Foreign Minister Max van der Stoel, State Secretary for Defence Wim van Eekelen, and Christian Democrat Joep Mommersteeg coordinated an official appeal for support for the OWI's Post-Helsinki Monitor Project to the Foreign Ministry on 1 March 1978, followed by an appeal for 200,000 guilders for the to-be-created CEVS.[126] The plan for the CEVS was more or less the Interdoc plan adapted to a new era: an information and documentation "clearing house" for partners at both the national and international levels and the issuing of a regular bulletin on developments, with research tasks and conference services to build on the connections. The Van den Heuvel–Alting von Geusau–Jurrjens triumvirate (Jurrjens also joined the CEVS board) was now backed by a significant cross-section of political supporters. Crucial to the presentation of this set-up was that it would facilitate Dutch foreign policy goals within the context of pursuing progress towards genuine change in settlement on European security issues. There was plenty of criticism coming from both East and West (this had marked the Belgrade conference), but "realistic, concrete and thought-through suggestions are completely absent".[127]

Never before had Van den Heuvel been so much at the centre of a mainstream political movement. As he admitted to Dake, he was aware that both his presence and the growing visibility of the OWI (and Van Stolkweg 10) could cause others to assume that "something secretive" lay behind it all.[128] True to form, when a press release was drafted that stated that European security and cooperation "was not only a matter for governments but above all for the people" and "what should or could happen", some members of the initiating committee (in particular Van der Stoel) soon began to question whether the CEVS was planning to go beyond what they had originally been led to believe.[129] Coordination with other institutes proved difficult, not just because of suspicions but also because of the fear of giving up terrain to a newcomer – the same problem that the OWI had faced since its inception. The Defence Study Centre, which had reacted hot and cold towards Van den Heuvel since the 1950s, depending on who was the director, avoided contact once again despite the efforts of middleman Ernst van der Beugel. Attempts to bring in the Dutch Society for International Affairs via Jerome Heldring were rebuffed due to the "political goals" of the CEVS.[130]

Money inevitably proved a problem. The Foreign Minister, Chris van der Klaauw, granted an initial 50,000 guilders in September 1978 and for subsequent years, but expected other ministries to fill the remaining gap. The Ministry of Defence did eventually match this with another 50,000 in 1981, but the Ministry of Economics proved unwilling. A detailed proposal to the Ministry of Culture, which fitted perfectly within the Ministry's outlook of managing cultural contacts with the East, never received much attention. The proposal made the point that the lack of reliable information from the East was hampering a successful implementation of Basket III. The coordinating activities of CEVS through East–West conferences, research groups, and meetings of Helsinki monitoring organizations would actually promote the development of democratic values and a vibrant interlinked European civil society. The defensive–offensive approach of Interdoc – strengthen Western values while at the same time softening the hard edges of communist thinking – was still very much present in this document.[131] The Dake family's Haëlla Foundation brought in an extra 30,000 guilders, but despite the presence on the advisory board of Shell's president-commissioner Gerrit Wagner (who had supported Interdoc ventures in the past) other business sources proved elusive. An attempt to gain Ford Foundation support – including a trip by Van den Heuvel to New York in June 1980 for a personal appeal – once again failed to rouse the philanthropists' interest.[132]

Internationalization was an essential aspect of this strategy. From the beginning, all publications were issued in English. As early as March 1978 plans were made to bring together the main Western Helsinki monitoring organizations for a coordination conference at Van den Heuvel's trusted location in Noordwijk (Huis ter Duin). Belonging to this group were familiar partners from earlier (Haus Rissen, Radio Free Europe, NATO) along with new institutions (the Aspen Institute in Berlin, the American Commission for European Security and Cooperation, the Swiss Europäische Helsinki Gruppe, and the Council of Europe's secretariat).[133] By 1980 internationalization was really a case of Europeanization: the best possibility lay in mobilizing the European Community (EC) to back CEVS as a further extension of European integration. With this in mind it was even envisaged that the Centre would move to Maastricht in the future to link up better with other EC organizations. A conference of Helsinki monitoring organizations was held in The Hague in May 1980 to pave the way, followed up by a conference on the promotion of human rights at the University of Leuven in February 1981.[134] An American journalist, Robert Weitzel, was hired, and funds from the UIRD veterans' network were used to support him at the Madrid conference during 1980–83, where he produced a newsletter under the CEVS logo (*CSCE Weekly*

Review) with the latest information on developments. Tracking the conference every day, Weitzel gained access to all sides in Madrid, and the *Review* was recognized as a useful service by the Dutch delegation and the international media itself. Meanwhile in The Hague, budgets of 500,000–600,000 guilders were floated as necessary to provide these services on a European scale.[135]

Yet by the end of 1981 the financial situation was desperate. Despite an impressive list of activities, it had been impossible to convince the various ministries that they should provide sufficient funds. The production of the *CSCE Weekly Review* alone took up 100,000 guilders a year.[136] Rapid internationalization was the only option, but this required a stable base in the Netherlands, a Catch-22 situation. In mid-1981 the board lamented that "it is still the case that our Centre is the only institution in the world that provides weekly information on the successes and failures of the CSCE Accords".[137] Neither did the return of Max van der Stoel as Foreign Minister in September 1981 signal any increase in support from the Ministry. On 1 April 1982 CEVS was effectively mothballed. A subsequent 50,000 guilders produced by Minister-President Dries van Agt in May plus another 25,000 from the General Lottery Fund were enough to keep Weitzel operational in Madrid through 1982 and fuel a last-ditch attempt to generate extra funds from within the EC (Van den Heuvel made several trips to London, Paris, Bonn, and Brussels in this period). Yet even though Emile Noël, the Secretary General of the European Commission, announced a one-off subsidy of around 10,000 guilders in December, it was too late to revive the project. Van den Heuvel, by then directing his attention to the Memorial Cross project, decided to drop it. In contrast Pieter van Dijk, Professor of the Law of International Organizations at the University of Utrecht and a member of the CEVS board, did receive a major government subsidy to start a Helsinki Monitor group after the Centrum had been closed down. The strong indication is that Van den Heuvel had once again been closed out by government officials mistrustful of his intentions.[138]

On another front, Praaning led the Atlantic Committee for ten years through the 1980s as a dynamic, relevant institution in the Dutch security debate. From Dake and Van den Heuvel he had picked up the sense of danger that, purely left to its own devices, Western public opinion could easily abandon the Atlantic alliance. Praaning lamented that "it is a sad fact that a washing powder enjoys so much more public interest than the context of peace and security without which the washing powder would have scarcely any relevance".[139] In these circumstance agitation was essential. The timing was right: in December 1979 NATO announced its Twin-Track decision on the deployment of medium-range nuclear missiles in Western Europe alongside the search for a disarmament agreement with the Soviet Union, and Dutch politics and society was deeply divided on the issue. Looking to widen the Committee's impact and present the facts to the public, Van den Heuvel used his media contacts to allow Praaning to create a series of group tours for Dutch journalists, first to the Royal United Services Institute for Defence Studies in London in April 1979 and then in 1980 and 1981 to Washington, DC. Subsidized by NATO's Information Service, the tours aimed to get the media to understand the implications of the deployment decision for the alliance as a whole and not just as a bitter dispute in Dutch politics. The attitude in much of the Dutch media was either sceptical or negative, and it was admitted that "the number of journalists that can be brought into these activities is quite limited". As a result these trips were important to strengthen those who were prepared to speak out in favour, but Praaning (and the journalists) were embarrassed when an internal report making this point was leaked to *Vrij Nederland*.[140] The links with Poland were also revived through an exchange of teachers and students in 1979–80 around the theme of "Peace and Security Education in East and West", designed to trigger reflection on how NATO was treated in schools on both sides. High-profile events such as the Round Table Conference in May 1985 on "European Defence or the Defence of Europe" that included Henry Kissinger, Zbigniew Brzezinski, and NATO Secretary General Lord Carrington were major coups. JASON was also a very active youth organization in this period, financial support from the Dutch corporate world being generated through board members Wim van Eekelen (then State Secretary for Foreign Affairs) and J. Spinoza Catella of Philips.[141]

Praaning followed Van den Heuvel's credo and always reached out to critics on the left, giving an interview to the Communist Party's *De Waarheid* and including their journalists on the tours, but, as he explained later, taking leftist academics by train through the GDR to Poland was also a deliberately confrontational move to expose their ideological thinking. Van den Heuvel had long known that the best way to defeat the communist cause was to use communist tactics, and Praaning understood fully how to "bring in the other side" and use them for other purposes, along the lines of the "popular front".[142] Nevertheless the standpoint of the AC was clear, and Praaning sought to emphasize it further by directly engaging with the main opposition movement, the Interkerkelijk Vredesberaad (IKV: Interdenominational Peace Commission), a conflict-resolution and peace campaign established by the Protestant Church and Pax Christi. Opinion poll data were used deliberately to undermine the IKV's claims to represent a majority of Dutch citizens. But there were limits to how far he could go. A plan for a national information campaign on NATO prior to the 1981 parliamentary elections would have turned the Committee into a partisan voice in a deeply divided political environment. Between 1981 and 1984 Dake, supported by Van den Heuvel and Praaning, led the charge to back away from "objectivity" and have the AC openly declare its support in favour of deployment, but this divisive step was blocked by those who demanded that the Committee hold on to its consensus-driven politically neutral "platform function".[143]

Blocked within the Atlantic Committee, Praaning assisted in the creation of a new venture that was able to engage directly in partisan politics. On 5 May 1981 (using the deliberate symbolism of the anniversary of the end of World War II) the Foundation for Peace Politics (SVP: Stichting Vredespolitiek) was established, a gathering of pro-deployment civil society groups designed to operate as a high-profile amplifier for voices opposed to unilateral disarmament. In contrast to the AC's caution, the SVP would meet the IKV head on by arguing that only a strong and united NATO could force Moscow to the negotiating table and achieve results, a rerun of the "Peace through Strength" line that had been the basis for the transatlantic alliance's approach towards the East since the early 1950s. The frontman during the movement's first year was chairperson Joris Voorhoeve, at the time a young researcher with the Liberal Party's think tank (Teldersstichting). Voorhoeve agreed with Praaning that the precarious political situation in the Netherlands required a greater role from pro-NATO activists in civil society, since the government was unable to take a stand. Although the SVP presented itself as above party politics and not aimed at any opponent, as Voorhoeve remarked later, "something needed to be done to balance the increasing influence of the IKV", whose promotion of unilateral disarmament had become the "dominant story". Working groups were set up to examine the IKV's message and organization (including its finances) and produce a detailed overview of opinion within the Catholic and Protestant churches.[144] The SVP was joined by the Interkerkelijk Comité Tweezijdige Ontwapening (ICTO: Interdenominational Committee for Bilateral Disarmament), an initiative of Groningen academic Paul Teunissen to mobilize opposition to the IKV within the Catholic and Protestant communities. The central message was that the churches should avoid taking controversial standpoints on unilateral disarmament and instead redirect their attention to the lack of human rights in the East. It was a symbiotic relationship: "ICTO took care of the numbers, SVP did the thinking."[145]

While Van den Heuvel was not directly connected with the SVP, his influence is written all over it. He provided support from the Institute for Psychological Defence (Geestelijke Weerbaarheid) and the veterans' groups (NFR), and the SVP's outlook reflected their call to defend the freedoms that were fought for in World War II. UN's Universal Declaration of Human Rights was a fundamental text, cloaking the SVP under the mantle of defending basic freedoms in Western society. It would coordinate other groups operating in this field and function as a "clearing house" for public information on security policy and nuclear weapons. Its secretariat would gather supporters in the media and "screen" the press for factual inaccuracies, which would then be responded to. In the end the SVP–ICTO movement never captured the imagination as the IKV did. At the end of 1981 the ICTO could only claim 3500 members, while the IKV and allied organizations could bring hundreds of thousands on to the streets for anti-nuclear demonstrations in

1981 and 1983. The choice of flamboyant right-wing politician Jim Jansen van Raaij to lead ICTO was a mistake, among other things because he was a public supporter of the apartheid regime in South Africa and a representative of High Frontier, the Strategic Defense Initiative lobby group. Three advertisements in four national newspapers in 1981 resulted, after deduction of costs, in an income of only 3000 guilders.[146]

Voorhoeve's clever public relations, with comments such as "it's not about numbers, but about arguments" and "peace is too important to be left to the pacifists", were not enough to swing the momentum their way.[147] The shadow of being a front for pro-nuclear forces also seemed to be confirmed when it emerged that the conference "Churches at the Crossroads", held in Wolfheze in September 1983, benefited from financial support from the Washington, DC-based Ethics and Public Policy Center (EPPC), itself contracted by the United States Information Agency to assist opposition to the European peace movement. Support also came via Shell's former chairman, Gerrit Wagner.[148] By one report, at a particularly cash-strapped moment 10,000 Dutch guilders was provided by the US Embassy – ten crisp 1000-guilder banknotes in a brown paper bag.[149] A British newspaper report later claimed that from 1983 the ISoC had also channelled money to pro-NATO groups in the Netherlands. Although both the SVP and the ICTO would have been prime candidates for such support, there is up till now no solid evidence for this.[150] But neither side was blameless in this regard.[151] The SVP continued with its public campaign throughout the decade, picking up enough support from political and press sympathizers for it to claim that it spoke for the "silent majority" of the Dutch public and never letting up on the message that apparent shifts in Soviet policy had to be tested before being trusted. In assessing the SVP–ICTO it is essential to recall one of Van den Heuvel's credos, which lay at the basis of psychological warfare thinking in both East and West: it is above all important to give the *impression* of a mass movement, and the *image* of citizens mobilized not by personal gain but by values worth defending. The more organizations that are created, the more the sense that there is something happening. And from this angle it succeeded.[152] Praaning, who had ambitions to join the NATO Information Service after he left the Atlantic Commission, went on to become a successful international consultant, first with Praaning-Meines in 1993 and then with his own business, PA Europe, based in Brussels.[153]

The collapse of the CEVS effectively marked the end of Van den Heuvel's contribution to the anti-communist cause at the international level, but during the 1980s he was more active than ever with some unfinished national business. After World War II it had been decreed by the Dutch government that it was not possible to award decorations to members of the resistance due to difficulties in identifying who would be eligible. The issue remained a sore point within the veterans' organizations, until in 1979 Van den Heuvel, together with three others, created a committee to push for a reversal of this official standpoint. Backed by the British Special Forces Club, the unofficial international centre for World War II resistance veterans, the committee found support from the Secretary General of the Ministry of Defence, Van den Heuvel's old friend Gerard Peijnenburg. Peijnenburg, on the advisory board for both the Netherlands–US Foundation and the SVP, had been a vital source of support for Van den Heuvel's many projects through the 1970s, channelling SFMO money to JASON and the ICTO, among others. In December 1980 it was agreed that a resistance memorial cross (Verzetsherdenkingskruis) would be awarded. A one-off subsidy of 400,000 guilders was provided to achieve it, a considerable sum. Around 10,000 recipients were anticipated, but the final total came to 15,300, keeping the committee and its 50-strong back-up staff busy up to 1985. Inevitably, the organization was run from the "humming beehive" of Van Stolkweg 10.[154] It was the culmination of Van den Heuvel's decades of work in keeping the legacies of World War II alive.

Conclusion: Assessing the Legacy

> Some time ago someone asked me "what is Interdoc really?" and he started firing many questions at me. Is it an anti-communist organization? Is it an organization to defend basic Western values? Is it just an information centre on East–West affairs? Is it an extention-piece [sic.] of certain intelligence- and security-services? Is it a covered psychological warfare branch of government or industry? Is it a new political movement?
>
> Cees van den Heuvel, 1964[1]

> A communist has a right also to live in this world.
>
> Cees van den Heuvel, 2002[2]

In January 1979 Van den Heuvel contacted his solicitor to make some changes to the Interdoc statutes. It was a sombre tale:

> Here are the articles of association of a foundation that has been reduced to a fraction of its original size. Concerning the board...: the secretary and treasurer have recently passed away; the chairman is over 80 and recently suffered a brain haemorrhage; there exists no contact with the foreign board members in relation to the foundation. Only Mr Hornix remains.[3]

Interdoc did continue to exist – albeit "on paper" – with Van den Heuvel, Hornix, and Dake as board members, as a kind of useful "holding company" for projects increasingly connected to the veterans' network. Barnett and Mott had already left, the last notation of common action between the two Americans, Crozier, and Van den Heuvel being their attendance at the International Freedom conference held by the Libertas group in Oslo in October 1977.[4] The German link no longer needed to be officially maintained, giving Interdoc a purely Dutch identity, which was somehow fitting considering the pioneering role of Einthoven and Van den Heuvel in launching Interdoc in the late 1950s. But by the mid-80s even this had outlived its use, and in November 1986 it was decided to wind it up for good. As was explained to the legal office, "the goal of the foundation [...] – documentation and information about international issues – can no longer be sufficiently carried out due to lack of resources".[5] Van den Heuvel had reached the age of 65 in 1983, and his supporters rallied round to engineer a one-off subsidy of 100,000 guilders from the Algemene Loterij Nederland (National Lottery) in 1984 to clear all remaining debts. A new umbrella organization, Stichting Dienstcentrum 1945–2000, was established to maintain the remaining strands of the network (Institute for Psychological Defence, Netherlands–America Foundation, Civis Mundi, the Memorial Cross administration, and George Embree's journalism operations), and its location was shifted from Van Stolkweg to temporary premises at Scheveningseweg 11, opposite the Peace Palace in The Hague. By 1989 this final foothold was also given up, due to Van den Heuvel's poor health, and the various parts of the network still functioning went their separate ways.[6]

Interdoc's aim to create itself as a central point for "positive anti-communism" and East–West contacts had proved no easy task. It needed to chart a path between the hard-line anti-communism that rejected all recognition of the Soviet bloc's legitimacy, and the anti-communism that was prepared to accept the normalization of relations between East and West with few reservations. In contrast, Interdoc wanted to engage the East while still emphasizing the continuing threat posed by peaceful coexistence to the political stability and unity of the West. As Van den Heuvel explained to a German colleague, "in this way Interdoc occupied a central position, distancing itself from the Cold War on one side, and from gullibility, naivety, and wishful thinking on the other".[7] Peaceful coexistence had to be taken up for what it really was – an ideological challenge – by meeting Moscow's call for greater East–West interaction head on. Contacts with the East were to be conducted with, as the Dutch say, an *open geest* (open spirit), accepting the opportunities (and the risks) in order to influence opinion and, bit by bit, take the hard edges off communist thinking. The Interdoc story shows that it was sections of the West European intelligence and security services – normally the most cautious when it came to advocating contacts with the enemy – who were some of the strongest proponents of this open approach. Yet, as the story shows, the obstacles to achieving such coordination were overwhelming, ranging from national sovereignty to institutional spheres of influence and individual intransigence.

In terms of the Cold War as an ideological contest, Interdoc's significance comes from its defensive–offensive outlook, which sought to guide opinion and manipulate discourse both in the East and in the West. This was a comprehensive approach. As Van den Heuvel wrote in July 1960, the aim "is a psychological influencing of the opponent party, *one's own party*, friend and neutral, in the interests of the own warfare [sic]".[8] This was intended to be achieved on a relatively small budget, proving to the Americans that this was possible so long as the goals were clear and the team was committed. While the CIA spent millions running the Congress for Cultural Freedom and many other ventures to influence opinion abroad, in the 1960s Interdoc was being run on a combination of funding from the BND and business corporations, and in the 1970s the commercial approach was emphasized even more. In this way Western society – specifically, the sections of it that had most to lose from communist agitation, such as large business concerns – would pay for its own "psychological defence" via Interdoc's services. International cooperation was anyway easier to achieve on a small scale, as the Helsinki and Strasbourg/Luxembourg Groups proved. US financial largesse may at times have seemed all-powerful, but it could easily cause resentment.

It is noteworthy that the British were very sceptical about American dominance. Even Brigadier Thompson stated that "of its kind INTERDOC is unique in being not only European based but having also predominantly European financial support", and Ellis was "most anxious that Interdoc should be predominantly European". Bell went further: "I am more than ever suspicious of bodies like NSIC", he wrote in 1976, "because they must depend so much for funds on the armament people."[9] In contrast, Interdoc could never be accused of throwing its money around. Van den Heuvel sometimes indulged in shameless bravado: he announced to *Vrij Nederland* in 1979 that "I'm working now with a budget of 200,000 guilders a year. In the past it was a few million a year. West Germany contributed as well, but that stopped when Willy Brandt initiated *Ostpolitik* and such support didn't fit their concept any more. There was also less money coming from Britain and America."[10] Geyer's entire unit ran on only DM 2 million a year, out of which Interdoc was funded. There was never any substantial funding from Britain. At the heart of the operation lay the Geyer–Van den Heuvel link. Geyer, given free rein by Gehlen, took up where Foertsch left off and became the brains behind the BND's approach, taking full responsibility for IIIF and Interdoc. In these circumstances it was inevitable that Geyer would take the fall when the SPD assumed power, since the free-wheeling Interdoc operation would have looked dangerously reckless from the perspective of the careful political manoeuvring of Brandt and Bahr. Yet Geyer's philosophical style was not to everyone's taste. Commenting on Geyer's paper for the Deidesheim conference on "Neutrality and Détente" in September 1969, Ellis admitted that "after reading it 17 times and reducing it to half a dozen simple points I have finally grasped it".[11]

World War II laid the basis for the world view of the original Interdoc circle. The factor that united the Dutch and the German was anti-communism, and the Dutch and the East European were united by anti-Nazism. For Van den Heuvel the task was both to pass on the meaning of the wartime experience to the younger generation as a guiding moral code, and to use it to build bridges with erstwhile Cold War adversaries. As he put it, "the many tests of the war made it clear to everyone what they were worth [...] The resistance brought out the best in people: people fought with total conviction against an all-seeing enemy that was the clear embodiment of everything evil. This was a powerful, motivational force that one often missed later in life."[12] This drive connected all the strands of his thinking. Even in the late 1970s the Centre for Active Democracy's vision of democratic citizenship was linked with support for NATO as the essential protector of the West's free societies. Self-belief was key, in the words of Couwenberg:

> I said from the 60s that communism is a danger, is an enemy, but I am not afraid of that enemy, I will communicate with him and I will fight with him with ideas and arguments.[13]

Or, as Van den Heuvel put it: "I have nothing against communism. I am only opposed to the expansion drive of communism."[14]

Up till now Interdoc has been largely absent from Cold War history. The long-running focus on governmental decision-making and "high politics" – legitimate in itself – has obscured much of the socio-political history of the Cold War. It has only been in the last decade or two that this space has been opened up by a new generation of historians who have reframed the Cold War as a psychological contest of ideas and messages.[15] Thanks to this shift, Interdoc's role can now be more fully appreciated. References to Interdoc in the past generally placed it within the suspect pantheon of right-wing anti-communism. Yet the records show that a line was sometimes drawn. The mistrust of the Democratic Alliance in Scandinavia was just one example, and that of Common Cause in Britain was another. As Van den Heuvel wrote to Ellis in 1967, "I am convinced that the Common Cause voice should be heard, but again I wonder if it is wise to combine their anti-communist efforts with ours, which – to my opinion – are more sophisticated. Therefore underground we may cooperate, but co-operation overground may harm the activities of both parties concerned."[16] Those who did not change their views were dismissed as "1950s anti-communists", such as the Belgian Roger Cosyns-Verhaegen:

> he was regarded as an expert on subversion and psychological warfare during the time of the "cold war". As so many of his colleagues he did not develop and is still thinking in old conception. Subversion and psywar have taken so different forms that representatives of the West should have developed adequate forms to meet this new challenge. They either stick to old concepts or they give in to Soviet demands. What we need now are new Western conceptions in this field [...][17]

The ambition all along was to create a clearing house functioning above the dense network of existing Western anti-communist institutions, coordinating and facilitating and not simply becoming another name on a list. By the end of the 1960s the Interdoc publications distribution list had increased from 1300 individuals and institutions in 100 countries in 1968 to a peak of 2204 contacts across 119 countries in 1970.[18] Many of these contacts were themselves press or publishing ventures that recycled the Interdoc materials, often unattributed, through their own channels. Interdoc itself therefore did not have a clear idea of how large its audience actually was, but it was clearly global in scope. As Van den Heuvel delicately explained in 1973 to the head of the World Anti-Communist League, who requested a public statement of support, "a good deal of our effort is not meant for the converted but for those who doubt, and that demands different ways and means".[19]

This was appreciated by some: as Bertil Häggman saw it, the value of Interdoc was "the inspiration from meeting other anti-communists, maybe even stronger organizations than in Sweden that opposed communist tyranny".[20] Applying the Münzenberg strategy of front organizations at will, Van den Heuvel was constantly creating new outlets – often with the same members switching positions between them – to promote activities as required. The possibility of "dirty tricks" was never discounted. The May 1972 Interdoc board meeting still refers to unspecified "Special Operations" for which a sum of 10,000 guilders had been reserved.[21] Van den Heuvel moved with the times, creating new alliances and finding new sources of income along the way. Commenting on this in 1979, he noted:

> I have changed. I am known as a progressive on East–West relations, but a conservative on NATO [...] The underlying mistrust [of NATO] still exists. I am above all interested in the psychological aspect of this. How do you overcome that mistrust? I think also through contacts and exchanges.[22]

But such flexibility also caused problems. At the end of the 1970s Van den Heuvel seemed to be accepting Soviet-bloc pronouncements on the Helsinki Accords as if they were fact, precisely the kind of attitude which in previous decades he had warned against. This generated both uncertainty and criticism from the outside world. As Couwenberg put it much later, "the problem with Cees and me is that it was very difficult to close us up in a category".[23]

Did Interdoc achieve its hoped-for role as the central point for Western anti-communism – a privatized alternative to psychological warfare being run out of NATO? It is true that the level of international cooperation did not meet the original ambition. The Netherlands was certainly the best location through which to attempt such a trans-European/transatlantic apparatus. Explaining the value of the Dutch psyche behind Interdoc, Van den Heuvel and Hornix saw it as an advantage that the Dutch were influenced by three larger neighbours, because in this way the Netherlands was the prime site for blending all three and crafting its own practical response in the process.[24] Van den Heuvel managed to remain an independent operator, shifting from one project and anti-communist coalition to another, matching the "free agent" identity of Brian Crozier. But this required a constant balancing act between partners. The cool pragmatism of the British, close to the Dutch outlook, "could form a counterbalance to the German more philosophical, ideological approach".[25] But the British – along with the Italians, the Belgians, the Swiss, the Scandinavians, and to some extent the Americans – never became full partners, either holding Interdoc at arm's length or simply being unable to form the national committees as direct partners with SOEV/OWI and the Verein. Instead it was the Germans who dominated in the first decade, although from 1965 onwards Interdoc successfully developed its "platform" function, plugged into a diverse range of anti-communist networks and working closely with specific individuals and institutions on a more ad hoc project-by-project basis. The suspicion may well remain that Interdoc – via the Dutch – was little more than another CIA ploy to control West European activities. Yet the evidence points towards a more subtle conclusion: that the Americans (in the beginning at least, in the form of Allen Dulles) encouraged the Europeans to *organize themselves* in order to increase the effectiveness of their anti-communist activities, and the Dutch were the most likely to succeed as point-men for guiding such an operation. This would place the origins of Interdoc within the context of the general American support for European integration in the late 1950s and early 1960s. Such a conclusion would also fit with the fact that at the heart of Interdoc lay Franco-German rapprochement. Similar to what happened with European integration as a whole, transatlantic and trans-European relations in the 1960s and 1970s did not really work out as any of the parties had originally hoped.

The flexibility this allowed was in many ways more effective, and it tied in more with the needs of the loose alliance of anti-communist activists spread across the West and beyond that it linked together. Somehow this approach fitted better with the democratic principles that it was supposed to be defending than the more static framework of the early period. It was simply impossible to coordinate Western anti-communism fully – this was no mirror-image response to Moscow's apparatus. Interdoc did hold together a "network of networks" that would otherwise not have coalesced, due to different purposes or different shades of anti-communism. Admittedly Interdoc was never able to escape its public reputation as an affiliate of Western intelligence. Domestic politics and bureaucratic divisions meant that it was not utilized as fully by Western governments as it could have been. It functioned according to a media/communications model that looks somewhat dated in the internet age. It exposed along the way the severe obstacles that lay in the way of European integration in the security field, a legacy that is still being acted out today. Yet these limitations should not obscure Interdoc's contribution to the ideological contest that was the Cold War.

The protection and promotion of Western values – exemplified by the UN Declaration of Human Rights – was central to the Interdoc enterprise from beginning to end. Neither did this egalitarian stance shy away from engaging in self-criticism, even though the demands of facing a communist adversary often obscured this. Interdoc's association with right-wing anti-communism should not erase its progressive (if admittedly patriarchal) social outlook. It was precisely out of this progressiveness that a vision of how the Cold War could end emerged. Like most visions, it was only partly realized, but its significance for any consideration of intelligence and security liaison, and more broadly the links between ideas and power, remains relevant today.

Appendix I: Interdoc Conferences

List of all Interdoc meetings:

1. Jouy-en-Josas (France), 2 - 5 october, 1958
   Theme: "La guerre psychologique"

2. Wolfheze (Netherlands), 16 - 19 april, 1959
   Theme: "Communism and Religion"

3. Ettal (Germany), 25 - 27 september, 1959
   Theme: "Das Wertbewusstsein und der Einfluss des kommunistischen Denkens und Wirkens"

4. Aix-en-Provence (France), 24 - 27 march, 1960
   Theme: "Des systèmes économiques comme porteurs de valeurs"

5. Heelsum (Netherlands), 20 september - 2 october, 1960
   Theme: "L'influence de la coexistance pacifique communisme sur le monde non-communiste"

6. Bad Soden (Germany), 13 - 16 april, 1961
   Themes: - Gedanken zum Begriff Praxis als philosophisches Element der kommunistischen Aktion;
   - Faschismus, Nationalsozialismus, Kommunismus;
   - Die Rolle der Entwicklungsländer im kalten Krieg.

7. Barbizon (France), 5 - 8 october, 1961
   Theme: "La formation de cadres"

8. Mont Saint-Michel (France), 29 march - 1 april, 1962
   Theme: "Lattitude des cadres de l'industrie devant les problèmes posés par une société en transformation";
   "Les possibilités concrètes d'une action générale de réflexion"

250

9. Noordwijk aan Zee (Netherlands), 27 - 30 september, 1962
   Theme: "Möglichkeiten einer Zusammenarbeit zwischen Erziehungswesen und Industrie zur Förderung der staatsbürgerlichen Erziehung der Führungskräfte"

10. Bad Godesberg (Germany), 28 - 31 march, 1963
    Theme: "Die verschiedenen Aspekte der Aspekte der Situation des zweigeteilten Deutschlands im Rahmen der Ost-West-Auseinandersetzung"

11. Oxford (England), 25 - 28 september, 1963
    Theme: "Britain and the Commonwealth and East-West problems"

12. Lunteren (Netherlands), 6 - 9 may, 1964
    Theme: "Youth and Communism"

13. Eschwege (Germany), 1 - 4 october, 1964
    Theme: "Gedanken über eine aktive Politik des Friedens"

14. Locarno (Switzerland), 8 - 11 april 1965
    Theme: "Practical experiences in regard to East-West contacts"

15. Zandvoort (Netherlands), 24 - 25 september, 1965
    Theme: "Preparation for East-West Contacts"

16. Cambridge (England), 22 - 23 september, 1966
    Theme: "Africa: East-West confrontation"

17. Bad Tönisstein, Eifel (Germany), 22-23 september 1967
    Theme: "Communist Reassessment of Capitalism; Its Resultant Strategy and the Western Response"

- Noordwijk (Nederland), maart 1968.
"The Armed Forces in the Psycho-Political East-West Confrontation".

- Zandvoort (Nederland), september 1968.
"The New Left".

- Deidesheim (BRD), september 1969.
"Neutrality and East-West Détente - wishful thinking or reality?"

- Noordwijk (Nederland), april 1970.
"Radicalism and Security".

- Rimini (Italië), oktober 1970.
"Soviet Activities in the Mediterranean".

- Noordwijk (Nederland), juni 1971.
"Guerrilla Warfare in Asia".

- Brighton (Engeland), september 1971.
"The Policies of Western Europe and North America towards the Soviet Bloc"

- Valley Forge (VS), november 1972.
"American-European Relations vis à vis Communist Objectives in Europe".

- Noordwijk (Nederland), september 1973.
"Development of East-West Relations through freer movement of people, ideas and information."

- Noordwijk (Nederland), september 1974.
"Europe and the North Atlantic Alliance".

- Noordwijk (Nederland), september 1974
"Verteidigungsbereitschaft".

- Noordwijk (Nederland), september 1976.
"Implementation of the Conference on Security and Co-operation in Europe".

Appendix II: Interdoc Publications

II. INTERDOC PUBLICATIONS

Series on East-West Relations

1. Tasks for the Free World Today; (*)
   contributions by various writers;
   Mohn & Co., G.m.b.H, Gütersloh, F.R.G.;
   1964 - 93 pp. Hfl. 3,--

2. The Challenge of Coexistence; (*)
   contributions by various writers;
   Ampersand Ltd., London;
   1965 - 130 pp. Hfl. 3,--

3. East-West Contacts in Practice;
   contributions by various writers;
   Interdoc, The Hague;
   1965 - 60 pp. Hfl. 3,--

4. Communist Reassessment of Capitalism,
   Its Resultant Strategy and the Western Response; (*)
   contributions by various writers;
   Interdoc, The Hague;
   1967 - 68 pp. Hfl. 3,--

5. War and Peace in Communist Thinking;
   by C.C. van den Heuvel;
   Interdoc, The Hague;
   1967 - 22 pp. Hfl. 1,50

6. Neutralism and East-West Détente -
   Wishful Thinking or Reality ?
   contributions by various writers;
   Interdoc, The Hague;
   1969 - 95 pp. Hfl. 3,50

7. National Views on Neutralism and East-West Détente;
   contributions by various writers;
   Interdoc, The Hague;
   1970 - 109 pp. Hfl. 3,50

(*) = out of stock

(Series on East-West Relations - contd.)

8. Soviet Foreign Policy and Ideology;
   by C.C. van den Heuvel;
   Interdoc, The Hague;
   1972 - 15 pp. Hfl. 1,50

9. American-European Relations vis-à-vis
   Communist Objectives in Europe; (*)
   Interdoc, The Hague;
   1972 - 52 pp. Hfl. 7,50

10. Development of East-West Relations Through
    Freer Movement of People, Ideas and Information;
    contributions by various writers;
    Interdoc, The Hague;
    1973 - 57 pp. Hfl. 6,50

11. The Soviet Conception of Coexistence and the Conference
    on Security and Cooperation in Europe (CSCE);
    by Boris Meissner;
    East-West Institute, the Hague;
    1975 - 59 pp. Hfl. 6,50

12. Implementation of the Conference on Security and
    Cooperation in Europe (CSCE), Part I.
    by C.C. van den Heuvel, R.D. Praaning and F.Z.R. Wijchers;
    East-West Institute, the Hague;
    1976 - 45 pp. f 6,--

Series on the New Left

1. The New Left;
   contributions by various writers;
   Interdoc, The Hague;
   1969 - 52 pp. Hfl. 3,50

2. The New Left in the United States of America,
   Great Britain and the Federal Republic of Germany;
   contributions by various writers;
   Interdoc, The Hague;
   1969 - 77 pp. Hfl. 3,50

(*) = out of stock

(Series on the New Left - contd.)

3. La Crise de l'Enseignement Supérieur en France;
by Claude Harmel;
Interdoc, The Hague;
1970 - 35 pp. Hfl. 1,50

4. Student Revolutionaries of the Sixties;
by Karel van Wolferen;
Interdoc, The Hague;
1971 - 60 pp. Hfl. 4,50

Series on Asian Problems

1. Cambodia - Problems of Neutrality and Independence;
Interdoc, The Hague;
1970 - 16 pp. Hfl. 1,50

2. South Vietnam Takes the Offensive - Lam Son 719;
Interdoc, The Hague;
1971 - 12 pp. Hfl. 1,50

3. Activities of the G.D.R. in India;
Interdoc, The Hague;
1971 - 39 pp. Hfl. 1,50

4. The Indonesian Communist Party (PKI) and Its Relations with the Soviet Union and the People's Republic of China;
by C. van Dijk;
Interdoc, The Hague;
1972 - 76 pp. Hfl. 3,50

5. Soviet Aid to India; (*)
Interdoc, The Hague;
1973 - 39 pp. Hfl. 4,50

6. Soviet Views on Japanese Expansion;
Editor: Dr.H.A. van Oort;
Interdoc, The Hague;
1973 - 113 pp. Hfl. 6,--

(*) = out of stock

(Series on Asian Problems - contd.)

7. The Devious Dalang
   Editor R.S. Karni;
   Interdoc, The Hague;
   1974 - 211 pp. Hfl. 9,--

Series on Vietnam

1. Vietnam, Aspects of a Tragedy;
   contributions by various writers;
   1967 - 136 pp. Hfl. 4,50

2. Viet-nam, Aspects d'une Tragédie;
   contributions by various writers;
   1967 - 136 pp. Hfl. 4,50

3. Vietnam is Our World;
   by Max Nord;
   1970 - 125 pp. Hfl. 8,--

Series on African Problems

1. East-West Confrontation in Africa (*)
   contributions by various writers;
   Interdoc, The Hague;
   1966 - 83 pp. Hfl. 3,--

Series on Guerrilla Warfare

1. Tupamaros - A Pattern for Urban Guerrilla Warfare
   in Latin America;
   by Alphonse Max;
   Interdoc, The Hague;
   1970 - 16 pp. Hfl. 1,50

2. Guerrillas in Latin America;
   by Alphonse Max;
   Interdoc, The Hague;
   1971 - 100 pp. hfl. 3,50

(*) = out of stock

(Series on Guerrilla Warfare - contd.)

3. Guerrilla Warfare in Asia;
contributions by various writers;
1971 - 90 pp. Hfl. 3,50
Interdoc, The Hague

Series on Neutralism and Détente

1. Neutralism and East-West Détente - Wishful Thinking or Reality?
contributions by various writers;
Interdoc, The Hague;
1969 - 96 pp. Hfl. 3,50

2. National Views on Neutralism and East West Détente;
contributions by various writers;
Interdoc, The Hague;
1969 - 109 pp. Hfl. 3,50

Series on International Communist Front Organizations

1. The International Student Movement - History and Background
by G. van Maanen;
1966 - 350 pp. Hfl. 8,--

2. F.I.R. - History and Background;
by A. Heldring;
1969 - 120 pp. Hfl. 3,50

3. F.I.R. - Histoire et Actualité;
by A. Heldring;
1969 - 120 pp. Hfl. 3,50

Series on Defence Problems

1. The Armed Forces in the Psychopolitical East-West Confrontation;
contributions by various writers;
Interdoc, The Hague;
1968 - 70 pp. Hfl. 3,50

2. Radicalism and Security;
contributions by various writers;
Interdoc, The Hague;
1970 - 134 pp. Hfl. 3,50

Additional Publications

1. A Soviet Dilemma: Soviet Jews (A study in Jewish Emigration from the Soviet Union)
   by R.I. Weitzel
   The Hague 1980 - 43 pp.

2. Afghanistan is our world
   by G. Pietersen
   Interdoc, The Hague;
   1981 - 51 pp.

Bijlage bij blz.3.

13. Implementation of the Conference on Security and Cooperation
    in Europe, Part II
    by C.C.van den Heuvel, R.D.Praaning, P.Vaillant, F.Z.R.Wijchers;
    East-West Institute, the Hague.
    1977 - 102 pp, Hfl.7,50
14. Implementation of the Conference on Security and Cooperation
    in Europe, Part III
    by F.Z.R.Wijchers;
    East-West Institute, the Hague.
    1977 - 97 pp, Hfl. 7,50
15. Soviet Perceptions of Western Realities
    by C.C.van den Heuvel;
    American Bar Association, Chicago(USA)
    1977 - 43 pp.
16. The Belgrade Conference, Progress or Regression?
    Ed.C.C.van den Heuvel, R.D.Praaning.
    Contributions: Dr.G.Wettig, American Commission on Security and
                   Cooperation in Europe, Dr.V.Lomeiko, Dr.L.Aćimović.
                   C.C.van den Heuvel.
    New Rhine Publishers, Leyden.
    1978 - 60 pp, Hfl. 9,50

Gestopte reeksen uitgebracht doot het Oost-West Instituut/Interdoc:

a. Activities of the Communist World Organizations (quarterly)
b. The Communist Parties (once a year)
c. Religion and Church in the Communist Orbit (monthly)
d. Review of Communist Scientific and Political Publications (monthly)
e. East-West Contacts (bimonthly)
f. Economic East-West relations (monthly)
g. Africa in the light of Soviet Russian publications (quarterly)
h. Essays on the Psycho-political Situation in the Eastern Bloc
   Countries of Europe (10 times a year)
j. The psychological situation in East Germany (quarterly)
k. Notes on Communist and Communist-sponsored Activities as reported
   by Communist sources (weekly)
l. Handbuch der kommunistische Weltorganisationen (loose-leaf collectic
m. Red China (monthly)
n. Pro-Chinese Newspapers and Periodicals (once a year)

Nagenoeg alle series uitgebracht in Engels, Duits, Frans en Spaans.
Bovendien werden i.s.m. "Die Deutsche Arbeitsgruppe für Ost-West
Beziehungen e.V." (München), "das Institut für Gesellschaft und Wissen-
schaft in Mitteldeutschland", Erlangen,Stichting Volk en Verdediging
(Nederland), verschillende andere reeksen, brochures, boeken, en
ook conferenties uitgebracht en georganiseerd.

Appendix III: Interdoc Contacts in Eastern Europe

V. Instituten waarmee contacten worden onderhouden:

Soviet Union

1. Institute for World Economy and International Relations of the USSR
   Academy of Sciences
   adress: Yaroslavskaya Ulitsa 13,
   Moscow L-243
   tel. 283.50.40

2. Soviet Committee for European Security and Cooperation
   adress: Moscow G-34
   3, Kropotkinstr.

3. Institute for the United States of America and Canada
   of the USSR Academy of Sciences
   adress: Khlebny Pereulde 2/3
   Mosco K-9
   tel. 290.58.75

Yugoslavia

Institute for International Politics and Economics
adress: Makedonska 25
   11000 Beograd

Poland

Polish Institute of International Affairs
adress: 1a, Warecka street
   00-950 Warsaw
   tel. 28.82.51

German Democratic Republic

1. Institute for International Politics and Economics
   adress: 102 East Berlin
      Breitestrasse 11

2. G.D.R. Committee for European Security and Cooperation
   in Europe
   adress: 102 East Berlin
           Breitestrasse 11

Hungary

Committé National pour la Sécurité Europeenne
adress: Szeceenyi Rakpart 19
        Budapest 5

Romania

Association for International Law and International Relations
of the Socialist Republic of Romania
adress: 47 Kiseleff Avenue, Sector 1
        Bucharest

Bulgaria

Institute for International Relations and Socialist Integration
Moslowska Str. 21
Sofia

National Committee for European Security and Cooperation
Dobromir Hriz str. 7
Sofia

The Institute for International Relations and Foreign Policy
Dr.Janko Vekilov
Dr.Georgi Stefanov

The Bulgarian Committee for European Security and Cooperation
Mr.Guero Grozev, president

Soviet War Veterans Committee
Gogolevsky Bulvar 4
121019 Moscow
USSR

Zwiazek Bojownikow o Wolnosc i Demokracje - SBoWid
Aleje Ujazdowskie Nr 6 a
00 - 461 Warsaw

Komitee der Antifaschistischen Widerstandskampfer
in der Deutschen Demokratischen Republik
Unter den Linden 12
DDR 108 Berlin

SUBNOR (Savez Udruzenja Boraca Narodnooslobodilackog Rata Jugoslavije
Federation of Veterans' Associations of the People's Liberation
War in Yugoslavia
Bulevar Lenjina 6
BEOGRAD

Notes

Introduction: The Communist Challenge

1. Rolf Geyer, 'Conclusions', in *Communist Reassessment of Capitalism, Its Resultant Strategy and the Western Response* (The Hague: Interdoc, 1968), p. 68.
2. George F. Kennan, *Memoirs 1925–1950* (Boston: Bantam, 1969), p. 588; Reagan's 8 March 1983 speech to the National Association of Evangelicals in Orlando, Florida, is his first recorded use of the phrase 'evil empire'.
3. Melvyn P. Leffler, *For the Soul of Mankind: The United States, the Soviet Union, and the Cold War* (New York: Hill & Wang, 2007), p. 8.
4. Odd Arne Westad, *The Global Cold War* (Cambridge: Cambridge University Press, 2007), p. 4.
5. Vladislav M. Zubok, *A Failed Empire: The Soviet Union in the Cold War from Stalin to Gorbachev* (Chapel Hill, NC: University of North Carolina Press, 2007), p. 6.
6. Philip Taylor, *Munitions of the Mind: A History of Propaganda from the Ancient World to the Present Day* (Manchester: Manchester University Press, 2003), p. 250.
7. Nigel Gould-Davis, 'The Logic of Soviet Cultural Diplomacy', *Diplomatic History*, 27 (April 2003), p. 195.
8. Wyn Rees and Richard J. Aldrich, 'European and US Approaches to Counterterrorism: Two Contrasting Cultures?' in Ronald Tiersky and Erik Jones (eds), *Europe Today: A Twenty-First Century Introduction* (Lanham, MA: Rowman & Littlefield, 2007) pp. 441–442.
9. See Hugh Wilford, *The Mighty Wurlitzer: How the CIA Played America* (Cambridge, MA: Harvard University Press, 2008).
10. Richard J. Aldrich, *The Hidden Hand: Britain, America and Cold War Secret Intelligence* (London: John Murray, 2001), p. 5.
11. Stella Rimington (Director General of MI5 1992–1996), quoted in Aldrich, *Hidden Hand*, p. 9.
12. See H. Bradford Westerfield, 'America and the World of Intelligence Liaison', *Intelligence and National Security* 11 (1996), pp. 523–560; Chris Clough, 'Quid Pro Quo: The Challenges of International Strategic Intelligence Cooperation', *International Journal of Intelligence and CounterIntelligence*, 17 (2004), pp. 601–613; Jennifer E. Syms, 'Foreign Intelligence Liaison: Devils, Deals, and Details', *International Journal of Intelligence and CounterIntelligence* 19 (2006), pp. 195–217.
13. Wesley Wark, 'The Origins of Intelligence Cooperation between the United States and West Germany', in Detlef Junker (ed.), *The United States and Germany in the Era of the Cold War, 1945–1968*, Vol. 1 (Washington, DC: German Historical Institute, 2004), p. 248.
14. See Giles Scott-Smith, 'Not a NATO Responsibility? Psychological Warfare, the Berlin Crisis, and the formation of Interdoc', in A. Locher and C. Nuenlist (eds), *Challenges Beyond Deterrence: NATO in the 1960s* (London: Routledge, 2006), pp. 31–49; Linda Risso, ' "Enlightening Public Opinion": A Study of NATO's Information Policies between 1949 and 1959 based on Recently Declassified Documents', *Cold War History* 7 (February 2007), pp. 45–74; Valérie Aubourg, 'Creating the Texture of the Atlantic Community: The NATO Information Service, Private

Atlantic Networks and the Atlantic Community in the 1950s', in V. Aubourg et al. (eds), *European Community, Atlantic Community?* (Paris: Soleb, 2008), pp. 390–415.
15. Sean McMeekin, *The Red Millionaire: A Political Biography of Willi Münzenberg* (New Haven, CT: Yale University Press, 2003); Martin Ceadel, 'The First Communist "Peace Society": The British Anti-War Movement 1932–1935', *Twentieth Century British History* 1 (1990), pp. 58–86.
16. 'Report by the National Security Council on Coordination of Foreign Information Measures', NSC 4, 17 December 1947, Document 252 in C. Thomas Thorne Jr. and David S. Patterson (eds), *Foreign Relations of the United States 1945–1952: Emergence of the Intelligence Establishment* (Washington, DC: US Government Printing Office, 1996), pp. 640–641.
17. Christopher Andrew and Vasili Mitrokhin, *The Mitrokhin Archive: The KGB in Europe and the West* (London: Allen Lane, 1999), p. 361.
18. Marshall Shulman, *Stalin's Foreign Policy Reappraised* (Cambridge, MA: Harvard University Press, 1963), pp. 80–103.
19. Zubok, *A Failed Empire*, p. 102.
20. See Rolf Steininger, *The German Question: The Stalin Note of 1952 and the Problem of Reunification* (New York: Columbia University, 1990); Klaus Larres and Ken Osgood (eds), *The Cold War after Stalin's Death: A Missed Opportunity for Peace?* (Lanham, MD: Rowman & Littlefield, 2006).
21. Quote taken from a report submitted by Soviet atomic scientists to the Politburo in March 1954. See Wilfried Loth, *Overcoming the Cold War: A History of Détente 1950–1991* (Basingstoke: Palgrave Macmillan, 2002), p. 34.
22. Robert Tucker, *The Soviet Political Mind: Studies in Stalinism and Post-Stalin Change* (London: Pall Mall Press, 1963), pp. 180–222.
23. Khrushchev, 'Peaceful Coexistence', *Foreign Affairs* (October 1959), pp.126–128.
24. Ken Osgood, *Total Cold War: Eisenhower's Secret Propaganda Battle at Home and Abroad* (Laurence, KA: University Press of Kansas, 2006), p. 24; Ken Osgood, 'The Perils of Coexistence: Peace and Propaganda in Eisenhower's Foreign Policy', in Larres and Osgood (eds), *The Cold War after Stalin's Death*, pp. 40, 41–42; see also Blanche Wiesen Cook, *The Declassified Eisenhower* (Harmondsworth: Penguin, 1981), pp. 149–183.
25. Evron Kirkpatrick (ed.), *Year of Crisis: Communist Propaganda Activities in 1956* (New York: Macmillan, 1957), p. 7. This book was prepared with material from USIA's Office of Research and Information.
26. See 'Statement of Policy on East-West Exchanges', NSC-5607, *Foreign Relations of the United States 1955–57*, Vol. XXIV: Soviet Union; Eastern Mediterranean, pp. 243–246.
27. Sir Humphrey Trevelyan (Foreign Office) to M.A.M. Robb (British Embassy, Washington, DC), 19 February 1962, FO 1110/1489, Papers of the Information Research Department, National Archives, London (hereafter IRD NAL); 'The Answer to Peaceful Co-Existence', n.d. [1962], FO 1110/1489, IRD NAL; Christopher Mayhew, *Coexistence-Plus: A Positive Approach to World Peace* (London: Bodley Head, 1962). See also Lynn Smith, 'Covert British Propaganda: The Information Research Department, 1947–77', *Millennium* 9/1 (1980), pp. 67–83.
28. M.A.M. Robb to Sir Humphrey Trevelyan, 1 March 1962, FO 1110/1489, IRD NAL.
29. Sir Humphrey Trevelyan (Foreign Office) to M.A.M. Robb (British Embassy, Washington, DC), 19 February 1962, FO 1110/1489, IRD NAL.
30. M.A.M. Robb to Sir Humphrey Trevelyan, 1 March 1962, FO 1110/1489, IRD NAL.

31. National Security Action Memorandum No. 61, 'An Effective Counter Theme to "Peaceful Coexistence"', 14 July 1961, National Security Action Memoranda, Meetings and Memoranda Series, National Security Files, John F. Kennedy Presidential Library, Boston, MA.
32. Lucius Battle, oral history interview, 23 June 1971, Oral History Collection, Harry S. Truman Presidential Library.
33. Von Dellingshausen (Ministerium für Gesamtdeutsche Fragen), "Geistig-Politische Auseinandersetzung mit dem Kommunismus in Deutschland," 15 October 1957, File B 137, Collection 16429, National Archives, Koblenz (hereafter NAK).
34. Uwe Holl, interview with the author, Cologne, 18 December 2005.
35. "Maar bovenal was internationale samenwerking noodzakelijk om te komen tot een uitwisseling van gegevens over een wereldomvattende beweging, die vanuit enkele centrale punten (Moskou en later Peking) gedirigeerd wordt." Louis Einthoven, *Tegen de Stroom In* (Apeldoorn: Semper Agindo, 1974), p. 200.
36. Details of Geyer's biography from Michel Garder, Rolf Geyer et al., *Einstellung zum Krieg in West und Ost* (Kopernicus Verlag: München, 1980), p. 144; Gunhild Bohm-Geyer, interview with the author, Würthsee, 4 July 2008 and correspondence thereafter.
37. Rio Praaning et al. in *Strijdbaar Toen en Nu: Vriendenbundel bij de 80ste verjaardag van Kees van den Heuvel*; Pieter Koerts, interviews with the author, Amsterdam, 2 June 2004, and Leiden, 24 June 2009.
38. On the Albrecht Group see C.M. Schulten, *'En verpletterd werd het juk': Verzet in Nederland 1940–1945* (The Hague: Sdu, 1995); J.W.M. Linssen, 'De Albrechtgroep: een fenomeen ontleed', in P. Koedijk et al. (eds), *Verspreiders voor het Vaderland* (The Hague: Sdu, 1996), pp. 37–84; Anon., *Albrecht meldt zich* (Wageningen: Zomer en Keunings, 1946).
39. Rens Broekhuis, Chris Vos et al., *De Geheime Dienst: Verhalen over de BVD* (Amsterdam: Boom, 2005), pp. 13, 34–35. As former BVD officer Frits Hoekstra put it, the World War II experience defined the outlook of both the Christians and the communists: 'they were each other's mirror image' ("zij waren elkaars spiegelbeeld"). Herman Veenhof, 'Hoofdrol orthodoxe christenen in BVD', available online at http://intel.web-log.nl/intel/2006/07/hoofdrol_orthod.html (accessed 22 June 2011).
40. Anthony Dake, interview with the author, The Hague, 27 July 2011.
41. C.C. van den Heuvel, interview with the author, The Hague, 6 August 2002.
42. C.C. van den Heuvel, 'De Psychologische Oorlogvoering van het Communisme in het Kader van de Koude Oorlog', n.d. [1954–1955], Inzagedossier: Psychologische Oorlogvoering, Freedom of Information request (Wet Openbaar Bestuur) to Ministry of Justice / AIVD, 12 December 2005.
43. On Van den Heuvel's "dirty tricks" campaign against the Dutch Communist Party see Dick Engelen, *Geschiedenis van de Binnenlandse Veiligheidsdienst* (The Hague: Sdu, 1995), pp. 222–224. A similar campaign was successfully waged against the Danish Communist Party: see Peer Henrik Hansen, 'Upstairs and Downstairs: The Forgotten CIA Operations in Copenhagen', *International Journal of Intelligence and CounterIntelligence* 19 (2006–2007), pp. 685–701.
44. Isaiah Berlin, 'Soviet Russian Culture', in Berlin (ed. Henry Hardy), *The Soviet Mind: Russian Culture under Communism* (Washington, DC: Brookings Institution, 2004), p. 155.

45. C.C. van den Heuvel et. al., 'Possibilities of Psychological Defence against Soviet Influence' (study group report on the US (The Hague, Netherlands) April 1959), p. 3.
46. C.C. van den Heuvel, *East-West Confrontation: A Psychological Strategy* (The Hague: Interdoc, 1967), p. 5.
47. "Das INTERDOK ist der Ansicht, daß zur geistigen Auseinandersetzung mit dem Weltkommunismus und zur politischen und wirtschaftlichen Verteidigung der demokratischen Staats-, Gesellschafts- und Wirtschaftsordnung gegen der Angriff des totalitären Weltkommunismus auch die Vervollkommnung der eigenen freiheitlichen Ordnungen gehört. Die Sicherung, Bewahrung, Entwicklung und Verteidigung unserer Lebensordnungen ist der beste Anti-Kommunismus." 'Merkblatt über Veranlassung, Vorgeschichte und Aufgabe des INTERDOK', March 1963, File: B 137, Collection: 16431, archive of the Bundesministerium für Gesamtdeutsche Fragen, NAK.
48. See David Engerman, *Know Your Enemy: The Rise and Fall of America's Soviet Experts* (Oxford: Oxford University Press, 2009). The phrase "military-intellectual complex" is taken from Ron Robin, *The Making of the Cold War Enemy: Culture and Politics in the Military-Intellectual Complex* (Princeton: Princeton University Press, 2001).
49. Quoted in Tucker, *The Soviet Political Mind*, p. 206.
50. S.W. Couwenberg, *Oost en West op de drempel van een nieuw tijdperk* (The Hague: Pax Nederland, 1966), pp. 188–199.
51. 'Oost-West Instituut Jaarverslag 1965', p. 6.
52. Van den Heuvel to Dr Laureano Lopez Rodo, 28 December 1964, File: 166 Spanje 1964–1974, Overige West-Europese Landen (1964–1976), archive of C.C. van den Heuvel, National Archives, The Hague (hereafter CC NAH).
53. For instance, correspondence shows that Helmut Gruber, 'Willi Münzenberg's Communist Propaganda Empire 1921–1933', *Journal of Modern History* 38 (1966), pp. 278–297, was on the Interdoc reading list.
54. See W. Scott Lucas, 'Mobilizing Culture: The State-Private Network and the CIA in the Early Cold War', in Dale Carter (ed.), *War and Cold War in American Foreign Policy 1942–1962* (New York: Palgrave Macmillan, 2002) pp. 83–107; Scott Lucas, *Freedom's War: The American Crusade against the Soviet Union* (New York: New York University Press, 1999).
55. See Frances Stonor Saunders, *Who Paid the Piper? The CIA and the Cultural Cold War* (London: Granta, 1999); Giles Scott-Smith, *The Politics of Apolitical Culture: The CIA, the Congress for Cultural Freedom, and Post-war American Hegemony* (London: Routledge, 2002); Hugh Wilford, *The CIA, the British Left and the Cold War* (London: Frank Cass, 2003), pp. 193–224, 262–296.
56. Ian Richardson et al., *Bilderberg People: Elite Power and Consensus in World Affairs* (London: Routledge, 2011), p. 18.
57. Wolfram Kaiser, 'Transnational Networks in European Governance', in Wolfram Kaiser et al. (eds), *The History of the European Union: Origins of a Trans- and Supranational Polity 1950–72* (London: Routledge, 2009), p. 15; Wolfram Kaiser et al., 'Transnational Networks in European Integration Governance: Historical Perspectives on an Elusive Phenomenon', in Kaiser et al. (eds), *Transnational Networks in Regional Integration: Governing Europe 1945–83* (London: Palgrave Macmillan, 2010), p. 2.
58. Ken Osgood, 'Hearts and Minds: The Unconventional Cold War', *Journal of Cold War History* 4 (Spring 2002), p. 86.

59. On CEDI and CIDCC see Johannes Grossman, 'Ein Europa der "Hintergründigen": Antikommunistische christliche Organisationen, konservative Elitenzirkel und private Außenpolitik in Westeuropa nach dem Zweiten Weltkrieg', in Johannes Wienand and Christianne Wienand (eds), *Die kulturelle integration Europas* (Wiesbaden: Springer, 2010), pp. 303–340; on the Pinay Circle see David Teacher, *Rogue Agents: Habsburg, Pinay, and the Private Cold War 1951–1991*, available online at www.cryptome.org/2012/01/cercle-pinay-6i.pdf.
60. Hugh Wilford, *The CIA, the British Left, and the Cold War: Calling the Tune?* (London: Frank Cass, 2003), p. 254.
61. C.C. van den Heuvel to Hernandez, 26 February 1968, File: 180 Zuid-Korea 1966–1975, Diverse Oost-Aziatische Landen (1963–1975), CC NAH.
62. 'die Diversifizierung, Privatisierung und wachsende Komplexität außenpolitischer Entscheidungsprozesse'. Grossman, 'Ein Europa der "Hintergründigen"', p. 320.

1 Anti-Communism and PsyWar in the 1950s

1. 'Why Communists are Dangerous', n.d. [1963], background briefing paper contained in Maclaren to diplomatic posts, 13 February 1963, FO 1110/1712, papers of the Information Research Department, National Archives, London (hereafter IRD NAL).
2. William Glenn Gray, *Germany's Cold War: The Global Campaign to Isolate East Germany, 19491–969* (Chapel Hill: University of North Carolina Press, 2003), pp. 10–12, 25, 38.
3. Ibid., p. 18.
4. Ibid., p. 40.
5. Laszlo Görgey, *Bonn's Eastern Policy 19641–971* (Hamden: Archon, 1972), pp. 8–11, 13, 26.
6. Mary Ellen Reese, *General Reinhard Gehlen: The CIA Connection* (Fairfax: George Mason University Press, 1990), pp. 12–13, 17.
7. See Wolfgang Krieger, 'German–American Intelligence Relations, 1945–1956: New Evidence on the Origins of the BND', *Diplomacy & Statecraft* 22 (2011), pp. 28–43, for the latest revelations on the US relationship with Gehlen, which raises doubts about Gehlen's original motives. See also James H. Critchfield, *Partners at the Creation: The Men behind Postwar Germany's Defense and Intelligence Establishments* (Annapolis: Naval Institute Press, 2003), pp. 24–27.
8. Critchfield, pp. 31–32, 45.
9. Ibid., p. 47.
10. Ibid., p. 87. Eric Waldman stated much the same thing in Reese, *General Reinhard Gehlen*, pp. 94–95.
11. Galloway (assistant director of special operations) quoted in Krieger, 'German-American Intelligence Relations', p. 35.
12. Reese, *General Reinhard Gehlen*, pp. 110, 118, 129.
13. Patrick Major, *The Death of the KPD: Communism and Anti-Communism in West Germany, 1945–1956* (Oxford: Clarendon Press, 1997), p. 258.
14. This led to the formation by the employers' association and the Ministry of the Interior of the privately run Beratungsstelle für Betriebsschutz in April 1951, which became the Gemeinschaft zum Schutze der deutschen Wirtschaft in 1959, located in Essen. 'Geistige Auseinandersetzung mit dem Kommunismus und psychologische Verteidigung', 31 March 1960, File: 16430, Collection: B 137,

Bundesministerium für gesamtdeutsche Fragen, National Archives, Koblenz (hereafter NAK).
15. 'Stellungnahme zu Fragen der psychologischen Kriegführung und zur Strategie des kalten Krieges', 3 December 1952, File: 16428, Collection: B 137, NAK.
16. "der Pflege des gesamtdeutschen Bewußtseins": 'Zur geistig-politischen Auseinandersetzung mit dem Kommunismus', 14 January 1966, File: 16431, Collection: B 137, NAK.
17. On these private organizations see Stefan Creuzberger, *Kampf für die Einheit: Das gesamtdeutsche Ministerium und die politische Kultur des Kalten Krieges 1949–1969* (Düsseldorf: Droste, 2008), pp. 141–153; Ernst Nolte, *Deutschland und der Kalte Krieg* (Munich: R. Piper Verlag, 1974), pp. 403–404. Nolte describes the Ministry as not so much an *"Überministerium"* but a "sphere of activity" (*Betätigungsfeld*), albeit an important one.
18. 'Vorschlag zur Bildung einer zentralen Propagandaorganisation zur Abwehr der kommunistischen Infiltration', 12 October 1953, File: 16428, Collection: B 137, NAK.
19. Deborah Kisatsky, *The United States and the European Right 1945–1955* (Columbus, OH: Ohio State University Press, 2005), pp. 59–85. In Daniele Ganser, *NATO's Secret Armies: Operation Gladio and Terrorism in Western Europe* (London: Frank Cass, 2005), Daniele Ganser records how the BDJ–TD set-up was also closely linked to the Gehlen Organization, pp. 189–211.
20. 'Statement of Intentions vis-à-vis Resistance Groups', 12 October 1954, File: 16428, Collection: B 137, NAK.
21. For a detailed discussion of the negotiations with the CIA see Creuzberger, *Kampf für die Einheit*, pp. 197–223.
22. 'Telegram from the Secretary of State to the Department of State', 17 December 1955, *Foreign Relations of the United States* (hereafter *FRUS*), 1955–1957 Volume IV: Western European Security and Integration, p. 37.
23. Geistig-Politische Auseinandersetzung mit dem Kommunismus in Deutschland', 15 October 1957, File: 16429, Collection: B 137, NAK. Through CIA liaison officer Seymour Bolton, von Dellingshausen was influenced by US thinking on Rollback during the early to mid-1950s, although this mindset faded out by the end of the decade. See Creuzberger, *Kampf für die Einheit*, p. 140.
24. On the formation and activities of the NATO Information Service (NATIS) see Linda Risso, ' "Enlightening Public Opinion": A Study of NATO's Information Policies between 1949 and 1959 based on Recently Declassified Documents', *Cold War History 7* (February 2007), pp. 45–74; Valérie Aubourg, 'Creating the Texture of the Atlantic Community: The NATO Information Service, private Atlantic networks and the Atlantic Community in the 1950s', in Valérie Aubourg, Gérard Bossuat, and Giles Scott-Smith (eds), *European Community, Atlantic Community?* (Paris: Soleb, 2008), pp. 390–415.
25. General H.J. Kruls, *Vrede of Oorlog: De Wereld, West-Europa en de Benelux onder de Dreiging van onze Tijd* (The Hague: Stok, 1952), p. 237; C.C. van den Heuvel, 'Psychologische Oorlogvoering', *Militair Spectator*, 131/1 (1962), p. 22.
26. 16 February 1951, D-R(51)10, NATO archive, Brussels (hereafter NATO).
27. 'Proposed Advisory Committee on NATO Information', 8 November 1951, D-D(51)277, NATO.
28. The PSB was never able to fulfil its role due to internecine struggles between the various government departments. Brandon Trissler, 'The Psychological Strategy Board: Psychological Operations and Policy Coordination, 1951–1953',

MA thesis, University of Missouri Columbia, 1995; Scott Lucas, 'Campaigns of Truth: The Psychological Strategy Board and American Ideology, 1951–1953', *International History Review*, 18/2 (May 1996), pp. 279–302.
29. Eric Duhamel, 'Jean-Paul David et le Mouvement Paix et Liberté, un Anticommuniste Radical', in J. Delmas and J. Kessler (eds), *Renseignement et Propagande pendant la Guerre Froide (1947–1953)* (Brussels: Editions Complexe, 1999), pp. 198–199, 201. See also René Sommer, 'Paix et liberté: La Quatrième République contre le PC', *L'Histoire* 40 (December 1981), pp. 26–35.
30. On Taubert and the VFF in the 1950s and 1960s see Bernhard Ludwig, 'La Propagande Anticommuniste en Allemagne Fédérale: Le VFF pendant Allemand de Paix et Liberté?' *Vingtième Siècle: Revue d'histoire* 80 (October–December 2003), pp. 33–42.
31. Affiliated groups were active in Britain, Switzerland, Norway, Denmark, Greece, Turkey, Australia, Canada, Mexico, Israel, Korea, South Africa, Taiwan, Vietnam, and Japan. It is important not to overestimate the level of coordination between these groups, which were often linked by correspondence only. Bernard Ludwig, 'Le Comité européen et international Paix et Liberté: "Internationale" ou réseau de l'anticommunisme?' *Bulletin de l'Institut Pierre Renouvin* 20 (Autumn, 2004), pp. 15–22; Philippe Régnier, 'La Propagande Anticommuniste de Paix et Liberté, France, 1950–1956', Ph.D. thesis, Université Libre, Brussels, 1987, pp. 1–44, 52.
32. Regnier, pp. 45–46; Paul Koedijk, 'Van "Vrede en Vrijheid" tot "Volk en Verdediging": Veranderingen in Anti-communistische Psychologische Oorlogvoering in Nederland 1950–1965', in B. Schoenmaker and J.A.M.M. Janssen (eds), *In de Schaduw van de Muur: Maatschappij en Krijgsmacht rond 1960* (The Hague: Sdu, 1997), p. 70.
33. It was reported that "David is spending two weeks in the United States as guest of the National Committee for a Free Europe", 'French Anti-Communist Visits in Washington', *New York Times*, 1 February 1952.
34. H.F. Eschauzier to M, 8 September 1953, File 11728, BVC, Ministeries AOK en AZ, Kabinet van de Minister-President (1944) 1945–1979, National Archives, The Hague (hereafter NAH).
35. Bernard Ludwig, 'Le Comité européen et international Paix et Liberté: "Internationale" ou réseau de l'anticommunisme (1950–1970)?', *Bulletin de l'Institut Pierre Renouvin* 20 (Autumn 2004), pp. 30–31; Bernard Ludwig, 'Guerre psychologique et propagande anticommuniste: espoirs et illusions d'une "communauté atlantique"', in Aubourg, Bossuat, and Scott-Smith (eds), *European Community, Atlantic Community?* pp. 426–431.
36. Duhamel, 'Jean-Paul David et le Mouvement Paix et Liberté', p. 210. The Dutch report of September 1953 does state that "it cannot be denied that the movement in France is mainly sustained from American funds" but does not say what information this remark is based on. Régnier contends that even if American funding was involved it must have been a small percentage of the overall budget provided by French professional and employers' organizations, Régnier, 'La Propagande Anticommuniste', p. 55–56.
37. Thomas de Jonge, 'Anticommunistische propaganda of gewoon De Echte Waarheid? Het anticommunistische geluid in Nederland 1945–1965,' MA thesis, Leiden university, p. 54.
38. 'Statuten van de Stichting "Vrede en Vrijheid",' Inzagedossier: Psychologische Oorlogvoering, Freedom of Information request (Wet Openbaar Bestuur) to Ministry of Justice / AIVD, 12 December 2005.

39. Koedijk, 'Van "Vrede en Vrijheid"...', pp. 65, 66.
40. 'Persconferentie te Eindhoven door "Vrede en Vrijheid"', 12 June 1953, Ibid.
41. Paul Koedijk, 'De Koude burgeroorlog in Nederland', *Vrij Nederland*, 18 July 1992.
42. Ludwig, 'Le Comité européen', pp. 22, 31.
43. C-M(52)110, approved in C-R(52)31, NATO. The records of AC/46 remain classified.
44. 'Positive Information Policy towards Peoples of NATO Countries', 24 September 1952, AC/24-D/7, NATO; 'Counter-Propaganda', 24 September 1952, AC/24-D/8, NATO.
45. Report of the Committee of Three on Non-Military Cooperation in NATO, 13 December 1956, available online at http://www.nato.int/docu/basictxt/b561213a.html (22 June 2010). See also Joseph P. Sinasac, 'The Three Wise Men: The Effects of the 1956 Committee of Three on NATO', in Margaret O. MacMillan and David S. Sorenson (eds), *Canada and NATO: Uneasy Past, Uncertain Future* (Waterloo: University of Waterloo Press, 1990), pp. 27–46.
46. Lord Ismay, *NATO: The First Five Years, 1949–1954* (Utrecht: Bosch, 1955), p. 155.
47. Thomas Gijswijt, 'Uniting the West: the Bilderberg Group, the Cold War and European Integration 1952–1966', Ph.D. dissertation, Heidelberg University, 2008, pp. 74–75.
48. Prince Bernhard to Einthoven, 13 May 1955, Box 187, Bilderberg Papers, NAH.
49. Corinna Unger, *Ostforschung in Westdeutschland: Die Erforschung des europäischen Ostens und die Deutsche Forschungsgemeinschaft, 1945–1975* (Stuttgart: Franz Steiner, 2007), pp. 206–215.
50. State Secretary of the Bundeskanzleramt to State Secretaries Thedieck (BMG) and von Lex (Ministry of the Interior), 11 April 1956, File: 16428, Collection: B 137, NAK; Ministry of the Interior to Chancellor Adenauer, 3 May 1956, File: 16428, Collection: B 137, NAK.
51. Minister of the Interior Schröder to Chancellor Adenauer, 3 May 1956, File: 16429, Collection: B 137, NAK.
52. Krieger, 'German–American Intelligence Relations', pp. 38–39.
53. 'Geistig-Politische Auseinandersetzung mit dem Kommunismus in Deutschland', 15 October 1957, File: 16429, Collection: B 137, NAK.
54. Interesting in this respect is the general lack of knowledge within the German government of some of the anti-communist refugee organizations active within the Federal Republic. On Croat groups see Alexander Clarkson, 'Home and Away: Immigration and Political Violence in the Federal Republic of Germany, 1945–90', *Cold War History* 8 (2008), pp. 1–21.
55. Unger, *Ostforschung in Westdeutschland*, pp. 250–251.
56. Critchfield, *Partners at the Creation*, pp. 100–101.
57. Heldring remembered that Hornix, Van den Heuvel, and BVD communism expert W.A.H. (Ad) de Jonge were also present. Heldring had already met Van den Heuvel at a Defence Study Centre course in 1955. J.L. Heldring, interview with the author, The Hague, 6 May 2011.
58. Paul Villatoux and Marie-Catherine Villatoux, *La République et son armée face au 'péril subversif': Guerre et action psychologiques en France 1945–1960* (Paris: Les Indes Savantes, 2005), p. 359.
59. According to Brian Crozier, Bonnemaison's office was a basement on a back street off rue des Capucines, in the 9th Arrondissement. According to Bonnemaison's letterhead, however, in 1960 he was running his activities from

the rue de la Pépinière. See Brian Crozier, *Free Agent: The Unseen War 1941–1991* (London: HarperCollins, 1993), pp. 30–31.
60. 'Achtergrond van onze bemoeiingen inzake de psychologische beïnvloeding', H.K.O (Hoofd Kader Opleiding) (Van den Heuvel), 4 November 1958, File: Voorgeschiedenis Interdoc (hereafter VI). My thanks to Paul Koedijk for providing this material.
61. Crozier, *Free Agent*, p. 32.
62. Roger Faligot and Pascal Krop, *La Piscine: The French Secret Service since 1944* (Oxford: Basil Blackwell, 1989), p. 141.
63. Klaus Schwabe, 'West Germany between French and American Conceptions of European Unity and Atlantic Partnership 1949–1960', in Valérie Aubourg, Gérard Bossuat, and Giles Scott-Smith (eds), *European Community, Atlantic Community?* (Paris: Soleb, 2008), pp. 165–166, 168–169.
64. Critchfield, *Partners at the Creation*, p. 149.
65. See Mathilde von Bülow, 'The Telefunken Affair and the Internationalisation of the Algerian War, 1957–59', *Journal of Strategic Studies* 28 (2005), pp. 703–729, and 'Myth or Reality? The Red Hand and French Covert Action in Federal Germany during the Algerian War, 1956–61', *Intelligence and National Security* 22 (2007), pp. 787–820.
66. 'Strauss hat große Pläne mit der Abwehr,' *Frankfurter Allgemeine Zeitung*, 16 August 1958.
67. Willi Peters, 'Propagandakrieg gegen wen?', 16 August 1958, File: 16429, Collection: B 137, NAK.
68. Gray, *Germany's Cold War*, pp. 74, 87.
69. 'Vermerk: Geisteige Auseinandersetzung mit dem Kommunismus und psychologische Verteidigung', 31 March 1960, File: 16430, Collection: B 137, NAK.
70. 'Achtergrond van onze bemoeiingen…' VI; von Dellingshausen, 'Geistig-Politische Auseinandersetzung mit dem Kommunismus in Deutschland', 15 October 1957, File: 16429, Collection: B 137, NAK.
71. "… nach Dänemark, wo ein internationales Gespräch des Studienburos Berlin (von Dellingshausen) stattfindet." Van den Heuvel to Baron von Hahn, 19 April 1963, File: 238 baron W. Von Hahn, Persoonsdossiers, archive of C.C. van den Heuvel, National Archives, The Hague (hereafter CC NAH).
72. Von Dellingshausen, 'Geistig-Politische Auseinandersetzung mit dem Kommunismus in Deutschland', 15 October 1957, File: 16429, Collection: B 137, NAK.
73. 'Bericht über das VI Internationale Gespräch des Studienbüro Berlin vom 25 bis 28 September 1961 in Berlin', File: 16431, Collection: B 137, NAK. Among the Germans was Günter Triesch. International participants included Van den Heuvel, Colonel Ivar Göthberg (Sweden), Colonel Huber and Dr Hans Kopp (Switzerland), Konrad Seine (Norway), and Harry Welton (IRD, Britain). So no Americans, and no French.
74. "die Beinflussung der Westdeutsche Bevölkerung durch den Sowjetblock auf dem Umweg über westliche Länder": 'Aktennotiz: Arbeitsgruppe VII', 12 February 1957, File: 16429, Collection: B 137, NAK.
75. Linda Risso, 'A Difficult Compromise: British and American Plans for a Common Anti-Communist Propaganda Response in Western Europe, 1948–1958', *Intelligence and National Security* 26 (2011), pp. 330–354.

Notes 273

76. 'Morele Herbewapening', 14 June 1954, Inzagedossier: Psychologische Oorlogvoering, Freedom of Information request (Wet Openbaar Bestuur) to Ministry of Justice / AIVD, 12 December 2005.
77. Dick Engelen, *Geschiedenis van de Binnenlandse Veiligheidsdienst* (Mepperl: Ten Brink, 1995), pp. 218–234; Koedijk, 'Van "Vrede en Vrijheid"...', p. 71. Interesting in this respect is that Einthoven clearly had no confidence in Minister President Willem Drees: "Drees is hopeloos": 'Bespreking H.BVD [Einthoven] en H.KO [van den Heuvel] op 10-12-58', VI.
78. *Tasks for the Free World Today* (The Hague: Interdoc, 1963), p. 93; Louis Einthoven, *Tegen De Stroom In* (Apeldoorn: Semper Agendo, 1974), pp. 235–238; Crozier, *Free Agent: The Unseen War 1914–1991* (London: Harper Collins, 1993), pp. 30–33.
79. 'Überlegungen zur weiteren Arbeit des französisch-holländisch-deutschen Arbeitskreises', n.d. [1958], VI. Van den Heuvel remarked that the Foertsch proposal was more useful than "the suggestions which Bonnemaison originally made available". The subjects Bonnemaison put forward were quite specialized: communist infiltration in the Protestant and Catholic churches; communist influence in sub-Saharan Africa; and Soviet psychological warfare with Muslim peoples.
80. 'Bespreking H.BVD en H.KO op 10-12-58', VI. Einthoven had already been fully informed by CIA officer James Critchfield about the poor relations between Gehlen's BND and the Bundesamt für Verfassungsschutz (office for the protection of the constitution, the domestic intelligence and security service), a not inconsequential detail for future cooperation.
81. Cees van den Heuvel, 'De "Vreedzame Coëxistentie" in Nederland', n.d. [1959–60], in author's possession.
82. Ibid.
83. 'Possibilities of Psychological Defense against Soviet Influence' (US study trip report), April 1959, p. 27.
84. Bonnemaison to Einthoven, 2 December 1959, File: 130 Algemeen 1959–1961 – Italië (1959–1975), CC NAH. There is no record of Aron's participation to be found in his papers. The only direct contact with Bonnemaison appears to be a postcard sent to console Aron at the time of the latter's illness, 9 May 1977, correspondance personnelle (1928–1983), Box 212: 1977–1980, NAF 28060, Archive of Raymond Aron, Bibliothèque Nationale, Paris.
85. 'Verslag van de reis naar Duitsland van 29 november tot 6 december 1958 door een aantal functionarissen uit de grootste Nederlandse bedrijven', Cees van den Heuvel, 17 December 1958, File: 59 Haus der Zukunft, Duitsland (1958–1978), CC NAH.
86. 'Bericht über die Tätigkeit des Hauses der Zukunft 1956 und 1957' and 'Verslag van de reis naar Duitsland...', Cees van den Heuvel, 17 December 1958, File: 59 Haus der Zukunft, Duitsland (1958–1978), CC NAH; 'Rapport', G. Diepenhorst, Centraal Sociaal Werkgevers Verbond (Central Social Employers' Union), December 1958, File: 59 Haus der Zukunft, Duitsland (1958–1978), CC NAH. The CSWV focused on generating positive industrial relations in a broad sense, and it hired Diepenhorst, formerly with the BVD, to focus on countering communist influence and maintain close links with business security officers, the BVD, Vrede en Vrijheid, the Economic League, and the Deutsches Industrie-Institut in Cologne.
87. Van den Heuvel's son Christiaan did visit the Haus in 1966 to follow two summer courses. Van den Heuvel to H. Jöhren, 16 September 1966; Van den Heuvel

to Jöhren, 2 January 1968, File: 59 Haus der Zukunft, Duitsland (1958–1978), CC NAH.
88. J.H. van den Berg, *Metabletica, of Leer der Veranderingen: Beginsel van een Historische Psychologie* (Nijkerk: Callenbach, 1956).
89. The Bataviche Petroleum Maatschappij (BPM) was a division of Royal Dutch Shell. Koedijk, 'Van "Volk en Verdediging"...' p. 72; Einthoven–Den Hollander memo, 22 October 1958; HKO (Van den Heuvel) to HBVD (Einthoven), 14 January 1959, File: 301 1959, Beschouwingen en Verslagen, CC NAH.
90. 'Possibilities of Psychological Defense against Soviet Influence' (US trip report), April 1959, p. 47.
91. J.H. van den Berg, interview with the author, Antwerp, 6 March 2004.
92. 'Bespreking H.BVD en H.KO op 101-25-8', VI. Gittinger's main contribution to mind control was the development, with a $1 million budget and 29,000 subjects for questionnaires, of the Personality Assessment System for predicting future behaviour. By 1963 he was running the system for corporate clients via Psychological Assessment Associates in Washington, DC. SIHE also funded Ewen Cameron's highly controversial electro-convulsive therapy, "psychic driving", and sensory deprivation experiments on patients at McGill University. See Gordon Thomas, *Journey into Madness: The True Story of Secret CIA Mind Control and Medical Abuse* (New York: Bantam, 1989), pp. 239–240; Dominic Streatfield, *Brainwash: The Secret History of Mind Control* (London: Hodder, 2006).
93. John Marks, *The Search for the Manchurian Candidate: The CIA and Mind Control* (New York: W.W. Norton, 1979), p. 159. The Society became the Human Ecology Fund in 1961 and was eventually closed down in 1965. Contact between the Society and the Netherlands was already in progress in 1958, when a grant of $15,000 was paid to Nijmegen University for a study of Hungarian refugees as part of a wider research programme on what led people to defect.
94. See Edward Hunter, *Brainwashing: The Story of Men Who Defied It* (New York: Pyramid, 1956).
95. 1957 Annual Report, p. 9.
96. See Susan Carruthers, '"The Manchurian Candidate" (1962) and the Cold War Brainwashing Scare', *Historical Journal of Film, Radio and Television* 18 (1998), pp. 75–94; Susan Carruthers, 'Not Just Washed but Dry-Cleaned: Korea and the "Brainwashing" Scare of the 1950s', in Gary Rawnsley (ed.), *Cold War Propaganda in the 1950s* (Basingstoke: Macmillan, 1999), pp. 47–66.
97. 'Geistig-Politische Auseinandersetzung mit dem Kommunismus in Deutschland', 15 October 1957, File: 16429, Collection: B 137, NAK.
98. Monroe to Einthoven, 9 December 1958, File: 42 Society for the Investigation of Human Ecology 1958–1964, Verenigde Staten (1958–1979), CC NAH.
99. Van den Heuvel to Monroe, 27 January 1959, File: 42 Society for the Investigation of Human Ecology 1958–1964, Verenigde Staten (1958–1979), CC NAH.
100. J.H. van den Berg, interview with the author, Antwerp, 6 March 2004.
101. 'Possibilities of Psychological Defense', p. 13.
102. Ibid., p. 67.
103. Ibid., p. 69. This comment was provoked by the evidence presented in William Sargant, *Battle for the Mind* (London: William Heinemann, 1957), which covered the many and varied "mechanics of indoctrination" used through history.
104. 'Possibilities of Psychological Defense', p. 17.
105. The overly positive picture of American society given at Du Pont led Van den Berg to complain to the speaker that "this is not heaven". J.H. van den Berg, interview with the author, Antwerp, 6 March 2004.

Notes 275

106. Ken Osgood, *Total Cold War: Eisenhower's Secret Propaganda Battle at Home and Abroad* (Lawrence, KS: University Press of Kansas, 2006), p. 314.
107. Ibid., p. 321.
108. 'Possibilities of Psychological Defense', pp. 36, 42, 44–46.
109. Galantière to Monroe, 24 August 1959; Perry to Monroe, 8 September 1959; Irving Gitlin to Monroe, 1 October 1959; HBVD [Einthoven] to HKO [Van den Heuvel], 20 October 1959, File: 42 Society for the Investigation of Human Ecology 1958–1964, Verenigde Staten (1958–1979), CC NAH.
110. The Nijmegen project was a study of Hungarian refugees paid for by SIHE and run through the Gemeenschappelijk instituut voor toegepaste psychologie (GITP) based at the university there. See 'Nederlands onderzoek via CIA betaald', *NRC Handelsblad*, 1 August 1979.
111. Monroe to Van den Heuvel, 10 November 1959, 42 Society for the Investigation of Human Ecology 1958–1964, Verenigde Staten (1958–1979), CC NAH.
112. Van den Heuvel to Monroe, 3 December 1959, and Van den Heuvel to Monroe, 30 May 1960, ibid.
113. Monroe to Van den Heuvel, 28 July 1960, ibid.
114. Van den Heuvel to Monroe, 7 January 1961, and Einthoven to Monroe, 18 December 1961, ibid.
115. Monroe to Van den Heuvel, 18 January 1962, and Walter Pasternak to Van den Heuvel, 5 October 1963, ibid.
116. 'The Story of the Economic League', n.d. [1958], File: 90 Economic League 1959–1978, Groot-Brittannië (1959–1985), CC NAH.
117. 'Rapport', G. Diepenhorst, 25 November 1959, ibid.
118. Van den Heuvel to Dettmer, 28 January 1961, and Van den Heuvel to Dettmer, 31 August 1961, ibid.
119. Scott Anthony, ' "Tate not State": The Aims of Industry and British Public Relations in the Cold War', paper given at the conference 'Public Relations of the Cold War', Cambridge University, 2–4 December 2011.
120. Cees van den Heuvel, 'Enkele Gegevens over de Psychologische Verdediging in de VS en Engeland', March 1960, in author's possession; SOEV Annual Report (Jaarverslag) 1960, p. 12.
121. Cees van den Heuvel, 'Some outlines of an international institute for combating psychological warfare of communism', October 1959, VI.
122. 'Gedanken zur Errichtung einer Zentrale für Dokumentation und Information im Anschluss an den französisch-holländisch-deutschen Arbeitskreis', October 1959, VI.
123. 'Einige möglichen Aktivitäten im Rahmen einer psychologischen Kriegsführung gegen den Kommunismus', n.d. [1959–60], VI.
124. 'De invloed van de vreedzame coëxistentie-propaganda in Nederland', in 'De "Vreedzame Coëxistentie" in Nederland', n.d. [1959–60], in author's possession. Einthoven also argued within Dutch government circles for loosening the restrictive visa policies to allow more visitors from the East to have direct contact with the freedoms of Western society. See Einthoven, *Tegen De Stroom In*, pp. 240–241.
125. 'NOTE sur les PROPOSITIONS de la DELEGATION FRANCAISE à la séance de TRAVAIL de la HAYE (5 mai 1960)', 28 April 1960, VI.
126. 'Merkblatt über die Gründung eines Internationalen Dokumentationszentrums im HAAG zur psychologischen Bekämpfung des Weltkommunismus', n.d. [1963], File: 16431, Collection: B 137, NAK.

127. Record of Secretary of State Dulles' Press Conference, 26 November 1958, *Foreign Relations of the United States* (hereafter *FRUS*), 1958–1960, vol. VIII, p. 125; Adenauer to Dulles, 30 January 1959, *FRUS*, 1958–1960, vol. VIII, p. 310; Bruce to State Department, 10 August 1959, *FRUS*, 1959–1960, vol. IX, p. 2; Richard J. Barnet, *The Alliance: America–Europe–Japan, Makers of the Postwar World* (New York: Simon and Schuster, 1983), p. 181.
128. Bruce to State Department, 10 August 1959, *FRUS*, 1959–1960, vol. IX, p. 3; Kohler to Secretary of State, February 1960, *FRUS*, 1959–1960, vol. IX, p. 83.
129. C-M(60)22, 9 March 1960, NATO.
130. Ibid.
131. 'Vermerk: Psychologisch-politische Verteidigung des freien Westens im Rahmen der NATO', File: 16430, Collection: B 137, NAK.
132. Interestingly enough, the nature of the expert groups was deliberately concealed behind the anodyne title Ad Hoc Study Group to avoid any complications. For details see Giles Scott-Smith, 'Not a NATO Responsibility? Psychological Warfare, the Berlin Crisis, and the Formation of Interdoc', in A. Wenger, C. Nuenlist, and A. Locher (eds), *Transforming NATO in the Cold War: Challenges beyond Deterrence in the 1960s* (London: Routledge, 2007), pp. 31–49; 'Sitzung der ad hoc-Arbeitsgruppe "Psychologische Aktion" in der NATO', 27 March 1961, File: 16430, Collection: B 137, NAK.
133. 'Besprechung mit amerikanischen Herren über allgemeine Fragen der psychologischen Kriegführung', 25 June 1958, File: 16429, Collection: B 137, NAK. Whereas the CIA officers stated the intention to continue with the Free Jurists (Untersuchungsausschuss Freiheitlicher Juristen), the Kampfgruppe was in a state of "dissolution" ("Auflösung").
134. Reinhard Gehlen, *The Service* (New York: World Publishing, 1972), pp. 195–196.
135. Critchfield, *Partners at the Creation*, pp. 133, 177; Reese, *General Reinhard Gehlen*, p. 176; Wesley Wark, 'The Origins of Intelligence Cooperation between the United States and West Germany', in Detlef Junker (ed.), *The United States and Germany in the Era of the Cold War, 1945–1968*, Vol. 1 (Washington, DC: German Historical Institute/Cambridge University Press, 2004), pp. 251–252.
136. Critchfield, *Partners at the Creation*, p. 209.
137. On Königswinter see Christian Haase, *Pragmatic Peacemakers: Institutes of International Affairs and the Liberalization of West Germany 1945–1973* (Augsburg: Wißner, 2007), pp. 125–131.
138. Information obtained from East European émigré groups was one product the BND hoped to use to raise its status in the eyes of the Americans. And, as the Curveball saga in the run-up to the Iraq invasion of 2003 demonstrates, the same motivations continue to apply in the twenty-first century. See Unger, *Ostforschung in Westdeutschland*, p. 208; Bob Drogin, *Curveball: Spies, Lies, and the Con Man Who Caused a War* (New York: Random House, 2007).
139. Richard Deacon, *The French Secret Service* (London: Grafton, 1990), p. 191.
140. "die Autorität eines oder mehrer 'großer Förderer' (Persönlichkeit der kath. Kirche, prominente jüdische Persönlichkeit, kein Amerikaner)": 'Gedanken zur Errichtung einer Zentrale...' October 1959, VI.
141. 'Enkele aantekeningen bij het voorstel van de Generaal Foertsch m.b.t. een "Zentrale für Dokumentation und Information"', 16 November 1959, in 'Hoofdlijnen van een internationaal instituut ter bestrijding van de psychologische oorlogvoering van het communisme', in author's possession.

142. Einthoven to Bernhard, 15 January 1962, File: 254 Prins Bernhard 1962–1986, Nederland, CC NAH.
143. Fritz Hoekstra, 'The Dutch BVD and Transatlantic Co-operation during the Cold War Era: Some Experiences', *Journal of Intelligence History* 3/1 (Summer 2003) p. 48.
144. CIA funding for the BVD was officially terminated in 1967, although it lingered on due to various long-term arrangements. See Bob de Graaff and Cees Wiebes, 'Intelligence and the Cold War behind the Dykes: The Relationship between the American and Dutch Intelligence Communities 1946–1994', in Rhodri Jeffreys-Jones and Christopher Andrew (eds), *Eternal Vigilance: 50 years of the CIA* (London: Frank Cass, 1997) pp. 44–45.

2 Building the Network

1. Einthoven to Vaccari, 23 May 1961, File: 130 Algemeen 1959–1961, Italië (1959–1975), archive of C.C. van den Heuvel, National Archives, The Hague (hereafter CC NAH).
2. On the debates in West Germany on this issue see for instance Anselm Doering-Manteuffel, *Wie westlich sind die Deutschen: Amerikanisierung und Westernisierung im 20. Jahrhundert* (Göttingen: Vandenbroeck & Ruprecht, 1999).
3. Louis Einthoven, *Tegen de Stroom In* (Apeldoorn: SemperAgendo, 1974), p. 225.
4. Paul Koedijk, 'Van "Vrede en Vrijheid" tot "Volk en Verdediging": Veranderingen in Anti-communistische Psychologische Oorlogvoering in Nederland 1950–1965', in B. Schoenmaker and J.A.M.M. Janssen (eds), *In de Schaduw van de Muur: Maatschappij en Krijgsmacht rond 1960* (The Hague: Sdu, 1997), p. 71.
5. Einthoven, *Tegen de Stroom In*, p. 226.
6. File 96: Courses 1953–56, File 97: Course 1954, File 98: Courses 1954–1955, File 128: Curatorium 1955–59, Defensie Studie Centrum, Archive of the Ministry of Defence, Inventory No. 2.13.188, National Archives, The Hague; 'Achtergrond van onze bemoeiingen inzake de psychologische beïnvloeding medegedeeld door H.KO op 4 november 1958', File: Voorgeschiedenis Interdoc (hereafter VI), in author's possession. Mathon received an invitation to attend the Studienbüro in 1957 but was unable to go. Seizing the opportunity, Einthoven sent Van den Heuvel in his place.
7. 'Bespreking H.BVD en H.KO op 10-12-58', VI.
8. Although Van den Berg claimed that after the US trip he had no further contact with Van den Heuvel, he is referred to as an "adviser" in the OWI's annual reports right up to 1974. J.H. van den Berg, interview with the author, Antwerp, 6 March 2004.
9. Einthoven, *Tegen de Stroom In*, p. 233.
10. Cees van den Heuvel, 'Het communisme als "ideologie" en de relatie tussen theorie en praktijk in het communisme', July 1960, in author's possession.
11. J.M.M. Hornix and C.C. van den Heuvel, 'Een karakteristiek van de waarden van het westen, alsmede enkele gedachten over de mogelijkheden van bevordering van een blijvende invloed van deze waarden', September 1959, in author's possession.
12. Hornix and Van den Heuvel, 'Syllabus: Waarden van het Westen', 1961, in author's possession; 'Ten Geleide', *Oost-West* 1 (March–April 1962), p. 2.
13. Hornix and Van den Heuvel, 'Een karakteristiek van de waarden van het westen', September 1959, in author's possession.

14. Ibid.
15. Jackson to National Security Advisor Robert Cutler, 26 February 1957, quoted in Scott Lucas, *Freedom's War: The American Crusade against the Soviet Union* (Manchester: Manchester University Press, 1999), p. 266; quote from Max Millikan, Quantico Meetings, 2nd Panel, 25 September 1955, Declassified Documents Reference System, Roosevelt Study Center, The Netherlands.
16. 'Geistig-Politische Auseinandersetzung mit dem Kommunismus in Deutschland', 15 October 1957, File B 137, Collection 16429, National Archives, Koblenz (hereafter NAK).
17. C.C. van den Heuvel, 'Bevordering van het Waardenbesef', 1961, in author's possession.
18. C.C. van den Heuvel, *East–West Confrontation: A Psychological Strategy* (The Hague: Interdoc, 1967), p. 8.
19. 'Possibilities of Psychological Defense against Soviet Influence' (US study trip report), April 1959, p. 42; Prof. Wim Couwenberg, interview with the author, Middelburg, 18 September 2002.
20. C.C. van den Heuvel, 'De psychologische oorlogvoering in verband met de BVD-taak', and 'Het gebruik van de inlichtingen van een veiligheidsdienst ten behoeve van de psychologische oorlogvoering tegen het communisme', n.d. [1958–59], File: 301 1959, Beschouwingen en Verslagen, CC NAH.
21. C.C. van den Heuvel, 'Morele Herbewapening', 14 June 1954, Inzagedossier: Psychologische Oorlogvoering, Freedom of Information request (Wet Openbaar Bestuur) to Ministry of Justice / AIVD, 12 December 2005.
22. Ibid.
23. 'De psychologische oorlogvoering in verband met de BVD-taak', File: 301 1959, Beschouwingen en Verslagen, CC NAH.
24. 'Fact-Finding', 24 October 1961, VI.
25. 'Stichting voor Onderzoek van Ecologische Vraagstukken', File 305: Correspondence 1961–72, Stichting Geestelijke Weerbaarheid, archive of the Nationale Federatieve Raad van het Voormalig Verzet Nederland, Netherlands Institute for War Documentation, Amsterdam (hereafter NFR NIOD).
26. Cees van den Heuvel, 'Enkele nadere gegevens m.b.t. de mogelijkheid van een instituut in Nederland ter bestudering van de psychologische verdediging tegen Sowjet-beïnvloeding', 15 March 1960, in author's possession.
27. SOEV Annual Report (Jaarverslag) 1960, p. 7, 8.
28. 'Possibilities of Psychological Defense...', p. 50.
29. 'De motivering, alsmede de onderwerpen van een programma "Staatsburgelijke Vorming" voor kaders in het bedrijfsleven', VI.
30. "Op politiek terrein volgt hieruit tolerantie, als houding van onzekerheid." SOEV Annual Report (Jaarverslag), 1960, p. 14.
31. SOEV Annual Report (Jaarverslag) 1961, pp. 10–11.
32. Frans Kluiters, *De Nederlandse Inlichtingen en Veiligheidsdiensten* (The Hague: Sdu, 1993), p. 34.
33. On Les Galeries and Shell see Max van Rooy, *Honderdzes adressen in Den Haag: De Koninklijke en de Residentie* (The Hague: Shell International Petroleum Company, 1986), p. 71.
34. Lyda de Bree, interview with the author, 22 January 2011; Anneke Landheer-Roelants, *Romantisch buiten wonen in de stad: 125 jaar Van Stolkpark* (Utrecht: Stichting Matrijs, 1999), p. 80.

35. Herman Mennes, 'Inleiding voor een programma ter bevordering van westerse waarden', August 1961, File: 306 Syllabus 1961, Beschouwingen en Verslagen, CC NAH.
36. S.W. Couwenberg, *De Vereenzaming van de Moderne Mens: Een nieuwe formulering van het sociale vraagstuk* (The Hague: Pax, 1956).
37. Professor S.W. Couwenberg, interview with the author, Middelburg, 7 November 2002.
38. 'Waarden van het Westen', August 1961, File: 306 Syllabus 1961, Beschouwingen en Verslagen, CC NAH.
39. Ibid.
40. 'Waarden van het Westen', 1961 (contributions by Hornix and Van den Heuvel), in author's possession.
41. Jean-Marie Domenach, 'Leninist Propaganda', *Public Opinion Quarterly* 15 (Summer 1951), p. 272.
42. Eric Hobsbawm, 'Cadres', *London Review of Books*, 26 April 2007, p. 24.
43. Robert Service, 'Introduction', in V.I. Lenin, *What is to be Done?* (London: Penguin, 1989), pp. 25–26.
44. Brian Crozier, *Free Agent: The Unseen War 1941–1991* (London: HarperCollins, 1993), p. 33.
45. C.C. van den Heuvel, 'De psychologische oorlogvoering in verband met de BVD-taak', File: 301 1959, Beschouwingen en Verslagen, CC NAH.
46. Einthoven to Bernhard, 24 July 1962, and Einthoven to Bernhard, 22 July 1963, File: 254 Prins Bernhard 1962–1986, Nederland, CC NAH.
47. 'Aan de leden van het Hoofdbestuur', 5 August 1958, File 305: Correspondence 1961–72, Stichting Geestelijke Weerbaarheid, NFR NIOD.
48. Algemene Vergadering, 30 May 1959, and Jaarverslag 1959, File 66, NFR, NIOD.
49. Jaarverslag 1960, File 66, NFR, NIOD.
50. 'Aan de leden…', File 305: Correspondence 1961–72, Stichting Geestelijke Weerbaarheid, NFR, NIOD.
51. Jaarverslag 1961, File 66, NFR, NIOD.
52. Cees van den Heuvel, 'Suggesties SOEV ten aanzien van het orgaan G.W.', 21 December 1965, File 305: Correspondence 1961–72, Stichting Geestelijke Weerbaarheid, NFR, NIOD.
53. Besluit No. 1041/Afdeling Kabinet, Ministerie van Binnenlandse Zaken, 19 August 1950; 'Het verkrijgen en gebruik van agenten', n.d., File 2: Spoorwegrecherche, Archive of the Nederlandse Spoorwegen, Collectie 938, Utrechts Archief, Utrecht (hereafter NS).
54. Memoranda, 6 March 1956 and 3 May 1956, File 4: Stafvergaderingen 1954–65, NS.
55. File 15: Jaarverslagen, NS.
56. Memoranda, 21 June 1960, 23 November 1961, and 6 February 1962, File 4: Stafvergaderingen 19546–5, NS.
57. 'Stichting bestudeert de koude oorlog', *Trouw*, 3 February 1962, p. 9.
58. C.C. van den Heuvel, 'Psychologische Oorlogvoering', *Militaire Spectator* 131/1 (1962), pp. 22–25.
59. Koedijk, 'Van "Vrede en Vrijheid…," pp. 79–80. Koedijk notes that around this time Hornix also became secretary of the Nationale Raad Welzijn Militairen, an advisory board for the Ministry of Defence that focused on the (social and psychological) welfare – literally, the *geestelijke weerbaarheid* – of military personnel.

60. 'Some aspects of an International Documentation Centre for Psychological Action against Communism', March 1960, VI.
61. Draft statutes, 13 August 1960, VI.
62. 'Documentatiecentrum in maximale opzet', n.d. VI.
63. 'INTERDOC: International centre for the psychological struggle against world communism', September 1960, VI.
64. 'Documentatiecentrum in maximale opzet', n.d. VI.
65. 'Rapport van het werkcomité ter onderzoek van de mogelijkheden van een documentatiecentrum', 1 September 1960, VI.
66. Van den Heuvel to C.R.C. Wijckerheid Bisdom (solicitor), 7 October 1960; Wijckerheid Bisdom to Van den Heuvel, 10 October 1960; Van den Heuvel to Einthoven, 24 October 1960, VI.
67. 'Vergadering van het Werkcomité op 7 december 1960', VI.
68. 'Entwurf eines Aktionsplanes', 23 December 1960, File B 137, Collection 16430, NAK.
69. 'OAK Staff Comments on Precis on INTERDOC', 30 March 1961, VI.
70. 'Nadere omschrijving opleidingstaak i.v.m. vorming van kaders in het bedrijfsleven', July 1961; 'Nadere omschrijving documentatie-taak Interdoc', July 1961; 'Training as the primary task of Interdoc', n.d.; 'De motivering, alsmede de onderwerpen van een programma "Staatsburgerlijke Vorming" voor kaders in het bedrijfsleven", n.d., VI.
71. 'Werkplan Interdoc 1962', July 1961, VI.
72. Van den Heuvel to James L. Monroe, 21 July 1961, File: 42 Society for the Investigation of Human Ecology 1958–1964, Verenigde Staten (1958–1979), CC NAH.
73. 'Stand en Toekomst Interdoc', 5 July 1961, VI.
74. 'Vorschlag des BND vom 12 Juli 1961 für die Behandlung der grundsätzlichen Themen in der Auseinandersetzung mit dem Kommunismus', 19 Juli 1961, File: B 137, Collection 16430, NAK.
75. 'Besprechung am 22 September 1961', Ministry of the Interior, 27 September 1961, File: B 137, Collection 16430, NAK. Both Josef Bochenski (University of Fribourg) and Boris Meissner (Ostkolleg, Cologne), soon to be part of the wider Interdoc network, were important participants in these "Action Plan" discussion meetings. On von Mende see Corinna Unger, *Ostforschung in Westdeutschland: Die Erforschung des europäischen Ostens und die Deutsche Forschungsgemeinschaft, 1945–1975* (Stuttgart: Franz Steiner Verlag, 2007), pp. 206–207.
76. 'Bezoeken aan Parijs', n.d. [1961], VI. Rostini's link with SDECE comes from a handwritten note by Van den Heuvel in the margin of a letter from Frank Trehern (Common Cause), 23 November 1967, File: 107 Common Cause 1964–1971, Groot-Britannië (1959–1985), CC NAH.
77. On Albertini see Jean Lévy, *Le Dossier Georges Albertini* (Paris: Editions L'Harmattan, 1992); Pierre Assouline, 'Un expert en anticommunisme, Georges Albertini', in *Le Temps de la guerre froide* (Paris: Seuil, 1994), pp. 243–263
78. 'Bezoeken aan Parijs', n.d. [1961], VI.
79. Ibid.
80. Ibid.
81. Ibid.
82. "j'ai la presque certitude de la disposition des Allemands à participer largement au financement de l'Interdoc". 'Voyage en Allemagne du 13 au 15 septembre 1961', VI.

83. 'Verslag Mr. L. Einthoven in Barbizon 7 Oct. 61', VI.
84. Ibid.
85. 'Fact-Finding', 24 October 1961, VI.
86. 'Verslag Mr. L. Einthoven in Barbizon 7 Oct. 61', VI; Einthoven, *Tegen de Stroom In*, p. 233
87. Ibid.
88. Louis Einthoven, closing words at the Barbizon *colloque*, 7 October 1961, VI.
89. Einthoven to Dick Ellis (head of MI6), 20 October 1961, Einthoven to C.H. (Dick) Ellis, 3 November 1961, File: 92 C.H. (Dick) Ellis 1961–1963, Groot-Britannië (1959–1985), CC NAH.
90. 'Fact-Finding', 24 October 1961, VI.
91. Crozier, *Free Agent*, pp. 29–33.
92. Crawley was the author of a series of articles in the *Sunday Times* between 28 October and 18 November 1962 entitled 'The Hidden Face of British Communism'. Crozier to Bonnemaison, 1 September 1961, Van den Heuvel to Crozier, 8 September 1961, Crozier to Van den Heuvel, 12 September 1961, File: 91 Brian Crozier 1961–1976, Groot-Britannië (1959–1985), CC NAH; Van den Heuvel to John Dettmer (Economic League), 31 August 1961, File: 90 Economic League 1959–1978, Groot-Britannië (1959–1985), CC NAH; 'Engelse delegatie in Barbizon', n.d. [1961], File: 83 Algemeen 1961–1964, Groot-Britannië (1959–1985), CC NAH.
93. William Stevenson, *Intrepid's Last Case* (London: Michael Joseph, 1984), pp. 238–249; Stephen Dorril, *MI6: Fifty Years of Special Operations* (London: Fourth Estate, 2000), pp. 189–191.
94. Stevenson, *Intrepid's Last Case*, p. 251.
95. See Chapman Pincher, *Their Trade Is Treachery* (London: Sidgwick & Jackson, 1981), pp. 192–205; Chapman Pincher, *Too Secret Too Long* (London: Sidgwick & Jackson, 1984); Peter Wright, *Spycatcher* (New York: Viking, 1987), pp. 325–330.
96. Ellis to Van den Heuvel, 27 December 1967, in author's possession.
97. Jos Hagers, 'Ook hier opschudding over spionnenboek, *De Telegraaf*, 1 August 1987.
98. Einthoven to White, 8 June 1961, File: 92 C.H. (Dick) Ellis 1961–1963, Groot-Britannië (1959–1985), CC NAH; White to Einthoven, 28 June 1961, File: 83 Algemeen 1961–1964, Groot-Britannië (1959–1985), CC NAH; Stevenson, *Intrepid's Last Case*, p. 253.
99. 'Engeland', n.d. [1961], File: 83 Algemeen 1961–1964, Groot-Britannië (1959–1985), CC NAH.
100. 'Fact-Finding', 24 October 1961, VI.
101. 'Gesprek met C.H. Ellis op 26 april 1962', 'Gesprek met Ellis 27 juli 1962', and 'Gesprek CC van den Heuvel met CH Ellis op 13 en 14-9-1962', File: 92 C.H. (Dick) Ellis 1961–1963, Groot-Britannië (1959–1985), CC NAH.
102. 'Gesprek C.C. van den Heuvel met C.H. Ellis op 13 en 14-9-1962', File: 92 C.H. (Dick) Ellis 1961–1963, Groot-Britannië (1959–1985), CC NAH.
103. Stevenson, *Intrepid's Last Case*, p. 253.
104. Ellis to Van den Heuvel, 7 January 1963, File: 92 C.H. (Dick) Ellis 1961–1963, Groot-Britannië (1959–1985), CC NAH.
105. 'US Information Policy with regard to Anti-American Propaganda', 1 December 1947, FO 1110/24, and 'Communism – New Publicity Policy', 12 February 1948,

282 Notes

FO 1110/24, Papers of the Information Research Department (hereafter IRD), National Archives, London (hereafter NAL).
106. See Andrew Defty, *Britain, America and Anti-Communist Propaganda 1945–53* (London: Routledge, 2004).
107. 'I.R.D. Imprint Policy', n.d., FO 1110/1614; 'Use of IRD Written Material', September 1961, FO 1110/1355, IRD NAL.
108. "The [UK] Delegation [to NATO] receives IRD's entire output automatically", since "There is no counter-propaganda organ in NATO with executive responsibilities like the counter-subversion office in CENTO." T.C. Barker, 'NATO: Notes on IRD Role,' 9 April 1962, FO 1110/1596, IRD NAL.
109. 'Information Research Department', n.d. [1963], PR 101/205G, IRD NAL.
110. H.A.H. Cortazzi (IRD) to M.I. Mackie (British Embassy The Hague), 11 November 1957, FO 1110/1014, IRD NAL.
111. D.C. (Donald) Hopson (director of IRD) to R.G.A. (Gordon) Etherington-Smith (British Embassy The Hague), 12 September 1958, Etherington-Smith to Hopson, 21 October 1960, FO 1110/1124, IRD NAL.
112. G.A. Carey-Foster (British Embassy The Hague) to D.C. Hopson, 13 April 1961, FO 1110/1380, IRD NAL.
113. 'Information about Communism in the Netherlands', in T.H. Gillson to H.H. Tucker, 5 May 1961, FO 1110/1380, IRD NAL.
114. H.H. Tucker to G.A. Carey-Foster, 25 April 1961, FO 1110/1380, IRD NAL.
115. T.H. Gillson to H.H. Tucker, 29 June 1961, FO 1110/1380, IRD NAL.
116. 'Die Schweiz', n.d. [1961], File: 151 Reisverslagen Zwitserland 1961–1967, Zwitserland (1961–1975), CC NAH.
117. Einthoven to Bernhard, 22 July 1963, File: 254 Prins Bernhard 1962–1986, Nederland, CC NAH.
118. 'Niederschrift über die Sitzung am 15 März 1962 über die geistig-politische Auseinandersetzung mit dem Kommunismus im Bundesministerium des Innern in Bonn', archive of the Bundesministeriums für gesamtdeutsche Fragen, File: 16431, Collection: B 137, NAK. See also Einthoven, *Tegen de Stroom In*, pp. 237–238.
119. 'Reise nach Genf – 21/22 Juli 1961,' 'Schweizersiche Ost-Institut', and 'Schweizerischer Aufklärungsdienst', File: 151 Reisverslagen Zwitserland 1961–1967, Zwitserland (1961–1975), CC NAH.
120. Einthoven to Déonna, 20 December 1961, File: 150 Algemeen 1961–1970, Zwitserland (1961–1975), CC NAH; '24 Januari Peter Sager (Bern)', and '26 januari 1962. Déonna Genève', File: 151 Reisverslagen Zwitserland 1961–1967, Zwitserland (1961–1975), CC NAH; Einthoven to Sager, 22 September 1961, Einthoven to Sager, 28 December 1961, and Einthoven to Sager, 3 August 1962, File: 152 Schweizerisches Ost-Institut 1961–1965, Zwitserland (1961–1975), CC NAH.
121. 'Vermerk über die Besprechung mit Herrn Huber am 10.9.1964', File: 150 Algemeen 1961–1970, Zwitserland (1961–1975), CC NAH.
122. 'Gesprek met Procureur-generaal Fürst', 25 January 1962, File: 151 Reisverslagen Zwitserland 1961–1967, Zwitserland (1961–1975), CC NAH.
123. 'Bezoek bij Dr. Albert Münst in Zürich op 31 oktober 1963', File: 156 Liga für Freiheit 1963–1965, Zwitserland (1961–1975), CC NAH.
124. Van den Heuvel was impressed enough by materials from Aktion Freier Staatsbürger to initiate a combined action between Münst and Vrede en Vrijheid's Van Dam van Isselt on the seventh anniversary of the Hungarian

revolution. Van den Heuvel to Münst, 10 October 1963, File: 156 Liga für Freiheit 1963–1965, Zwitserland (1961–1975), CC NAH.
125. See Leopoldo Nuti, 'The United States, Italy, and the Opening to the Left', *Journal of Cold War Studies* 4 (Summer 2002), pp. 36–55.
126. Battista to Einthoven, 13 April 1960, File: 130 Algemeen 1959–1961, Italië (1959–1975), CC NAH. Others involved at the time were Dr Signorelli (director of *Prospettive Meridionali*), Dr Ugo Sciascia (director-general of Comitato Civico), and Lieutenant Colonel di Lorenzo.
127. Bonnemaison to Einthoven, 2 December 1959, and Einthoven to Colonel di Lorenzo (Ministry of Defence), 25 August 1960, File: Italy 7 (19606–1), CC NAH.
128. 'Reis naar Rome 16–21 juni 1961', File: 130 Algemeen 1959–61, Italië (1959–1975), CC NAH.
129. 'Fact-Finding', VI.
130. Vaccari to Einthoven, 12 October 1960, File: 130 Algemeen 1959–1961, Italië (1959–1975), CC NAH.
131. Vaccari to Einthoven, 2 January 1961, File: 130 Algemeen 1959–1961, Italië (1959–1975), CC NAH.
132. Einthoven to Guicciardi, 16 February 1961, File: 130 Algemeen 1959–1961, Italië (1959–1975), CC NAH.
133. Einthoven also tried to use Alfrink's influence as chairman of the board to create a Chair in Soviet Studies at the University of Nijmegen for Zacharias. 'Gesprek met Kardinaal Alfrink', 8 June 1961, File: 130 Algemeen 1959–1961, Italië (1959–1975), CC NAH.
134. 'Reise nach Rom (nur für B.N.D., der Bruder einbegriffen)', File: 130 Algemeen 1959–1961, Italië (1959–1975), CC NAH.
135. 'Contact Report', 16 September 1966, Gehlen, Reinhard, Vol. 5, Box 40, Entry ZZ-18, RG 263 Records of the Central Intelligence Agency, National Archives, College Park.
136. 'Reis naar Rome 16–21 juni 1961', File: 130 Algemeen 1959–1961, Italië (1959–1975), CC NAH. On Gedda see F. Cassata, 'Against UNESCO: Gedda, Gini, and American Scientific Racism', *Med Secoli* 20 (2008), pp. 907–935.
137. Einthoven was almost pushed by one of his hosts into a meeting with Minister of Defence Giulio Andreotti, which he was strongly unenthusiastic about considering the weak attitude of the Christian Democrat government towards anti-communist action. Fortunately the minister proved to be unavailable. 'Visit to Rome', File: 130 Algemeen 1959–1961, Italië (1959–1975), CC NAH.
138. As Einthoven remarked in his autobiography, "this caused a reaction from the employers: Look how hypocritical the Jesuits are; in Rome they warn against communism, while in Milan they stir up the workers!" Einthoven, *Tegen de Stroom In*, p. 237.
139. Nicla Buonasorte, *Siri: Tradizione e Novecento* (Bologna: Il Mulino, 2006).
140. *Rerum Novarum* (Of New Things) was an encyclical that expressed concern about the desperate conditions of the working classes. *Mater et Magistra*, issued seventy years later as a follow-up encyclical on the same theme, pleaded for greater working-class influence in the workplace and more aid for the developing world.
141. 'Bezoek aan Kardinaal Siri – Genua – 11 augustus 1961', File: 130 Algemeen 1959–1961, Italië (1959–1975), CC NAH.
142. Einthoven to Vaccari, 14 August 1961, File: 130 Algemeen 1959–1961, Italië (1959–1975), CC NAH.

143. Einthoven to Van Gestel, 26 October 1961, and Einthoven to Van Gestel, 26 October 1961, File: 130 Algemeen 1959–1961, Italië (1959–1975), CC NAH.
144. 'Rome Reis 4–8 september 1961', File: 130 Algemeen 1959–1961, Italië (1959–1975), CC NAH.
145. 'Bezoek Vaccari 29 november 1961', File: 130 Algemeen 1959–1961, Italië (1959–1975), CC NAH.
146. Einthoven to Vaccari, 1 March 1962, 'Bezoek Rome 22 maart/27 maart 1962 van de Heer Einthoven', Guicciardi to Einthoven, 10 October 1962, and Einthoven to Guicciardi, 13 November 1962, File: 131 Algemeen 1962–1963, Italië (1959–1975), CC NAH; 'Fact-Finding', VI.'
147. C.C. van den Heuvel, 'Hoofdlijnen van een internationaal instituut ter bestrijding van de psychologische oorlogvoering van het communisme', 16 November 1959, in author's possession; CC NAH; Van den Heuvel, 'Psychologische Oorlogvoering', *Militaire Spectator* 131/1 (1962), pp. 22–23.
148. 'Rome Reis 4–8 September 1961', File: 130 Algemeen 1959–1961, Italië (1959–1975), CC NAH.
149. 'Aufzeichnung' (Koordinierungszentrum), 29 May 1961, 'Gedanken über das zu bildende Informationszentrum' (BND), 27 June 1961, and 'Koordinierungsausschuss Bundeskanzleramt' (Ministry of the Interior), 19 July 1961, File B 137, Collection 16430, NAK.
150. As an example of what the BND was up to, Gehlen handed the CIA men a copy of *Ost-West-Begegnung in Frage und Antwort*, produced under Geyer's supervision, a 300-page compendium offering opinion on the most common questions related to East–West contacts. 'Contact Report', 16 September 1966, Gehlen, Reinhard, Vol. 5, Box 40, Entry ZZ-18, RG 263 Records of the Central Intelligence Agency, National Archives, College Park.
151. 'Reis Amsterdam-München-Zürich-Bern-Genève-Amsterdam', January 1962, File: 151 Reisverslagen 1961–1967, Zwitserland (1961–1975), CC NAH; "also möglichst in Hintergrund wirken": 'Aufgabenstellung INTERDOK', 7 February 1962, VI.
152. 'Reis Amsterdam-München-Zürich-Bern-Genève-Amsterdam', January 1962, File: 151 Reisverslagen 1961–1967, Zwitserland (1961–1975), CC NAH.
153. Richard Deacon, *The French Secret Service* (London: Grafton, 1990), pp. 184–193.
154. 'Programme d'un Colloque Français-Allemand-Hollandais sur l'Attitude de l'Industrie en face de la Propagande diffuse du Marxisme-Léninisme auprès de ses Cadres', 'The role and the formation of the industrial cadres in competitive coexistence', and 'Concept de l'Agression et Principe de Riposte', File: 138 Mont Saint Michel, Italië (1959–1975), CC NAH.
155. 'The role and the formation of the industrial cadres in competitive coexistence', File: 138 Mont Saint Michel, Italië (1959–1975), CC NAH.
156. Writing to Guicciardi, Einthoven let drop that Bonnemaison was "a close friend of Charron's", indicating that the offices of Shell in France were also of major importance. Einthoven to Guicciardi, 16 February 1961, File: 130 Algemeen 1959–1961, Italië (1959–1975), CC NAH.
157. On the Büro – the former "Gruppe Siefart" – see Stefan Creuzberger, *Kampf für die Einheit: Das gesamtdeutsche Ministerium und die politische Kultur des Kalten Krieges 1949–1969* (Düsseldorf: Droste, 2008), p. 150.
158. Gehlen knew von Dellingshausen's family, and Andreas von Weiß, part of Geyer's IIIF in the BND, was von Dellingshausen's cousin. See Creuzberger, *Kampf für die Einheit*, p. 139.

159. 'Vermerk' (Einthoven/Van den Heuvel/von Dellingshausen/Scheffler, 2 May 1962), File: 16431, Collection: B 137, NAK.
160. The Verein's early membership can be judged from a meeting held in January 1963 on the 'Krise des Antikommunismus': Geyer and IIIF members Krause, von Weiss, and Herbert Ruoff, the Verein's chief von Grote, Lades, Kernig, Hiltmann, influential BND "associates" Professor Otto Rögele (editor of *Rheinischer Merkur*, chairman of the Society for Catholic Publishers, director of the Institute for Newspaper Journalism, and a member of the College for Television and Film) and Springer journalist Winfried Martini (once referred to as Gehlen's press "bodyguard"), and General (retired) Eberbach from the Evangelische Akademie. 'Zusammenkunft des Vereins am 12. Januar 1963', File: 16431, Collection: B 137, NAK; Erich Schmidt-Eenboom, *Geheimdienst Politik und Medien* (Berlin: Kai Homilius Verlag, 2004), pp. 148–149, 211–212.
161. Von Dellingshausen to Worgitski (BND), 23 May 1962, and von Dellingshausen to Dr Mercker (Chancellery), 24 May 1962, File: 16431, Collection: B 137, NAK.
162. 'Aktennotiz' (von Dellingshausen–Geyer), 3 July 1962, and 'Betr.: Interdok', 9 July 1962, File: 16431, Collection: B 137, NAK.
163. "Eine Orientierung des französischen Gesprächspartners erfolgt sowohl durch Dr. Einthoven wie durch Herrn Geyer." Dutch–German agreement, 28 June 1962, VI; 'Reis Amsterdam–München–Zürich–Bern–Genève–Amsterdam', File: 151 Reisverslagen 1961–1967, Zwitserland (1961–1975), CC NAH.
164. 'Merkblatt über die Gründung eines Internationalen Dokumentationszentrums im HAAG zur psychologischen Bekämpfung des Weltkommunismus', n.d. [1962], File: 16431, Collection: B 137, NAK.
165. Einthoven to Bernhard, 15 January 1962, File: 254 Prins Bernhard 1962–1986, Nederland, CC NAH.
166. Memo, n.d. [February 1962], ibid.
167. Einthoven to Bernhard, 24 July 1962, ibid.
168. Geyer to Van den Heuvel, 3 August 1962; Geyer to Van den Heuvel, 31 August 1962, VI.
169. 'Gesprek tussen de heer Geyer enerzijds en het bestuur SOEV alsmede de heer Einthoven anderzijds, dd. 28 september 1962', VI.
170. Einthoven to Bernhard, 15 January 1962, File: 254 Prins Bernhard 1962–1986, Nederland, CC NAH.
171. See Ellen Reese, *General Reinhard Gehlen: The CIA Connection* (Fairfax: George Mason University Press, 1990), pp. 143–167.
172. Einthoven to Bernhard, 22 July 1963, File: 254 Prins Bernhard 1962–1986, Nederland, CC NAH. Borchenski had already told Einthoven in 1961 that the Ford Foundation "ganz anti-anticommunistisch war": 'Besuch Prof. J.M. Borchenski – Freiburg – 15-8-1961', File: 151 Reisverslagen Zwitserland 1961–1967, Zwitserland (1961–1975), CC NAH. There is a record card in Einthoven's name of his approach to the Ford Foundation, dated 1962, with the heading "educational program in Europe to immunize citizens against communism", but no actual letter or proposal has been kept by the Ford archive.
173. Van den Heuvel to Monroe, 18 January 1961, and memo concerning Eugene Metz of the Free Europe Committee, n.d. [January 1961], File: 42 Society for the Investigation of Human Ecology, Verenigde Staten (1958–1979), CC NAH.
174. 'De dialoog tussen West en Oost', n.d. [Autumn 1962], File: 254 Prins Bernhard 1962–1986, Nederland, CC NAH.

175. Memo, n.d. [February 1963] and Einthoven to Bernhard, 19 August 1963, File: 254 Prins Bernhard 1962–1986, Nederland, CC NAH.
176. Einthoven to Bernhard, 19 August 1963; ibid.
177. Einthoven to Bernhard, 22 July 1963; ibid.
178. File: 224 Statutes 1962–1987, Organisatie, CC NAH.
179. 'INTERDOC', January 1963, File: 83 Algemeen 1961–1964, Groot Britannië (1959-1985), CC NAH.
180. Reinhard Gehlen, *The Service* (New York: World Publishing, 1972), p. 258.
181. Crozier, *Free Agent*, pp. 48–49; Einthoven to Pirenne, 14 June 1965, File: 142 J-H Pirenne 1965–1966, België (1961–1977), CC NAH. Thanks partly to the support from Shell, by this time Bonnemaison had an entrance into French business circles and was financed by, among others, Air Liquide. In 1965 he gave two lectures in the Netherlands on *"les clubs"*, according to Einthoven *"avec beaucoup de succès"*.
182. 'Interdoc', January 1963, File: 103 L. Sheridan 1963–1964, Groot-Britannië (1959–1985), CC NAH.
183. Van den Heuvel to von Hahn, 9 May 1963, File: 65 Baron von Hahn 1963–1968, Duitsland (1958–1978), CC NAH; Einthoven to Rijks, 7 October 1966, in author's possession.
184. Einthoven to Lemonnier, 2 July 1964, File: 137 Cronaca Politica 1964–1968, Italië (1959–1975), CC NAH; Ellis to Van den Heuvel, 25 February 1966, File: 95 C.H. (Dick) Ellis 1966, Groot-Britannië (1959–1985), CC NAH.
185. 'Extension de Notre Travail sur le Plan International', 4 June 1964, Archive of Georges Albertini, Box 13 Folder 7, Hoover Institution Archives, Stanford. This document also refers to contacts in the Dutch Ministry of Foreign Affairs and at the University of Leiden.
186. Roger Faligot and Pascal Krop, *La Piscine: The French Secret Service since 1944* (Oxford: Basil Blackwell, 1989), pp. 151–152.
187. Brian Crozier, interview with the author, London, 4 November 2004.
188. "Die einzigen Gruppen, die sich mit Kommunismus befassten, seien ganz rechts-stehende Katholiken." 'Protokoll der Interdok-Vortstandssitzung in Freiburg/Brsg "Schauinsland" am 27 April 1967', File: 224 Statutes 1962–1987, Organisatie, CC NAH.
189. Van den Heuvel to Geyer, 14 February 1966 and 5 May 1966, in author's possession; 'Visit to London, 12–15 February 1964', File: 89 Reisverslagen 1963–1968, Groot Britannië (1959–1985), CC NAH.

3 A Dutch–German Cabal

1. "The fields are ripe for harvest but the labourers are few." Van den Heuvel to Geyer, 14 February 1966, File: 66 H.J. Geyer 1965–1972, Duitsland (1958–1978), archive of C.C. van den Heuvel, National Archives, The Hague (hereafter CC NAH).
2. *Tasks* was originally produced in German (*Aufgaben der Freien Welt – heute*, Cologne: Verlag Wissenschaft und Politik, 1964) and translated into English by Rachel van der Wilden-Fall, an MI6 officer married to Van den Heuvel's old BVD colleague, Joop van der Wilden. She would translate several Interdoc/Ampersand titles, including Douglas Hyde's *United We Fall* and Karl Anders' *Murder to Order*.

Van den Heuvel to Ellis, 6 April 1964; Rachel van der Wilden-Fall, interview with the author, Rijswijk, 26 July 2005.
3. Van den Heuvel, 'Introduction', in *Tasks for the Free World Today: Thoughts on Positive Anti-Communism* (Gütersloh: Mohn & Co, 1964), pp. 7–8; Baron von Hahn to Alfred Münst, 19 December 1963, File: 156 Liga für Freiheit 1963–1965, Zwitserland (1961–1975), CC NAH.
4. Van den Heuvel, 'Notes on Terminology', *Tasks*, p. 9.
5. Van den Heuvel to Lamberty, 24 July 1963, File: 141 M. Lamberty 1962–1966, België (1961–1977), CC NAH.
6. M. Lamberty, 'Western Values and Positive Anti-Communism', and A. Münst, 'Thoughts on East–West Conflict', *Tasks*, pp. 11, 61.
7. S.W. Couwenberg, 'Changing Attitudes Towards Communism', and C.C. van den Heuvel, 'The Answer of the West to the Challenge of "Peaceful Coexistence"', *Tasks*, p. 35, 83.
8. Von Hahn to Renato Mieli, 27 October 1964, File: 136 CESES 1961–1975, Italië (1959–1975), CC NAH.
9. C.C. van den Heuvel, 'Introduction', in *The Challenge of Coexistence* (London: Ampersand, 1965), p. 11.
10. A. Avtorkhanov, 'Strategy for Freedom', *Challenge*, p. 37. Avtorkhanov is described as a graduate of Moscow's Institute of Red Professors who left the Soviet Union during World War II. The other authors were former *Daily Worker* editor Joseph Clark, *Deutsche Welle* journalist Ernest Salter, the Hungarian Vincent Savarius (pseudonym for Béla Szász), and former British Communist Party ideologue Douglas Hyde. Several others had been asked, but either failed to deliver (Mieli) or produced something of poor quality (Swedish socialist Ture Nerman).
11. Those involved in preparing this project were Hornix, Zacharias, and professors Baudet (Groningen), Kuypers (Free University Amsterdam), and Barents (Amsterdam). 'Notulen van de Vergadering van de Stichting Vrede en Vrijheid, gehouden op 8 September 1960 te 's-Gravenhage', 'Samenvatting van de Conclusies der Redactievergadering inzake de Uitgave van een Nieuw Maandblad, opgesteld door de Hoofdredacteur, De Heer L. Hanekroot', n.d. [1960], Van den Heuvel to Prof. Albregts, 8 October 1960, and 'Afspraken Betreffende Digest', 11 July 1961, File: Oost-West '1961–1971', in author's possession (with thanks to Professor Couwenberg for providing this material).
12. 'Oost-West', 17 January 1962, VI. The first editorial board did include Van Dam van Isselt and L. Hanekroot from Vrede en Vrijheid, but the journal soon came fully under the SOEV-dominated East–West Foundation.
13. Annual Report 1962, SOEV, File: Voorgeschiedenis Interdoc (hereafter VI), in author's possession.
14. The statutes for the new Foundation refer only to Van den Heuvel, Couwenberg, and Bart van der Laan. By the end of 1962 it would consist of Chair: Peter Koets (former editor of *Het Parool*), Treasurer: Van den Heuvel, Secretary: Couwenberg, Board members: Spits, Prof. Henri Baudet (Social History, Groningen), Prof. Ivan Gadourek (Sociology, Groningen), Constant Smits (journalist with the *Nieuwe Rotterdamse Courant*), Prof. Lamberty (Political Philosophy, Ghent) and Prof. Devolder (Social History, Leuven). This information was eventually made public in the January 1963 issue of *Oost-West*. 'Verslag van de Vergadering van het Bestuur van de SOEV', 3 May 1962, and 'Vergadering op 17 November 1962', File: Oost-West '1961–1971'.

15. Albregts to Couwenberg, February 1962, and Banning to Couwenberg, 24 March 1962, File: Oost-West '1961–1971'.
16. 'Vergadering op 21 mei 1962 van het Bestuur van de Stichting ter Voorlichting over de Oost-West Verhouding', File: Oost-West '1961–1971'.
17. It is also noticeable that few Dutch intellectuals participated in the CCF. See Tity de Vries, 'The Absent Dutch', in G. Scott-Smith and H. Krabbendam (eds), *The Cultural Cold War in Western Europe 1945–1960* (London: Frank Cass, 2003), pp. 254–266.
18. 'Ten Geleide', *Oost-West* 1 (March–April 1962), p. 2.
19. 'Oost-West', *De Brug*, 30 June 1962, p. 5.
20. Willem Couwenberg, interview with the author, Rotterdam, 21 October 2004.
21. HKO (Van Rest) to HBVD (Sinninghe Damsté), 13 July 1962, Inzagedossier: geheime memoirs van Louis Einthoven, Freedom of Information request (Wet Openbaar Bestuur) to Ministry of Justice / AIVD, 25 February 2009.
22. 'Vergadering op 17 november 1962 van het Bestuur van de Stichting ter Voorlichting over de Oost-West Verhouding', File: Oost-West '1961–1971'.
23. Wim Couwenberg, interview with the author, Middelburg, 7 November 2002.
24. 'Vergadering op 3 december 1963', File: Oost-West '1961–1971'.
25. 'Stichting Oost-West', n.d. [1964], File: Oost-West '1961–1971'.
26. Its main direct competitor was *Internationale Spectator*, published by the prestigious the Netherlands Society for International Affairs, a group that could raise large sums from advertising revenue and as a result produce a more attractive journal than the sober if high quality *Oost-West*.
27. While the ZWO gave a straight no, the Ministry showed interest but never converted this into a subsidy. 'Gesprek CC van den Heuvel en SW Couwenberg met Drs. M van Loosdrecht', 7 November 1963, and J.H. Bannier to Couwenberg, 21 June 1965, 'Nota voor Ir. HJ Rijks in verband met eventueel bezoek aan Minister O en W', n.d. [1965], File: Oost-West '1961–1971'; Wim Couwenberg, interview with the author, Middelburg, 7 November 2002.
28. 'Nota inzake een nieuwe opzet van onze stichting', n.d. [1965], and Van den Heuvel to SOEV staff, n.d. [1965], File: Oost-West '1961–1971'.
29. Those present at the meeting were Sinninghe Damsté, the head of Section A (Administration/Juridical Matters), Van den Heuvel, and Nico van Rest. 'Taakafbakening BVD en SOEV', 18 December 1961, Inzagedossier: geheime memoirs van Louis Einthoven, Freedom of Information request (Wet Openbaar Bestuur) to Ministry of Justice / AIVD, 25 February 2009.
30. My thanks to Constant Hijzen for providing this piece of information from the BVD 'Aurora' reports.
31. Joop van der Wilden, interview with the author, Rijswijk, 26 July 2005.
32. Peter Keller, interview with the author, Brussels, 23 April 2008. Keller was himself head of training for the BVD in the 1970s.
33. This clash had nothing to do with Van den Heuvel's activities. See Bob de Graaff and Cees Wiebes, *Villa Maarheeze: De Geschiedenis van de Inlichtingendienst Buitenland* (The Hague: Sdu, 1998), pp. 327–328.
34. Dick Engelen, *Geschiedenis van de Binnenlandse Veiligheidsdienst* (Den Haag: Sdu, 1995), pp. 30–31.
35. 'Stichting Oost en West', 3 March 1967, Inzagedossier: geheime memoirs van Louis Einthoven, Freedom of Information request (Wet Openbaar Bestuur) to Ministry of Justice / AIVD, 25 February 2009.

36. Wolfgang Buchow, interview with the author, Neuss, 10 January 2007.
37. Einthoven to Bernhard, 22 July 1963, File: 254 Prins Bernhard 1962–1986, Nederland, CC NAH.
38. W.G. Wieringa to A.J. Guépin, 2 January 1962, PCA 25: 936 Oost-West Instituut vh Stichting Onderzoek Ecologische Vraagstukken [SOEV], archives of Philips International BV (hereafter Philips).
39. 'Stichting voor Onderzoek van Ecologische Vraagstukken: Staat van baten en lasten over 1963', dated February 1964, Philips.
40. The visit reveals that at the time twelve people were active at Van Stolkweg for SOEV and Interdoc. 'Kort Verslag van de Bespreking op 3.3.1964 over Ecologische Vraagstukken', 20 March 1964, and memo I.T.M. Snellen to J.R. Schaafsma, 24 March 1964, Philips.
41. J.L.J.M. v.d. Does de Willebois and I.T.H.M. Snellen, 'Notitie voor Mr. Schaafsma – R.v.B.' 9 August 1965, Philips.
42. Statutes of WCDE, File: 291 Stichting Werkcomité voor Opvoeding tot Democratie 1962–1964, Nederland, CC NAH.
43. Van den Heuvel to E.H.F. van der Lely, 22 February 1962, C.C. van den Heuvel: 'Gesprek met Dr. E.H.F. van der Lely op 5 april 1962', and Van den Heuvel to W. Hogeveen (WCDE), 6 March 1964, File: 289 Werkcomité voor Opvoeding tot Democratie 1961–1969, Nederland, CC NAH; Van den Heuvel to Hogeveen, 16 March 1965, File: 294 Geestelijke Weerbaarheid en Centrum voor Actieve Democratie, Nederland, CC NAH.
44. 'Notitie voor Mr. Schaafsma – R.v.B.' 9 August 1965, I.T.M. Snellen to Bavinck, v.d. Does de Willebois, Dronkers, and Schaafsma, 6 October 1965, and 'Notitie voor Mr. J.R. Schaafsma – R.v.B.', 4 November 1965, Philips.
45. For example, through the conference on Mass Media and Citizenship held in November 1969, which called for a critical understanding of the effects of the commercial media on the individual's political awareness. 'Mededelingen', 7 August 1967, and Couwenberg to *Oost-West* Advisory Council, 13 August 1970, File: Oost-West 1961–1971.
46. 'Verslag van de cursus 11–17 september 1966 aan het Ostkolleg te Keulen', File: 63 Ostkolleg 1965–1972, Duitsland (1958–1978), CC NAH. According to Alexander Heldring (whose aunt was a member of the BVD), Van Oort had also belonged to the BVD circle (Van den Heuvel, Mennes, and Couwenberg) at the centre of Van Stolkweg, but he was more likely to have been military intelligence.
47. Memorandum, 27 July 1962, File 4: Stafvergaderingen 1954–65, Archive of the Nederlandse Spoorwegen, Collectie 938, Utrechts Archief, Utrecht (hereafter NS).
48. Memoranda, 2 July 1963 and 17 March 1964, File 4: Stafvergaderingen 1954–65, NS.
49. SOEV Annual Report (Jaarverslag) 1964, pp. 5–6; "daadwerkelijk in het Oost-West verkeer betrokken is": SOEV Annual Report 1965, p. 14; 'Gesprek directeur met penningmeester op 16 juli 1965', in author's possession. This document demonstrates the ongoing tension between Munich and The Hague over finances.
50. The conference was intended to take place in 1964, but there is no evidence that it went further than the drawing board. 'Gesprek Mr. L. Einthoven met ZKH Prins Bernhard, d.d. 12-11-1963', File: 254 Prins Bernhard 1962–1986, Nederland, CC NAH.

51. Van den Heuvel would apply to the Fund several times between 1963 and 1981, only once being successful: a 5000 guilder grant towards a conference in The Hague in May 1970 of the Union Internationale de la Résistance et de la Déportation. File: 245 Prins Bernhard Fonds 1963–1981, Financieel beheer, CC NAH.
52. Christiaan van den Heuvel, interview with the author, Rockanje, 20 June 2009.
53. The InVoLu staff, predominantly Catholic officers, included a young Jaap de Hoop Scheffer. J.J.M. Penders to Ernst van der Beugel, 9 December 1966, File 7: Private Correspondence 1963–67, Archive of E.H. van der Beugel, Inventory No. 2.21.183.08, Collection 357, National Archives, the Hague; Dirk Barth (InVoLu 1969–70), interview with the author, Middelburg, 27 November 2007; Jos van Gennip (InVoLu 1963–67), interview with the author, The Hague, 3 December 2007.
54. There is no hint from the correspondence that anyone enquired who exactly the foreign benefactor was, but that was probably too indiscreet to commit to paper. C.C. van den Heuvel to W. den Toom (Minister of Defence), 4 January 1968, W. den Toom to Van den Heuvel, 13 March 1968, Van den Heuvel to P. de Jong, 9 May 1968, H. Bos (coordinator of intelligence and security services, Minister-President's office) to W. den Toom, 7 June 1968, Subsidie-aanvraag OWI 1967–68, Archive of the Minister of Defence, Dossier 317.300, Centraal Archieven Depot, Ministry of Defence, Rijswijk.
55. Jaarverslag van de secretaris Binnenland, January 1967, File 67: Jaarverslagen 1963–72, archive of the Nationale Federatieve Raad van het Voormalig Verzet Nederland, Netherlands Institute for War Documentation, Amsterdam (hereafter NFR NIOD).
56. Statutes, 8 September 1969, File 305: Correspondence 1961–72, Stichting Geestelijke Weerbaarheid, NFR NIOD.
57. Cees van den Heuvel, 'Het heden en de geestelijke weerbaarheid', *Basis*, 25 December 1970; Cees van den Heuvel, 'Eerste stap is gezet', *Basis*, 1 January 1970.
58. This was a controversial move, because the Veteranen Legioen Nederland included Dutch military personnel who had served for the Germans in World War II – obviously an unacceptable group for the NFR's former resistance fighters. See Igor Cornelissen, 'Het moreel van de troep in Urk', *Vrij Nederland*, 21 September 1968.
59. A report in the *Haagsche Courant* included this remarkable exchange – Q: Are you subsidized by the CIA? A [Van den Heuvel]: No. If a condition for such a subsidy was that I had to infiltrate student and labour circles, I would refuse it. But without such a condition I would certainly welcome a subsidy from the CIA. 'Mening van eigenaars grond van Nationaal Monument moet meetellen', *Haagsche Courant*, 23 September 1970. See also 'Overschakelen van verzet op geestelijke weerbaarheid', *Algemeen Handelsblad*, 4 April 1968; 'Een beetje autoritair gezag werkt zeer heilzaam voor de zuidelijke landen', *De Nieuwe Linie*, 30 August 1969; P.J. Kat, 'Niet wachten tot je door het extremisme van links verzwolgen bent', *Algemeen Handelsblad*, 3 September 1969; Eelke de Jong, 'De wanorde van deze tijd daadwerkelijk corrigeren', *Spiegel*, 20 September 1969; 'Geestelijke Weerbaarheid II', *Vrij Nederland*, 30 May 1970; 'Wij luiden zo nodig de bel!' *De Telegraaf*, 3 February 1972.

60. C.C. van den Heuvel, Curriculum Vitae, File: 220 Einde Interdok 1970–1973, Overige Dossiers betreffende Interdoc, CC NAH; 'Psychologische Verdediging', n.d. [1971–72], File: 38 'Jeugd en Verzet' 1970–1974, Internationale Jeugdzaken, CC NAH.
61. Van den Heuvel to Geyer, 30 November 1962, VI. Hiltmann did continue his association as a member of von Grote's Verein/Arbeitsgruppe.
62. Curriculum Vitae; von Hahn to Van den Heuvel, 19 February 1963, File: 65 Baron W. von Hahn 1963–1968, Duitsland (1958–1978), CC NAH.
63. The Institut für Sowjetologie was officially established as the Bundesinstitut zur Erforschung des Marxismus-Leninismus in 1961, changing its name to the Bundesinstitut für ostwissenschaftliche und internationale Studien in May 1966. Its purpose was to examine the entire theoretical and practical reality of the "communist phenomenon", and its staff, led by its first directors Boris Meissner and Karl Thalheim, played an important role in the Ostkolleg. Its initial budget was DM 1.2 million. See Corinna Unger, *Ostforschung in Westdeutschland: Die Erforschung des europäischen Ostens und die Deutsche Forschungsgemeinschaft, 1945–1975* (Stuttgart: Franz Steiner, 2007), pp. 245–246.
64. SOEV board meeting: minutes, 5 February 1964 (Verslag no. 25), File: 65 Baron W. von Hahn 1963–1968, Duitsland (1958–1978), CC NAH.
65. The Netherlands was the only West European country with a Communist Party that directed its ire principally at West Germany instead of the US. Despite lingering resentment from World War II, the survey found that the Dutch, aside from some determined anti-German sentiment among certain intellectuals, were largely immune to CPN attempts to profit from this. 'The Effect of Soviet Propaganda regarding West Germany in a Number of West European Countries: The Netherlands', September 1966, author's copy.
66. Gunhild Bohm-Geyer, interview with the author, Würthsee, 4 July 2008.
67. 'Reis Amsterdam-München-Zürich-Bern-Genève-Amsterdam', January 1962, File: 151 Reisverslagen 1961–1967, Zwitserland (1961–1975), CC NAH.
68. Peter Becker, interview with the author, Tutzing, 9 April 2006; Dietmar Töppel, interview with the author, Munich, 3 July 2008. Töppel (code name Thorberg) ran IIIF's analysis on trends in world communism, while Becker (code name Zeussel) worked under Theodor Krause (code name Krebs), covering the Soviet Union for *Orientierung*, *Bundesrepublik im Spiegel der sowjetischen Presse*, and other outlets. Von Weiss (code name Weber) ran the Polish section.
69. Dethleffsen had moved from the military after the war to head an economic research institute in Frankfurt, through which he was well known within the German business world.
70. Curiously enough, Volker Foertsch was suspected of being an informer, but this was never proved. Peter Becker, interviews with the author, Tutzing, 9 April 2006, and subsequent discussions in Middelburg and Munich; Dietmar Töppel, interview with the author, Munich, 3 July 2008; Gunhild Bohm-Geyer, interview with the author, Würthsee, 12 July 2011.
71. Rolf Geyer, 'Ansprache zur Weihnachtsfeier 1968', personal papers of Gunhild Bohm-Geyer.
72. General Foertsch, 'Gedanken zur Errichtung einer Zentrale für Dokumentation und Information im Anschluss an den französisch-holländisch-deutschen Arbeitskreis', October 1959, in C.C. van den Heuvel, 'Hoofdlijnen van een Internationaal Instituut ter Bestrijding van de Psychologische Oorlogvoering van het Communisme', 16 November 1959, in author's possession.

292   Notes

73. "Insofern war unser Budget illusorisch." Von Hahn to Van den Heuvel, 22 May 1963, File: 65 Baron W. von Hahn 1963–1968, Duitsland (1958–1978), CC NAH.
74. As von Hahn put it, "wir sollten Geyer die Möglichkeit geben zu zeigen, that we were very good boys" to strengthen his position. Von Hahn to Van den Heuvel, 22 May 1963, File: 65 Baron W. von Hahn 1963–1968, Duitsland (1958–1978), CC NAH.
75. "Finanzierung: keine Regierungskontrolle": 'Entstehung von Interdok – Geschichte – Aufbau – Zielsetzung', 17 June 1965, File: 238 Baron W. von Hahn 1965–1966, Persoonsdossiers, CC NAH.
76. Rijks to Einthoven and Van den Heuvel, 6 August 1966, and Einthoven to Rijks, 7 October 1966, in author's possession.
77. File: 220 Einde Interdok 1970–1973, Overige Dossiers betreffende Interdoc, CC NAH. The guilder: deutschmark exchange rate was about 1:1 at the time.
78. Von Hahn to Van den Heuvel, 14 August 1964, File: 65 Baron W. von Hahn 1963–1968, Duitsland (1958–1978), CC NAH.
79. Geyer to Van den Heuvel, 8 September 1965, File: 66 H.J. Geyer 1965–1972, Duitsland (1958–1978), CC NAH.
80. Van den Heuvel to Geyer, 13 September 1965 and 14 December 1965; ibid.
81. Dietmar Töppel, interview with the author, Munich, 3 July 2008.
82. SOEV Annual Report (Jaarverslag) 1963, p. 10.
83. H.K.O. (Van den Heuvel) to H.B.V.D. (Einthoven), 18 June 1960, File: 61 Ostkolleg 1960–1962, Duitsland (1958–1978), CC NAH.
84. 'Bezoek Ost-Kolleg 31 januari 1962', File: 61 Ostkolleg 1960–1962, Duitsland (1958–1978), CC NAH.
85. 'Gesprek in Ostkolleg met Bahro en Nitsche op 16 januari 1963', File: 62 Ostkolleg 1963–1964, Duitsland (1958–1978), CC NAH.
86. Van den Heuvel to Geyer, 24 October 1962, VI.
87. Von Hahn to Van den Heuvel, 2 December 1963, File: 65 Baron W. von Hahn 1963–1968, Duitsland (1958–1978), CC NAH.
88. Von Hahn to von Dellingshausen, 3 September 1964, File: 64 Bundesministerium für gesamtdeutsche Fragen 1961–1968, Duitsland (1958–1978), CC NAH.
89. See Unger, *Ostforschung in Westdeutschland*, p. 248.
90. Von Hahn to Buchholz, 5 October 1964, File: 64 Bundesministerium für gesamtdeutsche Fragen 1961–1968, Duitsland (1958–1978), CC NAH. Buchholz's *Der Kampf um die bessere Welt* (Stuttgart: Deutsche Verlags-Anstalt, 1961) was translated into Dutch as *De Dialoog tussen Oost en West* (Amsterdam: Wetenschappelijke Uitgeverij, 1966).
91. 'Gesprek in Ostkolleg met Bahro en Nitsche op 16 januari 1963', File: 62 Ostkolleg 1963–1964, Duitsland (1958–1978), CC NAH.
92. 'Rapport over de OSTKOLLEG cursus 13 mei–20 mei 1962', File: 61 Ostkolleg 1960–1962, Duitsland (1958–1978), CC NAH. In that first year other Dutch participants included Marine Attaché A.J.J. Benist, Lieutenant Colonel S. van der Pol, and journalist J.R.G. Verreijdt.
93. Banning told Van der Laan that there was much suspicion within both Kerk en Wereld and the Roman Catholic study centre De Hostink towards SOEV and one of its principal associates, Prof. Dr Zacharias Anthonisse from the University of Nijmegen. He recommended that the name "Ecology" be dropped because it was an unknown term in the Netherlands and appeared too much like a cover for suspicious psychological warfare activities. 'Onderhoud d.d. 15 mei te

Driebergen met Prof. Dr. W. Banning', File: 61 Ostkolleg 1960–1962, Duitsland (1958–1978), CC NAH.
94. 'Verslag van een Bezoek van 14 okt t/m 20 okt '62 aan het OstKolleg', 23 October 1962, File: 61 Ostkolleg 1960–1962, Duitsland (1958–1978), CC NAH.
95. Heldring to Van den Heuvel, 28 December 1962, File: 61 Ostkolleg 1960–62, Duitsland (1958–1978), CC NAH; J.L. Heldring, interview with the author, The Hague, 6 May 2011.
96. 'Cursus aan het OstKolleg te Keulen, van 14 tot 20 oktober 1962', File: 61 Ostkolleg 1960–62, Duitsland (1958–1978), CC NAH.
97. Mennes to J.A. Offermans (Utrechts Studenten Faculteiten), 20 February 1964, File: 62 Ostkolleg 1963–1964, Duitsland (1958–1978), CC NAH.
98. Britain, France, Italy, Sweden, Denmark, Norway, Portugal, Greece, Switzerland, the Netherlands, and the US provided delegates.
99. Georg von Rauch to Van den Heuvel, 16 September 1964, File: 62 Ostkolleg 1963–1964, Duitsland (1958–1978), CC NAH.
100. 'Kurzreferate über Methoden der Behandlung von Ostfragen in der politischen Bildung, gehalten am 15. Dezember 1964', File: 63 Ostkolleg 1965–1972, Duitsland (1958–1978), CC NAH.
101. Peter Foster to J.C. Edmonds (Foreign Office), 16 December 1964, FO 1110/1860, papers of the Information Research Department, National Archives, London (hereafter IRD NAL); 'Internationale Tagung im Ostkolleg vom 14 bis 16 Dezember 1964 in Köln', File: 75 Ostkolleg 1960–1978, Duitsland (1958–1978), CC NAH; 'Ostforschung und politische Bildung', File: 62 Ostkolleg 1963–1964, Duitsland (1958–1978), CC NAH.
102. Edmonds to Foster, 23 December 1964, FO 1110/1860, IRD NAL.
103. Geyer to Van den Heuvel, 8 September 1965, File: 66 H.J. Geyer 1965–1972, Duitsland (1958–1978), CC NAH.
104. See Ulrich von Hassell, *The von Hassell Diaries: The Story of the Forces against Hitler Inside Germany* (London: Hamish Hamilton, 1948). Von Hassell was executed on 8 September 1944 for his involvement in the 20 July plot to assassinate Hitler.
105. 'Abendland: Die Missionäre Monarchie', *Der Spiegel*, 10 August 1955, pp. 12–14.
106. 'Aufgaben von Frau R. von Hassell in Den Haag', n.d. [1966], File: 239 R. Von Hassell-von Caprivi, Persoonsdossiers, CC NAH.
107. Van den Heuvel to Geyer, 22 December 1966, File: 66 H.J. Geyer 1965–1972, Duitsland (1958–1978), CC NAH.

4 The European Web

1. C.C. van den Heuvel, 'Enkele hoofdlijnen van een internationaal instituut ter bestrijding van de psychologische oorlogvoering van het communisme', 10 October 1959, in author's possession.
2. 'Verslag Reis Engeland 19–21 februari 1962', File: 83 Algemeen 1961–1964, Groot-Britannië (1959–1985), archive of C.C. van den Heuvel, National Archives, The Hague (hereafter CC NAH).
3. Noble to Glass (Foreign Office), 24 August 1962, FO 1110/1488, papers of the Information Research Department, National Archives, London (hereafter IRD NAL).
4. Barclay to Noble, 18 September 1962, FO 1110/1488, IRD NAL.
5. Minutes (Mr McWilliams), 19 November 1962, FO 1110/1488, IRD NAL.

6. The resentment mentioned here apparently came directly from Einthoven. Minutes (Miss Allott), 4 September 1962, FO 1110/1488, IRD NAL.
7. Josephine O'Connor Howe, interview with the author, Charing, 20 July 2007.
8. Noble to Barclay, 3 November 1962, Barclay to Noble, 10 December 1962, FO 1110/1488, IRD NAL.
9. Josephine O'Connor Howe, interview with the author, Charing, 20 July 2007.
10. 'Besprekingen i.v.m. Interdoc in Engeland van 21–23 januari 1963', File: 89 Reisverslagen 1963–1968, Groot-Britannië (1959–1985), CC NAH; Van den Heuvel to Ellis, 4 February 1963, File: 92 C.H. (Dick) Ellis 1961–1963, Groot-Britannië (1959–1985), CC NAH.
11. 'Gesprek met Dettmer en Baker White op 17 juli 1962', File: 90 Economic League 1959–1978, Groot-Britannië (1959–1985), CC NAH.
12. 'Gesprek met Economic League (Dettmer en Baker White) op 21 jan. 1963', File: 90 Economic League 1959–1978, Groot-Britannië (1959–1985), CC NAH.
13. 'Visit to London and Oxford 4–7 March 1963', File: 89 Reisverslagen 1963–1968, Groot-Britannië (1959–1985), CC NAH.
14. 'Gesprek met Economic League (Dettmer en Baker White) op 21 jan. 1963', File: 90 Economic League 1959–1978, Groot-Britannië (1959–1985), CC NAH; 'INTERDOC', January 1963, File: 83 Algemeen 1961–1964, Groot-Britannië (1959–1985), CC NAH. While Shell supported the Economic League financially, it proved difficult to expand this funding base. Unilever turned down Dettmer's approaches, saying that these kinds of anti-communist activities should be carried out by the government.
15. 'Bezoek aan Engeland, 25–30 april 1963', File: Reisverslagen 1963–1968, Groot-Britannië (1959–1985), CC NAH.
16. Van den Heuvel to David Footman, 14 August 1962, and Footman to Van den Heuvel, 2 September 1962, File: 101 St. Antony's College 1962–1964, Groot-Britannië (1959–1985), CC NAH.
17. Christ Church was at the time an all-male college, somehow appropriate for the Interdoc clientele. Von Grote's intention to attend with Gräfin Fugger von Babenhausen therefore caused serious embarrassment to Ellis as host. Ellis to Einthoven, 24 July 1963, File: 92 C.H. (Dick) Ellis 1961–1963, Groot-Britannië (1959–1985), CC NAH.
18. 'Common Cause Ltd', Interdoc memo, n.d., File: 107 Common Cause 1964–1971, Groot-Britannië (1959–1985), CC NAH.
19. 'Visit to London from February 24th to March 3rd 1965', File: 89 Reisverslagen 1963–1968, Groot-Britannië (1959–1985), CC NAH.
20. But contacts were kept at a distance. Ellis mentioned in passing the links between Common Cause and Belgian banker Marcel De Roover, a member of the right-wing Centre Européen de Documentation et d'Information (CEDI), founded in 1948 by Archduke Otto von Habsburg, and the World Anti-Communist League (WACL). Van den Heuvel and Geyer did not follow up on Common Cause's wish to invite De Roover and other CIAS figures to Christ Church. 'Reis Londen 18 en 19 november 1963', File: 89 Reisverslagen 1963–1968, Groot-Britannië (1959–1985), CC NAH; Van den Heuvel to Ellis, 4 April 1963, 'Visit to England 25–30 April 1963', and Ellis to Van den Heuvel, 23 May 1963, File: 92 C.H. (Dick) Ellis 1961–1963, Groot-Britannië (1959–1985), CC NAH; David Teacher, Rogue Agents: The Cercle Pinay Complex 1951–1991 (2008), available online at www.cryptome.org/2012/01/cercle-pinay-6i.pdf.

21. 'Visit to England 25–30 April 1963', File: 89 Reisverslagen 1963–1968, Groot-Britannië (1959–1985), CC NAH.
22. "in het algemeen zeer gunstig": 'Bespreking C.C. van den Heuvel met L. Sheridan en C.H. Ellis […]' 30 September 1963, File: 92 C.H. (Dick) Ellis 1961–1963, Groot-Britannië (1959–1985), CC NAH; Richard Aldrich, *The Hidden Hand: Britain, America and Cold War Secret Intelligence* (London: John Murray, 2001), pp. 455, 458.
23. Van den Heuvel to Ellis, 30 August 1963 and 'Gesprek CC van den Heuvel met L Sheridan, 30 augustus 1963', File: 103 L. Sheridan 1963–1964, Groot-Britannië (1959–1985), CC NAH.
24. 'Bespreking C.C. van den Heuvel met L. Sheridan en C.H. Ellis […]' 30 September 1963, File: 92 C.H. (Dick) Ellis 1961–1963, Groot-Britannië (1959–1985), CC NAH.
25. Ellis to Van den Heuvel, 30 October 1963 and 31 October 1963, File: 92 C.H. (Dick) Ellis 1961–1963, Groot-Britannië (1959–1985), CC NAH.
26. Van den Heuvel to Ellis, 1 February 1964, File: UK 1 Leslie Sheridan, CC NAH. Possible alternatives included Guy Hadley, head of the research department at the Conservative Party's central office. Contacts in this period also included the leaders of the Young Conservatives, John MacGregor and Nicholas Scott, both of whom went on to become MPs.
27. 'Interdoc and Interdoc-UK', 16 July 1964, File: 105 Oprichting 1964, Groot-Britannië (1959–1985), CC NAH.
28. 'Interdoc-UK', 20 July 1964, File: 105 Oprichting 1964, Groot-Britannië (1959–1985), CC NAH; Van den Heuvel to Ellis, 7 July 1964, File: 93 C.H. (Dick) Ellis 1964, Groot-Britannië (1959–1985), CC NAH.
29. Invitation to prospective Interdoc UK board members, C.H. Ellis, 4 June 1964, File: 89 Reisverslagen 1963–1968, Groot-Britannië (1959–1985), CC NAH.
30. 'Interdoc-UK [van den Heuvel notes]', n.d. (July 1964), File: 105 Oprichting 1964, Groot-Britannië (1959–1985), CC NAH.
31. Stephen Howarth and Joost Jonker, *Geschiedenis van Koninklijke Shell*, deel 2 (1939–1973), (Amsterdam: Boom, 2007), p. 191.
32. D.G. Stewart-Smith (with foreword by Julian Amery), *No Vision Here: Non-Military Warfare in Britain* (Foreign Affairs: Petersham, 1966).
33. Ellis to Van den Heuvel, 26 August 1964 and 29 June 1964, File: 93 C.H. (Dick) Ellis 1964, Groot-Britannië (1959–1985), CC NAH.
34. 'Report on a visit to Interdoc UK on 7 and 8 December 1966', File: 89 Reisverslagen 1963–1968, Groot-Britannië (1959–1985), CC NAH.
35. 'Visit to London 12–15 February 1964', File: 89 Reisverslagen 1963–1968, Groot-Britannië (1959–1985), CC NAH; File: 104 J. Josten 1963–1974, Groot-Britannië (1959–1985), CC NAH. It was later claimed by Czech defector Major Josef Frolik that Josten was twice singled out as a potential assassination target. See *The Times*, 25 January 1974, and East West Digest, 10 (December 1974).
36. 'Reise nach England – vom 2 bis 4 November 1964', File: 89 Reisverslagen 1963–1968, Groot-Britannië (1959–1985), CC NAH; Ellis to Van den Heuvel, 8 October 1964, File: 93 C.H. (Dick) Ellis 1964, Groot-Britannië (1959–1985), CC NAH.
37. 'Reis naar Londen' and 'Gesprek met Ellis in Londen op dinsdag 18 augustus 1964', File: 89 Reisverslagen 1963–1968, Groot-Britannië (1959–1985), CC NAH; Van den Heuvel to Ellis, 13 October 1964, File: 93 C.H. (Dick) Ellis 1964, Groot-Britannië (1959–1985), CC NAH.

38. Van den Heuvel to Ellis, 11 August 1965, File: 106 Financiën 1964–1969, Groot-Britannië (1959–1985), CC NAH.
39. Van den Heuvel to Sheridan, 3 December 1963, File: 103 L. Sheridan 1963–1964, Groot-Britannië (1959–1985), CC NAH.
40. German participants in 1961 included Felix von Eckhardt (head of the Bundespresseamt/Federal Press and Information Office) and Dr Wickert (Legionsrat/First Secretary of the Eastern Department of the West German Foreign Ministry). Wickert was the specialist on international student issues.
41. H.A.H. Cortazzi (British Embassy Bonn) to John Jeaffreson (IRD), 8 April 1961, FO 1110/1372, IRD NAL. Cortazzi identified three anti-communist organizations: Rettet die Freiheit ("very new […] must be treated with the greatest circumspection"), the CIDCC, and CIAS's German affiliate, the VFF. The last, financed from the BMG and the "Reptilienfund" of the Chancellery, was deemed to offer the most useful opportunities.
42. J.L.W. Price (British Embassy Bonn), 4 July 1963, FO 1110/1633, IRD NAL; 'Report on a visit to Interdoc UK on 7 and 8 December 1966', File: 89 Reisverslagen 1963–1968, Groot-Britannië (1959–1985), CC NAH.
43. 'Current Trends in Soviet Policy', August 1960, FO 1110/1738, IRD NAL.
44. In 1964–65 IRD's budget via the Secret Vote was £900,000, compared to the £2 million dispensed by the overt information departments of the Foreign Office. Secretary of State to Sir John Nichols, 20 March 1964; Sir John Nichols to Secretary of State, 21 April 1964, FO 1110/1738, IRD NAL.
45. 'Communist Policy and our Counter-Propaganda', Circular No. 70, 29 May 1964, FO 1110/1738, IRD NAL.
46. Minutes of 89th Meeting of the Permanent Under-Secretary's Steering Committee, 8 December 1966; J.H. Peck to Permanent Under-Secretary, 7 December 1966, FO 1110/2004, IRD NAL.
47. 'Bericht von Herrn van den Heuvel über seine Reise nach England vom 19 bis 23 Juli 1965', File: 84 Algemeen 1965, Groot-Britannië (1959–1985), CC NAH; Ellis to Van den Heuvel, 1 January 1965, File: 94 C.H. (Dick) Ellis 1965, Groot-Britannië (1959–1985), CC NAH.
48. 'Reise von Herrn van den Heuvel nach Londen am 18 und 19 November 1963', File: 89 Reisverslagen 1963–1968, Groot-Britannië (1959–1985), CC NAH.
49. Van den Heuvel to Ellis, 11 August 1965, File: 106 Financiën 1964–1969, Groot-Britannië (1959–1985), CC NAH; 'Visit to London from February 24th to March 3rd 1965', File: 89 Reisverslagen 1963–1968, Groot-Britannië (1959–1985), CC NAH.
50. Ellis to Van den Heuvel, 12 June 1964, and Van den Heuvel to Ellis, 26 October 1964, File: 93 C.H. (Dick) Ellis 1964, Groot-Britannië (1959–1985), CC NAH; Ellis to Van den Heuvel, 6 March 1965 and 5 July 1965, File: 94 C.H. (Dick) Ellis 1965, Groot-Britannië (1959–1985), CC NAH.
51. Even Cees de Niet visited Shell UK during this period to try to generate interest. 'Reise nach England – vom 9 bis 11 Dezember 1964', File: 89 Reisverslagen 1963–1968, Groot-Britannië (1959–1985), CC NAH.
52. For this reason the Association, initially open to invitations from Van den Heuvel, soon shied away from contact with Interdoc to avoid being seen as an anti-communist organization. 'Anlage zum Reisbericht England (2–4 Nov. 1964)', 'Reise nach England – vom 9 bis 11 Dezember 1964', 'Visit to London from February 24th to March 3rd 1965', and 'Reise nach England

am 3 und 4 Mai 1965', File: 89 Reisverslagen 1963–1968, Groot-Britannië (1959–1985), CC NAH.
53. Van den Heuvel to Geyer, 13 September 1965, File: 66 H.J. Geyer 1965–1972, Duitsland (1958–1978), CC NAH.
54. 'Visit to London 14–17 February 1966', File: 89 Reisverslagen 1963–1968, Groot-Britannië (1959–1985), CC NAH.
55. In 1961–63 Sager was embroiled in a court case against the Social Democrat member of parliament Hans Oprecht, due to Oprecht accusing Sager of "politische Schizophrenie" for opposing cultural contacts with the Soviet block in Klare Blick while simultaneously promoting East–West trade through the Ost-Institut's Wirtschaftsdienst. Sager eventually lost the case.
56. Sager instead applied to the Ford Foundation for $70,000 a year for five years. Einthoven report on discussions, June 1964, File: 151 Reisverslagen Zwitserland 1961–1967, Zwitserland (1961–1975), CC NAH; Einthoven to Sager, 3 July 1964, File: 150 Algemeen 1961–1970, Zwitserland (1961–1975), CC NAH; 'The Swiss Eastern Institute', n.d. [1964], File: 160 Schweizerisches Ost-Institut 1961–1972, Zwitserland (1961–1975), CC NAH.
57. 'Rapport reis naar Zwitserland 18 en 19 januari 1965', File: 151 Reisverslagen Zwitserland 1961–1967, Zwitserland (1961–1975), CC NAH. The contact with the *Zeitung* had a remarkable follow-up when Einthoven visited the chief editor in June 1965 to try to persuade the paper to run a strongly worded critique of de Gaulle's foreign policy and how he was undermining the Western alliance. Einthoven went so far as to compare the 1960s with the 1930s, although he admitted that "the parallel between Hitler and de Gaulle is of course not exact in every detail [...]" The Swiss seemed unmoved. Written in English, the report of this meeting must have been meant for American eyes, raising interesting questions about the extent to which the CIA – the most obvious candidate – would make use of Einthoven's contacts.
58. 'Reise in die Schweiz am 14 und 15 Februar 1965', File: 151 Reisverslagen 1961–1967, Zwitserland (1961–1975), CC NAH.
59. 'Gespräch mit Professor Dr. Hofer am 12 April 1965', File: 151 Reisverslagen 1961–1967, Zwitserland (1961–1975), CC NAH. Ming's associate W.P. Renschler told Einthoven and Van den Heuvel in June 1965 that the level of cooperation with the Swiss intelligence and security service was not ideal. 'Reise in die Schweiz und nach Italien in der Zeit vom 1 bis 5 juni '65', ibid.
60. Gasteyger was willing to provide useful contacts but was not further connected with the manoeuvrings in Switzerland itself. Van den Heuvel was also irritated by Gasteyger's judgements of others and inability to appreciate the problematic differences of opinion in his own country. 'Reise nach England – vom 9 bis 11 Dezember 1964', and 'Visit to London from February 24th to March 3rd 1965', File: 89 Reisverslagen 1963–1968, Groot-Britannië (1959–1985), CC NAH.
61. Walter Renschler, Elizabeth Kopp, and Max Frenkel, *la suisse = Switzerland*, (Zurich: Aktionskomitee Wahret die Freiheit, 1962).
62. 'Besprechungen von Herrn van den Heuvel in der Schweiz', April 1965, and 'Gespräch mit Herrn Dr. Münst am 14 April 1965', File: 150 Algemeen 1961–1970, Zwitserland (1961–1975), CC NAH.
63. 'Reise in die Schweiz und nach Italien in der Zeit vom 1 bis 5 Juni 65', File: 151 Reisverslagen 1961–1967, Zwitserland (1961–1975), CC NAH; 'Zusammenfassende Widergabe des Reiseberichtes von Herrn van den Heuvel

über seine Reise in die Schweiz und nach Italien in der Zeit vom 2 bis 4 Juni 1965', File: 132 Algemeen 1964–1965, Italië (1959–1975), CC NAH.
64. 'Gesprek met Dr. Sager op 17 november 1965 in Bern', File: 152 Schweizerisches Ost-Institut 1961–1965, Zwitserland (1961–1975), CC NAH.
65. Van den Heuvel to Sager, 24 December 1965, File: 152 Schweizerisches Ost-Institut 1961–1965, Zwitserland (1961–1975), CC NAH. It involved seven publications: *Notes on Communist and Communist-sponsored Activities as Reported by Communist Sources* (weekly); *Activities of International Communist Organisations* (quarterly); *Beiträge zur psychopolitischen Lage der europäischen Ostblockländer* (monthly/bimonthly); *Die psychopolitische Lage in der S.B.Z.* (monthly/bimonthly); *Spiegel der kommunistischen wissenschaftlichpolitischen Publizistik* (monthly); *Religion und Kirche im kommunistischen Einflussbereich* (monthly); *Interdoc Information Bulletin* (every two or three months).
66. 'Gesprek met Graf (president Wahret die Freiheit) op 20 aug. 1965', Van den Heuvel to Graf, 13 October 1965, 'Gesprek met Graf op 16 november 1965 te Zürich', File: 155 Aktionskomitee Wahret die Freiheit 1962–1969, Zwitserland (1961–1975), CC NAH. Einthoven also persevered with Sager, arranging via Schepers' successor as Shell director, Gerrit Wagner, to bring the Swiss to London to meet "one of the big managers", R.G. Searight. This led to the strong possibility that Shell UK would finance an Arabic press service at the Ost-Institut. Einthoven to Sager, 17 June 1965, and Sager to Einthoven, 23 July 1965, File: 152 Schweizerisches Ost-Institut 1961–1965, Zwitserland (1961–1975), CC NAH.
67. Von Hahn clearly knew Gianbattista Zanchi of Ideal-Standard very well, and it was Zanchi who opened the doors to both the Associazione and Confindustria. 'Einige Bemerkungen zu den Gesprächen in Mailand und Rom', 25 October 1963, File: 134 Reisverslagen 1961–1964, Italië (1959–1975), CC NAH; von Hahn to Zanchi, 30 August 1963, and von Hahn to Zanchi, 11 November 1963, File: 131 Algemeen 1962–1963, Italië (1959–1975), CC NAH.
68. Einthoven to Pavetto, 20 August 1962, and Van den Heuvel to Pavetto, 25 October 1963, File: 136 CESES 1961–1975, Italië (1959–1975), CC NAH.
69. 'Vermerk für Herrn van den Heuvel', 25 October 1963, 'Aufzeichnung', n.d. [31 October 1963], File: 134 Reisverslagen 1961–1964, Italië (1959–1975), CC NAH.
70. Pavetto to Van den Heuvel, 3 December 1963, Van den Heuvel to Dettmer, n.d. [January 1964], File: 136 CESES 1961–1975, Italië (1959–1975), CC NAH.
71. Biographical details, File: 136 CESES 1961–1975, Italië (1959–1975), CC NAH.
72. 'Vermerk', 9 January 1964, File: 136 CESES 1961–1975, Italië (1959–1975), CC NAH.
73. Geyer had literally warned that Bonnemaison should not conduct business at Van Stolkweg. His trip was not secret, since the Frenchman had fully briefed Colonel Mareuil on its purpose beforehand. Von Hahn to Geyer, 14 January 1964, File: 136 CESES 1961–1975, Italië (1959–1975), CC NAH.
74. Van den Heuvel to Vaccari, 2 March 1964, File: 132 Algemeen 1964–1965, Italië (1959–1975), CC NAH.
75. 'Visit Milan 25-3-1964', File: 134 Reisverslagen 1961–1964, Italië (1959–1975), CC NAH.
76. Einthoven to Mieli, 23 March 1965, Einthoven to Guicciardi, 23 March 1965, and Einthoven to Mieli, 9 July 1965, File: 136 CESES 1961–1975, Italië (1959–1975), CC NAH.

Notes 299

77. 'Visit to Britain 29/5–3/6/1964', File: 89 Reisverslagen 1963–1968, Groot-Britannië (1959–1985), CC NAH.
78. Von Grote to Van den Heuvel, 16 November 1964, File: 136 CESES 1961–1975, Italië (1959–1975), CC NAH.
79. 'Seminar on the Problems of Soviet Planning', 12–13 November 1964, File: 136 CESES 1961–1975, Italië (1959–1975), CC NAH.
80. Once again von Hahn's Italian connections played a role. The first candidate was Count Lucca Pietromarchi, a former diplomat with excellent business connections who was renowned for refusing to cooperate with German authorities concerning the deportation of Jews from Italian-occupied territories during the war. Pietromarchi was later Ambassador in Moscow. Von Hahn knew him from his days with the League of Nations in Geneva. See Jonathan Steinberg, *All or Nothing: The Axis and the Holocaust* 1941–1943 (London: Routledge, 1990) pp. 60–61.
81. Van den Heuvel to Lamberty, 22 April 1965, File: 142 J.H. Pirenne 1965–1966, België (1961–1977), CC NAH.
82. 'Reise nach England am 3 und 4 Mai 1965', File: 89 Reisverslagen 1963–1968, Groot-Britannië (1959–1985), CC NAH.
83. 'Bezoek G. Zucchini d.d. 25 mei 1965', File: 136 CESES 1961–1975, Italië (1959–1975), CC NAH.
84. Alongside established Interdoc colleagues such as John Baker White (UK), von Grote (Federal Republic), and Caeymaex (Belgium – using the pseudonym Benoit), Herman Mennes wrote the Dutch, French (as "Pierre Mendès"), and Finnish (as "Pentti Mennelekki") contributions.
85. Von Hahn to Mieli, 7 September 1965, File: 136 CESES 1961–1975, Italië (1959–1975), CC NAH.
86. 'Visit to Zurich-Bern-Milano 20–23 March 1967', File: 136 CESES 1961–1975, Italië (1959–1975), CC NAH.
87. 'Vermerk für Herrn van den Heuvel', 18 August 1965, File: 132 Algemeen 1964–1965, Italië (1959–1975), CC NAH.
88. Einthoven to Van Gestel, 25 November 1965, and von Hahn to Galletti (UCID), 26 October 1965, File: 132 Algemeen 1964–1965, Italië (1959–1975), CC NAH. One of the Italian participants at Locarno, Società Edison's Luigi Craici, even told von Hahn at this time that CESES was so successful it made Interdoc unnecessary.
89. Von Hahn to Zanchi, 11 January 1966, File: 133 Algemeen 1966–1967, Italië (1959–1975), CC NAH.
90. Vaccari even reported in 1966 that Giulio Andreotti, whom he had tried to link up with Einthoven in 1961, was (as Minister for Industry) still interested in the Interdoc enterprise. Vaccari to Van den Heuvel, 13 July 1966, File: 133 Algemeen 1966–1967, Italië (1959–1975), CC NAH.
91. Vaccari to Van den Heuvel, 1 June 1966, File: 133 Algemeen 1966–1967, Italië (1959–1975), CC NAH. Madiran (real name Arfel) had been pro-Vichy during the war and would gain notoriety again in the 1980s, when the newspaper he co-founded, *Présent*, became a source of inspiration for the Front National.
92. Einthoven to Rijks, 7 October 1966, in author's possession; 'Reis Amsterdam-München-Zürich-Bern-Genève-Amsterdam', 22–26 January 1962, File: 151 Reisverslagen 1961–1967, Zwitserland (1961–1975), CC NAH.

93. In the words of von Hahn, "Madame Labin représente l'aile extrèmement gauche socialiste. Entre le groupe Labin et nous aucune cooperation existe. Madame Labin n'appartient pas au groupe français avec lequel nous coopérons." It is curious that von Hahn refers to Labin as extreme left, not right. Von Hahn to Philipe Mottu, 14 December 1964, File: 150 Algemeen 1961–1970, Zwitserland (1961–1975), CC NAH.
94. Margot to Einthoven, 25 May 1962, File: 140 Algemeen 1961–1972, België (1961–1977), CC NAH. Margot, who was connected with the Belgian Gladio network, had complained before of too much American dominance in intelligence and security affairs. See Hugo Gijsels, *Netwerk Gladio* (Leuven: Kritak, 1991), p. 80.
95. 'Bezoek aan Professor Devolder op 31 Mei 1961', File: 140 Algemeen 1961–1972, België (1961–1977), CC NAH. Devolder confirmed the opportunism of Belgian business, such that employers would send their sons to study in Moscow in the hope of reaping economic rewards afterwards.
96. On Lamberty's importance within Belgian-Flemish intellectual circles see Fanny Leys, *Max Lamberty* (Antwerp: Nederlandsche Boekhandel, 1977); Eva Schandevyl, 'Max Lamberty en het ontstaan van de Stichting Lodewijk de Raet', in K. van Goethem and E. Schandevyl (eds), 50 *Jaar Stichting Lodewijk de Raet* (Brussels: Stichting Lodewijk de Raet, 2002).
97. In the end he only succeeded in publishing an updated version in Dutch, Grondslagen van de Westerse Cultuur, in 1966.
98. Max Lamberty, 'Dialoog met de Sowjets?' I (September–October 1963) and II (November–December 1963), *Oost-West*.
99. Lamberty to Van den Heuvel, 27 September 1964, File: 141 Max Lamberty 1962–1966, België (1961–1977), CC NAH.
100. Lamberty to Van den Heuvel, 30 November 1963, Van den Heuvel to Lamberty, 23 January 1964, and Lamberty to Van den Heuvel, 29 May 1964, File: 141 Max Lamberty 1962–1966, België (1961–1977), CC NAH.
101. 'Bezoek D.G. Stewart-Smith en Dr. F.J. Thomson, 24 juli 1964' and 'Gesprek met Professor Dr. Emmanuel Coppetiers en Dr. Thomson in Antwerpen op 1 december 1964', File: 140 Algemeen 1961–1972, België (1961–1977), CC NAH; Van Gestel to Lamberty, 12 October 1964, Lamberty to Van den Heuvel, 8 January 1965, and Van den Heuvel to Lamberty, 16 March 1965 and 22 March 1965, File: 141 Max Lamberty 1962–1966, België (1961–1977), CC NAH; 'Report on the meeting with Prof. Dr. M. Lamberty and Dr. J.H. Pirenne, on January 21, 1965', and Van den Heuvel to Pirenne, 19 February 1965, File: 142 J.H. Pirenne 1965–1966, België (1961–1977), CC NAH.
102. Pirenne's views are to be found in 'Une dimension nouvelle du problème atlantique et des relations Est-Ouest?' *Le Phare*, 25 April 1965. Van den Heuvel to Lamberty, 16 March 1965, File: 141 Max Lamberty 1962–1966, België (1961–1977), CC NAH.
103. Pirenne to Van den Heuvel, 2 April 1965, and 'Programme Interdoc-Belgique', 10 April 1965, File: 142 J.H. Pirenne 1965–1966, België (1961–1977), CC NAH.
104. Van den Heuvel to Lamberty, 22 April 1965, File: 142 J.H. Pirenne 1965–1966, België (1961–1977), CC NAH; Lamberty to Van den Heuvel, 7 April 1965, File: 141 Max Lamberty 1962–1966, België (1961–1977), CC NAH.
105. Van den Heuvel to Pirenne, 27 April 1965, and Shell memo [Einthoven], 29 April 1965, File: 142 J.H. Pirenne 1965–1966, België (1961–1977), CC NAH.

106. J.H. Pirenne, 'Rapport: Problèmes actuels des Relations Est-Ouest', and Van den Heuvel to Pirenne, 19 May 1965, File: 142 J.H. Pirenne 1965–1966, België (1961–1977), CC NAH.
107. Pirenne to Van den Heuvel, 25 May 1965, File: 142 J.H. Pirenne 1965–1966, België (1961–1977), CC NAH.
108. 'Bezoek aan de heer J.H. Pirenne te Brussel op woensdag 2 juni 1965', File: 142 J.H. Pirenne 1965–1966, België (1961–1977), CC NAH.
109. Lamberty to Van den Heuvel, 14 July 1965, File: 141 Max Lamberty 1962–1966, België (1961–1977), CC NAH.
110. 'Unterrednung mit Herrn Prof. Dr. M. Lamberty am 6 August 1965 in Brüssel', Lamberty to Van den Heuvel, 28 September 1965, and 'Gesprek CC van den Heuvel met Prof. Dr. M. Lamberty, d.d. 8-10-65', File: 142 J.H. Pirenne 1965–1966, België (1961–1977), CC NAH.
111. Van den Heuvel to Lamberty, 25 October 1965, File: 141 Max Lamberty 1962–1966, België (1961–1977) CC NAH.
112. 'Bericht über die Sitzung in Brüssel am 5 November 1965', File: 142 J.H. Pirenne 1965–1966, België (1961–1977), CC NAH.
113. Geyer to Van den Heuvel, 28 October 1965, File: 66 H.J. Geyer 1965–1972, Duitsland (1958–1978), CC NAH.
114. In 1966 in Brussels Einthoven shared his dismay about the situation with Jim O'Ryan, the former CIA station chief in The Hague (1955–61). O'Ryan would suggest other individuals to lead the Belgian operation. Van den Heuvel to Geyer, 14 February 1966, File: 66 H.J. Geyer 1965–1972, Duitsland (1958–1978), CC NAH; in author's possession; Van den Heuvel to Lamberty, 28 January 1966, and Van den Heuvel to Lamberty, 3 November 1966, File: 141 Max Lamberty 1962–1966, België (1961–1977), CC NAH; Van den Heuvel to Fosty, 1 November 1966, File: 140 Algemeen 1961–1972, België (1961–1977), CC NAH; Einthoven to Ellis, 29 March 1966, File: 95 C.H. (Dick) Ellis 1966, Groot Britannië (1959–1985), CC NAH; L. Einthoven, Memo, 4 March 1966, File: 140 Algemeen 1961–1972, België (1961–1977), CC NAH.
115. Peeters to Van den Heuvel, 17 February 1967, File: 143 F. Peeters 1965–1970, België (1961–1977), CC NAH.
116. 'Verslag van bezoek van de heer Mennes aan Prof Peeters op 19 en 20 oktober en 30 oktober 1967', File: 143 F. Peeters 1965–1970, België (1961–1977), CC NAH.
117. Van den Heuvel admitted to already having asked the Ligue for clandestine help on two occasions, both times with satisfactory results. 'Besuch bei der "Ligue Internationale de la Liberté" und dem "Centre de Défense Nationale" in Brüssel am 14 Januar 1970', File: 144 Ligue Internationale de la Liberté 1967–1971, België (1961–1977), CC NAH.
118. Teacher, Rogue Agents.
119. Van den Heuvel to Göthberg, 12 December 1958, Van den Heuvel to Göthberg, 18 March 1961, and Göthberg to Van den Heuvel, 6 October 1961, File: 81 I. Göthberg 1958–1963, Zweden (1958–1978), CC NAH.
120. The group's principal members were Per-Eric Jangvert, Bertil Häggman, and Sten Pålsson.
121. 'Het algemeen verslag van de 15th International Student Course at Lund University 25 augustus–8 september 1963', and 'A Conference on the Communist Menace to the West in Lund/Sweden', File: 79 Algemeen 1962–1966, Zweden (1958–1978), CC NAH.

302 Notes

122. 'Op maandag 16 november 1964 kregen wij bezoek van Dr. Birger Hagard', November 1964, Hagård to Van den Heuvel, 31 December 1964, Van den Heuvel to Häggman, 6 January 1965, File: 79 Algemeen 1962–1966, Zweden (1958–1978), CC NAH.
123. 'Bezoek Mr. B Häggman – Zweden – 7 januari 1965, Den Haag', File: 79 Algemeen 1962–1966, Zweden (1958–1978), CC NAH.
124. "der erste schwedische Kontakt 'von Niveau' zu sein": 'Besprechung mit Herrn Dr. Ake Sparring (Schwede) am 11.3.1965', Sparring to von Hassell, 2 February 1967, File: 82 Ake Sparring 1965–1967, Zweden (1958–1978), CC NAH.
125. 'Bezoek Mr. B. Häggman – Zweden – 7 januari 1965, Den Haag', 'Meeting with Mr. S. Pålsson, Luxemburg, January 21, 1965', and 'Interdoc Contacts in Sweden', February 1965, File: 79 Algemeen 1962–1966, Zweden (1958–1978), CC NAH. On the origins of the Baltic Committee see Mikail Nilsson, 'The Professor and the CIA: Herbert Tingsten and the Congress for Cultural Freedom, a Symbiotic Relationship', *European Review of History* 18 (April 2011), pp. 147–174.
126. See Fredrik Logevall, 'The Swedish–American Conflict over Vietnam', *Diplomatic History* 17 (1993), pp. 421–445.
127. Bertil Häggman, telephone interview with the author, 4 December 2008.
128. Armfelt himself describes this complicated incident as follows: the Swedish Count von Rosen had provided Finland with its first warplane in 1918, and had had part of the von Rosen crest – a swastika, widely used in India as a Hindu, Buddhist, and Jainist decorative symbol, as well as in Egypt and in medieval Nordic culture – painted on the tail-wing. It was duly adopted as the air force's symbol. Armfelt's arrest in December 1941 came through the discovery of a photo of his father wearing Finnish Air Force regalia, including a swastika. Armfelt's attempt to join the Finnish Air Force in 1939 was also later seen as suspicious, since by 1941 it would mean "fighting against a great friend of the USA" – the USSR. 'Information on the Armfelt Family', n.d., File: 321 C.G. Armfelt, CC NAH.
129. 'De Zweedse Connectie', *De Groene Amsterdammer*, 31 January 1996. Neither Armfelt nor Sweden feature in Daniele Ganser's *NATO's Secret Armies: Operation Gladio and Terrorism in Western Europe* (London: Frank Cass, 2005).
130. Bertil Wedin, 'En djärv antikommunists spännande liv', *Contra* 209 (2010), pp. 20–24.
131. 'Op maandag 16 november 1964 kregen wij bezoek van Dr. Birger Hagard', November 1964, File: 79 Algemeen 1962–1966, Zweden (1958–1978), CC NAH.
132. Ellis to Van den Heuvel, 15 August 1967, File: 96 C.H. (Dick) Ellis 1967, Groot-Britannië (1959–1985), CC NAH; Tom Bower, *The Perfect English Spy: Sir Dick White and the Secret War 1935–90* (London: Mandarin, 1996), pp. 205–207.
133. Bertil Häggman, telephone interview with the author, 4 December 2008; Armfelt to Wedin and Häggman, 3 June 1969, File: 320 C. Armfelt Reports 1968–1970, CC NAH.
134. Ellis to Van den Heuvel, 14 May 1965, File: 94 C.H. (Dick) Ellis 1965, Groot-Britannië (1959–1985), CC NAH; Ellis to Van den Heuvel, 6 July 1967 and 15 August 1967, File: 96 C.H. (Dick) Ellis 1967, Groot-Britannië (1959–1985), CC NAH; Ellis to Van den Heuvel, 25 February 1969, File: 98 C.H. (Dick) Ellis 1969, Groot-Britannië (1959–1985), CC NAH.
135. Freedom Studies Center opened in Virginia, *Svoboda, The Ukrainian Weekly*, 1 October 1966; Ellis to Van den Heuvel, 27 February 1969, in author's possession. Ellis had first come into contact with Armfelt in December 1964, when the

Notes 303

Swede came to London "claiming to be in charge of an organisation specialising in counter-acting communist subversion": Ellis to Van den Heuvel, 7 December 1964, File: 104 J. Josten 1963–1974, Groot-Britannië (1959–1985), CC NAH.
136. File: 320 C. Armfelt Reports 1968–1970, CC NAH.
137. René de Bok, 'KGB drong door in de Tweede Kamer', *Elsevier Magazine*, 24 April 1976; 'De Zweedse Connectie', *De Groene Amsterdammer*, 31 January 1996.
138. Wedin, 'En djärv antikommunists spännande liv', pp. 20–24.
139. *Strijdbaar toen en nu: Vriendenbundel bij de 80ste verjaardag van Kees van den Heuvel* (1998), pp. 3–4. Armfelt, attending a dinner with Margaret Thatcher in 1992, took the opportunity to thank her "for putting a lid on the Dickey Ellis rumours and charges" (in relation to her opposition to Peter Wright's *Spycatcher*). Armfelt to Van den Heuvel, 20 September 1992, File: 322 C. Armfelt 1989–1999, CC NAH.
140. Bertil Häggman, interview with the author, Copenhagen, 30 September 2011.
141. Sheridan to John Dettmer, 9 October 1963, File: 103 L. Sheridan 1963–1964, Groot-Britannië (1959–1985), CC NAH.
142. On Sejr and the Firm see Ingeborg Philipsen, 'Out of Tune: The Congress for Cultural Freedom in Denmark 1953–1960', in G. Scott-Smith and Hans Krabbendam (eds), *The Cultural Cold War in Western Europe 1945–1960* (London: Frank Cass, 2003), pp. 237–253; Peer Henrik Hansen, *Second to None: US Intelligence Activities in Northern Europe 1943–1946* (Dordrecht: Republic of Letters, 2011).
143. Van den Heuvel to E[rik].N[orman]. Svendsen, 22 May 1964, where Van den Heuvel indicates that Sejr was invited to the Lunteren *colloque* that year but never replied. File: Italy 5, Cronaca Politica 1964–1968, CC NAH. Svendsen, who insisted on receiving all correspondence under the cover name "F. Nielsen", was an important figure in the Danish Protestant Church. He supplied an article on communism in Denmark for *Cronaca Politica* in 1965, using the pseudonym "Eric Christiaansen", and later turned up on the board of International Analyse. See distribution list for Peter Sager's *De Klare Blick*, 1 June 1965, File: 152 Schweizerisches Ost-Institut 1961–1965, Zwitserland (1961–1975), CC NAH.
144. 'Interdoc: Report on Activities 1967' refers to Frihed og Folkestyre as the only Danish contact, whereas Sweden listed the following: Høgerns Ungdomsførbund [literally 'right-wing youth organization'], Utrikespolitiska Institutet, Stockholm, Göteborgsstudenternas Internationella Stipendiefond, Free Asia Committee in Scandinavia [Häggman].
145. It was revealed later that the Alliance was covertly supported by the Politiets Efterretningstjeneste (PET), the Danish domestic intelligence and security service. 'Kurzreferate über Methoden der Behandlung von Ostfragen in der politischen Bildung', Ostkolleg, 15 December 1964, File: 63 Ostkolleg 1965–1972, Duitsland (1958–1978), CC NAH; 'Interdoc: Report on Activities 1967', p. 12, in author's possession; PET's Overvågning af den Antiimperialistiske Venstrefløj 1945–1989, PET-Kommissionens Beretning Bind 9 (Copenhagen: Ministry of Justice, 2008); Bertil Häggman, interview with the author, Copenhagen, 30 September 2011.
146. 'Internationale Tagung im Ostkolleg der Bundeszentrale für politische Bildung vom 14. Bis 16. Dezember 1964 in Köln,' File: 62 Ostkolleg 1963–1964, Duitsland (1958–1978), CC NAH; P.A. Heegård-Poulsen, 'Focus På Ungdoms Oprøret', *International Analyse* 11 (1970).

147. Paust to Holl, 9 October 1968, and Van den Heuvel to Ørvik, 3 October 1967, File: 163 Algemeen 1967–1976, Noorwegen (1967–1978), CC NAH.
148. See Frédéric Laurent, *L'Orchestre Noir* (Paris: Stock, 1978), pp. 120–138 & ff.
149. See for instance von Hassell to Guérin-Sérac, 7 May 1969, and Guérin-Sérac to von Hassell, 20 May 1969, File: 168 Portugal 1967–1976, Overige West-Europese Landen (1964–1976), CC NAH.
150. Van den Heuvel to Van der Stoel, 27 March 1975, 'J. (Jan) Habets', 5 December 1975, and Habets to Van den Heuvel, 6 September 1976, File: 168 Portugal 1967–1976, Overige West-Europese Landen (1964–1976), CC NAH.
151. Van den Heuvel to General Pierre Nicolopoulos, 24 March 1969, File: 170 Greece 1967–1971, Overige West-Europese Landen (1964–1976), CC NAH. Van den Heuvel was criticized in the Dutch press for his links with Nicolopoulos, seen as further evidence of Interdoc's right-wing identity.

5 East–West Engagement and Interdoc Youth

1. Einthoven to Sager, 3 August 1962, File: 152 Schweizerisches Ost-Institut 1961–1965, Zwitserland (1961–1975), archive of C.C. van den Heuvel, National Archives, The Hague (hereafter CC NAH).
2. Jeremi Suri, *Power and Protest: Global Revolution and the Rise of Détente* (Cambridge, MA: Harvard University Press, 2003); Martin Klimke, *The Other Alliance: Global Protest and Student Unrest in West Germany and the US, 1962–1972* (Princeton: Princeton University Press, 2009).
3. 'INTERDOC', January 1963, File: 83 Algemeen 1961–1964, Groot-Britannië (1959–1985), CC NAH.
4. On the early festivals and the West's response see Joel Kotek, 'Youth Organizations as a Battlefield in the Cold War', in G. Scott-Smith and H. Krabbendam (eds), *The Cultural Cold War in Western Europe 1945–1960* (London: Frank Cass, 2003) pp. 168–191.
5. Joni Krekola, 'Peace and Friendship or Freedom? Meaning of the Slogans at the World Youth Festival in Helsinki, 1962', paper presented at 'Cold War Interactions Reconsidered', a conference held at Helsinki University, 29–31 October 2009. On Moscow 1957 see Pia Koivunen, 'The Moscow 1957 Youth Festival: Propagating a New Peaceful Image of the Soviet Union', in M. Ilic and J. Smith (eds), *Soviet State and Society under Nikita Khrushchev* (London: Routledge, 2009), pp. 46–65.
6. Jarkko Vesikansa, ' "Kommunismi uhkaa maatamme": Kommunisminvastainen porvarillinen aktivismi ja järjestötoiminta Suomessa 1950–1968', Ph.D. dissertation, Helsinki University, 2004, p. 368.
7. 'World Youth Festivals', International Youth Service, Norway, n.d. [1962], CIA-RDP79-01194A000200030001-1, CREST (CIA Records Search Tool), National Archives, College Park, Washington, DC.
8. David Baad, 'Discussions with Pennti Mahlamaki, the President of SYL Finland, primarily concerning developments on the 8th World Festival for Youth and Students', n.d. [November 1960], Box F/9/20a: World Festival of Youth and Students: General, archive of the International Student Conference/Coordinating Secretariat, International Institute of Social History, Amsterdam.
9. On the Independent Research Service and NSA see Richard Cummings, *The Pied Piper: Allard Lowenstein and the Liberal Dream* (New York: Grove Press, 1985);

On American efforts to coordinate anti-festival activities see Joni Krekola and Simo Mikkonen, 'Backlash of the Free World: The US presence at the World Youth Festival in Helsinki, 1962,' *Scandinavian Journal of History* 36 (2011), pp. 230–255.
10. 'VIIIth World Youth Festival – Helsinki – 29th July to 6th August 1962', Cees van den Heuvel, pp. 1, 2; Drs. J.M.M. Hornix and C.C. van den Heuvel, 'Een Karakteristiek van de Waarden van het Westen, alsmede enkele Gedachten over de Mogelijkheden van Bevordering van een Blijvende Invloed van deze Waarden', September 1959, in author's possession.
11. 'Vermerk' (The Hague meeting: Einthoven/Van den Heuvel/von Dellingshausen/ Scheffler, 2 May 1962), archive of the Bundesministerium für gesamtdeutsche Fragen, File: 16431, Collection: B 137, National Archives, Koblenz (hereafter NAK).
12. 'Communist World Youth Festival Helsinki', 17 February 1962, File: 132 Algemeen 1964–1965, Italië (1959–1975), CC NAH.
13. Van den Heuvel to John Baker White, 13 February 1962, File: 90 Economic League 1959–1978, Groot-Britannië (1959–1985), CC NAH; 'Verslag Reis Engeland 19–21 februari 1962', File: 83 Algemeen 1961–1964, Groot-Britannië (1959–1985), CC NAH.
14. 'Reis naar Italie in Maart 1962 (Hr Einthoven)', File: File: 132 Algemeen 1964–1965, Italië (1959–1975), CC NAH.
15. Hans Peter Ming to Van den Heuvel, 16 July 1962, File: 155 Aktionskomitee Wahret die Freiheit 1962–1969, Zwitserland (1961–1975), CC NAH.
16. Erwin Bresslein, *Drushba! Freundschaft? Von der communistische Jugendinternationale zu den Weltjugendfestspielen* (Frankfurt: M. Fischer, 1973), p. 121; Sydney Stern, *Gloria Steinum: Her Passions, Politics, and Mystique* (Secaucus: Birch Lane Press, 1997), pp. 129–130.
17. Hans Beuker, interview with the author, Houten, 3 September 2003; Hans Beuker, 'Wereld jeugdfestival Helsinki 1962', in *Strijdbaar toen en nu: Vriendenbundel bij de 80ste verjaardag van Kees van den Heuvel* (1998), p. 6.
18. Van den Heuvel to Ellis, 7 February 1962, File: 92 C.H. (Dick) Ellis 1961–1963, Groot-Britannië (1959–1985), CC NAH.
19. Hans Beuker, interview with the author, Houten, 3 September 2003; Pieter Koerts, interview with the author, Amsterdam, 2 June 2004.
20. 'VIIIth World Youth Festival', p. 7; 'Communist World Youth Festival Helsinki', 17 February 1962, File: 132 Algemeen 1964–1965, Italië (1959–1975), CC NAH.
21. Van den Heuvel to Ellis, 16 May 1962, File: 92 C.H. (Dick) Ellis 1961–1963, Groot-Britannië (1959–1985), CC NAH.
22. This was run through several members of the NSR's foreign affairs committee, and was to be funded by Shell, Philips, and Unilever, but lack of preparation prevented it from happening. Chel Mertens, interview with the author, Amsterdam, 9 December 2003; Hans Beuker, interview with the author, Houten, 3 September 2003.
23. Hans Beuker, interview with the author, Houten, 3 September 2003.
24. Ibid. Since the festival "disciplinary service" (Finnish communists) "kept very strict watch at the debates, discussions and seminars", it was a major slip that Beuker was allowed to speak. 'VIIIth World Youth Festival', p. 11.
25. Chel Mertens, interview with the author, 9 December 2003. Mertens also said he was not prepared to give an anti-Russian speech when there were negative aspects to both East and West.

306   Notes

26. The full title of the colloquium at which Beuker spoke was 'The Role of Students in the Struggle for National Independence and for Solving the Political, Economic, and Social Problems of the Colonial and Underdeveloped Nations.'
27. 'Niederschrift über die Sitzung am 15 März 1962 über die geistig-politische Ausseinandersetzung mit dem Kommunismus im Bundesministerium des Innern in Bonn', File: 16431, Collection: B 137, NAK.
28. In April 1964 Einthoven wrote to Caeymaex about a suspicious car accident the previous month that killed the Dutchman Josef Roeloffzen, a former World Alliance for Student Cooperation activist who had carried out very important anti-communist propaganda ("een zeer belangrijke anticommunistische propaganda heeft gevoerd") in Helsinki. Roeloffzen had been spokesperson for the WASC café on board the Dutch ship *Mathilde* located in Helsinki harbour. Einthoven clearly felt the two incidents were connected. Einthoven to Caeymaex, 17 April 1964, File: 137 Cronaca Politica 1964–1968, Italië (1959–1975), CC NAH.
29. 'Colonialism stirs wrath at youth rally', *New York Herald Tribune*, 4–5 August 1962; *Pravda* article translated in *Vrij Nederland*, 18 August 1962; 'Afgevaardigden vermaken zich', *Het Binnenhof*, 6 August 1962; 'Nederlander bespreekt Russisch kolonialisme', *Het Vaderland*, 6 August 1962; 'Jong Anti-Communist', *Het Parool*, 25 August 1962; 'Paniek in Helsinki', *Panorama*, 1 September 1962; '20th Century', CBS, 3 February 1963.
30. Hans Beuker, interview with the author, Houten, 3 September 2003.
31. 'Paniek in Helsinki', *De Waarheid*, 1 September 1962.
32. LFr. (L. Frijda), 'Hypocrisie van het absoluut gelijk', *Pharetra*, October 1962.
33. Hans Beuker, 'Hypocrisie van het absoluut gelijk', and L. Frijda, 'Rancune van het absoluut gelijk', *Pharetra*, 7 November 1962. Frijda and Mertens clearly shared the same viewpoint on this, so it could have been Mertens who provided the information on the SOEV link from Helsinki. Mertens said later that Beuker had told him about the plans on the train journey there: "He learnt I knew Russian so he thought I must be a good guy." Chel Mertens, interview with the author, Amsterdam, 9 December 2003.
34. This was Jerome Heldring's viewpoint in the *NRC* following the festival. Referring to Beuker, Heldring wrote: "dat betekent dat deelnemers uit het Westen, willen zij enige vat krijgen op de jeugd uit de ongebonden landen, hun terminologie en hun optreden althans enigzins zullen moeten aanpassen aan de voor ons onlogische criteria van deze jeugd".
35. 'Ecologie', *Vrij Nederland*, 18 May 1963.
36. 'VIIIth World Youth Festival', pp. 2–3, 10, 15, 32.
37. *Frieden und Freundschaft? Weltjugendfestspiele, Funktion und Wirkung* (Bonn: Walter Lütz, 1963). Beuker's speech is included on p. 159.
38. Ellis to Van den Heuvel, 13 May 1965, and Van den Heuvel to Ellis, 11 March 1965, File: 94 C.H. (Dick) Ellis 1965, Groot-Britannië (1959–1985), CC NAH.
39. Sten Pållson, telephone interviews with the author, 29 June 2012 and 13 July 2012; Van den Heuvel to Hagård, 7 October 1964 and 19 October 1964, File: 79 Algemeen 1962–1966, Zweden (1958–1978), CC NAH.
40. Irja Berendson (secretary, SYS) to Interdoc, 16 March 1965, and Hagård to Van den Heuvel, 31 December 1964, File: 79 Algemeen 1962–1966, Zweden (1958–1978), CC NAH.
41. 'VIIIth World Youth Festival', p. 30.
42. Pieter Koerts, interview with the author, Leiden 24 June 2009.

43. Gert van Maanen, interviews with the author, Leidschendam, 14 May 2004, 1 November 2006, and 8 April 2009. Correspondence from Van der Beugel himself lists Van den Heuvel as a member in October 1966, and a BVD report from June 1968 includes the claim that he was still an active member of the group. Yet both Van Maanen and his successor as NSR president, Frans Duynstee, have contested this claim. Van der Beugel to R. Samkalden (NSR International Secretary), 12 October 1966, File 7: Private Correspondence 1963–67, Archive of E.H. van der Beugel, Inventory No. 2.21.183.08, Collection 357, National Archives, the Hague; Minutes, 'Aurora' meeting, 21 June 1968, Inzagedossier: Psychologische Oorlogvoering, Freedom of Information request (Wet Openbaar Bestuur) to Ministry of Justice/AIVD, 12 December 2005.
44. Minutes, 'Aurora' meeting, 23 December 1964, Inzagedossier: Psychologische Oorlogvoering, Freedom of Information request (Wet Openbaar Bestuur) to Ministry of Justice/AIVD, 12 December 2005. Freedom of Information Act (Wet Openbaar Bestuur) request to the AIVD, 2005.
45. G.H.O. van Maanen, 'A Dutch view on East–West student exchanges', and [C.C. van den Heuvel] 'Summary', in *East–West contacts in practice* (The Hague: Interdoc, 1965), pp. 49–58, quotes on pp. 59–60.
46. G.H.O. van Maanen, 'De Nederlandse student en het Oost-West contact', *Internationale Spectator*, 19 (8 June 1965), p. 921; Gert van Maanen, interview with the author, Leidschendam, 14 May 2004.
47. There are indications that Van Maanen was still involved in activities opposing the New Left in Dutch student politics during 1968. He was probably involved with the study 'The European Syndicalist Student Movement', an exposé of the leftist student scene submitted without attribution to *Accord* in March 1968.
48. Gert van Maanen, *The International Student Movement: History and Background* (The Hague: Interdoc, 1966). Van Maanen later recalled visiting the Fund for Youth and Student Affairs in New York to research his book, and encountering their "very thin files". As he later carefully said about the CIA link, "I knew enough to know that it could be true", but he remained adamant that despite the CIA the ISC was an "open house" apparatus in comparison with its competitor, the IUS, a blatant Soviet front. He even approached the Ministry of Foreign Affairs to see if they would provide "bridge finance" to enable the ISC to overcome the CIA revelations and refashion itself, but it was a lost cause. Gert van Maanen, interviews with the author, Leidschendam, 1 November 2006 and 8 April 2009.
49. Ellis did take around 600 copies for various outlets in Britain. How many ended up with MI6 is not stated. 'Report on a visit to Interdoc UK on 7 and 8 December 1966', and 'Points of discussion with Mr. Ellis on 1–2 March 1967 in London', File: 89 Reisverslagen 1963–1968, Groot-Britannië (1959–1985), CC NAH; Van den Heuvel to Ellis, 24 May 1965, File: 94 C.H. (Dick) Ellis 1965, Groot-Britannië (1959–1985), CC NAH.
50. 'Bericht bezüglich des Nennens von Interdok in der Öffentlichkeit und in Studentenkreisen aufgrund der letzten Enthüllungen über CIA', n.d., File: 96 C.H. (Dick) Ellis 1967, Groot-Britannië (1959–1985), CC NAH.
51. For more recent research see Karen Paget, 'From Stockholm to Leiden', in G. Scott-Smith and Hans Krabbendam (eds), *The Cultural Cold War in Western Europe* (London: Frank Cass, 2003), pp. 134–167, and her forthcoming book on the history of the National Student Association and its relationship with the CIA.

52. Van den Heuvel to Ellis, 5 November 1963, File: 92 C.H. (Dick) Ellis 1961–1963, Groot-Britannië (1959–1985), CC NAH; Van den Heuvel to Aureli Argeo, 21 October 1963, File: 135 Comitato Civico 1960–1965, Italië (1959–1975), CC NAH. Van den Heuvel to Mieli, 18 February 1964, File: 136 CESES 1961–1975, Italië (1959–1975), CC NAH; 'Bezoek bij Dr. Albert Münst in Zürich op 31 oktober 1963', and Münst to von Hahn, 24 February 1964, File: 156 Liga für Freiheit 1963–1965, Zwitserland (1961–1975), CC NAH. Van den Heuvel reported afterwards that Mennes and Hess formed a good team in Florence.
53. Pieter Koerts, interview with the author, Amsterdam, 2 June 2004.
54. Van den Heuvel to Ellis, 3 March 1964 and 6 April 1964, File: 93 C.H. (Dick) Ellis 1964, Groot-Britannië (1959–1985), CC NAH; Van den Heuvel, 'Interdoc', n.d. [1964], File: Voorgeschiedenis Interdoc, in author's possession (hereafter VI).
55. Hess to Mennes, 7 March 1964, File: 157 Aare-Verlag 1964–1965, Zwitserland (1961–1975), CC NAH; 'Vermerk über die Besprechung mit Peter Hess am 9.9.1964 in Zürich', File: 150 Algemeen 1961–1970, Zwitserland (1961–1975), CC NAH.
56. Despite this fact, Koerts has denied that he was connected with the Strasbourg/Luxembourg Group.
57. Pieter Koerts, interviews with the author, Amsterdam, 2 June 2004, and Leiden, 24 June 2009.
58. Ming to Van den Heuvel, 13 November 1962, File: 155 Aktionskomitee Wahret die Freiheit 1962–1969, Zwitserland (1961–1975), CC NAH.
59. 'Vermerk über die Besprechung mit Herrn Dr. Münst und Vertretern der Schweizer Studentenorganisationen', 9 September 1964, File: 150 Algemeen 1961–1970, Zwitserland (1961–1975), CC NAH.
60. Van den Heuvel to von Dellingshausen, 18 August 1964, File: 64 Bundesministerium für gesamtdeutsche Fragen 1961–1968, Duitsland (1958–1978), CC NAH.
61. 'Anglo-German Information Talks: Notes for IRD Discussions with Herr Wickert', 15 February 1963, FO 1110/1633, papers of the Information Research Department, National Archives, London IRD NAL.
62. Mennes to Ming, 1 December 1964, File: 155 Aktionskomitee Wahret die Freiheit 1962–1969, Zwitserland (1961–1975), CC NAH. The letter refers to the (confidential) protocols of the group, but the only specific detail mentioned covers the coordination of documentation and information materials.
63. Van den Heuvel to Mieli, 29 January 1965, File: 136 CESES 1961–1975, Italië (1959–1975), CC NAH.
64. 'Anlage zum Reisebericht England (2–4 Nov. 1964)', File: 89 Reisverslagen 1963–1968, Groot-Britannië (1959–1985), CC NAH.
65. Correspondence with Gert van Maanen, International Secretary (1962–63) and President (1963–64) of the National Student Council, 21 November 2006; Van den Heuvel to Ellis, 11 May 1965, File: 84 Algemeen 1965, Groot-Britannië (1959–1985), CC NAH.
66. H. Graf to Bundesministerium für Familien und Jugendfragen, 9 June 1965, File: 150 Algemeen 1961–1970, Zwitserland (1961–1975), CC NAH. Other partners in this venture were the London-based Ariel Foundation (an assumed MI6 front active in Africa – see Stephen Dorril, *MI6* (London: Fourth Estate, 2000) p. 470ff.) – and Piet van Engelen, secretary of the Dutch Catholic Party's youth wing (KVPJO).

67. Van den Heuvel to Ellis, 24 June 1965, File: 94 C.H. (Dick) Ellis 1965, Groot-Britannië (1959–1985), CC NAH.
68. 'Gesprek met Graf (president Wahret die Freiheit) op 20 aug. 1965', Graf to Van den Heuvel, 17 August 1965, 'Gesprek met Graf op 16 november 1965 te Zürich', and Graf to Van den Heuvel, 29 December 1965, File: 155 Aktionskomitee Wahret die Freiheit 1962–1969, Zwitserland (1961–1975), CC NAH.
69. Pålsson has since stated that by 1966 he was doing military service and Häggman had started his legal career, making them both unavailable. 'Visit to London 14–17 February 1966', File: 89 Reisverslagen 1963–1968, Groot-Britannië (1959–1985), CC NAH.
70. Ellis to Van den Heuvel, 28 June 1968, File: 97 C.H. (Dick) Ellis 1968, Groot-Britannië (1959–1985), CC NAH.
71. 'Visit to Zürich-Bern-Milano 20–23 March 1967', File: 155 Aktionskomitee Wahret die Freiheit 1962–1969, Zwitserland (1961–1975), CC NAH; 'A Short Account of International Student Politics and the Cold War, with particular reference to NSA, CIA, etc.', *Ramparts*, March 1967, pp. 29–38.
72. Alexander Heldring to Graf, 31 May 1968, Graf to Van den Heuvel, 2 June 1968, and Van den Heuvel to Graf, 18 July 1968, File: 155 Aktionskomitee Wahret die Freiheit 1962–1969, Zwitserland (1961–1975), CC NAH; 'Personalia', File: 34 Sofia 1967–1968, Internationale jeugdzaken, CC NAH; 'Angstpsychose voor de BVD: Twist en tweespalt op Rood Festival in Sofia', *De Telegraaf*, 10 August 1968; Nick Rutter, 'The Better Germans: The German Rivalry at the World Youth Festival 1951–1973', unpublished paper; Alexander Heldring, interview with the author, The Hague, 30 June 2004; Antoinette Gosses, interview with the author, Brussels, 23 April 2008.
73. 'Talk with Dr. Kassel, 12-4-73', File: 35 Berlijn 1973, Internationale jeugdzaken, CC NAH.
74. Van den Heuvel explained to Häggman that this procedure had already been carried out with British, German, French, Belgian, and Dutch institutions in the past. The Berlin publications were "Points of View" (contesting Moscow's line on European security, human rights, peaceful coexistence, and pollution) and "Two from Our Generation" (contrasting Angela Davis and Soviet dissident poet Yri Galanskov). Van den Heuvel to Häggman, 16 June 1973 and 20 August 1973, File: 80 Algemeen 1973–1978, Zweden (1958–1978), CC NAH.
75. Christiaan van den Heuvel, interview with the author, The Hague, 27 May 2009. He later wrote his Master's thesis on the event: 'Nederland en het 11de Wereldjeugdfestival', February 1979.
76. Van den Heuvel to Häggman, 20 August 1973, File: 80 Algemeen 1973–1978, Zweden (1958–1978), CC NAH.
77. 'Jeugd Festival: aanslag op de detente', *Elsevier Magazine*, 11 August 1973.
78. 'Bericht über das VI Internationale Gespräch des Studienbüro Berlin vom 25 bis 28 September 1961 in Berlin', Collection B 137, File 16431, NAK.
79. SOEV Annual Report (Jaarverslag) 1963, pp. 2–3.
80. Einthoven to Bernhard, 19 August 1963, File: 254 Prins Bernhard 1962–1986, Nederland, CC NAH.
81. Von Hahn to von Grote, 5 June 1964, File: 136 CESES 1961–1975, Italië (1959–1975), CC NAH.
82. Rolf Geyer, 'Die Strategie des Friedens', n.d. [1964], in author's possession. See W.W. Rostow, *The Stages of Economic Growth* (Cambridge: Cambridge University Press, 1960) and 'The Third Round', *Foreign Affairs* 42 (October 1963), pp. 1–10.

83. "die Menschen des Sowjetblocks mit der Fülle des westlichen geistig-politischen Lebens zu konfrontieren": Geyer, 'Die Strategie des Friedens', p. 24.
84. Van den Heuvel to Mieli, 11 June 1964, File: 136 CESES 1961–1975, Italië (1959–1975), CC NAH. Van den Heuvel wrote almost exactly the same words to Ellis, suggesting that he was conducting major damage control following Eschwege.
85. Geyer to Mieli, 28 July 1964, File: 136 CESES 1961–1975, Italië (1959–1975), CC NAH.
86. Brzezinski's work, which Van den Heuvel described as "so good", was the subject of much discussion at Interdoc and Verein meetings in late 1965. Van den Heuvel to Ellis, 20 October 1965, File: 94 C.H. (Dick) Ellis 1965, Groot-Britannië (1959–1985), CC NAH; Zbigniew Brzezinski, 'Het Westen en de onenigheid in de communistische wereld', *Oost-West* 2 (March-April 1963), pp. 36–40 (this article was a translation of the original from the CCF journal *China Quarterly*).
87. Zbigniew Brzezinski, *Alternative to Partition: For a Broader Conception of America's Role in Europe* (New York: McGraw-Hill, 1965), p. 136.
88. Ibid., p. 152.
89. Van den Heuvel to Ernst Kux, 20 February 1965, File: 150 Algemeen 1961–1970, Zwitserland (1961–1975), CC NAH.
90. R. Dubs, 'A Swiss view on East–West contacts', in *East–West contacts in practice*, Interdoc conference, Locarno, 9–10 April 1965, p. 46.
91. P.R. Dubien, 'Some French experiences on East-West contacts', *East–West contacts in practice*, p. 32; 'Ausführungen Dr. Mielis während Interdok-Tagung am 19.6.64', File: 136 CESES 1961–1975, Italië (1959–1975), CC NAH.
92. R. Dubs, 'A Swiss view on East–West contacts', p. 47.
93. Ellis to Van den Heuvel, 15 October 1965, File: 94 C.H. (Dick) Ellis 1965, Groot-Britannië (1959–1985), CC NAH.
94. Von Hahn to Pietro Quarani (head of Italian state broadcasting), 26 June 1964, File: 132 Algemeen 1964–1965, Italië (1959–1975), CC NAH.
95. 'Entstehung von Interdok – Geschichte – Aufbau – Zielsetzung', 17 June 1965, File: 65 Baron W. von Hahn 1963–1968, Duitsland (1958–1978), CC NAH.
96. 'Entstehung von Interdok – Geschichte – Aufbau – Zielsetzung', 17 June 1965, File: 65 Baron W. von Hahn 1963–1968, Duitsland (1958–1978), CC NAH.
97. *Preparation for East–West Contacts*, Interdoc conference, Zandvoort, 24–25 September 1965, pp. 11–12.
98. Geyer to Van den Heuvel, 8 September 1965, File: 66 H.J. Geyer 1965–1972, Duitsland (1958–1978), CC NAH.
99. Van den Heuvel to Geyer, 14 December 1965, File: 66 H.J. Geyer 1965–1972, Duitsland (1958–1978), CC NAH.
100. Van den Heuvel to Ellis, 11 August 1965, File: 106 Financiën 1964–1969, Groot-Britannië (1959–1985), CC NAH.
101. 'Free Europe Committee,' March 1965, and Van den Heuvel to Ellis, 18 June 1965, File: 84 Algemeen 1965, Groot-Britannië (1959–1985), CC NAH.
102. 'Subversion and Counter-Subversion,' preparatory notes and speech, Oxford, 22 July 1965, File: 84 Algemeen 1965, Groot-Britannië (1959–1985), CC NAH.
103. Von Hahn to von Grote, 6 December 1965, File: 150 Algemeen 1961–1970, Zwitserland (1961–1975), CC NAH. There were limits to the kind of publicity Interdoc sought, and von Hahn had to dissuade one of the staff officers visiting Van Stolkweg from writing about the visit in the *NATO Letter*.
104. See Peter Grose, 'Soviet Trying Briton as Agent of Exiles', *New York Times*, 22 July 1965.

105. Ellis to Van den Heuvel, 5 May 1965, and Van den Heuvel to Ellis, 11 May 1965, File: 84 Algemeen 1965, Groot-Britannië (1959–1985), CC NAH.
106. Interdoc: Progress Report 1968, p. 8; on Cram see Bob de Graaff and Cees Wiebes, *Villa Maarheeze: De Geschiedenis van de Inlichtingendienst Buitenland* (The Hague: Sdu, 1998), p. 328.
107. *The New Left* (The Hague: Interdoc, 1968); *The New Left in The United States of America, Britain, The Federal Republic of Germany* (The Hague: Interdoc, 1969), with chapters by Milorad M. Drachkovitch, C.H. Ellis, and Hans Joachim Woehl; Claude Harmel, *La Crise de l'Enseignement Supérieur en France* (The Hague: Interdoc, 1970).
108. Brian Crozier, 'The New Inspirers of Violence', in *The New Left*, p. 40; Nils-Eric Brodin, 'Right & Left-Wing Radicalism and Security in the United States', Stephen Kreppel, 'Political Radicalism and Defence: The British Situation', and Hans Joachim Wohl, 'Left-Wing Radicalism and Defence in the Federal Republic of Germany', in *Radicalism and Security* (The Hague: Interdoc, 1970), pp. 73, 78, 111.
109. Von Weiss would subsequently produce a book-length study, *Die Neue Linke: Kritische Analyse* (Boppard: Harald Boldt Verlag, 1969).
110. A. von Weiss, 'Ideological Foundations of the New Left', C.D. Kernig, 'An Analysis of the Motives and Aims of the Student Movement', Cees van den Heuvel, 'International Aspects of the Radical Student Movement and Relations with Communism', in *The New Left*, pp. 14, 15, 50; Ivan Matteo Lombardo, 'Radicalism and Security', in *Radicalism and Security*, p. 131.
111. N. von Grote, 'Conclusions', *The New Left*, p. 51.
112. Karel van Wolferen, *Student Revolutionaries of the 1960s* (The Hague: Interdoc, 1970). A summary of an Interdoc board meeting, probably in summer 1968, mentions that the European bureau of *Reader's Digest* in Paris had approached Interdoc for assistance with a study on leftist radicalism. Interdoc Berlin and other contacts were put at the periodical's disposal.
113. Ibid., p. 33.
114. Significantly enough, Van Wolferen states that Couwenberg and to a certain extent Van den Heuvel were themselves sceptical of the hard-line German opinions expressed at Noordwijk. Karel van Wolferen, interviews with the author, 12 January 2005 and 21 April 2011.
115. *The Armed Forces in the Psycho-Political East–West Confrontation* (The Hague: Interdoc, 1968), with contributions by Geyer (Introduction), Spits (communist strategy), Wing Commander E.S. Williams (Britain), Dr Günther Wagenlehner (West Germany), Ivan Matteo Lombardo (Italy), Nils Ørvik (Scandinavia), G. Bruderer (Switzerland), and L. van der Put (Netherlands). Lombardo, who had close relations with Interdoc during 1968–71, went so far as to propose creating a "'parallel' General Staff" for the purpose of running clandestine resistance operations in the event of a "revolutionary insurrection", something very close to the principles of Gladio.
116. "Holland könne als neutrale Ebene eine vermittelnde Funktion ausüben." 'Protokoll der Interdok-Vorstandssitzung in Freiburg/Brsg. "Schauinsland" am 27 April 1967', File: 224 Statutes 1962–1987, Organisatie, CC NAH.
117. Among the speakers in Amersfoort were Ernst van der Beugel (transatlantic relations) and Alfred Mozer (European integration). Van den Heuvel to Geyer, 3 May 1968, in author's possession; 3 May 1968, File: 66 H.J. Geyer 1965–1972, Duitsland (1958–1978), CC NAH; File: 155 Aktionskomitee Wahret die

312 Notes

Freiheit 1962–1969, Zwitserland (1961–1975), CC NAH; Van den Heuvel to Mozer, 7 February 1968, File: 140 Algemeen 1961–1972, België (1961–1972), CC NAH.

118. Holl recalled that following an Interdoc meeting in Munich the group went to see the musical *Hair* (probably Geyer's idea). This was not to everyone's liking, and Ellis "suffered terribly". Uwe Holl, telephone interview, 7 July 2006.
119. Uwe Holl, interview with the author, Cologne, 18 December 2005; Uwe Holl, telephone interview, 7 July 2006.
120. 'Besprechung am 22 September 1961', Ministry of the Interior, 27 September 1961, File: B 137, Collection 16430, NAK.
121. Gunhild Bohm-Geyer, interview with the author, Würthsee, 4 July 2008.
122. Appendix 4, 'International Conference: Interdoc Youth', 29–30 March 1969, The Hague, File: 219 Interdoc Youth 1969–1970, CC NAH.
123. Wolfgang Buchow, interview with the author, Neuss, 10 January 2007.
124. 'Interdoc Youth: Aims and Activities', File: Interdoc Youth – Correspondence, in author's possession (hereafter IY).
125. Holl to Ellis, 15 April 1969, IY.
126. 'International Conference: Interdoc Youth', 29–30 March 1969, The Hague, and 'Organisation von Interdok der Jugend', Hans Graf, 25 March 1969, File: 219 Interdoc Youth 1969–1970, CC NAH; Holl to von Geyso, 17 April 1969, IY.
127. "den Pfad der Tugend": Geyer to Van den Heuvel, 6 June 1969, File: 66 H.J. Geyer 1965–1972, Duitsland (1958–1978), CC NAH.
128. Alexander Heldring, *FIR: Histoire et Actualité de la Fédération Internationale des Résistants* (The Hague: Interdoc, 1969).
129. Alexander Heldring, interview with the author, The Hague, 30 June 2004. According to Heldring it was actually the Ministry of Foreign Affairs itself that rejected his participation in Sofia. His replacements, Antoinette Gosses and Michiel Verschoor van Nisse, were friends from his Leiden student house.
130. As Holl put it once, "Im Falle Frankreichs sind wir besonders an der Ausweitung unserer Kontakte interessiert, da wir dort bisher noch etwas 'unterbesetzt' sind." The only sign of an attempt to involve the Italians concerns a trip, paid for by IY, made by Jim Daly, Per Paust, and Henri Starckx, three of the most active IY board members, to Milan in mid-October 1970, only two weeks before the Interdoc Rimini conference. The purpose of this trip is not clear, but it may have involved some form of liaison with CESES. Holl to Herrn Fuchs, 19 June 1970, and Holl to INTRANED travel agency, 2 October 1970, IY.
131. Holl to Ernst Riggert (Volk und Verteidigung), 25 June 1969, and Holl to S. Stenderup, 13 August 1969, IY.
132. Holl to Howarth, 19 December 1969, and Holl to Eduard Kaan, 24 September 1970, IY.
133. Paust to Holl, 9 October 1968, Paust to Van den Heuvel, 28 January 1969, and Holl to Paust, 4 February 1969, File: 163 Algemeen 1967–1976, Noorwegen (1967–1978), CC NAH.
134. Holl to Geyso, 13 June 1969, IY.
135. Ulmer to Van den Heuvel, 20 March 1969, File: 154 Schweizerischer Aufklärungsdienst 1961–1974, Zwitserland (1961–1975), CC NAH.
136. Holl to E.J. de Roo, 27 May 1969, 'Projekt Russlandreise SIB', 16 October 1969, and 'Extraordinary Board Meeting of Interdoc Youth', 29 May 1970, IY. IY provided 8000 guilders (40 per cent of the costs) for the SIB, and 2000 guilders

for the Free University. It was the intention to adapt the reports for inclusion in a new Interdoc booklet Oost-West Begegnung *in Frage und Antwort* or the forthcoming *Youth Forum*.
137. Holl to W.H. van Claassen (SIB president), 9 September 1969, IY. 'Students unite to fight rebels', *Daily Telegraph*, 25 August 1969.
138. Visit of Miss v.d. Pijl (study secretary, NJG), 11 September 1969, IY. It is evident that after the exposure of the ISC as a CIA front, the WAY took on a renewed significance as an international contact network.
139. 'Bericht zum Gespräch', 9 June 1969, IY; Ellis to Holl, 4 February 1969, Ellis to Van den Heuvel, 7 March 1969, and 'Comment by James Daly: Berlin meeting 24–26 February 1969', File: 98 C.H. (Dick) Ellis 1969, Groot-Brittannië (1959–1985), CC NAH. The Transport House group included Gwyn Morgan (formerly NUS and general secretary of ISC), Daly (formerly NUS and ISC), T. McNally (formerly NUS and ISC), and John Smith (formerly NUS and Common Cause). Daly went on to work for the Greater London Council and stayed in touch via Walter Bell through the 1970s.
140. 'Visit of Mr. S.N. Khare', 9 September 1969, IY.
141. Holle to Iversen, 11 June 1969, IY.
142. The meeting was organized by Jim Daly and had originally been planned for the National Coal Board College in Chalfont St Giles, Buckinghamshire, with an opening speech by Lord Robens. The location was switched in August when the college, for reasons unknown, cancelled the arrangement. 'Interdoc Seminar for Young Professionals, Executives, Academics and Students', 16 May 1969, IY.
143. Rolf Geyer, 'The Situation of the Youth in West and East', International Interdoc Youth Conference, 18–19 October 1969, in author's possession.
144. Holl to Etsuo Kohtani, 29 October 1969, IY.
145. 'Telefon von Herrn Claasman', 23 September 1969, IY. Van den Heuvel had already emphasized the need for an official press release announcing Interdoc Youth, but this was to be prepared only at the Deidesheim Interdoc *colloque* in September 1969. The KRO were therefore upsetting the plan.
146. 'Working Paper for IY Board Meeting, Strasbourg, 14 March 1970', IY.
147. Holl to Oberst Preusker, 22 December 1969, and Holl to H.J. Woehl, 29 January 1970, IY.
148. An interesting contact for this event, provided by General Dethleffsen, was Dr G.A. Krapf, a personal adviser to Kenneth Kaunda in Zambia.
149. Wolfgang Buchow, interview with the author, Neuss, 10 January 2007.
150. Holl to Godson, 24 September 1969, IY.
151. Holl to Brown, 21 January 1970, and 'Working Paper for IY Board Meeting, Strasbourg, 14 March 1970', IY. When Godson's plan fell through Van den Heuvel stepped in to offer advice to Bertil Wedin on how to disrupt the conference by playing up in the media the differences between the pro-Soviet World Council of Peace and the Trotskyist Bertrand Russell Peace Foundation and the International War Crimes Tribunal. "Promoting antagonism" in this way could "at least frustrate the maximum goals of the conference" by showing the left to be more interested in fighting among themselves than opposing the war. Van den Heuvel to Wedin, 24 March 1970, IY.
152. Holl to Godson, 29 June 1970, Holl to Ministry of the Interior (Bonn), 13 July 1970, 'Filmprojekt', 17 August 1970, and Holl to Godson, 19 August 1970, IY.
153. Wolfgang Buchow, interview with the author, Neuss, 10 January 2007.
154. 'Declaration of Interdoc Youth', 1 December 1969, IY.

314 Notes

155. Holl to Raoul Syts, 4 February 1970, IY.
156. Holl to Godson, 29 January 1970, Holl to Wolfgang Buchow, 12 February 1970, Holl to Godson, 18 February 1970, and Holl to Jim Daly, 18 February 1970, IY.
157. Holl to Heikki von Hertzen, 9 July 1970, IY. Starckx, who attended the European Union of Christian Democratic and Conservative Students (ECCS) conference in Vienna in early July, came away disillusioned because the national representatives were completely unaware of developments outside of their own countries and spent most of their time on organizational issues instead of being able "to make use of the possibilities on international coordination". Originally formed as the International Union of Christian-Democratic and Conservative Students (ICCS) in 1961, it changed its name in 1970 to reflect a greater focus on European unity. One of ECCS's goals was also "to counter the influence of the extremist left at the universities". Since Starckx obtained Belgian membership of ECCS (as representative of the Katholiek Vlaams Hoogstudenten Verbond Gent) he then attended the executive committee meeting in Copenhagen in October. Once again ECCS came across as a badly organized group split down the middle on whether to support or oppose Ostpolitik. Although the intention was to focus more on EEC-related issues and "offer a new alternative to the youth of Europe as a counterbalance against SDS [Students for a Democratic Society] alternatives", Starckx found ECCS to be "rather conservative", reflecting "limited political interest", and that "great things cannot be expected" beyond it being a useful base for contacts in Germany and Scandinavia. 'Report on the ECCS Annual Conference, Vienna, 3–10 July 1970', and 'Executive Committee Meeting (EC) of ECCS,' Copenhagen, 23–25 October 1970, File: IY; 'ECCS – a short introduction', File: 37 ICCS-ECCS-EDS 1970–1977, Internationale Jeugdzaken, CC NAH.
158. Holl to Captain O.E. Saebøe, 11 March 1970, Holl to von Geyso, 25 May 1970, and 'Extraordinary Board Meeting of Interdoc Youth', 29 May 1970, IY.
159. 'Berlinseminar vom 25–30 Mai 1970', IY. This core group consisted of Mennes, Holl, W. Buchow (West Germany), Bütikofer (Switzerland), Henri Starckx and Raoul Syts (Belgium), and Wedin (Sweden), along with guests Niels Aasheim (Norway), Wolfgang Gläsker (Europahaus), and two students from Erlangen. In the end Wedin failed to make it. Aasheim, together with Jon Skard, produced an occasional periodical at Oslo University on Cold War issues, *Fri informasjon*, that was sent out to around 10,000 "politically interested youth in Norway". 'Extraordinary Board Meeting of Interdoc Youth', 29 May 1970, IY.
160. Holl to IY conference participants, 14 May 1970, IY.
161. Holl to Wolfgang Buchow, 5 June 1970, and Holl to IY board members, 31 August 1970, IY.
162. Uwe Holl, interview with the author, Cologne, 18 December 2005.

6 The Fallout from *Ostpolitik*

1. Van den Heuvel to Geyer, 22 December 1966, File: 66 H.J. Geyer 1965–1972, Duitsland (1958–1978), archive of C.C. van den Heuvel, National Archives, The Hague (hereafter CC NAH).
2. 'Protokoll der Sitzung mit Herrn Wiggers am 2.6.1970', File: 220 Einde Interdoc 1970–1973, Overige Dossiers betreffende Interdoc, CC NAH.
3. Geyer to Van den Heuvel, 8 September 1965, File: 66 H.J. Geyer 1965–1972, Duitsland (1958–1978), CC NAH.

4. Wilfried Loth, *Overcoming the Cold War: A History of Détente* (Basingstoke: Palgrave Macmillan, 2002), pp. 80–82; David Ryan, *The United States and Europe in the Twentieth Century* (London: Pearson Longman, 2003), pp. 79–85.
5. Lyndon B. Johnson, 'Remarks in Lexington at the Dedication of the George C. Marshall Research Library', 23 May 1964, *Public Papers of the Presidents of the United States, Lyndon B. Johnson, 1963–64 I* (Washington, DC: US Government Printing Office, 1965), pp. 708–710; 'Remarks in New York City before the National Conference of Editorial Writers', 7 October 1966, *Public Papers of the Presidents of the United States, Lyndon B. Johnson, 1966 II* (Washington, DC: US Government Printing Office, 1967), pp. 1125–1130.
6. 'Bridges to Eastern Europe', Memo for Director of Central Intelligence, 25 June 1964, available online via CIA Freedom of Information Act Electronic Reading Room, at http://www.foia.cia.gov/ (accessed 24 June 2011).
7. See Zbigniew Brzezinski and William Griffith, 'Peaceful Engagement in Eastern Europe', *Foreign Affairs* 39 (July 1961), pp. 642–654; Bennett Kovrig, *Of Walls and Bridges: The United States and Eastern Europe* (New York: New York University Press, 1991), pp. 107–109.
8. Stephan Kieninger, 'Zbigniew Brzezinski, the Crisis of Superpower Détente and NATO's Dual-Track Decision 1979', paper delivered at the Transatlantic Studies Association, Canterbury, 13–16 July 2009.
9. Gottfried Niedhart, 'The East–West Problem as seen from Berlin: Willy Brandt's Early Ostpolitik', in Wilfried Loth (ed.), *Europe, Cold War and Coexistence 1953–1965* (London: Frank Cass, 2004), pp. 285–296.
10. See Jeremi Suri, *Power and Protest: Global Revolution and the Rise of Détente* (Cambridge, MA: Harvard University Press, 2003), pp. 216–218; Gottfried Niedhart, 'Ostpolitik: Phases, Short-Term Objectives, and Grand Design', *GHI Bulletin Supplement* 1 (2003), pp 118–136; Oliver Bange, 'Ostpolitik as a source of intra-bloc tensions', paper presented at the Lemnitzer Centre for NATO Studies/Ohio State University, available online at http://detente.de/ostpolitik/publications/index.html (accessed 23 June 2011); Egon Bahr's speech available online at http://germanhistorydocs.ghi-dc.org/sub_document.cfm?document_id=81 (accessed 23 June 2011).
11. See Peter Bender, *Offensive Entspannung* (Cologne: Kiepenheuer & Witsch, 1964); Ludwig Raiser, 'Deutsche Ostpolitik im Lichte der Denkschrift der Evangelischen Kirke', *Europa-Archiv* 21 (1966), pp. 195–208; Gottfried Erb, 'Das Memorandum des Bensberger Kreises zur Polenpolitik', in Werner Plum (ed.), *Ungewöhnliche Normalisierung: Beziehungen der Bundesrepublik Deutschland zu Polen* (Bonn: Verlag Neue Gesellschaft, 1984), pp. 179–190.
12. Gerhard Schröder, 'Germany looks at Eastern Europe', *Foreign Affairs*, 44 (October 1965), p. 17.
13. László Görgey, *Bonn's Eastern Policy 1964–1971: Evolution and Limitations* (Hamden: Archon, 1972), pp. 3–28.
14. 'Bonn Looks Eastward', 10 November 1964, CIA: Office of National Estimates, Reel 2, CIA Research Reports: Western Europe 1946–1976, University Publications of America.
15. William Glenn Gray, *Germany's Cold War: The Global Campaign to Isolate East Germany, 1949–1969* (Chapel Hill, NC: University of North Carolina Press, 2003), p. 193.
16. See Ronald J. Granieri, 'Odd Man Out? The CDU–CSU, Ostpolitik, and the Atlantic Alliance', in Matthias Schulz and Thomas Schwartz (eds), *The Strained*

Alliance: US–European Relations from Nixon to Carter (Cambridge: Cambridge University Press, 2010), pp. 83–101.
17. Reinhard Gehlen, *The Service: The Memoirs of General Reinhard Gehlen* (New York: World Publishing, 1972), p. 278.
18. Van den Heuvel to H.J. Rijks, 11 January 1967, in author's possession.
19. 'The Effect of Soviet Propaganda regarding West Germany in a Number of West European Countries', Interdoc survey, September 1966, author's copy.
20. Uwe Holl, interview with the author, Cologne, 18 December 2005.
21. Von Hahn to Zanchi, 25 August 1966, File: 133 Algemeen 1966–1967, Italië (1959–1975), CC NAH.
22. Rolf Geyer, 'Some Thoughts on Communist Policy', in *Communist Reassessment of Capitalism, its Resultant Strategy and the Western Response*, Interdoc conference, 1967.
23. 'Einzel-Information über die Struktur, die Tätigkeit und die Zielsetzung des Internationalen Dokumentations- und Informationszentrums (Interdok), Den Haag', Ministerium für Staatsicherheit (hereafter MfS), HVA-139, Bundesbeauftragter für die Unterlagen des Staatssicherheitsdienstes der ehemaligen Deutschen Demokratischen Republik, Berlin (hereafter BstU). The source for this report is probably Ludwig Bress, a Stasi IM (*Inoffizieller Mitarbeiter*) who was working for Kernig at the time.
24. "Aufklärung einer verstärkten Koordinierung gegnerischer geheimdienstlicher, militärischer und staatlicher Stellen mit den Zentren und Einrichtungen der politisch-ideologischen Diversion und eine erhöhte Einflussnahme auf diese sowie besondere Aktivitäten der Hetze und Verleumdung gegen die DDR und andere sozialistische Staaten": 'Befehl Nr. 40/68 über die Durchführung politisch-operativer Maßnahmen zur Ausschaltung des Überraschungsmomentes und zum rechtzeitigen Erkennen einer akuten Kriegsgefahr', 2 December 1968, MfS-BdL, Dok-1509, BstU; 'Interdok Den Haag', 16 July 1969, MfS-HA II, No. 33802, BStU.
25. Henry Kissinger, *The White House Years* (Boston: Little, Brown, 1979), p. 99.
26. See Stefanie Waske, *Mehr Liaison als Kontrolle: Die Kontrolle des BND durch Parlament und Regierung* (Wiesbaden: VS Verlag, 2008); Erich Schmidt-Eenboom, *Der BND* (Berlin: ECON Verlag, 1993); Paul Maddrell, 'The Western secret services, the East German Ministry for State Security, and the building of the Berlin Wall', *Intelligence and National Security*, 21 (2006), pp. 829–847; Eberhard Blum (code name Hartwig), 'Einleitung und Vorschlag für Neuordnung', 24 July 1968, archive of the Forschungsinstitut für Friedenspolitik e.V., Welheim, Germany.
27. *East–West Confrontation in Africa* (The Hague: Interdoc, 1966) included contributions from David Morison (Central Asian Research Centre, London), Roswitha Zastrow, Pieter Lessing, Pierre Alexandre, and A.G. Aukes (Africa Institute, The Hague).
28. 'Accounts' and 'International Interdoc Conference, Cambridge, 22–23 September 1966', File: 95 C.H. (Dick) Ellis 1966, Groot-Britannië (1959–1985), CC NAH.
29. Meeting with Johnson's representative, 'Report on visit to London on the 30th and 31st of May, 1967', File: 89 Reisverslagen 1961–1968, Groot-Britannië (1959–1985), CC NAH.
30. Ellis to Van den Heuvel, 7 November 1969, in author's possession.

31. 'Liaison between Power/Johnson & Interdoc', 7 November 1967, File: 89 Reisverslagen 1961–1968, Groot-Britannië (1959–1985), CC NAH; 'Joint Management Committee: Special Agenda 31st May 1967', File: 107 Common Cause 1964–1971, Groot-Britannië (1959–1985), CC NAH.
32. Ellis to Van den Heuvel, 19 January 1968, File: 97 C.H. (Dick) Ellis 1968, Groot-Britannië (1959–1985), CC NAH.
33. 'Distribution of Interdoc material', n.d. [1968], File: 106 Financiën 1964–1969, Groot-Britannië (1959–1985), CC NAH; Ellis to Van den Heuvel, 8 March 1969, File: 98 C.H. (Dick) Ellis 1969, Groot-Britannië (1959–1985), CC NAH.
34. 'Visit of Mr Ellis to The Hague on the 14th of February 1968', 'Visit to London 21–23 March 1968', and 'Visit to London on the 30th and 31st of May 1968', File: 89 Reisverslagen 1961–1968, Groot-Britannië (1959–1985), CC NAH; Hesmondhalgh to Van den Heuvel, 26 June 1968, File: 97 C.H. (Dick) Ellis 1968, Groot-Britannië (1959–1985), CC NAH.
35. 'Interdoc UK: Meeting of Board 18.12.68', File: 97 C.H. (Dick) Ellis 1968, Groot-Britannië (1959–1985), CC NAH.
36. British Embassy The Hague to IRD, 13 August 1968; O'Connor Howe to Maclaren, 16 August 1968; H.H. Tucker (IRD Editorial Section) to T.J. Trout (British Embassy The Hague), 5 September 1968, FCO 96/87, papers of the Information Research Department, National Archives, London (hereafter IRD NAL).
37. T.J. Trout to Maclaren, 31 December 1968, FCO 95/448, IRD NAL.
38. Colin Maclaren to A.H. Campbell (British Embassy Paris),13 March 1969, FCO 95/503, IRD NAL.
39. P. Garran (British Embassy The Hague) to B.R. Curson (Foreign Office), 6 June 1969; Colin Maclaren to R.J.T. Trout (British Embassy The Hague), 7 July 1969; Trout to Maclaren, 8 October 1969, FCO 95/531, IRD NAL; Ellis to Van den Heuvel, 28 January 1969, File: 98 C.H. (Dick) Ellis 1969, Groot-Britannië (1959–1985), CC NAH. IRD material continued to be sent direct to the wider Interdoc circle: Tony Dake, Hornix, De Niet, Mennes, Van Oort, the academic Alting von Geusau, and the journalists Jerome Heldring and Henk Hofland.
40. 'Interdoc', FCO 95/907, IRD NAL. Interestingly Ellis mentions a possible meeting with the Ministry of Defence as well, suggesting that Geyer is redirecting his attention towards the effects of student radicalism on attitudes towards the armed forces. This theme occupied Interdoc – together with the German Ministry of Defence – in the early 1970s.
41. 'Interdoc UK: Report on Progress Sept 1969', File: 98 C.H. (Dick) Ellis 1969, Groot-Britannië (1959–1985), CC NAH; Ellis to Van den Heuvel, 3 June 1969, File: 113 Walter Bell 1969–70, Groot-Britannië (1959–1985), CC NAH; Uwe Holl, interview with the author, Cologne, 18 December 2005; Stephen Dorril, *MI6* (London: Fourth Estate, 2000), p. 51.
42. Ellis to Van den Heuvel, 30 December 1969, in author's possession.
43. Whether Geyer did actually influence the course of events is another matter, but it is clear that he had an opportunity at the New Left experts meeting in Murnau in March 1968 to discuss this with someone from MI6. Geyer to von Grote, 21 February 1968, File: 112 W.B. Hesmondhalgh 1968, Groot-Britannië (1959–1985), CC NAH; Geyer to Van den Heuvel, 12 February 1970, File: 66 H.J. Geyer 1965–1972, Duitsland (1958–1978), CC NAH.
44. Brian Crozier, *Free Agent: The Unseen War 1941–1991* (London: HarperCollins, 1993), pp. 104–105

45. Ibid., p. 81.
46. Van den Heuvel to Dr N. Ørvik, 20 February 1970, File: 163 Algemeen 1967–1976, Noorwegen (1967–1978), CC NAH. In a letter to Peeters, Van den Heuvel literally asked him to speak up for those who opposed the recognition of the GDR at the conference, to balance the majority who would be in favour – a sign of the times. Van den Heuvel to Peeters, 20 February 1970, File: 143 F. Peeters 1965–1970, België (1961–1977), CC NAH.
47. Gunhild Bohm-Geyer, interviews with the author, Würthsee, 4 July 2008 and 12 July 2011. See Rolf Geyer, *Entspannung, Neutralität, Sicherheit* (Osnabruck: Verlag A. Fromm, 1970) and 'Der Deutsche im Spannungsfeld psychopolitischer Vorgänge', *Politische Studien: Monatschrift für Zeitgeschichte und Politik* (1975), pp. 369–376 for a concise outline of Geyer's thinking on the negative consequences for the West of a détente process that was largely orientated towards Soviet-bloc interests.
48. Geyer to Van den Heuvel, 20 December 1972, File: 66 H.J. Geyer 1965–1972, Duitsland (1958–1978), CC NAH.
49. Dietmar Töppel became chief of staff of the GDR section at BND HQ, while Peter Becker, who regarded the decision to disband IIIF as an arrogant mistake on the part of the SPD, undertook operational training and subsequently held posts in Hong Kong, Taiwan, Cairo, and Beijing. On the Stiftung see Albrecht Zunker, 'Stiftung Wissenschaft und Politik: Die Neu-Berlinerin', *Handbuch Politikberatung* II (2006), pp. 363–373.
50. 'Betr.: Interdok', 13 April 1970, and 'Gesprek met K. op 14 april 1970 in bijzijn van Dr. Von Grote en Frau von Hassell', File: 220 Einde Interdoc 1970–1973, Overige Dossiers betreffende Interdoc, CC NAH.
51. Blötz to C.E. Riggert (Volk und Verteidigung), 15 May 1970, archive of the Forschungsinstitut für Friedenspolitiek e.V., Welheim, Germany.
52. Geyer to Van den Heuvel, 11 May 1970, File: 66 H.J. Geyer 1965–1972, Duitsland (1958–1978), CC NAH.
53. 'Protokoll der Sitzung mit Herrn Wiggers am 2.6.1970, 11.00 Uhr,' and Wiggers to Van den Heuvel, 12 June 1970, File: 220 Einde Interdoc 1970–1973, Overige Dossiers betreffende Interdoc, CC NAH.
54. The document for the meeting shows that sums of money were being used for 'Interdoc India' (4000 guilders) and Interdoc Canada (2000 guilders). 'Protokoll der Sitzung mit Herrn Wiggers am 2.6.1970, 11.00 Uhr', File: 220 Einde Interdoc 1970–1973, Overige Dossiers betreffende Interdoc, CC NAH.
55. 'Reorganisation Interdok', September 1970, File: 220 Einde Interdoc 1970–1973, Overige Dossiers betreffende Interdoc, CC NAH.
56. Van den Heuvel to de Biasi, 22 November 1963, File: 136 CESES 1961–1971, Italië (1959–1975), CC NAH.
57. See File: 23 EDIZ [Europäisches Dokumentations- und Informations-Zentrum] 1960, Internationale Organisaties, CC NAH.
58. Interdoc never developed a foothold in Spain despite this meeting, which included University of Madrid philosophy professor Muñoz-Alonso, General Staff officer Joaquín Sánchez Gabriel, and the communication/information chiefs of the Ministry of Information, the trade unions, and Movimiento. De Carranza moved on to become an ambassador and could only provide contacts at a distance, one of which led Van den Heuvel to write to the King of Spain, Don Juan Carlos de Borbón y Borbón, offering to send him Interdoc periodicals (at an

annual subscription rate of 12 guilders). Van den Heuvel to Don Juan Carlos, 11 November 1971, and 'Visit to Madrid from 4–6 February 1969 made by CC van den Heuvel', File: 166 Spanje 1964–1974, Overige West-Europese Landen (1964–1976), CC NAH.
59. Lombardo had come into the Interdoc circle via the link with the Belgian Florent Peeters.
60. Waldman's papers included 'Canada's Attitude towards Detente and Neutralism' (Conference: National Views on Neutralism and East–West Détente, Deidesheim, September 1969) and 'Political Radicalism and Defence: The Situation in North America' (Conference: Radicalism and Security, Noordwijk, April 1970). On Waldman and Gehlen see James Critchfield, *Partners at the Creation: The Men behind Postwar Germany's Defense and Intelligence Establishments* (Annapolis, MA: Naval Institute Press, 2003), pp. 31–41.
61. Wolfgang Höpker, *Wie rot ist das Mittelmeer? – Europas gefährdete Südflanke* (Stuttgart: Seewald, 1968)
62. 'Soviet Activities in the Mediterranean', International Interdoc Conference, Rimini, Italy, 16–18 October 1970, in author's possession.
63. Those present were Kernig, Lades, Hoheisel, Holl, von Hassell, IIIF researcher Albert von Weiss, Rolf Buchow, von Grote, the Arbeitsgruppe secretary von Freier, Hornix, Van den Heuvel, De Niet, Elles, and Bell. Dick Ellis was forced to miss the meeting due to his wife's poor health. 'Protokoll der ordentlichen Vorstandssitzung von Interdok in Rimini am 19 Oktober 1970 9.00-11.00 Uhr', File: 220 Einde Interdoc 1970–1973, Overige Dossiers betreffende Interdoc, CC NAH.
64. Van den Heuvel to Ulmer, 8 October 1970, File: 154 Schweizerischer Aufklärungsdienst 1961–1974, Zwitserland (1961–1975), CC NAH.
65. "Ich bin daher auch der Auffassung, dass sich die Ziele von Interdok gut in die Gedanken der deutschen Ostpolitik hineinfügen, indem sie auf der einen Seite eine realistische Analyse der Ost-West-Problematik und auf der anderen Seite eine Förderung der Ost-West-Kontakte beinhalten." Van den Heuvel to Ehmke, 10 November 1970, and Schlichter (Chancellery) to Van den Heuvel, 3 December 1970, File: 220 Einde Interdoc 1970–1973, Overige Dossiers betreffende Interdoc, CC NAH.
66. 'Besprechung mit dem Präsidenten des BND am 3.12.1970, 17.10-17.40 Uhr', Van den Heuvel to Wessel, 10 December 1970, and Wessel to Van den Heuvel, 14 February 1972, File: 220 Einde Interdoc 1970–1973, Overige Dossiers betreffende Interdoc, CC NAH.
67. Couwenberg held the chair, which continues thanks to funding from the Civis Mundi foundation, 1971 to 1995.
68. 'Information über die finanzielle Situation und analytische Materialen des Internationalen Dokumentations- und Informationszentrums (Interdok), Den Haag', 1971, MfS, HVA 180, BstU.
69. Van den Heuvel to Kernig, 11 January 1972, in author's possession.
70. 'Memorandum m.t.b. de huidige precaire financiële situatie van Interdoc (en daardoor ook het Oost-West Instituut)', and Van den Heuvel to Hoheisel, 1 August 1972, File: 220 Einde Interdok 1970–1973, Overige Dossiers betreffende Interdoc, CC NAH; Van den Heuvel to Bell, 18 July 1972, File: 115 Walter Bell 1972, Groot-Britannië (1959–1985), CC NAH.
71. Einthoven to Bernhard, 4 September 1972, Van den Heuvel to Thompson, 1 August 1972, and Van den Heuvel to Ehmke, 10 August 1972, File: 220 Einde Interdok 1970–1973, Overige Dossiers betreffende Interdoc, CC NAH.

72. Ehmke to Van den Heuvel, 26 September 1972, File: 220 Einde Interdok 1970–1973, Overige Dossiers betreffende Interdoc, CC NAH. The story did not stop there. A year later it was discovered that Ehmke had withdrawn DM 50,000 from a secret fund controlled by the Chancellor's office, a day before this same amount was paid to a CDU politician in 1972 as a bribe to gain his support for the Brandt coalition. The *International Herald Tribune* report on the events included the strong suspicion that the fund "was earmarked for covert intelligence operations" and noted Ehmke's inability to fully explain his action. It is possible that this could have been the money Ehmke used to save Interdoc. 'Ehmke Admits Using Secret Funds', *IHT* 6 September 1973.
73. An overview from the end of 1972 reports two amounts coming from West Germany: 60,000 guilders (Ehmke) and 30,000 guilders (probably Kernig). Income was 233,000 guilders for the year, against costs of 270,000. 'Kort Verslag Oost-West Instituut/Interdoc', 31 December 1972, File: 246 Financiën OWI 1969–1979, Financieel beheer, CC NAH.
74. 'Financial Report 1972/1973', File: 220 Einde Interdok 1970–1973, Overige Dossiers betreffende Interdoc, CC NAH.
75. 'Geistig-Politische Auseinandersetzung mit dem Kommunismus in Deutschland', 15 October 1957, and 'Aufgaben der Arbeitsgruppe VII (als Beispiel für das vorgeschlagene Studienbüro)', File B 137, Collection 16429, Bundesministerium für gesamtdeutsche Fragen, National Archives, Koblenz (hereafter NAK).
76. 'Anglo-German Information Talks', 23–24 October 1961, FO 1110/1372, IRD NAL. Although the Wall drastically reduced the number of refugees from the GDR, thus cutting off a valuable intelligence source, it did on the other hand raise the status of radio broadcasting out of West Berlin as the prime means of reaching out to East Germans. R.M. Russell, 'Berlin as A Centre for Information Operations', 1 November 1961, FO 1110/1372, IRD NAL.
77. SOEV Annual Report: 1963, p. 10.
78. Wolfgang Buchow, interview with the author, Neuss, 10 January 2007.
79. 'Reis Amsterdam-München-Zürich-Bern-Genève-Amsterdam', January 1962, File: 151 Reisverslagen 1961–1967, Zwitserland (1961–1975), CC NAH.
80. Creuzberger, *Kampf für die Einheit: Das gesamtdeutsche Ministerium und die politische Kultur des Kalten Krieges 1949–1969* (Düsseldorf: Droste, 2008), pp. 279–286; Sonja Krämer, 'Westdeutsche Propaganda im Kalten Krieg: Organisationen und Akteure', in Jürgen Wilke (ed.), *Pressepolitik und Propaganda: Historische Studien vom Vormärz bis zum Kalten Krieg* (Cologne: Böhlau, 1997), pp. 333–371.
81. 'Auszug aus dem GM Bericht "Heinz"', n.d. [1953], 'Auszug aus dem Bericht des GM "Heinz"', n.d. [1954], 'Bericht über die technische Durchführung der Verteilung von SED-Oppositions-Material nach dem Gebiet der DDR', n.d. [1955?], MfS, AOP 110/61 und 110/61 Teilvorgang 5, BStU.
82. "Herr Buchow ist von Natur aus sehr verschlossener Mensch, mehr ein wissenschaftlicher Analytiker und sagt nie mehr, als zur direkten Arbeit notwendig ist." 'Bericht über die Arbeit der Arbeitsgemeinschaft für Ostfragen ev. (liquidiert) und der SED Opposition', 5 December 1955, MfS, 110/61 Teilvorgang 5, BStU.
83. 'Anhang zum Beschluss über das Anlegen des zentralen Operativ-Vorganges "Reichskanzler"', n.d., 'Bearbeitung von verdächtigen Personen', 29 June 1959,

'Teilvorgang V des Zentralen Operativvorganges "Reichskanzler" ', 23 July 1962, MfS, 110/61 and 110/61 Teilvorgang 5, BStU.
84. Wolfgang Buchow, interview with the author, Neuss, 10 January 2007.
85. Holl to H. Schiffer, 5 March 1970, File: Interdoc Youth – Correspondence, in author's possession (hereafter IY).
86. Oost-West Instituut: Jaarverslag 1969, p. 26. The Danes were especially active, with several groups of politicians, journalists, trade unionists, military officers and the home defence force, and academics (the Nordic Agricultural College in Odense, an institution that had close connections with developing countries) making use of the Berlin seminars during 1968–69.
87. Holl to J.H.R.D. van Roijen (exam commission for the diplomatic service), 5 June 1970, IY.
88. Rolf Buchow to Deutsche Arbeitsgruppe, 3 May 1968, File: 68 Interdoc Berlin 1967–1968, Duitsland (1958–1978), CC NAH. There are signs that the Dutch students saw the trips as little more than a holiday opportunity. Holl felt the need to inform Engelorp-Gastelaars, responsible for the SIB's East–West relations (and who went to study with Lades in Erlangen in late 1969), that "with sending groups in the future the leader of the group must sustain greater discipline (punctuality, attendance at the sessions) than was the case in July 1969". Holl to Engelorp-Gastelaars, 10 September 1969, IY.
89. Rolf Buchow to Deutsche Arbeitsgruppe, 3 May 1968, File: 68 Interdoc Berlin 1967–1968, Duitsland (1958–1978), CC NAH; Van den Heuvel to Dr Krätschell, 29 April 1976, File: 72 Europäische Akademie 1974–1976, Duitsland (1958–1978), CC NAH.
90. Interdoc: Progress Report 1969, The Hague, p. 9.
91. Holl to Henri Starckx, 13 January 1969, IY.
92. Holl to Löwenthal, 3 September 1970, and Holl to K. Gould (BBC), 18 September 1970, IY. Bad Marienberg was set up through Herbert Scheffler, a board member of the Europa-Haus organization and head of the German section of Deutsche Welle. Scheffler had shown genuine interest in IY and was planning to attend the conference himself.
93. Holl to von Geyso, 29 October 1970, IY
94. Uwe Holl, interview with the author, Cologne, 18 December 2005.
95. 'Probleme im Zusammenhang mit Interdok-Jugend', 21 September 1970, File: 220 Einde Interdok 1970–1973, Duitsland (1958–1978), CC NAH.
96. Holl to von Geyso, 29 October 1970, IY.
97. Holl to IY board members, 11 November 1970, IY.
98. 'Draft for Interdoc Youth's possible activities after 1st January 1971', November 1970, IY.
99. Holl to Paust, 12 November 1970, IY.
100. Holl to G. Scheer, 16 December 1970, and 'Protocol of the meeting in Erlangen', 11 December 1970, File: 219 Interdoc Youth 1969–1970, Overige Dossiers betreffende Interdoc, CC NAH.
101. Wolfgang Buchow remembers a meeting around 1980 "to try a new start" with the IY concept, but the details of this meeting, which apparently took place in the Netherlands, are uncertain. Wolfgang Buchow, interview with the author, Neuss, 10 January 2007.
102. 'Report on a Visit to Berlin, July 10–11, 1972', File: 220 Einde Interdok 1970–1973, Duitsland (1958–1978), CC NAH.
103. Wolfgang Buchow, interview with the author, Neuss, 10 January 2007.

7 Bringing the Americans Back In

1. C.C. van den Heuvel, interview with the author, The Hague, 18 September 2002.
2. 'National Strategy Information Center Inc', undated pamphlet. See also RightWeb, run by Political Research Associates, available online at http://rightweb.irc-online.org/gw/2806.html (accessed 12 February 2009).
3. Frank R. Barnett, 'A Proposal for Political Warfare', *Military Review* (March 1961), p. 3.
4. Ellis to Van den Heuvel, 20 February 1966, File: 95 C.H. (Dick) Ellis 1966, Groot-Britannië (1959–1985), archive of C.C. van den Heuvel, National Archives, The Hague (hereafter CC NAH). Ellis had also maintained his contact with 'Intrepid' William Stephenson during the latter's post-WW-II sojourn on Bermuda and did try to build links between the former British Security Coordination man and Interdoc in relation to Cuban activities and Black Power movements in the Caribbean.
5. Van den Heuvel to Geyer, 5 May 1966, File: 66 H.J. Geyer 1965–1972, Duitsland (1958–1978), CC NAH; Van den Heuvel to Ellis, 25 March 1966, File: 95 C.H. (Dick) Ellis 1966, Groot-Britannië (1959–1985), CC NAH.
6. Vaccari to Van den Heuvel, 11 November 1964, File: 132 Algemeen 1964–1965, Italië (1959–1975), CC NAH; A memo in author's possession to Van den Heuvel dated 1 June 1966, probably from Cleveland Cram, CIA station chief in The Hague at the time, states that "Barnett has had a long career of professional anti-Communism and was one of the most ardent proponents of the Free Slavic Legion in the early 1950s".
7. Van den Heuvel to Vaccari, 23 June 1966, File: 133 Algemeen 1966–1967, Italië (1959–1975), CC NAH.
8. Van den Heuvel to Ellis, 25 July 1966, File: 95 C.H. (Dick) Ellis 1966, Groot-Britannië (1959–1985), CC NAH.
9. Uwe Holl, interview with the author, Cologne, 18 December 2005; Bell to Van den Heuvel, 21 April 1972, File: 115 Walter Bell 1972, Groot-Britannië (1959–1985), CC NAH.
10. Ellis to Van den Heuvel, 17 November 1966, File: 95 C.H. (Dick) Ellis 1966, Groot-Britannië (1959–1985), CC NAH; Van den Heuvel to Baeder, 11 October 1966, File: 150 Algemeen 1961–1970, Zwitserland (1961–1975), CC NAH.
11. 'Bezoek Vaccari 6 oktober 1966', and Van den Heuvel to Vaccari, 10 October 1966, File: 133 Algemeen 1966–1967, Italië (1959–1975), CC NAH.
12. Van den Heuvel to Ellis, 14 November 1966, File: 95 C.H. (Dick) Ellis 1966, Groot-Britannië (1959–1985), CC NAH.
13. 'Report on a visit to Interdoc UK on 7 and 8 December 1966', File: 89 Reisverslagen 1963–1968, Groot-Britannië (1959–1985), CC NAH.
14. Ellis to Van den Heuvel, 17 November 1966, File: 95 C.H. (Dick) Ellis 1966, Groot-Britannië (1959–1985), CC NAH; Brian Crozier, *Free Agent: The Unseen War 1941–1991* (London: HarperCollins, 1993), p. 90. On Scaife see Karen Rothmeyer, 'Citizen Scaife', in David Weir and Dan Noyes, *Raising Hell* (Reading, MA: Addison-Wesley, 1983), pp. 53–90.
15. 'Background Paper: East–West Trade, Visit of Chancellor Erhard, December 28–29 1963', 19 December 1963, document released 31 May 1984, Declassified Documents Reference System (hereafter DDRS); Ian Jackson, *The Economic Cold War: America, Britain, and East–West Trade* (Basingstoke: Palgrave Macmillan, 2001).

16. Zbigniew Brzezinski, interview with Paige Mulhollan, 12 November 1971, Reel 5, Part I: White House and Executive Departments, Oral Histories of the Johnson Administration 1963–1969, University Publications of America.
17. John Dumbrell, *President Lyndon Johnson and Soviet Communism* (Manchester: Manchester University Press, 2004), pp. 33, 44–45, 165–166.
18. 'Economic Pressure for Change in Eastern Europe', CIA Intelligence Memorandum, March 1968, document released 7 September 2000, DDRS.
19. Bennett Kovrig, *Of Walls and Bridges: The United States and Eastern Europe* (New York: New York University Press, 1991), pp. 109, 247–251.
20. J. Wilczynski, *The Economics and Politics of East–West Trade* (London: Macmillan, 1969), p. 21.
21. Although they were growing, US exports to Eastern Europe represented only 0.3 per cent of global exports to the region in 1967. See Kovrig, *Of Walls and Bridges*, p. 251.
22. Mose Harvey, *East–West Trade and United States Policy* (New York: National Association of Manufacturers, 1966), pp. 121–128, 155–171.
23. Van den Heuvel to Hesmondhalgh, 11 July 1968, File: 112 W.B. Hesmondhalgh 1968, Groot-Britannië (1959–1985), CC NAH.
24. The study still remarked that "To this day US policy is characterized by a dogmatic attitude" largely caused by the war in Vietnam. Pieter Koerts and Jean de Vries, *East–West Trade: Problems and Prospects* (The Hague: Oost-West Instituut, 1967), p. 14.
25. Ellis to Van den Heuvel, 6 February 1967, File: 96 C.H. (Dick) Ellis 1967, Groot-Britannië (1959–1985), CC NAH.
26. Ellis to Van den Heuvel, 15 February 1967, File: 96 C.H. (Dick) Ellis 1967, Groot-Britannië (1959–1985), CC NAH.
27. Ellis to Van den Heuvel, 15 May 1967, File: 96 C.H. (Dick) Ellis 1967, Groot-Britannië (1959–1985), CC NAH; 'Visit to Zürich-Bern-Milano 20–23 March 1967', File: 151 Reisverslagen 1961–1967, Zwitserland (1961–1975), CC NAH. See also Ellis to Van den Heuvel, 28 January 1969, File: 98 C.H. (Dick) Ellis 1969, Groot-Britannië (1959–1985), CC NAH, where Ellis again refers to a proposed East–West trade meeting in The Hague.
28. On the circumstances of his participation in the Program see G. Scott-Smith, *Networks of Empire: The US State Department's Foreign Leader Program in the Netherlands, France, and Britain 1950–1970* (Brussels: Peter Lang, 2008) pp. 296–297.
29. C.C. van den Heuvel, interview with the author, The Hague, 6 August 2002.
30. Donald Norland, correspondence with the author, 3 July 2002.
31. US Embassy to Department of State, 17 April 1967, and 'Planning Mr Cornelis C. van den Heuvel,' 29 May 1967, Grantee File: C.C. van den Heuvel, archive of the Governmental Affairs Institute, Washington, DC (hereafter GAI).
32. C.C. van den Heuvel, 'Report on a visit to the United States', 26 June–5 August 1967, GAI.
33. Ibid., p. 26.
34. 'Visit of Mr C.C. van den Heuvel', 8 August 1967, File: General Correspondence 1967, Reel C1556, archive of the Ford Foundation, New York.
35. Mennes to F.Th. Witkamp, 19 August 1964, and Witkamp to SOEV, 19 October 1964, File: 256 Nederlands Centrum van Directeuren 1963–1964, Nederland, CC NAH; 'Delegatie van NCD naar Sowjetunie', 4 September 1964; F.Th. Witkamp and H.J. Aben, *Oriëntatie in de Sowjetunie* (NCD, 1965); Corinna Unger, *Ostforschung in Westdeutschland: Die Erforschung des europäischen Ostens und*

die Deutsche Forschungsgemeinschaft, 1945–1975 (Stuttgart: Franz Steiner Verlag, 2007), pp. 147, 181.

36. Van den Heuvel had reported to the Studienbüro in 1961 that the first Dutch trade mission to the Soviet Union had gone there in the previous year to try to redress the Netherlands' trade deficit with Moscow. The general attitude of the Dutch business world was that trade could facilitate the convergence of the West and the Soviet Union, and that anyway it was China that represented the greater threat. 'Bericht Niederlande', n.d. [September 1961], File: 16431, Collection: B 137, archive of the Bundesministerium für gesamtdeutsche Fragen, National Archives, Koblenz.
37. Robert Hutchinson, *Their Kingdom Come: Inside the Secret World of Opus Dei* (NY: Doubleday, 1997) pp. 153–158.
38. C.C. van den Heuvel, 'Report on a visit to the United States', 26 June–5 August 1967, GAI.
39. "Beslist gevaarlijk vind ik zijn neiging om rechtse bewegingen als naziorganisaties te bestempelen. Dat doen de communisten ook!" Interestingly enough the Radicalism issue proved popular with Shell, which bought up 115 copies to be distributed among its management. 'Aan C van H', 6 August 1970, File: Oost-West 1961–1971, in author's possession.
40. 'Contact Report', 11 October 1966, Gehlen, Reinhard, Vol. 5, Box 40, Entry ZZ-18, RG 263 Records of the Central Intelligence Agency, National Archives, College Park.
41. Van den Heuvel to Ellis, 29 December 1966, File: 95 C.H. (Dick) Ellis 1966, Groot-Britannië (1959–1985), CC NAH.
42. C.C. van den Heuvel (ed.), *Vietnam: Aspects of a Tragedy* (Alphen aan de Rijn: Samson, 1967)
43. M.J.W.M. Broekmeijer, *South Vietnam: Victim of Misunderstanding* (Bilthoven: H. Nelissen, 1967).
44. Max Nord, *Vietnam is our World* (The Hague: Interdoc, 1970).
45. Van Oort to South Vietnamese Ambassador to Britain, 1 April 1968, File: AK Internationale South Vietnam, CC NAH; Van Oort to Ernst van der Beugel, 16 February 1968, File 7: Private Correspondence 1963–67, Archive of E.H. van der Beugel, Inventory No. 2.21.183.08, Collection 357, National Archives, the Hague.
46. File: 262 Stichting Azië Instituut 1968–1975, Nederland, CC NAH; Oost-West Instituut: Jaarverslag 1969, p. 12.
47. 'Memorandum', 15 December 1972, and Van Ketwich Verschuur to Van den Heuvel, 24 May 1973, File: 273 Sun Yat Sen Center 1972–1973, CC NAH; George Embree, interview with the author, The Hague, 21 October 2004.
48. Van den Heuvel to Hernandez, 26 February 1968, File: 180 South Korea 1966–1975, Diverse Oost-Aziatische Landen (1963–1975), CC NAH.
49. A full study of the WACL still needs to be written. Scott Anderson and Jon Lee Anderson, *Inside the League: The Shocking Exposé of How Terrorists, Nazis, and Latin American Death Squads Have Infiltrated The World Anti-Communist League* (New York: Dodd, Mead & Co, 1986); Ross Koen, *The China Lobby in American Politics* (New York: Harper & Row, 1974 [1960]); Correspondence with Pierre Abramovici, 28 November 2011 and 10 January 2012.
50. Early contacts were made with Professor D.G. Kotzé at the University of Stellenbosch and the National Council against Communism, an action committee set up in 1964 by representatives of the Protestant churches. In July 1969

an arrangement was made via Einthoven with General van den Bergh, the head of the Bureau of State Security (BOSS), for Interdoc periodicals to be sent to the South African service via the Embassy in The Hague. See 'Bezoek van de heren M.C.W. Geldenhuys en Brand, Zuidafrika, op 9-7-69 aan de heer Einthoven in Lunteren', File: 201 Zuid Afrika 1962–1979, Afrika (1962–1979), CC NAH.

51. Pater van Gestel to Einthoven, 29 March 1962, File: 206 Latijns Amerika 1962–1974, Overige Niet-Communistische Landen (1962–1974), CC NAH.
52. Interdoc: Progress Report 1968, The Hague, p. 3; Interdoc: Progress Report 1969, The Hague, p. 1.
53. Chamieh to von Hassell, 22 December 1967, File: 198 Libanon 1967–1973, Overige Aziatische Landen (1966–1976), CC NAH.
54. The only brochure that was available was *The Muslim Peoples in the Soviet Union* by Abdullah Al-Qadiri (probably a pseudonym for a BND researcher), which Chamieh regarded as useful but outdated. Chamieh to von Hassell, 24 February 1968, Chamieh to Van den Heuvel, 6 March 1968, and Van den Heuvel to Chamieh, 29 April 1968, File: 198 Libanon 1967–1973, Overige Aziatische Landen (1966–1976), CC NAH.
55. 'Soviet Activities in the Mediterranean', International Interdoc Conference, Rimini, Italy, 16–18 October 1970, in author's possession.
56. See Etsuo Kohtani, *The Recent International Communist Movement: Review of the Khrushchev Line* (Tokyo: Public Security Investigation Agency, 1962).
57. See File: 179 Etsuo Kohtani 1967–1973, Japan (1963–1973), CC NAH.
58. William Glenn Gray, *Germany's Cold War: The Global Campaign to Isolate East Germany, 1949–1969* (Chapel Hill, NC: University of North Carolina Press, 2003), p. 215.
59. "Sein Material ist begrenzt verwertbar": 'Protokoll der Interdok-Vorstandssitzung in Freiburg/Brsg. "Schauinsland" am 27. April 1967', File: 224 Statutes 1962–1987, Organisatie, CC NAH. Swarup was listed as one of the speakers for the aborted *Inform* conference of September 1963.
60. Agarwala was not the only person from this region to publish in *Orientierung*. Nirmal Singh, the director of Sikkim's Namgyal Institute of Tibetology, also contributed the article 'How Chinese was China's Tibet Region?' See Files: 188 Algemeen 1967–1968 and 190 Rama Swarup 1967–1969, India (1967–1976); 195 Sikkim 1967–1970, CC NAH.
61. 'Protokoll der Interdok-Vorstandssitzung in Freiburg/Brsg. "Schauinsland" am 27. April 1967', File: 224 Statutes 1962–1987, Organisatie, CC NAH.
62. Einthoven to Ellis, 29 October 1968, File: 97 C.H. (Dick) Ellis 1968, Groot-Britannië, CC NAH.
63. H. Sitompoel, 'Memo', 14 January 1969, Dharmawan Tjondonegro and Domingus Nanlohy, 'Outline', n.d. [1970], and 'Report by Hasan Sastraatmadja' [chief editor of *Nusantara*], June 1970, File: 175 Nusantara 1967–1970, Indonesië (1966–1977), CC NAH.
64. 'Program Proposal for Mr. Oejeng Soewargana', 12 May 1969, Soewargana to Einthoven and Broekmeijer, 24 August 1970, and A.C.A. Dake to Soewargana, 27 February 1971, File: 176 Oejeng Soewargana 1968–1977, Indonesië (1966–1977), CC NAH. Dake, a close associate of Van den Heuvel in the 1970s, arranged for 2000 guilders via the Stichting Vredesfonds (of which he was treasurer at the time) for Soewargana's Dutch trip, and another 2000 came from Interdoc funds.

65. 'Indonesië-Conferentie van het Oost-West Instituut', File: Oost-West 1961–1971, in author's possession; Louis Einthoven, *Tegen de Stroom In* (Apeldoorn: Semper Agendo, 1974), pp 243–244.
66. Van den Heuvel to Vaccari, 21 November 1967, File: 133 Algemeen 1966–1967, Italië (1959–1975), CC NAH.
67. Reports from earlier in 1968 indicate that a British delegation (with Professor Michael Kaser as the main speaker) was being prepared for "the Vienna conference", but after that Van den Heuvel becomes evasive when asked for more details and the trail goes dead. 'Visit to London on the 30th and 31st of May 1968', File: 89 Reisverslagen 1963–968, Groot-Britannië (1959–1985), CC NAH; Hesmondhalgh to Van den Heuvel, 16 August 1968, File: 112 W.B. Hesmondhalgh 1968, Groot-Britannië (1959–1985), CC NAH.
68. Crozier to Donald Tyerman, 20 December 1963, Box 2: Personal Correspondence 1958–65, archive of Brian Crozier, Hoover Institution Archives.
69. Crozier, *Free Agent*, p. 90.
70. See 'Conflicting Accounts', *Time Out*, 29 August–4 September 1975, pp. 5–6, for a useful account of ISoC's founding and circle.
71. Dietmar Töppel, interview with the author, Munich, 3 July 2008. Gunhild Bohn-Geyer also confirmed that Geyer had been to the US and met Allen Dulles, but there are no further details as to exactly when. Gunhild Bohm-Geyer, interview with the author, Würthsee, 4 July 2008.
72. Van den Heuvel to Hesmondhalgh, 5 November 1968, File: 112 W.B. Hesmondhalgh 1968, Groot-Britannië (1959–1985), CC NAH; "een aantal concrete samenwerkings-objecten": Oost-West Instituut: Jaarverslag 1967, p. 26. On Lovink see Hans Meijer, ' "Op de drempel tussen twee werelden." A.H.J. Lovink, de laatste landvoogd van Indonesië', *BMGN / Low Countries Historical Review*, 144 (1999), pp. 39–60.
73. Interdoc Progress Report 1968, The Hague, p. 4.
74. Interdoc Progress Report 1969, The Hague, p.6.
75. Van den Heuvel to Ellis, 17 June 1970, File: 100 C.H. (Dick) Ellis 1969–75, Groot-Britannië (1959–1985), CC NAH.
76. Van den Heuvel to Crozier, 18 December 1968, and Crozier to Van den Heuvel, 31 December 1968, File: 91 Brian Crozier 1961–1976, Groot-Britannië (1959–1985), CC NAH.
77. Crozier, *Free Agent*, p. 90.
78. Brian Crozier (ed.), *We Will Bury You: A Study in Left-Wing Subversion Today* (London: Tom Stacey, 1970). Ellis contributed a chapter on Soviet imperialism but there was no further Interdoc input. A guest list for a Common Cause reception on 21 October 1968 includes an impressive cross-section of British CEOs from the construction and manufacturing industries, see File: 97 C.H. (Dick) Ellis 1968, Groot-Britannië (1959–1985), CC NAH. On Common Cause's background and connections – particularly the strong likelihood that it was linked to the CIA – see Robin Ramsay, *The Clandestine Caucus* (Hull: Lobster, 1996) pp. 8–10.
79. For a time in the late 1960s Mott's daughter, the future Colorado-based novelist Diane Mott Davidson, also worked at Van Stolkweg 10.
80. 'Report on a visit to the United States from 11–20 November 1970', File: 220 Einde Interdoc 1970–1973, Overige Dossiers betreffende Interdoc, CC NAH.
81. See 'Conflict Confab', The Times, 12 December 1970.

82. Crozier to Van den Heuvel, 9 July 1971, File: 91 Brian Crozier 1961–1976, Groot-Britannië (1959–1985), CC NAH.
83. 'Conférence Interdoc', 27 September 1971, Archive of Georges Albertini, Box 8 Folder 3, Hoover Institution Archives, Stanford. Van den Heuvel wrote to Walter Bell in late 1973 that the French could be providing 20,000 guilders for future Interdoc operations, but this is nowhere confirmed. Van den Heuvel to Bell, File: 116 Walter Bell 1973–74, Groot-Britannië (1959–1985), CC NAH.
84. Barnett to Van den Heuvel, 20 January 1971, Van den Heuvel to Frank Trager (AAEE), 26 January 1971, Trager to Van den Heuvel, 4 February 1971, Van den Heuvel to Trager, 11 February 1971, and Trager to Van den Heuvel, 5 March 1971, File: 116 Walter Bell 1973–74, Groot-Britannië (1959–1985), CC NAH.
85. Frank N. Trager, 'The Wars going on in South East Asia', in *Guerrilla Warfare in Asia* (The Hague: Interdoc, 1971), p. 83.
86. Van den Heuvel to Ellis, 6 April and 2 June 1971, File: 100 C.H. (Dick) Ellis 1969–75, Groot-Britannië (1959–1985), CC NAH.
87. 'Minutes of the Interdoc Board Meeting in The Hague May 12, 1972', File: 220 Einde Interdoc 1970–1973, Overige Dossiers betreffende Interdoc, CC NAH.
88. McMichael to Van den Heuvel, 3 August 1972, File: 220 Einde Interdoc 1970–1973, Overige Dossiers betreffende Interdoc, CC NAH.
89. Van den Heuvel to Kernig, 11 January 1972, in author's possession.
90. Van den Heuvel to Crozier, 11 October 1971, File: 91 Brian Crozier 1961–1976, Groot-Britannië (1959–1985), CC NAH.
91. Thompson to Mott, 23 November 1972, File: 120 Brigadier W.F.K. Thompson 1971–1978, Groot-Britannië (1959–1985), CC NAH.
92. None were able to attend, Luns tactfully declining because "I think it would be inappropriate for a responsible NATO official to speak on the subject 'Frictions within the Alliance'". Van den Heuvel to W.F.K. Thompson, 1 August 1972, File: 220 Einde Interdoc 1970–1973, Overige Dossiers betreffende Interdoc, CC NAH; Luns to Van den Heuvel, 4 September 1972, File: Reis Amerika 16–19 November 1972 Valley Forge, in author's possession.
93. The Germans included Helmut Bohn of Markus-Verlag, Günther Lauterbach of Lades' Institut für Gesellschaft und Wissenschaft, Gerhard Merzyn of Haus Rissen, Günther Scheer of the Deutscher Gewerkschaftsbund, Rudolf Rothe of the Ministry of Defence, the writer Manfred Obst, and Holl. The Dutch were Couwenberg, Dake, Van Eeghen, Van Ketwich Verschuur, Hornix, and De Niet. The British were Bell, Anthony Hartley, the Economist's Kenneth MacKenzie, Carol Mather MP, S.W.B. (Paddy) Menaul, Michael Niblock of the Conservative Party's research centre, Jeremy Russell of Shell, Alan Lee Williams, Harry Welton of the Economic League, W.F.K. Thompson, Ernest Wistrich of the European Movement, Crozier's deputy at the ISoC Michael Goodwin, and student organizer turned stockbroker Ian Taylor.
94. 'East–West Negotiations', *Burlington Free Press*, 30 November 1972.
95. "die Stärke und Einheit der westlichen Allianz eine entscheidende Voraussetzung für erfolgreiche Verhandlungen mit dem Osten sei": 'Information über Situation und Aktivitäten von Interdok', 1972, MfS Hauptverwaltung Aufklärung-90, Bundesbeauftragter für die Unterlagen des Staatssicherheitsdienstes der ehemaligen Deutschen Demokratischen Republik, Berlin.
96. 'American–European Relations vis-a-vis Communist Objectives in Europe', 17–18 November 1972, conference booklet, pp.33–34; Bell to Van den Heuvel, 21 April 1972, File: 115 Walter Bell 1972, Groot-Britannië (1959–1985), CC NAH; Van den

Heuvel to Kernig, Lades, and von Grote, 4 December 1972, File: Reis Amerika 16–19 November 1972 Valley Forge, in author's possession.

8 Interdoc Reconfigures: The 1970s and Détente

1. C.C. van den Heuvel, *East–West Confrontation: A Psychological Strategy* (The Hague: Interdoc, 1967), p. 8.
2. Ibid., p. 1.
3. For the American side of this story see Sarah Snyder, *Human Rights Activism and the End of the Cold War: A Transnational History of the Helsinki Network* (Cambridge: Cambridge University Press, 2011).
4. Van den Heuvel to Crozier, 2 May 1975, File: 91 Brian Crozier 1961–1976, Groot-Britannië (1959–1985), archive of C.C. van den Heuvel, National Archives, The Hague (hereafter CC NAH); Oost-West Instituut, Annual Report (Jaarverslag) 1973, p. 3. The declaration that Interdoc would be reduced to the international section of the OWI was stated only in the Dutch-language version and *not* in the English-language version of the 1973 Annual Report.
5. W.F.K. Thompson, 'Dealing with the wolf in the fold', *Daily Telegraph*, 28 August 1972.
6. 'Minutes of the Interdoc Board Meeting in The Hague May 12, 1972', File: 220 Einde Interdoc 1970–1973, Overige Dossiers betreffende Interdoc, CC NAH.
7. Van den Heuvel to Hoheisel, 1 August 1972, File: 220 Einde Interdoc 1970–1973, Overige Dossiers betreffende Interdoc, CC NAH.
8. The Arbeitskreis had close relations with the Arbeitsgruppe Volk und Verteidigung, the "sister organization" to Hornix's Volk en Verdediging, which aimed to unite citizens with the military.
9. Oost-West Institut, Annual Report (Jaarverslag) 1973, p. 4; Van den Heuvel to J. Kortenhorst (chair, Atlantische Commissie), 3 September 1974, File 40: Correspondence 1974–76, archive of the Atlantische Commissie, Semi-Statische Archiefdiensten, Ministry of Defence, Rijswijk (hereafter AC).
10. The final accounts for 1978 show a total of 40,000 guilders from Dutch companies instead of the proposed 45,000, indicating that one or other of them cut back on their contribution. 'Begroting 1978' and 'Staat van Baten en Lasten 1978', File: 246 Financiën OWI 1969–1979, Financieel beheer, CC NAH.
11. 'Gesprek met de Secretaris-Generaal van Defensie op 26 Jan. 1971', File: 277 Ministerie van Defensie, Nederland, CC NAH; Micha Kat and Tom Nierop, 'Gegoochel met Geld voor Oorlogsinvaliden', *De Krant op Zondag*, 6 January 1991, p. 9. In 1973 the internal communications department of the Dutch Navy contracted OWI to contribute to its training programme for the first time.
12. Dan McMichael let it be known in March 1976 that "I am not certain just how we can be helpful to your various enterprises", indicating a lack of consensus on Van den Heuvel's activities. Another source may have come through Edward J. Rozek of the Edward Teller Foundation, a contact of Shell's Jeremy Russell, but it is not clear if the Foundation ever provided funding. File: 246 Financiën OWI 1969–1979, Financieel beheer, CC NAH; Van den Heuvel to Bell, 6 July 1973, and Van den Heuvel to Bell, 30 July 1974, File: 116 Walter Bell 1973–74, Groot-Britannië (1959–1985), CC NAH; McMichael to Van den Heuvel, 29 March 1976, File: 117 Walter Bell 1975–80, Groot-Britannië (1959–1985), CC NAH.

13. 'Nederlands Instituut voor Studie van en Informatie over Oost-West Betrekkingen (Oost-West Instituut)', n.d. [1978], in author's possession; Bell to Van den Heuvel, 10 November 1973, File: 116 Walter Bell 1973–74, Groot-Britannië (1959–1985), CC NAH; Van den Heuvel to Bell, 8 March 1978, File: 117 Walter Bell 1975–80, Groot-Britannië (1959–1985), CC NAH.
14. 'INTERDOC', pamphlet, 1973.
15. 'Staat van Baten en Lasten 1976', File: 246 Financiën OWI 1969–1979, Financieel beheer, CC NAH.
16. On van Eeghen see Willem Oltmans, *Zaken Doen: notities van een ooggetuige* (Baarn: In den Toren, 1986). The Voorhees reference then follows this. On Dartmouth see James Voorhees, *Dialogue Sustained: The Multilevel Peace Process and the Dartmouth Conference* (Washington, DC: United States Institute of Peace Press, 2002).
17. Oost-West Instituut, Annual Report (Jaarverslag) 1973, p. 4. The Institute was formed in 1970 and has been primarily focused on forging transatlantic contacts. Its major sponsors include the Federation of German Industry and the Swiss–American Chamber of Commerce.
18. Van den Heuvel to Häggman, 1 November 1973, File: 80 Algemeen 1973–1978, Zweden (1958–1978), CC NAH; File: 145 ASIS 1972–1974, België (1961–1977), CC NAH. Häggman supplied Major Per Lindgren as a counter-infiltration expert for the Esso meeting. ASIS was founded in 1955 as an organization dedicated to professionalizing and improving the effectiveness of corporate security systems: see http://www.asisonline.org/about/history/index.xml (accessed 11 January 2012).
19. Other names had been suggested over the years: *Atlantica*, *Ontmoeting* (Meeting), *Dialoog*, and *Vrede en Ontwikkeling* (Peace and Development). 'Aanvulling: Toekomst "Oost-West"', n.d. [1969], 'Kort verslag van de Raad van Advies op 26 februari 1970', 2 March 1970, 'Concentratie van periodieken op het terrein van nationale en mondiale burgerschapsvorming', File: Oost-West 1961–1971, in author's possession.
20. 'Oprichting vereniging Civis Mundi', n.d. [1970], 'Mededelingen', 10 November 1970, and 'Kort verslag vergadering Raad van Advies op 17 december 1970', File: Oost-West 1961–1971.
21. Oost-West Instituut, Annual Report (Jaarverslag) 1971, pp. 21–22; Oost-West Instituut, Annual Report (Jaarverslag) 1974, p. 4; Willem Couwenberg, interview with the author, Rotterdam, 21 October 2004.
22. On the formation of the ATA see Valérie Aubourg, 'Creating the Texture of the Atlantic Community: The NATO Information Service, private Atlantic networks and the Atlantic Community in the 1950s', in V. Aubourg, G. Bossuat, and G. Scott-Smith (eds), *European Community, Atlantic Community?* (Paris: Soleb, 2008), pp. 404–405.
23. Anthony Dake, interview with the author, The Hague, 26 July 2005.
24. Remco van Diepen, *'Beschaafd ageren voor de NAVO': 50 Jaar Atlantische Commissie* (The Hague: Atlantische Commissie, 2002), pp. 62–69.
25. 'Nota van Voorlichtingsadviseur Atlantische Commissie', 1 October 1975, and J. Kortenhorst (Secretary) to Atlantic Committee board members, 30 August 1974, File: 269 Atlantische Commissie 1974–87, Nederland, CC NAH; L.J. Meiresonne, 'Defensievoorlichting Doorgelicht', 3 February 1973, File: 266 Volk en Verdediging 1971–1978, Nederland, CC NAH; A.C.A. Dake, 'Information tasks of members of ATA', September 1972, Box 9: 1971–73 & 1976–77, AC;

Henk Aben, 'Storm om de Atlantische Commissie', *Algemeen Dagblad*, 30 August 1975.
26. 'De Geloofwaardigheid van de NAVO', April 1974, File: 269 Atlantische Commissie 1974–87, Nederland, CC NAH; 'Verslag van het plenaire vergadering', 18 November 1974, Box 10: 1974–79, AC.
27. 'Verslag van de vergadering van het Dagelijks Bestuur', 28 June 1976, Box 10: 1974–79, AC.
28. 'Verslag van de vergadering van de Onderwijs Commissie', 3 December 1976, Box 10: 1974–79, AC.
29. 'Verslag van de vergadering van het Dagelijks Bestuur', 8 November 1977, Box 9: 1971–73 & 1976–77, AC.
30. 'Voorlichtingsactiviteiten die van 1 September 1974 af door het Oost-West Instituut verzorgd zullen worden', 30 August 1974, 'Richtlijnen Voorlichting t.b.v. Atlantische Commissie', 1 October 1974, and 'Detente and the Information Policy of the Atlantic Alliance', File: 269 Atlantische Commissie 1974–87, Nederland, CC NAH; 'Verslag van de Vergadering van het Dagelijks Bestuur', 6 June 1977, Box 9: 1971–73 & 1976–77, AC; Van Diepen, *Beschaafd ageren voor de NAVO*, p. 76.
31. 'Visit to London, 7–9 July 1966', File: 89 Reisverslagen 1963–1968, Groot-Britannië (1959–1985), CC NAH; Van den Heuvel to Ellis, 25 July 1966, File: 95 C.H. (Dick) Ellis 1966, Groot-Britannië (1959–1985), CC NAH.
32. 'Verslag van de Vergadering van het Dagelijks Bestuur', 8 December 1977, Box 9: 1971–73, 1976–77, AC; Van den Heuvel to Bell, 4 September 1972, File: 220 Einde Interdoc 1970–1973, Overige Dossiers betreffende Interdoc, CC NAH.
33. Van den Heuvel to Bell, 15 March 1976, File: 117 Walter Bell 1975–78.
34. 'Nota Activiteit Voorlichtingsadviseur Atlantische Commissie', 28 October 1975, File: 269 Atlantische Commissie 1974–87, Nederland, CC NAH; 'Doel, taak en opzet van de Atlantische Commissie', Informatiemap, 1975, File: 268 Atlantische Commissie 1971–75, Nederland, CC NAH; 'Advisory Committee on Conference Matters', October 1977, Box 9: 1971–73 & 1976–77, AC; C.C. van den Heuvel, 'Veranderende Oost-West-Verhoudingen en Percepties', *JASON*, 1 (December 1975), p. 15; 'Curriculum Vitae', File: 242 Rio Praaning 1975–1990, Persoonsdossier, CC NAH; Rio Praaning, interview with the author, Brussels, 7 November 2005.
35. One of the early JASON newsletters included an article by Pacifist–Socialist MP Fred van de Spek on the military–industrial complex which drew a critical phone call from NATO's Information Service in Brussels. Winfried van den Muisenbergh, interview with the author, Middelburg, 9 January 2009.
36. *Jasonde* (report on JASON activities), 1976, Box 11: 1971–76, AC.
37. 'Verslag van de Vergadering van het Dagelijks Bestuur', 22 December 1980, Box 12: 1978, 1980–81, AC.
38. Praaning to Barend Biesheuvel (Chairperson AC), 17 December 1976, Box 10: 1974–79, AC.
39. Max van Weezel, 'ALCM, ICBM, MBFR, Ach, ik heb er zelf ook altijd een zakboekje bij', *Vrij Nederland*, 8 December 1979. In this detailed, carefully worded but clearly politically motivated article Van Weezel sketched Praaning's role and the Committtee's location fully in terms of the context of the OWI and Interdoc.
40. Neither, interestingly enough, had Leonid Brezhnev. See William Bundy, *A Tangled Web: The Making of Foreign Policy in the Nixon Presidency* (New York: Hill & Wang, 1998), pp. 255–259.

Notes 331

41. Crozier to Van den Heuvel, 5 October 1971, and Van den Heuvel to Crozier, 11 October 1971, File: 91 Brian Crozier 1961–1976, Groot-Britannië (1959–1985), CC NAH.
42. 'Minutes of the Interdoc Board Meeting in The Hague May 12, 1972,' File: 220 Einde Interdoc 1970–1973, Overige Dossiers betreffende Interdoc, CC NAH.
43. Raymond Aron to Alain Peyrefitte, n.d. [early 1973], Box 113: Hollande – Amsterdam, Section: Conférences/*colloques* (invitations refusées), archive of Raymond Aron, NAF 28060, Bibliothèque Nationale, Paris (hereafter Aron).
44. Bell to Van den Heuvel, 20 September 1972, File: 115 Walter Bell 1972, Groot-Britannië (1959–1985), CC NAH.
45. Henk Hergarden, interview with the author, Berlicum, 30 July 2005; Henk Hergarden, 'Met beide benen op de grond', in *Strijdbaar toen en nu: Vriendenbundel bij de 80ste verjaardag van Kees van den Heuvel*, p. 38; Pieter Koerts, interviews with the author, Leiden, 24 June 2009 and 29 June 2011.
46. A brochure, 'America the Beautiful', was produced by the foundation in 1976 advertising transatlantic offers by KLM. As Van den Heuvel remarked in the foreword: "There is widespread misunderstanding about America. Providing correct information can help to counteract this."
47. 'Stichting Nederland-Verenigde Staten: Informatiebulletin', 1973, personal archive of H.G. Groenewald (hereafter HG).
48. Henk Hergarden, interview with the author, Berlicum, 30 July 2005; Henk Hergarden, 'Met beide benen op de grond', in *Strijdbaar toen en nu: Vriendenbundel bij de 80ste verjaardag van Kees van den Heuvel*, p. 38; and 'De Stichting Nederland-Verenigde Staten', unpublished memoir.
49. C.C. van den Heuvel, 'Terugblik en Toekomst', 22 November 1977, HG; "ter bevordering van een blijvende aanwezigheid van de Verenigde Staten in Europe": C.C. van den Heuvel, 'Solidariteit met VS moet bevorderd', *NRC Handelsblad*, 19 November 1973.
50. Jantiena Fieyra, interview with the author, Amsterdam, 26 June 2009.
51. Casey to Groenewald, 17 January 1975, HG; 'Federation of European–American Organizations', August 1977, HG; 'Report of the FEAO Assembly Meeting, 21–23 October 21–22–23 1977, Bordeaux, France', HG; FEAO, 'A Declaration of Principles and Objectives', 15 January 1977, HG; Roger Beardwood to Prince Cyrille Makinsky, 25 November 1977, HG; 'Minutes of the Meeting, FEAO Board of Governors, Paris, July 11, 1978', HG; Henk Hergarden, interview with the author, Berlicum, 30 July 2005.
52. Two other veterans' organizations for former resistance members existed, representing each side of the Cold War divide. The World Veterans Federation, founded in Paris in November 1950, represented West European, North and South American, and African nations (the Dutch representative was Van den Heuvel's close friend Willem van Lanschot). The Fédération Internationale des Résistants (FIR), formed in response in Vienna in 1951, was dominated by communist sympathizers and included members from the Soviet bloc.
53. The conference, whose participants included Simon Wiesenthal, featured on its programme a dinner offered by 'Interdoc' in The Hague on 25 May. For a report of the event see 'La VIIIme conférence internationale de la Résistance et de la Déportation', *Le Soir*, 2 June 1970.
54. 'Resistance and Youth', Berlin Congress 17–20 July 1974, File: 38 Jeugd en Verzet 1970–1974, Internationale jeugdzaken, CC NAH.

55. Alphonse Max, *Tupamaros: A Pattern for Urban Guerrilla Warfare in Latin America* (The Hague: Interdoc, 1970), and *Guerrillas in Latin America* (The Hague: Interdoc, 1971).
56. Van den Heuvel to Dr N. Ørvik, 20 February 1970, File: 163 Algemeen 1967–1976, Noorwegen (1967–1978), Norway, CC NAH.
57. Oost-West Instituut: Jaarverslag 1971, pp. 16–17. This was also picked up by the press, which asked whether the New Left was now being targeted by the government as a threat to the state. See 'Staatsgevaarlijk?', *Het Vrije Volk*, 8 March 1971.
58. Crozier to Van den Heuvel, 19 April 1972, and Van den Heuvel to Crozier, 29 June 1972. Crozier was also in touch with former OWI employee Bart van der Laan, who was at the time with the Dutch Ministry of Defence. The list of contacts Van den Heuvel provided for Crozier's Study Group gives an interesting insight into his links at this time. On Germany: Hoheisel; on Italy: Ligue Internationale de la Liberté's Ivan Matteo Lombardo; on Belgium: Hubert Halin, secretary general of the UIRD; on Switzerland: Hans Ulmer of the Schweizerischer Aufklärungsdienst; on Denmark: former IY contact P.A. Heegaard-Poulsen; on Sweden: former IY contact Bertil Häggman. File: 91 Brian Crozier 1961–1976, Groot-Britannië (1959–1985), CC NAH.
59. Ellis to Van den Heuvel, 21 January 1969, File: 98 C.H. (Dick) Ellis 1969, Groot-Britannië (1959–1985), CC NAH.
60. On the military career of Thompson, who died in 1980, see http://www.unithistories.com/officers/1AirbDiv_officersT.htm (accessed 19 February 2009).
61. 'Politics, Violence, and the Threat to International Law and Order: Summary', G.L. [Gordon Lett], File 38 Jeugd en Verzet 1970–1974, Internationale Jeugdzaken, CC NAH.
62. Lett's explanation of the need for this anti-subversion campaign drew direct links between the experience of resistance movements in World War II and the continuation of that form of irregular warfare by certain units in Europe: the Norwegians, the Danish Home Guard (which trained with the SAS), Luxembourg, and Belgium, "where much attention is given in the training of Reserve Forces to 'stay behind' operations reminiscent of the underground rescue and escape lines that served their purpose so well during the last war". 'Politics, Violence, and the Threat to International Law and Order,' G.L. [Gordon Lett], File 38 Jeugd en Verzet 1970–1974, Internationale Jeugdzaken, CC NAH.
63. Handwritten note, n.d., ibid.
64. Bell to Van den Heuvel, 16 October 1972, File 38 Jeugd en Verzet 1970–1974, Internationale Jeugdzaken, CC NAH.
65. Van den Heuvel to Häggman, 6 January 1965, File: 79 Algemeen 1962–1966, Zweden (1958–1978), CC NAH.
66. See for instance B. Häggman, *Sweden's Maoist Subversives: A Case Study* (London: Institute for the Study of Conflict, 1975). Bertil Häggman, *For Freedom against Totalitarianism: The Great Triumph*, self-published memoir, 2000; Häggman to Mennes, 3 January 1966, File: 79 Algemeen 1962–1966, Zweden (1958–1978), CC NAH; Bertil Häggman, telephone interview with the author, 4 December 2008; 'How to improve America's Image in Sweden', n.d. [1966], personal papers of Bertil Häggman; Bertil Häggman, interview with the author, Copenhagen, 30 September 2011.

67. Van den Heuvel to Häggman, 22 December 1975, 'Film on Left Wing Extremism,' February 1976, and 'Bertil Häggman', File: 80 Algemeen 1973–1978, Zweden (1958–1978), CC NAH.
68. Rolf Geyer, 'Some Thoughts on Communist Policy', Hans Lades, 'Reform as a form of revolution', and C.C. van den Heuvel, 'Suggestions for a Western Response', in *Communist Reassessment of Capitalism, its Resultant Strategy and the Western Response* (The Hague: Interdoc, 1968).
69. C.C. van den Heuvel, 'Oost-Europa en Ontspanning en Veiligheid', September 1969, in author's possession.
70. Rolf Geyer, 'Neutralism and East–West Détente: Wishful Thinking or Reality?' in *Neutralism and East–West Détente: Wishful Thinking or Reality?* (The Hague: Interdoc, 1969), pp. 16, 19.
71. Rolf Geyer, 'Summary', in *National Views on Neutralism and East–West Détente* (The Hague: Interdoc, 1970), pp. 108, 109. The conference booklet included contributions from Gerald Steibel (US), Alan Lee Williams (UK), Nicolas Lang (France), Hans Lades (West Germany), A. Camponeschi (Italy), Eric Waldman (Canada), P.A. Heegaard-Poulsen (Scandinavia), F.C. Spits (Netherlands), Hans Graf (Switzerland), Etsuo Kohtani (Japan/Asia), and Uwe Holl (Interdoc Youth).
72. Uwe Holl, interview with the author, Cologne, 18 December 2005.
73. C.C. van den Heuvel, R.D. Praaning, and F.Z.R. Wijchers, *Implementation of the Conference on Security and Cooperation in Europe Part I* (The Hague: East–West Institute, 1976), pp. 3–4.
74. See Matthew Evangelista, *Unarmed Forces: The Transnational Movement to End the Cold War* (Ithaca, NY: Cornell University Press, 1999).
75. File: 275 Bijeenkomsten en Lezingen 1974–1985, Nederland, CC NAH.
76. 'Overzicht van binnengekomen bedragen voor Interdoc conferentie Noordwijk, 21/22 september 1973', File: 247 Noordwijk 1973, Financieel beheer, CC NAH.
77. Van den Heuvel to Ellis, 30 October 1973, File: 98 C.H. (Dick) Ellis 1969, Groot-Britannië (1959–1985), CC NAH; C.C. van den Heuvel (ed.), *Development of East–West Relations through Freer Movement of People, Ideas and Information* (The Hague: Interdoc, 1973), pp. 7, 11, 14, 18, 31, 54. The line-up in the publication was Berkhouwer, Kuznetsov, J. van der Valk (Dutch Ministry of Foreign Affairs), Meissner, and Reverend Michael Bordeaux (Director, Centre for the Study of Religion and Communism, UK). Berkhouwer had actually been third choice behind Foreign Minister Max van der Stoel and NATO Secretary General Joseph Luns, neither of whom could make it. Kuznetsov's contribution was also written up in the *Economist*'s Foreign Report (26 September 1973) via Noordwijk participant Kenneth Mackenzie.
78. Van den Heuvel to Ambassador A.I. Romanov, 6 May 1974, Van den Heuvel to G.J. van Hattum (Bureau Oost-Europa), 4 October 1974, and Van den Heuvel to Ambassador A.I. Romanov, 5 November 1974, File: 210 Moskou 1974, Sovjet-Unie (1974–1985), CC NAH; Van den Heuvel to Bell, 14 October 1974, File: 116 Walter Bell 1973–74, CC NAH.
79. 'Soviet Perceptions of the West and NATO', 10 November 1974, File: 210 Moskou 1974, Sovjet Unie (1974–1985), CC NAH.
80. Ibid.; Van den Heuvel to Bell, 31 October 1974, File: UK 4b, Walter Bell 1973–74, Groot-Britannië (1959–1985), CC NAH.
81. For instance, 'Voorlichting Atlantische Commissie', *Economisch Dagblad*, 7 January 1975, which included a long quote from his Moscow report, was written by "special contact" W. Schaap at that newspaper following a prompting

letter from Van den Heuvel. See list of media contacts in File: 269 Atlantische Commissie 1974–87, Nederland, CC NAH.
82. Rio Praaning, interview with the author, Brussels, 7 November 2005.
83. Van den Heuvel to Geyer, 3 May 1968, File: 66 H.J. Geyer 1965–1972, Duitsland (1958–1978), CC NAH.
84. For instance, the Polish ambassador to the Netherlands in the early 1970s was Włodzimierz Lechowicz, a former resistance fighter.
85. SUBNOR stood for Savez Udruzenjan Boraca Narodno Oslobodilackog Rata Jugoslavije (Federation of War Veterans of the People's Liberation of Yugoslavia). In May 1975 Van den Heuvel would also link up with a Soviet veterans' delegation that visited the Netherlands for the 30th anniversary of the end of World War II. Van den Heuvel to Tarik Ajanovic (Ambassador to the Netherlands), 8 August 1975, File: 214 Jugoslavië 1975–1979, Overige Communistische Landen (1973–1985), CC NAH.
86. Van den Heuvel to Prof. M. Dobrosielski, 30 August 1976, File: 215 Polen 1975–1985, Overige Communistische Landen (1973–1985), CC NAH; Van den Heuvel to Dr M. Sahovic, 31 August 1976, File: 214 Jugoslavië 1975–1979, Overige Communistische Landen (1973–1985), CC NAH.
87. Van den Heuvel to Henk Aben, 3 September 1979, File: 216 Bulgarije 1977–1979, Overige Communistische Landen (1973–1985), CC NAH.
88. 'Visit at Polski Instytut Spraw Miedzynarodowyck (Polish Institute of International Relations)', September 1977, File: 215 Polen 1975–1985, Overige Communistische Landen (1973–1985), CC NAH.
89. Van den Heuvel claimed to Ellis that "we had our hand in the invitation" to Professor Leontiev of the Moscow Economics Academy to deliver a lecture in Tilburg on Russian industrial development in June 1965, which Mieli attended. Van den Heuvel to Ellis, 11 August 1965, File: 106 Financiën 1964–1969, Groot-Britannië (1959–1985), CC NAH.
90. Frans Alting von Geusau, interview with the author, Leiden, 11 March 2009.
91. 'Second Report', p. 2, File: JFK Circulaires 1966 tot 1-9-1967, archive of the JFK Institute, Tilburg University (hereafter JFK).
92. Ibid., p. 8.
93. Willem Couwenberg, interview with the author, Rotterdam, 21 October 2004; Rio Praaning, interview with the author, Brussels, 7 November 2005.
94. Embree, who appeared on the scene in 1962 out of curiosity over who was producing *Oost-West*, ended up paying rent from 1966 onwards for office space at Van Stolkweg. By all accounts he remained an independent operator running his own press bureau. Willem Couwenberg, interview with the author, Rotterdam, 21 October 2004; Rio Praaning, interview with the author, Brussels, 7 November 2005; George Embree, interviews with the author, The Hague, 15 March 2004 and 21 October 2004.
95. Van den Heuvel to Geyer, 3 May 1968, and Geyer to Van den Heuvel, 15 May 1968, File: 66 H.J. Geyer 1965–1972, Duitsland (1958–1978), CC NAH.
96. 'Mededelingen', 10 November 1970, File: Oost-West 1961–1971; Oost-West Instituut: Jaarverslag 1970, pp. 22–23.
97. Alting von Geusau, 'First Report on Activities', August 1966, File: Correspondentie 1-4-1967 tot 1-7-1967, JFK.
98. Frans Alting von Geusau, interview with the author, Oisterwijk, 5 June 2002.
99. Alting von Geusau, March 1968, File: JFK Circulaires 11-9-1967 tot 1-9-1968, JFK.
100. File: JFK Circulaires 1-9-1967 tot 1-9-1968, JFK.

101. Jurrjens to Raymond Aron, 28 January 1975, Box 113: Hollande – Amsterdam, Section: Conférences/*colloques* (invitations refusées), Aron.
102. The closest he came to doing so is in the recent publication F.A.H. Alting von Geusau, *Cultural Diplomacy: Waging War by other Means?* (Nijmegen: Wolf, 2009).
103. Max van Weezel, 'ALCM, ICBM, MBFR, Ach, ik heb er zelf ook altijd een zakboekje bij', *Vrij Nederland*, 8 December 1979.
104. Frans Alting von Geusau, interview with the author, Oisterwijk, 16 February 2011.
105. Rudolf Jurrjens, 'The Free Flow: People, Ideas and Information in Soviet Ideology and Politics', Ph.D. dissertation, Free Vrij Universiteit, Amsterdam, 1978, p. 14.
106. There is a letter from Van den Heuvel to Damman declining the invitation for himself and Mennes to attend an Académie conference in Antibes in September 1972. With the US conference only two months away and money in short supply in 1972, Van den Heuvel had plenty of reasons to turn it down, but it also fits his caution against becoming too embroiled in the networks of rightwing anti-communism – unless, as with the WACL, he could tap into their networks for his own purposes. Van den Heuvel to Damman, 25 August 1972, 'For a True and Lasting Peace', Pinay Circle Declaration, January 1973, 'Un Appel de l'Académie Européenne de Sciences Politiques sur la Sécurité Européenne', *Le Monde*, 21 June 1973, File: 146 Académie Européenne de Sciences Politiques 1972–1977, België (1961–1977), CC NAH; Johannes Grossman, 'Ein Europa der "Hintergründigen": Antikommunistische christliche Organisationen, konservative Elitenzirkel und private Außenpolitik in Westeuropa nach dem Zweiten Weltkrieg', in Johannes Wienand and Christianne Wienand (eds), *Die kulturelle Integration Europas* (Springer: VS Verlag, 2010), pp. 335–336.
107. 'Ultra rechts lonkt naar Nederland', *Het Vrije Volk*, 12 January 1984.
108. Brian Crozier, Max Beloff, and Robert Conquest, *European Security and the Soviet Problem* (London: Institute for the Study of Conflict, 1970), pp. 14, 39; Brian Crozier, *Free Agent: The Unseen War 1941–1991* (London: HarperCollins, 1993), pp. 82, 96.
109. Bell to Van den Heuvel, 16 October 1974, File: 116 Walter Bell 1973–1974, Groot-Britannië (1959–1985), CC NAH; Bell to Van den Heuvel, n.d. [1976], File: 117 Walter Bell 1975–80, Groot-Britannië (1959–1985), CC NAH. Mott remained a valuable if erratic contact. In 1977 the OWI and the American Bar Association published *Soviet Perceptions of Western Realities*, a translation of an official Soviet handbook, for which Mott overruled opposition on the ABA board after Crozier had rejected the project.
110. 'The New Concept of Security for Europe', March 1974, and conference programme, File: 122 Ditchley Park 1974–1975, Groot-Britannië (1959–1985), CC NAH; Van den Heuvel to Crozier, 2 May 1975, File: 91 Brian Crozier 1961–1976, Groot-Britannië (1959–1985), CC NAH.
111. Boris Meissner, *The Soviet Conception of Coexistence and the Conference on Security and Cooperation in Europe* (The Hague: East–West Institute, 1974), p. 14; Zacharias Anthonisse, *Communistische Vreedzame Coëxistentie* (The Hague: SOEV, 1963).
112. "Naar de opvattingen van degenen die internationale betrekkingen bestuderen, wordt in toenemende mate geluisterd." 'Détente, het Oost-West Instituut en enkele Projecten', n.d. [1975], in author's possession
113. Crozier, *Free Agent*, p. 104.

114. Van Eeghen's letter was dictated by Van den Heuvel himself. Van Eeghen to Barnett, 30 November 1976, and Couwenberg to G.J.B. Kleinsman, 30 November 1976, File: 91 Brian Crozier 1961–1976, Groot-Britannië (1959–1985), CC NAH; Van den Heuvel to Bell, 30 November 1976, File: 117 Walter Bell 1975–80, Groot-Britannië (1959–1985), CC NAH.
115. Bertil Häggman, telephone interview with the author, 4 December 2008.
116. The Soviets were not the only ones interested. In 1973 a positive article about the OWI was published in the Polish *Studia Nauk Politycznych*, 14/4.
117. The Dutch group consisted of Van den Heuvel, Couwenberg, Mennes, journalist George Embree, businessman Ernst H. van Eeghen, the chairman of the Netherlands Association for the UN H.E. Scheffer, and international law researcher Wallis de Vries. 'Meeting Soviet Committee for European Security and Cooperation with East–West Institute on 21 November 1974', File: 211 Sovjet-Comité voor Europese Weiligheid en Samenwerking, Sovjet-Unie (1974–1985), CC NAH; Questionnaire for SCESC visit, November 1974, File: 210 Moskou 1974, Sovjet-Unie (1974–1985), CC NAH.
118. 'Détente, het Oost-West Instituut en enkele Projecten', n.d. [1975], in author's possession; Van den Heuvel to N. Pankov (Soviet Committee for European Security and Cooperation), 2 May 1977, File: 211 Sovjet Comité voor Europese Veiligheid en Samenwerking, Sovjet-Unie (1974–1985), CC NAH. In 1978 the volume *The Belgrade Conference: Progress or Regression?*, edited by Van den Heuvel and Rio Praaning, was published with contributions from Gerhard Wettig, the US Congress's American Commission on Security and Cooperation in Europe, Soviet researcher Dr V. Lomeiko, and Dr L. Acimovic of the Yugoslav Institute for International Relations.
119. C.C. van den Heuvel, R.D. Praaning, & F.Z.R. Wijchers, *Implementation of the Conference on Security and Cooperation in Europe, Part I* (The Hague: OWI, 1976); C.C. van den Heuvel, R.D. Praaning, P. Vaillant, & F.Z.R. Wijchers, *Part II* (1977); F.Z.R. Wijchers, *Part III* (1977).
120. 'Meeting with Delegation of Soviet Committee for Security and Cooperation in Europe, Tuesday June 6 1978', File: 275 Bijeenkomsten en Lezingen 1974–1985, Nederland, CC NAH.
121. J.W. van der Meulen, 'Commentaar: Het Oost-West Instituut als spreekbuis van het Kremlin', *Internationale Spectator*, 30 (December 1976), pp. 748–750. See the subsequent sharp exchange between Van den Heuvel and Van der Meulen in 'Commentaar: Een merkwaardige insinuatie', *Internationale Spectator*, 31 (February 1977), pp. 122–125.
122. Gerrit Pietersen, *Afghanistan is Our World* (The Hague: Interdoc, 1981), pp. 7–8. It was intended to be a direct riposte to *The Truth about Afghanistan* (Moscow: Novosty Press Agency, 1980).
123. Bildt to Interdoc, 14 February 1974, Van den Heuvel to Bildt, 1 March 1974, Maltby to Van den Heuvel, 12 November 1974, 'Gesprek met twee vertegenwoordigers van ECCS op 12 december 1974', Bildt to Van den Heuvel, 9 August 1975, and 'Talk with Carl BILDT', 27 August 1975, File: 37 ICCS EDS ECCS 1970–1977, Internationale jeugdzaken, CC NAH.
124. Van den Heuvel to Bell, 6 July 1977, File: 117 Walter Bell 1975–80, Groot-Britannië (1959–1985), CC NAH.
125. Floribert Baudet, ' "Het heeft onze aandacht": Nederland en de Rechten van de Mens in Oost-Europa en Joegoslavië 1971–1989', Ph.D. Dissertation, Utrecht University, 2001, pp. 259, 262; 'De rechten van de mens in het

buitenlands beleid', Tweede Kamer der Staten-Generaal, zitting 1978–79, 15 571 nrs. 1–2.
126. 'Toelichting', n.d. [1978], and 'Centrum voor CVSE-Informatie', n.d. [1978], File: CEVS, CC NAH.
The appeal for finance went out under the names of van der Stoel (Labour Party), Laurens Jan Brinkhorst (Democrats 66), Ad Ploeg (Liberal Party, VVD), and Joep Mommersteeg (Christian Democratic Party, CDA).
127. 'Secretariaat/Centrum CVSE Informatie', n.d. [1978], File: CEVS, CC NAH.
128. Van den Heuvel to Dake, 1 November 1978, File: CEVS, CC NAH.
129. 'Persbericht' and 'Verslag van de Vergadering van de Initiatiefgroep Centrum Europese Veiligheid en Samenwerking', 23 November 1978, File: CEVS, CC NAH.
130. Minutes of board meeting, 16 August 1979, File: CEVS Bestuursvergaderingen 1979–82, CC NAH.
131. 'Suggesties n.a.v. Nota betreffende de Internationale Culturele Betrekkingen', 3 January 1979, File: CEVS, CC NAH.
132. 'Activiteiten Rapport: Voorbereiding CVSE Centrum', 5 October 1978, File: CEVS, CC NAH; Minutes of board meeting, 24 June 1980, File: CEVS Bestuursvergaderingen 1979–82, CC NAH.
133. 'Conferentie Helsinki Monitor Instellingen', n.d. [1978], File: CEVS, CC NAH.
134. Minutes of board meeting, 23 July 1980, File: CEVS Bestuursvergaderingen 1979–82, CC NAH.
135. 'Centre for European Security and Cooperation (internationalization)', n.d. [1980], File: CEVS, CC NAH; Robert Weitzel, interview with the author, Amsterdam, 11 July 2006. Weitzel would also contribute one of the last 'Interdoc' publications, *A Soviet Dilemma: Soviet Jews, A Study in Jewish Emigration from the Soviet Union* (The Hague: CEVS, 1980).
136. Minutes of board meeting, 24 June 1980, File: CEVS Bestuursvergaderingen 1979–82, CC NAH.
137. Minutes of board meeting, 23 July 1980, File: CEVS Bestuursvergaderingen 1979–82, CC NAH.
138. Weitzel recalled later that Van der Stoel was probably to blame for the final collapse of CEVS: "we had a problem with him". C.C. van den Heuvel to board, 23 December 1982, File: CEVS Bestuursvergaderingen 1979–82, CC NAH; Noel to Van den Heuvel, 17 December 1982, and Van den Heuvel to C. Trajan (EC Commission), 14 February 1983, File: Algemene Correspondentie 1983, CC NAH; Robert Weitzel, interview with the author, Amsterdam, 11 July 2006. See also Arie Bloed and P. van Dijk (eds), *Essays on Human Rights in the Helsinki Process* (Leiden: Martinus Nijhoff, 1985).
139. 'De Nederlandse Atlantische Commissie: Schets van Voorlichtingstaal', Box 10: 1974–79, AC.
140. 'Aanzet tot een Beleidsnota van de Stichting Atlantische Commissie', 13 August 1980, Box 12: 1978, 1980–81, AC; 'Atlantische Eenheidsworst', *Vrij Nederland*, 5 July 1980; Joep Bik, interview with the author, The Hague, 1 February 2008. Bik, who went on the 1981 journalists' trip to Washington, DC, and several other tours organized by the US Embassy and NATO, was at the time diplomatic editor of the *NRC Handelsblad*, where the editorial staff was deeply divided on the deployment issue. Together with Rob Meines Bik was a key supporter of the NATO decision on the paper's editorial board.
141. Frank van den Heuvel (JASON executive board 1984–87), interview with the author, Middelburg, 13 June 2008.

338 Notes

142. *De Waarheid*, 29 October 1983; Rio Praaning, interview with the author, Brussels, 7 November 2005.
143. Dake wanted the Committee to function "as independently as possible" rather than strictly "objectively", giving it more leeway for political activism against its opponents. 'Verslag van de Vergadering van het Dagelijks Bestuur', 22 December 1980, Box 12: 1978, 1980–81, AC; Van Diepen, *Beschaafd ageren voor de NAVO*, pp. 76–77, 95–114.
144. 'Stichting Vredespolitiek', 5 May 1981, and 'Vrede is Duur' advertisement, *Trouw*, *Volkskrant* et al., 23 May 1981, Box 213: Overzicht Stichting Vredespolitiek, AC; Joris Voorhoeve, interview with the author, The Hague, 23 June 2010.
145. Teunissen to Praaning, 19 March 1981, and Praaning to Voorhoeve and Nederlof, 25 April 1981, Box 213: Overzicht Stichting Vredespolitiek, AC; Joris Voorhoeve, interview with the author, The Hague, 23 June 2010.
146. 'Enkele opmerkingen over mogelijke SVP-activiteiten,' n.d. [1981], 'Plan de Campagne', 1 April 1982, Box 213: Overzicht Stichting Vredespolitiek, AC; Winfried van den Muisenbergh, interview with the author, Middelburg, 9 January 2009.
147. 'Concurrentie bewegingen bestrijden monopolie van IKV', *NRC Handelsblad*, 10 October 1983; 'De opmars van rechts in de vredesbeweging', *Week-Uit*, 22 October 1983.
148. The EPPC was led by its founder, the conservative Ernest W. Lefever, who was notorious for opposing President Carter's human rights policy. The Dutch press picked up that USIA had given the EPPC at least $190,000 for its European activities. The SVP's total budget was reported to be 150,000 guilders a year in 1983. 'Concurrentie bewegingen bestrijden monopolie van IKV', *NRC Handelsblad*, 10 October 1983; 'VVD-Kamerlid Voorhoeve hekelt horizontale theologie', *Trouw*, 17 September 1983.
149. Winfried van den Muijsenbergh (SVP treasurer), interview with the author, Middelburg, 9 January 2009. Van den Heuvel did set up a splinter group of Geestelijke Weerbaarheid at this time called Order and Freedom (Gezag en Vrijheid), but this was a short-lived venture, too right-wing in outlook. The SVP's events calendar for late 1982 reports that the group's proposed demonstration against violence and terror in Amsterdam that October had to be cancelled because the mayor could not guarantee the safety of the participants.
150. See 'Dutch missile groups "financed from London" ', *The Guardian*, 26 June 1987, p. 3. SVP treasurer Winfried van den Muisenbergh does not recall any funding from London, but he does not exclude the possibility that a secret channel was opened up via SVP director (and former naval officer) Fred de Bree. Crozier had handed over the ISoC to former Ampersand Books editor Michael Goodwin in 1979.
151. The IKV was actually supported via Dutch government subsidies for development cooperation. On Soviet and GDR efforts to influence the Dutch debate on nuclear weapons see 'Nederland geliefd doelwit van communistische infiltratie', *Reformatorisch Dagblad*, Part I 15 July 1981, Part II 16 July 1981; Beatrice de Graaf, *Over de Muur: De DDR de Nederlandse Kerken en de Vredesbeweging* (Amsterdam: Boom, 2004).
152. For positive commentary see for instance 'Alternatief vredesberaad', *Het Parool*, 28 September 1982. The SVP's last event was the conference 'Perestroika – Opportunities for Real Détente?', held in September 1988. Voorhoeve was again a keynote speaker.

153. See 'Waar zakenwereld en wereld diplomatie 'samenvloeien', *Focus*, 8 March 2007, pp. 56–59. Praaning's NATO ambitions (he hoped for a position with the Information Service) were cut short due to his previous links with Eastern-bloc representatives – yet another indication of official suspicion of Van den Heuvel's "unorthodox" methods. One of Praaning's important customers as a consultant has always been the Sultanate of Oman. His first contact with that nation also came via Van den Heuvel. In 1976 Tony Ashworth, a UK diplomat, quit the Foreign Office to become a public relations adviser to Sultan Qaboos bin Said and himself hired former IRD official Hans Welser as his London-based associate. Welser was tasked to "select suitable visitors from the field of politics, academics, writers, and members of international bodies" for visits to Oman in order to promote greater appreciation of this rich oil state. Welser duly contacted Van den Heuvel, who, having his hands full with the OWI Post-Helsinki Monitor Project, passed the responsibility over to Praaning. He organized a visit of nine Dutch students (including JASON board member and future diplomat Kees Nederlof) to Oman in December 1977. Such were the relations between the Sultan and the Shah of Iran that, while there, the group were transported around by an Iranian military plane. The group's members were well aware of the propaganda nature of their trip. See Bell to Van den Heuvel, 3 October 1976 and Welser to Van den Heuvel, 16 May 1977, File: 123 J.L. Welser 1976–1978, Groot-Britannië (1959–1985), CC NAH; Winfried van den Muisenbergh, interview with the author, Middelburg, 9 January 2009.
154. The other members of the committee were Willem Ch.J.M. van Lanschot, E. Roest, and H.J. Teengs Gerritsen (a close friend of Prince Bernhard). *Gedenkboek Verzetsherdenkingskruis* (The Hague, Samson, 1985), pp. 15–20, 25–33; Micha Kat and Tom Nierop, 'Gegoochel met Geld voor Oorlogsinvaliden', *De Krant op Zondag*, 6 January 1991, p. 9.

Conclusion: Assessing the Legacy

1. C.C. van den Heuvel, 'Interdoc', n.d. [1964], File: Voorgeschiedenis Interdoc, in author's possession.
2. C.C. van den Heuvel, interview with the author, The Hague, 6 August 2002.
3. Van den Heuvel to G.L. Maaldrink, 25 January 1979, File: 224 Statutes 1962–1987, Organisatie, archive of C.C. van den Heuvel, National Archives, The Hague (hereafter CC NAH).
4. File: 164 Libertas 1975–1978, Noorwegen (1967–1978), CC NAH.
5. "Interdoc besteht noch immer auf Papier": Van den Heuvel to Kernig, 20 February 1979, and document winding up the Interdoc Foundation, 11 November 1986, File: 224 Statutes 1962–1987, Organisatie, CC NAH.
6. H.J. Teengs Gerritsen, W.J.C. Tensen, and J. Glaser to Algemene Loterij Nederland, 9 April 1984, A. van Emden to Van Stolkweg 10, 29 May 1984, and C.C. van den Heuvel, 'Memorandum: Dienstcentrum Organisaties Tweede Wereldoorlog Nederland,' 15 September 1986, File: 251 Dienstencentrum 1984–1990, Financieel beheer, CC NAH. There would be one final rift in this ageing network. In 1989 Van den Heuvel gave an interview in *Vrij Nederland* in which he suggested that there should be no special status for those who were imprisoned during World War II. Meant as a comment on the different experiences of resistance fighters and those who were arrested and ended up in the camps, it caused a storm of protest from those who thought he was belittling the torment

of the Jews. In fact he was only commenting on the internal divisions within the veterans' organizations.
7. "Dabei hat Interdok stets eine Zentrumposition eingenommen, d.h. Distanzierung vom Kalten Krieg einerzeits, allerdings andererzeits auch von Gutgläubigkeit, Naivität und Wunschdenken." Van den Heuvel to Brigadegeneraal Dr J. Gerber (Chancellery), 14 August 1972, File: 220 Einde Interdoc 1970–1973, Overige Dossiers betreffende Interdoc, CC NAH.
8. Discussion document, File: 308 psychologische oorlogvoering 1960–1967, Beschouwingen en Verslagen, CC NAH.
9. Thompson to Van den Heuvel, 16 June 1972, File: 120 Brigadier W.F.K. Thompson 1971–1980, Groot-Britannië (1959–1985), CC NAH; Ellis to Van den Heuvel, 26 September 1971, in author's possession; Bell to Van den Heuvel, 10 July 1976, File: 117 Walter Bell 1975–1980, Groot-Britannië (1959–1985), CC NAH.
10. Max van Weezel, 'ALCM, ICBM, MBFR. Ach, ik heb er zelf ook altijd een zakboekje bij', *Vrij Nederland*, 8 December 1979.
11. Ellis to Van den Heuvel, 10 September 2011, File: 98 C.H. (Dick) Ellis 1969, Groot-Britannië (1959–1985), CC NAH.
12. 'Comité Résistance et Jeunesse: Verantwoording voor Congres U.I.R.D. West-Berlijn, 1974', June 1974, File: 38 Jeugd en Verzet 1970–1974, Internationale jeugdzaken, CC NAH.
13. Professor W. Couwenberg, interview with the author, Middelburg, 7 November 2002.
14. 'Een beetje autoritair gezag werkt zeer heilzaam voor de zuidelijke landen', *De Nieuwe Linie*, 30 August 1969.
15. In particular Scott Lucas, *Freedom's War: America's Crusade against the Soviet Union* (Manchester: Manchester University Press, 1999); Frances Stonor Saunders, *Who Paid the Piper? The CIA and the Cultural Cold War* (London: Granta, 1999); Volker Berghahn, *America and the Intellectual Cold Wars in Europe* (New York: Berghahn Books, 2002).
16. Van den Heuvel to Ellis, 2 October 1967, File: 96 C.H. (Dick) Ellis 1967, Groot-Britannië (1959–1985), CC NAH.
17. Van den Heuvel to Häggman, 20 July 1976, File: 80 Algemeen 1973–1978, Zweden (1958–1978), CC NAH. Cosyns-Verhaegen was the author of many books on communist infiltration, including *Theory of Subversive Action* (Brussels: Les Ours, 1968).
18. Interdoc Progress Report 1968, p. 3; Oost-West Instituut: Jaarverslag 1970, The Hague, p. 24.
19. Van den Heuvel to Ku Cheng-Kang (WACL chairman), 20 August 1973, File: 9 WACL/APACL 1968–1976, Internationale Organisaties, CC NAH.
20. Bertil Häggman, telephone interview with the author, 4 December 2008.
21. 'Minutes of the Interdoc Board Meeting in The Hague May 12, 1972', File: 220 Einde Interdoc 1970–1973, Overige Dossiers betreffende Interdoc, CC NAH.
22. Max van Weezel, 'ALCM, ICBM, MBFR, Ach, ik heb er zelf ook altijd een zakboekje bij', *Vrij Nederland*, 8 December 1979.
23. Professor W. Couwenberg, interview with the author, Middelburg 7 November 2002.
24. J.M.M. Hornix and C.C. van den Heuvel, 'Een karakteristiek van de waarden van het westen, alsmede enkele gedachten over de mogelijkheden van bevordering van een blijvende invloed van deze waarden', September 1959, author's copy.
25. Van den Heuvel to Ellis, 10 April 1967, File: 96 C.H. (Dick) Ellis 1967, Groot-Britannië (1959–1985), CC NAH.

Bibliography

Interviews

F.A.M. Alting von Geusau, Oisterwijk, 5 June 2002 & 11 March 2009
Dirk Barth, Middelburg, 27 November 2007
Peter Becker, Tutzing, 9 April 2006
J.H. van den Berg, Antwerp, 6 March 2004
Hans Beuker, Houten, 3 September 2003
Gunhild Bohm-Geyer, Würthsee, 4 July 2008
M. Bolten, Wassenaar, 13 July 2006
Lyda van der Bree, The Hague, 22 January 2011
Wolfgang Buchow, Neuss, 10 January 2007
Wim Couwenberg, Middelburg, 7 November 2002, Rotterdam, 21 October 2004
Brian Crozier, London, 4 November 2004
Anthony Dake, The Hague, 26 July 2005
George Embree, The Hague, 15 March 2004 & 21 October 2004
Jantiena Fieyra, Amsterdam, 26 June 2009
Jos van Gennip, The Hague, 3 December 2007
Antoinette Gosses, Brussels, 23 April 2008
Edo Groenewald, Amsterdam, 16 June 2009
Bertil Häggman, Copenhagen, 30 September 2011
Alexander Heldring, The Hague, 30 June 2004
Henk Hergarden, Berlicum, 30 July 2005
Christiaan van den Heuvel, The Hague, 27 May 2009, Rockanje, 27 May 2009
C.C. (Cees) van den Heuvel, The Hague, 6 August 2002 & 18 September 2002
Frank van den Heuvel, Middelburg, 13 June 2008
Uwe Holl, Cologne, 18 December 2005 & 7 July 2006
Peter Keller, Brussels, 23 April 2008
Pieter Koerts, Amsterdam, 2 June 2004, Leiden, 24 June 2009
Gerd van Maanen, Leidschendam, 14 May 2004, 1 November 2006, & 8 April 2009
Chel Mertens, Amsterdam, 9 December 2003
Winfried van den Muisenbergh, Middelburg, 9 January 2009
Josephine O'Connor Howe, Charing, 20 July 2007
Sten Pålsson, telephone, 29 June 2012 & 13 July 2012
Rio Praaning, Brussels, 7 November 2005
Dietmar Töppel, Munich, 3 July 2008
Joris Voorhoeve, The Hague, 23 June 2010
Robert Weitzel, Amsterdam, 11 July 2006
Joop van der Wilden, The Hague, 26 July 2005
Karel van Wolferen, Amsterdam, 12 January 2005

Archives

Nationaal Archief, The Hague:

Papers of C.C. van den Heuvel

Papers of the Cabinet of the Minister-President (1944) 1945–1979
Papers of the Bilderberg Meetings
Papers of the Defensie Studie Centrum
Papers of E.H. van der Beugel

Royal Dutch Shell, The Hague:

Archive of Royal Dutch Shell

Algemene Inlichtingen en Veiligheidsdienst, The Hague:

Papers of the BVD (Freedom of Information Act requests)

Centraal Archieven Depot, Ministry of Defence, Rijswijk:

Archive of the Minister of Defence
Papers of the Atlantic Committee

Netherlands Institute for War Documentation, Amsterdam:

Papers of the National Federal Council for the Former Resistance in the Netherlands

International Institute of Social History, Amsterdam:

Papers of the International Student Conference Coordinating Secretariat (COSEC)

Utrecht Archive, Utrecht:

Papers of the Dutch Railways

Philips, Eindhoven:

Papers of Philips International

Tilburg University, Tilburg:

Papers of the JFK Institute

National Archives, Koblenz:

Papers of the Bundesministerium für gesamtdeutsche Fragen

Bundesbeauftragter für die Unterlagen des Staatssicherheitsdienstes der ehemaligen Deutschen Demokratischen Republik (BstU), Berlin:

Papers of the Ministerium für Staatsicherheit

National Archives, London:

Papers of the Information Research Department

Bibliothèque Nationale, Paris:

Papers of Raymond Aron

NATO Headquarters, Brussels:

Archive of NATO

National Archives, College Park, Washington, DC:

RG 263 Records of the Central Intelligence Agency
CREST database (CIA Records Search Tool)

Meridian International, Washington, DC:

Papers of the Governmental Affairs Institute

Ford Foundation, New York:

Papers of the Ford Foundation

Hoover Institution, Stanford, CA:

Papers of Brian Crozier
Papers of Georges Albertini

Books

Albrecht meldt zich (Wageningen: Zomer en Keunings, 1946).
Richard J. Aldrich, *The Hidden Hand: Britain, America and Cold War Secret Intelligence* (London: John Murray, 2001).
F.A.H. Alting von Geusau, *Cultural Diplomacy: Waging War by Other Means?* (Nijmegen: Wolf, 2009).
Scott Anderson and Jon Lee Anderson, *Inside the League: The Shocking Expose of How Terrorists, Nazis, and Latin American Death Squads Have Infiltrated the World Anti-Communist League* (New York: Dodd, Mead & Co, 1986).
Christopher Andrew and Vasili Mitrokhin, *The Mitrokhin Archive: The KGB in Europe and the West* (London: Allen Lane, 1999).
Valérie Aubourg, Gérard Bossuat, and Giles Scott-Smith (eds), *European Community, Atlantic Community?* (Paris: Soleb, 2008).
Oliver Bange and Gottfried Niedhart (eds), *Helsinki 1975 and the Transformation of Europe* (New York: Berghahn Books, 2008).

Richard J. Barnet, *The Alliance: America–Europe–Japan, Makers of the Postwar World* (New York: Simon and Schuster, 1983).
Peter Bender, *Offensive Entspannung* (Cologne: Kiepenheuer & Witsch, 1964).
Volker Berghahn, *America and the Intellectual Cold Wars in Europe* (New York: Berghahn Books, 2002).
J.H. van den Berg, *Metabletica, of Leer der Veranderingen: Beginsel van een Historische Psychologie* (Nijkerk: Callenbach, 1956).
Tom Bower, *The Perfect English Spy: Sir Dick White and the Secret War 1935–90* (London: Mandarin, 1996).
Erwin Bresslein, *Drushba! Freundschaft? Von der communistische Jugendinternationale zu den Weltjugendfestspielen* (Frankfurt: M. Fischer, 1973).
M.J.W.M. Broekmeijer, *South Vietnam: Victim of Misunderstanding* (Bilthoven: H. Nelissen, 1967).
Zbigniew Brzezinski, *Alternative to Partition: For a Broader Conception of America's Role in Europe* (New York: McGraw-Hill, 1965).
William Bundy, *A Tangled Web: The Making of Foreign Policy in the Nixon Presidency* (New York: Hill & Wang, 1998).
Nicla Buonasorte, *Siri: Tradizione e Novecento* (Bologna: Il Mulino, 2006).
Blanche Wiesen Cook, *The Declassified Eisenhower* (Harmondsworth: Penguin, 1981).
S.W. Couwenberg, *De Vereenzaming van de Moderne Mens: Een nieuwe formulering van het sociale vraagstuk* (The Hague: Pax, 1956).
S.W. Couwenberg, *Oost en West: Op de Drempel van een Nieuwe Tijdperk* (The Hague: Pax Nederland, 1966).
Stefan Creuzberger, *Kampf für die Einheit: Das gesamtdeutsche Ministerium und die politische Kultur des Kalten Krieges 1949–1969* (Düsseldorf: Droste, 2008).
James H. Critchfield, *Partners at the Creation: The Men behind Postwar Germany's Defense and Intelligence Establishments* (Annapolis: Naval Institute Press, 2003).
Brian Crozier (ed.), *We Will Bury You: A Study in Left-Wing Subversion Today* (London: Tom Stacey, 1970).
Brian Crozier, *Free Agent: The Unseen War 1941–1991* (London: HarperCollins, 1993).
Brian Crozier, Max Beloff, and Robert Conquest, *European Security and the Soviet Problem* (London: Institute for the Study of Conflict, 1970).
Richard Cummings, *The Pied Piper: Allard Lowenstein and the Liberal Dream* (New York: Grove Press, 1985).
Richard Deacon, *The French Secret Service* (London: Grafton, 1990).
Andrew Defty Britain, *America and Anti-Communist Propaganda 1945–53* (London: Routledge, 2004).
Remco van Diepen, *'Beschaafd ageren voor de NAVO': 50 Jaar Atlantische Commissie* (The Hague: Atlantische Commissie, 2002).
Anselm Doering-Manteuffel, *Wie westlich sind die Deutschen: Amerikanisierung und Westernisierung im 20. Jahrhundert* (Göttingen: Vandenbroeck & Ruprecht, 1999).
Stephen Dorril, *MI6: Fifty Years of Special Operations* (London: Fourth Estate, 2000).
Bob Drogin, *Curveball: Spies, Lies, and the Con Man who Caused a War* (New York: Random House, 2007).
John Dumbrell, *President Lyndon Johnson and Soviet Communism* (Manchester: Manchester University Press, 2004).
Louis Einthoven, *Tegen de Stroom In* (Apeldoorn: Semper Agindo, 1974).
Dick Engelen, *Geschiedenis van de Binnenlandse Veiligheidsdienst* (The Hague: Sdu, 1995).

David Engerman, *Know Your Enemy: The Rise and Fall of America's Soviet Experts* (Oxford: Oxford University Press, 2009).
Matthew Evangelista, *Unarmed Forces: The Transnational Movement to End the Cold War* (Ithaca, NY: Cornell University Press, 1999).
Roger Faligot and Pascal Krop, *La Piscine: The French Secret Service since 1944* (Oxford: Basil Blackwell, 1989).
Frieden und Freundschaft, *Weltjugendfestspiele, Funktion und Wirkung* (Bonn: Walter Lütz, 1963).
Daniele Ganser, *NATO's Secret Armies: Operation Gladio and Terrorism in Western Europe* (London: Frank Cass, 2005).
Gedenkboek Verzetsherdenkingskruis (The Hague: Samson, 1985).
Reinhard Gehlen, *The Service* (New York: World Publishing, 1972).
Rolf Geyer, *Entspannung, Neutralität, Sicherheit* (Osnabruck: Verlag A. Fromm, 1970).
Hugo Gijsels, *Netwerk Gladio* (Leuven: Kritak, 1991).
László Görgey, *Bonn's Eastern Policy 1964–1971: Evolution and Limitations* (Hamden: Archon, 1972).
Beatrice de Graaf, *Over de Muur: De DDR de Nederlandse Kerken en de Vredesbeweging* (Amsterdam: Boom, 2004).
Bob de Graaff and Cees Wiebes, *Villa Maarheeze: De Geschiedenis van de Inlichtingendienst Buitenland* (The Hague: Sdu, 1998).
William Glenn Gray, *Germany's Cold War: The Global Campaign to Isolate East Germany, 1949–1969* (Chapel Hill, NC: University of North Carolina Press, 2003).
Christian Haase, *Pragmatic Peacemakers: Institutes of International Affairs and the Liberalization of West Germany 1945–1973* (Augsburg: Wißner, 2007).
Bertil Häggman, *Sweden's Maoist Subversives: A Case Study* (London: Institute for the Study of Conflict, 1975).
Mose Harvey, *East–West Trade and United States Policy* (New York: National Association of Manufacturers, 1966).
Ulrich von Hassell, *The von Hassell Diaries: The Story of the Forces against Hitler inside Germany* (London: Hamish Hamilton, 1948).
Wolfgang Höpker, *Wie rot ist das Mittelmeer? – Europas gefährdete Südflanke* (Stuttgart: Seewald, 1968).
Stephen Howarth and Joost Jonker, *Geschiedenis van Koninklijke Shell*, Pt 2 (1939–1973), (Amsterdam: Boom, 2007).
Edward Hunter, *Brainwashing: The Story of Men Who Defied It* (New York: Pyramid, 1956).
Robert Hutchinson, *Their Kingdom Come: Inside the Secret World of Opus Dei* (New York: Doubleday, 1997).
Lord Ismay, *NATO: The First Five Years, 1949–1954* (Utrecht: Bosch, 1955).
Ian Jackson, *The Economic Cold War: America, Britain, and East–West Trade* (Basingstoke: Palgrave Macmillan, 2001).
George F. Kennan, *Memoirs 1925–1950* (Boston, MA: Bantam, 1969).
Deborah Kisatsky, *The United States and the European Right 1945–1955* (Columbus: Ohio State University Press, 2005).
Henry Kissinger, *The White House Years* (Boston: Little, Brown, 1979).
Martin Klimke, *The Other Alliance: Global Protest and Student Unrest in West Germany and the US, 1962–1972* (Princeton: Princeton University Press, 2009).
Frans Kluiters, *De Nederlandse Inlichtingen en Veiligheidsdiensten* (The Hague: Sdu, 1993).

Ross Koen, *The China Lobby in American Politics* (New York: Harper & Row, 1974
Bennett Kovrig, *Of Walls and Bridges: The United States and Eastern Europe* (New York: New York University Press, 1991).
General H.J. Kruls, *Vrede of Oorlog: De Wereld, West-Europa en de Benelux onder de Dreiging van onze Tijd* (The Hague: Stok, 1952).
Anneke Landheer-Roelants, *Romantisch buiten wonen in de stad: 125 jaar Van Stolkpark* (Utrecht: Stichting Matrijs, 1999).
Klaus Larres and Ken Osgood (eds), *The Cold War after Stalin's Death: A Missed Opportunity for Peace?* (Lanham: Rowman & Littlefield, 2006).
Frédéric Laurent, *L'Orchestre Noir* (Paris: Stock, 1978).
Melvyn P. Leffler, *For the Soul of Mankind: The United States, the Soviet Union, and the Cold War* (New York: Hill & Wang, 2007).
V.I. Lenin, *What is to be Done?* with introduction by Robert Service (London: Penguin, 1989).
Jean Levy, *Le Dossier Georges Albertini* (Paris: Editions L'Harmattan, 1992).
Fanny Leys, *Max Lamberty* (Antwerp: Nederlandsche Boekhandel, 1977).
Wilfried Loth, *Overcoming the Cold War: A History of Détente 1950–1991* (Basingstoke: Palgrave, 2002).
Wilfried Loth (ed.), *Europe, Cold War and Coexistence 1953–1965* (London: Frank Cass, 2004).
Scott Lucas, *Freedom's War: The American Crusade against the Soviet Union* (New York: New York University Press, 1999).
Sean McMeekin, *The Red Millionaire: A Political Biography of Willi Münzenberg* (New Haven: Yale University Press, 2003).
Patrick Major, *The Death of the KPD: Communism and Anti-Communism in West Germany, 1945–1956* (Oxford: Clarendon Press, 1997).
John Marks, *The Search for the Manchurian Candidate: The CIA and Mind Control* (New York: W.W. Norton, 1979).
Christopher Mayhew, *Coexistence-Plus: A Positive Approach to World Peace* (London: Bodley Head, 1962).
Ernst Nolte, *Deutschland und der Kalte Krieg* (Munich: R. Piper Verlag, 1974).
PET's Overvågning af den Antiimperialistiske Venstrefløj 1945–1989, PET-Kommissionens Beretning Bind 9 (Copenhagen: Ministry of Justice, 2008).
Gerrit Pietersen, *Afghanistan Is Our World* (The Hague: Interdoc, 1981).
Chapman Pincher, *Their Trade Is Treachery* (London: Sidgwick & Jackson, 1981).
Robin Ramsay, *The Clandestine Caucus* (Hull: Lobster, 1996).
Mary Ellen Reese, *General Reinhard Gehlen: The CIA Connection* (Fairfax: George Mason University Press, 1990).
Ian Richardson, Andrew Kakabadse, and Nada Kakabadse, *Bilderberg People: Elite Power and Consensus in World Affairs* (London: Routledge, 2011).
Ron Robin, *The Making of the Cold War Enemy: Culture and Politics in the Military–Intellectual Complex* (Princeton: Princeton University Press, 2001).
Max van Rooy, *Honderdzes adressen in Den Haag: De Koninklijke en de Residentie* (The Hague: Shell International Petroleum Company, 1986).
W.W. Rostow, *The Stages of Economic Growth* (Cambridge: Cambridge University Press, 1960).
David Ryan, *The United States and Europe in the Twentieth Century* (London: Pearson Longman, 2003).
William Sargant, *Battle for the Mind* (London: William Heinemann, 1957).
M.E. Sarotte, *Dealing with the Devil: East Germany, Détente, and Ostpolitik 1969–1973* (Chapel Hill, NC: University of North Carolina Press, 2001).

Frances Stonor Saunders, *Who Paid the Piper? The CIA and the Cultural Cold War* (London: Granta, 1999).
Erich Schmidt-Eenboom, *Der BND* (Berlin: ECON Verlag, 1993).
Erich Schmidt-Eenboom, *Geheimdienst Politik und Medien* (Berlin: Kai Homilius Verlag, 2004).
C.M. Schulten, *'En verpletterd werd het juk': Verzet in Nederland 1940–1945* (The Hague: Sdu, 1995).
Matthias Schulz and Thomas Schwartz (eds), *The Strained Alliance: US–European Relations from Nixon to Carter* (Cambridge: Cambridge University Press, 2010).
Giles Scott-Smith, *The Politics of Apolitical Culture: The CIA, the Congress for Cultural Freedom, and Post-war American Hegemony* (London: Routledge, 2002).
G. Scott-Smith, *Networks of Empire: The US State Department's Foreign Leader Program in the Netherlands, France, and Britain 1950–1970* (Brussels: Peter Lang, 2008).
G. Scott-Smith and Hans Krabbendam (eds), *The Cultural Cold War in Western Europe 1945–1960* (London: Frank Cass, 2003).
Marshall Shulman, *Stalin's Foreign Policy Reappraised* (Cambridge: Harvard University Press, 1963).
Sarah Snyder, *Human Rights Activism and the End of the Cold War: A Transnational History of the Helsinki Network* (Cambridge: Cambridge University Press, 2011).
Sydney Stern, *Gloria Steinum: Her Passions, Politics, and Mystique* (Secaucus: Birch Lane Press, 1997).
Jonathan Steinberg, *All or Nothing: The Axis and the Holocaust 1941–1943* (London: Routledge, 1990).
Rolf Steininger, *The German Question: The Stalin Note of 1952 and the Problem of Reunification* (New York: Columbia University, 1990).
William Stevenson, *Intrepid's Last Case* (London: Michael Joseph, 1984).
D.G. Stewart-Smith (with foreword by Julian Amery), *No Vision Here: Non-Military Warfare in Britain* (Foreign Affairs: Petersham, 1966).
Dominic Streatfield, *Brainwash: The Secret History of Mind Control* (London: Hodder & Stoughton, 2006).
Jeremi Suri, *Power and Protest: Global Revolution and the Rise of Détente* (Cambridge: Harvard University Press, 2003).
Philip Taylor, *Munitions of the Mind: A History of Propaganda from the Ancient World to the Present Day* (Manchester: Manchester University Press, 2003).
David Teacher, *Rogue Agents: Habsburg, Pinay, and the Private Cold War 1951–1991*, available online at www.cryptome.org/2012/01/cercle-pinay-6i.pdf
Gordon Thomas, *Journey into Madness: The True Story of Secret CIA Mind Control and Medical Abuse* (New York: Bantam, 1989).
Robert Tucker, *The Soviet Political Mind: Studies in Stalinism and Post-Stalin Change* (London: Pall Mall Press, 1963).
Corinna Unger, *Ostforschung in Westdeutschland: Die Erforschung des europäischen Ostens und die Deutsche Forschungsgemeinschaft, 1945–1975* (Stuttgart: Franz Steiner, 2007).
Paul Villatoux and Marie-Catherine Villatoux, *La République et son armée face au 'péril subversif': Guerre et action psychologiques en France 1945–1960* (Paris: Les Indes Savantes, 2005).
James Voorhees, *Dialogue Sustained: The Multilevel Peace Process and the Dartmouth Conference* (Washington: United States Institute of Peace Press, 2002).
Chris Vos, Rens Broekhuis, Lies Janssen, and Barbara Mounier, *De Geheime Dienst: Verhalen over de BVD* (Amsterdam: Boom, 2005).

Stefanie Waske, *Mehr Liaison als Kontrolle: Die Kontrolle des BND durch Parlament und Regierung* (Wiesbaden: VS Verlag, 2008).
Andreas von Weiss, *Die Neue Linke: Kritische Analyse* (Boppard: Harald Boldt Verlag, 1969).
Andreas Wenger, Vojtech Mastny and Christian Nuenlist (eds), *Origins of the European Security System: The Helsinki Process Revisited, 1965–75*(London: Routledge, 2008).
Odd Arne Westad, *The Global Cold War* (Cambridge: Cambridge University Press, 2007).
J. Wilczynski, *The Economics and Politics of East–West Trade* (London: Macmillan, 1969).
Hugh Wilford, *The CIA, the British Left and the Cold War* (London: Frank Cass, 2003).
Hugh Wilford, *The Mighty Wurlitzer: How the CIA Played America* (Cambridge: Harvard University Press, 2008).
Karel van Wolferen, *Student Revolutionaries of the 1960s* (The Hague: Interdoc, 1970).
Peter Wright, *Spycatcher* (New York: Viking, 1987).
Vladislav Zubok, *A Failed Empire: The Soviet Union in the Cold War from Stalin to Gorbachev* (Chapel Hill, NC: University of North Carolina Press, 2007).

Articles/Book chapters

Pierre Assouline, 'Un expert en anticommunisme, Georges Albertini', in *Le Temps de la guerre froide* (Paris: Seuil, 1994), pp. 243–261.
Frank R. Barnett, 'A Proposal for Political Warfare', *Military Review* (March 1961), pp. 2–10.
H. Bradford Westerfield, 'America and the World of Intelligence Liaison', *Intelligence and National Security* 11 (1996), pp. 523–560.
Zbigniew Brzezinski and William Griffith, 'Peaceful Engagement in Eastern Europe', *Foreign Affairs* 39 (July 1961), pp. 642–654.
Mathilde von Bülow, 'The Telefunken Affair and the Internationalisation of the Algerian War, 1957–59', *Journal of Strategic Studies* 28 (2005), pp. 703–729.
Mathilde von Bülow, 'Myth or Reality? The Red Hand and French Covert Action in Federal Germany during the Algerian War, 1956–61', *Intelligence and National Security* 22 (2007), pp. 787–820.
Susan Carruthers, 'Not Just Washed bu Dry-Cleaned: Korea and the "Brainwashing" Scare of the 1950s', in Gary Rawnsley (ed.), *Cold War Propaganda in the 1950s* (Basingstoke: Macmillan, 1999), pp. 47–66.
Martin Ceadel, 'The First Communist "Peace Society": The British Anti-War Movement 1932–1935', *Twentieth Century British History* 1 (1990), pp. 58–86.
Alexander Clarkson, 'Home and Away: Immigration and Political Violence in the Federal Republic of Germany, 1945–90', *Cold War History* 8 (2008), pp. 1–21.
Chris Clough, 'Quid Pro Quo: The Challenges of International Strategic Intelligence Cooperation', *International Journal of Intelligence and CounterIntelligence* 17 (2004), pp. 601–613.
Jean-Marie Domenach, 'Leninist Propaganda', *Public Opinion Quarterly* 15 (Summer 1951), pp. 265–273.
Eric Duhamel, 'Jean-Paul David et le Mouvement Paix et Liberté, un Anticommuniste Radical', in J. Delmas and J. Kessler (eds), *Renseignement et Propagande pendant la Guerre Froide (1947–1953)* (Brussels: Editions Complexe, 1999), pp. 195–216.
Gottfried Erb, 'Das Memorandum des Bensberger Kreises zur Polenpolitik', in Werner Plum (ed.), *Ungewöhnliche Normalisierung: Beziehungen der Bundesrepublik Deutschland zu Polen* (Bonn: Verlag Neue Gesellschaft, 1984), pp. 179–190.

Rolf Geyer, 'Der Deutsche im Spannungsfeld psychopolitischer Vorgänge', *Politische Studien: Monatschrift für Zeitgeschichte und Politik* (1975), pp. 369–376.

Nigel Gould-Davis, 'The Logic of Soviet Cultural Diplomacy', *Diplomatic History* 27 (April 2003), pp. 193–214.

Bob de Graaff and Cees Wiebes, 'Intelligence and the Cold War behind the Dykes: The Relationship between the American and Dutch Intelligence Communities 1946–1994', in Rhodri Jeffreys-Jones and Christopher Andrew (eds), *Eternal Vigilance: 50 years of the CIA* (London: Frank Cass, 1997), pp. 41–58.

Johannes Grossman, 'Ein Europa der "Hintergründigen": Antikommunistische christliche Organisationen, konservative Elitenzirkel und private Außenpolitik in Westeuropa nach dem Zweiten Weltkrieg', in Johannes Wienand and Christianne Wienand (eds), *Die kulturelle Integration Europas* (Springer: VS Verlag, 2010), pp. 303–340.

Peer Henrik Hansen, 'Upstairs and Downstairs: The Forgotten CIA Operations in Copenhagen', *International Journal of Intelligence and Counter Intelligence* 19 (2006–2007), pp. 685–701.

C.C. van den Heuvel, 'Psychologische Oorlogvoering', *Militaire Spectator* 131 (1962), pp. 22–25.

Eric Hobsbawm, 'Cadres', *London Review of Books*, 26 April 2007.

Fritz Hoekstra, 'The Dutch BVD and Transatlantic Co-operation during the Cold War Era: Some Experiences', *Journal of Intelligence History* 3 (Summer 2003), pp. 47–54.

Wolfram Kaiser, 'Transnational Networks in European Governance', in Wolfram Kaiser, Brigitte Leucht, and Morten Rasmussen (eds), *The History of the European Union: Origins of a Trans- and Supranational Polity 1950–72* (London: Routledge, 2009), pp. 12–33.

Wolfram Kaiser, Brigitte Leucht, and Michael Gehler, 'Transnational Networks in European Integration Governance: Historical Perspectives on an Elusive Phenomenon', in Kaiser, Leucht, and Michael Gehler (eds), *Transnational Networks in Regional Integration: Governing Europe 1945–83* (London: Palgrave Macmillan, 2010), pp. 1–17.

Paul Koedijk, 'Van "Vrede en Vrijheid" tot "Volk en Verdediging": Veranderingen in Anti-communistische Psychologische Oorlogvoering in Nederland 1950–1965', in B. Schoenmaker and J.A.M.M. Janssen (eds), *De Schaduw van de Muur: Maatschappij en Krijgsmacht rond 1960* (The Hague: Sdu, 1997), pp. 57–81.

Pia Koivunen, 'The Moscow 1957 Youth Festival: Propagating a New Peaceful Image of the Soviet Union', in M. Ilic and J. Smith (eds), *Soviet State and Soviety under Nikita Khrushchev* (London: Routledge, 2009), pp. 46–65.

Sonja Krämer, 'Westdeutsche Propaganda im Kalten Krieg: Organisationen und Akteure', in Jürgen Wilke (ed.), *Pressepolitik und Propaganda: Historische Studien vom Vormärz bis zum Kalten Krieg* (Cologne: Böhlau 1997), pp. 333–371.

Joni Krekola and Simo Mikkonen, 'Backlash of the Free World: The US presence at the World Youth Festival in Helsinki, 1962', *Scandinavian Journal of History* 36 (2011), pp. 230–255.

Wolfgang Krieger, 'German–American Intelligence Relations, 1945–1956: New Evidence on the Origins of the BND,' *Diplomacy & Statecraft* 22 (2011), pp. 28–43.

J.W.M. Linssen, 'De Albrechtgroep: een fenomeen ontleed', in P. Koedijk, J. Linssen, and D. Engelen (eds), *Verspreiders voor het Vaderland* (The Hague: Sdu, 1996), pp. 37–84.

Fredrik Logevall, 'The Swedish–American Conflict over Vietnam', *Diplomatic History* 17 (1993), pp. 421–445.

Scott Lucas, 'Campaigns of Truth: The Psychological Strategy Board and American Ideology, 1951–1953', *International History Review,* 18 (May 1996), pp. 279–302.

Scott Lucas, 'Mobilizing Culture: The State–Private Network and the CIA in the Early Cold War', in Dale Carter (ed.), *War and Cold War in American Foreign Policy 1942–1962* (New York: Palgrave Macmillan, 2002), pp. 83–107.

Bernhard Ludwig, 'La Propagande Anticommuniste en Allemagne Fédérale: Le VFF pendant Allemand de Paix et Liberté?' *Vingtième Siècle: Revue d'histoire* 80 (October–December 2003), pp. 33–42.

G.H.O. van Maanen, 'De Nederlandse student en het Oost-West contact', *Internationale Spectator* 19 (8 June 1965), pp. 914–931.

Paul Maddrell, 'The Western secret services, the East German Ministry for State Security, and the building of the Berlin Wall', *Intelligence and National Security* 21 (2006), pp. 829–847.

Jeffrey H. Michaels, 'Waging Protracted Conflict Behind-the-Scenes: The Cold War Activism of Fran R. Barnett,' paper given at the HOTCUS annual conference, Roosevelt Study Center, Middelburg, The Netherlands, 22 June 2012.

Mikail Nilsson, 'The Professor and the CIA: Herbert Tingsten and the Congress for Cultural Freedom, a Symbiotic Relationship', *European Review of History* 18 (April 2011), pp. 147–174.

Leopoldo Nuti, 'The United States, Italy, and the Opening to the Left', *Journal of Cold War Studies* 4 (Summer 2002), pp. 36–55.

Ken Osgood, 'Hearts and Minds: The Unconventional Cold War', *Journal of Cold War History* 4 (Spring 2002), pp. 85–107.

Ludwig Raiser, 'Deutsche Ostpolitik im Lichte der Denkschrift der Evangelischen Kirke', *Europa-Archiv* 21 (1966), pp. 195–208.

Wyn Rees and Richard J. Aldrich, 'European and US Approaches to Counterterrorism: Two Contrasting Cultures?' in Ronald Tiersky and Erik Jones (eds), *Europe Today: A Twenty-First Century Introduction* (Lanham: Rowman & Littlefield, 2007), pp. 437–464.

Linda Risso, ' "Enlightening Public Opinion": A Study of NATO's Information Policies between 1949 and 1959 based on Recently Declassified Documents', *Cold War History* 7 (February 2007), pp. 45–74.

Linda Risso, 'A Difficult Compromise: British and American Plans for a Common Anti-Communist Propaganda Response in Western Europe, 1948–1958', *Intelligence and National Security* 26 (2011), pp. 330–354.

W.W. Rostow, 'The Third Round', *Foreign Affairs* 42 (October 1963), pp. 1–10.

Karen Rothmeyer, 'Citizen Scaife', in David Weir and Dan Noyes (eds), *Raising Hell* (Reading MA: Addison-Wesley, 1983), pp. 53–90.

Peter Sager, 'L'URSS à l'heure de la coexistence,' bulletin no. 4, Centre d'Etudes Avancées, Strasbourg-Robertsau, 1955.

Eva Schandevyl, 'Max Lamberty en het ontstaan van de Stichting Lodewijk de Raet', in K. van Goethem and E. Schandevyl (eds), *50 Jaar Stichting Lodewijk de Raet* (Brussels: Stichting Lodewijk de Raet, 2002), pp. 8–13.

Gerhard Schröder, 'Germany looks at Eastern Europe', *Foreign Affairs,* 44 (October 1965), pp. 15–25.

Giles Scott-Smith, 'Not a NATO Responsibility? Psychological Warfare, the Berlin Crisis, and the formation of Interdoc', in A. Locher and C. Nuenlist (eds), *Challenges Beyond Deterrence: NATO in the 1960s* (London: Routledge, 2006), pp. 31–49.

Giles Scott-Smith, 'Interdoc, Peaceful Coexistence, and Positive Anti-Communism: West European Cooperation in Psychological Warfare 1963–1972', *Cold War History,* 7 (February 2007), pp. 19–43.

Giles Scott-Smith, 'Interdoc and West European Psychological Warfare: The American Connection', *Intelligence and National Security*, 26 (2011), pp. 355–376.
Giles Scott-Smith, 'Psychological Warfare for the West: Interdoc, the West European Intelligence Services, and the International Student Movements of the 1960s' in Kathrin Fahlenbrach, Martin Klimke, Joachim Scharloth, and Laura Wong (eds), *The Establishment Responds: Power, Politics, and Protest since 1945* (New York: Palgrave Macmillan, 2012), pp. 123–138.
Joseph P. Sinasac, 'The Three Wise Men: The Effects of the 1956 Committee of Three on NATO', in Margaret O. MacMillan and David S. Sorenson (eds), *Canada and NATO: Uneasy Past, Uncertain Future* (Waterloo: University of Waterloo Press, 1990), pp. 27–46.
Lynn Smith, 'Covert British Propaganda: The Information Research Department, 1947–77', *Millennium* 9 (1980), pp. 67–83.
René Sommer, 'Paix et liberté: La Quatrième République contre le PC', *L'Histoire*, 40 (December 1981), pp. 26–35.
Jennifer E. Syms, 'Foreign Intelligence Liaison: Devils, Deals, and Details', *International Journal of Intelligence and CounterIntelligence*, 19 (2006), pp. 195–217.
Wesley Wark, 'The Origins of Intelligence Cooperation between the United States and West Germany', in Detlef Junker (ed.), *The United States and Germany in the Era of the Cold War, 1945–1968*, Vol. 1 (Washington, DC: German Historical Institute/Cambridge University Press, 2004), pp. 248–254.
Albrecht Zunker, 'Stiftung Wissenschaft und Politik: Die Neu-Berlinerin', *Handbuch Politikberatung* Vol. II (2006), pp. 363–373.

Ph.D. Dissertations

Thomas Gijswijt, 'Uniting the West: the Bilderberg Group, the Cold War and European Integration 1952–1966', Ph.D. dissertation, Heidelberg University, 2008.
Philippe Régnier, 'La Propagande Anticommuniste de Paix et Liberté, France, 1950–1956', Ph.D. thesis, Université Libre, Brussels, 1987.

Index

Note: Locators followed by 'n' refer to notes.

Académie Européenne de Sciences Politiques (AESP), 127, 232
Adenauer, Konrad, 13, 14, 19, 20, 26, 40, 170
Aginter Press, 133
Aktionskomitee Wahret die Freiheit (AWF), 116–17, 136, 141, 144, 145–6
Albertini, Georges, 6, 56, 60, 83, 179, 205
American Bar Association, 206, 211, 335 n.109
Ampersand (publishing house), 110, 113
Andreotti, Giulio, 283 n.137, 299 n.90
Arbatov, Gyorgy, 226, 231
Armfelt, Carl, 6, 129–31, 141, 302 n.128, 302 n.135, 303 n.139
Aron, Raymond, 32, 273 n.84
Atlantic Treaty Association (ATA), 214, 216–17
Atlantische Commissie (AC), 214–17, 239

Barnett, Frank, 165, 190–2, 194–6, 203–8, 210, 218, 222, 243
  see also National Strategy Information Center (NSIC)
Bell, Walter, 176–7, 180, 208, 210, 222, 245, 327 n.83
Bensberger Kreis, 170
Bilderberg meetings, 24–5, 81
Bildt, Carl, 235
Binnenlandse Veiligheidsdienst (BVD), 7–8, 23, 25, 30–1, 32, 33, 38, 41, 43, 44–5, 48–9, 51–2, 55, 59, 62, 67, 80, 88–90, 92–3, 104–5, 137, 139, 140, 142, 147, 161, 186, 214, 215
Blötz, Dieter, 173, 178
Bochenski, Professor Josef, 68–9, 70, 77, 106, 232, 280 n.75, 285 n.172
Bonnemaison, Antoine, 6, 27, 60, 61, 71, 76, 83, 271 n.59, 286 n.181
brainwashing, 34–5

British Reserve Forces Association (BRFA), 221–2, 332 n.62
Broger, Colonel John, 36
Brooke, Gerald, 155
Brufina, 125, 126
Brzezinski, Zbigniew, 150, 169, 195, 231, 310 n.86
Buchow, Rolf, 33, 68, 160, 166, 183–5, 186, 188
  see also Interdoc Berlin
Bund Deutscher Jugend (BDJ), 19
Bundesnachrichtendienst (BND), 6, 7, 15–17, 27–8, 29, 31, 42, 56, 58, 61, 63, 66, 72, 75–6, 78–9, 81, 98–103, 104–5, 128, 134, 152, 157, 158, 161, 171, 173, 177–85, 186, 201, 207, 210, 245
Bureau of State Security (BOSS), 325 n.50
Büro für politische Studien (Bonn), 29, 78

cadre training, 50, 53, 59, 77
Caeymaex, Ludovicus, 122, 125, 127, 299 n.84, 306 n.28
Carstens, Karl, 173
Casey, William J., 190, 204, 219
Catholic Action, 72, 74, 117
Central Intelligence Agency (CIA), 7–8, 10, 16, 19, 27, 34, 41–2, 43, 58, 70, 71, 75, 81, 90, 92, 119, 139, 169, 170, 189, 194, 197, 203, 248, 290 n.59
Centre Européen de Documentation et d'Information (CEDI), 12, 127, 131, 179, 211
Centro di studi e ricerche sui problemi economico–sociali (CESES), 119–22, 299 n.88, 312 n.130
Chaban-Delmas, Jacques, 219–20
Challenge of Coexistence, The (1965), 87, 113, 287 n.9
Chamieh, Jebran, 200

Clive, Nigel, 176–7
Comitato Civico, 72, 74, 117, 136, 144
Comité International d'Information et d'Action Sociale (CIAS), 12, 23, 68, 110, 199
Comité International pour la Défense de la Civilisation Chrétienne (CIDCC), 12, 113, 296 n.41
Common Cause (CC), 109–10, 111, 112, 174, 294 n.20, 326 n.78
Confindustria, 118–21
Congress for Cultural Freedom (CCF), 10, 11, 89–90, 132
Cram, Cleveland (CIA), 155, 322 n.6
Critchfield, James, 16
Crozier, Brian, 6, 64, 83, 110, 155, 177, 179, 192, 203–5, 218, 221, 232–4, 243, 332 n.58
see also Institute for the Study of Conflict (ISoC)
Cuneo, Ernest, 191

Damman, Florimond, 127, 232, 335 n.106
David, Jean Paul, 21
Von Dellingshausen, Ewert, 20, 26–7, 29, 34, 48, 61, 78–9, 104, 284 n.158
Deutsche Arbeitsgruppe für West-Ost Beziehungen, 107
Dulles, Allen, 6, 43, 72, 81–2, 100, 190

East-West trade, 150, 170, 192–4, 324 n.36
Economic League (EL), 38–9, 64, 111, 112, 114, 136, 294 n.14
Ehmke, Horst, 173, 180–1, 182, 320 n.72
Einthoven, Louis, 6, 23, 25, 27, 30, 38, 43, 44, 56, 59–64, 65, 66, 71–4, 80–2, 83, 91, 93, 104, 122, 128, 136, 180–1, 182, 199, 201–2, 221, 275 n.124, 283 n.133, 283 n.137, 283 n.138, 297 n.57, 297 n.59
Ellis, Charles Howard (Dick), 64–6, 83, 109, 111, 113, 131, 174, 177, 191, 194, 317 n.42
Erhard, Ludwig, 170
Ethics and Public Policy Center (EPPC), 241, 338 n.148

European Union of Christian Democratic and Conservative Students (ECCS), 235, 314 n.157
Federal Bureau of Investigation (FBI), 37
Federation of European-American Organizations (FEAO), 219–20
Fédération Internationale des Résistants (FIR), 161, 331 n.52
see also Union Internationale de la Résistance et de la Déportation (UIRD); World Veterans Federation (WVF)
Felfe, Heinz, 81
Foertsch, Herman, 26–7, 31, 39, 57, 59, 75
Ford Foundation, 39, 81, 191, 195–6, 204, 230, 285 n.172, 297 n.56
Free Europe Committee, 81, 141, 153–4
Frihed og Folkestyr (Denmark), 132, 303 n.144

Galantière, Lewis, 37
Gasteyger, Curt, 109, 115, 116, 207, 216, 297 n.60
De Gaulle, Charles, 27, 41, 60, 76
Gedda, Luigi, 72–3
Gehlen, Reinhard, 15–17, 26, 28, 31, 42, 72, 75, 197, 284 n.150
Geyer, Rolf, 7, 63, 75, 78–9, 83, 99–100, 101–3, 107, 114, 126, 149–50, 153, 161, 163–4, 168, 177–8, 203–4, 223–4, 229, 245, 294 n.20, 317 n.40, 317 n.43
Globke, Hans, 18, 26–7
Godson, Roy, 164, 165, 218, 222–3
God That Failed, The (1949), 87
Grote, Nicolas von, 79, 82, 86, 87, 99, 100–3, 107, 109–10, 156, 158, 161, 168, 174, 177, 178, 183, 185, 187, 196, 201, 202, 208, 225, 294 n.17
Guicciardi, Luigi, 71, 74

Häggman, Bertil, 128–9, 141, 176, 201, 222–3, 234, 247, 309 n.74, 329 n.18
Von Hahn, Baron W., 98–9, 101–5, 117–18, 121–2, 126, 151–2, 154, 171, 298 n.67, 299 n.80, 300 n.93, 310 n.103
Hallstein doctrine, 13, 14, 28

354 Index

Haus der Zukunft (West Berlin), 29, 32, 33
Haus Rissen (Gesellschaft für Wirtschafts- und Sozialpolitik), 29, 32, 210, 211
Heath, Edward, 182
Hoover Institution (Stanford), 191, 211

Independent Research Service, 135, 136, 146, 192
Information Research Department (IRD), 5, 30, 66–8, 108–15, 136, 141, 144, 145, 155, 173–7, 296 n.44
Institute for the Study of Conflict (ISoC), 203–6, 211, 221, 222, 232
Interdoc Berlin, 33, 172, 185, 186, 311 n.112
 see also Buchow, Rolf
International Student Conference (ISC), 67, 135–6, 143, 147, 163, 307 n.48, 313 n.139
International Union of Christian Democratic and Conservative Students (ICCS), 162, 314 n.157
International Union of Students (IUS), 135

Jackson, Charles Douglas (C.D.), 48
John F. Kennedy Institute (Tilburg), 228–31
Johnson, President Lyndon B., 168–9, 193
Josten, Josef, 112

Kampfgruppe gegen Unmenschlichkeit, 20, 25, 276 n.133
Kelly, Crosby, 196–7
Kernig, Professor Claus, 64, 79, 82, 156, 178, 181, 182, 210
Khrushchev, Nikita, 4, 9, 28, 222
Kohtani, Etsuo, 200, 333 n.71
Krause, Theodor (BND), 56, 61
Kuznetsov, Vladimir, 225–6, 332 n.77

Labin, Suzanne, 123, 127, 300 n.93
Lades, Professor Hans, 79, 157, 159, 187, 210, 224, 333 n.71
De Lagarde, Georges, 61, 110
Lamberty, Max, 123–6

Leninism, 3, 53
von Lippe-Biesterfeld, Prince Bernhard, 25, 43, 68, 80, 93, 149, 182, 218, 219
Lombardo, Ivan Matteo, 133, 156, 179, 311 n.115
Luns, Joseph, 207
Luxembourg Group, 140–1, 146–7

de Marenches, Alexandre, 205
Meissner, Professor Boris, 105, 232, 233, 280 n.75, 291 n.63
Menaul, Stewart 'Paddy', 210, 222, 233, 327 n.93
MI6, 27, 42, 64–6, 68, 110, 111, 114, 115, 136, 144, 174–5, 194
Mieli, Renato, 118–21, 144, 151, 228
Militant Liberty, 36, 52
Mollet, Guy, 60–1
Mont Pelerin Society, 212
Moral Rearmament (Caux), 30, 54
Münzenberg, Willi, 3, 247

National Alliance of Russian Solidarists (NTS), 112, 130, 155
National Association of Manufacturers (NAM), 191–3, 195–7
Nationale Federatieve Raad van het Voormalige Verzet Nederland (NFR), 54–5, 290 n.58
National Security Council (NSC), 3
National Strategy Information Center (NSIC), 38, 164, 165, 179, 190, 211, 233
New Left, 155–7
North Atlantic Treaty Organization (NATO), 20–5, 41, 74, 154, 216

Oost-West (periodical), 88–90, 91, 95–6, 123, 213, 229, 287 n.14, 288 n.26
Operations Coordinating Board, 22, 26
Orientierung (periodical), 27, 88, 100, 201, 291 n.68, 325 n.60
O'Ryan, Jim (CIA), 301 n.114
Ost-Institut, Bern (OI), 62, 63, 68, 69–70, 115, 117, 179, 205, 211
 see also Sager, Peter

Ostkolleg (Cologne), 60, 62, 104–6
Ostpolitik, 169–71, 180

Paix et Liberté, 12, 21–3, 270 n.31, 270 n. 36
Palme, Olof, 129, 131
Peaceful Coexistence, 4–5, 40
Peeters, Professor Florent, 124, 127
Philips (company), 39, 45, 55, 70, 80, 93–5
Philips, Frits J., 33, 61, 98
Pirenne, Jacques-Henri, 124–6
policy networks, 11
positive anti-communism, 48, 86
Praaning, Rio, 216–17, 238–9, 241, 330 n.39, 338 n.142
Psychological Strategy Board (PSB), 21, 22

Ratzinger, Josef, 118, 170
De Roover, Marcel, 125, 127, 131, 294 n.20
Royal Dutch Shell, 39, 45, 50–1, 61, 74, 78, 80, 93, 202, 210, 298 n.66, 324 n.39
  Shell Belgium, 125
  Shell Italy, 71, 120
  Shell UK, 109–10, 111, 114, 174–5, 207, 294 n.14, 327 n.93, 328 n.12

Sager, Peter, 62, 63, 68, 69–70, 115, 117, 297 n.56, 297 n.55, 298 n.66, 303 n.143
  see also Ost-Institut, Bern (OI)
Scaife, Richard Mellon, 192, 203, 211
Scheffler, Herbert, 113, 141, 321 n.92
Sejr, Arne, 132
Service de Documentation Extérieure et de Contre-Espionage (SDECE), 23, 27, 42, 64, 76, 83, 119, 205
Siri, Cardinal Guiseppe, 73, 121
Sitompoel, H., 201
Society for the Investigation of Human Ecology (SIHE), 34–8, 49, 70, 274 n.92, 274 n.93, 275 n.110
Stasi (Ministerium für Staatssicherheit), 172–3, 181–2, 184, 207
state-private networks, 10–11

Stewart-Smith, Geoffrey, 6, 111–12, 124, 232
Stichting voor Onderzoek van Ecologische Vraagstukken (SOEV), 49–51, 53–4, 79, 82, 88, 91, 92, 93, 95–6, 106, 136–7, 148, 183, 292 n.93
Strauss, Franz-Josef, 28, 41
Studienbüro Berlin, 29, 31, 79, 131, 183, 277 n.6
Swarup, Rana, 201
Symonides, Janusz, 228

Tasks for the Free World (1964), 85–7, 90, 113, 123, 287 n.3
Thatcher, Margaret, 303 n.139
Thompson, Brigadier W.F.K., 179, 182, 206, 207, 210, 245, 327 n.93
Triesch, Günter (Deutsches Industrie-Institut), 56, 61, 72, 79, 104, 172, 181, 187, 202

Union Internationale de la Résistance et de la Déportation (UIRD), 220, 221, 227, 290 n.51
  see also Fédération Internationale des Résistants (FIR); World Veterans Federation (WVF)
Unione Cristiana Imprenditori Dirigenti (UCID), 62, 71–2, 74, 117, 120, 133, 191
Universal Declaration of Human Rights (UDHR), 10, 47, 86, 90, 220

Vankerkhoven, Paul, 127, 232
Verein zur Erforschung sozialpolitischer Verhältnisse im Ausland e.V., 78–9, 98, 285 n.160
Violet, Jean, 83, 122, 232
Volk en Verdediging, 56, 128, 160, 210
Volk und Verteidigung, 128, 160, 186
Volksbund für Frieden und Freiheit (VFF), 20, 22, 25, 32, 296 n.41
  see also Comité International d'Information et d'Action Sociale (CIAS)
Voorhoeve, Joris, 240–1
Vrede en Vrijheid, 23, 30, 32, 45, 88, 282 n.124

Waldman, Eric, 15, 16, 319 n.60
Wedin, Bertil, 130, 161, 164, 313 n.151, 314 n.159
Wendland, Horst (BND), 76
Wessel, Gerhard (BND), 173, 180–1
Western values, 46–8, 52–3
White, Dick (MI6), 65, 112, 174
World Alliance for Student Cooperation (WASC), 141
World Anti-Communist League (WACL), 12, 128, 131, 179, 199, 211, 247, 294 n.20

World Federation of Democratic Youth (WFDY), 135, 145, 235
World Veterans Federation (WVF), 225, 227, 331 n.52
see also Fédération Internationale des Résistants (FIR); Union Internationale de la Résistance et de lar Déportation (UIRD)
World Youth Festival
East Berlin (1972), 148
Helsinki (1962), 135–40
Sofia (1968), 147